2019–2020
CIVIL PROCEDURE SUPPLEMENT
FOR USE WITH ALL PLEADING AND PROCEDURE CASEBOOKS

JACK H. FRIEDENTHAL

Edward F. Howrey Professor of Law Emeritus and Former Dean
George Washington University

ARTHUR R. MILLER

University Professor
New York University
Former Bruce Bromley Professor of Law
Harvard University

JOHN E. SEXTON

President Emeritus, Former Dean, and Benjamin Butler Professor of Law
New York University

HELEN HERSHKOFF

Herbert M. and Svetlana Wachtell
Professor of Constitutional Law and Civil Liberties
New York University

WEST
ACADEMIC
PUBLISHING

COPYRIGHT © 1985, 1987, 1989–1991, JACK H. FRIEDENTHAL, ARTHUR R. MILLER & JOHN E. SEXTON
COPYRIGHT © 1993–1996 West Publishing Company
© West, a Thomson business, 1997–2008
© 2009–2012 Thomson Reuters
© 2013 LEG, Inc. d/b/a West Academic Publishing
© 2014–2018 LEG, Inc. d/b/a West Academic
© 2019 LEG, Inc. d/b/a West Academic
    444 Cedar Street, Suite 700
    St. Paul, MN 55101
    1-877-888-1330

Printed in the United States of America

ISBN: 978-1-68467-144-1

[No claim of copyright is made for official U.S. government statutes, rules or regulations.]

TABLE OF CONTENTS

2019–2020
CIVIL PROCEDURE SUPPLEMENT
FOR USE WITH ALL PLEADING AND PROCEDURE CASEBOOKS

Flow Chart of a Civil Action

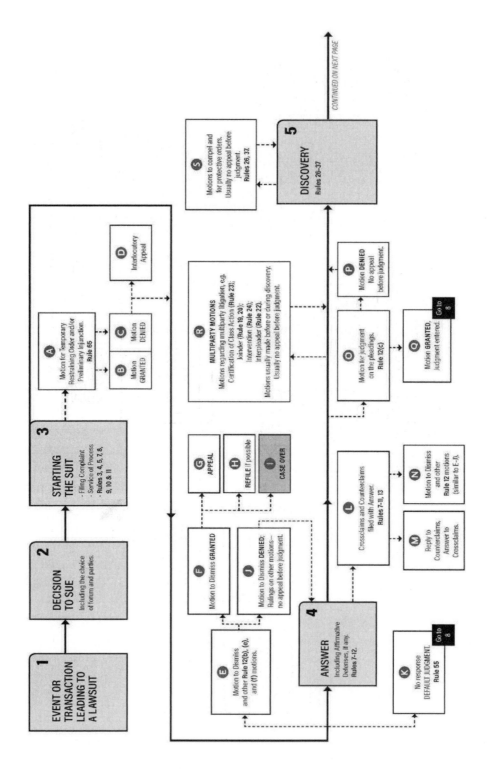

Flow Chart of a Civil Action

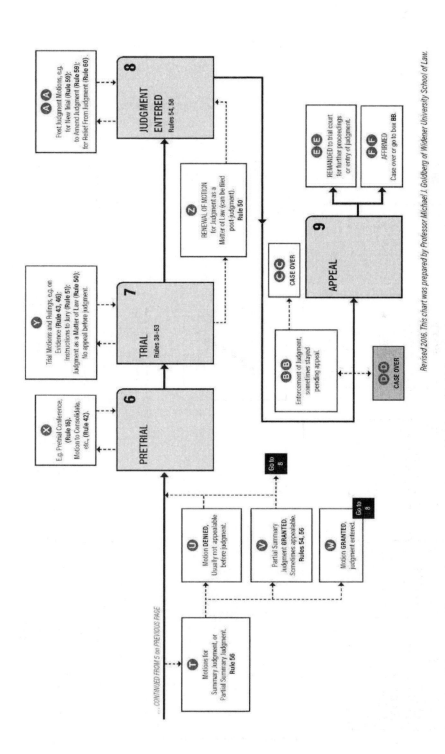

Revised 2016. This chart was prepared by Professor Michael J. Goldberg of Widener University School of Law.

PART I

Federal Rules of Civil Procedure for the United States District Courts

and

Comparative Federal and State Provisions

and

Appendix of Abrogated Forms

and

Supplemental Rules for Admiralty or Maritime Claims and Asset Forfeiture Actions

---

TABLE OF CONTENTS
Federal Rules of Civil Procedure

I.   Scope of Rules—One Form of Action

FEDERAL RULES OF CIVIL PROCEDURE

III. Pleadings and Motions

FEDERAL RULES OF CIVIL PROCEDURE

IV. Parties

FEDERAL RULES OF CIVIL PROCEDURE

V. Disclosures and Discovery

FEDERAL RULES OF CIVIL PROCEDURE

VII. Judgment

VIII. Provisional and Final Remedies

FEDERAL RULES OF CIVIL PROCEDURE

Appendix of Abrogated Forms

Supplemental Rules for Admiralty or Maritime Claims and Asset Forfeiture Actions

Rule

———

TITLE I. SCOPE OF RULES—ONE FORM OF ACTION

Rule 1. Scope and Purpose

These rules govern the procedure in all civil actions and proceedings in the United States district courts, except as stated in Rule 81. They should be construed and administered and employed by the court and the parties to secure the just, speedy, and inexpensive determination of every action and proceeding.

Rule 2. One Form of Action

There is one form of action—the civil action.

TITLE II. COMMENCING OF ACTION; SERVICE OF PROCESS, PLEADINGS, MOTIONS, AND ORDERS

Rule 3. Commencing an Action

A civil action is commenced by filing a complaint with the court.

Comparative State Provision

Kansas Statutes Annotated § 60–203(a)

A civil action is commenced at the time of: (1) Filing a petition with the court, if service of process is obtained or the first publication is made for service by publication within 90 days after the petition is filed, except that the court may extend that time an additional 30 days upon a showing of good cause by the plaintiff; or (2) service of process or first publication, if service of process or first publication is not made within the time specified by paragraph (1).

Rule 4. Summons

(a) Contents; Amendments.

(1) *Contents.* A summons must:

(A) name the court and the parties;

(B) be directed to the defendant;

(C) state the name and address of the plaintiff's attorney or—if unrepresented—of the plaintiff;

(D) state the time within which the defendant must appear and defend;

(E) notify the defendant that a failure to appear and defend will result in a default judgment against the defendant for the relief demanded in the complaint;

(F) be signed by the clerk; and

(G) bear the court's seal.

(2) *Amendments.* The court may permit a summons to be amended.

(b) Issuance. On or after filing the complaint, the plaintiff may present a summons to the clerk for signature and seal. If the summons is properly completed, the clerk must sign, seal, and issue it to the plaintiff for service on the defendant. A summons—or a copy of a summons that is addressed to multiple defendants—must be issued for each defendant to be served.

(c) Service.

(1) *In General.* A summons must be served with a copy of the complaint. The plaintiff is responsible for having the summons and complaint served within the time allowed by Rule 4(m) and must furnish the necessary copies to the person who makes service.

(2) *By Whom.* Any person who is at least 18 years old and not a party may serve a summons and complaint.

(3) *By a Marshal or Someone Specially Appointed.* At the plaintiff's request, the court may order that service be made by a United States marshal or deputy marshal or by a person specially appointed by the court. The court must so order if the plaintiff is authorized to proceed in forma pauperis under 28 U.S.C. § 1915 or as a seaman under 28 U.S.C. § 1916.

(d) Waiving Service.

(1) *Requesting a Waiver.* An individual, corporation, or association that is subject to service under Rule 4(e), (f), or (h) has a duty to avoid unnecessary expenses of serving the summons. The plaintiff may notify such a defendant that an action has been commenced and request that the defendant waive service of a summons. The notice and request must:

(A) be in writing and be addressed:

(i) to the individual defendant; or

(ii) for a defendant subject to service under Rule 4(h), to an officer, a managing or general agent, or any other agent authorized by appointment or by law to receive service of process;

(B) name the court where the complaint was filed;

(C) be accompanied by a copy of the complaint, 2 copies of the waiver form appended to this Rule 4, and a prepaid means for returning the form;

(D) inform the defendant, using the form appended to this Rule 4, of the consequences of waiving and not waiving service;

(E) state the date when the request is sent;

(F) give the defendant a reasonable time of at least 30 days after the request was sent—or at least 60 days if sent to the defendant outside any judicial district of the United States—to return the waiver; and

(G) be sent by first-class mail or other reliable means.

(2) *Failure to Waive.* If a defendant located within the United States fails, without good cause, to sign and return a waiver requested by a plaintiff located within the United States, the court must impose on the defendant:

(A) the expenses later incurred in making service; and

(B) the reasonable expenses, including attorney's fees, of any motion required to collect those service expenses.

(3) *Time to Answer After a Waiver.* A defendant who, before being served with process, timely returns a waiver need not serve an answer to the complaint until 60 days after the request was sent—or until 90 days after it was sent to the defendant outside any judicial district of the United States.

(4) *Results of Filing a Waiver.* When the plaintiff files a waiver, proof of service is not required and these rules apply as if a summons and complaint had been served at the time of filing the waiver.

(5) *Jurisdiction and Venue Not Waived.* Waiving service of a summons does not waive any objection to personal jurisdiction or to venue.

(e) **Serving an Individual Within a Judicial District of the United States.** Unless federal law provides otherwise, an individual—other than a minor, an incompetent person, or a person whose waiver has been filed—may be served in a judicial district of the United States by:

(1) following state law for serving a summons in an action brought in courts of general jurisdiction in the state where the district court is located or where service is made; or

(2) doing any of the following:

(A) delivering a copy of the summons and of the complaint to the individual personally;

(B) leaving a copy of each at the individual's dwelling or usual place of abode with someone of suitable age and discretion who resides there; or

(C) delivering a copy of each to an agent authorized by appointment or by law to receive service of process.

(f) **Serving an Individual in a Foreign Country.** Unless federal law provides otherwise, an individual—other than a minor, an incompetent person, or a person whose waiver has been filed—may be served at a place not within any judicial district of the United States:

(1) by any internationally agreed means of service that is reasonably calculated to give notice, such as those authorized by the Hague Convention on the Service Abroad of Judicial and Extrajudicial Documents;

(2) if there is no internationally agreed means, or if an international agreement allows but does not specify other means, by a method that is reasonably calculated to give notice:

(A) as prescribed by the foreign country's law for service in that country in an action in its courts of general jurisdiction;

(B) as the foreign authority directs in response to a letter rogatory or letter of request; or

(C) unless prohibited by the foreign country's law, by:

(i) delivering a copy of the summons and of the complaint to the individual personally; or

(ii) using any form of mail that the clerk addresses and sends to the individual and that requires a signed receipt; or

(3) by other means not prohibited by international agreement, as the court orders.

(g) Serving a Minor or an Incompetent Person. A minor or an incompetent person in a judicial district of the United States must be served by following state law for serving a summons or like process on such a defendant in an action brought in the courts of general jurisdiction of the state where service is made. A minor or an incompetent person who is not within any judicial district of the United States must be served in the manner prescribed by Rule 4(f)(2)(A), (f)(2)(B), or (f)(3).

(h) Serving a Corporation, Partnership, or Association. Unless federal law provides otherwise or the defendant's waiver has been filed, a domestic or foreign corporation, or a partnership or other unincorporated association that is subject to suit under a common name, must be served:

(1) in a judicial district of the United States:

(A) in the manner prescribed by Rule 4(e)(1) for serving an individual; or

(B) by delivering a copy of the summons and of the complaint to an officer, a managing or general agent, or any other agent authorized by appointment or by law to receive service of process and—if the agent is one authorized by statute and the statute so requires—by also mailing a copy of each to the defendant; or

(2) at a place not within any judicial district of the United States, in any manner prescribed by Rule 4(f) for serving an individual, except personal delivery under (f)(2)(C)(i).

(i) Serving the United States and Its Agencies, Corporations, Officers, or Employees.

(1) *United States.* To serve the United States, a party must:

(A) (i) deliver a copy of the summons and of the complaint to the United States attorney for the district where the action is brought—or to an assistant United States attorney or clerical employee whom the United States attorney designates in a writing filed with the court clerk—or

(ii) send a copy of each by registered or certified mail to the civil-process clerk at the United States attorney's office;

(B) send a copy of each by registered or certified mail to the Attorney General of the United States at Washington, D.C.; and

(C) if the action challenges an order of a nonparty agency or officer of the United States, send a copy of each by registered or certified mail to the agency or officer.

(2) *Agency; Corporation; Officer or Employee Sued in an Official Capacity.* To serve a United States agency or corporation, or a United States officer or employee sued only in an official capacity, a party must serve the United States and also send a copy of the summons and of the complaint by registered or certified mail to the agency, corporation, officer, or employee.

(3) *Officer or Employee Sued Individually.* To serve a United States officer or employee sued in an individual capacity for an act or omission occurring in connection with duties performed on the United States' behalf (whether or not the officer or employee is also sued in an official capacity), a party must serve the United States and also serve the officer or employee under Rule 4(e), (f), or (g).

(4) *Extending Time.* The court must allow a party a reasonable time to cure its failure to:

    (A) serve a person required to be served under Rule 4(i)(2), if the party has served either the United States attorney or the Attorney General of the United States; or

    (B) serve the United States under Rule 4(i)(3), if the party has served the United States officer or employee.

(j) **Serving a Foreign, State, or Local Government.**

    (1) *Foreign State.* A foreign state or its political subdivision, agency, or instrumentality must be served in accordance with 28 U.S.C. § 1608.

    (2) *State or Local Government.* A state, a municipal corporation, or any other state-created governmental organization that is subject to suit must be served by:

        (A) delivering a copy of the summons and of the complaint to its chief executive officer; or

        (B) serving a copy of each in the manner prescribed by that state's law for serving a summons or like process on such a defendant.

(k) **Territorial Limits of Effective Service.**

    (1) *In General.* Serving a summons or filing a waiver of service establishes personal jurisdiction over a defendant:

        (A) who is subject to the jurisdiction of a court of general jurisdiction in the state where the district court is located;

        (B) who is a party joined under Rule 14 or 19 and is served within a judicial district of the United States and not more than 100 miles from where the summons was issued;

        (C) when authorized by a federal statute.

    (2) *Federal Claim Outside State-Court Jurisdiction.* For a claim that arises under federal law, serving a summons or filing a waiver of service establishes personal jurisdiction over a defendant if:

        (A) the defendant is not subject to jurisdiction in any state's courts of general jurisdiction; and

        (B) exercising jurisdiction is consistent with the United States Constitution and laws.

(*l*) **Proving Service.**

    (1) *Affidavit Required.* Unless service is waived, proof of service must be made to the court. Except for service by a United States marshal or deputy marshal, proof must be by the server's affidavit.

    (2) *Service Outside the United States.* Service not within any judicial district of the United States must be proved as follows:

        (A) if made under Rule 4(f)(1), as provided in the applicable treaty or convention; or

        (B) if made under Rule 4(f)(2) or (f)(3), by a receipt signed by the addressee, or by other evidence satisfying the court that the summons and complaint were delivered to the addressee.

    (3) *Validity of Service; Amending Proof.* Failure to prove service does not affect the validity of service. The court may permit proof of service to be amended.

(m) **Time Limit for Service.**

If a defendant is not served within 90 days after the complaint is filed, the court—on motion or on its own after notice to the plaintiff—must dismiss the action without prejudice against that defendant or order the service to be made within a specified time. But if the plaintiff shows good cause for the failure, the court must extend the time for service for an appropriate period. This subdivision (m) does not apply to service in a foreign country under Rule 4(f), 4(h)(2), or 4(j)(1), or to service of a notice under Rule 71.1(d)(3)(A).

(n) Asserting Jurisdiction Over Property or Assets.

(1) *Federal Law.* The court may assert jurisdiction over property if authorized by a federal statute. Notice to claimants of the property must be given as provided in the statute or by serving a summons under this rule.

(2) *State Law.* On a showing that personal jurisdiction over a defendant cannot be obtained in the district where the action is brought by reasonable efforts to serve a summons under this rule, the court may assert jurisdiction over the defendant's assets found in the district. Jurisdiction is acquired by seizing the assets under the circumstances and in the manner provided by state law in that district.

Rule 4 Notice of a Lawsuit and Request to Waive Service of Summons

[Note that the Rule 4 Notice and the following Rule 4 Waiver of the Service of Summons had been Forms 5 and 6 of the Federal Forms that were abrogated in 2015. They now are "directly incorporated into Rule 4." Committee Notes on Rules—2015 Amendment.]

(Caption)

To (name the defendant or—if the defendant is a corporation, partnership of association—name an officer or agent authorized to receive service):

Why are you getting this?

A lawsuit has been filed against you, or the entity you represent, in this court under the number shown above. A copy of the complaint is attached.

This is not a summons, or an official notice from the court. It is a request that, to avoid expenses, you waive formal service of a summons by signing and returning the enclosed waiver. To avoid these expenses, you must return the assigned waiver within ___ days (give at least 30 days or at least 60 days if the defendant is outside any judicial district of the United States) from the date shown below, which is the date this notice was sent. Two copies of the waiver form are enclosed, along with a stamped, self-addressed envelope or other prepaid means for returning one copy.

What happens next?

If you return the signed waiver, I will file it with the court. The action will then proceed as if you had been served on the date the waiver is filed, but no summons will be served on you and you will have 60 days from the date this notice is sent (see the date below) to answer the complaint (or 90 days if this notice is sent to you outside any judicial district of the United States).

If you do not return the signed waiver within the time indicated, I will arrange to have the summons and complaint served on you. And I will ask the court to require you, or the entity you represent, to pay the expenses of making service.

Please read the enclosed statement about the duty to avoid unnecessary expenses.

I certify that this request is being sent to you on the date below.

Date: _____

_____
(Signature of the attorney or unrepresented party)

_____
(Printed name)

_____
(Address)

_____
(E-mail address)
_____
(Telephone number)

Rule 4 Waiver of the Service of Summons

(Caption)

To (Name of the plaintiff's attorney or the unrepresented plaintiff)

I have received your request to waive service of a summons in this action along with a copy of the complaint, two copies of this waiver form, and prepaid means of returning one signed copy of the form to you.

I, or the entity I represent, agree to save the expense of serving a summons and complaint in this case.

I understand that I, or the entity I represent, will keep all defenses or objections to the lawsuit, the court's jurisdiction, and the venue of the action, but that I waive an objections to the absence of a summons or to service.

I also understand that I, or the entity I represent, must file and serve an answer or a motion under Rule 12 within 60 days from _____, the date when this request was sent (or 90 days if it was sent outside the United States). If I fail to do so, a default judgment will be entered against me or the entity I represent.

Date: _____

_____
(Signature of the attorney or unrepresented party)
_____
(Printed name)
_____
(Address)
_____
(E-mail address)
_____
(Telephone number)

Duty to Avoid Unnecessary Expenses of Serving a Summons

Rule 4 of the Federal Rules of Civil Procedure requires certain defendants to cooperate in saving unnecessary expenses of serving a summons and complaint. A defendant who is located in the United States and who fails to return a signed waiver of service requested by a plaintiff located in the United States will be required to pay the expenses of service, unless the defendant shows good cause for the failure.

"Good cause" does *not* include a belief that the lawsuit is groundless, or that it has been brought in an improper venue, or that the court has no jurisdiction over this matter or over the defendant or the defendant's property.

If the waiver is signed and returned, you can still make these and all other defenses and objections, but you cannot object to the absence of a summons or of service.

If you waive service, then you must, within the time specified on the waiver form, serve an answer or a motion under Rule 12 on the plaintiff and file a copy with the court. By signing and returning the waiver form, you are allowed more time to respond than if a summons had been served.

Notes on Amendments to Federal Rule 4 and Comparative State Provisions

(a)   *Amendments in 1993*

The 1993 Amendments provided significant changes and updates to Rule 4. Instead of requiring that the form of a summons follow local rules and statutes, the amendment, set out in Rule 4(a), implemented a uniform summons form and procedure to be used by all federal courts. Furthermore, the amendment broadened the reach of the federal courts under Rule 4(e) by allowing service to be effected anywhere within the United States. Moreover, with respect to actions based on a federal claim, the amendment (now Rule 4(k)(2)) provides that a federal court shall obtain federal jurisdiction over a defendant who is not subject to the jurisdiction of any single state to the fullest extent permitted by United States Constitution and laws. Finally, Rule 4(f) states a preference for the use of international agreements permitting service of process to be effected on individuals in a foreign country by "any internationally agreed means * * * such as means authorized by the Hague Convention on the Service Abroad of Judicial and Extrajudicial Documents * * *."

(b)   *Comparative State Provisions—The Illinois Scheme for Issuing and Serving Process*

1.   *Issuance of process*

Illinois Compiled Statutes ch. 735, 5/2–201(a)

Every action, unless otherwise expressly provided by statute, shall be commenced by the filing of a complaint. The clerk shall issue summons upon request of the plaintiff. The form and substance of the summons, and of all other process, and the issuance of alias process and the service of copies of pleadings shall be according to rules.

2.   *By whom served*

Illinois Compiled Statutes ch. 735, 5/2–202

(a)   Process shall be served by a sheriff, or if the sheriff is disqualified, by a coroner of some county of the State. * * * A sheriff of a county with a population of less than 2,000,000 may employ civilian personnel to serve process * * *. The court may, in its discretion upon motion, order service to be made by a private person over 18 years of age and not a party to the action. It is not necessary that service be made by a sheriff or coroner of the county in which service is made. If served or sought to be served by a sheriff or coroner, he or she shall endorse his or her return thereon, and if by a private person the return shall be by affidavit.

* * *

(b)   Summons may be served upon the defendants wherever they may be found in the State, by any person authorized to serve process. An officer may serve summons in his or her official capacity outside his or her county, but fees for mileage outside the county of the officer cannot be taxed as costs. The person serving the process in a foreign county may make return by mail.

(c)   If any sheriff, coroner, or other person to whom any process is delivered, neglects or refuses to make return of the same, the plaintiff may petition the court to enter a rule requiring the sheriff, coroner, or other person, to make return of the process on a day to be fixed by the court, or to show cause on that day why that person should not be attached for contempt of the court. The plaintiff shall then cause a written notice of the rule to be served on the sheriff, coroner, or other person. If good and sufficient cause be not shown to excuse the officer or other person, the court shall adjudge him or her guilty of a contempt, and shall impose punishment as in other cases of contempt.

* * *

3.   *Personal service within the state*

Illinois Compiled Statutes ch. 735, 5/2–203(a)

Except as otherwise expressly provided, service of summons upon an individual defendant shall be made (1) by leaving a copy of the summons with the defendant personally, (2) by leaving a copy at the defendant's usual place of abode, with some person of the family or a person residing there, of the age of 13 years or upwards, and informing that person of the contents of the summons, provided the officer or other person making service shall also send a copy of the summons in a sealed envelope with postage fully prepaid, addressed to the defendant at his or her usual place of abode, or (3) as provided in section 1–2–9.2 of the Illinois Municipal Code with respect to violation of an ordinance governing parking or standing of vehicles in cities with a population over 500,000. The certificate of the officer or affidavit of the person that he or she has sent the copy in pursuance of this Section is evidence that he or she has done so. * * *

Illinois Compiled Statutes ch. 735, 5/2–204

A private corporation may be served (1) by leaving a copy of the process with its registered agent or any officer or agent of the corporation found anywhere in the State; or (2) in any other manner now or hereafter permitted by law. A private corporation may also be notified by publication and mail in like manner and with like effect as individuals.

Illinois Compiled Statutes ch. 735, 5/2–205

(a)   A partnership sued in its firm name may be served by leaving a copy of the process with any partner personally or with any agent of the partnership found anywhere in the State. A partnership sued in its firm name may also be notified by publication and mail in like manner and with like effect as individuals.

(b)   When a personal judgment is sought against a known partner for a partnership liability the partner may be served (1) in any manner provided for service on individuals or (2) by leaving a copy of the summons for him or her with any other partner and mailing a copy of the summons in a sealed envelope with postage prepaid, addressed to the partner against whom the judgment is sought at his or her usual place of abode as shown by an affidavit filed in the cause. The certificate of the officer or the affidavit of the other person making service that he or she has mailed the copy in pursuance of this section is evidence that he or she has done so. Service on a nonresident partner against whom a personal judgment is sought may be made by leaving a copy with any other partner, and mailing, as provided herein, only if the cause of action sued on is a partnership liability arising out of the transaction of business within the State.

(c)   When a personal judgment is sought against an unknown owner in an action authorized under Section 6 of "An Act in relation to the use of an assumed name in the conduct or transaction of business in this State", approved July 17, 1941, as amended, service may be made by leaving a copy of the summons with any agent of the business and publishing notice in the manner provided by Section 2–206 of this Act. (Footnote omitted.)

Illinois Compiled Statutes ch. 735, 5/2–205.1

A voluntary unincorporated association sued in its own name may be served by leaving a copy of the process with any officer of the association personally or by leaving a copy of the process at the office of the association with an agent of the association. A voluntary unincorporated association sued in its own name may also be notified by publication and mail in like manner and with like effect as individuals.

Illinois Compiled Statutes ch. 735, 5/2–211

In actions against public, municipal, governmental or quasi-municipal corporations, summons may be served by leaving a copy with the chairperson of the county board or county clerk in the case of a county, with the mayor or city clerk in the case of a city, with the president of the board of trustees or village clerk in the case of a village, with the supervisor or town clerk in the case of a town, and with the president or clerk or other officer corresponding thereto in the case of any other public, municipal, governmental or quasi-municipal corporation or body.

Illinois Compiled Statutes ch. 735, 5/2–212

Any trustee of a corporation or its property or any receiver may be served with summons (1) in any manner provided for service on individuals or corporations, as is appropriate, or (2) by leaving a copy thereof with any agent in the employ of the trustee or receiver anywhere in the State. The trustee or receiver may also be notified by publication and mail in like manner and with like effect as individuals.

4. *Personal service on party not inhabitant of or found within state*

Illinois Compiled Statutes ch. 735, 5/2–208

(a)   Personal service of summons may be made upon any party outside the State. If upon a citizen or resident of this State or upon a person who has submitted to the jurisdiction of the courts of this State, it shall have the force and effect of personal service of summons within this State; otherwise it shall have the force and effect of service by publication.

(b)   The service of summons shall be made in like manner as service within this State, by any person over 18 years of age not a party to the action. No order of court is required. An affidavit of the server shall be filed stating the time, manner and place of service. The court may consider the affidavit, or any other competent proofs, in determining whether service has been properly made.

(c)   No default shall be entered until the expiration of at least 30 days after service. A default judgment entered on such service may be set aside only on a showing which would be timely and sufficient to set aside a default judgment entered on personal service within this State.

5. *Service by publication*

Illinois Compiled Statutes ch. 735, 5/2–206(a)

Whenever, in any action affecting property or status within the jurisdiction of the court, including an action to obtain the specific performance, reformation, or rescission of a contract for the conveyance of land, plaintiff or his or her attorney shall file, at the office of the clerk of the court in which the action is pending, an affidavit showing that the defendant resides or has gone out of this State, or on due inquiry cannot be found, or is concealed within this State, so that process cannot be served upon him or her and stating the place of residence of the defendant, if known, or that upon diligent inquiry his or her place of residence cannot be ascertained, the clerk shall cause publication to be made in some newspaper published in the county in which the action is pending. If there is no newspaper published in that county, then the publication shall be in a newspaper published in an adjoining county in this State, having a circulation in the county in which action is pending. The publication shall contain notice of the pendency of the action, the title of the court, the title of the case, showing the names of the first named plaintiff and the first named defendant, the number of the case, the names of the parties to be served by publication, and the date on or after which default may be entered against such party. The clerk shall also, within 10 days of the first publication of the notice, send a copy thereof by mail, addressed to each defendant whose place of residence is stated in such affidavit. The certificate of the clerk that he or she has sent the copy in pursuance of this Section is evidence that he or she has done so.

Illinois Compiled Statutes ch. 735, 5/2–207

The notice required in the preceding section may be given at any time after the commencement of the action, and shall be published at least once in each week for 3 successive weeks. No default or proceeding shall be taken against any defendant not served with summons, or a copy of the complaint, and not appearing, unless the first publication be at least 30 days prior to the time when the default or other proceeding is sought to be taken.

6. *Service when action based on attachment*

Illinois Compiled Statutes ch. 735, 5/4–101

In any court having competent jurisdiction, a creditor having a money claim, whether liquidated or unliquidated, and whether sounding in contract or tort or based upon a statutory cause of action created by law in favor of the People of the State of Illinois, or any agency of the State, may have an attachment against the property of his or her debtor, or that of any one or more of several debtors, either at the time of commencement of the action or thereafter, when the claim exceeds $20, in any one of the following cases:

1.   Where the debtor is not a resident of this State.

2. When the debtor conceals himself or herself or stands in defiance of an officer, so that process cannot be served upon him or her.

3. Where the debtor has departed from this State with the intention of having his or her effects removed from this State.

4. Where the debtor is about to depart from this State with the intention of having his or her effects removed from this State.

5. Where the debtor is about to remove his or her property from this State to the injury of such creditor.

6. Where the debtor has within 2 years preceding the filing of the affidavit required, fraudulently conveyed or assigned his or her effects, or a part thereof, so as to hinder or delay his or her creditors.

7. Where the debtor has, within 2 years prior to the filing of such affidavit, fraudulently concealed or disposed of his or her property so as to hinder or delay his or her creditors.

8. Where the debtor is about fraudulently to conceal, assign, or otherwise dispose of his or her property or effects, so as to hinder or delay his or her creditors.

9. Where the debt sued for was fraudulently contracted on the part of the debtor. The statements of the debtor, his or her agent or attorney, which constitute the fraud, shall have been reduced to writing, and his or her signature attached thereto, by himself or herself, agent or attorney.

10. When the debtor is a person convicted of first degree murder or * * * [other serious] felony, or found not guilty by reason of insanity or guilty but mentally ill of first degree murder or * * * [such other felony], against the creditor and that crime makes the creditor a "victim" under the Criminal Victims' Asset Discovery Act.

11. When the debtor is referred by the Department of Corrections to the Attorney General under Section 3–7–6 of the Unified Code of Corrections to recover the expenses incurred as a result of that debtor's cost of incarceration.

Illinois Compiled Statutes ch. 735, 5/4–126

The sheriff or any other person authorized to serve summons shall, in like manner as summons are served in ordinary civil cases, summon, wherever they may be found in the State, the persons mentioned in such order of attachment as garnishees and all other persons whom the creditor shall designate as having any property, effects, choses in action or credits in their possession or power, belonging to the defendant, or who are in any way indebted to such defendant, the same as if their names had been inserted in such order for attachment. The persons so summoned shall be considered as garnishees. The return shall state the names of all persons so summoned, and the date of such service on each.

Persons summoned as garnishees shall thereafter hold any property, effects, choses in action or credits in their possession or power belonging to the defendant which are not exempt, subject to the court's order in such proceeding, and shall not pay to the defendant any indebtedness owed to him or her subject to such order, and such property, effects, choses in action, credits and debts shall be considered to have been attached and the plaintiff's claim to have become a lien thereon pending such action.

(c) *Comparative State Provisions—California*
Provision for Service of Summons by Mail

California Civil Procedure Code § 415.30

(a) A summons may be served by mail as provided in this section. A copy of the summons and of the complaint shall be mailed (by first-class mail or airmail, postage prepaid) to the person to be served, together with two copies of the notice and acknowledgment provided for in subdivision (b) and a return envelope, postage prepaid, addressed to the sender.

(b) The notice specified in subdivision (a) shall be in substantially the following form:

(Title of court and cause, with action number, to
be inserted by the sender prior to mailing)

NOTICE

To: (Here state the name of the person to be served.)

This summons is served pursuant to Section 415.30 of the California Code of Civil Procedure. Failure to complete this form and return it to the sender within 20 days may subject you (or the party on whose behalf you are being served) to liability for the payment of any expenses incurred in serving a summons upon you in any other manner permitted by law. If you are served on behalf of a corporation, unincorporated association (including a partnership), or other entity, this form must be signed in the name of such entity by you or by a person authorized to receive service of process on behalf of such entity. In all other cases, this form must be signed by you personally or by a person authorized by you to acknowledge receipt of summons. Section 415.30 provides that this summons is deemed served on the date of execution of an acknowledgment of receipt of summons.

....
Signature of sender

ACKNOWLEDGMENT OF RECEIPT OF SUMMONS

This acknowledges receipt on (insert date) of a copy of the summons and of the complaint at (insert address).

Date: ....
(Date this acknowledgment is executed)

....
Signature of person acknowledging receipt, with
title if acknowledgment is made on behalf of
another person

(c) Service of a summons pursuant to this section is deemed complete on the date a written acknowledgment of receipt of summons is executed, if such acknowledgment thereafter is returned to the sender.

(d) If the person to whom a copy of the summons and of the complaint are mailed pursuant to this section fails to complete and return the acknowledgment form set forth in subdivision (b) within 20 days from the date of such mailing, the party to whom the summons was mailed shall be liable for reasonable expenses thereafter incurred in serving or attempting to serve the party by another method permitted by this chapter, and, except for good cause shown, the court in which the action is pending, upon motion, with or without notice, shall award the party such expenses whether or not he is otherwise entitled to recover his costs in the action.

(e) A notice or acknowledgment of receipt in form approved by the Judicial Council is deemed to comply with this section.

Rule 4.1. Serving Other Process

(a) **In General.** Process—other than a summons under Rule 4 or a subpoena under Rule 45— must be served by a United States marshal or deputy marshal or by a person specially appointed for that purpose. It may be served anywhere within the territorial limits of the state where the district court is located and, if authorized by a federal statute, beyond those limits. Proof of service must be made under Rule 4(*l*).

(b) **Enforcing Orders: Committing for Civil Contempt.** An order committing a person for civil contempt of a decree or injunction issued to enforce federal law may be served and enforced in any district. Any other order in a civil-contempt proceeding may be served only in the state where the issuing court is located or elsewhere in the United States within 100 miles from where the order was issued.

Rule 5. Serving and Filing Pleadings and Other Papers

(a) Service: When Required.

(1) *In General.* Unless these rules provide otherwise, each of the following papers must be served on every party:

(A) an order stating that service is required;

(B) a pleading filed after the original complaint, unless the court orders otherwise under Rule 5(c) because there are numerous defendants;

(C) a discovery paper required to be served on a party, unless the court orders otherwise;

(D) a written motion, except one that may be heard ex parte; and

(E) a written notice, appearance, demand, or offer of judgment, or any similar paper.

(2) *If a Party Fails to Appear.* No service is required on a party who is in default for failing to appear. But a pleading that asserts a new claim for relief against such a party must be served on that party under Rule 4.

(3) *Seizing Property.* If an action is begun by seizing property and no person is or need be named as a defendant, any service required before the filing of an appearance, answer, or claim must be made on the person who had custody or possession of the property when it was seized.

(b) Service: How Made.

(1) *Serving an Attorney.* If a party is represented by an attorney, service under this rule must be made on the attorney unless the court orders service on the party.

(2) *Service in General.* A paper is served under this rule by:

(A) handing it to the person;

(B) leaving it:

(i) at the person's office with a clerk or other person in charge or, if no one is in charge, in a conspicuous place in the office; or

(ii) if the person has no office or the office is closed, at the person's dwelling or usual place of abode with someone of suitable age and discretion who resides there;

(C) mailing it to the person's last known address—in which event service is complete upon mailing;

(D) leaving it with the court clerk if the person has no known address;

(E) sending it to a registered user by filing it with the court's electronic-filing system or sending it by other electronic means that the person consented to in writing—in either of which events service is complete upon filing or sending, but is not effective if the filer or sender learns that it did not reach the person to be served; or

(F) delivering it by any other means that the person consented to in writing—in which event service is complete when the person making service delivers it to the agency designated to make delivery.

(3) *Using Court Facilities.* [Abrogated.]

(c) Serving Numerous Defendants.

(1) *In General.* If an action involves an unusually large number of defendants, the court may, on motion or on its own, order that:

(A) defendants' pleadings and replies to them need not be served on other defendants;

(B) any crossclaim, counterclaim, avoidance, or affirmative defense in those pleadings and replies to them will be treated as denied or avoided by all other parties; and

(C) filing any such pleading and serving it on the plaintiff constitutes notice of the pleading to all parties.

(2) *Notifying Parties.* A copy of every such order must be served on the parties as the court directs.

(d) Filing.

(1) *Required Filings; Certificate of Service.*

(A) *Papers After the Complaint.* Any paper after the complaint that is required to be served must be filed no later than a reasonable time after service. But disclosures under Rule 26(a)(1) or (2) and the following discovery requests and responses must not be filed until they are used in the proceedings or the court orders filing: depositions, interrogatories, requests for documents or tangible things or to permit entry onto land, and requests for admission.

(B) *Certificate of Service.* No certificate of service is required when a paper is served by filing it with the court's electronic-filing system. When a paper that is required to be served is served by other means:

(i) if the paper is filed, a certificate of service must be filed with it or within a reasonable time after service; and

(ii) if the paper is not filed, a certificate of service need not be filed unless filing is required by court order or by local rule.

(2) *Nonelectronic Filing.* A paper not filed electronically is filed by delivering it:

(A) to the clerk; or

(B) to a judge who agrees to accept it for filing and who must then note the filing date on the paper and promptly send it to the clerk.

(3) *Electronic Filing and Signing.*

(A) *By a Represented Person—Generally Required; Exceptions.* A person represented by an attorney must file electronically unless nonelectronic filing is allowed by the court for good cause or is allowed or required by local rule.

(B) *By an Unrepresented Person—When Allowed or Required.* A person not represented by an attorney:

(i) may file electronically only if allowed by court order or local rule; and

(ii) may be required to file electronically only by court order, or by local rule that includes reasonable exceptions.

(C) *Signing.* A filing made through a person's electronic-filing account and authorized by that person, together with that person's name on a signature block, constitutes the person's signature.

(D) *Same as a Written Paper.* A paper filed electronically is a written paper for purposes of these rules.

(4) *Acceptance by the Clerk.* The clerk must not refuse to file a paper solely because it is not in the form prescribed by these rules or by a local rule or practice.

Note on 2001 Amendments to Federal Rule 5(b)

The amended rule added a new provision, [now 5(b)(2)(E)], permitting service by electronic means, but only with the consent of the person served. The latter requirement is in recognition of the fact that entry into the world of electronic communication is not yet universal. Consent must be in writing. Consent should include the identity of the person or persons to whom transmissions may be sent, their electronic addresses, the format to be used, and the scope and duration of the consent. When electronic means are used, service is effective, as in the case of mailing, upon transmission.

The rule provides that if the party making service becomes aware that the attempted electronic service did not reach the person to be served, the service is not effective. Unfortunately the rule fails to provide a time limit during which the party making service must learn that the service was ineffective. This could raise a serious problem long after a matter has been completed.

Rule 5.1. Constitutional Challenge to a Statute—Notice, Certification, and Intervention

(a) Notice by a Party. A party that files a pleading, written motion, or other paper drawing into question the constitutionality of a federal or state statute must promptly:

(1) file a notice of constitutional question stating the question and identifying the paper that raises it, if:

(A) a federal statute is questioned and the parties do not include the United States, one of its agencies, or one of its officers or employees in an official capacity; or

(B) a state statute is questioned and the parties do not include the state, one of its agencies, or one of its officers or employees in an official capacity; and

(2) serve the notice and paper on the Attorney General of the United States if a federal statute is questioned—or on the state attorney general if a state statute is questioned—either by certified or registered mail or by sending it to an electronic address designated by the attorney general for this purpose.

(b) Certification by the Court. The court must, under 28 U.S.C. § 2403, certify to the appropriate attorney general that a statute has been questioned.

(c) Intervention; Final Decision on the Merits. Unless the court sets a later time, the attorney general may intervene within 60 days after the notice is filed or after the court certifies the challenge, whichever is earlier. Before the time to intervene expires, the court may reject the constitutional challenge, but may not enter a final judgment holding the statute unconstitutional.

(d) No Forfeiture. A party's failure to file and serve the notice, or the court's failure to certify, does not forfeit a constitutional claim or defense that is otherwise timely asserted.

Rule 5.2. Privacy Protection For Filings Made With the Court

(a) Redacted Filings. Unless the court orders otherwise, in an electronic or paper filing with the court that contains an individual's social-security number, taxpayer-identification number, or birth date, the name of an individual known to be a minor, or a financial-account number, a party or nonparty making the filing may include only:

(1) the last four digits of the social-security number and taxpayer-identification number;

(2) the year of the individual's birth;

(3) the minor's initials; and

(4) the last four digits of the financial-account number.

(b) Exemptions from the Redaction Requirement. The redaction requirement does not apply to the following:

(1) a financial-account number that identifies the property allegedly subject to forfeiture in a forfeiture proceeding;

(2) the record of an administrative or agency proceeding;

(3) the official record of a state-court proceeding;

(4) the record of a court or tribunal, if that record was not subject to the redaction requirement when originally filed;

(5) a filing covered by Rule 5.2(c) or (d); and

(6) a pro se filing in an action brought under 28 U.S.C. §§ 2241, 2254, or 2255.

(c) Limitations on Remote Access to Electronic Files; Social-Security Appeals and Immigration Cases. Unless the court orders otherwise, in an action for benefits under the Social Security Act, and in an action or proceeding relating to an order of removal, to relief from removal, or to immigration benefits or detention, access to an electronic file is authorized as follows:

(1) the parties and their attorneys may have remote electronic access to any part of the case file, including the administrative record;

(2) any other person may have electronic access to the full record at the courthouse, but may have remote electronic access only to:

(A) the docket maintained by the court; and

(B) an opinion, order, judgment, or other disposition of the court, but not any other part of the case file or the administrative record.

(d) Filings Made Under Seal. The court may order that a filing be made under seal without redaction. The court may later unseal the filing or order the person who made the filing to file a redacted version for the public record.

(e) Protective Orders. For good cause, the court may by order in a case:

(1) require redaction of additional information; or

(2) limit or prohibit a nonparty's remote electronic access to a document filed with the court.

(f) Option for Additional Unredacted Filing Under Seal. A person making a redacted filing may also file an unredacted copy under seal. The court must retain the unredacted copy as part of the record.

(g) Option for Filing a Reference List. A filing that contains redacted information may be filed together with a reference list that identifies each item of redacted information and specifies an appropriate identifier that uniquely corresponds to each item listed. The list must be filed under seal and may be amended as of right. Any reference in the case to a listed identifier will be construed to refer to the corresponding item of information.

(h) Waiver of Protection of Identifiers. A person waives the protection of Rule 5.2(a) as to the person's own information by filing it without redaction and not under seal.

Rule 6. Computing and Extending Time; Time for Motion Papers

(a) Computing Time. The following rules apply in computing any time period specified in these rules, in any local rule or court order, or any statute that does not specify a method of computing time.

(1) *Period Stated in Days or a Longer Unit.* When the period is stated in days or a longer unit of time:

(A) exclude the day of the event that triggers the period;

(B) count every day, including intermediate Saturdays, Sundays, and legal holidays; and

(C) include the last day of the period, but if the last day is a Saturday, Sunday, or legal holiday, the period continues to run until the end of the next day that is not a Saturday, Sunday, or legal holiday.

(2) *Period Stated in Hours.* When the period is stated in hours:

(A) begin counting immediately on the occurrence of the event that triggers the period;

(B) count every hour, including hours during intermediate Saturdays, Sundays, and legal holidays; and

(C) if the period would end on a Saturday, Sunday, or legal holiday, the period continues to run until the same time on the next day that is not a Saturday, Sunday, or legal holiday.

(3) *Inaccessibility of the Clerk's Office.* Unless the court orders otherwise, if the clerk's office is inaccessible:

(A) on the last day for filing under Rule 6(a)(1), then the time for filing is extended to the first accessible day that is not a Saturday, Sunday, or legal holiday; or

(B) during the last hour for filing under Rule 6(a)(2), then the time for filing is extended to the same time on the first accessible day that is not a Saturday, Sunday, or legal holiday.

(4) *"Last Day" Defined.* Unless a different time is set by a statute, local rule, or court order, the last day ends:

(A) for electronic filing, at midnight in the court's time zone; and

(B) for filing by other means, when the clerk's office is scheduled to close.

(5) *"Next Day" Defined.* The "next day" is determined by continuing to count forward when the period is measured after an event and backward when measured before an event.

(6) *"Legal Holiday" Defined.* As used in these rules, "legal holiday" means:

(A) the day set aside by statute for observing New Year's Day, Martin Luther King Jr.'s Birthday, Washington's Birthday, Memorial Day, Independence Day, Labor Day, Columbus Day, Veterans' Day, Thanksgiving Day, or Christmas Day; and

(B) any day declared a holiday by the President or Congress; and

(C) for periods that are measured after an event, any other day declared a holiday by the state where the district court is located.

(b) Extending Time.

(1) *In General.* When an act may or must be done within a specified time, the court may, for good cause, extend the time:

(A) with or without motion or notice if the court acts, or if a request is made, before the original time or its extension expires; or

(B) on motion made after the time has expired if the party failed to act because of excusable neglect.

(2) *Exceptions.* A court must not extend the time to act under Rules 50(b) and (d), 52(b), 59(b), (d), and (e), and 60(b).

(c) Motions, Notices of Hearing, and Affidavits.

(1) *In General.* A written motion and notice of the hearing must be served at least 14 days before the time specified for the hearing, with the following exceptions:

(A) when the motion may be heard ex parte;

(B) when these rules set a different time; or

(C) when a court order—which a party may, for good cause, apply for ex parte—sets a different time.

(2) *Supporting Affidavit.* Any affidavit supporting a motion must be served with the motion. Except as Rule 59(c) provides otherwise, any opposing affidavit must be served at least 7 days before the hearing, unless the court permits service at another time.

(d) Additional Time After Certain Kinds of Service. When a party may or must act within a specified time after being served and service is made under Rule 5(b)(2)(C) (mail), D (leaving with the clerk), or F (other methods consented to), 3 days are added after the period would otherwise expire under Rule 6(a).

TITLE III. PLEADINGS AND MOTIONS

Rule 7. Pleadings Allowed; Form of Motions and Other Papers

(a) Pleadings. Only these pleadings are allowed:

(1) a complaint;

(2) an answer to a complaint;

(3) an answer to a counterclaim designated as a counterclaim;

(4) an answer to a crossclaim;

(5) a third-party complaint;

(6) an answer to a third-party complaint; and

(7) if the court orders one, a reply to an answer.

(b) Motions and Other Papers.

(1) *In General.* A request for a court order must be made by motion. The motion must:

(A) be in writing unless made during a hearing or trial;

(B) state with particularity the grounds for seeking the order; and

(C) state the relief sought.

(2) *Form.* The rules governing captions and other matters of form in pleadings apply to motions and other papers.

Comparative State Provisions

Pennsylvania Rules of Civil Procedure 1017(a)

(a)   Except as provided by Rule 1041.1, the pleadings in an action are limited to

(1)   a complaint and an answer thereto,

(2)   a reply if the answer contains new matter, a counterclaim or a crossclaim,

(3)   a counter-reply if the reply to a counterclaim or crossclaim contains new matter,

(4)   a preliminary objection and a response thereto.

Pennsylvania Rules of Civil Procedure 1029(b) & (d)

(b)   Averments in a pleading to which a responsive pleading is required are admitted when not denied specifically or by necessary implication. * * *

(d)   Averments in a pleading to which no responsive pleading is required shall be deemed to be denied.

Rule 7.1. Disclosure Statement

(a) Who Must File; Contents. A nongovernmental corporate party must file two copies of a disclosure statement that:

(1) identifies any parent corporation and any publicly held corporation owning 10% or more of its stock; or

(2) states that there is no such corporation.

(b) Time to File; Supplemental Filing. A party must:

(1) file the disclosure statement with its first appearance, pleading, petition, motion, response, or other request addressed to the court; and

(2) promptly file a supplemental statement if any required information changes.

Rule 8. General Rules of Pleading

(a) Claim for Relief. A pleading that states a claim for relief must contain:

(1) a short and plain statement of the grounds for the court's jurisdiction, unless the court already has jurisdiction and the claim needs no new jurisdictional support;

(2) a short and plain statement of the claim showing that the pleader is entitled to relief; and

(3) a demand for the relief sought, which may include relief in the alternative or different types of relief.

(b) Defenses; Admissions and Denials.

(1) *In General.* In responding to a pleading, a party must:

(A) state in short and plain terms its defenses to each claim asserted against it; and

(B) admit or deny the allegations asserted against it by an opposing party.

(2) *Denials—Responding to the Substance.* A denial must fairly respond to the substance of the allegation.

(3) *General and Specific Denials.* A party that intends in good faith to deny all the allegations of a pleading—including the jurisdictional grounds—may do so by a general denial. A party that does not intend to deny all the allegations must either specifically deny designated allegations or generally deny all except those specifically admitted.

(4) *Denying Part of an Allegation.* A party that intends in good faith to deny only part of an allegation must admit the part that is true and deny the rest.

(5) *Lacking Knowledge or Information.* A party that lacks knowledge or information sufficient to form a belief about the truth of an allegation must so state, and the statement has the effect of a denial.

(6) *Effect of Failing to Deny.* An allegation—other than one relating to the amount of damages—is admitted if a responsive pleading is required and the allegation is not denied. If a responsive pleading is not required, an allegation is considered denied or avoided.

(c) Affirmative Defenses.

(1) *In General.* In responding to a pleading, a party must affirmatively state any avoidance or affirmative defense, including:

- accord and satisfaction;

- arbitration and award;

- assumption of risk;

- contributory negligence;

- duress;

- estoppel;

- failure of consideration;

- fraud;

- illegality;

- injury by fellow servant;

- laches;

- license;

- payment;

- release;

- res judicata;

- statute of frauds;

- statute of limitations; and

- waiver.

(2) *Mistaken Designation.* If a party mistakenly designates a defense as a counterclaim, or a counterclaim as a defense, the court must, if justice requires, treat the pleading as though it were correctly designated, and may impose terms for doing so.

(d) **Pleading to Be Concise and Direct; Alternative Statements; Inconsistency.**

(1) *In General.* Each allegation must be simple, concise, and direct. No technical form is required.

(2) *Alternative Statements of a Claim or Defense.* A party may set out two or more statements of a claim or defense alternatively or hypothetically, either in a single count or defense or in separate ones. If a party makes alternative statements, the pleading is sufficient if any one of them is sufficient.

(3) *Inconsistent Claims or Defenses.* A party may state as many separate claims or defenses as it has, regardless of consistency.

(e) **Construing Pleadings.** Pleadings must be construed so as to do justice.

Comparative State Provisions

(a)   *Rule 8(a)*

1.   *Stating a right to relief*

California Civil Procedure Code § 425.10(a)(1)

A complaint or crosscomplaint shall contain * * * the following:

(1)   A statement of the facts constituting the cause of action, in ordinary and concise language.

New York Civil Practice Law and Rules 3013

Statements in a pleading shall be sufficiently particular to give the court and parties notice of the transactions, occurrences, or series of transactions or occurrences, intended to be proved and the material elements of each cause of action or defense.

New York Civil Practice Law and Rules 3041

Any party may require any other party to give a bill of particulars of such party's claim, or a copy of the items of the account alleged in a pleading. * * *

New York Civil Practice Law and Rules 3043

(a) Specified particulars. In actions to recover for personal injuries the following particulars may be required:

(1)   The date and approximate time of day of the occurrence;

(2)   Its approximate location;

(3)   General statement of the acts or omissions constituting the negligence claimed;

(4)   Where notice of a condition is a prerequisite, whether actual or constructive notice is claimed;

(5)   If actual notice is claimed, a statement of when and to whom it was given;

(6)   Statement of the injuries and description of those claimed to be permanent, and in an action designated in * * * [§ 5104(a)] of the insurance law, for personal injuries arising out of negligence in the use or operation of a motor vehicle in this state, in what respect plaintiff has sustained a serious injury, as defined in * * * [§ 5102(d)] of the insurance law, or economic loss greater than basic economic loss, as defined in * * * [§ 5102(a)] of the insurance law;

(7)   Length of time confined to bed and to house;

(8)   Length of time incapacitated from employment; and

(9)   Total amounts claimed as special damages for physicians' services and medical supplies; loss of earnings, with name and address of the employer; hospital expenses; nurses' services.

(b) Supplemental bill of particulars without leave. A party may serve a supplemental bill of particulars with respect to claims of continuing special damages and disabilities without leave of court at any time, but not less than thirty days prior to trial. Provided however that no new cause of action may be alleged or new injury claimed * * *.

(c) Discretion of court. Nothing contained in the foregoing shall be deemed to limit the court in denying in a proper case, any one or more of the foregoing particulars, or in a proper case, in granting other, further or different particulars.

North Carolina Rules of Civil Procedure, Rule 84. Forms (3) Complaint for Negligence

1.   On _____, ___, at [name of place where accident occurred], defendant negligently drove a motor vehicle against plaintiff who was then crossing said street.

2.   Defendant was negligent in that:

(a)   Defendant drove at an excessive speed.

(b)   Defendant drove through a red light.

(c)   Defendant failed to yield the right-of-way to plaintiff in a marked crosswalk.

3.   As a result plaintiff was thrown down and had his leg broken and was otherwise injured, was prevented from transacting his business, suffered great pain of body and mind, and incurred expenses for medical attention and hospitalization [in the sum of one thousand dollars] (or) [in an amount not yet determined].

Wherefore, plaintiff demands judgment against defendant in the sum of _____ dollars and costs.

2.   *Pleading the relief sought*

California Civil Procedure Code § 425.10(a)(2), (b)

[A complaint or cross-complaint shall contain:]

(a)(2) A demand for judgment for the relief to which the pleader claims to be entitled. If the recovery of money or damages is demanded, the amount demanded shall be stated.

(b)   Notwithstanding subdivision (a), where an action is brought to recover actual or punitive damages for personal injury or wrongful death, the amount demanded shall not be stated * * *.

Florida Statutes Annotated § 768.72(1)

In any civil action, no claim for punitive damages shall be permitted unless there is a reasonable showing by evidence in the record or proffered by the claimant which would provide a reasonable basis for recovery of such damages. The claimant may move to amend her or his complaint to assert a claim for punitive damages as allowed by the rules of civil procedure. The rules of civil procedure shall be liberally construed so as to allow the claimant discovery of evidence which appears reasonably calculated to lead to admissible evidence on the issue of punitive damages. No discovery of financial worth shall proceed until after the pleading concerning punitive damages is permitted.

Georgia Code Annotated § 9–11–8(a)(2)(B)

[An original complaint shall contain:]

A demand for judgment for the relief to which the pleader deems himself entitled; provided, however, that in actions for medical malpractice, as defined in this Code section, in which a claim for unliquidated damages is made for $10,000.00 or less, the pleadings shall contain a demand for judgment in a sum certain; and, in actions for medical malpractice in which a claim for unliquidated damages is made for a sum exceeding $10,000.00, the demand for judgment shall state that the pleader "demands judgment in excess of $10,000.00," and no further monetary amount shall be stated. Relief in the alternative or of several different types may be demanded.

Illinois Compiled Statutes ch. 735, 5/2–604

Every count in every complaint and counterclaim shall contain specific prayers for the relief to which the pleader deems himself or herself entitled except that in actions for injury to the person, no ad damnum may be pleaded except to the minimum extent necessary to comply with the circuit rules of assignment where the claim is filed. Relief may be requested in the alternative. Prayers for relief which the allegations of the pleadings do not sustain may be objected to on motion or in the answering pleading. In actions for injury to the person, any complaint filed which contains an ad damnum, except to the minimum extent necessary to comply with the circuit rules of assignment where the claim is filed, shall, on motion of a defendant or on the court's own motion, be dismissed without prejudice. Except in case of default, the prayer for relief does not limit the relief obtainable, but where other relief is sought the court shall, by proper orders, and upon terms that may be just, protect the adverse party against prejudice by reason of surprise. In case of default, if relief is sought, whether by amendment, counterclaim, or otherwise, beyond that prayed in the pleading to which the party is in default, notice shall be given the defaulted party as provided by rule.

Nothing in this Section shall be construed as prohibiting the defendant from requesting of the plaintiff by interrogatory the amount of damages which will be sought.

New York Civil Practice Law and Rules 3017(c)

In an action to recover damages for personal injuries or wrongful death, the complaint, counterclaim, crossclaim, interpleader complaint, and third-party complaint shall contain a prayer for general relief but shall not state the amount of damages to which the pleader deems himself entitled. If the action is brought in the supreme court, the pleading shall also state whether or not the amount of damages sought exceeds the jurisdictional limits of all lower courts which would otherwise have jurisdiction. Provided, however, that a party against whom an action to recover damages for personal injuries or wrongful death is brought, may at any time request a supplemental demand setting forth the total damages to which the pleader deems himself entitled. A supplemental demand shall be provided by the party bringing the action within fifteen days of the request. In the event the supplemental demand is not served within fifteen days, the court, on motion, may order that it be served. * * *

(b) Rule 8(b)(1)–(4)

1.   *In general*

Illinois Compiled Statutes ch. 735, 5/2–610

(a)   Every answer and subsequent pleading shall contain an explicit admission or denial of each allegation of the pleading to which it relates.

(b)   Every allegation, except allegations of damages, not explicitly denied is admitted, unless the party states in his or her pleading that he or she has no knowledge thereof sufficient to form a belief, and attaches an affidavit of the truth of the statement of want of knowledge, or unless the party has had no opportunity to deny.

(c)   Denials must not be evasive, but must fairly answer the substance of the allegation denied.

(d)   If a party wishes to raise an issue as to the amount of damages only, he or she may do so by stating in his or her pleading that he or she desires to contest only the amount of the damages.

2.   *Importance of verification*

California Civil Procedure Code § 431.30(d)

If the complaint is * * * not verified, a general denial is sufficient but only puts in issue the material allegations of the complaint. If the complaint is verified, * * * [then, with exceptions for certain actions,] the denial of the allegations shall be made positively or according to the information and belief of the defendant. * * *

California Civil Procedure Code § 446(a)

Every pleading shall be subscribed by the party or his or her attorney. * * * When the complaint is verified, the answer shall be verified. * * *

(c) Rule 8(b)(5)–(6)

New York Civil Practice Law and Rules 3018(a)

A party shall deny those statements known or believed by him to be untrue. He shall specify those statements as to the truth of which he lacks knowledge or information sufficient to form a belief and this shall have the effect of a denial. All other statements of a pleading are deemed admitted, except that where no responsive pleading is permitted they are deemed denied or avoided.

(d) Rule 8(c)

New York Civil Practice Law and Rules 3018(b)

A party shall plead all matters which if not pleaded would be likely to take the adverse party by surprise or would raise issues of fact not appearing on the face of a prior pleading such as arbitration and award, collateral estoppel, culpable conduct claimed in diminution of damages * * *, discharge in bankruptcy, facts showing illegality either by statute or common law, fraud, infancy or other disability of the party defending, payment, release, res judicata, statute of frauds, or statute of limitation. The application of this subdivision shall not be confined to the instances enumerated.

(e) Rule 8(d)(1)

Colorado Rule of Civil Procedure 8(e)(1)

Each averment of a pleading shall be simple, concise, and direct. When a pleader is without direct knowledge, allegations may be made upon information and belief. No technical forms of pleading or motions are required. Pleadings otherwise meeting the requirements of these rules shall not be considered objectionable for failure to state ultimate facts as distinguished from conclusions of law.

(f) Rule 8(d)(2)–(3)

Georgia Code Annotated § 9–11–8(e)(2)

A party may set forth two or more statements of a claim or defense alternatively or hypothetically, either in one count or defense or in separate counts or defenses. When two or more statements are made in the alternative and one of them, if made independently, would be sufficient, the pleading is not made insufficient by the insufficiency of one or more of the alternative statements. A party may also state as many separate claims or defenses as he has, regardless of consistency and whether based on legal or on equitable grounds or on both. * * *

Rule 9. Pleading Special Matters

(a) Capacity or Authority to Sue; Legal Existence.

(1) *In General.* Except when required to show that the court has jurisdiction, a pleading need not allege:

(A) a party's capacity to sue or be sued;

(B) a party's authority to sue or be sued in a representative capacity; or

(C) the legal existence of an organized association of persons that is made a party.

(2) *Raising Those Issues.* To raise any of those issues, a party must do so by a specific denial, which must state any supporting facts that are peculiarly within the party's knowledge.

(b) Fraud or Mistake; Conditions of Mind. In alleging fraud or mistake, a party must state with particularity the circumstances constituting fraud or mistake. Malice, intent, knowledge, and other conditions of a person's mind may be alleged generally.

(c) Conditions Precedent. In pleading conditions precedent, it suffices to allege generally that all conditions precedent have occurred or been performed. But when denying that a condition precedent has occurred or been performed, a party must do so with particularity.

(d) Official Document or Act. In pleading an official document or official act, it suffices to allege that the document was legally issued or the act legally done.

(e) Judgment. In pleading a judgment or decision of a domestic or foreign court, a judicial or quasi-judicial tribunal, or a board or officer, it suffices to plead the judgment or decision without showing jurisdiction to render it.

(f) Time and Place. An allegation of time or place is material when testing the sufficiency of a pleading.

(g) Special Damages. If an item of special damage is claimed, it must be specifically stated.

(h) Admiralty or Maritime Claim.

(1) *How Designated.* If a claim for relief is within the admiralty or maritime jurisdiction and also within the court's subject-matter jurisdiction on some other ground, the pleading may designate the claim as an admiralty or maritime claim for purposes of Rules 14(c), 38(e), and 82 and the Supplemental Rules for Admiralty or Maritime Claims and Asset Forfeiture Actions. A claim cognizable only in the admiralty or maritime jurisdiction is an admiralty or maritime claim for those purposes, whether or not so designated.

(2) *Designation for Appeal.* A case that includes an admiralty or maritime claim within this subdivision (h) is an admiralty case within 28 U.S.C. § 1292(a)(3).

Comparative State Provisions

(a) *In General*

New York Civil Practice Law and Rules 3015

(a) **Conditions precedent.** The performance or occurrence of a condition precedent in a contract need not be pleaded. A denial of performance or occurrence shall be made specifically and with particularity. In case of such denial, the party relying upon the performance or occurrence shall be required to prove on the trial only such performance or occurrence as shall have been so specified.

(b) **Corporate status.** Where any party is a corporation, the complaint shall so state and, where known, it shall specify the state, country or government by or under whose laws the party was created.

(c) **Judgment, decision or determination.** A judgment, decision or other determination of a court, judicial or quasi-judicial tribunal, or of a board or officer, may be pleaded without stating matter showing jurisdiction to render it.

(d) **Signatures.** Unless specifically denied in the pleadings each signature on a negotiable instrument is admitted.

* * *

New York Civil Practice Law and Rules 3016

(a) **Libel or slander.** In an action for libel or slander, the particular words complained of shall be set forth in the complaint, but their application to the plaintiff may be stated generally.

(b) **Fraud or mistake.** Where a cause of action or defense is based upon misrepresentation, fraud, mistake, wilful default, breach of trust or undue influence, the circumstances constituting the wrong shall be stated in detail.

(c) **Separation or divorce.** In an action for separation or divorce, the nature and circumstances of a party's alleged misconduct, if any, and the time and place of each act complained of, if any, shall be specified in the complaint or counterclaim as the case may be.

(d) **Judgment.** In an action on a judgment, the complaint shall state the extent to which any judgment recovered by the plaintiff against the defendant, or against a person jointly liable with the defendant, on the same cause of action has been satisfied.

(e) **Law of foreign country.** Where a cause of action or defense is based upon the law of a foreign country or its political subdivision, the substance of the foreign law relied upon shall be stated.

(f) **Sale and delivery of goods or performing of labor or services.** In an action involving the sale and delivery of goods, or the performing of labor or services, or the furnishing of materials, the plaintiff may set forth and number in his verified complaint the items of his claim and the reasonable value or agreed price of each. Thereupon the defendant by his verified answer shall indicate specifically those items he disputes and whether in respect of delivery or performance, reasonable value or agreed price.

* * *

(b) *Rule 9(c)*

New Jersey Civil Practice Rule 4:5–8(b)

In pleading the performance or occurrence of conditions precedent, it is sufficient to allege generally that all such conditions have been performed or have occurred. A denial of performance or occurrence shall be made specifically and with particularity, but when so made the party pleading the performance or occurrence has the burden of establishing it.

See also New York Civil Practice Law and Rules 3015(a), supra.

(c)   *Requirement of Affidavit of Merit in Specific Types of Cases*

Illinois Compiled Statutes ch. 735, 5/2–622(a)

In any action, whether in tort, contract or otherwise, in which the plaintiff seeks damages for injuries or death by reason of medical, hospital, or other healing art malpractice, the plaintiff's attorney * * * shall file an affidavit, attached to the original and all copies of the complaint, declaring * * *;

That the affiant has consulted and reviewed the facts of the case with a health professional who the affiant reasonably believes; (i) is knowledgeable in the relevant issues involved in the particular action; (ii) practices or has practiced within the last 6 years or teaches or has taught within the last 6 years in the same area of health care or medicine that is at issue in the particular action; and (iii) is qualified by experience or demonstrated competence in the subject of the case; that the reviewing health professional has determined in a written report, after a review of the medical record and other relevant material involved in the particular action that there is reasonable and meritorious cause for the filing of such action. * * * [Note that the statute goes on to exempt this requirement in special circumstances.]

[See also Colorado Rev. Stat. § 13–20–602 (malpractice suits against acupuncturists).]

Rule 10. Form of Pleadings

(a) Caption; Names of Parties. Every pleading must have a caption with the court's name, a title, a file number, and a Rule 7(a) designation. The title of the complaint must name all the parties; the title of other pleadings, after naming the first party on each side, may refer generally to other parties.

(b) Paragraphs; Separate Statements. A party must state its claims or defenses in numbered paragraphs, each limited as far as practicable to a single set of circumstances. A later pleading may refer by number to a paragraph in an earlier pleading. If doing so would promote clarity, each claim founded on a separate transaction or occurrence—and each defense other than a denial—must be stated in a separate count or defense.

(c) Adoption by Reference; Exhibits. A statement in a pleading may be adopted by reference elsewhere in the same pleading or in any other pleading or motion. A copy of a written instrument that is an exhibit to a pleading is a part of the pleading for all purposes.

Comparative State Provisions

(a)   *Rule 10(b)*

Illinois Compiled Statutes ch. 735, 5/2–613(a)

Parties may plead as many causes of action, counterclaims, defenses, and matters in reply as they may have, and each shall be separately designated and numbered.

Illinois Compiled Statutes ch. 735, 5/2–603(b)

Each separate cause of action upon which a separate recovery might be had shall be stated in a separate count or counterclaim, as the case may be and each count, counterclaim, defense or reply, shall be separately pleaded, designated and numbered, and each shall be divided into paragraphs numbered consecutively, each paragraph containing, as nearly as may be, a separate allegation.

(b)   *Rule 10(c)*

Michigan Court Rule 2.113(F)

Exhibits; Written Instruments.

    (1)   If a claim or defense is based on a written instrument, a copy of the instrument or its pertinent parts must be attached to the pleading as an exhibit unless the instrument is

        (a)   a matter of public record in the county in which the action is commenced and its location in the record is stated in the pleading;

(b)   in the possession of the adverse party and the pleading so states;

(c)   inaccessible to the pleader and the pleading so states, giving the reason; or

(d)   of a nature that attaching the instrument would be unnecessary or impractical and the pleading so states, giving the reason.

(2)   An exhibit attached or referred to under subrule (F)(1)(a) or (b) is a part of the pleading for all purposes.

Michigan Court Rule 2.113(G)

Adoption by Reference. Statements in a pleading may be adopted by reference only in another part of the same pleading.

Rule 11. Signing Pleadings, Motions, and Other Papers; Representations to the Court; Sanctions

(a) Signature. Every pleading, written motion, and other paper must be signed by at least one attorney of record in the attorney's name—or by a party personally if the party is unrepresented. The paper must state the signer's address, e-mail address, and telephone number. Unless a rule or statute specifically states otherwise, a pleading need not be verified or accompanied by an affidavit. The court must strike an unsigned paper unless the omission is promptly corrected after being called to the attorney's or party's attention.

(b) Representations to the Court. By presenting to the court a pleading, written motion, or other paper—whether by signing, filing, submitting, or later advocating it—an attorney or unrepresented party certifies that to the best of the person's knowledge, information, and belief, formed after an inquiry reasonable under the circumstances:

(1)   it is not being presented for any improper purpose, such as to harass, cause unnecessary delay, or needlessly increase the cost of litigation;

(2)   the claims, defenses, and other legal contentions are warranted by existing law or by a nonfrivolous argument for extending, modifying, or reversing existing law or for establishing new law;

(3)   the factual contentions have evidentiary support or, if specifically so identified, will likely have evidentiary support after a reasonable opportunity for further investigation or discovery; and

(4)   the denials of factual contentions are warranted on the evidence or, if specifically so identified, are reasonably based on belief or a lack of information.

(c) Sanctions.

(1) *In General.* If, after notice and a reasonable opportunity to respond, the court determines that Rule 11(b) has been violated, the court may impose an appropriate sanction on any attorney, law firm, or party that violated the rule or is responsible for the violation. Absent exceptional circumstances, a law firm must be held jointly responsible for a violation committed by its partner, associate, or employee.

(2) *Motion for Sanctions.* A motion for sanctions must be made separately from any other motion and must describe the specific conduct that allegedly violates Rule 11(b). The motion must be served under Rule 5, but it must not be filed or be presented to the court if the challenged paper, claim, defense, contention, or denial is withdrawn or appropriately corrected within 21 days after service or within another time the court sets. If warranted, the court may award to the prevailing party the reasonable expenses, including attorney's fees, incurred for the motion.

(3) *On the Court's Initiative.* On its own, the court may order an attorney, law firm, or party to show cause why conduct specifically described in the order has not violated Rule 11(b).

(4) *Nature of a Sanction.* A sanction imposed under this rule must be limited to what suffices to deter repetition of the conduct or comparable conduct by others similarly situated. The sanction may include nonmonetary directives; an order to pay a penalty into court; or, if imposed on motion and warranted for effective deterrence, an order directing payment to the movant of part or all of the reasonable attorney's fees and other expenses directly resulting from the violation.

(5) *Limitations on Monetary Sanctions.* The court must not impose a monetary sanction:

(A) against a represented party for violating Rule 11(b)(2); or

(B) on its own, unless it issued the show-cause order under Rule 11(c)(3) before voluntary dismissal or settlement of the claims made by or against the party that is, or whose attorneys are, to be sanctioned.

(6) *Requirements for an Order.* An order imposing a sanction must describe the sanctioned conduct and explain the basis for the sanction.

(d) Inapplicability to Discovery. This rule does not apply to disclosures and discovery requests, responses, objections, and motions under Rules 26 through 37.

Note on Amendments to Federal Rule 11 and Comparative State Provisions

(a)   *Amendment in 2007 to Federal Rule 11(b)(4)*

The rule, as amended, permits denials of factual contentions "reasonably based on belief *or* a lack of information." (Emphasis added.) The rule previously had allowed denials "reasonably based on a lack of information *and* belief." (Emphasis added.) Arguably the amended rule expands the bases for denials.

(b)   *Amendments in 1993 to Federal Rule 11*

Several revisions to Rule 11 were adopted in 1993 to address problems that had arisen from application of the 1983 amendments to the Rule. While the purpose of the Rule, to provide sanctions for litigants and attorneys who attempt to thwart the goals of the Federal Rules of Civil Procedure set forth in Rule 1, remained the same, the Rule was altered to attempt to reduce the large number of motions for sanctions presented under the old Rule.

The amended Rule broadened the duty of an attorney or pro se litigant to warrant that representations to the court, by any means and at any time, are proper, as defined in subdivision (b)(1)–(4). The inclusion of the phrase "later advocating" in subdivision (b) makes clear that the duty to make truthful representations to the court is an ongoing one. Therefore, factual contentions in initial pleadings which fail to be sustained by information obtained through discovery may not, under the new Rule, continue to be advocated. The pleading party making such a contention, however, need only cease advocating the unsustainable contention and is under no duty to formally amend the initial pleading.

Another major change to Rule 11 is that sanctions, whether prompted by motion or issued at the court's own initiative, are no longer mandatory. Subdivision (c) states that "If * * * the court determines that Rule 11(b) has been violated, the court may impose an appropriate sanction." The former rule required that a court "shall impose" appropriate sanctions if a violation of the rule occurred. Additionally, the new rule makes clear that not only the attorney in violation of the rule, but also that attorney's firm, may be sanctioned, in effect overturning the Supreme Court's decision in Pavelic & Leflore v. Marvel Entertainment Group, 493 U.S. 120, 110 S. Ct. 456, 107 L. Ed.2d 438 (1989).

Finally, the language contained in subdivision (d) of the revised rule has been added to make clear that the provisions of Rule 11 are inapplicable to discovery. Certification standards for discovery are contained in Rules 26(g) and 37.

(c)   *Comparative State Provisions*

Georgia Code Annotated § 9–11–11(b)

Except when otherwise specifically provided by rule or statute, pleadings need not be verified or accompanied by affidavit.

Georgia Code Annotated § 9–10–111

In all cases where the plaintiff files a pleading with an affidavit attached to the effect that the facts stated in the pleading are true to the best of his knowledge and belief, the defendant shall in like manner verify any answer. If the defendant is a corporation, the affidavit may be made by the president, vice-president, superintendent, or any officer or agent who knows, or whose official duty it is to know, about the matters set out in the answer.

Georgia Code Annotated § 19–5–5(a)

The action for divorce shall be brought by written petition and process, the petition being verified by the petitioner.

Pennsylvania Rule of Civil Procedure 1024

(a)   Every pleading containing an averment of fact not appearing of record in the action or containing a denial of fact shall state that the averment or denial is true upon the signer's personal knowledge or information and belief and shall be verified. The signer need not aver the source of the information or expectation of ability to prove the averment or denial at the trial. A pleading may be verified upon personal knowledge as to a part and upon information and belief as to the remainder.

(b)   If a pleading contains averments which are inconsistent in fact, the verification shall state that the signer has been unable after reasonable investigation to ascertain which of the inconsistent averments, specifying them, are true but that the signer has knowledge or information sufficient to form a belief that one of them is true.

(c)   The verification shall be made by one or more of the parties filing the pleading unless all the parties (1) lack sufficient knowledge or information, or (2) are outside the jurisdiction of the court and the verification of none of them can be obtained within the time allowed for filing the pleading. In such cases, the verification may be made by any person having sufficient knowledge or information and belief and shall set forth the source of the person's information as to matters not stated upon his or her own knowledge and the reason why the verification is not made by a party.

Rule 12. Defenses and Objections: When and How Presented; Motion for Judgment on the Pleadings; Consolidating Motions; Waiving Defenses; Pretrial Hearing

(a)   Time to Serve a Responsive Pleading.

(1)   *In General.* Unless another time is specified by this rule or a federal statute, the time for serving a responsive pleading is as follows:

(A)   A defendant must serve an answer:

(i)   within 21 days after being served with the summons and complaint; or

(ii)   if it has timely waived service under Rule 4(d), within 60 days after the request for a waiver was sent, or within 90 days after it was sent to the defendant outside any judicial district of the United States.

(B)   A party must serve an answer to a counterclaim or crossclaim within 21 days after being served with the pleading that states the counterclaim or crossclaim.

(C)   A party must serve a reply to an answer within 21 days after being served with an order to reply, unless the order specifies a different time.

(2)   *United States and Its Agencies, Officers, or Employees Sued in an Official Capacity.* The United States, a United States agency, or a United States officer or employee sued only in an official capacity must serve an answer to a complaint, counterclaim, or crossclaim within 60 days after service on the United States attorney.

(3) *United States Officers or Employees Sued in an Individual Capacity.* A United States officer or employee sued in an individual capacity for an act or omission occurring in connection with duties performed on the United States' behalf must serve an answer to a complaint, counterclaim, or crossclaim within 60 days after service on the officer or employee or service on the United States attorney, whichever is later.

(4) *Effect of a Motion.* Unless the court sets a different time, serving a motion under this rule alters these periods as follows:

    (A) if the court denies the motion or postpones its disposition until trial, the responsive pleading must be served within 14 days after notice of the court's action; or

    (B) if the court grants a motion for a more definite statement, the responsive pleading must be served within 14 days after the more definite statement is served.

(b) How to Present Defenses. Every defense to a claim for relief in any pleading must be asserted in the responsive pleading if one is required. But a party may assert the following defenses by motion:

    (1) lack of subject-matter jurisdiction;

    (2) lack of personal jurisdiction;

    (3) improper venue;

    (4) insufficient process;

    (5) insufficient service of process;

    (6) failure to state a claim upon which relief can be granted; and

    (7) failure to join a party under Rule 19.

A motion asserting any of these defenses must be made before pleading if a responsive pleading is allowed. If a pleading sets out a claim for relief that does not require a responsive pleading, an opposing party may assert at trial any defense to that claim. No defense or objection is waived by joining it with one or more other defenses or objections in a responsive pleading or in a motion.

(c) Motion for Judgment on the Pleadings. After the pleadings are closed—but early enough not to delay trial—a party may move for judgment on the pleadings.

(d) Result of Presenting Matters Outside the Pleadings. If, on a motion under Rule 12(b)(6) or 12(c), matters outside the pleadings are presented to and not excluded by the court, the motion must be treated as one for summary judgment under Rule 56. All parties must be given a reasonable opportunity to present all the material that is pertinent to the motion.

(e) Motion for a More Definite Statement. A party may move for a more definite statement of a pleading to which a responsive pleading is allowed but which is so vague or ambiguous that the party cannot reasonably prepare a response. The motion must be made before filing a responsive pleading and must point out the defects complained of and the details desired. If the court orders a more definite statement and the order is not obeyed within 14 days after notice of the order or within the time the court sets, the court may strike the pleading or issue any other appropriate order.

(f) Motion to Strike. The court may strike from a pleading an insufficient defense or any redundant, immaterial, impertinent, or scandalous matter. The court may act:

    (1) on its own; or

    (2) on motion made by a party either before responding to the pleading or, if a response is not allowed, within 21 days after being served with the pleading.

(g) Joining Motions.

(1) *Right to Join.* A motion under this rule may be joined with any other motion allowed by this rule.

(2) *Limitation on Further Motions.* Except as provided in Rule 12(h)(2) or (3), a party that makes a motion under this rule must not make another motion under this rule raising a defense or objection that was available to the party but omitted from its earlier motion.

(h) Waiving and Preserving Certain Defenses.

(1) *When Some Are Waived.* A party waives any defense listed in Rule 12(b)(2)–(5) by:

(A) omitting it from a motion in the circumstances described in Rule 12(g)(2); or

(B) failing to either:

(i) make it by motion under this rule; or

(ii) include it in a responsive pleading or in an amendment allowed by Rule 15(a)(1) as a matter of course.

(2) *When to Raise Others.* Failure to state a claim upon which relief can be granted, to join a person required by Rule 19(b), or to state a legal defense to a claim may be raised:

(A) in any pleading allowed or ordered under Rule 7(a);

(B) by a motion under Rule 12(c); or

(C) at trial.

(3) *Lack of Subject-Matter Jurisdiction.* If the court determines at any time that it lacks subject-matter jurisdiction, the court must dismiss the action.

(i) Hearing Before Trial. If a party so moves, any defense listed in Rule 12(b)(1)–(7)—whether made in a pleading or by motion—and a motion under Rule 12(c) must be heard and decided before trial unless the court orders a deferral until trial.

Comparative State Provisions and Notes on Amendments to Federal Rule 12

(a)   *Rule 12(a)*

Maryland Rule 2–321

(a) General Rule. A party shall file an answer to an original complaint, counterclaim, crossclaim, or third-party claim within 30 days after being served, except as provided by sections (b) and (c) of this Rule.

(b) Exceptions.

(1)   A defendant who is served with an original pleading outside of the State but within the United States shall file an answer within 60 days after being served.

(2)   A defendant who is served with an original pleading by publication or posting, pursuant to Rule 2–122, shall file an answer within the time specified in the notice.

(3)   A person [whose required agent is] * * * served with an original pleading by service upon the State Department of Assessments and Taxation, the Insurance Commissioner, or some other agency of the State authorized by statute to receive process shall file an answer within 60 days after being served.

(4)   The United States or an officer or agency of the United States served with an original pleading pursuant to Rule 2–124(m) or (n) shall file an answer within 60 days after being served.

(5)   A defendant who is served with an original pleading outside of the United States shall file an answer within 90 days after being served.

(6)   If rules for special proceedings, or statutes of this State or of the United States, provide for a different time to answer, the answer shall be filed as provided by those rules or statutes.

(c)   Automatic Extension. When a motion is filed pursuant to Rule 2–322 or when a matter is remanded from an appellate court or a federal court, the time for filing an answer is extended without special order to 15 days after entry of the court's order on the motion or remand or, if the court grants a motion for a more definite statement, to 15 days after the service of the more definite statement.

Missouri Rule of Civil Procedure 55.25(a)

A defendant shall file an answer within thirty days after the service of the summons and petition, except where service by mail is had, in which event a defendant shall file an answer within thirty days after the acknowledgment of receipt of summons and petition or return registered or certified mail receipt is filed in the case, or within forty-five days after the first publication of notice if neither personal service nor service by mail is had.

(b)   Rule 12(b)

1.   *In general*

California Civil Procedure Code § 430.10

The party against whom a complaint or cross-complaint has been filed may object by demurrer or answer * * * to the pleading on any one or more of the following grounds:

(a)   The court has no jurisdiction of the subject of the cause of action alleged in the pleading.

(b)   The person who filed the pleading does not have the legal capacity to sue.

(c)   There is another action pending between the same parties on the same cause of action.

(d)   There is a defect or misjoinder of parties.

(e)   The pleading does not state facts sufficient to constitute a cause of action.

(f)   The pleading is uncertain. * * * "[U]ncertain" includes ambiguous and unintelligible.

(g)   In an action founded upon a contract, it cannot be ascertained from the pleading whether the contract is written, is oral, or is implied by conduct.

* * *

California Civil Procedure Code § 430.30

(a)   When any ground for objection to a complaint, cross-complaint, or answer appears on the face thereof, or from any matter of which the court is required to or may take judicial notice, the objection on that ground may be taken by a demurrer to the pleading.

(b)   When any ground for objection to a complaint or cross-complaint does not appear on the face of the pleading, the objection may be taken by answer.

(c)   A party objecting to a complaint or cross-complaint may demur and answer at the same time.

California Civil Procedure Code § 430.60

A demurrer shall distinctly specify the grounds upon which any of the objections to the complaint, cross-complaint, or answer are taken. Unless it does so, it may be disregarded.

California Civil Procedure Code § 430.80(b)

If the party against whom an answer has been filed fails to demur thereto, that party is deemed to have waived the objection unless it is an objection that the answer does not state facts sufficient to constitute a defense.

2.   *Challenging jurisdiction over the subject matter*

Pennsylvania Rule of Civil Procedure 213(f)

When an action is commenced in a court which has no jurisdiction over the subject matter of the action it shall not be dismissed if there is another court of appropriate jurisdiction within the

Commonwealth in which the action could have originally been brought but the court shall transfer the action at the cost of the plaintiff to the court of appropriate jurisdiction. * * *

3.   *Challenging venue*

Illinois Compiled Statutes ch. 735, 5/2–104(b)

All objections of improper venue are waived by a defendant unless a motion to transfer to a proper venue is made by the defendant on or before the date upon which he or she is required to appear or within any further time that may be granted him or her to answer or move with respect to the complaint, except that if a defendant upon whose residence venue depends is dismissed upon motion of plaintiff, a remaining defendant may promptly move for transfer as though the dismissed defendant had not been a party.

4.   *Challenging personal jurisdiction, process, and service of process*

Illinois Compiled Statutes ch. 735, 5/2–301

(a)   Prior to the filing of any other pleading or motion other than as set forth in subsection (a-6), a party may object to the court's jurisdiction over the party's person, either on the ground that the party is not amenable to process of a court of this State or on the ground of insufficiency of process or insufficiency of service of process, by filing a motion to dismiss the entire proceeding or any cause of action involved in the proceeding or by filing a motion to quash service of process. Such a motion may be made singly or included with others in a combined motion, but the parts of a combined motion must be identified in the manner described in Section 2–619.1. Unless the facts that constitute the basis for the objection are apparent from papers already on file in the case, the motion must be supported by an affidavit setting forth those facts.

* * *

(a-6)   A party filing any other pleading or motion prior to the filing of a motion objecting to the court's jurisdiction over the party's person * * * waives all objections to the court's jurisdiction over the party's person prospectively, unless the initial motion filed is one of the following:

   (1)   A motion for an extension of time to answer or otherwise plead.

   (2)   [A motion for relief from a judgment or for a judgment based on the pleadings.]

(b)   In disposing of a motion objecting to the court's jurisdiction over the person of the objecting party, the court shall consider all matters apparent from the papers on file in the case, affidavits submitted by any party, and any evidence adduced upon contested issues of fact. The court shall enter an appropriate order sustaining or overruling the objection. No determination of any issue of fact in connection with the objection is a determination of the merits of the case or any aspect thereof. A decision adverse to the objector does not preclude the objector from making any motion or defense which he or she might otherwise have made.

(c)   Error in ruling against the objecting party on the objection is waived by the party's taking part in further proceedings unless the objection is on the ground that the party is not amenable to process issued by a court of this State.

Minnesota Rule of Civil Procedure 4.04(a)(2)(B)

* * *

When quasi in rem jurisdiction has been obtained, a party defending the action thereby submits personally to the jurisdiction of the court. An appearance solely to contest the validity of quasi in rem jurisdiction is not such a submission.

(c)   *Rule 12(i)*

California Civil Procedure Code § 597

When the answer pleads that the action is barred by the statute of limitations, or by a prior judgment, or that another action is pending upon the same cause of action, or sets up any other defense not involving the merits of the plaintiff's cause of action but constituting a bar or ground of abatement

42

to the prosecution thereof, the court may, either upon its own motion or upon the motion of any party, proceed to the trial of the special defense or defenses before the trial of any other issue in the case * * *.

California Civil Procedure Code § 597.5

[In a malpractice action against a doctor, dentist, nurse, or other medical professional] * * * if the answer pleads that the action is barred by the statute of limitations, and if any party so moves or the court upon its own motion requires, the issues raised thereby must be tried separately and before any other issues in the case are tried. * * *

(d)   Rule 12(e)

California Civil Procedure Code § 430.10

The party against whom a complaint or cross-complaint has been filed may object, by demurrer or answer as provided in Section 430.30, to the pleading on any one or more of the following grounds:

* * *

(f)   The pleading is uncertain. * * * "[U]ncertain" includes ambiguous and unintelligible.

(g)   In an action founded upon a contract, it cannot be ascertained from the pleading whether the contract is written, is oral, or is implied by conduct.

* * *

(e)   Rule 12(g)(2) and (h)—Comments

Subdivisions (g)(2) and (h) state that certain specified defenses which were available to a party when she made a preanswer motion, but which she omitted from the motion, are waived. The specified defenses are lack of jurisdiction over the person, improper venue, insufficiency of process, and insufficiency of service of process (see Rule 12(b)(2)–(5)). A party who by motion invites the court to pass upon a threshold defense should bring forward all the specified defenses she then has and thus allow the court to do a reasonably complete job. The specified defenses are of such a character that they should not be delayed and brought up for the first time by means of an application to the court to amend the responsive pleading. Successive motions are forbidden.

Rule 13. Counterclaim and Crossclaim

(a) Compulsory Counterclaim.

(1) *In General.* A pleading must state as a counterclaim any claim that—at the time of its service—the pleader has against an opposing party if the claim:

(A) arises out of the transaction or occurrence that is the subject matter of the opposing party's claim; and

(B) does not require adding another party over whom the court cannot acquire jurisdiction.

(2) *Exceptions.* The pleader need not state the claim if:

(A) when the action was commenced, the claim was the subject of another pending action; or

(B) the opposing party sued on its claim by attachment or other process that did not establish personal jurisdiction over the pleader on that claim, and the pleader does not assert any counterclaim under this rule.

(b) Permissive Counterclaim. A pleading may state as a counterclaim against an opposing party any claim that is not compulsory.

(c) Relief Sought in a Counterclaim. A counterclaim need not diminish or defeat the recovery sought by the opposing party. It may request relief that exceeds in amount or differs in kind from the relief sought by the opposing party.

(d) Counterclaim Against the United States. These rules do not expand the right to assert a counterclaim—or to claim a credit—against the United States or a United States officer or agency.

(e) Counterclaim Maturing or Acquired After Pleading. The court may permit a party to file a supplemental pleading asserting a counterclaim that matured or was acquired by the party after serving an earlier pleading.

(f) [Abrogated.]

(g) Crossclaim Against a Coparty. A pleading may state as a crossclaim any claim by one party against a coparty if the claim arises out of the transaction or occurrence that is the subject matter of the original action or of a counterclaim, or if the claim relates to any property that is the subject matter of the original action. The crossclaim may include a claim that the coparty is or may be liable to the crossclaimant for all or part of a claim asserted in the action against the crossclaimant.

(h) Joining Additional Parties. Rules 19 and 20 govern the addition of a person as a party to a counterclaim or crossclaim.

(i) Separate Trials; Separate Judgments. If the court orders separate trials under Rule 42(b), it may enter judgment on a counterclaim or crossclaim under Rule 54(b) when it has jurisdiction to do so, even if the opposing party's claims have been dismissed or otherwise resolved.

Comparative State Provisions

(a) *Rules 13(a) and 13(b)*

Michigan Court Rule 2.203(B)

A pleader may join as either independent or alternate claims as many claims, legal or equitable, as the pleader has against an opposing party. If a claim is one previously cognizable only after another claim has been prosecuted to a conclusion, the two claims may be joined in a single action; but the court may grant relief only in accordance with the substantive rights of the parties.

(b) *Rule 13(g)*

New York Civil Practice Law and Rules 3019(b)

A cross-claim may be any cause of action in favor of one or more defendants or a person whom a defendant represents against one or more defendants, a person whom a defendant represents or a defendant and other persons alleged to be liable. A cross-claim may include a claim that the party against whom it is asserted is or may be liable to the cross-claimant for all or part of a claim asserted in the action against the cross-claimant.

Rule 14. Third-Party Practice

(a) When a Defending Party May Bring in a Third Party.

(1) *Timing of the Summons and Complaint.* A defending party may, as third-party plaintiff, serve a summons and complaint on a nonparty who is or may be liable to it for all or part of the claim against it. But the third-party plaintiff must, by motion, obtain the court's leave if it files the third-party complaint more than 14 days after serving its original answer.

(2) *Third-Party Defendant's Claims and Defenses.* The person served with the summons and third-party complaint—the "third-party defendant":

(A) must assert any defense against the third-party plaintiff's claim under Rule 12;

(B) must assert any counterclaim against the third-party plaintiff under Rule 13(a), and may assert any counterclaim against the third-party plaintiff under Rule 13(b) or any crossclaim against another third-party defendant under Rule 13(g);

(C) may assert against the plaintiff any defense that the third-party plaintiff has to the plaintiff's claim; and

(D) may also assert against the plaintiff any claim arising out of the transaction or occurrence that is the subject matter of the plaintiff's claim against the third-party plaintiff.

(3) *Plaintiff's Claims Against a Third-Party Defendant.* The plaintiff may assert against the third-party defendant any claim arising out of the transaction or occurrence that is the subject matter of the plaintiff's claim against the third-party plaintiff. The third-party defendant must then assert any defense under Rule 12 and any counterclaim under Rule 13(a), and may assert any counterclaim under Rule 13(b) or any crossclaim under Rule 13(g).

(4) *Motion to Strike, Sever, or Try Separately.* Any party may move to strike the third-party claim, to sever it, or to try it separately.

(5) *Third-Party Defendant's Claim Against a Nonparty.* A third-party defendant may proceed under this rule against a nonparty who is or may be liable to the third-party defendant for all or part of any claim against it.

(6) *Third-Party Complaint In Rem.* If it is within the admiralty or maritime jurisdiction, a third-party complaint may be in rem. In that event, a reference in this rule to the "summons" includes the warrant of arrest, and a reference to the defendant or third-party plaintiff includes, when appropriate, a person who asserts a right under Supplemental Rule C(6)(a)(i) in the property arrested.

(b) When a Plaintiff May Bring in a Third Party. When a claim is asserted against a plaintiff, the plaintiff may bring in a third party if this rule would allow a defendant to do so.

(c) Admiralty or Maritime Claim.

(1) *Scope of Impleader.* If a plaintiff asserts an admiralty or maritime claim under Rule 9(h), the defendant or a person who asserts a right under Supplemental Rule C(6)(a)(i) may, as a third-party plaintiff, bring in a third-party defendant who may be wholly or partly liable—either to the plaintiff or to the third-party plaintiff—for remedy over, contribution, or otherwise on account of the same transaction, occurrence, or series of transactions or occurrences.

(2) *Defending Against a Demand for Judgment for the Plaintiff.* The third-party plaintiff may demand judgment in the plaintiff's favor against the third-party defendant. In that event, the third-party defendant must defend under Rule 12 against the plaintiff's claim as well as the third-party plaintiff's claim; and the action proceeds as if the plaintiff had sued both the third-party defendant and the third-party plaintiff.

Note on the 2007 Amendment to Federal Rule 14(b)

Previously the rule permitted a plaintiff against whom a "counterclaim" had been asserted to bring in a third party. The amendment changed the word "counterclaim" to "claim" since there is no reason not to permit a plaintiff to utilize the provisions of Rule 14 regardless of the nature of the claim against her.

Rule 15. Amended and Supplemental Pleadings

(a) Amendments Before Trial.

(1) *Amending as a Matter of Course.* A party may amend its pleading once as a matter of course within:

(A) 21 days after serving it, or

(B) if the pleading is one to which a responsive pleading is required, 21 days after service of a responsive pleading or 21 days after service of a motion under Rule 12(b), (e), or (f), whichever is earlier.

(2) *Other Amendments.* In all other cases, a party may amend its pleading only with the opposing party's written consent or the court's leave. The court should freely give leave when justice so requires.

(3)   ***Time to Respond.*** Unless the court orders otherwise, any required response to an amended pleading must be made within the time remaining to respond to the original pleading or within 14 days after service of the amended pleading, whichever is later.

(b)   Amendments During and After Trial.

(1)   ***Based on an Objection at Trial.*** If, at trial, a party objects that evidence is not within the issues raised in the pleadings, the court may permit the pleadings to be amended. The court should freely permit an amendment when doing so will aid in presenting the merits and the objecting party fails to satisfy the court that the evidence would prejudice that party's action or defense on the merits. The court may grant a continuance to enable the objecting party to meet the evidence.

(2)   ***For Issues Tried by Consent.*** When an issue not raised by the pleadings is tried by the parties' express or implied consent, it must be treated in all respects as if raised in the pleadings. A party may move—at any time, even after judgment—to amend the pleadings to conform them to the evidence and to raise an unpleaded issue. But failure to amend does not affect the result of the trial of that issue.

(c)   Relation Back of Amendments.

(1)   ***When an Amendment Relates Back.*** An amendment to a pleading relates back to the date of the original pleading when:

    (A)   the law that provides the applicable statute of limitations allows relation back;

    (B)   the amendment asserts a claim or defense that arose out of the conduct, transaction, or occurrence set out—or attempted to be set out—in the original pleading; or

    (C)   the amendment changes the party or the naming of the party against whom a claim is asserted, if Rule 15(c)(1)(B) is satisfied and if, within the period provided by Rule 4(m) for serving the summons and complaint, the party to be brought in by amendment:

        (i)   received such notice of the action that it will not be prejudiced in defending on the merits; and

        (ii)   knew or should have known that the action would have been brought against it, but for a mistake concerning the proper party's identity.

(2)   ***Notice to the United States.*** When the United States or a United States officer or agency is added as a defendant by amendment, the notice requirements of Rule 15(c)(1)(C)(i) and (ii) are satisfied if, during the stated period, process was delivered or mailed to the United States attorney or the United States attorney's designee, to the Attorney General of the United States, or to the officer or agency.

(d)   Supplemental Pleadings. On motion and reasonable notice, the court may, on just terms, permit a party to serve a supplemental pleading setting out any transaction, occurrence, or event that happened after the date of the pleading to be supplemented. The court may permit supplementation even though the original pleading is defective in stating a claim or defense. The court may order that the opposing party plead to the supplemental pleading within a specified time.

Comparative State Provisions

(a)   Rule 15(a)

New York Civil Practice Law and Rules 3025(a) & (b)

(a)   A party may amend his pleading once without leave of court within twenty days after its service, or at any time before the period for responding to it expires, or within twenty days after service of a pleading responding to it.

(b)   A party may amend his or her pleading, or supplement it by setting forth additional or subsequent transactions or occurrences, at any time by leave of court or by stipulation of all parties.

Leave shall be freely given upon such terms as may be just including the granting of costs and continuances. Any motion to amend or supplement pleadings shall be accompanied by the proposed amended or supplemental pleading clearly showing the changes or additions to be made to the pleading.

(b)   Rule 15(b)

California Civil Procedure Code § 469

Variance between the allegation in a pleading and the proof shall not be deemed material, unless it has actually misled the adverse party to his prejudice in maintaining his or her action or defense upon the merits. If it appears that a party has been so misled, the Court may order the pleading to be amended upon such terms as may be just.

California Civil Procedure Code § 470

Where the variance is not material, as provided in Section 469 the Court may direct the fact to be found according to the evidence, or may order an immediate amendment, without costs.

California Civil Procedure Code § 471

Where, however, the allegation of the claim or defense to which the proof is directed, is unproved, not in some particular or particulars only, but in its general scope and meaning, it is not to be deemed a case of variance, within the meaning of Sections 469 and 470, but a failure of proof.

(c)   Rule 15(c)

New Jersey Civil Practice Rule 4:9–3

Whenever the claim or defense asserted in the amended pleading arose out of the conduct, transaction or occurrence set forth or attempted to be set forth in the original pleading, the amendment relates back to the date of the original pleading; but the court, in addition to its power to allow amendments may, upon terms, permit the statement of a new or different claim or defense in the pleading. * * *

(d)   Rule 15(d)

[See New York Civil Practice Law and Rules 3025(b) as set out in connection with Federal Rule 15(a), supra.]

Rule 16. Pretrial Conferences; Scheduling; Management

(a)   Purposes of a Pretrial Conference. In any action, the court may order the attorneys and any unrepresented parties to appear for one or more pretrial conferences for such purposes as:

(1)   expediting disposition of the action;

(2)   establishing early and continuing control so that the case will not be protracted because of lack of management;

(3)   discouraging wasteful pretrial activities;

(4)   improving the quality of the trial through more thorough preparation; and

(5)   facilitating settlement.

(b)   Scheduling.

(1)   *Scheduling Order.* Except in categories of actions exempted by local rule, the district judge—or a magistrate judge when authorized by local rule—must issue a scheduling order:

(A)   after receiving the parties' report under Rule 26(f); or

(B)   after consulting with the parties' attorneys and any unrepresented parties at a scheduling conference.

(2) *Time to Issue.* The judge must issue the scheduling order as soon as practicable, but, unless the judge finds good cause for delay, the judge must issue it within the earlier of 90 days after any defendant has been served with the complaint or 60 days after any defendant has appeared.

(3) *Contents of the Order.*

(A) *Required Contents.* The scheduling order must: limit the time to join other parties, amend the pleadings, complete discovery, and file motions.

(B) *Permitted Contents.* The scheduling order may:

(i) modify the timing of disclosures under Rules 26(a) and 26(e)(1);

(ii) modify the extent of discovery;

(iii) provide for disclosure, discovery, or preservation of electronically stored information;

(iv) include any agreements the parties reach for asserting claims of privilege or of protection as trial-preparation material after information is produced, including agreements reached under Federal Rule of Evidence 502;

(v) direct that before moving for an order relating to discovery, the movant must request a conference with the court;

(vi) set dates for pretrial conferences and for trial; and

(vii) include other appropriate matters.

(4) *Modifying a Schedule.* A schedule may be modified only for good cause and with the judge's consent.

(c) **Attendance and Matters for Consideration at a Pretrial Conference.**

(1) *Attendance.* A represented party must authorize at least one of its attorneys to make stipulations and admissions about all matters that can reasonably be anticipated for discussion at a pretrial conference. If appropriate, the court may require that a party or its representative be present or reasonably available by other means to consider possible settlement.

(2) *Matters for Consideration.* At any pretrial conference, the court may consider and take appropriate action on the following matters:

(A) formulating and simplifying the issues, and eliminating frivolous claims or defenses;

(B) amending the pleadings if necessary or desirable;

(C) obtaining admissions and stipulations about facts and documents to avoid unnecessary proof, and ruling in advance on the admissibility of evidence;

(D) avoiding unnecessary proof and cumulative evidence, and limiting the use of testimony under Federal Rule of Evidence 702;

(E) determining the appropriateness and timing of summary adjudication under Rule 56;

(F) controlling and scheduling discovery, including orders affecting disclosures and discovery under Rule 26 and Rules 29 through 37;

(G) identifying witnesses and documents, scheduling the filing and exchange of any pretrial briefs, and setting dates for further conferences and for trial;

(H) referring matters to a magistrate judge or a master;

(I) settling the case and using special procedures to assist in resolving the dispute when authorized by statute or local rule;

(J) determining the form and content of the pretrial order;

(K) disposing of pending motions;

(L) adopting special procedures for managing potentially difficult or protracted actions that may involve complex issues, multiple parties, difficult legal questions, or unusual proof problems;

(M) ordering a separate trial under Rule 42(b) of a claim, counterclaim, crossclaim, third-party claim, or particular issue;

(N) ordering the presentation of evidence early in the trial on a manageable issue that might, on the evidence, be the basis for a judgment as a matter of law under Rule 50(a) or a judgment on partial findings under Rule 52(c);

(O) establishing a reasonable limit on the time allowed to present evidence; and

(P) facilitating in other ways the just, speedy, and inexpensive disposition of the action.

(d) Pretrial Orders. After any conference under this rule, the court should issue an order reciting the action taken. This order controls the course of the action unless the court modifies it.

(e) Final Pretrial Conference and Orders. The court may hold a final pretrial conference to formulate a trial plan, including a plan to facilitate the admission of evidence. The conference must be held as close to the start of trial as is reasonable, and must be attended by at least one attorney who will conduct the trial for each party and by any unrepresented party. The court may modify the order issued after a final pretrial conference only to prevent manifest injustice.

(f) Sanctions.

(1) *In General.* On motion or on its own, the court may issue any just orders, including those authorized by Rule 37(b)(2)(A)(ii)–(vii), if a party or its attorney:

(A) fails to appear at a scheduling or other pretrial conference;

(B) is substantially unprepared to participate—or does not participate in good faith—in the conference; or

(C) fails to obey a scheduling or other pretrial order.

(2) *Imposing Fees and Costs.* Instead of or in addition to any other sanction, the court must order the party, its attorney, or both to pay the reasonable expenses—including attorney's fees—incurred because of any noncompliance with this rule, unless the noncompliance was substantially justified or other circumstances make an award of expenses unjust.

Notes on Amendments to Federal Rule 16 and Comparative State Provisions

(a) *Amendments in 1983 and 1993 to Federal Rule 16*

The purpose of the 1983 changes was to alter the focus of pretrial conferences to encompass all aspects of case management and not merely the conduct of the trial. The most dramatic addition was the mandatory scheduling order that must be prepared even in the absence of a formal pretrial conference (unless the case is exempted by local rule).

In 1993, the rule was modified to broaden the scope of what may be considered at pretrial conferences. What is now paragraph (c)(2)(E) was added to allow parties to discuss at pretrial conferences the possibility of summary judgment under Rule 56. Paragraph (c)(2)(I) was revised to refer to alternative dispute resolution techniques, especially those authorized by local rule or statute.

(b)   *Comparative State Provisions*

New Jersey Civil Practice Rule 4:25–1

(a)   Actions to Be Pretried. Pretrial conferences in contested actions may be held in the discretion of the court either on its own motion or upon a party's written request. The request of a party for a pretrial conference shall include a statement of the facts and reasons supporting the request. * * *

(b)   Pretrial Order. Immediately upon the conclusion of the conference, the court shall enter a pretrial order to be signed forthwith by the attorneys, which shall recite specifically:

(1)   A concise descriptive statement of the nature of the action.

(2)   The admissions or stipulations of the parties with respect to the cause of action pleaded by plaintiff or defendant-counterclaimant.

(3)   The factual and legal contentions of the plaintiff as to the liability of the defendant.

(4)   The factual and legal contentions of the defendant as to non-liability and affirmative defenses.

(5)   All claims as to damages and the extent of injury, and admissions or stipulations with respect thereto, and this shall limit the claims thereto at the trial. * * *

(6)   Any amendments to the pleadings made at the conference * * *.

(7)   A specification of the issues to be determined at the trial including all special evidence problems to be determined at trial * * *.

(8)   A specification of the legal issues raised by the pleadings which are abandoned or otherwise disposed of. * * *

(9)   A list of the exhibits marked in evidence by consent.

(10)   Any limitation on the number of expert witnesses.

(11)   Any direction with respect to the filing of briefs. * * *

(12)   In special circumstances the order of opening and closing to the jury at the trial.

(13)   Any other matters which have been agreed upon in order to expedite the disposition of the case.

(14)   In the event that a particular member or associate of a firm is to try a case, or if outside trial counsel is to try the case, the name must be specifically set forth. No change in such designated trial counsel shall be made without leave of court if such change will interfere with the trial schedule. * * *

(15)   The estimated length of the trial.

(16)   When the case shall be placed on the weekly call.

When entered, the pretrial order becomes part of the record, supersedes the pleadings where inconsistent therewith, and controls the subsequent course of action unless modified at or before the trial or pursuant to R. 4:9–2 to prevent manifest injustice. The matter of settlement may be discussed at the sidebar, but it shall not be mentioned in the order.

* * *

TITLE IV. PARTIES

Rule 17.   Plaintiff and Defendant; Capacity; Public Officers

(a)   Real Party in Interest.

(1)   *Designation in General.* An action must be prosecuted in the name of the real party in interest. The following may sue in their own names without joining the person for whose benefit the action is brought:

(A) an executor;

(B) an administrator;

(C) a guardian;

(D) a bailee;

(E) a trustee of an express trust;

(F) a party with whom or in whose name a contract has been made for another's benefit; and

(G) a party authorized by statute.

(2) *Action in the Name of the United States for Another's Use or Benefit.* When a federal statute so provides, an action for another's use or benefit must be brought in the name of the United States.

(3) *Joinder of the Real Party in Interest.* The court may not dismiss an action for failure to prosecute in the name of the real party in interest until, after an objection, a reasonable time has been allowed for the real party in interest to ratify, join, or be substituted into the action. After ratification, joinder, or substitution, the action proceeds as if it had been originally commenced by the real party in interest.

(b) Capacity to Sue or Be Sued. Capacity to sue or be sued is determined as follows:

(1) for an individual who is not acting in a representative capacity, by the law of the individual's domicile;

(2) for a corporation by the law under which it was organized; and

(3) for all other parties by the law of the state where the court is located, except that:

(A) a partnership or other unincorporated association with no such capacity under that state's law may sue or be sued in its common name to enforce a substantive right existing under the United States Constitution or laws; and

(B) 28 U.S.C. §§ 754 and 959(a) govern the capacity of a receiver appointed by a United States court to sue or be sued in a United States court.

(c) Minor or Incompetent Person.

(1) *With a Representative.* The following representatives may sue or defend on behalf of a minor or an incompetent person:

(A) a general guardian;

(B) a committee;

(C) a conservator; or

(D) a like fiduciary.

(2) *Without a Representative.* A minor or an incompetent person who does not have a duly appointed representative may sue by a next friend or by a guardian ad litem. The court must appoint a guardian ad litem—or issue another appropriate order—to protect a minor or incompetent person who is unrepresented in an action.

(d) Public Officer's Title and Name. A public officer who sues or is sued in an official capacity may be designated by official title rather than by name, but the court may order that the officer's name be added.

Notes on Amendments in 1966 to Federal Rule 17(a)

In 1966 Federal Rule 17(a) was amended to add the provision prohibiting dismissal until a reasonable time has been allowed for ratification, joinder, or substitution of the real party in interest.

The Advisory Committee commented on this provision as follows:

This provision keeps pace with the law as it is actually developing. Modern decisions are inclined to be lenient when an honest mistake has been made in choosing the party in whose name the action is to be filed * * *. The provision should not be misunderstood or distorted. It is intended to prevent forfeiture when determination of the proper party to sue is difficult or when an understandable mistake has been made. It does not mean, for example, that, following an airplane crash in which all aboard were killed, an action may be filed in the name of John Doe (a fictitious person), as personal representative of Richard Roe (another fictitious person), in the hope that at a later time the attorney filing the action may substitute the real name of the real personal representative of a real victim, and have the benefit of suspension of the limitation period. * * *

Rule 18. Joinder of Claims

(a) In General. A party asserting a claim, counterclaim, crossclaim, or third-party claim may join, as independent or alternative claims, as many claims as it has against an opposing party.

(b) Joinder of Contingent Claims. A party may join two claims even though one of them is contingent on the disposition of the other; but the court may grant relief only in accordance with the parties' relative substantive rights. In particular, a plaintiff may state a claim for money and a claim to set aside a conveyance that is fraudulent as to that plaintiff, without first obtaining a judgment for the money.

Comparative State Provision

Michigan Court Rule 2.203

(A) Compulsory Joinder. In a pleading that states a claim against an opposing party, the pleader must join every claim that the pleader has against that opposing party at the time of serving the pleading, if it arises out of the transaction or occurrence that is the subject matter of the action and does not require for its adjudication the presence of third parties over whom the court cannot acquire jurisdiction.

(B) Permissive Joinder. A pleader may join as either independent or alternate claims as many claims, legal or equitable, as the pleader has against an opposing party. If a claim is one previously cognizable only after another claim has been prosecuted to a conclusion, the two claims may be joined in a single action; but the court may grant relief only in accordance with the substantive rights of the parties.

* * *

Rule 19. Required Joinder of Parties

(a) Persons Required to Be Joined if Feasible.

(1) *Required Party.* A person who is subject to service of process and whose joinder will not deprive the court of subject-matter jurisdiction must be joined as a party if:

(A) in that person's absence, the court cannot accord complete relief among existing parties; or

(B) that person claims an interest relating to the subject of the action and is so situated that disposing of the action in the person's absence may:

(i) as a practical matter impair or impede the person's ability to protect the interest; or

(ii) leave an existing party subject to a substantial risk of incurring double, multiple, or otherwise inconsistent obligations because of the interest.

(2) *Joinder by Court Order.* If a person has not been joined as required, the court must order that the person be made a party. A person who refuses to join as a plaintiff may be made either a defendant or, in a proper case, an involuntary plaintiff.

(3) *Venue.* If a joined party objects to venue and the joinder would make venue improper, the court must dismiss that party.

(b) When Joinder Is Not Feasible. If a person who is required to be joined if feasible cannot be joined, the court must determine whether, in equity and good conscience, the action should proceed among the existing parties or should be dismissed. The factors for the court to consider include:

(1) the extent to which a judgment rendered in the person's absence might prejudice that person or the existing parties;

(2) the extent to which any prejudice could be lessened or avoided by:

(A) protective provisions in the judgment;

(B) shaping the relief; or

(C) other measures;

(3) whether a judgment rendered in the person's absence would be adequate; and

(4) whether the plaintiff would have an adequate remedy if the action were dismissed for nonjoinder.

(c) Pleading the Reasons for Nonjoinder. When asserting a claim for relief, a party must state:

(1) the name, if known, of any person who is required to be joined if feasible but is not joined; and

(2) the reasons for not joining that person.

(d) Exception for Class Actions. This rule is subject to Rule 23.

Notes on Federal Rule 19 and Comparative State Provisions

(a)   *Comments on Rule 19*

Subdivision (a) now defines the persons whose joinder in the action is desirable. The provision stresses the desirability of joining those persons in whose absence the court would be obliged to grant partial or "hollow" rather than complete relief to the parties before the court. The interests that are being furthered here are not only those of the parties, but also that of the public in avoiding repeated lawsuits on the same essential subject matter. The provision also recognizes the importance of protecting the person whose joinder is in question against the practical prejudice to him which may arise through a disposition of the action in his absence and recognizes the need for considering whether a party may be left, after the adjudication, in a position where a person not joined can subject him to a double or otherwise inconsistent liability.

Subdivision (b). When a person as described in subdivision (a) cannot be made a party, the court is to determine whether in equity and good conscience the action should proceed among the parties already before it, or should be dismissed. That this decision is to be made in the light of pragmatic considerations has often been acknowledged by the courts. See *Roos v. Texas Co.,* 23 F.2d 171 (2d Cir. 1927), *cert. denied,* 277 U.S. 587 (1928); *Niles-Bement-Pond Co. v. Iron Moulders' Union,* 254 U.S. 77, 80 (1920). The subdivision sets out four relevant considerations drawn from the experience revealed in the decided cases. The factors are to a certain extent overlapping, and they are not intended to exclude other considerations which may be applicable in particular situations.

(b)   State Mandatory Joinder Provisions in Specific Cases

Pennsylvania Rule of Civil Procedure 2228

(a)   If an injury, not resulting in death, is inflicted upon the person of a husband or a wife, and causes of action therefor accrue to both, they shall be enforced in one action brought by the husband and the wife.

(b)   If an injury, not resulting in death, is inflicted upon the person of a minor, and causes of action therefor accrue to the minor and also to the parent or parents of the minor, they shall be enforced in one action brought by the parent or parents and the child. Either parent may sue therefor in the name of both * * *.

Wisconsin Statutes Annotated § 803.03(2)

A party asserting a claim for affirmative relief shall join as parties to the action all parties who at the commencement of the action have claims based upon subrogation to the rights of the party asserting the principal claim, derivation from the principal claim, or assignment of part of the principal claim. * * *

Rule 20. Permissive Joinder of Parties

(a)   Persons Who May Join or Be Joined.

(1) *Plaintiffs.* Persons may join in one action as plaintiffs if:

(A) they assert any right to relief jointly, severally, or in the alternative with respect to or arising out of the same transaction, occurrence, or series of transactions or occurrences; and

(B) any question of law or fact common to all plaintiffs will arise in the action.

(2) *Defendants.* Persons—as well as a vessel, cargo, or other property subject to admiralty process in rem—may be joined in one action as defendants if:

(A) any right to relief is asserted against them jointly, severally, or in the alternative with respect to or arising out of the same transaction, occurrence, or series of transactions or occurrences; and

(B) any question of law or fact common to all defendants will arise in the action.

(3) *Extent of Relief.* Neither a plaintiff nor a defendant need be interested in obtaining or defending against all the relief demanded. The court may grant judgment to one or more plaintiffs according to their rights, and against one or more defendants according to their liabilities.

(b)   Protective Measures. The court may issue orders—including an order for separate trials—to protect a party against embarrassment, delay, expense, or other prejudice that arises from including a person against whom the party asserts no claim and who asserts no claim against the party.

Comparative State Provisions

Michigan Court Rule 2.206(A)

(1)   All persons may join in one action as plaintiffs

(a)   if they assert a right to relief jointly, severally, or in the alternative, in respect of or arising out of the same transaction, occurrence, or series of transactions or occurrences and if a question of law or fact common to all of the plaintiffs will arise in the action; or

(b)   if their presence in the action will promote the convenient administration of justice.

(2)   All persons may be joined in one action as defendants

(a)   if there is asserted against them jointly, severally, or in the alternative, a right to relief in respect of or arising out of the same transaction, occurrence, or series of transactions or occurrences and if a question of law or fact common to all of the defendants will arise in the action; or

      (b)   if their presence in the action will promote the convenient administration of justice.

    (3)   A plaintiff or defendant need not be interested in obtaining or defending against all the relief demanded. Judgment may be rendered for one or more of the parties against one or more of the parties as the rights and liabilities of the parties are determined.

New York Civil Practice Law and Rules 1002(a) & (b)

    (a)   Persons who assert any right to relief jointly, severally, or in the alternative arising out of the same transaction, occurrence, or series of transactions or occurrences, may join in one action as plaintiffs if any common question of law or fact would arise.

    (b)   Persons against whom there is asserted any right to relief jointly, severally, or in the alternative, arising out of the same transaction, occurrence, or series of transactions or occurrences, may be joined in one action as defendants if any common question of law or fact would arise.

* * *

Rule 21. Misjoinder and Nonjoinder of Parties

Misjoinder of parties is not a ground for dismissing an action. On motion or on its own, the court may at any time, on just terms, add or drop a party. The court may also sever any claim against a party.

Rule 22. Interpleader

(a) Grounds.

    (1) ***By a Plaintiff.*** Persons with claims that may expose a plaintiff to double or multiple liability may be joined as defendants and required to interplead. Joinder for interpleader is proper even though:

      (A)   the claims of the several claimants, or the titles on which their claims depend, lack a common origin or are adverse and independent rather than identical; or

      (B)   the plaintiff denies liability in whole or in part to any or all of the claimants.

    (2) ***By a Defendant.*** A defendant exposed to similar liability may seek interpleader through a crossclaim or counterclaim.

    (b) **Relation to Other Rules and Statutes.** This rule supplements—and does not limit—the joinder of parties allowed by Rule 20. The remedy this rule provides is in addition to—and does not supersede or limit—the remedy provided by 28 U.S.C. §§ 1335, 1397, and 2361. An action under those statutes must be conducted under these rules.

Comparative State Provision

California Civil Procedure Code § 386

    (a)   A defendant, against whom an action is pending upon a contract, or for specific personal property, may, at any time before answer, upon affidavit that a person not a party to the action makes against him, and without any collusion with him, a demand upon such contract, or for such property, upon notice to such person and the adverse party, apply to the court for an order to substitute such person in his place, and discharge him from liability to either party, on his depositing in court the amount claimed on the contract, or delivering the property or its value to such person as the court may direct; and the court may, in its discretion, make the order; or such defendant may file a verified cross-complaint in interpleader, admitting that he has no interest in such amount or such property claimed, or in a portion of such amount or such property and alleging that all or such portion of the amount or property is demanded by parties to such action or cross-action and apply to the court upon notice to such parties for an order to deliver such property or portion thereof or its value to such person as the court shall direct. And whenever conflicting claims are or may be made upon a person for or relating to personal property, or the performance of an obligation, or any portion thereof, such person may bring an action against the conflicting claimants to compel them to interplead and litigate their several claims. The order of substitution may be made and the action of interpleader may be maintained, and the applicant or interpleading party be discharged from liability to all or any of the conflicting claimants, although their titles or claims have not a common origin, or are not identical but are adverse to and independent of one another.

(b) Any person, firm, corporation, association or other entity against whom double or multiple claims are made, or may be made, by two or more persons which are such that they may give rise to double or multiple liability, may bring an action against the claimants to compel them to interplead and litigate their several claims.

When the person, firm, corporation, association or other entity against whom such claims are made, or may be made, is a defendant in an action brought upon one or more of such claims, it may either file a verified cross-complaint in interpleader, admitting that it has no interest in the money or property claimed, or in only a portion thereof, and alleging that all or such portion is demanded by parties to such action, and apply to the court upon notice to such parties for an order to deliver such money or property or such portion thereof to such person as the court shall direct; or may bring a separate action against the claimants to compel them to interplead and litigate their several claims. The action of interpleader may be maintained although the claims have not a common origin, are not identical but are adverse to and independent of one another, or the claims are unliquidated and no liability on the part of the party bringing the action or filing the cross-complaint has arisen. The applicant or interpleading party may deny liability in whole or in part to any or all of the claimants. The applicant or interpleading party may join as a defendant in such action any other party against whom claims are made by one or more of the claimants or such other party may interplead by cross-complaint; provided, however, that such claims arise out of the same transaction or occurrence.

* * *

Rule 23. Class Actions

[See the various provisions of the Class Action Fairness Act of 2005 in Part II, infra, as follows: 28 U.S.C. § 1332(d) (federal jurisdiction over class actions), 28 U.S.C. § 1453 (removal of interstate class actions to federal court), and 28 U.S.C. §§ 1711–1715 (control of class-action settlements). See also 28 U.S.C. § 1369, in Part II, infra.]

(a) **Prerequisites.** One or more members of a class may sue or be sued as representative parties on behalf of all members only if:

(1) the class is so numerous that joinder of all members is impracticable;

(2) there are questions of law or fact common to the class;

(3) the claims or defenses of the representative parties are typical of the claims or defenses of the class; and

(4) the representative parties will fairly and adequately protect the interests of the class.

(b) **Types of Class Actions.** A class action may be maintained if Rule 23(a) is satisfied and if:

(1) prosecuting separate actions by or against individual class members would create a risk of:

(A) inconsistent or varying adjudications with respect to individual class members that would establish incompatible standards of conduct for the party opposing the class; or

(B) adjudications with respect to individual class members that, as a practical matter, would be dispositive of the interests of the other members not parties to the individual adjudications or would substantially impair or impede their ability to protect their interests;

(2) the party opposing the class has acted or refused to act on grounds that apply generally to the class, so that final injunctive relief or corresponding declaratory relief is appropriate respecting the class as a whole; or

(3) the court finds that the questions of law or fact common to class members predominate over any questions affecting only individual members, and that a class action is superior to other available methods for fairly and efficiently adjudicating the controversy. The matters pertinent to these findings include:

(A) the class members' interests in individually controlling the prosecution or defense of separate actions;

(B) the extent and nature of any litigation concerning the controversy already begun by or against class members;

(C) the desirability or undesirability of concentrating the litigation of the claims in the particular forum; and

(D) the likely difficulties in managing a class action.

(c) Certification Order; Notice to Class Members; Judgment; Issues Classes; Subclasses.

(1) *Certification Order.*

(A) *Time to Issue.* At an early practicable time after a person sues or is sued as a class representative, the court must determine by order whether to certify the action as a class action.

(B) *Defining the Class; Appointing Class Counsel.* An order that certifies a class action must define the class and the class claims, issues, or defenses, and must appoint class counsel under Rule 23(g).

(C) *Altering or Amending the Order.* An order that grants or denies class certification may be altered or amended before final judgment.

(2) *Notice.*

(A) *For (b)(1) or (b)(2) Classes.* For any class certified under Rule 23(b) or (b)(2), the court may direct appropriate notice to the class.

(B) *For (b)(3) Classes.* For any class certified under Rule 23(b)(3)—or upon ordering notice under Rule 23(e)(1) to a class proposed to be certified for purposes of settlement under Rule 23(b)(3)—the court must direct to class members the best notice that is practicable under the circumstances, including individual notice to all members who can be identified through reasonable effort. The notice may be by one or more of the following: United States mail, electronic means, or other appropriate means. The notice must clearly and concisely state in plain, easily understood language:

(i) the nature of the action;

(ii) the definition of the class certified;

(iii) the class claims, issues, or defenses;

(iv) that a class member may enter an appearance through an attorney if the member so desires;

(v) that the court will exclude from the class any member who requests exclusion;

(vi) the time and manner for requesting exclusion; and

(vii) the binding effect of a class judgment on members under Rule 23(c)(3).

(3) *Judgment.* Whether or not favorable to the class, the judgment in a class action must:

(A) for any class certified under Rule 23(b)(1) or (b)(2), include and describe those whom the court finds to be class members; and

(B) for any class certified under Rule 23(b)(3), include and specify or describe those to whom the Rule 23(c)(2) notice was directed, who have not requested exclusion, and whom the court finds to be class members.

(4) *Particular Issues.* When appropriate, an action may be brought or maintained as a class action with respect to particular issues.

(5) *Subclasses.* When appropriate, a class may be divided into subclasses that are each treated as a class under this rule.

(d) Conducting the Action.

(1) *In General.* In conducting an action under this rule, the court may issue orders that:

(A) determine the course of proceedings or prescribe measures to prevent undue repetition or complication in presenting evidence or argument;

(B) require—to protect class members and fairly conduct the action—giving appropriate notice to some or all class members of:

(i) any step in the action;

(ii) the proposed extent of the judgment; or

(iii) the members' opportunity to signify whether they consider the representation fair and adequate, to intervene and present claims or defenses, or to otherwise come into the action;

(C) impose conditions on the representative parties or on intervenors;

(D) require that the pleadings be amended to eliminate allegations about representation of absent persons and that the action proceed accordingly; or

(E) deal with similar procedural matters.

(2) *Combining and Amending Orders.* An order under Rule 23(d)(1) may be altered or amended from time to time and may be combined with an order under Rule 16.

(e) Settlement, Voluntary Dismissal, or Compromise. The claims, issues, or defenses of a certified class—or a class proposed to be certified for purposes of settlement—may be settled, voluntarily dismissed, or compromised only with the court's approval. The following procedures apply to a proposed settlement, voluntary dismissal, or compromise:

(1) *Notice to the Class.*

(A) *Information That Parties Must Provide to the Court.* The parties must provide the court with information sufficient to enable it to determine whether to give notice of the proposal to the class.

(B) *Grounds for a Decision to Give Notice.* The court must direct notice in a reasonable manner to all class members who would be bound by the proposal if giving notice is justified by the parties' showing that the court will likely be able to:

(i) approve the proposal under Rule 23(e)(2); and

(ii) certify the class for purposes of judgment on the proposal.

(2) *Approval of the Proposal.* If the proposal would bind class members, the court may approve it only after a hearing and only on finding that it is fair, reasonable, and adequate after considering whether:

(A) the class representatives and class counsel have adequately represented the class;

(B) the proposal was negotiated at arm's length;

(C) the relief provided for the class is adequate, taking into account:

    (i) the costs, risks, and delay of trial and appeal;

    (ii) the effectiveness of any proposed method of distributing relief to the class, including the method of processing class-members claims;

    (iii) the terms of any proposed award of attorney's fees, including timing of payment; and

    (iv) any agreement required to be identified under Rule 23(e)(3); and

(D) the proposal treats class members equitably relative to each other.

(3) *Identifying Agreements.* The parties seeking approval must file a statement identifying any agreement made in connection with the proposal.

(4) *New Opportunity to Be Excluded.* If the class action was previously certified under Rule 23(b)(3), the court may refuse to approve a settlement unless it affords a new opportunity to request exclusion to individual class members who had an earlier opportunity to request exclusion but did not do so.

(5) *Class-Member Objections.*

(A) *In General.* Any class member may object to the proposal if it requires court approval under this subdivision (e). The objection must state whether it applies only to the objector, to a specific subset of the class, or to the entire class, and also state with specificity the grounds for the objection.

(B) *Court Approval Required for Payment in Connection with an Objection.* Unless approved by the court after a hearing, no payment or other consideration may be provided in connection with:

    (i) forgoing or withdrawing an objection, or

    (ii) forgoing, dismissing, or abandoning an appeal from a judgment approving the proposal.

    (C) *Procedure for Approval After an Appeal.* If approval under Rule 23(e)(5)(B) has not been obtained before an appeal is docketed in the court of appeals, the procedure of Rule 62.1 applies while the appeal remains pending.

(f) **Appeals.** A court of appeals may permit an appeal from an order granting or denying class-action certification under this rule, but not from an order under Rule 23(e)(1). A party must file a petition for permission to appeal with the circuit clerk within 14 days after the order is entered, or within 45 days after the order is entered if any party is the United States, a United States agency, or a United States officer or employee sued for an act or omission occurring in connection with duties performed on the United States' behalf. An appeal does not stay proceedings in the district court unless the district judge or the court of appeals so orders.

(g) **Class Counsel.**

(1) *Appointing Class Counsel.* Unless a statute provides otherwise, a court that certifies a class must appoint class counsel. In appointing class counsel, the court:

(A) must consider:

    (i) the work counsel has done in identifying or investigating potential claims in the action;

    (ii) counsel's experience in handling class actions, other complex litigation, and the types of claims asserted in the action;

    (iii) counsel's knowledge of the applicable law; and

    (iv) the resources that counsel will commit to representing the class;

  (B) may consider any other matter pertinent to counsel's ability to fairly and adequately represent the interests of the class;

  (C) may order potential class counsel to provide information on any subject pertinent to the appointment and to propose terms for attorney's fees and nontaxable costs;

  (D) may include in the appointing order provisions about the award of attorney's fees or nontaxable costs under Rule 23(h); and

  (E) may make further orders in connection with the appointment.

  (2) *Standard for Appointing Class Counsel.* When one applicant seeks appointment as class counsel, the court may appoint that applicant only if the applicant is adequate under Rule 23(g)(1) and (4). If more than one adequate applicant seeks appointment, the court must appoint the applicant best able to represent the interests of the class.

  (3) *Interim Counsel.* The court may designate interim counsel to act on behalf of a putative class before determining whether to certify the action as a class action.

  (4) *Duty of Class Counsel.* Class counsel must fairly and adequately represent the interests of the class.

(h) Attorney's Fees and Nontaxable Costs. In a certified class action, the court may award reasonable attorney's fees and nontaxable costs that are authorized by law or by the parties' agreement. The following procedures apply:

  (1) A claim for an award must be made by motion under Rule 54(d)(2), subject to the provisions of this subdivision (h), at a time the court sets. Notice of the motion must be served on all parties and, for motions by class counsel, directed to class members in a reasonable manner.

  (2) A class member, or a party from whom payment is sought, may object to the motion.

  (3) The court may hold a hearing and must find the facts and state its legal conclusions under Rule 52(a).

  (4) The court may refer issues related to the amount of the award to a special master or a magistrate judge, as provided in Rule 54(d)(2)(D).

Notes on Amendments to Federal Rule 23 and Comparative State Provision

(a)   *Amendments in 2003 Altering Subsections (c)*
and (e) and Adding Subsections (g) and (h)

The 2003 amendments to Rule 23 were designed to give greater protection to class members, in particular members of 23(b)(3) classes. Subsections (c)(2)(B) and (e) were designed to provide additional protections by prescribing detailed requirements of notice upon class certification, by giving those who would be bound notice and an opportunity to be heard regarding the adequacy of a proposed settlement, and by providing the right of individual class members to opt out of settlement even though they had refused the right to opt out at an earlier point in the case.

Subsection (g) was added to specify the details of the appointment of a class counsel. A problem exists when members of a class have individual lawyers who vie for the position of class counsel, i.e. the lawyer who will be in charge of the litigation, and who, as a result, will be the primary recipient of the fees (often very large) engendered by the case.

Subsection (h) was added to require notice and an opportunity for class members to object to the awarding of the amount of attorney fees and costs sought in the case.

(b)   *Comparative State Provision*

California Civil Procedure Code § 382

* * * [W]hen the question is one of a common or general interest, of many persons, or when the parties are numerous, and it is impracticable to bring them all before the court, one or more may sue or defend for the benefit of all.

Rule 23.1. Derivative Actions

(a) Prerequisites. This rule applies when one or more shareholders or members of a corporation or an unincorporated association bring a derivative action to enforce a right that the corporation or association may properly assert but has failed to enforce. The derivative action may not be maintained if it appears that the plaintiff does not fairly and adequately represent the interests of shareholders or members who are similarly situated in enforcing the right of the corporation or association.

(b) Pleading Requirements. The complaint must be verified and must:

(1)   allege that the plaintiff was a shareholder or member at the time of the transaction complained of, or that the plaintiff's share or membership later devolved on it by operation of law;

(2)   allege that the action is not a collusive one to confer jurisdiction that the court would otherwise lack; and

(3)   state with particularity:

(A) any effort by the plaintiff to obtain the desired action from the directors or comparable authority and, if necessary, from the shareholders or members; and

(B) the reasons for not obtaining the action or not making the effort.

(c) Settlement, Dismissal, and Compromise. A derivative action may be settled, voluntarily dismissed, or compromised only with the court's approval. Notice of a proposed settlement, voluntary dismissal, or compromise must be given to shareholders or members in the manner that the court orders.

Rule 23.2. Actions Relating to Unincorporated Associations

This rule applies to an action brought by or against the members of an unincorporated association as a class by naming certain members as representative parties. The action may be maintained only if it appears that those parties will fairly and adequately protect the interests of the association and its members. In conducting the action, the court may issue any appropriate orders corresponding with those in Rule 23(d), and the procedure for settlement, voluntary dismissal, or compromise must correspond with the procedure in Rule 23(e).

Note on the Adoption in 1966 of Federal Rule 23.2

The substance of Rule 23.2 was not directly treated prior to its addition in 1966. The Advisory Committee's Note to the Rule reads as follows:

Although an action by or against representatives of the membership of an unincorporated association has often been viewed as a class action, the real or main purpose of this characterization has been to give "entity treatment" to the association when for formal reasons it cannot sue or be sued as a jural person under Rule 17(b). See Louisell & Hazard, *Pleading and Procedure: State and Federal* 718 (1962); 3 *Moore's Federal Practice* ¶ 23.08 (2d ed. 1963) * * *. Rule 23.2 deals separately with these actions, referring where appropriate to Rule 23.

Rule 24. Intervention

(a) Intervention of Right. On timely motion, the court must permit anyone to intervene who:

(1) is given an unconditional right to intervene by a federal statute; or

(2) claims an interest relating to the property or transaction that is the subject of the action, and is so situated that disposing of the action may as a practical matter impair or impede the movant's ability to protect its interest, unless existing parties adequately represent that interest.

(b) Permissive Intervention.

(1) *In General.* On timely motion, the court may permit anyone to intervene who:

(A) is given a conditional right to intervene by a federal statute; or

(B) has a claim or defense that shares with the main action a common question of law or fact.

(2) *By a Government Officer or Agency.* On timely motion, the court may permit a federal or state governmental officer or agency to intervene if a party's claim or defense is based on:

(A) a statute or executive order administered by the officer or agency; or

(B) any regulation, order, requirement, or agreement issued or made under the statute or executive order.

(3) *Delay or Prejudice.* In exercising its discretion, the court must consider whether the intervention will unduly delay or prejudice the adjudication of the original parties' rights.

(c) Notice and Pleading Required. A motion to intervene must be served on the parties as provided in Rule 5. The motion must state the grounds for intervention and be accompanied by a pleading that sets out the claim or defense for which intervention is sought.

Rule 25. Substitution of Parties

(a) Death.

(1) *Substitution if the Claim Is Not Extinguished.* If a party dies and the claim is not extinguished, the court may order substitution of the proper party. A motion for substitution may be made by any party or by the decedent's successor or representative. If the motion is not made within 90 days after service of a statement noting the death, the action by or against the decedent must be dismissed.

(2) *Continuation Among the Remaining Parties.* After a party's death, if the right sought to be enforced survives only to or against the remaining parties, the action does not abate, but proceeds in favor of or against the remaining parties. The death should be noted on the record.

(3) *Service.* A motion to substitute, together with a notice of hearing, must be served on the parties as provided in Rule 5 and on nonparties as provided in Rule 4. A statement noting death must be served in the same manner. Service may be made in any judicial district.

(b) Incompetency. If a party becomes incompetent, the court may, on motion, permit the action to be continued by or against the party's representative. The motion must be served as provided in Rule 25(a)(3).

(c) Transfer of Interest. If an interest is transferred, the action may be continued by or against the original party unless the court, on motion, orders the transferee to be substituted in the action or joined with the original party. The motion must be served as provided in Rule 25(a)(3).

(d) Public Officers; Death or Separation from Office. An action does not abate when a public officer who is a party in an official capacity dies, resigns, or otherwise ceases to hold office while the action is pending. The officer's successor is automatically substituted as a party. Later proceedings should be in the substituted party's name, but any misnomer not affecting the parties' substantial rights must be disregarded. The court may order substitution at any time, but the absence of such an order does not affect the substitution.

TITLE V. DISCLOSURES AND DISCOVERY

Rule 26. Duty to Disclose; General Provisions Governing Discovery

(a) **Required Disclosures.**

  (1) *Initial Disclosure.*

    (A) *In General.* Except as exempted by Rule 26(a)(1)(B) or as otherwise stipulated or ordered by the court, a party must, without awaiting a discovery request, provide to the other parties:

      (i) the name and, if known, the address and telephone number of each individual likely to have discoverable information—along with the subjects of that information—that the disclosing party may use to support its claims or defenses, unless the use would be solely for impeachment;

      (ii) a copy—or a description by category and location—of all documents, electronically stored information, and tangible things that the disclosing party has in its possession, custody, or control and may use to support its claims or defenses, unless the use would be solely for impeachment;

      (iii) a computation of each category of damages claimed by the disclosing party—who must also make available for inspection and copying as under Rule 34 the documents or other evidentiary material, unless privileged or protected from disclosure, on which each computation is based, including materials bearing on the nature and extent of injuries suffered; and

      (iv) for inspection and copying as under Rule 34, any insurance agreement under which an insurance business may be liable to satisfy all or part of a possible judgment in the action or to indemnify or reimburse for payments made to satisfy the judgment.

    (B) *Proceedings Exempt from Initial Disclosure.* The following proceedings are exempt from initial disclosure:

      (i) an action for review on an administrative record;

      (ii) a forfeiture action in rem arising from a federal statute;

      (iii) a petition for habeas corpus or any other proceeding to challenge a criminal conviction or sentence;

      (iv) an action brought without an attorney by a person in the custody of the United States, a state, or a state subdivision;

      (v) an action to enforce or quash an administrative summons or subpoena;

      (vi) an action by the United States to recover benefit payments;

      (vii) an action by the United States to collect on a student loan guaranteed by the United States;

      (viii) a proceeding ancillary to a proceeding in another court; and

      (ix) an action to enforce an arbitration award.

    (C) *Time for Initial Disclosures—In General.* A party must make the initial disclosures at or within 14 days after the parties' Rule 26(f) conference unless a different time is set by stipulation or court order, or unless a party objects during the conference that initial disclosures are not appropriate in this action and states the objection in the proposed discovery plan. In ruling on the objection, the court must determine what disclosures, if any, are to be made and must set the time for disclosure.

(D) *Time for Initial Disclosures—For Parties Served or Joined Later.* A party that is first served or otherwise joined after the Rule 26(f) conference must make the initial disclosures within 30 days after being served or joined, unless a different time is set by stipulation or court order.

(E) *Basis for Initial Disclosure; Unacceptable Excuses.* A party must make its initial disclosures based on the information then reasonably available to it. A party is not excused from making its disclosures because it has not fully investigated the case or because it challenges the sufficiency of another party's disclosures or because another party has not made its disclosures.

(2) *Disclosure of Expert Testimony.*

(A) *In General.* In addition to the disclosures required by Rule 26(a)(1), a party must disclose to the other parties the identity of any witness it may use at trial to present evidence under Federal Rule of Evidence 702, 703, or 705.

(B) *Witnesses Who Must Provide a Written Report.* Unless otherwise stipulated or ordered by the court, this disclosure must be accompanied by a written report—prepared and signed by the witness—if the witness is one retained or specially employed to provide expert testimony in the case or one whose duties as the party's employee regularly involve giving expert testimony. The report must contain:

    (i) a complete statement of all opinions the witness will express and the basis and reasons for them;

    (ii) the facts or data considered by the witness in forming them;

    (iii) any exhibits that will be used to summarize or support them;

    (iv) the witness's qualifications, including a list of all publications authored in the previous 10 years;

    (v) a list of all other cases in which, during the previous four years, the witness testified as an expert at trial or by deposition; and

    (vi) a statement of the compensation to be paid for the study and testimony in the case.

(C) *Witnesses Who Do Not Provide a Written Report.* Unless otherwise stipulated or otherwise ordered by the court, if the witness is not required to provide a written report, this disclosure must state:

    (i) the subject matter on which the witness is expected to present evidence under Federal Rule of Evidence 702, 703, or 705; and

    (ii) a summary of the facts and opinions to which the witness is expected to testify.

(D) *Time to Disclose Expert Testimony.* A party must make these disclosures at the times and in the sequence that the court orders. Absent a stipulation or a court order, the disclosures must be made:

    (i) at least 90 days before the date set for trial or for the case to be ready for trial; or

    (ii) if the evidence is intended solely to contradict or rebut evidence on the same subject matter identified by another party under Rule 26(a)(2)(B) or (C), within 30 days after the other party's disclosure.

(E) *Supplementing the Disclosure.* The parties must supplement these disclosures when required under Rule 26(e).

(3) *Pretrial Disclosures.*

(A) *In General.* In addition to the disclosures required by Rule 26(a)(1) and (2), a party must provide to the other parties and promptly file the following information about the evidence that it may present at trial other than solely for impeachment:

(i) the name and, if not previously provided, the address and telephone number of each witness—separately identifying those the party expects to present and those it may call if the need arises;

(ii) the designation of those witnesses whose testimony the party expects to present by deposition and, if not taken stenographically, a transcript of the pertinent parts of the deposition; and

(iii) an identification of each document or other exhibit, including summaries of other evidence—separately identifying those items the party expects to offer and those it may offer if the need arises.

(B) *Time for Pretrial Disclosures; Objections.* Unless the court orders otherwise, these disclosures must be made at least 30 days before trial. Within 14 days after they are made, unless the court sets a different time, a party may serve and promptly file a list of the following objections: any objections to the use under Rule 32(a) of a deposition designated by another party under Rule 26(a)(3)(A)(ii); and any objection, together with the grounds for it, that may be made to the admissibility of materials identified under Rule 26(a)(3)(A)(iii). An objection not so made—except for one under Federal Rule of Evidence 402 or 403—is waived unless excused by the court for good cause.

(4) *Form of Disclosures.* Unless the court orders otherwise, all disclosures under Rule 26(a) must be in writing, signed, and served.

(b) **Discovery Scope and Limits.**

(1) *Scope in General.* Unless otherwise limited by court order, the scope of discovery is as follows: Parties may obtain discovery regarding any nonprivileged matter that is relevant to any party's claim or defense and proportional to the needs of the case, considering the importance of the issues at stake in the action, the amount in controversy, the parties' relative access to relevant information, the parties' resources, the importance of the discovery in resolving the issues, and whether the burden or expense of the proposed discovery outweighs its likely benefit. Information within this scope of discovery need not be admissible in evidence to be discoverable.

(2) *Limitations on Frequency and Extent.*

(A) *When Permitted.* By order, the court may alter the limits in these rules on the number of depositions and interrogatories or on the length of depositions under Rule 30. By order or local rule, the court may also limit the number of requests under Rule 36.

(B) *Specific Limitations on Electronically Stored Information.* A party need not provide discovery of electronically stored information from sources that the party identifies as not reasonably accessible because of undue burden or cost. On motion to compel discovery or for a protective order, the party from whom discovery is sought must show that the information is not reasonably accessible because of undue burden or cost. If that showing is made, the court may nonetheless order discovery from such sources if the requesting party shows good cause, considering the limitations of Rule 26(b)(2)(C). The court may specify conditions for the discovery.

(C) *When Required.* On motion or on its own, the court must limit the frequency or extent of discovery otherwise allowed by these rules or by local rule if it determines that:

(i) the discovery sought is unreasonably cumulative or duplicative, or can be obtained from some other source that is more convenient, less burdensome, or less expensive;

(ii) the party seeking discovery has had ample opportunity to obtain the information by discovery in the action; or

(iii) the proposed discovery is outside the scope permitted by Rule 26(b)(1).

(3) *Trial Preparation: Materials.*

(A) *Documents and Tangible Things.* Ordinarily, a party may not discover documents and tangible things that are prepared in anticipation of litigation or for trial by or for another party or its representative (including the other party's attorney, consultant, surety, indemnitor, insurer, or agent). But, subject to Rule 26(b)(4), those materials may be discovered if:

(i) they are otherwise discoverable under Rule 26(b)(1); and

(ii) the party shows that it has substantial need for the materials to prepare its case and cannot, without undue hardship, obtain their substantial equivalent by other means.

(B) *Protection Against Disclosure.* If the court orders discovery of those materials, it must protect against disclosure of the mental impressions, conclusions, opinions, or legal theories of a party's attorney or other representative concerning the litigation.

(C) *Previous Statement.* Any party or other person may, on request and without the required showing, obtain the person's own previous statement about the action or its subject matter. If the request is refused, the person may move for a court order, and Rule 37(a)(5) applies to the award of expenses. A previous statement is either:

(i) a written statement that the person has signed or otherwise adopted or approved; or

(ii) a contemporaneous stenographic, mechanical, electrical, or other recording— or a transcription of it—that recites substantially verbatim the person's oral statement.

(4) *Trial Preparation: Experts.*

(A) *Deposition of an Expert Who May Testify.* A party may depose any person who has been identified as an expert whose opinions may be presented at trial. If Rule 26(a)(2)(B) requires a report from the expert, the deposition may be conducted only after the report is provided.

(B) *Trial-Preparation Protection for Draft Reports or Disclosures.* Rules 26(b)(3)(A) and (B) protect drafts of any report or disclosure required under Rule 26(a)(2), regardless of the form in which the draft is recorded.

(C) *Trial-Preparation Protection for Communications Between a Party's Attorney and Expert Witnesses.* Rules 26(b)(3)(A) and (B) protect communications between the party's attorney and any witness required to provide a report under Rule 26(a)(2)(B), regardless of the form of the communications, except to the extent that the communications:

(i) relate to compensation for the expert's study or testimony;

(ii) identify facts or data that the party's attorney provided and that the expert considered in forming the opinions to be expressed; or

(iii) identify assumptions that the party's attorney provided and that the expert relied on in forming the opinions to be expressed.

(D) *Expert Employed Only for Trial Preparation.* Ordinarily, a party may not, by interrogatories or deposition, discover facts known or opinions held by an expert who has been retained or specially employed by another party in anticipation of litigation or to prepare for trial and who is not expected to be called as a witness at trial. But a party may do so only:

>**(i)**   as provided in Rule 35(b); or

>**(ii)**   on showing exceptional circumstances under which it is impracticable for the party to obtain facts or opinions on the same subject by other means.

(E) *Payment.* Unless manifest injustice would result, the court must require that the party seeking discovery:

>**(i)**   pay the expert a reasonable fee for time spent in responding to discovery under Rule 26(b)(4)(A) or (D); and

>**(ii)**   for discovery under (D), also pay the other party a fair portion of the fees and expenses it reasonably incurred in obtaining the expert's facts and opinions.

(5) *Claiming Privilege or Protecting Trial-Preparation Materials.*

(A) *Information Withheld.* When a party withholds information otherwise discoverable by claiming that the information is privileged or subject to protection as trial-preparation material, the party must:

>**(i)**   expressly make the claim; and

>**(ii)**   describe the nature of the documents, communications, or tangible things not produced or disclosed—and do so in a manner that, without revealing information itself privileged or protected, will enable other parties to assess the claim.

(B) *Information Produced.* If information produced in discovery is subject to a claim of privilege or of protection as trial-preparation material, the party making the claim may notify any party that received the information of the claim and the basis for it. After being notified, a party must promptly return, sequester, or destroy the specified information and any copies it has; must not use or disclose the information until the claim is resolved; must take reasonable steps to retrieve the information if the party disclosed it before being notified; and may promptly present the information to the court under seal for a determination of the claim. The producing party must preserve the information until the claim is resolved.

(c) Protective Orders.

(1) *In General.* A party or any person from whom discovery is sought may move for a protective order in the court where the action is pending—or as an alternative on matters relating to a deposition, in the court for the district where the deposition will be taken. The motion must include a certification that the movant has in good faith conferred or attempted to confer with other affected parties in an effort to resolve the dispute without court action. The court may, for good cause, issue an order to protect a party or person from annoyance, embarrassment, oppression, or undue burden or expense, including one or more of the following:

>**(A)**   forbidding the disclosure or discovery;

>**(B)**   specifying terms, including time and place or the allocation of expenses, for the disclosure or discovery;

>**(C)**   prescribing a discovery method other than the one selected by the party seeking discovery;

>**(D)**   forbidding inquiry into certain matters, or limiting the scope of disclosure or discovery to certain matters;

(E) designating the persons who may be present while the discovery is conducted;

(F) requiring that a deposition be sealed and opened only on court order;

(G) requiring that a trade secret or other confidential research, development, or commercial information not be revealed or be revealed only in a specified way; and

(H) requiring that the parties simultaneously file specified documents or information in sealed envelopes, to be opened as the court directs.

(2) *Ordering Discovery.* If a motion for a protective order is wholly or partly denied, the court may, on just terms, order that any party or person provide or permit discovery.

(3) *Awarding Expenses.* Rule 37(a)(5) applies to the award of expenses.

(d) Timing and Sequence of Discovery.

(1) *Timing.* A party may not seek discovery from any source before the parties have conferred as required by Rule 26(f), except in a proceeding exempted from initial disclosure under Rule 26(a)(1)(B), or when authorized by these rules, by stipulation, or by court order.

(2) *Early Rule 34 Requests.*

(A) *Time to Deliver.* More than 21 days after the summons and complaint are served on a party, a request under Rule 34 may be delivered:

(i) to that party by any other party, and

(ii) by that party to any plaintiff or to any other party that has been served.

(B) *When Considered Served.* The request is considered to have been served at the first Rule 26(f) conference.

(3) *Sequence.* Unless the parties stipulate or the court orders otherwise for the parties' and witnesses' convenience and in the interests of justice:

(A) methods of discovery may be used in any sequence; and

(B) discovery by one party does not require any other party to delay its discovery.

(e) Supplementing Disclosures and Responses.

(1) *In General.* A party who has made a disclosure under Rule 26(a)—or who has responded to an interrogatory, request for production, or request for admission—must supplement or correct its disclosure or response:

(A) in a timely manner if the party learns that in some material respect the disclosure or response is incomplete or incorrect, and if the additional or corrective information has not otherwise been made known to the other parties during the discovery process or in writing; or

(B) as ordered by the court.

(2) *Expert Witness.* For an expert whose report must be disclosed under Rule 26(a)(2)(B), the party's duty to supplement extends both to information included in the report and to information given during the expert's deposition. Any additions or changes to this information must be disclosed by the time the party's pretrial disclosures under Rule 26(a)(3) are due.

(f) Conference of the Parties; Planning for Discovery.

(1) *Conference Timing.* Except in a proceeding exempted from initial disclosure under Rule 26(a)(1)(B) or when the court orders otherwise, the parties must confer as soon as practicable—and in any event at least 21 days before a scheduling conference is to be held or a scheduling order is due under Rule 16(b).

(2) ***Conference Content; Parties' Responsibilities.*** In conferring, the parties must consider the nature and basis of their claims and defenses and the possibilities for promptly settling or resolving the case; make or arrange for the disclosures required by Rule 26(a)(1); discuss any issues about preserving discoverable information; and develop a proposed discovery plan. The attorneys of record and all unrepresented parties that have appeared in the case are jointly responsible for arranging the conference, for attempting in good faith to agree on the proposed discovery plan, and for submitting to the court within 14 days after the conference a written report outlining the plan. The court may order the parties or attorneys to attend the conference in person.

(3) ***Discovery Plan.*** A discovery plan must state the parties' views and proposals on:

(A) what changes should be made in the timing, form, or requirement for disclosures under Rule 26(a), including a statement of when initial disclosures were made or will be made;

(B) the subjects on which discovery may be needed, when discovery should be completed, and whether discovery should be conducted in phases or be limited to or focused on particular issues;

(C) any issues about disclosure or discovery or preservation of electronically stored information, including the form or forms in which it should be produced;

(D) any issues about claims of privilege or of protection as trial-preparation materials, including—if the parties agree on a procedure to assert these claims after production— whether to ask the court to include their agreement in an order under Federal Rule of Evidence 502;

(E) what changes should be made in the limitations on discovery imposed under these rules or by local rule, and what other limitations should be imposed; and

(F) any other orders that the court should issue under Rule 26(c) or under Rule 16(b) and (c).

(4) ***Expedited Schedule.*** If necessary to comply with its expedited schedule for Rule 16(b) conferences, a court may by local rule:

(A) require the parties' conference to occur less than 21 days before the scheduling conference is held or a scheduling order is due under Rule 16(b); and

(B) require the written report outlining the discovery plan to be filed less than 14 days after the parties' conference, or excuse the parties from submitting a written report and permit them to report orally on their discovery plan at the Rule 16(b) conference.

(g) Signing Disclosures and Discovery Requests, Responses, and Objections.

(1) ***Signature Required; Effect of Signature.*** Every disclosure under Rule 26(a)(1) or (a)(3) and every discovery request, response, or objection must be signed by at least one attorney of record in the attorney's own name—or by the party personally, if unrepresented—and must state the signer's address, e-mail address, and telephone number. By signing, an attorney or party certifies that to the best of the person's knowledge, information, and belief formed after a reasonable inquiry:

(A) with respect to a disclosure, it is complete and correct as of the time it is made; and

(B) with respect to a discovery request, response, or objection, it is:

(i) consistent with these rules and warranted by existing law or by a nonfrivolous argument for extending, modifying, or reversing existing law, or for establishing new law;

(ii) not interposed for any improper purpose, such as to harass, cause unnecessary delay, or needlessly increase the cost of litigation; and

(iii) neither unreasonable nor unduly burdensome or expensive, considering the needs of the case, prior discovery in the case, the amount in controversy, and the importance of the issues at stake in the action.

(2) *Failure to Sign.* Other parties have no duty to act on an unsigned disclosure, request, response, or objection until it is signed, and the court must strike it unless a signature is promptly supplied after the omission is called to the attorney's or party's attention.

(3) *Sanction for Improper Certification.* If a certification violates this rule without substantial justification, the court, on motion or on its own, must impose an appropriate sanction on the signer, the party on whose behalf the signer was acting, or both. The sanction may include an order to pay the reasonable expenses, including attorney's fees, caused by the violation.

Notes on Amendments to Federal Rule 26 and Comparative State Provisions

(a)   *Amendment in 2015 to Federal Rule 26(b)(1) Designed to Control Discovery Abuse*

Concern about the overuse of discovery leading to injustice, whether or not employed in good faith, resulted in a revised Rule 26(b)(1). Much of the substance of the revised rule had already been included in former Rule 26(b)(2)(C) which stated, "On motion, or on its own, the court must limit the frequency or extent of discovery otherwise allowed by these rules or by local rule if it determines that: * * * (iii) the burden or expense of the proposed discovery outweighs its likely benefit, considering the needs of the case, the amount of controversy, the parties' resources, the importance of the issues at stake in the action, and the importance of the discovery in resolving the issues."

The significance of the revision appears to lie in the shift of the substance from a limitation rule to a rule defining the scope of discovery at the outset.

(b)   *Amendment in 2007 to Federal Rule 26(g)(1)(B)(i)*

The amendment added the words "or for establishing new law" to avoid denial of discovery when based on proposed changes to existing law.

(c)   *Amendments in 2006 to Federal Rule 26*

Several amendments to Rule 26 were designed to recognize the need to develop means of discovery of electronically stored information and for the protection of such information when covered by the attorney-client privilege or the work product doctrine. Changes in Rules 16, 33, 34, and 45 address the same issues.

(d)   *Amendments in 2000 to Rule 26 as restyled in 2007.*

Several major revisions to Rule 26 were adopted in 2000. First, subdivision (a)(1)(A) was altered to eliminate the power of a trial court to promulgate a standing local rule exempting cases from required automatic disclosures; a trial judge can still exempt a specific case when appropriate. Second, subdivision (a)(1)(B) specifies nine categories of cases that are now rendered exempt from the automatic disclosure requirements. As the Advisory Committee noted, these are matters "in which there is likely to be little or no discovery, or in which initial disclosure appears unlikely to contribute to the effective development of the case. * * * The Federal Judicial Center staff estimate that, nationwide, these categories total approximately one-third of all civil filings." These categories of cases are also exempt from the requirements of Rule 26(d) and (f) that the parties must confer to develop a plan of discovery and must do so prior to seeking discovery from any source.

Third, and of substantial significance, is the change in 26(a)(1)(A) narrowing initial automatic disclosures to identification of witnesses and documents "that the disclosing party may use to support its claims or defenses" and excluding information to be used "solely for impeachment." These changes replace the prior version of the rule that called for discoverable information or documents and other tangible things "relevant to the disputed facts alleged with particularity in the pleadings." According to the Advisory Committee, "A party is no longer obligated to disclose witnesses or documents that would harm its position." Just how far this goes, however, is not so clear because the Advisory

Committee goes on to state, "the disclosure obligation applies to 'claims and defenses,' and therefore requires a defendant to disclose information supporting its denials of the allegations or claims of another party."

The limitation regarding impeachment evidence merely makes obligations under Rule (a)(1) consistent with obligations already contained in Rule (a)(3) regarding pretrial disclosures of evidence that will or may be introduced at trial.

Fourth, under Rule 26(b)(1), the general scope of discovery is changed to limit it to "nonprivileged matter that is relevant to any party's claim or defense." This replaces broader language allowing discovery of "matter, not privileged, relevant to the subject matter involved in the pending action." The court has the power by order to expand discovery to include the broader scope.

Fifth, Rule 26(b)(2)(A) now bars a District Court from promulgating a standing rule limiting the number of interrogatories or the number or length of depositions, because limits now appear in the Federal Rules themselves. A court may issue a standard order regarding the number of Requests to Admit because Rule 36 does not contain such a limit.

(e)   *Comments of the Advisory Committee on 1993 Amendments to Federal Rule 26*

Subdivision (a) of Rule 26 was amended to include subparagraphs (1)–(4), which impose a duty to disclose basic information necessary for parties to prepare for trial. Subparagraph (1) states that parties must now automatically exchange information such as the names of witnesses, copies of pertinent documents, computations of damages and insurance data.

Subparagraph (2) imposes a duty to disclose information regarding expert testimony, usually within 90 days before the trial date. The revision clarifies the more vague requirement in old Rule 26 that the "substance" of expert testimony be revealed by requiring that experts retained to provide testimony submit detailed and complete written reports. This requirement, along with Rule 37(c)(1), which provides that ordinarily a party will be unable to use expert testimony not so disclosed, is intended to provide parties with basic information about the testimony of the expert. Revised Rule 26(b)(4)(A) now authorizes depositions of experts, but only after the expert's report has been served.

Subparagraph (3) requires that parties automatically exchange information regarding the use of witnesses, trial deposition testimony and exhibits at least 30 days before trial.

Subdivision (b) is substantially revised, in part for organizational clarity and in part to implement provisions which limit the discovery process. Of the substantive revisions, subparagraph (4)(A) is revised to show that experts may be deposed, but * * * only after the expert has submitted the required detailed report. * * *

Subparagraph (5) has been added to place upon a party an affirmative duty to disclose to other parties if it is withholding materials based on a claim of privilege or work product protection. The party claiming privilege must provide enough information to support its claim to enable other parties to evaluate the applicability of the claim. Sanctions may be imposed under Rule 37(b)(2) for violating this provision.

Subdivision (c) is revised to require parties to confer and attempt to resolve discovery disputes in good faith prior to seeking a protective order from the court.

Subdivision (d) is revised to prohibit the commencement of formal discovery until the parties have met pursuant to revised rule 26(f). Exceptions to this Rule are allowed under * * * [what is now Rule 30(a)(2)(A)(iii) (deposition of a person about to leave the country) and by local rule, order or stipulation].

Subdivision (e) provides that parties are subject to a continuing duty to supplement disclosures made pursuant to Rule 26(a) * * *. In addition, the revised rule clarifies that the duty to supplement formal discovery requests applies to interrogatories, requests for production, and requests for admissions, but not ordinarily to deposition testimony. Only when opinions expressed by an expert in deposition change is there a duty to supplement deposition responses.

Subdivision (f) is revised to remove provisions relating to a conference with the court regarding discovery. As noted by the Advisory Committee on Rules, "[t]his change does not signal any lessening of the importance of judicial supervision," but rather results from the relocation of such provisions to amended Rule 16 which addresses the court's role in directing the discovery process.

Subdivision (g), newly added, requires all disclosures to be signed. In keeping with the revisions to Rule 11, which state that that rule is no longer applicable to discovery matters, the signature requirement is now included directly in Rule 26.

(f)   *Comparative State Provisions*

1.   *Rule 26(a)—Required Disclosure*

Arizona Rule of Civil Procedure 26.1

(a)   Duty to Disclose, Disclosure Categories. Within the times set forth in Rule 26.1(f) or in a Scheduling Order or Case Management Order, each party must disclose in writing and serve on all other parties a disclosure statement setting forth:

(1)   the factual basis of each of the disclosing party's claims or defenses;

(2)   the legal theory on which each of the disclosing party's claims or defenses is based, including—if necessary for a reasonable understanding of the claim or defense—citations to relevant legal authorities;

(3)   the name, address, and telephone number of each witness whom the disclosing party expects to call at trial, and a description of the substance—and not merely the subject matter—of the testimony sufficient to fairly inform the other parties of each witness' expected testimony;

(4)   the name and address of each person whom the disclosing party believes may have knowledge or information relevant to the subject matter of the action, and a fair description of the nature of the knowledge or information each such person is believed to process;

(5)   the name and address of each person who has given a statement—as defined in Rule 26(b)(3)(C)(i) and (ii)—relevant to the subject matter of the action, and the custodian of each of those statements;

(6)   the anticipated subject areas of expert testimony;

(7)   a computation and measure of each category of damages alleged by the disclosing party, the documents and testimony on which such computation and measure are based, and the name, address, and telephone number of each witness whom the disclosing party expects to call at trial to testify on damages;

(8)   the existence, location, custodian, and general description of any tangible evidence, documents, or electronically stored information that the disclosing party plans to use at trial, including any material to be used for impeachment;

(9)   the existence, location, custodian, and general description of any tangible evidence, documents, or electronically stored information that may be relevant to the subject matter of the action; and

(10)   for any insurance policy, indemnity agreement, or suretyship agreement under which another person may be liable to satisfy part or all of the judgment entered in the action or to indemnify or reimburse for payments made to satisfy the judgment: (A) a copy—or if no copy is available, the existence and substance—of the insurance policy, indemnity agreement, or suretyship agreement; (B) a copy—or if no copy is available, the existence and basis—of any disclaimer, limitation, or denial of coverage or reservation of rights under the instance policy, indemnity agreement, or suretyship agreement; and (C) the remaining dollar limits of coverage under the insurance policy, indemnity agreement, or suretyship agreement. A party need only supplement its disclosure regarding the remaining dollar limits of coverage upon another party's written request made within 30 days before a settlement conference or mediation or within 30 days before trial. Within 10 days after such a request is served, a party must supplement its disclosure of the remaining dollar limits of coverage. For purposes of this rule, an insurance policy means a contract of or agreement for or effecting insurance, or the certificate memorializing it— by whatever name it is called—and includes all clauses, riders, endorsements, and papers

attached to, or a part of, it, but does not include an application for insurance. Information concerning an insurance policy, indemnity agreement, or suretyship agreement is not admissible in evidence merely because it is disclosed under this rule.

(b) Disclosure of Hard-Copy Documents. Subject to the limits of Rule(b)(1) or other good cause for not doing so, a party must serve with its disclosure a copy of any documents existing in hard copy that it has identified under Rule 26.1(a)(8), (9), and (10). If a party withholds any such hard-copy document from production, it must in its disclosure identify the document along with the name, telephone number, and address of the document's custodian. A party who produces hard-copy documents for inspection must produce them as they are kept in the usual course of business.

(c) Disclosure of Electronically Stored Information.

(1) *Duty to Confer.* When the existence of electronically stored information is disclosed or discovered, the parties must promptly confer and attempt to agree on matters relating to its disclosure and production, taking into account the limitations of Rule 26(b)(1) and (2). At the conference, each party must have at least one representative (which may include counsel) available who is reasonably familiar with the party's systems containing electronically stored information. Disputes must be presented under Rule 26(d). The following topics should be addressed, as applicable:

(A) the location and types of systems that are reasonably likely to contain electronically stored information within the permissible scope of discovery;

(B) whether it is appropriate to conduct discovery of electronically stored information in phases or stages as a method of reducing costs and burden, and if so, what the parties will include in the first phase;

(C) sources of electronically stored information that are less likely to contain discoverable information, and from which the parties will postpone or avoid discovery;

(D) search protocols or methods that will be used to identify discoverable information and filter out information not subject to discovery;

(E) the form in which the information will be produced;

(F) sharing or shifting of costs incurred by the parties for disclosing and producing the information;

(G) agreements on the preservation of electronically stored information; and

(H) whether the parties will enter a stipulation addressing inadvertent production of privileged information or will seek an order under Rule 502(d) of the Arizona Rules of Evidence addressing inadvertent production.

(2) *Production of Electronically Stored Information.* Unless the parties agree or the court orders otherwise, within 40 days after serving its initial disclosure statement, a party must produce the electronically stored information identified under Rule 26.1(a)(8) and (9). Absent good cause, no party need produce the same electronically stored information in more than one form.

(3) *Presumptive Form of Production.* Unless the parties agree or the court orders otherwise, a party must produce electronically stored information in the form requested by the receiving party. If the receiving party does not specify a form, the producing party may produce the electronically stored information in native form or in another reasonably usable form that will enable the receiving party to have the same ability to access, search, and display the information as the producing party.

(4) *Limits on Disclosure of Electronically Stored Information.* Rule 26(b)(2) applies to the disclosure of electronically stored information.

(d) Disclosure of Expert Testimony.

(1) *In General.* In addition to the disclosures required by Rule 26.1(a), a party must disclose the identity of any witness it may use at trial to present evidence under Arizona Rules of Evidence 702, 703, or 705.

(2) *Form of Expert Disclosures.* Unless the parties stipulate or the court orders otherwise, each party in an action assigned to Tier 3 must provide an expert report complying with Rule 26.1(d)(4) for any witness retained or specially employed to provide expert testimony in the action or one whose duties as the party's employee regularly involve giving expert testimony. On request of any party or on its own, the court may order an expert report in other actions if it determines that a written report will assist the court in determining if an expert's testimony satisfies the requirements of Arizona Rule of Evidence 702. In all other cases, expert disclosures must comply with Rule 26.1(d)(3). Any party contending that an expert report should be required in connection with a Rule 702 determination must raise the issue promptly after learning of the alleged need for the report. Disputes over the form or sufficiency of expert disclosures must be presented at the Rule 16(d) Scheduling Conference, or under Rule 26(d).

(3) *Expert Witnesses Who Do Not Provide a Written Report.* If an expert witness is not required to provide a written report, the disclosure must state:

    (A)   the expert's name, address, and qualifications;

    (B)   the subject matter on which the expert is expected to testify;

    (C)   the substance of the facts and opinions to which the expert is expected to testify;

    (D)   a summary of the grounds for each opinion;

    (E)   a statement of the compensation to be paid for the expert's work and testimony in the case; and

    (F)   a list of all other cases in which, during the previous 4 years, the witness testified as an expert at a hearing or trial.

(4) *Expert Witnesses Who Must Provide a Written Report.* If an expert is required to provide a signed written report, the report must contain:

    (A)   the expert's name, address, and qualifications, including a list of all publications authored in the previous 10 years;

    (B)   a complete statement of all opinions the expert will express and the basis and reasons for them;

    (C)   the facts or data considered by the expert in forming them;

    (D)   any exhibits that will be used to summarize or support them;

    (E)   identification of any publication within the scope of Arizona Rule of Evidence 803(18) on which the expert intends to rely for an opinion;

    (F)   a statement of the compensation to be paid for the expert's work and testimony in the case; and

    (G)   a list of all other cases in which, during the previous 4 years, the witness testified as an expert at a hearing or trial.

(e)   Purpose; Scope.

(1) *Purpose.* The purpose of the disclosure requirements of this Rule 26.1 is to ensure that all parties are fairly informed of the facts, legal theories, witnesses, documents, and other information relevant to the action.

(2) *Scope.* A party must include in its disclosures information and data in its possession, custody, and control as well as that which it can ascertain, learn, or acquire by reasonable inquiry and investigation.

(f)   Time for Disclosure; Continuing Duty.

(1) *Initial Disclosures.* Unless the parties agree or the court orders otherwise, a party seeking affirmative relief must serve its initial disclosure of information under Rule 26.1(a) as fully as then reasonably possible no later than 30 days after the filing of the first responsive pleading to the complaint, counterclaim, crossclaim, or third-party complaint that sets forth the party's claim for affirmative relief. Unless the parties agree or the court orders otherwise, a party filing a responsive pleading must serve its initial disclosure of information under Rule 26.1(a) as fully as then reasonably possible no later than 30 days after it files its responsive pleading.

(2) *Additional or Amended Disclosures.* The duty of disclosure prescribed in Rule 26.1(a) is a continuing duty, and each party must serve additional or amended disclosures when new or additional information is discovered or revealed. A party must serve such additional or amended disclosures in a timely manner, but in no event more than 30 days after the information is revealed to or discovered by the disclosing party. If a party obtains or discovers information that it knows reasonably should know is relevant to a hearing or deposition scheduled to occur in less than 30 days, the party must disclose such information reasonably in advance of the hearing or deposition. If the information is disclosed in a written discovery response or a deposition in a manner that reasonably informs all parties of the information, the information need not be presented in a supplemental disclosure statement. A party seeking to use information that it first disclosed later than the deadline set in a Scheduling Order or Case Management Order—or in the absence of such a deadline, later than 60 days before trial—must obtain leave of court to extend the time for disclosure as provided in Rule 37(c)(4) or (5).

(g) Signature Under Oath. Each disclosure must be in writing and signed under oath by the disclosing party.

(h) Claims of Privilege or Protection of Work-Product Materials.

(1) *Information Withheld.* When a party withholds information, a document, or electronically stored information from disclosure on a claim that it is privileged or subject to protection as work product, the party must promptly comply with Rule 26(b)(6)(A).

(2) *Inadvertent Production.* If a party contends that a document or electronically stored information subject to a claim or privilege or protection as work-product material has been inadvertently disclosed, the producing and receiving parties must comply with Rule 26(b)(6)(B).

2. *Rule 26(b)—Scope of Discovery*

New York Civil Practice Law and Rules 3101

(a) Generally. There shall be full disclosure of all matter material and necessary in the prosecution or defense of an action, regardless of the burden of proof, by:

(1) a party, or the officer, director, member, agent or employee of a party;

(2) a person who possessed a cause of action or defense asserted in the action;

(3) a person about to depart from the state, or without the state, or residing at a greater distance from the place of trial than one hundred miles, or so sick or infirm as to afford reasonable grounds of belief that he will not be able to attend the trial, or a person authorized to practice medicine, dentistry or podiatry who has provided medical, dental or podiatric care or diagnosis to the party demanding disclosure, or who has been retained by him as an expert witness; and

(4) any other person, upon notice stating the circumstances or reasons such disclosure is sought or required.

(b) Privileged matter. Upon objection by a person entitled to assert the privilege, privileged matter shall not be obtainable.

(c) Attorney's work product. The work product of an attorney shall not be obtainable.

(d) Trial preparation. 1. Experts. (i) Upon request, each party shall identify each person whom the party expects to call as an expert witness at trial and shall disclose in reasonable detail the subject matter on which each expert is expected to testify, the substance of the facts and opinions on which each expert is expected to testify, the qualifications of each expert witness and a summary of the grounds for each expert's opinion. However, where a party for good cause shown retains an expert an insufficient period of time before the commencement of trial to give appropriate notice thereof, the party shall not thereupon be precluded from introducing the expert's testimony at the trial solely on grounds of noncompliance with this paragraph. In that instance, upon motion of any party, made before or at trial, or on its own initiative, the court may make whatever order may be just. In an action for medical, dental or podiatric malpractice, a party, in responding to a request, may omit the names of medical, dental or podiatric experts but shall be required to disclose all other information concerning such experts otherwise required by this paragraph.

(ii)   In an action for medical, dental or podiatric malpractice, any party may, by written offer made to and served upon all other parties and filed with the court, offer to disclose the name of, and to make available for examination upon oral deposition, any person the party making the offer expects to call as an expert witness at trial. Within twenty days of service of the offer, a party shall accept or reject the offer by serving a written reply upon all parties and filing a copy thereof with the court. Failure to serve a reply within twenty days of service of the offer shall be deemed a rejection of the offer. If all parties accept the offer, each party shall be required to produce his or her expert witness for examination upon oral deposition upon receipt of a notice to take oral deposition in accordance with rule thirty-one hundred seven of this chapter. If any party, having made or accepted the offer, fails to make that party's expert available for oral deposition, that party shall be precluded from offering expert testimony at the trial of the action.

(iii)   Further disclosure concerning the expected testimony of any expert may be obtained only by court order upon a showing of special circumstances and subject to restrictions as to scope and provisions concerning fees and expenses as the court may deem appropriate. However, a party, without court order, may take the testimony of a person authorized to practice medicine or dentistry or podiatry who is the party's treating or retained expert, as described in paragraph three of subdivision (a) of this section, in which event any other party shall be entitled to the full disclosure authorized by this article with respect to that expert without court order.

* * *

2.   Materials. [Identical in substance to Federal Rule 26(b)(3)(A).]

(e)   **Party's statement.** A party may obtain a copy of his own statement.

(f)   **Contents of insurance agreement.** * * *

(g)   **Accident reports.** Except as otherwise provided by law, in addition to any other matter which may be subject to disclosure, there shall be full disclosure of any written report of an accident prepared in the regular course of business operations or practices of any person, firm, corporation, association or other public or private entity * * *.

(h)   * * *

(i)   In addition to any other matter which may be subject to disclosure, there shall be full disclosure of any films, photographs, video tapes or audio tapes, including transcripts or memoranda thereof, involving a person referred to in paragraph one of subdivision (a) of this section. There shall be disclosure of all portions of such material, including out-takes, rather than only those portions a party intends to use. * * *

3.   *Rule 26(c)—Discretionary Limits on Discovery*

Minnesota Rule of Civil Procedure 26.02(b)

(b)   **Scope and Limits.** Unless otherwise limited by court order, the scope of discovery is as follows. Parties may obtain discovery regarding any nonprivileged matter that is relevant to any party's claim or defense and proportional to the needs of the case, considering the importance of the issues at stake in the action, the amount in controversy, the parties' relative access to relevant information, the parties' resources, the importance of the discovery in resolving the issues, and whether the burden or expense of the proposed discovery outweighs its likely benefit[.] Information within this scope of discovery need not be admissible in evidence to be discoverable.

(1)   *Authority to Limit Frequency and Extent.* The court may establish or alter the limits on the number of depositions and interrogatories and may also limit the length of depositions under Rule 30 and the number of requests under Rule 36. The court may act upon its own initiative after reasonable notice or pursuant to a motion under Rule 26.03.

(2)   *Limits on Electronically Stored Evidence for Undue Burden or Cost.* A party need not provide discovery of electronically stored information from sources that the party identifies as not reasonably accessible because of undue burden or cost. On motion to compel discovery or for a protective order, the party from whom discovery is sought must show that the information is not reasonably accessible because of undue burden or cost. If that showing is made, the court may nonetheless order discovery from such sources if the requesting party shows good cause and proportionality, considering the limitations of Rule 26.02(b)(3). The court may specify conditions for the discovery.

(3)   *Limits Required When Cumulative; Duplicative; More Convenient Alternative; and Ample Prior Opportunity.* The frequency or extent of use of the discovery methods otherwise permitted under these rules shall be limited by the court if it determines that:

(i)   the discovery sought is unreasonably cumulative or duplicative, or is obtainable from some other source that is more convenient, less burdensome, or less expensive; or

(ii)   the party seeking discovery has had ample opportunity by discovery in the action to obtain the information sought; or

(iii)   the burden of proposed discovery is outside the scope permitted by Rule 26.02(b).

The court may act upon its own initiative after reasonable notice or pursuant to a motion under Rule 26.03.

4.   Rule 26(b)(5)(B)—Claiming Privilege or Protecting Trial-Preparation Materials—Limitations on Waiver

Federal Rule of Evidence 502. [Enacted into law on September 19, 2008. Restyled by the Supreme Court, April 26, 2011.]

The following provisions apply, in the circumstances set out, to disclosure of a communication or information covered by the attorney-client privilege or work-product protection.

(a)   Disclosure Made in a Federal Proceeding or to a Federal Office or Agency; Scope of a Waiver.—When the disclosure is made in a federal proceeding or to a federal office or agency and waives the attorney-client privilege or work-product protection, the waiver extends to an undisclosed communication or information in a Federal or State proceeding only if:

(1)   the waiver is intentional;

(2)   the disclosed and undisclosed communications or information concern the same subject matter; and

(3)   they ought in fairness to be considered together.

(b)   Inadvertent Disclosure.—When made in a federal proceeding or to a federal office or agency, the disclosure does not operate as a waiver in a federal or state proceeding if:

(1)   the disclosure is inadvertent;

(2)   the holder of the privilege or protection took reasonable steps to prevent disclosure; and

(3)   the holder promptly took reasonable steps to rectify the error, including (if applicable) following Federal Rule of Civil Procedure 26(b)(5)(B).

(c)   Disclosure Made in a State Proceeding.—When the disclosure is made in a state proceeding and is not the subject of a state-court order concerning waiver, the disclosure does not operate as a waiver in a federal proceeding if the disclosure:

(1)   would not be a waiver under this rule if it had been made in a federal proceeding; or

(2)   is not a waiver under the law of the state where the disclosure occurred.

(d) Controlling Effect of a Court Order.—A federal court may order that the privilege or protection is not waived by disclosure connected with the litigation pending before the court—in which event the disclosure is also not a waiver in any other federal or state proceeding.

(e) Controlling Effect of a Party Agreement.—An agreement on the effect of disclosure in a federal proceeding is binding only on the parties to the agreement, unless it is incorporated into a court order.

(f) Controlling Effect of this Rule.—Notwithstanding Rules 101 and 1101, this rule applies to state proceedings and to federal court-annexed and federal court-mandated arbitration proceedings, in the circumstances set out in the rule. And notwithstanding Rule 501, this rule applies even if state law provides the rule of decision.

(g) Definitions.—In this rule:

(1) "attorney-client privilege" means the protection that applicable law provides for confidential attorney-client communications; and

(2) "work-product protection" means the protection that applicable law provides for tangible material (or its intangible equivalent) prepared in anticipation of litigation or for trial.

5.   *Rule 26(d)—Sequence and Timing of Discovery*

New York Civil Practice Law and Rules 3106

(a) Normal priority. After an action is commenced, any party may take the testimony of any person by deposition upon oral or written questions. Leave of the court, granted on motion, shall be obtained if notice of the taking of the deposition of a party is served by the plaintiff before that party's time for serving a responsive pleading has expired.

(b) Witnesses. Where the person to be examined is not a party or a person who at the time of taking the deposition is an officer, director, member or employee of a party, he shall be served with a subpoena. Unless the court orders otherwise, on motion with or without notice, such subpoena shall be served at least twenty days before the examination. Where a motion for a protective order against such an examination is made, the witness shall be notified by the moving party that the examination is stayed.

(c) Prisoners. The deposition of a person confined under legal process may be taken only by leave of the court.

(d) Designation of deponent. A party desiring to take the deposition of a particular officer, director, member or employee of a person shall include in the notice or subpoena served upon such person the identity, description or title of such individual. Such person shall produce the individual so designated unless they shall have, no later than ten days prior to the scheduled deposition, notified the requesting party that another individual would instead be produced and the identity, description or title of such individual is specified. If timely notification has been so given, such other individual shall instead be produced.

6.   *Rule 26(e)—Supplementation of Responses*

New Jersey Civil Practice Rule 4:17–7

* * * [I]f a party who has furnished answers to interrogatories thereafter obtains information that renders such answers incomplete or inaccurate, amended answers shall be served not later than 20 days prior to the end of the discovery period, as fixed by the track assignment or subsequent order. Amendments may be allowed thereafter only if the party seeking to amend certifies therein that the information requiring the amendment was not reasonably available or discoverable by the exercise of due diligence prior to the discovery end date. * * * All amendments to answers to interrogatories shall be binding on the party submitting them * * *.

Rule 27. Depositions to Perpetuate Testimony

(a) Before an Action Is Filed.

(1) *Petition.* A person who wants to perpetuate testimony about any matter cognizable in a United States court may file a verified petition in the district court for the district where any expected adverse party resides. The petition must ask for an order authorizing the petitioner to depose the named persons in order to perpetuate their testimony. The petition must be titled in the petitioner's name and must show:

(A) that the petitioner expects to be a party to an action cognizable in a United States court but cannot presently bring it or cause it to be brought;

(B) the subject matter of the expected action and the petitioner's interest;

(C) the facts that the petitioner wants to establish by the proposed testimony and the reasons to perpetuate it;

(D) the names or a description of the persons whom the petitioner expects to be adverse parties and their addresses, so far as known; and

(E) the name, address, and expected substance of the testimony of each deponent.

(2) *Notice and Service.* At least 21 days before the hearing date, the petitioner must serve each expected adverse party with a copy of the petition and a notice stating the time and place of the hearing. The notice may be served either inside or outside the district or state in the manner provided in Rule 4. If that service cannot be made with reasonable diligence on an expected adverse party, the court may order service by publication or otherwise. The court must appoint an attorney to represent persons not served in the manner provided in Rule 4 and to cross-examine the deponent if an unserved person is not otherwise represented. If any expected adverse party is a minor or is incompetent, Rule 17(c) applies.

(3) *Order and Examination.* If satisfied that perpetuating the testimony may prevent a failure or delay of justice, the court must issue an order that designates or describes the persons whose depositions may be taken, specifies the subject matter of the examinations, and states whether the depositions will be taken orally or by written interrogatories. The depositions may then be taken under these rules, and the court may issue orders like those authorized by Rules 34 and 35. A reference in these rules to the court where an action is pending means, for purposes of this rule, the court where the petition for the deposition was filed.

(4) *Using the Deposition.* A deposition to perpetuate testimony may be used under Rule 32(a) in any later-filed district-court action involving the same subject matter if the deposition either was taken under these rules or, although not so taken, would be admissible in evidence in the courts of the state where it was taken.

(b) Pending Appeal.

(1) *In General.* The court where a judgment has been rendered may, if an appeal has been taken or may still be taken, permit a party to depose witnesses to perpetuate their testimony for use in the event of further proceedings in that court.

(2) *Motion.* The party who wants to perpetuate testimony may move for leave to take the depositions, on the same notice and service as if the action were pending in the district court. The motion must show:

(A) the name, address, and expected substance of the testimony of each deponent; and

(B) the reasons for perpetuating the testimony.

(3) *Court Order.* If the court finds that perpetuating the testimony may prevent a failure or delay of justice, the court may permit the depositions to be taken and may issue orders like those authorized by Rules 34 and 35. The depositions may be taken and used as any other deposition taken in a pending district-court action.

(c) Perpetuation by an Action. This rule does not limit a court's power to entertain an action to perpetuate testimony.

Comparative State Provision

Rule 27(a)(1), (3)

New York Civil Practice Law and Rules 3102(c)

Before an action is commenced, disclosure to aid in bringing an action, to preserve information or to aid in arbitration, may be obtained, but only by court order. The court may appoint a referee to take testimony.

Rule 28. Persons Before Whom Depositions May be Taken

(a) Within the United States.

(1) *In General.* Within the United States or a territory or insular possession subject to United States jurisdiction, a deposition must be taken before:

(A) an officer authorized to administer oaths either by federal law or by the law in the place of examination; or

(B) a person appointed by the court where the action is pending to administer oaths and take testimony.

(2) *Definition of "Officer".* The term "officer" in Rules 30, 31, and 32 includes a person appointed by the court under this rule or designated by the parties under Rule 29(a).

(b) In a Foreign Country.

(1) *In General.* A deposition may be taken in a foreign country:

(A) under an applicable treaty or convention;

(B) under a letter of request, whether or not captioned a "letter rogatory";

(C) on notice, before a person authorized to administer oaths either by federal law or by the law in the place of examination; or

(D) before a person commissioned by the court to administer any necessary oath and take testimony.

(2) *Issuing a Letter of Request or a Commission.* A letter of request, a commission, or both may be issued:

(A) on appropriate terms after an application and notice of it; and

(B) without a showing that taking the deposition in another manner is impracticable or inconvenient.

(3) *Form of a Request, Notice, or Commission.* When a letter of request or any other device is used according to a treaty or convention, it must be captioned in the form prescribed by that treaty or convention. A letter of request may be addressed "To the Appropriate Authority in [name of country]." A deposition notice or a commission must designate by name or descriptive title the person before whom the deposition is to be taken.

(4) *Letter of Request—Admitting Evidence.* Evidence obtained in response to a letter of request need not be excluded merely because it is not a verbatim transcript, because the testimony was not taken under oath, or because of any similar departure from the requirements for depositions taken within the United States.

(c) Disqualification. A deposition must not be taken before a person who is any party's relative, employee, or attorney; who is related to or employed by any party's attorney; or who is financially interested in the action.

Notes on Amendments to Federal Rule 28 and Related Federal and State Acts Providing Judicial Assistance to Foreign Tribunals

(a) *Amendments in 1993 and 1963 to Federal Rule 28(b)*

The 1993 changes were primarily linguistic, substituting the term "letter of request" for "letter rogatory" to conform to the Hague Convention.

It was in 1963 that Rule 28(b) was altered to facilitate the taking of depositions abroad. The Advisory Committee discussed the 1963 changes as follows:

> The amendment of clause (1) is designed to facilitate depositions in foreign countries by enlarging the class of persons before whom the depositions may be taken on notice. The class is no longer confined, as at present, to a secretary of embassy or legation, consul general, consul, vice consul, or consular agent of the United States. In a country that regards the taking of testimony by a foreign official in aid of litigation pending in a court of another country as an infringement upon its sovereignty, it will be expedient to notice depositions before officers of the country in which the examination is taken. * * *

> It has been held that a letter rogatory will not be issued unless the use of a notice or commission is shown to be impossible or impracticable. * * * The intent of * * * [clause (2)] is to overcome this judicial antipathy and to permit a sound choice between depositions under a letter rogatory and on notice or by commission in the light of all the circumstances. In a case in which the foreign country will compel a witness to attend or testify in aid of a letter rogatory but not in aid of a commission, a letter rogatory may be preferred on the ground that it is less expensive to execute, even if there is plainly no need for compulsory process. A letter rogatory may also be preferred when it cannot be demonstrated that a witness will be recalcitrant or when the witness states that he is willing to testify voluntarily, but the contingency exists that he will change his mind at the last moment. In the latter case, it may be advisable to issue both a commission and a letter rogatory, the latter to be executed if the former fails. The choice between a letter rogatory and a commission may be conditioned by other factors, including the nature and extent of the assistance that the foreign country will give to the execution of either.

> In executing a letter rogatory the courts of other countries may be expected to follow their customary procedure for taking testimony. See *United States* v. *Paraffin Wax, 2255 Bags,* 23 F.R.D. 289 (E.D.N.Y.1959). In many non-common-law countries the judge questions the witness, sometimes without first administering an oath, the attorneys put any supplemental questions either to the witness or through the judge, and the judge dictates a summary of the testimony, which the witness acknowledges as correct. * * * The last sentence of the amended subdivision provides, contrary to the implications of some authority, that evidence recorded in such a fashion need not be excluded on that account. * * * Whether or to what degree the value or weight of the evidence may be affected by the method of taking or recording the testimony is left for determination according to the circumstances of the particular case * * *; the testimony may indeed be so devoid of substance or probative value as to warrant its exclusion altogether.

> Some foreign countries are hostile to allowing a deposition to be taken in their country, especially by notice or commission, or to lending assistance in the taking of a deposition. Thus compliance with the terms of amended subdivision (b) may not in all cases ensure completion of a deposition abroad. Examination of the law and policy of the particular foreign country in advance of attempting a deposition is therefore advisable. See 4 *Moore's Federal Practice* ¶¶ 28.05–28.08 (2d ed. 1950).

(b) *Judicial Assistance to Foreign Tribunals*

See 28 U.S.C. § 1782(a) and the comparative state provision set forth in Part II, infra.

Rule 29. Stipulations About Discovery Procedure

Unless the court orders otherwise, the parties may stipulate that:

(a) a deposition may be taken before any person, at any time or place, on any notice, and in the manner specified—in which event it may be used in the same way as any other deposition; and

(b) other procedures governing or limiting discovery be modified—but a stipulation extending the time for any form of discovery must have court approval if it would interfere with the time set for completing discovery, for hearing a motion, or for trial.

Rule 30. Depositions by Oral Examination

(a) When a Deposition May Be Taken.

(1) *Without Leave.* A party may, by oral questions, depose any person, including a party, without leave of court except as provided in Rule 30(a)(2). The deponent's attendance may be compelled by subpoena under Rule 45.

(2) *With Leave.* A party must obtain leave of court, and the court must grant leave to the extent consistent with Rule 26(b)(1) and (2):

(A) if the parties have not stipulated to the deposition and:

(i) the deposition would result in more than 10 depositions being taken under this rule or Rule 31 by the plaintiffs, or by the defendants, or by the third-party defendants;

(ii) the deponent has already been deposed in the case; or

(iii) the party seeks to take the deposition before the time specified in Rule 26(d), unless the party certifies in the notice, with supporting facts, that the deponent is expected to leave the United States and be unavailable for examination in this country after that time; or

(B) if the deponent is confined in prison.

(b) Notice of the Deposition; Other Formal Requirements.

(1) *Notice in General.* A party who wants to depose a person by oral questions must give reasonable written notice to every other party. The notice must state the time and place of the deposition and, if known, the deponent's name and address. If the name is unknown, the notice must provide a general description sufficient to identify the person or the particular class or group to which the person belongs.

(2) *Producing Documents.* If a subpoena duces tecum is to be served on the deponent, the materials designated for production, as set out in the subpoena, must be listed in the notice or in an attachment. The notice to a party deponent may be accompanied by a request under Rule 34 to produce documents and tangible things at the deposition.

(3) *Method of Recording.*

(A) *Method Stated in the Notice.* The party who notices the deposition must state in the notice the method for recording the testimony. Unless the court orders otherwise, testimony may be recorded by audio, audiovisual, or stenographic means. The noticing party bears the recording costs. Any party may arrange to transcribe a deposition.

(B) *Additional Method.* With prior notice to the deponent and other parties, any party may designate another method for recording the testimony in addition to that specified in the original notice. That party bears the expense of the additional record or transcript unless the court orders otherwise.

(4) ***By Remote Means.*** The parties may stipulate—or the court may on motion order—that a deposition be taken by telephone or other remote means. For the purpose of this rule and Rules 28(a), 37(a)(2), and 37(b)(1), the deposition takes place where the deponent answers the questions.

(5) ***Officer's Duties.***

(A) *Before the Deposition.* Unless the parties stipulate otherwise, a deposition must be conducted before an officer appointed or designated under Rule 28. The officer must begin the deposition with an on-the-record statement that includes:

(i) the officer's name and business address;

(ii) the date, time, and place of the deposition;

(iii) the deponent's name;

(iv) the officer's administration of the oath or affirmation to the deponent; and

(v) the identity of all persons present.

(B) *Conducting the Deposition; Avoiding Distortion.* If the deposition is recorded nonstenographically, the officer must repeat the items in Rule 30(b)(5)(A)(i)–(iii) at the beginning of each unit of the recording medium. The deponent's and attorneys' appearance or demeanor must not be distorted through recording techniques.

(C) *After the Deposition.* At the end of a deposition, the officer must state on the record that the deposition is complete and must set out any stipulations made by the attorneys about custody of the transcript or recording and of the exhibits, or about any other pertinent matters.

(6) ***Notice or Subpoena Directed to an Organization.*** In its notice or subpoena, a party may name as the deponent a public or private corporation, a partnership, an association, a governmental agency, or other entity and must describe with reasonable particularity the matters for examination. The named organization must then designate one or more officers, directors, or managing agents, or designate other persons who consent to testify on its behalf; and it may set out the matters on which each person designated will testify. A subpoena must advise a nonparty organization of its duty to make this designation. The persons designated must testify about information known or reasonably available to the organization. This paragraph (6) does not preclude a deposition by any other procedure allowed by these rules.

(c) Examination and Cross-Examination; Record of the Examination; Objections; Written Questions.

(1) ***Examination and Cross-Examination.*** The examination and cross-examination of a deponent proceed as they would at trial under the Federal Rules of Evidence, except Rules 103 and 615. After putting the deponent under oath or affirmation, the officer must record the testimony by the method designated under Rule 30(b)(3)(A). The testimony must be recorded by the officer personally or by a person acting in the presence and under the direction of the officer.

(2) ***Objections.*** An objection at the time of the examination—whether to evidence, to a party's conduct, to the officer's qualifications, to the manner of taking the deposition, or to any other aspect of the deposition—must be noted on the record, but the examination still proceeds; the testimony is taken subject to any objection. An objection must be stated concisely in a nonargumentative and nonsuggestive manner. A person may instruct a deponent not to answer only when necessary to preserve a privilege, to enforce a limitation ordered by the court, or to present a motion under Rule 30(d)(3).

(3) ***Participating Through Written Questions.*** Instead of participating in the oral examination, a party may serve written questions in a sealed envelope on the party noticing the deposition, who must deliver them to the officer. The officer must ask the deponent those questions and record the answers verbatim.

(d)   Duration; Sanction; Motion to Terminate or Limit.

(1)   *Duration.* Unless otherwise stipulated or ordered by the court, a deposition is limited to 1 day of 7 hours. The court must allow additional time consistent with Rule 26(b)(1) and (2) if needed to fairly examine the deponent or if the deponent, another person, or any other circumstance impedes or delays the examination.

(2)   *Sanction.* The court may impose an appropriate sanction—including the reasonable expenses and attorney's fees incurred by any party—on a person who impedes, delays, or frustrates the fair examination of the deponent.

(3)   *Motion to Terminate or Limit.*

(A)   *Grounds.* At any time during a deposition, the deponent or a party may move to terminate or limit it on the ground that it is being conducted in bad faith or in a manner that unreasonably annoys, embarrasses, or oppresses the deponent or party. The motion may be filed in the court where the action is pending or the deposition is being taken. If the objecting deponent or party so demands, the deposition must be suspended for the time necessary to obtain an order.

(B)   *Order.* The court may order that the deposition be terminated or may limit its scope and manner as provided in Rule 26(c). If terminated, the deposition may be resumed only by order of the court where the action is pending.

(C)   *Award of Expenses.* Rule 37(a)(5) applies to the award of expenses.

(e)   Review by the Witness; Changes.

(1)   *Review; Statement of Changes.* On request by the deponent or a party before the deposition is completed, the deponent must be allowed 30 days after being notified by the officer that the transcript or recording is available in which:

(A)   to review the transcript or recording; and

(B)   if there are changes in form or substance, to sign a statement listing the changes and the reasons for making them.

(2)   *Changes Indicated in the Officer's Certificate.* The officer must note in the certificate prescribed by Rule 30(f)(1) whether a review was requested and, if so, must attach any changes the deponent makes during the 30-day period.

(f)   Certification and Delivery; Exhibits; Copies of the Transcript or Recording; Filing.

(1)   *Certification and Delivery.* The officer must certify in writing that the witness was duly sworn and that the deposition accurately records the witness's testimony. The certificate must accompany the record of the deposition. Unless the court orders otherwise, the officer must seal the deposition in an envelope or package bearing the title of the action and marked "Deposition of [witness's name]" and must promptly send it to the attorney who arranged for the transcript or recording. The attorney must store it under conditions that will protect it against loss, destruction, tampering, or deterioration.

(2)   *Documents and Tangible Things.*

(A)   *Originals and Copies.* Documents and tangible things produced for inspection during a deposition must, on a party's request, be marked for identification and attached to the deposition. Any party may inspect and copy them. But if the person who produced them wants to keep the originals, the person may:

(i) offer copies to be marked, attached to the deposition, and then used as originals—after giving all parties a fair opportunity to verify the copies by comparing them with the originals; or

(ii) give all parties a fair opportunity to inspect and copy the originals after they are marked—in which event the originals may be used as if attached to the deposition.

(B) *Order Regarding the Originals.* Any party may move for an order that the originals be attached to the deposition pending final disposition of the case.

(3) *Copies of the Transcript or Recording.* Unless otherwise stipulated or ordered by the court, the officer must retain the stenographic notes of a deposition taken stenographically or a copy of the recording of a deposition taken by another method. When paid reasonable charges, the officer must furnish a copy of the transcript or recording to any party or the deponent.

(4) *Notice of Filing.* A party who files the deposition must promptly notify all other parties of the filing.

(g) **Failure to Attend a Deposition or Serve a Subpoena; Expenses.** A party who, expecting a deposition to be taken, attends in person or by an attorney may recover reasonable expenses for attending, including attorney's fees, if the noticing party failed to:

(1) attend and proceed with the deposition; or

(2) serve a subpoena on a nonparty deponent, who consequently did not attend.

Notes on Amendments to Federal Rule 30

(a)   *Amendments in 2000 to Federal Rule 30*

Section 30(d) has been altered in two ways. First, subject to an extension by agreement of the parties and the deponent or by court order, a deposition is limited to one day of seven hours. Second, a person who impedes or frustrates an examination of a deponent may be sanctioned by the court.

(b)   *Amendments in 1993 to Federal Rule 30*

Rule 30, in an effort to limit costs of discovery, has been modified to limit the number of depositions. Paragraph (a)(2)(A), containing the new limit, provides that absent leave of court or stipulation among the parties, a party is limited to ten (10) depositions. Paragraph (a)(2)(A) also limits the number of times a witness may be deposed by requiring leave of court if a party wishes to depose a witness more than once.

Subdivision (b) has been revised to allow parties to record deposition testimony by nonstenographic means without first obtaining permission of other counsel. Parties choosing to record only by video- or audiotape should be cognizant that a transcript of such recordings will be required if the testimony is later offered as evidence at trial or on a dispositive motion under Rule 56, pursuant to Rules 26(a)(3)(B) and 32(c).

Subparagraph (b)(3) now allows parties, at their own expense, to record a deposition by any means, in addition to the method designated, and subparagraph (7) is revised to include technological improvements in the taking of depositions. In addition to the use of telephones, authorized by the 1980 Amendment to Rule 30, other remote electronic means such as satellite television are now allowed by stipulation or court order.

Subdivision (e) has been modified to require pre-filing review by the deponent only if requested before the deposition is completed. Recognizing the difficulty reporters often have in obtaining signatures for pre-filing review, such signatures are now waived unless review is requested and changes are made.

Rule 31. Depositions by Written Questions

(a) When a Deposition May Be Taken.

(1) *Without Leave.* A party may, by written questions, depose any person, including a party, without leave of court except as provided in Rule 31(a)(2). The deponent's attendance may be compelled by subpoena under Rule 45.

(2) *With Leave.* A party must obtain leave of court, and the court must grant leave to the extent consistent with Rule 26(b)(1) and (2):

(A) if the parties have not stipulated to the deposition and:

(i) the deposition would result in more than 10 depositions being taken under this rule or Rule 30 by the plaintiffs, or by the defendants, or by the third-party defendants;

(ii) the deponent has already been deposed in the case; or

(iii) the party seeks to take a deposition before the time specified in Rule 26(d); or

(B) if the deponent is confined in prison.

(3) *Service; Required Notice.* A party who wants to depose a person by written questions must serve them on every other party, with a notice stating, if known, the deponent's name and address. If the name is unknown, the notice must provide a general description sufficient to identify the person or the particular class or group to which the person belongs. The notice must also state the name or descriptive title and the address of the officer before whom the deposition will be taken.

(4) *Questions Directed to an Organization.* A public or private corporation, a partnership, an association, or a governmental agency may be deposed by written questions in accordance with Rule 30(b)(6).

(5) *Questions from Other Parties.* Any questions to the deponent from other parties must be served on all parties as follows: cross-questions, within 14 days after being served with the notice and direct questions; redirect questions, within 7 days after being served with cross-questions; and recross-questions, within 7 days after being served with redirect questions. The court may, for good cause, extend or shorten these times.

(b) Delivery to the Officer; Officer's Duties. The party who noticed the deposition must deliver to the officer a copy of all the questions served and of the notice. The officer must promptly proceed in the manner provided in Rule 30(c), (e), and (f) to:

(1) take the deponent's testimony in response to the questions;

(2) prepare and certify the deposition; and

(3) send it to the party, attaching a copy of the questions and of the notice.

(c) Notice of Completion or Filing.

(1) *Completion.* The party who noticed the deposition must notify all other parties when it is completed.

(2) *Filing.* A party who files the deposition must promptly notify all other parties of the filing.

Rule 32. Using Depositions in Court Proceedings

(a) Using Depositions.

(1) *In General.* At a hearing or trial, all or part of a deposition may be used against a party on these conditions:

(A) the party was present or represented at the taking of the deposition or had reasonable notice of it;

(B) it is used to the extent it would be admissible under the Federal Rules of Evidence if the deponent were present and testifying; and

(C) the use is allowed by Rule 32(a)(2) through (8).

(2) *Impeachment and Other Uses.* Any party may use a deposition to contradict or impeach the testimony given by the deponent as a witness, or for any other purpose allowed by the Federal Rules of Evidence.

(3) *Deposition of Party, Agent, or Designee.* An adverse party may use for any purpose the deposition of a party or anyone who, when deposed, was the party's officer, director, managing agent, or designee under Rule 30(b)(6) or 31(a)(4).

(4) *Unavailable Witness.* A party may use for any purpose the deposition of a witness, whether or not a party, if the court finds:

(A) that the witness is dead;

(B) that the witness is more than 100 miles from the place of hearing or trial or is outside the United States, unless it appears that the witness's absence was procured by the party offering the deposition;

(C) that the witness cannot attend or testify because of age, illness, infirmity, or imprisonment;

(D) that the party offering the deposition could not procure the witness's attendance by subpoena; or

(E) on motion and notice, that exceptional circumstances make it desirable—in the interest of justice and with due regard to the importance of live testimony in open court—to permit the deposition to be used.

(5) *Limitations on Use.*

(A) *Deposition Taken on Short Notice.* A deposition must not be used against a party who, having received less than 14 days' notice of the deposition, promptly moved for a protective order under Rule 26(c)(1)(B) requesting that it not be taken or be taken at a different time or place—and this motion was still pending when the deposition was taken.

(B) *Unavailable Deponent; Party Could Not Obtain an Attorney.* A deposition taken without leave of court under the unavailability provision of Rule 30(a)(2)(A)(iii) must not be used against a party who shows that, when served with the notice, it could not, despite diligent efforts, obtain an attorney to represent it at the deposition.

(6) *Using Part of a Deposition.* If a party offers in evidence only part of a deposition, an adverse party may require the offeror to introduce other parts that in fairness should be considered with the part introduced, and any party may itself introduce any other parts.

(7) *Substituting a Party.* Substituting a party under Rule 25 does not affect the right to use a deposition previously taken.

(8) *Deposition Taken in an Earlier Action.* A deposition lawfully taken and, if required, filed in any federal- or state-court action may be used in a later action involving the same subject matter between the same parties, or their representatives or successors in interest, to the same extent as if taken in the later action. A deposition previously taken may also be used as allowed by the Federal Rules of Evidence.

(b) Objections to Admissibility. Subject to Rules 28(b) and 32(d)(3), an objection may be made at a hearing or trial to the admission of any deposition testimony that would be inadmissible if the witness were present and testifying.

(c) Form of Presentation. Unless the court orders otherwise, a party must provide a transcript of any deposition testimony the party offers, but may provide the court with the testimony in nontranscript form as well. On any party's request, deposition testimony offered in a jury trial for any purpose other than impeachment must be presented in nontranscript form, if available, unless the court for good cause orders otherwise.

(d) Waiver of Objections.

(1) *To the Notice.* An objection to an error or irregularity in a deposition notice is waived unless promptly served in writing on the party giving the notice.

(2) *To the Officer's Qualification.* An objection based on disqualification of the officer before whom a deposition is to be taken is waived if not made:

(A) before the deposition begins; or

(B) promptly after the basis for disqualification becomes known or, with reasonable diligence, could have been known.

(3) *To the Taking of the Deposition.*

(A) *Objection to Competence, Relevance, or Materiality.* An objection to a deponent's competence—or to the competence, relevance, or materiality of testimony—is not waived by a failure to make the objection before or during the deposition, unless the ground for it might have been corrected at that time.

(B) *Objection to an Error or Irregularity.* An objection to an error or irregularity at an oral examination is waived if:

(i) it relates to the manner of taking the deposition, the form of a question or answer, the oath or affirmation, a party's conduct, or other matters that might have been corrected at that time; and

(ii) it is not timely made during the deposition.

(C) *Objection to a Written Question.* An objection to the form of a written question under Rule 31 is waived if not served in writing on the party submitting the question within the time for serving responsive questions or, if the question is a recross-question, within 7 days after being served with it.

(4) *To Completing and Returning the Deposition.* An objection to how the officer transcribed the testimony—or prepared, signed, certified, sealed, endorsed, sent, or otherwise dealt with the deposition—is waived unless a motion to suppress is made promptly after the error or irregularity becomes known or, with reasonable diligence, could have been known.

Comparative State Provisions

Rule 32(a)

Michigan Court Rule 2.302(B)(4)(d)

A party may depose a witness that he or she expects to call as an expert at trial. The deposition may be taken at any time before trial on reasonable notice to the opposite party, and may be offered as evidence at trial as provided in MCR 2.308(A). The court need not adjourn the trial because of the unavailability of expert witnesses or their depositions.

Michigan Court Rule 2.308(A)

Depositions or parts thereof shall be admissible at trial or on the hearing of a motion or in an interlocutory proceeding only as provided in the Michigan Rules of Evidence.

Rule 33. Interrogatories to Parties

(a) In General.

(1) *Number.* Unless otherwise stipulated or ordered by the court, a party may serve on any other party no more than 25 written interrogatories, including all discrete subparts. Leave to serve additional interrogatories may be granted to the extent consistent with Rule 26(b)(1) and (2).

(2) *Scope.* An interrogatory may relate to any matter that may be inquired into under Rule 26(b). An interrogatory is not objectionable merely because it asks for an opinion or contention that relates to fact or the application of law to fact, but the court may order that the interrogatory need not be answered until designated discovery is complete, or until a pretrial conference or some other time.

(b) Answers and Objections.

(1) *Responding Party.* The interrogatories must be answered:

(A) by the party to whom they are directed; or

(B) if that party is a public or private corporation, a partnership, an association, or a governmental agency, by any officer or agent, who must furnish the information available to the party.

(2) *Time to Respond.* The responding party must serve its answers and any objections within 30 days after being served with the interrogatories. A shorter or longer time may be stipulated to under Rule 29 or be ordered by the court.

(3) *Answering Each Interrogatory.* Each interrogatory must, to the extent it is not objected to, be answered separately and fully in writing under oath.

(4) *Objections.* The grounds for objecting to an interrogatory must be stated with specificity. Any ground not stated in a timely objection is waived unless the court, for good cause, excuses the failure.

(5) *Signature.* The person who makes the answers must sign them, and the attorney who objects must sign any objections.

(c) Use. An answer to an interrogatory may be used to the extent allowed by the Federal Rules of Evidence.

(d) Option to Produce Business Records. If the answer to an interrogatory may be determined by examining, auditing, compiling, abstracting, or summarizing a party's business records (including electronically stored information), and if the burden of deriving or ascertaining the answer will be substantially the same for either party, the responding party may answer by:

(1) specifying the records that must be reviewed, in sufficient detail to enable the interrogating party to locate and identify them as readily as the responding party could; and

(2) giving the interrogating party a reasonable opportunity to examine and audit the records and to make copies, compilations, abstracts, or summaries.

Notes on Amendments to Federal Rule 33 and Comparative Provisions

(a)   *Amendment in 1970 to Federal Rule 33*

The Advisory Committee commented on a 1970 amendment to Federal Rule 33 as follows:

*Subdivision * * * [(a)(2)].* There are numerous and conflicting decisions on the question whether and to what extent interrogatories are limited to matters "of fact," or may elicit opinions, contentions, and legal conclusions. * * *

Rule 33 is amended to provide that an interrogatory is not objectionable merely because it calls for an opinion or contention that relates to fact or the application of law to fact. Efforts to draw sharp lines between facts and opinions have invariably been unsuccessful, and the clear trend of the cases is to permit "factual" opinions. As to requests for opinions or contentions that call for the application of law to fact, they can be most useful in narrowing and sharpening the issues, which is a major purpose of discovery. * * * On the other hand, under the new language interrogatories may not extend to issues of "pure law," i.e., legal issues unrelated to the facts of the case. * * *

(b) *Amendment in 1980 to What Is Now Federal Rule 33(d)*

The last sentence of Rule 33(d) * * * was added in 1980. The Advisory Committee commented as follows:

> The Committee is advised that parties upon whom interrogatories are served have occasionally responded by directing the interrogating party to a mass of business records or by offering to make all of their records available, justifying the response by the option provided by this subdivision. Such practices are an abuse of the option. A party who is permitted by the terms of this subdivision to offer records for inspection in lieu of answering an interrogatory should offer them in a manner that permits the same direct and economical access that is available to the party. If the information sought exists in the form of compilations, abstracts or summaries then available to the responding party, those should be made available to the interrogating party.

(c) *Amendment in 1993 to Rule 33*

A revision to what now is Rule 33(a)(1) limits the number of interrogatories. The Advisory Committee on Rules, in commenting on the change, stated:

> Because Rule 26(a)(1) * * * requires disclosure of much of the information previously obtained by this form of discovery, there should be less occasion to use [Rule 33] * * *. Experience in over half of the district courts has confirmed that limitations on the number of interrogatories are useful and manageable.

(d) *Comparative State Provisions*

1. *Scope of Usage as to Claims and Parties*

New York Civil Practice Law and Rules 3130

    1.   Except as otherwise provided herein, after commencement of an action, any party may serve upon any other party written interrogatories. Except in a matrimonial action, a party may not serve written interrogatories on another party and also demand a bill of particulars of the same party pursuant to section 3041. In the case of an action to recover damages for personal injury, injury to property or wrongful death predicated solely on * * * negligence, a party shall not be permitted to serve interrogatories on and conduct a deposition of the same party * * * without leave of court.

    2.   After commencement of a matrimonial action or proceeding, upon motion brought by either party, upon such notice to the other party and to the non-party from whom financial disclosure is sought, and given in such manner as the court shall direct, the court may order a non-party to respond under oath to written interrogatories limited to furnishing financial information concerning a party, and further provided such information is both reasonable and necessary in the prosecution or the defense of such matrimonial action or proceeding.

2. *Limitations on Detail Required in Response*

California Civil Procedure Code § 2030.230

    If the answer to an interrogatory would necessitate the preparation or the making of a compilation, abstract, audit, or summary of or from the documents of the party to whom the interrogatory is directed, and if the burden or expense of preparing or making it would be substantially the same for the party propounding the interrogatory as for the responding party, it is a sufficient answer to that interrogatory to refer to this section and to specify the writings from which the answer may be derived or ascertained. This specification shall be in sufficient detail to permit the propounding party to locate and to identify, as readily as the responding party can, the documents from which the answer may be ascertained. The responding party shall then afford to the propounding party a reasonable opportunity to examine, audit, or inspect these documents and to make copies, compilations, abstracts, or summaries of them.

3. *Restriction on Number of Interrogatories Allowed*

Minnesota Rule of Civil Procedure 33.01(a)

Any party may serve written interrogatories upon any other party. Interrogatories may, without leave of court, be served upon any party after service of the summons and complaint. No party may serve more than a total of 50 interrogatories upon any other party unless permitted to do so by the court upon motion, notice and a showing of good cause. In computing the total number of interrogatories each subdivision of separate questions shall be counted as an interrogatory.

Rule 34. Producing Documents, Electronically Stored Information, and Tangible Things, or Entering onto Land, for Inspection and Other Purposes

(a) In General. A party may serve on any other party a request within the scope of Rule 26(b):

(1) to produce and permit the requesting party or its representative to inspect, copy, test, or sample the following items in the responding party's possession, custody, or control:

(A) any designated documents or electronically stored information—including writings, drawings, graphs, charts, photographs, sound recordings, images, and other data or data compilations—stored in any medium from which information can be obtained either directly or, if necessary, after translation by the responding party into a reasonably usable form; or

(B) any designated tangible things; or

(2) to permit entry onto designated land or other property possessed or controlled by the responding party, so that the requesting party may inspect, measure, survey, photograph, test, or sample the property or any designated object or operation on it.

(b) Procedure.

(1) *Contents of the Request.* The request:

(A) must describe with reasonable particularity each item or category of items to be inspected;

(B) must specify a reasonable time, place, and manner for the inspection and for performing the related acts; and

(C) may specify the form or forms in which electronically stored information is to be produced.

(2) *Responses and Objections.*

(A) *Time to Respond.* The party to whom the request is directed must respond in writing within 30 days after being served or—if the request was delivered under Rule 26(d)(2)—within 30 days after the parties' first Rule 26(f) conference. A shorter or longer time may be stipulated to under Rule 29 or be ordered by the court.

(B) *Responding to Each Item.* For each item or category, the response must either state that inspection and related activities will be permitted as requested or state with specificity the grounds for objecting to the request, including the reasons. The responding party may state that it will produce copies of documents or of electronically stored information instead of permitting inspection. The production must then be completed no later than the time for inspection specified in the request or another reasonable time specified in the response.

(C) *Objections.* An objection must state whether any responsive materials are being withheld on the basis of that objection. An objection to part of a request must specify the part and permit inspection of the rest.

(D) *Responding to a Request for Production of Electronically Stored Information.* The response may state an objection to a requested form for producing electronically stored information. If the responding party objects to a requested form—or if no form was specified in the request—the party must state the form or forms it intends to use.

(E) *Producing the Documents or Electronically Stored Information.* Unless otherwise stipulated or ordered by the court, these procedures apply to producing documents or electronically stored information:

(i) A party must produce documents as they are kept in the usual course of business or must organize and label them to correspond to the categories in the request;

(ii) If a request does not specify a form for producing electronically stored information, a party must produce it in a form or forms in which it is ordinarily maintained or in a reasonably usable form or forms; and

(iii) A party need not produce the same electronically stored information in more than one form.

(c) Nonparties. As provided in Rule 45, a nonparty may be compelled to produce documents and tangible things or to permit an inspection.

Notes on Amendments to Federal Rule 34 and Comparative State Provisions

(a)   *Amendments in 1970 to Federal Rule 34*

The Advisory Committee commented on the 1970 amendments to Rule 34 as follows:

Rule 34 is revised to accomplish the following major changes in the existing rule: (1) to eliminate the requirement of good cause; (2) to have the rule operate extrajudicially; (3) to include testing and sampling as well as inspecting or photographing tangible things; and (4) to make clear that the rule does not preclude an independent action for analogous discovery against persons not parties.

Subdivision (a). * * * The good cause requirement was originally inserted in Rule 34 as a general protective provision in the absence of experience with the specific problems that would arise thereunder. As the note to Rule 26(b)(3) on trial preparation materials makes clear, good cause has been applied differently to varying classes of documents, though not without confusion. It has often been said in court opinions that good cause requires a consideration of need for the materials and of alternative means of obtaining them, i.e., something more than relevance and lack of privilege. But the overwhelming proportion of the cases in which the formula of good cause has been applied to require a special showing are those involving trial preparation. In practice, the courts have not treated documents as having a special immunity to discovery simply because of their being documents. Protection may be afforded to claims of privacy or secrecy or of undue burden or expense under what is now Rule 26(c) (previously Rule 30(b)). To be sure, an appraisal of "undue" burden inevitably entails consideration of the needs of the party seeking discovery. With special provisions added to govern trial preparation materials and experts, there is no longer any occasion to retain the requirement of good cause.

The revision of Rule 34 to have it operate extrajudicially, rather than by court order, is to a large extent a reflection of existing law office practice. The Columbia Survey shows that of the litigants seeking inspection of documents or things, only about 25 percent filed motions for court orders. This minor fraction nevertheless accounted for a significant number of motions. About half of these motions were uncontested and in almost all instances the party seeking production ultimately prevailed. Although an extrajudicial procedure will not drastically alter existing practice under Rule 34—it will conform to it in most cases—it has the potential of saving court time in a substantial though proportionately small number of cases tried annually. * * *

(b)   *Amendments to Federal Rule 34(b)*

Current Rule 34(b)(2)(E) is the product of several amendments to proscribe the practice of some litigants of deliberately mixing critical documents with many others in order to obscure significance and to deal with the increasing importance of the discovery of electronically stored information.

New York Civil Practice Law and Rules 3120

1.   After commencement of an action, any party may serve on any other party a notice or on any other person a subpoena duces tecum:

(i)   to produce and permit the party seeking discovery, or someone acting on his behalf, to inspect, copy, test or photograph any designated documents or any things which are in the possession, custody or control of the party served; or

(ii)   to permit entry upon designated land or other property in the possession, custody or control of the party or person served for the purpose of inspecting, measuring, surveying, sampling, testing, photographing or recording by motion pictures or otherwise the property or any specifically designated object or operation thereon.

2.   The notice or subpoena duces tecum shall specify the time, which shall be not less than twenty days after service of the notice or subpoena, and the place and manner of making the inspection, copy, test or photograph, or of the entry upon the land or other property * * * .

* * *

Rule 35. Physical and Mental Examinations

(a)   Order for an Examination.

(1)   *In General.* The court where the action is pending may order a party whose mental or physical condition—including blood group—is in controversy to submit to a physical or mental examination by a suitably licensed or certified examiner. The court has the same authority to order a party to produce for examination a person who is in its custody or under its legal control.

(2)   *Motion and Notice; Contents of the Order.* The order:

(A)   may be made only on motion for good cause and on notice to all parties and the person to be examined; and

(B)   must specify the time, place, manner, conditions, and scope of the examination, as well as the person or persons who will perform it.

(b)   Examiner's Report.

(1)   *Request by the Party or Person Examined.* The party who moved for the examination must, on request, deliver to the requester a copy of the examiner's report, together with like reports of all earlier examinations of the same condition. The request may be made by the party against whom the examination order was issued or by the person examined.

(2)   *Contents.* The examiner's report must be in writing and must set out in detail the examiner's findings, including diagnoses, conclusions, and the results of any tests.

(3)   *Request by the Moving Party.* After delivering the reports, the party who moved for the examination may request—and is entitled to receive—from the party against whom the examination order was issued like reports of all earlier or later examinations of the same condition. But those reports need not be delivered by the party with custody or control of the person examined if the party shows that it could not obtain them.

(4)   *Waiver of Privilege.* By requesting and obtaining the examiner's report, or by deposing the examiner, the party examined waives any privilege it may have—in that action or any other action involving the same controversy—concerning testimony about all examinations of the same condition.

(5)   *Failure to Deliver a Report.* The court on motion may order—on just terms—that a party deliver the report of an examination. If the report is not provided, the court may exclude the examiner's testimony at trial.

(6) *Scope.* This subdivision (b) applies also to an examination made by the parties' agreement, unless the agreement states otherwise. This subdivision does not preclude obtaining an examiner's report or deposing an examiner under other rules.

Notes on Amendment to Federal Rule 35 and Comparative State Provisions

(a)   *Amendment in 1991 to Federal Rule 35*

The 1991 amendment eliminated the requirement that an examination be carried out by a physician, or, in the case of a mental examination, by a physician or psychologist. Instead, an order for an examination is proper if carried out "by a suitably licensed or certified examiner."

(b)   *Comparative State Provisions*

1.   *Rule 35(a)*

Minnesota Rule of Civil Procedure 35.01

In an action in which the physical or mental condition or the blood relationship of a party, or of an agent of a party, or of a person under control of a party, is in controversy, the court in which the action is pending may order the party to submit to, or produce such agent or person for a physical, mental or blood examination by a suitably licensed or certified examiner. The order may be made only on motion for good cause shown and upon notice to the party or person to be examined and to all other parties and shall specify the time, place, manner, conditions, and scope of the examination and the person or persons by whom it is made.

2.   *Rule 35(b)*

New York Civil Practice Law and Rules 3121(b)

A copy of a detailed written report of the examining physician setting out his findings and conclusions shall be delivered by the party seeking the examination to any party requesting to exchange therefor a copy of each report in his control of an examination made with respect to the mental or physical condition in controversy.

Rule 36. Requests for Admission

(a) Scope and Procedure.

(1) *Scope.* A party may serve on any other party a written request to admit, for purposes of the pending action only, the truth of any matters within the scope of Rule 26(b)(1) relating to:

> **(A)** facts, the application of law to fact, or opinions about either; and

> **(B)** the genuineness of any described documents.

(2) *Form; Copy of a Document.* Each matter must be separately stated. A request to admit the genuineness of a document must be accompanied by a copy of the document unless it is, or has been, otherwise furnished or made available for inspection and copying.

(3) *Time to Respond; Effect of Not Responding.* A matter is admitted unless, within 30 days after being served, the party to whom the request is directed serves on the requesting party a written answer or objection addressed to the matter and signed by the party or its attorney. A shorter or longer time for responding may be stipulated to under Rule 29 or be ordered by the court.

(4) *Answer.* If a matter is not admitted, the answer must specifically deny it or state in detail why the answering party cannot truthfully admit or deny it. A denial must fairly respond to the substance of the matter; and when good faith requires that a party qualify an answer or deny only a part of a matter, the answer must specify the part admitted and qualify or deny the rest. The answering party may assert lack of knowledge or information as a reason for failing to admit or deny only if the party states that it has made reasonable inquiry and that the information it knows or can readily obtain is insufficient to enable it to admit or deny.

(5) *Objections.* The grounds for objecting to a request must be stated. A party must not object solely on the ground that the request presents a genuine issue for trial.

(6) *Motion Regarding the Sufficiency of an Answer or Objection.* The requesting party may move to determine the sufficiency of an answer or objection. Unless the court finds an objection justified, it must order that an answer be served. On finding that an answer does not comply with this rule, the court may order either that the matter is admitted or that an amended answer be served. The court may defer its final decision until a pretrial conference or a specified time before trial. Rule 37(a)(5) applies to an award of expenses.

(b) Effect of an Admission; Withdrawing or Amending It. A matter admitted under this rule is conclusively established unless the court, on motion, permits the admission to be withdrawn or amended. Subject to Rule 16(e), the court may permit withdrawal or amendment if it would promote the presentation of the merits of the action and if the court is not persuaded that it would prejudice the requesting party in maintaining or defending the action on the merits. An admission under this rule is not an admission for any other purpose and cannot be used against the party in any other proceeding.

Note on Amendments to Federal Rule 36

In 1970, amendments made several important changes in Rule 36. The Advisory Committee commented on these changes as follows:

> *Subdivision (a).* As revised, the subdivision provides that a request may be made to admit any matters within the scope of Rule 26(b) that relate to statements or opinions of fact or of the application of law to fact. It thereby eliminates the requirement that the matters be "of fact." This change resolves conflicts in the court decisions as to whether a request to admit matters of "opinion" and matters involving "mixed law and fact" is proper under the rule. * * *

> Not only is it difficult as a practical matter to separate "fact" from "opinion," * * * but an admission on a matter of opinion may facilitate proof or narrow the issues or both. An admission of a matter involving the application of law to fact may, in a given case, even more clearly narrow the issues. For example, an admission that an employee acted in the scope of his employment may remove a major issue from the trial. * * *

> Courts have also divided on whether an answering party may properly object to request for admission as to matters which that party regards as "in dispute." * * * The proper response in such cases is an answer. The very purpose of the request is to ascertain whether the answering party is prepared to admit or regards the matter as presenting a genuine issue for trial. In his answer, the party may deny, or he may give as his reason for inability to admit or deny the existence of a genuine issue. The party runs no risk of sanctions if the matter is genuinely in issue, since Rule 37(c) provides a sanction of costs only when there are no good reasons for a failure to admit.

* * *

> Another sharp split of authority exists on the question whether a party may base his answer on lack of information or knowledge without seeking out additional information. One line of cases has held that a party may answer on the basis of such knowledge as he has at the time he answers. * * *

> The rule as revised adopts the majority view, as in keeping with a basic principle of the discovery rules that a reasonable burden may be imposed on the parties when its discharge will facilitate preparation for trial and ease the trial process. It has been argued against this view that one side should not have the burden of "proving" the other side's case. The revised rule requires only that the answering party make reasonable inquiry and secure such knowledge and information as are readily obtainable by him. In most instances, the investigation will be necessary either to his own case or to preparation for rebuttal. Even when it is not, the information may be close enough at hand to be "readily obtainable." Rule 36 requires only that the party state that he has taken these steps. The sanction for failure of a party to inform himself before he answers lies in the award of costs after trial, as provided in Rule 37(c). * * *

A problem peculiar to Rule 36 arises if the responding party serves answers that are not in conformity with the requirements of the rule—for example, a denial is not "specific," or the explanation of inability to admit or deny is not "in detail." Rule 36 now makes no provision for court scrutiny of such answers before trial, and it seems to contemplate that defective answers bring about admissions just as effectively as if no answer had been served. Some cases have so held. * * *

Giving a defective answer the automatic effect of an admission may cause unfair surprise. A responding party who purported to deny or to be unable to admit or deny will for the first time at trial confront the contention that he has made a binding admission. Since it is not always easy to know whether a denial is "specific" or an explanation is "in detail," neither party can know how the court will rule at trial and whether proof must be prepared. Some courts, therefore, have entertained motions to rule on defective answers. They have at times ordered that amended answers be served, when the defects were technical, and at other times have declared that the matter was admitted. * * * The rule as revised conforms to the latter practice.

Subdivision (b). The rule does not now indicate the extent to which a party is bound by his admission. Some courts view admissions as the equivalent of sworn testimony. * * * At least in some jurisdictions a party may rebut his own testimony, e.g., *Alamo v. Del Rosario,* 98 F.2d 328 (D.C.Cir.1938), and by analogy an admission made pursuant to Rule 36 may likewise be thought rebuttable. * * * In *McSparran v. Hanigan,* 225 F.Supp. 628, 636–637 (E.D.Pa.1963), the court held that an admission is conclusively binding, though noting the confusion created by prior decisions.

The new provisions give an admission a conclusively binding effect, for purposes only of the pending action, unless the admission is withdrawn or amended. In form and substance a Rule 36 admission is comparable to an admission in pleadings or a stipulation drafted by counsel for use at trial, rather than to an evidentiary admission of a party. * * *

Rule 37. Failure to Make Disclosures or to Cooperate in Discovery; Sanctions

(a) Motion for an Order Compelling Disclosure or Discovery.

(1) ***In General.*** On notice to other parties and all affected persons, a party may move for an order compelling disclosure or discovery. The motion must include a certification that the movant has in good faith conferred or attempted to confer with the person or party failing to make disclosure or discovery in an effort to obtain it without court action.

(2) ***Appropriate Court.*** A motion for an order to a party must be made in the court where the action is pending. A motion for an order to a nonparty must be made in the court where the discovery is or will be taken.

(3) ***Specific Motions.***

(A) *To Compel Disclosure.* If a party fails to make a disclosure required by Rule 26(a), any other party may move to compel disclosure and for appropriate sanctions.

(B) *To Compel a Discovery Response.* A party seeking discovery may move for an order compelling an answer, designation, production, or inspection. This motion may be made if:

(i) a deponent fails to answer a question asked under Rule 30 or 31;

(ii) a corporation or other entity fails to make a designation under Rule 30(b)(6) or 31(a)(4);

(iii) a party fails to answer an interrogatory submitted under Rule 33; or

(iv) a party fails to produce documents or fails to respond that inspection will be permitted—or fails to permit inspection—as requested under Rule 34.

(C) *Related to a Deposition.* When taking an oral deposition, the party asking a question may complete or adjourn the examination before moving for an order.

(4) *Evasive or Incomplete Disclosure, Answer, or Response.* For purposes of this subdivision (a), an evasive or incomplete disclosure, answer, or response must be treated as a failure to disclose, answer, or respond.

(5) *Payment of Expenses; Protective Orders.*

(A) *If the Motion Is Granted (or Disclosure or Discovery Is Provided After Filing).* If the motion is granted—or if the disclosure or requested discovery is provided after the motion was filed—the court must, after giving an opportunity to be heard, require the party or deponent whose conduct necessitated the motion, the party or attorney advising that conduct, or both to pay the movant's reasonable expenses incurred in making the motion, including attorney's fees. But the court must not order this payment if:

(i) the movant filed the motion before attempting in good faith to obtain the disclosure or discovery without court action;

(ii) the opposing party's nondisclosure, response, or objection was substantially justified; or

(iii) other circumstances make an award of expenses unjust.

(B) *If the Motion Is Denied.* If the motion is denied, the court may issue any protective order authorized under Rule 26(c) and must, after giving an opportunity to be heard, require the movant, the attorney filing the motion, or both to pay the party or deponent who opposed the motion its reasonable expenses incurred in opposing the motion, including attorney's fees. But the court must not order this payment if the motion was substantially justified or other circumstances make an award of expenses unjust.

(C) *If the Motion Is Granted in Part and Denied in Part.* If the motion is granted in part and denied in part, the court may issue any protective order authorized under Rule 26(c) and may, after giving an opportunity to be heard, apportion the reasonable expenses for the motion.

(b) **Failure to Comply With a Court Order.**

(1) *Sanctions Sought in the District Where the Deposition Is Taken.* If the court where the discovery is taken orders a deponent to be sworn or to answer a question and the deponent fails to obey, the failure may be treated as contempt of court. If a deposition-related motion is transferred to the court where the action is pending, and that court orders a deponent to be sworn or to answer a question and the deponent fails to obey, the failure may be treated as contempt of either the court where the discovery is taken or the court where the action is pending.

(2) *Sanctions Sought in the District Where the Action Is Pending.*

(A) *For Not Obeying a Discovery Order.* If a party or a party's officer, director, or managing agent—or a witness designated under Rule 30(b)(6) or 31(a)(4)—fails to obey an order to provide or permit discovery, including an order under Rule 26(f), 35, or 37(a), the court where the action is pending may issue further just orders. They may include the following:

(i) directing that the matters embraced in the order or other designated facts be taken as established for purposes of the action, as the prevailing party claims;

(ii) prohibiting the disobedient party from supporting or opposing designated claims or defenses, or from introducing designated matters in evidence;

(iii) striking pleadings in whole or in part;

(iv) staying further proceedings until the order is obeyed;

(v) dismissing the action or proceeding in whole or in part;

(vi) rendering a default judgment against the disobedient party; or

(vii) treating as contempt of court the failure to obey any order except an order to submit to a physical or mental examination.

(B) *For Not Producing a Person for Examination.* If a party fails to comply with an order under Rule 35(a) requiring it to produce another person for examination, the court may issue any of the orders listed in Rule 37(b)(2)(A)(i)–(vi), unless the disobedient party shows that it cannot produce the other person.

(C) *Payment of Expenses.* Instead of or in addition to the orders above, the court must order the disobedient party, the attorney advising that party, or both to pay the reasonable expenses, including attorney's fees, caused by the failure, unless the failure was substantially justified or other circumstances make an award of expenses unjust.

(c) **Failure to Disclose, to Supplement an Earlier Response, or to Admit.**

(1) *Failure to Disclose or Supplement.* If a party fails to provide information or identify a witness as required by Rule 26(a) or (e), the party is not allowed to use that information or witness to supply evidence on a motion, at a hearing, or at a trial, unless the failure was substantially justified or is harmless. In addition to or instead of this sanction, the court, on motion and after giving an opportunity to be heard:

(A) may order payment of the reasonable expenses, including attorney's fees, caused by the failure;

(B) may inform the jury of the party's failure; and

(C) may impose other appropriate sanctions, including any of the orders listed in Rule 37(b)(2)(A)(i)–(vi).

(2) *Failure to Admit.* If a party fails to admit what is requested under Rule 36 and if the requesting party later proves a document to be genuine or the matter true, the requesting party may move that the party who failed to admit pay the reasonable expenses, including attorney's fees, incurred in making that proof. The court must so order unless:

(A) the request was held objectionable under Rule 36(a);

(B) the admission sought was of no substantial importance;

(C) the party failing to admit had a reasonable ground to believe that it might prevail on the matter; or

(D) there was other good reason for the failure to admit.

(d) **Party's Failure to Attend Its Own Deposition, Serve Answers to Interrogatories, or Respond to a Request for Inspection.**

(1) *In General.*

(A) *Motion; Grounds for Sanctions.* The court where the action is pending may, on motion, order sanctions if:

(i) a party or a party's officer, director, or managing agent—or a person designated under Rule 30(b)(6) or 31(a)(4)—fails, after being served with proper notice, to appear for that person's deposition; or

(ii) a party, after being properly served with interrogatories under Rule 33 or a request for inspection under Rule 34, fails to serve its answers, objections, or written response.

(B) *Certification.* A motion for sanctions for failing to answer or respond must include a certification that the movant has in good faith conferred or attempted to confer with the party failing to act in an effort to obtain the answer or response without court action.

(2) *Unacceptable Excuse for Failing to Act.* A failure described in Rule 37(d)(1)(A) is not excused on the ground that the discovery sought was objectionable, unless the party failing to act has a pending motion for a protective order under Rule 26(c).

(3) *Types of Sanctions.* Sanctions may include any of the orders listed in Rule 37(b)(2)(A)(i)–(vi). Instead of or in addition to these sanctions, the court must require the party failing to act, the attorney advising that party, or both to pay the reasonable expenses, including attorney's fees, caused by the failure, unless the failure was substantially justified or other circumstances make an award of expenses unjust.

(e) Failure to Preserve Electronically Stored Information. If electronically stored information that should have been preserved in the anticipation or conduct of litigation is lost because a party failed to take reasonable steps to preserve it, and it cannot be restored or replaced through additional discovery, the court:

(1) upon finding prejudice to another party from loss of the information, may order measures no greater than necessary to cure the prejudice; or

(2) only upon finding that the party acted with the intent to deprive another party of the information's use in the litigation may:

(A) presume that the lost information was unfavorable to the party;

(B) instruct the jury that it may or must presume the information was unfavorable to the party; or

(C) dismiss the action or enter a default judgment.

(f) Failure to Participate in Framing a Discovery Plan. If a party or its attorney fails to participate in good faith in developing and submitting a proposed discovery plan as required by Rule 26(f), the court may, after giving an opportunity to be heard, require that party or attorney to pay to any other party the reasonable expenses, including attorney's fees, caused by the failure.

Notes on Amendments to Federal Rule 37 and Comparative Federal and State Provisions

(a)   *Amendments in 1993 to Federal Rule 37*

Rule 37 has been revised to reflect the revisions made to Rule 26(a) mandating the automatic exchange of information without formal discovery. Subdivision (a)(2)(A) [now Rule 37(a)(3)(A)] has been added to provide a method for compelling disclosure where a party fails to fully comply with Rule 26(a). Under (c)(1) of the revised rule, if the information is important evidence for the non-disclosing party, the party seeking to compel disclosure may, as an alternative measure, ask the court to exclude the evidence at trial.

Subdivision (c) provides that as a sanction for failing to automatically disclose information required by Rule 26(a) or 26(e)(1), a party will be prohibited from using such information at trial "unless the failure was substantially justified." Unlike the old version of the rule, this provision is self-executing and does not require the opposing party to make a motion. The exception from sanctions where the failure to disclose is harmless serves to mitigate the harshness of this rule.

(b)   *Comparative Provisions*

Rule 37(a)

1.   *Local Federal Rule*

United States District Court, District of Columbia, Civil Rule 7(m)

Duty to Confer on Nondispositive Motions. Before filing any nondispositive motion in a civil action, counsel shall discuss the anticipated motion with opposing counsel in a good-faith effort to determine whether there is any opposition to the relief sought and, if there is opposition, to narrow the areas of disagreement. The duty to confer also applies to non-incarcerated parties appearing pro se. A party shall include in its motion a statement that the required discussion occurred, and a statement as to whether the motion is opposed.

2. *Comparative State Provisions*

California Civil Procedure Code § 2023.010

Misuses of the discovery process include, but are not limited to, the following:

(a)   Persisting, over objection and without substantial justification, in an attempt to obtain information or materials that are outside the scope of permissible discovery.

(b)   Using a discovery method in a manner that does not comply with its specified procedures.

(c)   Employing a discovery method in a manner or to an extent that causes unwarranted annoyance, embarrassment, or oppression, or undue burden and expense.

(d)   Failing to respond or to submit to an authorized method of discovery.

(e)   Making, without substantial justification, an unmeritorious objection to discovery.

(f)   Making an evasive response to discovery.

(g)   Disobeying a court order to provide discovery.

(h)   Making or opposing, unsuccessfully and without substantial justification, a motion to compel or to limit discovery.

(i)   Failing to confer in person, by telephone, or by letter with an opposing party or attorney in a reasonable and good faith attempt to resolve informally any dispute concerning discovery, if the section governing a particular discovery motion requires the filing of a declaration stating facts showing that an attempt at informal resolution has been made.

California Civil Procedure Code § 2023.020

Notwithstanding the outcome of the particular discovery motion, the court shall impose a monetary sanction ordering that any party or attorney who fails to confer as required pay the reasonable expenses, including attorney's fees, incurred by anyone as a result of that conduct.

California Civil Procedure Code § 2023.030

To the extent authorized by the chapter governing any particular discovery method or any other provision of this title, the court, after notice to any affected party, person, or attorney, and after opportunity for hearing, may impose the following sanctions against anyone engaging in conduct that is a misuse of the discovery process:

     (a)   The court may impose a monetary sanction ordering that one engaging in the misuse of the discovery process, or any attorney advising that conduct, or both pay the reasonable expenses, including attorney's fees, incurred by anyone as a result of that conduct. The court may also impose this sanction on one unsuccessfully asserting that another has engaged in the misuse of the discovery process, or on any attorney who advised that assertion, or on both. If a monetary sanction is authorized by any provision of this article, the court shall impose that sanction unless it finds that the one subject to the sanction acted with substantial justification or that other circumstances make the imposition of the sanction unjust.

     (b)   The court may impose an issue sanction ordering that designed facts shall be taken as established in the action in accordance with the claim of the party adversely affected by the misuse of the discovery process. The court may also impose an issue sanction by an order prohibiting any party engaging in the misuse of the discovery process from supporting or opposing designated claims or defenses.

     (c)   The court may impose an evidence sanction by an order prohibiting any party engaging in the misuse of the discovery process from introducing designated matters in evidence.

     (d)   The court may impose a terminating sanction by one of the following orders:

(1)   An order striking out the pleadings or parts of the pleadings of any party engaging in the misuse of the discovery process.

(2)   An order staying further proceedings by that party until an order for discovery is obeyed.

(3)   An order dismissing the action, or any part of the action, of that party.

(4)   An order rendering a judgment by default against that party.

(e)   The court may impose a contempt sanction by an order treating the misuse of the discovery process as a contempt of court.

(f)   (1)   Notwithstanding subdivision (a), or any other section of this title, absent exceptional circumstances, the court shall not impose sanctions on a party or attorney for failure to provide electronically stored information that has been lost, damaged, altered, or overwritten as a result of the routine, good faith operation of an electronic information system.

(2)   This subdivision shall not be construed to alter any obligation to preserve discoverable information.

California Civil Procedure Code § 2023.040

A request for a sanction shall, in the notice of motion, identify every person, party, and attorney against whom the sanction is sought, and specify the type of sanction sought. The notice of motion shall be supported by a memorandum of points and authorities, and accompanied by a declaration setting forth facts supporting the amount of any monetary sanction sought.

TITLE VI. TRIALS

Rule 38. Right to a Jury Trial; Demand

(a)   **Right Preserved.** The right of trial by jury as declared by the Seventh Amendment to the Constitution—or as provided by a federal statute—is preserved to the parties inviolate.

(b)   **Demand.** On any issue triable of right by a jury, a party may demand a jury trial by:

(1)   serving the other parties with a written demand—which may be included in a pleading—no later than 14 days after the last pleading directed to the issue is served; and

(2)   filing the demand in accordance with Rule 5(d).

(c)   **Specifying Issues.** In its demand, a party may specify the issues that it wishes to have tried by a jury; otherwise, it is considered to have demanded a jury trial on all the issues so triable. If the party has demanded a jury trial on only some issues, any other party may—within 14 days after being served with the demand or within a shorter time ordered by the court—serve a demand for a jury trial on any other or all factual issues triable by jury.

(d)   **Waiver; Withdrawal.** A party waives a jury trial unless its demand is properly served and filed. A proper demand may be withdrawn only if the parties consent.

(e)   **Admiralty and Maritime Claims.** These rules do not create a right to a jury trial on issues in a claim that is an admiralty or maritime claim under Rule 9(h).

Federal and State Provisions Governing the Right to Jury Trial

(a)   *Constitutional Provisions*

United States Constitution, 7th Amendment

In Suits at common law, where the value in controversy shall exceed twenty dollars, the right of trial by jury shall be preserved, and no fact tried by a jury shall be otherwise re-examined in any Court of the United States, than according to the rules of the common law.

Pennsylvania Constitution Art. 1, § 6

Trial by jury shall be as heretofore, and the right thereof remain inviolate. The General Assembly may provide, however, by law, that a verdict may be rendered by not less than five-sixths of the jury in any civil case. * * *

Virginia Constitution Art. 1, § 11

* * *

That in controversies respecting property, and in suits between man and man, trial by jury is preferable to any other, and ought to be held sacred. The General Assembly may limit the number of jurors for civil cases in courts of record to not less than five.

* * *

(b)   *Federal Statute for Certain Title VII Cases*

42 U.S.C. § 1981a(c)

[This provision, enacted in 1991, provides for a jury trial in those Title VII suits in which respondent is alleged to have engaged in unlawful *intentional* discrimination.]

(c)   *State Statute on Demand and Waiver*

New York Civil Practice Law and Rules 4103

When it appears in the course of a trial by the court that the relief required, although not originally demanded by a party, entitles the adverse party to a trial by jury of certain issues of fact, the court shall give the adverse party an opportunity to demand a jury trial of such issues. Failure to make such demand within the time limited by the court shall be deemed a waiver of the right to trial by jury. Upon such demand, the court shall order a jury trial of any issues of fact which are required to be tried by jury.

Rule 39. Trial by Jury or by the Court

(a) When a Demand Is Made. When a jury trial has been demanded under Rule 38, the action must be designated on the docket as a jury action. The trial on all issues so demanded must be by jury unless:

    (1) the parties or their attorneys file a stipulation to a nonjury trial or so stipulate on the record; or

    (2) the court, on motion or on its own, finds that on some or all of those issues there is no federal right to a jury trial.

(b) When No Demand Is Made. Issues on which a jury trial is not properly demanded are to be tried by the court. But the court may, on motion, order a jury trial on any issue for which a jury might have been demanded.

(c) Advisory Jury; Jury Trial by Consent. In an action not triable of right by a jury, the court, on motion or on its own:

    (1) may try any issue with an advisory jury; or

    (2) may, with the parties' consent, try any issue by a jury whose verdict has the same effect as if a jury trial had been a matter of right, unless the action is against the United States and a federal statute provides for a nonjury trial.

Rule 40. Scheduling Cases for Trial

Each court must provide by rule for scheduling trials. The court must give priority to actions entitled to priority by a federal statute.

Rule 41. Dismissal of Actions

(a) Voluntary Dismissal.

    (1) *By the Plaintiff.*

        (A) *Without a Court Order.* Subject to Rules 23(e), 23.1(c), 23.2, and 66 and any applicable federal statute, the plaintiff may dismiss an action without a court order by filing:

            (i) a notice of dismissal before the opposing party serves either an answer or a motion for summary judgment; or

            (ii) a stipulation of dismissal signed by all parties who have appeared.

        (B) *Effect.* Unless the notice or stipulation states otherwise, the dismissal is without prejudice. But if the plaintiff previously dismissed any federal- or state-court action based on or including the same claim, a notice of dismissal operates as an adjudication on the merits.

    (2) *By Court Order; Effect.* Except as provided in Rule 41(a)(1), an action may be dismissed at the plaintiff's request only by court order, on terms that the court considers proper. If a defendant has pleaded a counterclaim before being served with the plaintiff's motion to dismiss, the action may be dismissed over the defendant's objection only if the counterclaim can remain pending for independent adjudication. Unless the order states otherwise, a dismissal under this paragraph (2) is without prejudice.

(b) Involuntary Dismissal; Effect. If the plaintiff fails to prosecute or to comply with these rules or a court order, a defendant may move to dismiss the action or any claim against it. Unless the dismissal order states otherwise, a dismissal under this subdivision (b) and any dismissal not under this rule—except one for lack of jurisdiction, improper venue, or failure to join a party under Rule 19—operates as an adjudication on the merits.

(c) Dismissing a Counterclaim, Crossclaim, or Third-Party Claim. This rule applies to a dismissal of any counterclaim, crossclaim, or third-party claim. A claimant's voluntary dismissal under Rule 41(a)(1)(A)(i) must be made:

    (1) before a responsive pleading is served; or

    (2) if there is no responsive pleading, before evidence is introduced at a hearing or trial.

(d) Costs of a Previously Dismissed Action. If a plaintiff who previously dismissed an action in any court files an action based on or including the same claim against the same defendant, the court:

    (1) may order the plaintiff to pay all or part of the costs of that previous action; and

    (2) may stay the proceedings until the plaintiff has complied.

Comparative Federal and State Provisions

(a)   *Rule 41(a)*

Illinois Compiled Statutes ch. 735, 5/2–1009(a), (c)

(a)   The plaintiff may, at any time before trial or hearing begins, upon notice to each party who has appeared or each such party's attorney, and upon payment of costs, dismiss his or her action or any part thereof as to any defendant, without prejudice, by order filed in the cause.

(c)   After trial or hearing begins, the plaintiff may dismiss, only on terms fixed by the court (1) upon filing a stipulation to that effect signed by the defendant, or (2) on motion specifying the ground for dismissal, which shall be supported by affidavit or other proof.

(b)   *Rule 41(b)*

1.   *Local Federal Rule*

United States District Court, District of Connecticut, Local Rule of Civil Procedure 41(a)

In civil actions in which no action has been taken by the parties for six (6) months or in which deadlines established by the Court pursuant to Rule 16 appear not to have been met, the Clerk shall give notice of proposed dismissal to counsel of record and self-represented parties, if any. If such notice has been given and no action has been taken in the action in the meantime and no satisfactory explanation is submitted to the Court within twenty-one (21) days thereafter, the Clerk shall enter an order of dismissal. Any such order entered by the Clerk under this Rule may be suspended, altered, or rescinded by the Court for cause shown.

2.   *Comparative State Provisions*

California Civil Procedure Code § 583.210

(a)   The summons and complaint shall be served upon a defendant within three years after the action is commenced against the defendant. For the purpose of this subdivision, an action is commenced at the time the complaint is filed.

(b)   Proof of service of the summons shall be filed within 60 days after the time the summons and complaint must be served upon a defendant.

California Civil Procedure Code § 583.310

An action shall be brought to trial within five years after the action is commenced against the defendant.

California Civil Procedure Code § 583.330

The parties may extend the time within which an action must be brought to trial pursuant to this article by the following means:

(a)   By written stipulation. The stipulation need not be filed but, if it is not filed, the stipulation shall be brought to the attention of the court if relevant to a motion for dismissal.

(b)   By oral agreement made in open court, if entered in the minutes of the court or a transcript is made.

California Civil Procedure Code § 583.360

(a)   An action shall be dismissed by the court on its own motion or on motion of the defendant, after notice to the parties, if the action is not brought to trial within the time prescribed in this article.

(b)   The requirements of this article are mandatory and are not subject to extension, excuse, or exception except as expressly provided by statute.

California Civil Procedure Code § 583.410(a)

The court may in its discretion dismiss an action for delay in prosecution pursuant to this article on its own motion or on motion of the defendant if to do so appears to the court appropriate under the circumstances of the case.

Indiana Rules of Trial Procedure, Rule 41(E)

Whenever there has been a failure to comply with these rules or when no action has been taken in a civil case for a period of sixty [60] days, the court, on motion of a party or on its own motion shall order a hearing for the purpose of dismissing such case. The court shall enter an order of dismissal at plaintiff's costs if the plaintiff shall not show sufficient cause at or before such hearing. Dismissal may be withheld or reinstatement of dismissal may be made subject to the condition that the plaintiff comply with these rules and diligently prosecute the action and upon such terms that the court in its discretion determines to be necessary to assure such diligent prosecution.

Rule 42. Consolidation; Separate Trials

(a) Consolidation. If actions before the court involve a common question of law or fact, the court may:

(1) join for hearing or trial any or all matters at issue in the actions;

(2) consolidate the actions; or

(3) issue any other orders to avoid unnecessary cost or delay.

(b) Separate Trials. For convenience, to avoid prejudice, or to expedite and economize, the court may order a separate trial of one or more separate issues, claims, crossclaims, counterclaims, or third-party claims. When ordering a separate trial, the court must preserve any federal right to a jury trial.

Comparative State Provisions

(a) *Rule 42(a)*

New York Civil Practice Law and Rules 602

(a) Generally. When actions involving a common question of law or fact are pending before a court, the court, upon motion, may order a joint trial of any or all the matters in issue, may order the actions consolidated, and may make such other orders concerning proceedings therein as may tend to avoid unnecessary costs or delay.

(b) Cases pending in different courts. Where an action is pending in the supreme court it may, upon motion, remove to itself an action pending in another court and consolidate it or have it tried together with that in the supreme court. Where an action is pending in the county court, it may, upon motion, remove to itself an action pending in a city, municipal, district or justice court in the county and consolidate it or have it tried together with that in the county court.

(b) *Rule 42(b)*

New York Civil Practice Law and Rules 1002(c)

It shall not be necessary that each plaintiff be interested in obtaining, or each defendant be interested in defending against, all the relief demanded or as to every claim included in an action; but the court may make such orders as will prevent a party from being embarrassed, delayed, or put to expense by the inclusion of a party against whom he asserts no claim and, who asserts no claim against him, and may order separate trials or make other orders to prevent prejudice.

Rule 43. Taking Testimony

(a) In Open Court. At trial, the witnesses' testimony must be taken in open court unless a federal statute, the Federal Rules of Evidence, these rules, or other rules adopted by the Supreme Court provide otherwise. For good cause in compelling circumstances and with appropriate safeguards, the court may permit testimony in open court by contemporaneous transmission from a different location.

(b) Affirmation Instead of an Oath. When these rules require an oath, a solemn affirmation suffices.

(c) Evidence on a Motion. When a motion relies on facts outside the record, the court may hear the matter on affidavits or may hear it wholly or partly on oral testimony or on depositions.

(d) Interpreter. The court may appoint an interpreter of its choosing; fix reasonable compensation to be paid from funds provided by law or by one or more parties; and tax the compensation as costs.

Rule 44. Proving an Official Record

(a) Means of Proving.

(1) *Domestic Record.* Each of the following evidences an official record—or an entry in it—that is otherwise admissible and is kept within the United States, any state, district, or commonwealth, or any territory subject to the administrative or judicial jurisdiction of the United States:

(A) an official publication of the record; or

(B) a copy attested by the officer with legal custody of the record—or by the officer's deputy—and accompanied by a certificate that the officer has custody. The certificate must be made under seal:

(i) by a judge of a court of record in the district or political subdivision where the record is kept; or

(ii) by any public officer with a seal of office and with official duties in the district or political subdivision where the record is kept.

(2) *Foreign Record.*

(A) *In General.* Each of the following evidences a foreign official record—or an entry in it—that is otherwise admissible:

(i) an official publication of the record; or

(ii) the record—or a copy—that is attested by an authorized person and is accompanied either by a final certification of genuineness or by a certification under a treaty or convention to which the United States and the country where the record is located are parties.

(B) *Final Certification of Genuineness.* A final certification must certify the genuineness of the signature and official position of the attester or of any foreign official whose certificate of genuineness relates to the attestation or is in a chain of certificates of genuineness relating to the attestation. A final certification may be made by a secretary of a United States embassy or legation; by a consul general, vice consul, or consular agent of the United States; or by a diplomatic or consular official of the foreign country assigned or accredited to the United States.

(C) *Other Means of Proof.* If all parties have had a reasonable opportunity to investigate a foreign record's authenticity and accuracy, the court may, for good cause, either:

(i) admit an attested copy without final certification; or

(ii) permit the record to be evidenced by an attested summary with or without a final certification.

(b) **Lack of a Record.** A written statement that a diligent search of designated records revealed no record or entry of a specified tenor is admissible as evidence that the records contain no such record or entry. For domestic records, the statement must be authenticated under Rule 44(a)(1). For foreign records, the statement must comply with (a)(2)(C)(ii).

(c) **Other Proof.** A party may prove an official record—or an entry or lack of an entry in it—by any other method authorized by law.

Rule 44.1. Determining Foreign Law

A party who intends to raise an issue about a foreign country's law must give notice by a pleading or other writing. In determining foreign law, the court may consider any relevant material or source, including testimony, whether or not submitted by a party or admissible under the Federal Rules of Evidence. The court's determination must be treated as a ruling on a question of law.

Notes by Advisory Committee on Adoption of Federal Rule 44.1

Rule 44.1 was added by amendment to furnish Federal courts with a uniform and effective procedure for raising and determining an issue concerning the law of a foreign country.

To avoid unfair surprise, the *first sentence* of the new rule requires that a party who intends to raise an issue of foreign law shall give notice thereof. The uncertainty under Rule 8(a) about whether foreign law must be pleaded * * * is eliminated by the provision that the notice shall be "written" and "reasonable." It may, but need not be, incorporated in the pleadings. In some situations the pertinence of foreign law is apparent from the outset; accordingly the necessary investigation of that law will have been accomplished by the party at the pleading stage, and the notice can be given conveniently in the pleadings. In other situations the pertinence of foreign law may remain doubtful until the case is further developed. A requirement that notice of foreign law be given only through the medium of the pleadings would tend in the latter instances to force the party to engage in a peculiarly burdensome type of investigation which might turn out to be unnecessary; and correspondingly the adversary would be forced into a possibly wasteful investigation. * * *

The *second sentence* of the new rule describes the materials to which the court may resort in determining an issue of foreign law. Heretofore the district courts, applying Rule 43(a), have looked in certain cases to State law to find the rules of evidence by which the content of foreign-country law is to be established. The State laws vary; some embody procedures which are inefficient, time consuming, and expensive. * * * In all events the ordinary rules of evidence are often inapposite to the problem of determining foreign law and have in the past prevented examination of material which could have provided a proper basis for the determination. * * *

The new rule refrains from imposing an obligation on the court to take "judicial notice" of foreign law because this would put an extreme burden on the court in many cases; and it avoids use of the concept of "judicial notice" in any form because of the uncertain meaning of that concept as applied to foreign law. See, *e.g.,* Stern, *Foreign Law in the Courts: Judicial Notice and Proof,* 45 Calif.L.Rev. 23, 43 (1957). Rather the rule provides flexible procedures for presenting and utilizing material on issues of foreign law by which a sound result can be achieved with fairness to the parties.

Under the *third sentence,* the court's determination of an issue of foreign law is to be treated as a ruling on a question of "law," not "fact," so that appellate review will not be narrowly confined by the "clearly erroneous" standard of Rule 52(a). * * *

Rule 45. Subpoena

(a) In General.

    (1) *Form and Contents.*

        (A) *Requirements—In General.* Every subpoena must:

            (i) state the court from which it issued;

            (ii) state the title of the action, the court in which it is pending, and its civil-action number;

            (iii) command each person to whom it is directed to do the following at a specified time and place: attend and testify; produce designated documents, electronically stored information, or tangible things in that person's possession, custody, or control; or permit the inspection of premises; and

            (iv) set out the text of Rule 45(d) and (e).

        (B) *Command to Attend a Deposition—Notice of the Recording Method.* A subpoena commanding attendance at a deposition must state the method for recording the testimony.

        (C) *Combining or Separating a Command to Produce or to Permit Inspection; Specifying the Form for Electronically Stored Information.* A command to produce documents, electronically stored information, or tangible things or to permit the inspection of premises may be included in a subpoena commanding attendance at a deposition, hearing, or trial, or may be set out in a separate subpoena. A subpoena may specify the form or forms in which electronically stored information is to be produced.

(D) *Command to Produce; Included Obligations.* A command in a subpoena to produce documents, electronically stored information, or tangible things requires the responding party to permit inspection, copying, testing, or sampling of the materials.

(2) *Issuing Court.* A subpoena must issue from the court where the action is pending.

(3) *Issued by Whom.* The clerk must issue a subpoena, signed but otherwise in blank, to a party who requests it. That party must complete it before service. An attorney also may issue and sign a subpoena if the attorney is authorized to practice in the issuing court.

(4) *Notice to Other Parties Before Service.* If the subpoena commands the production of documents, electronically stored information, or tangible things or the inspection of premises before trial, then before it is served on the person to whom it is directed, a notice and a copy of the subpoena must be served on each party.

(b) Service.

(1) *By Whom and How; Tendering Fees.* Any person who is at least 18 years old and not a party may serve a subpoena. Serving a subpoena requires delivering a copy to the named person and, if the subpoena requires that person's attendance, tendering the fees for 1 day's attendance and the mileage allowed by law. Fees and mileage need not be tendered when the subpoena issues on behalf of the United States or any of its officers or agencies.

(2) *Service in the United States*. A subpoena may be served at any place within the United States.

(3) *Service in a Foreign Country.* 28 U.S.C. § 1783 governs issuing and serving a subpoena directed to a United States national or resident who is in a foreign country.

(4) *Proof of Service.* Proving service, when necessary, requires filing with the issuing court a statement showing the date and manner of service and the names of the persons served. The statement must be certified by the server.

(c) Place of Compliance.

(1) *For a Trial, Hearing, or Deposition.* A subpoena may command a person to attend a trial, hearing, or deposition only as follows:

(A) within 100 miles of where the person resides, is employed, or regularly transacts business in person; or

(B) within the state where the person resides, is employed, or regularly transacts business in person, if the person

(i) is a party or a party's officer; or

(ii) is commanded to attend a trial and would not incur substantial expense.

(2) *For Other Discovery.* A subpoena may command:

(A) production of documents, electronically stored information, or tangible things at a place within 100 miles of where the person resides, is employed, or regularly transacts business in person; and

(B) inspection of premises at the premises to be inspected.

(d) Protecting a Person Subject to a Subpoena; Enforcement.

(1) *Avoiding Undue Burden or Expense; Sanctions.* A party or attorney responsible for issuing and serving a subpoena must take reasonable steps to avoid imposing undue burden or expense on a person subject to the subpoena. The court for the district where compliance is required must enforce this duty and impose an appropriate sanction—which may include lost earnings and reasonable attorney's fees—on a party or attorney who fails to comply.

(2) *Command to Produce Materials or Permit Inspection.*

(A) *Appearance Not Required.* A person commanded to produce documents, electronically stored information, or tangible things, or to permit the inspection of premises, need not appear in person at the place of production or inspection unless also commanded to appear for a deposition, hearing, or trial.

(B) *Objections.* A person commanded to produce documents or tangible things or to permit inspection may serve on the party or attorney designated in the subpoena a written objection to inspecting, copying, testing, or sampling any or all of the materials or to inspecting the premises—or to producing electronically stored information in the form or forms requested. The objection must be served before the earlier of the time specified for compliance or 14 days after the subpoena is served. If an objection is made, the following rules apply:

(i) At any time, on notice to the commanded person, the serving party may move the court for the district where compliance is required for an order compelling production or inspection.

(ii) These acts may be required only as directed in the order, and the order must protect a person who is neither a party nor a party's officer from significant expense resulting from compliance.

(3) *Quashing or Modifying a Subpoena.*

(A) *When required.* On timely motion, the court for the district where compliance is required must quash or modify a subpoena that:

(i) fails to allow a reasonable time to comply;

(ii) requires a person to comply beyond the geographical limits specified in Rule 45(c);

(iii) requires disclosure of privileged or other protected matter, if no exception or waiver applies; or

(iv) subjects a person to undue burden.

(B) *When Permitted.* To protect a person subject to or affected by a subpoena, the court for the district where compliance is required may, on motion, quash or modify the subpoena if it requires:

(i) disclosing a trade secret or other confidential research, development, or commercial information; or

(ii) disclosing an unretained expert's opinion or information that does not describe specific occurrences in dispute and results from the expert's study that was not requested by a party.

(C) *Specifying Conditions as an Alternative.* In the circumstances described in Rule 45(d)(3)(B), the court may, instead of quashing or modifying a subpoena, order appearance or production under specified conditions if the serving party:

(i) shows a substantial need for the testimony or material that cannot be otherwise met without undue hardship; and

(ii) ensures that the subpoenaed person will be reasonably compensated.

(e) Duties in Responding to a Subpoena.

(1) *Producing Documents or Electronically Stored Information.* These procedures apply to producing documents or electronically stored information:

(A) *Documents.* A person responding to a subpoena to produce documents must produce them as they are kept in the ordinary course of business or must organize and label them to correspond to the categories in the demand.

(B) *Form for Producing Electronically Stored Information Not Specified.* If a subpoena does not specify a form for producing electronically stored information, the person responding must produce it in a form or forms in which it is ordinarily maintained or in a reasonably usable form or forms.

(C) *Electronically Stored Information Produced in Only One Form.* The person responding need not produce the same electronically stored information in more than one form.

(D) *Inaccessible Electronically Stored Information.* The person responding need not provide discovery of electronically stored information from sources that the person identifies as not reasonably accessible because of undue burden or cost. On motion to compel discovery or for a protective order, the person responding must show that the information is not reasonably accessible because of undue burden or cost. If that showing is made, the court may nonetheless order discovery from such sources if the requesting party shows good cause, considering the limitations of Rule 26(b)(2)(C). The court may specify conditions for the discovery.

(2) *Claiming Privilege or Protection.*

(A) *Information Withheld.* A person withholding subpoenaed information under a claim that it is privileged or subject to protection as trial-preparation material must:

(i) expressly make the claim; and

(ii) describe the nature of the withheld documents, communications, or tangible things in a manner that, without revealing information itself privileged or protected, will enable the parties to assess the claim.

(B) *Information Produced.* If information produced in response to a subpoena is subject to a claim of privilege or of protection as trial-preparation material, the person making the claim may notify any party that received the information of the claim and the basis for it. After being notified, a party must promptly return, sequester, or destroy the specified information and any copies it has; must not use or disclose the information until the claim is resolved; must take reasonable steps to retrieve the information if the party disclosed it before being notified; and may promptly present the information under seal to the court for the district where compliance is required for a determination of the claim. The person who produced the information must preserve the information until the claim is resolved.

(f) Transferring a Subpoena-Related Motion. When the court where compliance is required did not issue the subpoena, it may transfer a motion under this rule to the issuing court if the person subject to the subpoena consents or if the court finds exceptional circumstances. Then, if the attorney for a person subject to a subpoena is authorized to practice in the court where the motion was made, the attorney may file papers and appear on the motion as an officer of the issuing court. To enforce its order, the issuing court may transfer the order to the court where the motion was made.

(g) Contempt. The court for the district where compliance is required—and also, after a motion is transferred, the issuing court—may hold in contempt a person who, having been served, fails without adequate excuse to obey the subpoena or an order related to it.

Notes on Amendments to Federal Rule 45 and Comparative State Provisions

(a) *Amendments in 2013 to Federal Rule 45*

Rule 45(a)(2) has been amended to provide that a subpoena is to be issued only by the court in which the action is pending. Previously a subpoena would be issued by the court where compliance was to take place. Rule 45(b)(2) eliminates limitations as to where a subpoena could be served and instead allows a subpoena to be served anywhere within the United States. Under Rule 45(d) the court in the district where compliance is to take place has control over the details of compliance and can limit or quash the subpoena as justice requires to protect the person subject to it. Under Rule 45(f) the court where compliance is to take place may transfer a motion regarding the subpoena or its enforcement to the court where the subpoena issued if the person subject to the subpoena consents or if the court finds exceptional circumstances.

(b) *Amendments in 1991 to Federal Rule 45*

In 1991 Rule 45 was modified in a number of significant respects. Rule 45(c)(2)(A) [now 45(d)(2)(A)] was added to provide that a subpoena may be issued for the production of documents and other items without requiring the person in possession to be summoned to a deposition as Rule 45 previously required. Indeed current Rule 45(c) [now 45(d)] was entirely new and was added to provide protection for any person who has been served with a subpoena. The purpose of the provision is to ensure that such a person be given reasonable time to comply and not be faced with other undue burdens.

(c) *Comparative State Provision*

Oregon Rule of Civil Procedure 55A

A subpoena is a writ or order directed to a person and may require the attendance of the person at a particular time and place to testify as a witness on behalf of a particular party therein mentioned or may require the person to produce books, papers, documents, or tangible things and permit inspection thereof at a particular time and place. A subpoena requiring attendance to testify as a witness requires that the witness remain until the testimony is closed unless sooner discharged but, at the end of each day's attendance, a witness may demand of the party, or the party's attorney, the payment of legal witness fees for the next following day and, if not then paid, the witness is not obliged to remain longer in attendance. Every subpoena shall state the name of the court, the case name, and the case number.

[See also New York Civil Practice Law and Rules 3120 as set out following Federal Rule 34, supra.]

Rule 46. Objecting to a Ruling or Order

A formal exception to a ruling or order is unnecessary. When the ruling or order is requested or made, a party need only state the action that it wants the court to take or objects to, along with the grounds for the request or objection. Failing to object does not prejudice a party who had no opportunity to do so when the ruling or order was made.

Rule 47. Selecting Jurors

(a) Examining Jurors. The court may permit the parties or their attorneys to examine prospective jurors or may itself do so. If the court examines the jurors, it must permit the parties or their attorneys to make any further inquiry it considers proper, or must itself ask any of their additional questions it considers proper.

(b) Peremptory Challenges. The court must allow the number of peremptory challenges provided by 28 U.S.C. § 1870.

(c) Excusing a Juror. During trial or deliberation, the court may excuse a juror for good cause.

Georgia Code Annotated § 15–12–133

In all civil cases, the parties thereto shall have the right to an individual examination of the panel of prospective jurors from which the jury is to be selected, without interposing any challenge. In all criminal cases, both the state and the accused shall have the right to an individual examination of each prospective juror from which the jury is to be selected prior to interposing a challenge. The examination shall be conducted after the administration of a preliminary oath to the panel or in criminal cases after the usual **voir dire** questions have been put by the court. In the examination, the counsel for either party shall have the right to inquire of the individual prospective jurors examined touching any matter or thing which would illustrate any interest of the prospective juror in the case, including any opinion as to which party ought to prevail, the relationship or acquaintance of the prospective juror with the parties or counsel therefor, any fact or circumstance indicating any inclination, leaning, or bias which the prospective juror might have respecting the subject matter of the action or the counsel or parties thereto, and the religious, social, and fraternal connections of the prospective juror.

South Carolina Code § 14–7–1020

The court shall, on motion of either party in the suit, examine on oath any person who is called as a juror to know whether he is related to either party, has any interest in the cause, has expressed or formed any opinion, or is sensible of any bias or prejudice therein, and the party objecting to the juror may introduce any other competent evidence in support of the objection. If it appears to the court that the juror is not indifferent in the cause, he must be placed aside as to the trial of that cause and another must be called.

Rule 48. Number of Jurors; Verdict; Polling

(a) **Number of Jurors.** A jury must begin with at least 6 and no more than 12 members, and each juror must participate in the verdict unless excused under Rule 47(c).

(b) **Verdict.** Unless the parties stipulate otherwise, the verdict must be unanimous and must be returned by a jury of at least 6 members.

(c) **Polling.** After a verdict is returned but before the jury is discharged, the court must on a party's request, or may on its own, poll the jurors individually. If the poll reveals a lack of unanimity or lack of assent by the number of jurors that the parties stipulated to, the court may direct the jury to deliberate further or may order a new trial.

Minnesota Constitution Art. 1, § 4

The right of trial by jury shall remain inviolate, and shall extend to all cases at law without regard to the amount in controversy. A jury trial may be waived by the parties in all cases in the manner prescribed by law. The legislature may provide that the agreement of five-sixths of a jury in a civil action or proceeding, after not less than six hours' deliberation, is a sufficient verdict. The legislature may provide for the number of jurors in a civil action or proceeding, provided that a jury have at least six members.

Virginia Code § 8.01–359

A.   Five persons from a panel of not less than 11 shall constitute a jury in a civil case when the amount involved exclusive of interest and costs does not exceed [specified] jurisdictional limits. * * * Seven persons from a panel of not less than 13 shall constitute a jury in all other civil cases except that when a special jury is allowed, 12 persons from a panel of not less than 20 shall constitute the jury.

* * *

D.   In any civil case in which the consent of the plaintiff and defendant shall be entered of record, it shall be lawful for the plaintiff to select one person who is eligible as a juror and for the defendant to select another, and for the two so selected to select a third of like qualifications, and the three so selected shall constitute a jury in the case. They shall take the oath required of jurors, and hear and determine the issue, and any two concurring shall render a verdict in like manner and with like effect as a jury of seven.

Rule 49. Special Verdict; General Verdict and Questions

(a) Special Verdict.

(1) *In General.* The court may require a jury to return only a special verdict in the form of a special written finding on each issue of fact. The court may do so by:

(A) submitting written questions susceptible of a categorical or other brief answer;

(B) submitting written forms of the special findings that might properly be made under the pleadings and evidence; or

(C) using any other method that the court considers appropriate.

(2) *Instructions.* The court must give the instructions and explanations necessary to enable the jury to make its findings on each submitted issue.

(3) *Issues Not Submitted.* A party waives the right to a jury trial on any issue of fact raised by the pleadings or evidence but not submitted to the jury unless, before the jury retires, the party demands its submission to the jury. If the party does not demand submission, the court may make a finding on the issue. If the court makes no finding, it is considered to have made a finding consistent with its judgment on the special verdict.

(b) General Verdict With Answers to Written Questions.

(1) *In General.* The court may submit to the jury forms for a general verdict, together with written questions on one or more issues of fact that the jury must decide. The court must give the instructions and explanations necessary to enable the jury to render a general verdict and answer the questions in writing, and must direct the jury to do both.

(2) *Verdict and Answers Consistent.* When the general verdict and the answers are consistent, the court must approve, for entry under Rule 58, an appropriate judgment on the verdict and answers.

(3) *Answers Inconsistent With the Verdict.* When the answers are consistent with each other but one or more is inconsistent with the general verdict, the court may:

(A) approve, for entry under Rule 58, an appropriate judgment according to the answers, notwithstanding the general verdict;

(B) direct the jury to further consider its answers and verdict; or

(C) order a new trial.

(4) *Answers Inconsistent With Each Other and the Verdict.* When the answers are inconsistent with each other and one or more is also inconsistent with the general verdict, judgment must not be entered; instead, the court must direct the jury to further consider its answers and verdict, or must order a new trial.

Comparative State Provisions

Wisconsin Statutes Annotated § 805.12(1)

Unless it orders otherwise, the court shall direct the jury to return a special verdict. The verdict shall be prepared by the court in the form of written questions relating only to material issues of ultimate fact and admitting a direct answer. The jury shall answer in writing. In cases founded upon negligence, the court need not submit separately any particular respect in which the party was allegedly negligent. The court may also direct the jury to find upon particular questions of fact.

Wisconsin Statutes Annotated § 805.12(2)

When some material issue of ultimate fact not brought to the attention of the trial court but essential to sustain the judgment is omitted from the verdict, the issue shall be deemed determined by the court in conformity with its judgment and the failure to request a finding by the jury on the issue shall be deemed a waiver of jury trial on that issue.

Rule 50. Judgment as a Matter of Law in a Jury Trial; Related Motion for a New Trial; Conditional Ruling

(a) Judgment as a Matter of Law.

(1) *In General.* If a party has been fully heard on an issue during a jury trial and the court finds that a reasonable jury would not have a legally sufficient evidentiary basis to find for the party on that issue, the court may:

(A) resolve the issue against the party; and

(B) grant a motion for judgment as a matter of law against the party on a claim or defense that, under the controlling law, can be maintained or defeated only with a favorable finding on that issue.

(2) *Motion.* A motion for judgment as a matter of law may be made at any time before the case is submitted to the jury. The motion must specify the judgment sought and the law and facts that entitle the movant to the judgment.

(b) Renewing the Motion After Trial; Alternative Motion for a New Trial. If the court does not grant a motion for judgment as a matter of law made under Rule 50(a), the court is considered to have submitted the action to the jury subject to the court's later deciding the legal questions raised by the motion. No later than 28 days after the entry of judgment—or if the motion addresses a jury issue not decided by a verdict, no later than 28 days after the jury was discharged—the movant may file a renewed motion for judgment as a matter of law and may include an alternative or joint request for a new trial under Rule 59. In ruling on the renewed motion, the court may:

(1) allow judgment on the verdict, if the jury returned a verdict;

(2) order a new trial; or

(3) direct the entry of judgment as a matter of law.

(c) Granting the Renewed Motion; Conditional Ruling on a Motion for a New Trial.

(1) *In General.* If the court grants a renewed motion for judgment as a matter of law, it must also conditionally rule on any motion for a new trial by determining whether a new trial should be granted if the judgment is later vacated or reversed. The court must state the grounds for conditionally granting or denying the motion for a new trial.

(2) *Effect of a Conditional Ruling.* Conditionally granting the motion for a new trial does not affect the judgment's finality; if the judgment is reversed, the new trial must proceed unless the appellate court orders otherwise. If the motion for a new trial is conditionally denied, the appellee may assert error in that denial; if the judgment is reversed, the case must proceed as the appellate court orders.

(d) Time for a Losing Party's New-Trial Motion. Any motion for a new trial under Rule 59 by a party against whom judgment as a matter of law is rendered must be filed no later than 28 days after the entry of the judgment.

(e) Denying the Motion for Judgment as a Matter of Law; Reversal on Appeal. If the court denies the motion for judgment as a matter of law, the prevailing party may, as appellee, assert grounds entitling it to a new trial should the appellate court conclude that the trial court erred in denying the motion. If the appellate court reverses the judgment, it may order a new trial, direct the trial court to determine whether a new trial should be granted, or direct the entry of judgment.

Comparative State Provisions and Notes on Amendments to Federal Rule 50

(a)   *Rules 50(a) and (b)—Comparative State Provisions*

New York Civil Practice Law and Rules 4404(a)

After a trial of a cause of action or issue triable of right by a jury, upon the motion of any party or on its own initiative, the court may set aside a verdict or any judgment entered thereon and direct that judgment be entered in favor of a party entitled to judgment as a matter of law or it may order a new trial of a cause of action or separable issue where the verdict is contrary to the weight of the evidence, in the interest of justice or where the jury cannot agree after being kept together for as long as is deemed reasonable by the court.

Indiana Rules of Trial Procedure, Rule 50(A) & (B)

(A)   Where all or some of the issues in a case tried before a jury or an advisory jury are not supported by sufficient evidence or a verdict thereon is clearly erroneous as contrary to the evidence because the evidence is insufficient to support it, the court shall withdraw such issues from the jury and enter judgment thereon or shall enter judgment thereon notwithstanding a verdict. * * *

(B)   Every case tried by a jury is made subject to the right of the court, before or after the jury is discharged, to enter final judgment on the evidence, without directing a verdict thereon.

(b)   *Notes on Amendments in 1963 Adding Federal Rule 50(c)*

The Advisory Committee commented on Rule 50(c) that was added in 1963, as follows:

Subdivision (c) deals with the situation where a party joins a motion for a new trial with his motion for judgment n.o.v., or prays for a new trial in the alternative, and the motion for judgment n.o.v. is granted. The procedure to be followed in making rulings on the motion for the new trial, and the consequences of the rulings thereon, were partly set out in *Montgomery Ward & Co. v. Duncan,* 311 U.S. 243, 253, 61 S.Ct. 189, 85 L.Ed. 147 (1940), and have been further elaborated in later cases. * * * However, courts as well as counsel have often misunderstood the procedure, and it will be helpful to summarize the proper practice in the text of the rule. The amendments do not alter the effects of a jury verdict or the scope of appellate review.

In the situation mentioned, *subdivision (c)(1)* requires that the court make a "conditional" ruling on the new-trial motion, *i.e.,* a ruling which goes on the assumption that the motion for judgment n. o. v. was erroneously granted and will be reversed or vacated; and the court is required to state its grounds for the conditional ruling. Subdivision * * * [(c)(2)] then spells out the consequences of a reversal of the judgment in the light of the conditional ruling on the new-trial motion.

If the motion for new trial has been conditionally granted, and the judgment is reversed, "the new trial shall proceed unless the appellate court has otherwise ordered." The party against whom the judgment n.o.v. was entered below may, as appellant, besides seeking to overthrow that judgment, also attack the conditional grant of the new trial. And the appellate court, if it reverses the judgment n. o. v., may in an appropriate case also reverse the conditional grant of the new trial and direct that judgment be entered on the verdict. * * *

If the motion for a new trial has been conditionally denied, and the judgment is reversed, "subsequent proceedings shall be in accordance with the order of the appellate court." The party in whose favor judgment n. o. v. was entered below may, as appellee, besides seeking to uphold that judgment, also urge on the appellate court that the trial court committed error in conditionally denying the new trial. The appellee may assert this error in his brief, without taking a cross-appeal. * * * If the appellate court concludes that the judgment cannot stand, but accepts the appellee's contention that there was error in the conditional denial of the new trial, it may order a new trial in lieu of directing the entry of judgment upon the verdict.

Rule 51. Instructions to the Jury; Objections; Preserving a Claim of Error

(a) Requests.

(1) *Before or at the Close of the Evidence.* At the close of the evidence or at any earlier reasonable time that the court orders, a party may file and furnish to every other party written requests for the jury instructions it wants the court to give.

(2) *After the Close of the Evidence.* After the close of the evidence, a party may:

(A) file requests for instructions on issues that could not reasonably have been anticipated by an earlier time that the court set for requests; and

(B) with the court's permission, file untimely requests for instructions on any issue.

(b) Instructions. The court:

(1) must inform the parties of its proposed instructions and proposed action on the requests before instructing the jury and before final jury arguments;

(2) must give the parties an opportunity to object on the record and out of the jury's hearing before the instructions and arguments are delivered; and

(3) may instruct the jury at any time before the jury is discharged.

(c) Objections.

(1) *How to Make.* A party who objects to an instruction or the failure to give an instruction must do so on the record, stating distinctly the matter objected to and the grounds for the objection.

(2) *When to Make.* An objection is timely if:

(A) a party objects at the opportunity provided under Rule 51(b)(2); or

(B) a party was not informed of an instruction or action on a request before that opportunity to object, and the party objects promptly after learning that the instruction or request will be, or has been, given or refused.

(d) Assigning Error; Plain Error.

(1) *Assigning Error.* A party may assign as error:

(A) an error in an instruction actually given, if that party properly objected; or

(B) a failure to give an instruction, if that party properly requested it and—unless the court rejected the request in a definitive ruling on the record—also properly objected.

(2) *Plain Error.* A court may consider a plain error in the instructions that has not been preserved as required by Rule 51(d)(1) if the error affects substantial rights.

Notes on Amendment to Federal Rule 51 and Comparative State Provisions

(a)   *1987 Amendment to Federal Rule 51*

In 1987, on recommendation of the Advisory Committee, Rule 51 was amended to give the court discretion to instruct the jury either before or after the argument. See generally Raymond, *Merits and Demerits of the Missouri System of Instructing Juries,* 5 St. Louis U. L.J. 317 (1959).

(b)   *Comparative State Provisions*

Georgia Code Annotated § 5–5–24

(a)   Except as otherwise provided in this Code section, in all civil cases, no party may complain of the giving or the failure to give an instruction to the jury unless he objects thereto before the jury returns its verdict, stating distinctly the matter to which he objects and the grounds of his objection. Opportunity shall be given to make the objection out of the hearing of the jury. Objection need not be made with the particularity formerly required of assignments of error and need only be as reasonably definite as the circumstances will permit. * * *

(b) In all cases, at the close of the evidence or at such earlier time during the trial as the court reasonably directs, any party may present to the court written requests that it instruct the jury on the law as set forth therein. Copies of requests shall be given to opposing counsel for their consideration prior to the charge of the court. The court shall inform counsel of its proposed action upon the requests prior to their arguments to the jury but shall instruct the jury after the arguments are completed. The trial judge shall file with the clerk all requests submitted to him, whether given in charge or not.

(c) Notwithstanding any other provision of this Code section, the appellate courts shall consider and review erroneous charges where there has been a substantial error in the charge which was harmful as a matter of law, regardless of whether objection was made hereunder or not.

Illinois Supreme Court Rule 239

(a) **Use of IPI Instructions; Requirements of Other Instructions.** Whenever Illinois Pattern Jury Instructions (IPI), Civil, contains an instruction applicable in a civil case, giving due consideration to the facts and the prevailing law, and the court determines that the jury should be instructed on the subject, the IPI instruction shall be used, unless the court determines that it does not accurately state the law. * * * Whenever IPI does not contain an instruction on a subject on which the court determines that the jury should be instructed, the instruction given in that subject should be simple, brief, impartial, and free from argument.

(b) **Court's Instructions.** At any time before or during the trial, the court may direct counsel to prepare designated instructions. Counsel shall comply with the direction and copies of instructions so prepared shall be marked "Court's Instruction." Counsel may object at the conference on instructions to any instruction prepared at the court's direction, regardless of who prepared it, and the court shall rule on these objections as well as objections to other instructions. The grounds of the objections shall be particularly specified.

(c) **Procedure.** Each instruction shall be accompanied by a copy, and a copy shall be delivered to opposing counsel. In addition to numbering the copies and indicating who tendered them, as required by section 2–1107 of the Code of Civil Procedure, the copy shall contain a notation substantially as follows:

"IPI No. _____" or "IPI No. _____ Modified" or "Not in IPI" as the case may be. All objections made at the conference and the rulings thereon shall be shown in the report of proceedings. The original instructions given by the court to the jury shall be taken by the jury to the jury room.

* * *

Mississippi Code Annotated § 11–7–155

The judge in any civil cause shall not sum up or comment on the testimony, or charge the jury as to the weight of evidence.

Rule 52. Findings and Conclusions by the Court; Judgment on Partial Findings

(a) **Findings and Conclusions.**

(1) *In General.* In an action tried on the facts without a jury or with an advisory jury, the court must find the facts specially and state its conclusions of law separately. The findings and conclusions may be stated on the record after the close of the evidence or may appear in an opinion or a memorandum of decision filed by the court. Judgment must be entered under Rule 58.

(2) *For an Interlocutory Injunction.* In granting or refusing an interlocutory injunction, the court must similarly state the findings and conclusions that support its action.

(3) *For a Motion.* The court is not required to state findings or conclusions when ruling on a motion under Rule 12 or 56 or, unless these rules provide otherwise, on any other motion.

(4) *Effect of a Master's Findings.* A master's findings, to the extent adopted by the court, must be considered the court's findings.

(5) *Questioning the Evidentiary Support.* A party may later question the sufficiency of the evidence supporting the findings, whether or not the party requested findings, objected to them, moved to amend them, or moved for partial findings.

(6) *Setting Aside the Findings.* Findings of fact, whether based on oral or other evidence, must not be set aside unless clearly erroneous, and the reviewing court must give due regard to the trial court's opportunity to judge the witnesses' credibility.

(b) Amended or Additional Findings. On a party's motion filed no later than 28 days after the entry of judgment, the court may amend its findings—or make additional findings—and may amend the judgment accordingly. The motion may accompany a motion for a new trial under Rule 59.

(c) Judgment on Partial Findings. If a party has been fully heard on an issue during a nonjury trial and the court finds against the party on that issue, the court may enter judgment against the party on a claim or defense that, under the controlling law, can be maintained or defeated only with a favorable finding on that issue. The court may, however, decline to render any judgment until the close of the evidence. A judgment on partial findings must be supported by findings of fact and conclusions of law as required by Rule 52(a).

Notes on Amendments to Federal Rule 52 and Comparative State Provision

(a)   *Amendment in 1985 to Federal Rule 52*

The purpose of the 1985 amendment was to make certain that the "clearly erroneous" standard applies when the trial court's decision is based solely on documentary evidence as well as when it is based on oral testimony. Previously, appellate courts were divided on the matter, some holding that the scope of review is broader when witness credibility is not involved. The change was designed to support the integrity of the trial court's findings of fact, thus to promote judicial economy by discouraging retrial at the appellate level.

(b)   *Amendment in 1983 to Federal Rule 52*

Rule 52(a) was amended to provide explicitly that the district judge may make the findings of fact and conclusions of law required in nonjury cases orally. The objective is to lighten the burden on the trial court in preparing findings in nonjury cases. It should also reduce the number of published district court opinions that embrace written findings.

(c)   *Comparative State Provision*

Oklahoma Statutes Annotated Tit. 12, § 611

Upon the trial of questions of fact by the court, it shall not be necessary for the court to state its findings, except generally, for the plaintiff or defendant, unless one of the parties request it, with the view of excepting to the decision of the court upon the questions of law involved in the trial; in which case the court shall state, in writing, the findings of fact found, separately from the conclusions of law.

Rule 53. Masters

(a) Appointment.

(1) *Scope.* Unless a statute provides otherwise, a court may appoint a master only to:

(A) perform duties consented to by the parties;

(B) hold trial proceedings and make or recommend findings of fact on issues to be decided without a jury if appointment is warranted by:

(i) some exceptional condition; or

(ii) the need to perform an accounting or resolve a difficult computation of damages; or

(C) address pretrial and posttrial matters that cannot be effectively and timely addressed by an available district judge or magistrate judge of the district.

(2) *Disqualification.* A master must not have a relationship to the parties, attorneys, action, or court that would require disqualification of a judge under 28 U.S.C. § 455, unless the parties, with the court's approval, consent to the appointment after the master discloses any potential grounds for disqualification.

(3) *Possible Expense or Delay.* In appointing a master, the court must consider the fairness of imposing the likely expenses on the parties and must protect against unreasonable expense or delay.

(b) Order Appointing a Master.

(1) *Notice.* Before appointing a master, the court must give the parties notice and an opportunity to be heard. Any party may suggest candidates for appointment.

(2) *Contents.* The appointing order must direct the master to proceed with all reasonable diligence and must state:

(A) the master's duties, including any investigation or enforcement duties, and any limits on the master's authority under Rule 53(c);

(B) the circumstances, if any, in which the master may communicate ex parte with the court or a party;

(C) the nature of the materials to be preserved and filed as the record of the master's activities;

(D) the time limits, method of filing the record, other procedures, and standards for reviewing the master's orders, findings, and recommendations; and

(E) the basis, terms, and procedure for fixing the master's compensation under Rule 53(g).

(3) *Issuing.* The court may issue the order only after:

(A) the master files an affidavit disclosing whether there is any ground for disqualification under 28 U.S.C. § 455; and

(B) if a ground is disclosed, the parties, with the court's approval, waive the disqualification.

(4) *Amending.* The order may be amended at any time after notice to the parties and an opportunity to be heard.

(c) Master's Authority.

(1) *In General.* Unless the appointing order directs otherwise, a master may:

(A) regulate all proceedings;

(B) take all appropriate measures to perform the assigned duties fairly and efficiently; and

(C) if conducting an evidentiary hearing, exercise the appointing court's power to compel, take, and record evidence.

(2) *Sanctions.* The master may by order impose on a party any noncontempt sanction provided by Rule 37 or 45, and may recommend a contempt sanction against a party and sanctions against a nonparty.

(d) Master's Orders. A master who issues an order must file it and promptly serve a copy on each party. The clerk must enter the order on the docket.

(e) Master's Reports. A master must report to the court as required by the appointing order. The master must file the report and promptly serve a copy on each party, unless the court orders otherwise.

(f) Action on the Master's Order, Report, or Recommendations.

(1) *Opportunity for a Hearing; Action in General.* In acting on a master's order, report, or recommendations, the court must give the parties notice and an opportunity to be heard; may receive evidence; and may adopt or affirm, modify, wholly or partly reject or reverse, or resubmit to the master with instructions.

(2) *Time to Object or Move to Adopt or Modify.* A party may file objections to—or a motion to adopt or modify—the master's order, report, or recommendations no later than 21 days after a copy is served, unless the court sets a different time.

(3) *Reviewing Factual Findings.* The court must decide de novo all objections to findings of fact made or recommended by a master, unless the parties, with the court's approval, stipulate that:

    (A) the findings will be reviewed for clear error; or

    (B) the findings of a master appointed under Rule 53(a)(1)(A) or (C) will be final.

(4) *Reviewing Legal Conclusions.* The court must decide de novo all objections to conclusions of law made or recommended by a master.

(5) *Reviewing Procedural Matters.* Unless the appointing order establishes a different standard of review, the court may set aside a master's ruling on a procedural matter only for an abuse of discretion.

(g) Compensation.

(1) *Fixing Compensation.* Before or after judgment, the court must fix the master's compensation on the basis and terms stated in the appointing order, but the court may set a new basis and terms after giving notice and an opportunity to be heard.

(2) *Payment.* The compensation must be paid either:

    (A) by a party or parties; or

    (B) from a fund or subject matter of the action within the court's control.

(3) *Allocating Payment.* The court must allocate payment among the parties after considering the nature and amount of the controversy, the parties' means, and the extent to which any party is more responsible than other parties for the reference to a master. An interim allocation may be amended to reflect a decision on the merits.

(h) Appointing a Magistrate Judge. A magistrate judge is subject to this rule only when the order referring a matter to the magistrate judge states that the reference is made under this rule.

Comparative State Provisions

(a)   *Rules 53(a) and (b)*

New York Civil Practice Law and Rules 4317

(a) Upon consent of the parties. The parties may stipulate that any issue shall be determined by a referee. Upon the filing of the stipulation with the clerk, the clerk shall forthwith enter an order referring the issue for trial to the referee named therein. * * *

(b) Without consent of the parties. On motion of any party or on its own initiative, the court may order a reference to determine a cause of action or an issue where the trial will require the examination of a long account, including actions to foreclose mechanic's liens; or to determine an issue of damages separately triable and not requiring a trial by jury; or where otherwise authorized by law.

* * *

(b)   *Rule 53(g)*

New Jersey Civil Practice Rule 4:41–5(b) & (c)

(b)   In Non-jury Actions. In an action to be tried without a jury the court shall accept the master's findings of fact unless contrary to the weight of the evidence. * * *

(c)   In Jury Actions. In an action to be tried by a jury the findings of the master upon the issues submitted are admissible as evidence of the matters found, and may together with the evidence taken before the master be read to the jury, subject to the ruling of the court upon objections to the report or the evidence.

TITLE VII. JUDGMENT

Rule 54. Judgment; Costs

(a)   Definition; Form. "Judgment" as used in these rules includes a decree and any order from which an appeal lies. A judgment should not include recitals of pleadings, a master's report, or a record of prior proceedings.

(b)   Judgment on Multiple Claims or Involving Multiple Parties. When an action presents more than one claim for relief—whether as a claim, counterclaim, crossclaim, or third-party claim— or when multiple parties are involved, the court may direct entry of a final judgment as to one or more, but fewer than all, claims or parties only if the court expressly determines that there is no just reason for delay. Otherwise, any order or other decision, however designated, that adjudicates fewer than all the claims or the rights and liabilities of fewer than all the parties does not end the action as to any of the claims or parties and may be revised at any time before the entry of a judgment adjudicating all the claims and all the parties' rights and liabilities.

(c)   Demand for Judgment; Relief to Be Granted. A default judgment must not differ in kind from, or exceed in amount, what is demanded in the pleadings. Every other final judgment should grant the relief to which each party is entitled, even if the party has not demanded that relief in its pleadings.

(d)   Costs; Attorney's Fees.

(1)   *Costs Other Than Attorney's Fees.* Unless a federal statute, these rules, or a court order provides otherwise, costs—other than attorney's fees—should be allowed to the prevailing party. But costs against the United States, its officers, and its agencies may be imposed only to the extent allowed by law. The clerk may tax costs on 14 days' notice. On motion served within the next 7 days, the court may review the clerk's action.

(2)   *Attorney's Fees.*

(A)   *Claim to Be by Motion.* A claim for attorney's fees and related nontaxable expenses must be made by motion unless the substantive law requires those fees to be proved at trial as an element of damages.

(B)   *Timing and Contents of the Motion.* Unless a statute or a court order provides otherwise, the motion must:

(i)   be filed no later than 14 days after the entry of judgment;

(ii)   specify the judgment and the statute, rule, or other grounds entitling the movant to the award;

(iii)   state the amount sought or provide a fair estimate of it; and

(iv)   disclose, if the court so orders, the terms of any agreement about fees for the services for which the claim is made.

121

(C) *Proceedings.* Subject to Rule 23(h), the court must, on a party's request, give an opportunity for adversary submissions on the motion in accordance with Rule 43(c) or 78. The court may decide issues of liability for fees before receiving submissions on the value of services. The court must find the facts and state its conclusions of law as provided in Rule 52(a).

(D) *Special Procedures by Local Rule; Reference to a Master or a Magistrate Judge.* By local rule, the court may establish special procedures to resolve fee-related issues without extensive evidentiary hearings. Also, the court may refer issues concerning the value of services to a special master under Rule 53 without regard to the limitations of Rule 53(a)(1), and may refer a motion for attorney's fees to a magistrate judge under Rule 72(b) as if it were a dispositive pretrial matter.

(E) *Exceptions.* Subparagraphs (A)–(D) do not apply to claims for fees and expenses as sanctions for violating these rules or as sanctions under 28 U.S.C. § 1927.

Comparative State Provisions

(a) *Rule 54(b)*

Texas Rule of Civil Procedure 301

* * * Only one final judgment shall be rendered in any cause except where it is otherwise specially provided by law. Judgment may, in a proper case, be given for or against one or more of several plaintiffs, and for or against one or more of several defendants or intervenors.

(b) *Rule 54(c)*

Georgia Code Annotated § 9–11–54(c)(1)

A judgment by default shall not be different in kind from or exceed in amount that prayed for in the demand for judgment. Except as to a party against whom a judgment is entered by default, every final judgment shall grant the relief to which the party in whose favor it is rendered is entitled, even if the party has not demanded such relief in his pleadings; but the court shall not give the successful party relief, though he may be entitled to it, where the propriety of the relief was not litigated and the opposing party had no opportunity to assert defenses to such relief.

Rule 55. Default; Default Judgment

(a) Entering a Default. When a party against whom a judgment for affirmative relief is sought has failed to plead or otherwise defend, and that failure is shown by affidavit or otherwise, the clerk must enter the party's default.

(b) Entering a Default Judgment.

(1) *By the Clerk.* If the plaintiff's claim is for a sum certain or a sum that can be made certain by computation, the clerk—on the plaintiff's request, with an affidavit showing the amount due—must enter judgment for that amount and costs against a defendant who has been defaulted for not appearing and who is neither a minor nor an incompetent person.

(2) *By the Court.* In all other cases, the party must apply to the court for a default judgment. A default judgment may be entered against a minor or incompetent person only if represented by a general guardian, conservator, or other like fiduciary who has appeared. If the party against whom a default judgment is sought has appeared personally or by a representative, that party or its representative must be served with written notice of the application at least 7 days before the hearing. The court may conduct hearings or make referrals—preserving any federal statutory right to a jury trial—when, to enter or effectuate judgment, it needs to:

    (A) conduct an accounting;

    (B) determine the amount of damages;

    (C) establish the truth of any allegation by evidence; or

(D) investigate any other matter.

(c) Setting Aside a Default or a Default Judgment. The court may set aside an entry of default for good cause, and it may set aside a final default judgment under Rule 60(b).

(d) Judgment Against the United States. A default judgment may be entered against the United States, its officers, or its agencies only if the claimant establishes a claim or right to relief by evidence that satisfies the court.

Rule 56. Summary Judgment

(a) Motion for Summary Judgment or Partial Summary Judgment. A party may move for summary judgment, identifying each claim or defense—or the part of each claim or defense—on which summary judgment is sought. The court shall grant summary judgment if the movant shows that there is no genuine dispute as to any material fact and the movant is entitled to judgment as a matter of law. The court should state on the record the reasons for granting or denying the motion.

(b) Time to File a Motion. Unless a different time is set by local rule or the court orders otherwise, a party may file a motion for summary judgment at any time until 30 days after the close of all discovery.

(c) Procedures.

(1) *Supporting Factual Positions.* A party asserting that a fact cannot be or is genuinely disputed must support the assertion by:

(A) citing to particular parts of materials in the record, including depositions, documents, electronically stored information, affidavits or declarations, stipulations (including those made for purposes of the motion only), admissions, interrogatory answers, or other materials; or

(B) showing that the materials cited do not establish the absence or presence of a genuine dispute, or that an adverse party cannot produce admissible evidence to support the fact.

(2) *Objection That a Fact Is Not Supported by Admissible Evidence.* A party may object that the material cited to support or dispute a fact cannot be presented in a form that would be admissible in evidence.

(3) *Materials Not Cited.* The court need consider only the cited materials, but it may consider other materials in the record.

(4) *Affidavits or Declarations.* An affidavit or declaration used to support or oppose a motion must be made on personal knowledge, set out facts that would be admissible in evidence, and show that the affiant or declarant is competent to testify on the matters stated.

(d) When Facts Are Unavailable to the Nonmovant. If a nonmovant shows by affidavit or declaration that, for specified reasons, it cannot present facts essential to justify its opposition, the court may:

(1) defer considering the motion or deny it;

(2) allow time to obtain affidavits or declarations or to take discovery; or

(3) issue any other appropriate order.

(e) Failing to Properly Support or Address a Fact. If a party fails to properly support an assertion of fact or fails to properly address another party's assertion of fact as required by Rule 56(c), the court may:

(1) give an opportunity to properly support or address the fact;

(2) consider the fact undisputed for purposes of the motion;

(3) grant summary judgment if the motion and supporting materials—including the facts considered undisputed—show that the movant is entitled to it; or

(4) issue any other appropriate order.

(f) Judgment Independent of the Motion. After giving notice and a reasonable time to respond, the court may:

(1) grant summary judgment for a nonmovant;

(2) grant the motion on grounds not raised by a party; or

(3) consider summary judgment on its own after identifying for the parties material facts that may not be genuinely is dispute.

(g) Failing to Grant All the Requested Relief. If the court does not grant all the relief requested by the motion, it may enter an order stating any material fact—including an item of damages or other relief—that is not genuinely in dispute and treating the fact as established in the case.

(h) Affidavit or Declaration Submitted in Bad Faith. If satisfied that an affidavit or declaration under this rule is submitted in bad faith or solely for delay, the court—after notice and a reasonable time to respond—may order the submitting party to pay the other party the reasonable expenses, including attorney's fees, it incurred as a result. An offending party or attorney may also be held in contempt or subjected to other appropriate sanctions.

Comparative State Provision

California Civil Procedure Code § 437c

(a)(1) A party may move for summary judgment in any action or proceeding if it is contended that the action has no merit or that there is no defense to the action or proceeding. The motion may be made at any time after 60 days have elapsed since the general appearance in the action or proceeding of each party against whom the motion is directed or at any earlier time after the general appearance that the court * * * may direct.

* * *

(b)(1) The motion shall be supported by affidavits, declarations, admissions, answers to interrogatories, depositions, and matters of which judicial notice shall or may be taken. The supporting papers shall include a separate statement setting forth plainly and concisely all material facts that the moving party contends are undisputed. Each of the material facts stated shall be followed by a reference to the supporting evidence. The failure to comply with this requirement of a separate statement may in the court's discretion constitute a sufficient ground for denial of the motion.

(2) An opposition to the motion shall be served and filed not less than 14 days preceding the noticed or continued date of hearing, unless the court for good cause orders otherwise. The opposition, where appropriate, shall consist of affidavits, declarations, admissions, answers to interrogatories, depositions, and matters of which judicial notice shall or may be taken.

(3) The opposition papers shall include a separate statement that responds to each of the material facts contended by the moving party to be undisputed, indicating if the opposing party agrees or disagrees that those facts are undisputed. The statement also shall set forth plainly and concisely any other material facts the opposing party contends are disputed. Each material fact contended by the opposing party to be disputed shall be followed by a reference to the supporting evidence. Failure to comply with this requirement of a separate statement may constitute a sufficient ground, in the court's discretion, for granting the motion.

(4) A reply to the opposition shall be served and filed by the moving party not less than five days preceding the noticed or continued date of hearing, unless the court for good cause orders otherwise.

(5) Evidentiary objections not made at the hearing shall be deemed waived.

(6)   * * *

(7)   An incorporation by reference of a matter in the court's file shall set forth with specificity the exact matter to which reference is being made and shall not incorporate the entire file.

(c)   The motion for summary judgment shall be granted if all the papers submitted show that there is no triable issue as to any material fact and that the moving party is entitled to a judgment as a matter of law. In determining if the papers show that there is no triable issue as to any material fact the court shall consider all of the evidence set forth in the papers, except the evidence to which objections have been made and sustained by the court, and all inferences reasonably deducible from the evidence, except summary judgment may not be granted by the court based on inferences reasonably deducible from the evidence if contradicted by other inferences or evidence, that raise a triable issue as to any material fact.

(d)   Supporting and opposing affidavits or declarations shall be made by a person on personal knowledge, shall set forth admissible evidence, and shall show affirmatively that the affiant is competent to testify to the matters stated in the affidavits or declarations. An objection based on the failure to comply with the requirements of this subdivision, if not made at the hearing, shall be deemed waived.

(e)   If a party is otherwise entitled to a summary judgment pursuant to this section, summary judgment shall not be denied on grounds of credibility or for want of cross-examination of witnesses furnishing affidavits or declarations in support of the summary judgment, except that summary judgment may be denied in the discretion of the court if the only proof of a material fact offered in support of the summary judgment is an affidavit or declaration made by an individual who was the sole witness to that fact; or if a material fact is an individual's state of mind, or lack thereof, and that fact is sought to be established solely by the individual's affirmation thereof.

(f)(1) A party may move for summary adjudication as to one or more causes of action within an action, one or more affirmative defenses, one or more claims for damages, or one or more issues of duty, if the party contends that the cause of action has no merit, that there is no affirmative defense to the cause of action, that there is no merit to an affirmative defense as to any cause of action, that there is no merit to a claim for damages, as specified in Section 3294 of the Civil Code, or that one or more defendants either owed or did not owe a duty to the plaintiff or plaintiffs. A motion for summary adjudication shall be granted only if it completely disposes of a cause of action, an affirmative defense, a claim for damages, or an issue of duty.

(2)   A motion for summary adjudication may be made by itself or as an alternative to a motion for summary judgment and shall proceed in all procedural respects as a motion for summary judgment. A party shall not move for summary judgment based on issues asserted in a prior motion for summary adjudication and denied by the court, unless that party establishes, to the satisfaction of the court, newly discovered facts or circumstances or a change of law supporting the issues reasserted in the summary judgment motion.

(g)   Upon the denial of a motion for summary judgment on the ground that there is a triable issue as to one or more material facts, the court shall, by written or oral order, specify one or more material facts raised by the motion that the court has determined there exists a triable controversy. This determination shall specifically refer to the evidence proffered in support of and in opposition to the motion that indicates that a triable controversy exists. Upon the grant of a motion for summary judgment on the ground that there is no triable issue of material fact, the court shall, by written or oral order, specify the reasons for its determination. The order shall specifically refer to the evidence proffered in support of, and, if applicable, in opposition to the motion that indicates that no triable issue exists. The court shall also state its reasons for any other determination. The court shall record its determination by court reporter or written order.

(h)   If it appears from the affidavits submitted in opposition to a motion for summary judgment or summary adjudication, or both, that facts essential to justify opposition may exist but cannot, for reasons stated, be presented, the court shall deny the motion, order a continuance to permit affidavits to be obtained or discovery to be had, or may make any other order as may be just. The application to continue the motion to obtain necessary discovery may also be made by ex parte motion at any time on or before the date the opposition response to the motion is due.

(i)   If, after granting a continuance to allow specified additional discovery, the court determines that the party seeking summary judgment has unreasonably failed to allow the discovery to be conducted, the court shall grant a continuance to permit the discovery to go forward or deny the motion for summary judgment or summary adjudication. This section does not affect or limit the ability of a party to compel discovery under the Civil Discovery Act * * *.

(j)   If the court determines at any time that an affidavit was presented in bad faith or solely for purposes of delay, the court shall order the party who presented the affidavit to pay the other party the amount of the reasonable expenses the filing of the affidavit caused the other party to incur. Sanctions shall not be imposed pursuant to this subdivision except on notice contained in a party's papers or on the court's own noticed motion, and after an opportunity to be heard.

(k)   Unless a separate judgment may properly be awarded in the action, a final judgment shall not be entered on a motion for summary judgment before the termination of the action, but the final judgment shall, in addition to any matters determined in the action, award judgment as established by the summary proceeding provided for in this section.

(*l*)   In an action arising out of an injury to the person or to property, if a motion for summary judgment is granted on the basis that the defendant was without fault, no other defendant during trial, over plaintiff's objection, may attempt to attribute fault to, or comment on, the absence or involvement of the defendant who was granted the motion.

(m)(1) A summary judgment entered under this section is an appealable judgment as in other cases. * * *

(2)   Before a reviewing court affirms an order granting summary judgment or summary adjudication on a ground not relied upon by the trial court, the reviewing court shall afford the parties an opportunity to present their views on the issue by submitting supplemental briefs. * * * The court may reverse or remand based upon the supplemental briefs to allow the parties to present additional evidence or to conduct discovery on the issue. * * *

(n)(1) If a motion for summary adjudication is granted, at the trial of the action, the cause or causes of action within the action, affirmative defense or defenses, claim for damages, or issue or issues of duty as to the motion that has been granted shall be deemed to be established and the action shall proceed as to the cause or causes of action, affirmative defense or defenses, claim for damages, or issue or issues of duty remaining.

(2)   In the trial of the action, the fact that a motion for summary adjudication is granted as to one or more causes of action, affirmative defenses, claims for damages, or issues of duty within the action shall not bar any cause of action, affirmative defense, claim for damages, or issue of duty as to which summary adjudication was either not sought or denied.

(3)   In the trial of an action, neither a party, a witness, nor the court shall comment to a jury upon the grant or denial of a motion for summary adjudication.

(o)   A cause of action has no merit if either of the following exists:

(1)   One or more of the elements of the cause of action cannot be separately established, even if that element is separately pleaded.

(2)   A defendant establishes an affirmative defense to that cause of action.

(p)   For purposes of motions for summary judgment and summary adjudication:

(1)   A plaintiff or cross-complainant has met his or her burden of showing that there is no defense to a cause of action if that party has proved each element of the cause of action entitling the party to judgment on the cause of action. Once the plaintiff or cross-complainant has met that burden, the burden shifts to the defendant or cross-defendant to show that a triable issue of one or more material facts exists as to the cause of action or a defense thereto. The defendant or cross-defendant shall not rely upon the allegations or denials of its pleadings to show that a triable issue of material fact exists

but, instead, shall set forth the specific facts showing that a triable issue of material fact exists as to the cause of action or a defense thereto.

(2) A defendant or cross-defendant has met his or her burden of showing that a cause of action has no merit if the party has shown that one or more elements of the cause of action, even if not separately pleaded, cannot be established, or that there is a complete defense to the cause of action. Once the defendant or cross-defendant has met that burden, the burden shifts to the plaintiff or cross-complainant to show that a triable issue of one or more material facts exists as to the cause of action or a defense thereto. The plaintiff or cross-complainant shall not rely upon the allegations or denials of its pleadings to show that a triable issue of material fact exists but, instead, shall set forth the specific facts showing that a triable issue of material fact exists as to the cause of action or a defense thereto.

(q) In granting or denying a motion for summary judgment or summary adjudication, the court need rule only on those objections to evidence that it deems material to its disposition of the motion. Objections to evidence that are not ruled on for purposes of the motion shall be preserved for appellate review.

(r) This section does not extend the period for trial provided by Section 1170.5.

(s) * * *

(t) Notwithstanding subdivision (f), a party may move for summary adjudication of a legal issue or a claim for damages other than punitive damages that does not completely dispose of a cause of action, affirmative defense, or issue of duty pursuant to this subdivision.

(1)(A) Before filing a motion pursuant to this subdivision, the parties whose claims or defenses are put at issue by the motion shall submit to the court both of the following:

(i) A joint stipulation stating the issue or issues to be adjudicated.

(ii) A declaration from each stipulating party that the motion will further the interest of judicial economy by decreasing trial time or significantly increasing the likelihood of settlement.

(B) The joint stipulation shall be served on any party to the civil action who is not also a party to the motion.

(2) Within 15 days of receipt of the stipulation and declarations, unless the court has good cause for extending the time, the court shall notify the stipulating parties if the motion may be filed. In making this determination, the court may consider objections by a nonstipulating party made within 10 days of the submission of the stipulation and declarations.

(3) If the court elects not to allow the filing of the motion, the stipulating parties may request, and upon request the court shall conduct, an informal conference with the stipulating parties to permit further evaluation of the proposed stipulation. The stipulating parties shall not file additional papers in support of the motion.

(4)(A) A motion for summary adjudication made pursuant to this subdivision shall contain a statement in the notice of motion that reads substantially similar to the following: "This motion is made pursuant to subdivision (t) of Section 437c of the Code of Civil Procedure. The parties to this motion stipulate that the court shall hear this motion and that the resolution of this motion will further the interest of judicial economy by decreasing trial time or significantly increasing the likelihood of settlement."

(B) The notice of motion shall be signed by counsel for all parties, and by those parties in propria persona, to the motion.

(5) A motion filed pursuant to this subdivision may be made by itself or as an alternative to a motion for summary judgment and shall proceed in all procedural respects as a motion for summary judgment.

(u) For the purposes of this section, a change in law does not include a later enacted statute without retroactive application.

California Civil Procedure Code § 436

The court may, upon a motion made pursuant to Section 435, or at any time in its discretion, and upon terms it deems proper:

(a)   Strike out any irrelevant, false, or improper matter inserted in any pleading.

(b)   Strike out all or any part of any pleading not drawn or filed in conformity with the laws of this state, a court rule, or an order of the court.

Rule 57. Declaratory Judgment

These rules govern the procedure for obtaining a declaratory judgment under 28 U.S.C. § 2201. Rules 38 and 39 govern a demand for a jury trial. The existence of another adequate remedy does not preclude a declaratory judgment that is otherwise appropriate. The court may order a speedy hearing of a declaratory-judgment action.

Rule 58. Entering Judgment

(a)   Separate Document. Every judgment and amended judgment must be set out in a separate document, but a separate document is not required for an order disposing of a motion:

(1)   for judgment under Rule 50(b);

(2)   to amend or make additional findings under Rule 52(b);

(3)   for attorney's fees under Rule 54;

(4)   for a new trial, or to alter or amend the judgment, under Rule 59; or

(5)   for relief under Rule 60.

(b)   Entering Judgment.

(1)   *Without the Court's Direction.* Subject to Rule 54(b) and unless the court orders otherwise, the clerk must, without awaiting the court's direction, promptly prepare, sign, and enter the judgment when:

(A)   the jury returns a general verdict;

(B)   the court awards only costs or a sum certain; or

(C)   the court denies all relief.

(2)   *Court's Approval Required.* Subject to Rule 54(b), the court must promptly approve the form of the judgment, which the clerk must promptly enter, when:

(A)   the jury returns a special verdict or a general verdict with answers to written questions; or

(B)   the court grants other relief not described in this subdivision (b).

(c)   Time of Entry. For purposes of these rules, judgment is entered at the following times:

(1)   if a separate document is not required, when the judgment is entered in the civil docket under Rule 79(a); or

(2)   if a separate document is required, when the judgment is entered in the civil docket under Rule 79(a) and the earlier of these events occurs:

(A)   it is set out in a separate document; or

(B)   150 days have run from the entry in the civil docket.

(d)   Request for Entry. A party may request that judgment be set out in a separate document as required by Rule 58(a).

(e) Cost or Fee Awards. Ordinarily, the entry of judgment may not be delayed, nor the time for appeal extended, in order to tax costs or award fees. But if a timely motion for attorney's fees is made under Rule 54(d)(2), the court may act before a notice of appeal has been filed and become effective to order that the motion have the same effect under Federal Rule of Appellate Procedure 4(a)(4) as a timely motion under Rule 59.

Notes on 2002 Amendments to Federal Rule 58

In 1963 Rule 58 was amended to clarify when a judgment was deemed entered. Unfortunately the amendment did not eliminate all controversy regarding Rule 58. Although it established the need for a separate document setting forth a judgment, it left uncertainty concerning decisions on certain orders under Rules 50(b), 52(b), 54, 59, and 60. The 2002 amendment, in (a)(1), specifically exempts these latter decisions from the separate document requirement thus making the requirement consistent with the provisions of Federal Rule of Appellate Procedure 4(a). In such situations judgment is deemed entered when the decision is entered in the civil docket under Rule 79(a). [See current Federal Rule 58(c)(1), supra.]

Another difficulty arose because the requirement of a separate document was frequently ignored, making it unclear whether a final judgment became effective, without a separate document, even though it was entered in the civil docket under Rule 79(a). The 2002 amendment deems such a docketed judgment as entered either when it is set forth in a separate document or when 150 days have run after it has been docketed. [See current Federal Rule 58(c)(2), supra.]

Rule 59. New Trial; Altering or Amending a Judgment

(a) In General.

(1) *Grounds for New Trial.* The court may, on motion, grant a new trial on all or some of the issues—and to any party—as follows:

(A) after a jury trial, for any reason for which a new trial has heretofore been granted in an action at law in federal court; or

(B) after a nonjury trial, for any reason for which a rehearing has heretofore been granted in a suit in equity in federal court.

(2) *Further Action After a Nonjury Trial.* After a nonjury trial, the court may, on motion for a new trial, open the judgment if one has been entered, take additional testimony, amend findings of fact and conclusions of law or make new ones, and direct the entry of a new judgment.

(b) Time to File a Motion for a New Trial. A motion for a new trial must be filed no later than 28 days after the entry of judgment.

(c) Time to Serve Affidavits. When a motion for a new trial is based on affidavits, they must be filed with the motion. The opposing party has 14 days after being served to file opposing affidavits. The court may permit reply affidavits.

(d) New Trial on the Court's Initiative or for Reasons Not in the Motion. No later than 28 days after the entry of judgment, the court, on its own, may order a new trial for any reason that would justify granting one on a party's motion. After giving the parties notice and an opportunity to be heard, the court may grant a timely motion for a new trial for a reason not stated in the motion. In either event, the court must specify the reasons in its order.

(e) Motion to Alter or Amend a Judgment. A motion to alter or amend a judgment must be filed no later than 28 days after the entry of the judgment.

Comparative State Provisions

(a)   *Rule 59(a)*

Minnesota Rule of Civil Procedure 59.01

A new trial may be granted to all or any of the parties and on all or part of the issues for any of the following causes:

(a)   Irregularity in the proceedings of the court, referee, jury, or prevailing party, or any order or abuse of discretion, whereby the moving party was deprived of a fair trial;

(b)   Misconduct of the jury or prevailing party;

(c)   Accident or surprise which could not have been prevented by ordinary prudence;

(d)   Material evidence, newly discovered, which with reasonable diligence could not have been found and produced at the trial;

(e)   Excessive or insufficient damages, appearing to have been given under the influence of passion or prejudice;

(f)   Errors of law occurring at the trial, and objected to at the time or, if no objection need have been made under Rules 46 and 51, plainly assigned in the notice of motion;

(g)   The verdict, decision, or report is not justified by the evidence, or is contrary to law; but, unless it be so expressly stated in the order granting a new trial, it shall not be presumed, on appeal, to have been made on the ground that the verdict, decision, or report was not justified by the evidence.

On a motion for a new trial in an action tried without a jury, the court may open the judgment if one has been entered, take additional testimony, amend findings of fact and conclusions of law or make new findings and conclusions, and direct entry of a new judgment.

Missouri Statutes Annotated § 510.330

A new trial may be granted for any of the reasons for which new trials have heretofore been granted. A new trial may be granted to all or any of the parties and on all or part of the issues after trial by jury, court or referee. On a motion for a new trial in an action tried without a jury, the court may open the judgment if one has been entered, take additional testimony, amend findings of fact or make new findings, and direct the entry of a new judgment. Only one new trial shall be allowed on the ground that the verdict is against the weight of the evidence. Every order allowing a new trial shall specify of record the ground or grounds on which said new trial is granted.

(b)   *Rule 59(b)*

Minnesota Rule of Civil Procedure 59.03

A notice of motion for a new trial shall be served within 30 days after a general verdict or service of notice by a party of the filing of the decision or order; and the motion shall be heard within 60 days after such general verdict or notice of filing, unless the time for hearing be extended by the court within the 60-day period for good cause shown.

Rule 60. Relief From a Judgment or Order

(a) Corrections Based on Clerical Mistakes; Oversights and Omissions. The court may correct a clerical mistake or a mistake arising from oversight or omission whenever one is found in a judgment, order, or other part of the record. The court may do so on motion or on its own, with or without notice. But after an appeal has been docketed in the appellate court and while it is pending, such a mistake may be corrected only with the appellate court's leave.

(b) Grounds for Relief From a Final Judgment, Order, or Proceeding. On motion and just terms, the court may relieve a party or its legal representative from a final judgment, order, or proceeding for the following reasons:

(1) mistake, inadvertence, surprise, or excusable neglect;

(2) newly discovered evidence that, with reasonable diligence, could not have been discovered in time to move for a new trial under Rule 59(b);

(3) fraud (whether previously called intrinsic or extrinsic), misrepresentation, or misconduct by an opposing party;

(4) the judgment is void;

(5) the judgment has been satisfied, released or discharged; it is based on an earlier judgment that has been reversed or vacated; or applying it prospectively is no longer equitable; or

(6) any other reason that justifies relief.

(c) **Timing and Effect of the Motion.**

(1) *Timing.* A motion under Rule 60(b) must be made within a reasonable time—and for reasons (1), (2), and (3) no more than a year after the entry of the judgment or order or the date of the proceeding.

(2) *Effect on Finality.* The motion does not affect the judgment's finality or suspend its operation.

(d) **Other Powers to Grant Relief.** This rule does not limit a court's power to:

(1) entertain an independent action to relieve a party from a judgment, order, or proceeding;

(2) grant relief under 28 U.S.C. § 1655 to a defendant who was not personally notified of the action; or

(3) set aside a judgment for fraud on the court.

(e) **Bills and Writs Abolished.** The following are abolished: bills of review, bills in the nature of bills of review, and writs of coram nobis, coram vobis, and audita querela.

Comparative State Provisions

Georgia Code Annotated § 9–11–60

(a) * * *

(b) **Methods of direct attack.** A judgment may be attacked by motion for a new trial or motion to set aside. Judgments may be attacked by motion only in the court of rendition.

(c) **Motion for new trial.** A motion for new trial must be predicated upon some intrinsic defect which does not appear upon the face of the record or pleadings.

(d) **Motion to set aside.** A motion may be brought to set aside a judgment based upon:

(1) Lack of jurisdiction over the person or the subject matter;

(2) Fraud, accident, or mistake or the acts of the adverse party unmixed with the negligence or fault of the movant; or

(3) A nonamendable defect which appears upon the face of the record or pleadings. Under this paragraph, it is not sufficient that the complaint or other pleading fails to state a claim upon which relief can be granted, but the pleadings must affirmatively show no claim in fact existed.

(e) **Complaint in equity.** The use of a complaint in equity to set aside a judgment is prohibited.

(f) **Procedure; time of relief.** * * * Motions for new trial must be brought within the time prescribed by law. In all other instances, all motions to set aside judgments shall be brought within three years from entry of the judgment complained of.

(g)   Clerical mistakes. Clerical mistakes in judgments, orders, or other parts of the record and errors therein arising from oversight or omission may be corrected by the court at any time of its own initiative or on the motion of any party and after such notice, if any, as the court orders.

(h)   Law of the case rule. The law of the case rule is abolished; but generally judgments and orders shall not be set aside or modified without just cause and, in setting aside or otherwise modifying judgments and orders, the court shall consider whether rights have vested thereunder and whether or not innocent parties would be injured thereby; provided, however, that any ruling by the Supreme Court or the Court of Appeals in a case shall be binding in all subsequent proceedings in that case in the lower court and in the Supreme Court or the Court of Appeals as the case may be.

Rule 61. Harmless Error

Unless justice requires otherwise, no error in admitting or excluding evidence—or any other error by the court or a party—is ground for granting a new trial, for setting aside a verdict, or for vacating, modifying, or otherwise disturbing a judgment or order. At every stage of the proceeding, the court must disregard all errors and defects that do not affect any party's substantial rights.

Rule 62. Stay of Proceedings to Enforce a Judgment

(a)   Automatic Stay. Except as provided in Rule 62(c) and (d), execution on a judgment and proceedings to enforce it are stayed for 30 days after its entry, unless the court orders otherwise.

(b)   Stay by Bond or Other Security. At any time after judgment is entered, a party may obtain a stay by providing a bond or other security. The stay takes effect when the court approves the bond or other security and remains in effect for the time specified in the bond or other security.

(c)   Stay of an Injunction, Receivership, or Patent Accounting Order. Unless the court orders otherwise, the following are not stayed after being entered, even if an appeal is taken:

　　(1)   an interlocutory or final judgment in an action for an injunction or receivership; or

　　(2)   a judgment or order that directs an accounting to an action for patent infringement.

(d)   Injunction Pending an Appeal. While an appeal is pending from an interlocutory order or final judgment that grants, continues, modifies, refuses, dissolves, or refuses to dissolve or modify an injunction, the court may suspend, modify, restore, or grant an injunction on terms for bond or other terms that secure the opposing party's rights. If the judgment appealed from is rendered by a statutory three-judge district court, the order must be made either:

　　(1)   by that court sitting in open session, or

　　(2)   by the assent of all its judges, as evidenced by their signatures.

(e)   Stay Without Bond on an Appeal by the United States, Its Officers, or Its Agencies. The court must not require a bond, obligation, or other security from the appellant when granting a stay on an appeal by the United States, its officers, or its agencies or on an appeal directed by a department of the federal government.

(f)   Stay in Favor of a Judgment Debtor Under State Law. If a judgment is a lien on the judgment debtor's property under the law of the state where the court is located, the judgment debtor is entitled to the same stay of execution the state court would give.

(g)   Appellate Court's Power Not Limited. This rule does not limit the power of the appellate court or one of its judges or justices:

　　(1)   to stay proceedings—or suspend, modify, restore, or grant an injunction—while an appeal is pending; or

　　(2)   to issue an order to preserve the status quo or the effectiveness of the judgment to be entered.

(h) Stay With Multiple Claims or Parties. A court may stay the enforcement of a final judgment entered under Rule 54(b) until it enters a later judgment or judgments, and may prescribe terms necessary to secure the benefit of the stayed judgment for the party in whose favor it was entered.

Rule 62.1. Indicative Ruling on a Motion for Relief That Is Barred by a Pending Appeal

(a) Relief Pending Appeal. If a timely motion is made for relief that the court lacks authority to grant because of an appeal that has been docketed and is pending, the court may:

    (1) defer considering the motion;

    (2) deny the motion; or

    (3) state either that it would grant the motion if the court of appeals remands for that purpose or that the motion raises a substantial issue.

(b) Notice to the Court of Appeals. The movant must promptly notify the circuit clerk under Federal Rule of Appellate Procedure 12.1 if the district court states that it would grant the motion or that the motion raises a substantial issue.

(c) Remand. The district court may decide the motion if the court of appeals remands for that purpose.

Rule 63. Judge's Inability to Proceed

If a judge conducting a hearing or trial is unable to proceed, any other judge may proceed upon certifying familiarity with the record and determining that the case may be completed without prejudice to the parties. In a hearing or a nonjury trial, the successor judge must, at a party's request, recall any witness whose testimony is material and disputed and who is available to testify again without undue burden. The successor judge may also recall any other witness.

TITLE VIII. PROVISIONAL AND FINAL REMEDIES

Rule 64. Seizing a Person or Property

(a) Remedies Under State Law—In General. At the commencement of and throughout an action, every remedy is available that, under the law of the state where the court is located, provides for seizing a person or property to secure satisfaction of the potential judgment. But a federal statute governs to the extent it applies.

(b) Specific Kinds of Remedies. The remedies available under this rule include the following—however designated and regardless of whether state procedure requires an independent action:

- arrest;
- attachment;
- garnishment;
- replevin;
- sequestration; and
- other corresponding or equivalent remedies.

Comparative State Provisions

New York Civil Practice Law and Rules 6201

An order of attachment may be granted in any action, except a matrimonial action, where the plaintiff has demanded and would be entitled, in whole or in part, or in the alternative, to a money judgment against one or more defendants, when:

1.   the defendant is a nondomiciliary residing within the state, or is a foreign corporation not qualified to do business in the state; or

2.   the defendant resides or is domiciled in the state and cannot be personally served despite diligent efforts to do so; or

3.   the defendant, with intent to defraud his creditors or frustrate the enforcement of a judgment that might be rendered in plaintiff's favor, has assigned, disposed of, encumbered or secreted property, or removed it from the state or is about to do any of these acts; or

4.   the action is brought by the victim * * * of a crime * * * to recover damages sustained as a result of such crime * * *.

5.   the cause of action is based on a judgment, decree or order of a court of the United States or of any other court which is entitled to full faith and credit in this state, or on a [recognized foreign] judgment * * *.

Rule 65. Injunctions and Restraining Orders

(a)   Preliminary Injunction.

(1)   *Notice.* The court may issue a preliminary injunction only on notice to the adverse party.

(2)   *Consolidating the Hearing With the Trial on the Merits.* Before or after beginning the hearing on a motion for a preliminary injunction, the court may advance the trial on the merits and consolidate it with the hearing. Even when consolidation is not ordered, evidence that is received on the motion and that would be admissible at trial becomes part of the trial record and need not be repeated at trial. But the court must preserve any party's right to a jury trial.

(b)   Temporary Restraining Order.

(1)   *Issuing Without Notice.* The court may issue a temporary restraining order without written or oral notice to the adverse party or its attorney only if:

(A)   specific facts in an affidavit or a verified complaint clearly show that immediate and irreparable injury, loss, or damage will result to the movant before the adverse party can be heard in opposition; and

(B)   the movant's attorney certifies in writing any efforts made to give notice and the reasons why it should not be required.

(2)   *Contents; Expiration.* Every temporary restraining order issued without notice must state the date and hour it was issued; describe the injury and state why it is irreparable; state why the order was issued without notice; and be promptly filed in the clerk's office and entered in the record. The order expires at the time after entry—not to exceed 14 days—that the court sets, unless before that time the court, for good cause, extends it for a like period or the adverse party consents to a longer extension. The reasons for an extension must be entered in the record.

(3)   *Expediting the Preliminary-Injunction Hearing.* If the order is issued without notice, the motion for a preliminary injunction must be set for hearing at the earliest possible time, taking precedence over all other matters except hearings on older matters of the same character. At the hearing, the party who obtained the order must proceed with the motion; if the party does not, the court must dissolve the order.

(4)   *Motion to Dissolve.* On 2 days' notice to the party who obtained the order without notice—or on shorter notice set by the court—the adverse party may appear and move to dissolve or modify the order. The court must then hear and decide the motion as promptly as justice requires.

(c)   Security. The court may issue a preliminary injunction or a temporary restraining order only if the movant gives security in an amount that the court considers proper to pay the costs and damages sustained by any party found to have been wrongfully enjoined or restrained. The United States, its officers, and its agencies are not required to give security.

(d) Contents and Scope of Every Injunction and Restraining Order.

(1) *Contents.* Every order granting an injunction and every restraining order must:

(A) state the reasons why it issued;

(B) state its terms specifically; and

(C) describe in reasonable detail—and not by referring to the complaint or other document—the act or acts restrained or required.

(2) *Persons Bound.* The order binds only the following who receive actual notice of it by personal service or otherwise:

(A) the parties;

(B) the parties' officers, agents, servants, employees, and attorneys; and

(C) other persons who are in active concert or participation with anyone described in Rule 65(d)(2)(A) or (B).

(e) Other Laws Not Modified. These rules do not modify the following:

(1) any federal statute relating to temporary restraining orders or preliminary injunctions in actions affecting employer and employee;

(2) 28 U.S.C. § 2361, which relates to preliminary injunctions in actions of interpleader or in the nature of interpleader; or

(3) 28 U.S.C. § 2284, which relates to actions that must be heard and decided by a three-judge district court.

(f) Copyright Impoundment. This rule applies to copyright-impoundment proceedings.

Comparative State Provision

New York Civil Practice Law and Rules 6301

A preliminary injunction may be granted in any action where it appears that the defendant threatens or is about to do, or is doing or procuring or suffering to be done, an act in violation of the plaintiffs' rights respecting the subject of the action, and tending to render the judgment ineffectual, or in any action where the plaintiff has demanded and would be entitled to a judgment restraining the defendant from the commission or continuance of an act, which, if committed or continued during the pendency of the action, would produce injury to the plaintiff. A temporary restraining order may be granted pending a hearing for a preliminary injunction where it appears that immediate and irreparable injury, loss or damage will result unless the defendant is restrained before the hearing can be had.

Rule 65.1. Proceedings Against a Security Provider

Whenever these rules (including the Supplemental Rules for Admiralty or Maritime Claims and Asset Forfeiture Actions) require or allow a party to give security, and security is given with one or more security providers, each provider submits to the court's jurisdiction and irrevocably appoints the court clerk as its agent for receiving service of any papers that affect its liability on the security. The security provider's liability may be enforced on motion without an independent action. The motion and any notice that the court orders may be served on the court clerk, who must promptly send a copy of each to every security provider whose address is known.

Rule 66. Receivers

These rules govern an action in which the appointment of a receiver is sought or a receiver sues or is sued. But the practice in administering an estate by a receiver or a similar court-appointed officer must accord with the historical practice in federal courts or with a local rule. An action in which a receiver has been appointed may be dismissed only by court order.

Comparative State Provision

New York Civil Practice Law and Rules 6401

(a)   Upon motion of a person having an apparent interest in property which is the subject of an action in the supreme or a county court, a temporary receiver of the property may be appointed, before or after service of summons and at any time prior to judgment, or during the pendency of an appeal, where there is danger that the property will be removed from the state, or lost, materially injured or destroyed. * * *

(b)   The court appointing a receiver may authorize him to take and hold real and personal property, and sue for, collect and sell debts or claims, upon such conditions and for such purposes as the court shall direct. A receiver shall have no power to employ counsel unless expressly so authorized by order of the court. Upon motion of the receiver or a party, powers granted to a temporary receiver may be extended or limited or the receivership may be extended to another action involving the property.

* * *

Rule 67. Deposit Into Court

(a)   **Depositing Property.** If any part of the relief sought is a money judgment or the disposition of a sum of money or some other deliverable thing, a party—on notice to every other party and by leave of court—may deposit with the court all or part of the money or thing, whether or not that party claims any of it. The depositing party must deliver to the clerk a copy of the order permitting deposit.

(b)   **Investing and Withdrawing Funds.** Money paid into court under this rule must be deposited and withdrawn in accordance with 28 U.S.C. §§ 2041 and 2042 and any like statute. The money must be deposited in an interest-bearing account or invested in a court-approved, interest-bearing instrument.

Rule 68. Offer of Judgment

(a)   **Making an Offer; Judgment on an Accepted Offer.** At least 14 days before the date set for trial, a party defending against a claim may serve on an opposing party an offer to allow judgment on specified terms, with the costs then accrued. If, within 14 days after being served, the opposing party serves written notice accepting the offer, either party may then file the offer and notice of acceptance, plus proof of service. The clerk must then enter judgment.

(b)   **Unaccepted Offer.** An unaccepted offer is considered withdrawn, but it does not preclude a later offer. Evidence of an unaccepted offer is not admissible except in a proceeding to determine costs.

(c)   **Offer After Liability Is Determined.** When one party's liability to another has been determined but the extent of liability remains to be determined by further proceedings, the party held liable may make an offer of judgment. It must be served within a reasonable time—but at least 14 days—before a hearing to determine the extent of liability.

(d)   **Paying Costs After an Unaccepted Offer.** If the judgment that the offeree finally obtains is not more favorable than the unaccepted offer, the offeree must pay the costs incurred after the offer was made.

Prior Proposed Amendment to Federal Rule 68 and Comparative State Provisions

(a) *Prior Proposed Amendment*

The Advisory Committee on the Federal Rules once circulated a draft proposal that would have altered the rule dramatically. In the main, the suggested rule provided for sanctions against any party who unreasonably refuses an offer to settle whether or not that party ultimately prevails in the action. The trial judge would be permitted to impose any "appropriate sanction" in light of all of the circumstances of the case.

(b) *Comparative State Provisions*

Michigan Court Rule 2.405

A.   Definitions. * * * "Average offer" means the sum of an offer and a counteroffer, divided by two. If no counteroffer is made, the offer shall be used as the average offer.

B.   Offer. Until 28 days before trial, a party may serve on an adverse party a written offer to stipulate to the entry of a judgment to the whole or part of the claim, including interest and costs then accrued. [Any counteroffer must be made within 21 days after service of the offer.]

C.   Acceptance of Offer [or Counteroffer]. * * * To accept, the adverse party, within 21 days of the service of the offer, must serve on the other parties a written notice of agreement to stipulate to the entry of the judgment offered and file the offer, the notice of acceptance, and proof of service of the notice with the court.

D.   Imposition of Costs Following Rejection of Offer. If an offer is rejected, costs are available as follows:

(1)   If the adjudicated verdict is more favorable to the offeror than the average verdict, the offeree must pay to the offeror the offeror's actual costs incurred in the prosecution or defense of the action.

(2)   If the adjudicated verdict is more favorable to the offeree than the average offer, the offeror must pay to the offeree the offeree's actual costs incurred in the prosecution or defense of the action. However, an offeree who has not made a counteroffer may not recover actual costs unless the offer was made less than 42 days before trial.

* * *

New York Civil Practice Law and Rules 3219

At any time not later than ten days before trial, any party against whom a cause of action based upon contract, expressed or implied, is asserted, and against whom a separate judgment may be taken, may, without court order, deposit with the clerk of the court for safekeeping, an amount deemed by him to be sufficient to satisfy the claim asserted against him, and serve upon the claimant a written tender of payment to satisfy such claim. * * * Within ten days after such deposit the claimant may withdraw the amount deposited upon filing a duly acknowledged statement that the withdrawal is in satisfaction of the claim. The clerk shall thereupon enter judgment dismissing the pleading setting forth the claim, without costs.

* * * If the tender is not accepted and the claimant fails to obtain a more favorable judgment, he shall not recover interest or costs from the time of the offer, but shall pay costs for defending against the claim from that time. A tender shall not be made known to the jury.

* * *

New York Civil Practice Law and Rules 3220

At any time not later than ten days before trial, any party against whom a cause of action based upon contract, express or implied, is asserted may serve upon the claimant a written offer to allow judgment to be taken against him for a sum therein specified, with costs then accrued, if the party against whom the claim is asserted fails in his defense. If within ten days thereafter the claimant serves a written notice that he accepts the offer, and damages are awarded to him on the trial, they shall be assessed in the sum specified in the offer. If the offer is not so accepted and the claimant fails to obtain a more favorable judgment, he shall pay the expenses necessarily incurred by the party against whom the claim is asserted, for trying the issue of damages from the time of the offer. The expenses shall be ascertained by the judge or referee before whom the case is tried. An offer under this rule shall not be made known to the jury.

New York Civil Practice Law and Rules 3221

Except in a matrimonial action, at any time not later than ten days before trial, any party against whom a claim is asserted, and against whom a separate judgment may be taken, may serve upon the claimant a written offer to allow judgment to be taken against him for a sum or property or to the effect therein specified, with costs then accrued. If within ten days thereafter the claimant serves a written notice that he accepts the offer, either party may file the summons, complaint and offer, with proof of acceptance, and thereupon the clerk shall enter judgment accordingly. If the offer is not accepted and the claimant fails to obtain a more favorable judgment, he shall not recover costs from the time of the offer, but shall pay costs from that time. An offer of judgment shall not be made known to the jury.

Rule 69. Execution

(a) In General.

(1) *Money Judgment; Applicable Procedure.* A money judgment is enforced by a writ of execution, unless the court directs otherwise. The procedure on execution—and in proceedings supplementary to and in aid of judgment or execution—must accord with the procedure of the state where the court is located, but a federal statute governs to the extent it applies.

(2) *Obtaining Discovery.* In aid of the judgment or execution, the judgment creditor or a successor in interest whose interest appears of record may obtain discovery from any person—including the judgment debtor—as provided in these rules or by the procedure of the state where the court is located.

(b) Against Certain Public Officers. When a judgment has been entered against a revenue officer in the circumstances stated in 28 U.S.C. § 2006, or against an officer of Congress in the circumstances stated in 2 U.S.C. § 118, the judgment must be satisfied as those statutes provide.

Comparative State Provisions Exempting Property From Execution

New York Civil Practice Law and Rules 5205

(a) Exemption for personal property. The following personal property when owned by any person is exempt from application to the satisfaction of a money judgment except where the judgment is for the purchase price of the exempt property or was recovered by a domestic, laboring person or mechanic for work performed by that person in such capacity:

1.   all stoves and home heating equipment kept for use in the judgment debtor's dwelling house and necessary fuel therefor for one hundred twenty days; one sewing machine with its appurtenances;

2.   religious texts, family pictures and portraits, and school books used by the judgment debtor or in the family; and other books, not exceeding five hundred dollars in value, kept and used as part of the family or judgment debtor's library;

3.   a seat or pew occupied by the judgment debtor or the family in a place of public worship;

4.   domestic animals with the necessary food for those animals for one hundred twenty days, provided that the total value of such animals and food does not exceed one thousand dollars; all necessary food actually provided for the use of the judgment debtor or his family for one hundred twenty days;

5.   all wearing apparel, household furniture, one mechanical, gas or electric refrigerator, one radio receiver, one television set, one computer and associated equipment, one cellphone, crockery, tableware and cooking utensils necessary for the judgment debtor and the family; all prescribed health aids;

6.   a wedding ring; a watch; jewelry and art not exceeding one thousand dollars in value; and

7.   tools of trade, necessary working tools and implements, including those of a mechanic, farm machinery, team, professional instruments, furniture and library, not exceeding three thousand dollars in value, together with the necessary food for the team for one hundred twenty days, provided, however, that the articles specified in this paragraph are necessary to the carrying on of the judgment debtor's profession or calling.

8.   one motor vehicle not exceeding four thousand dollars above liens and encumbrances of the debtor [but not applicable if the debt is for child support, spousal support, alimony or equitable distribution] * * * and

9.   if no homestead exemption is claimed, then one thousand dollars in personal property, bank accounts or cash.

(b)   Exemption of cause of action and damages for taking or injuring exempt personal property. A cause of action, to recover damages for taking or injuring personal property exempt from application to the satisfaction of a money judgment, is exempt from application to the satisfaction of a money judgment. A money judgment and its proceeds arising out of such a cause of action is exempt, for one year after the collection thereof, from application to the satisfaction of a money judgment.

(c)   Trust exemption. 1. * * * [A]ll property while held in trust for a judgment debtor, where the trust has been created by, or the fund so held in trust has proceeded from, a person other than the judgment debtor, is exempt from application to the satisfaction of a money judgment. * * *

(d)   Income exemptions. The following personal property is exempt from application to the satisfaction of a money judgment, except such part as a court determines to be unnecessary for the reasonable requirements of the judgment debtor and his dependents:

1.   ninety per cent of the income or other payments from a trust the principal of which is exempt under subdivision (c) * * * [and one hundred per cent of income from Keogh and other retirement plans];

2.   ninety per cent of the earnings of the judgment debtor for his personal services rendered within sixty days before, and at any time after, an income execution is delivered to the sheriff or a motion is made to secure the application of the judgment debtor's earnings to the satisfaction of the judgment; and

3.   payments pursuant to an award in a matrimonial action, for the support of a wife, where the wife is the judgment debtor, or for the support of a child, where the child is the judgment debtor; where the award was made by a court of the state, determination of the extent to which it is unnecessary shall be made by that court.

(e)   Exemptions to members of armed forces. The pay and bounty of a non-commissioned officer, musician or private in the armed forces of the United States or the state of New York; a land warrant, pension or other reward granted by the United States, or by a state, for services in the armed forces; a sword, horse, medal, emblem or device of any kind presented as a testimonial for services rendered in the armed forces of the United States or a state; and the uniform, arms and equipments which were used by a person in the service, are exempt from application to the satisfaction of a money judgment; provided, however, that the provisions of this subdivision shall not apply to the satisfaction of any order or money judgment for the support of a person's child, spouse, or former spouse.

(f)   Exemption for unpaid milk proceeds. Ninety per cent of any money or debt due or to become due to the judgment debtor for the sale of milk produced on a farm operated by him and delivered for his account to a milk dealer licensed pursuant to article twenty-one of the agriculture and markets law is exempt from application to the satisfaction of a money judgment.

(g)   Security deposit exemption. Money deposited as security for the rental of real property to be used as the residence of the judgment debtor or the judgment debtor's family; and money deposited as security with a gas, electric, water, steam, telegraph or telephone corporation, or a municipality rendering equivalent utility services, for services to judgment debtor's residence or the residence of judgment debtor's family, are exempt from application to the satisfaction of a money judgment.

(h) The following personal property is exempt from application to the satisfaction of money judgment, except such part as a court determines to be unnecessary for the reasonable requirements of the judgment debtor and his dependents:

1.   any and all medical and dental accessions to the human body and all personal property or equipment that is necessary or proper to maintain or assist in sustaining or maintaining one or more major life activities or is utilized to provide mobility for a person with a permanent disability; and

2.   any guide dog, service dog or hearing dog, as those terms are defined in section one hundred eight of the agriculture and markets law, or any animal trained to aid or assist a person with a permanent disability and actually being so used by such person, together with any and all food or feed for any such dog or other animal.

* * *

[The statute goes on to add other exemptions to those set out above.]

New York Civil Practice Law and Rules 5206

(a)   Exemption of homestead. Property of one of the following types, not exceeding * * * in value above liens and encumbrances, [one hundred fifty thousand dollars to seventy-five thousand dollars, depending upon the county where located,] owned and occupied as a principal residence, is exempt from application to the satisfaction of a money judgment, unless the judgment was recovered wholly for the purchase price thereof:

1.   a lot of land with a dwelling thereon,

2.   shares of stock in a cooperative apartment corporation,

3.   units of a condominium apartment, or

4.   a mobile home.

But no exempt homestead shall be exempt from taxation or from sale for nonpayment of taxes or assessments.

(b)   Homestead exemption after owner's death. The homestead exemption continues after the death of the person in whose favor the property was exempted for the benefit of the surviving spouse and surviving children until the majority of the youngest surviving child and until the death of the surviving spouse.

(c)   Suspension of occupation as affecting homestead. The homestead exemption ceases if the property ceases to be occupied as a residence by a person for whose benefit it may so continue, except where the suspension of occupation is for a period not exceeding one year, and occurs in consequence of injury to, or destruction of, the dwelling house upon the premises.

(d)   Exemption of homestead exceeding * * * in value [the amount specified in (a).] The exemption of a homestead is not void because the value of the property exceeds * * * [the amount specified in (a)] but the lien of a judgment attaches to the surplus.

(e)   Sale of homestead * * *. * * * Where the exemption of property sold as prescribed in this subdivision has been continued after the judgment debtor's death, or where he dies after the sale and before payment to him of his portion of the proceeds of the sale, the court may direct that portion of the proceeds which represents his interest be invested for the benefit of the person or persons entitled to the benefit of the exemption, or be otherwise disposed of as justice requires.

(f)   Exemption of burying ground. Land, set apart as a family or private burying ground, is exempt from application to the satisfaction of a money judgment, upon the following conditions only:

1.   a portion of it must have been actually used for that purpose;

2.   it must not exceed in extent one-fourth of an acre; and

3.   it must not contain any building or structure, except one or more vaults or other places of deposit for the dead, or mortuary monuments.

Rule 70. Enforcing a Judgment for a Specific Act

(a) Party's Failure to Act; Ordering Another to Act. If a judgment requires a party to convey land, to deliver a deed or other document, or to perform any other specific act and the party fails to comply within the time specified, the court may order the act to be done—at the disobedient party's expense—by another person appointed by the court. When done, the act has the same effect as if done by the party.

(b) Vesting Title. If the real or personal property is within the district, the court—instead of ordering a conveyance—may enter a judgment divesting any party's title and vesting it in others. That judgment has the effect of a legally executed conveyance.

(c) Obtaining a Writ of Attachment or Sequestration. On application by a party entitled to performance of an act, the clerk must issue a writ of attachment or sequestration against the disobedient party's property to compel obedience.

(d) Obtaining a Writ of Execution or Assistance. On application by a party who obtains a judgment or order for possession, the clerk must issue a writ of execution or assistance.

(e) Holding in Contempt. The court may also hold the disobedient party in contempt.

Rule 71. Enforcing Relief for or Against a Nonparty

When an order grants relief for a nonparty or may be enforced against a nonparty, the procedure for enforcing the order is the same as for a party.

TITLE IX. SPECIAL PROCEEDINGS

Rule 71.1. Condemning Real or Personal Property

(a) Applicability of Other Rules. These rules govern proceedings to condemn real and personal property by eminent domain, except as this rule provides otherwise.

(b) Joinder of Properties. The plaintiff may join separate pieces of property in a single action, no matter whether they are owned by the same persons or sought for the same use.

(c) Complaint.

(1) *Caption.* The complaint must contain a caption as provided in Rule 10(a). The plaintiff must, however, name as defendants both the property—designated generally by kind, quantity, and location—and at least one owner of some part of or interest in the property.

(2) *Contents.* The complaint must contain a short and plain statement of the following:

(A)   the authority for the taking;

(B)   the uses for which the property is to be taken;

(C)   a description sufficient to identify the property;

(D)   the interests to be acquired; and

(E)   for each piece of property, a designation of each defendant who has been joined as an owner or owner of an interest in it.

(3) *Parties.* When the action commences, the plaintiff need join as defendants only those persons who have or claim an interest in the property and whose names are then known. But before any hearing on compensation, the plaintiff must add as defendants all those persons who have or claim an interest and whose names have become known or can be found by a reasonably

diligent search of the records, considering both the property's character and value and the interests to be acquired. All others may be made defendants under the designation "Unknown Owners."

(4) *Procedure.* Notice must be served on all defendants as provided in Rule 71.1(d), whether they were named as defendants when the action commenced or were added later. A defendant may answer as provided in Rule 71.1(e). The court, meanwhile, may order any distribution of a deposit that the facts warrant.

(5) *Filing; Additional Copies.* In addition to filing the complaint, the plaintiff must give the clerk at least one copy for the defendants' use and additional copies at the request of the clerk or a defendant.

(d) **Process.**

(1) *Delivering Notice to the Clerk.* On filing a complaint, the plaintiff must promptly deliver to the clerk joint or several notices directed to the named defendants. When adding defendants, the plaintiff must deliver to the clerk additional notices directed to the new defendants.

(2) *Contents of the Notice.*

(A) *Main Contents.* Each notice must name the court, the title of the action, and the defendant to whom it is directed. It must describe the property sufficiently to identify it, but need not describe any property other than that to be taken from the named defendant. The notice must also state:

    (i) that the action is to condemn property;

    (ii) the interest to be taken;

    (iii) the authority for the taking;

    (iv) the uses for which the property is to be taken;

    (v) that the defendant may serve an answer on the plaintiff's attorney within 21 days after being served with the notice;

    (vi) that the failure to so serve an answer constitutes consent to the taking and to the court's authority to proceed with the action and fix the compensation; and

    (vii) that a defendant who does not serve an answer may file a notice of appearance.

(B) *Conclusion.* The notice must conclude with the name, telephone number, and e-mail address of the plaintiff's attorney and an address within the district in which the action is brought where the attorney may be served.

(3) *Serving the Notice.*

(A) *Personal Service.* When a defendant whose address is known resides within the United States or a territory subject to the administrative or judicial jurisdiction of the United States, personal service of the notice (without a copy of the complaint) must be made in accordance with Rule 4.

(B) *Service by Publication.*

    (i) A defendant may be served by publication only when the plaintiff's attorney files a certificate stating that the attorney believes the defendant cannot be personally served, because after diligent inquiry within the state where the complaint is filed, the defendant's place of residence is still unknown or, if known, that it is beyond the territorial limits of personal service. Service is then made by publishing the notice— once a week for at least three successive weeks—in a newspaper published in the county where the property is located or, if there is no such newspaper, in a newspaper with general circulation where the property is located. Before the last publication, a copy of the notice must also be mailed to every defendant who cannot be personally served but whose place of residence is then known. Unknown owners may be served by publication in the same manner by a notice addressed to "Unknown Owners."

(ii) Service by publication is complete on the date of the last publication. The plaintiff's attorney must prove publication and mailing by a certificate, attach a printed copy of the published notice, and mark on the copy the newspaper's name and the dates of publication.

(4) *Effect of Delivery and Service.* Delivering the notice to the clerk and serving it have the same effect as serving a summons under Rule 4.

(5) *Proof of Service; Amending the Proof or Notice.* Rule 4(*l*) governs proof of service. The court may permit the proof or the notice to be amended.

(e) **Appearance or Answer.**

(1) *Notice of Appearance.* A defendant that has no objection or defense to the taking of its property may serve a notice of appearance designating the property in which it claims an interest. The defendant must then be given notice of all later proceedings affecting the defendant.

(2) *Answer.* A defendant that has an objection or defense to the taking must serve an answer within 21 days after being served with the notice. The answer must:

(A) identify the property in which the defendant claims an interest;

(B) state the nature and extent of the interest; and

(C) state all the defendant's objections and defenses to the taking.

(3) *Waiver of Other Objections and Defenses; Evidence on Compensation.* A defendant waives all objections and defenses not stated in its answer. No other pleading or motion asserting an additional objection or defense is allowed. But at the trial on compensation, a defendant—whether or not it has previously appeared or answered—may present evidence on the amount of compensation to be paid and may share in the award.

(f) **Amending Pleadings.** Without leave of court, the plaintiff may—as often as it wants—amend the complaint at any time before the trial on compensation. But no amendment may be made if it would result in a dismissal inconsistent with Rule 71.1(i)(1) or (2). The plaintiff need not serve a copy of an amendment, but must serve notice of the filing, as provided in Rule 5(b), on every affected party who has appeared and, as provided in Rule 71.1(d), on every affected party who has not appeared. In addition, the plaintiff must give the clerk at least one copy of each amendment for the defendants' use, and additional copies at the request of the clerk or a defendant. A defendant may appear or answer in the time and manner and with the same effect as provided in Rule 71.1(e).

(g) **Substituting Parties.** If a defendant dies, becomes incompetent, or transfers an interest after being joined, the court may, on motion and notice of hearing, order that the proper party be substituted. Service of the motion and notice on a nonparty must be made as provided in Rule 71.1(d)(3).

(h) **Trial of the Issues.**

(1) *Issues Other Than Compensation; Compensation.* In an action involving eminent domain under federal law, the court tries all issues, including compensation, except when compensation must be determined:

(A) by any tribunal specially constituted by a federal statute to determine compensation; or

(B) if there is no such tribunal, by a jury when a party demands one within the time to answer or within any additional time the court sets, unless the court appoints a commission.

(2) *Appointing a Commission; Commission's Powers and Report.*

(A) *Reasons for Appointing.* If a party has demanded a jury, the court may instead appoint a three-person commission to determine compensation because of the character, location, or quantity of the property to be condemned or for other just reasons.

(B) *Alternate Commissioners.* The court may appoint up to two additional persons to serve as alternate commissioners to hear the case and replace commissioners who, before a decision is filed, the court finds unable or disqualified to perform their duties. Once the commission renders its final decision, the court must discharge any alternate who has not replaced a commissioner.

(C) *Examining the Prospective Commissioners.* Before making its appointments, the court must advise the parties of the identity and qualifications of each prospective commissioner and alternate, and may permit the parties to examine them. The parties may not suggest appointees, but for good cause may object to a prospective commissioner or alternate.

(D) *Commission's Powers and Report.* A commission has the powers of a master under Rule 53(c). Its action and report are determined by a majority. Rule 53(d), (e), and (f) apply to its action and report.

(i) Dismissal of the Action or a Defendant.

(1) *Dismissing the Action.*

(A) *By the Plaintiff.* If no compensation hearing on a piece of property has begun, and if the plaintiff has not acquired title or a lesser interest or taken possession, the plaintiff may, without a court order, dismiss the action as to that property by filing a notice of dismissal briefly describing the property.

(B) *By Stipulation.* Before a judgment is entered vesting the plaintiff with title or a lesser interest in or possession of property, the plaintiff and affected defendants may, without a court order, dismiss the action in whole or in part by filing a stipulation of dismissal. And if the parties so stipulate, the court may vacate a judgment already entered.

(C) *By Court Order.* At any time before compensation has been determined and paid, the court may, after a motion and hearing, dismiss the action as to a piece of property. But if the plaintiff has already taken title, a lesser interest, or possession as to any part of it, the court must award compensation for the title, lesser interest, or possession taken.

(2) *Dismissing a Defendant.* The court may at any time dismiss a defendant who was unnecessarily or improperly joined.

(3) *Effect.* A dismissal is without prejudice unless otherwise stated in the notice, stipulation, or court order.

(j) Deposit and Its Distribution.

(1) *Deposit.* The plaintiff must deposit with the court any money required by law as a condition to the exercise of eminent domain and may make a deposit when allowed by statute.

(2) *Distribution; Adjusting Distribution.* After a deposit, the court and attorneys must expedite the proceedings so as to distribute the deposit and to determine and pay compensation. If the compensation finally awarded to a defendant exceeds the amount distributed to that defendant, the court must enter judgment against the plaintiff for the deficiency. If the compensation awarded to a defendant is less than the amount distributed to that defendant, the court must enter judgment against that defendant for the overpayment.

(k) Condemnation Under a State's Power of Eminent Domain. This rule governs an action involving eminent domain under state law. But if state law provides for trying an issue by jury—or for trying the issue of compensation by jury or commission or both—that law governs.

(*l*) Costs. Costs are not subject to Rule 54(d).

Rule 72. Magistrate Judges: Pretrial Order

(a) Nondispositive Matters. When a pretrial matter not dispositive of a party's claim or defense is referred to a magistrate judge to hear and decide, the magistrate judge must promptly conduct the required proceedings and, when appropriate, issue a written order stating the decision. A party may serve and file objections to the order within 14 days after being served with a copy. A party may not assign as error a defect in the order not timely objected to. The district judge in the case must consider timely objections and modify or set aside any part of the order that is clearly erroneous or is contrary to law.

(b) Dispositive Motions and Prisoner Petitions.

    (1) *Findings and Recommendations.* A magistrate judge must promptly conduct the required proceedings when assigned, without the parties' consent, to hear a pretrial matter dispositive of a claim or defense or a prisoner petition challenging the conditions of confinement. A record must be made of all evidentiary proceedings and may, at the magistrate judge's discretion, be made of any other proceedings. The magistrate judge must enter a recommended disposition, including, if appropriate, proposed findings of fact. The clerk must promptly mail a copy to each party.

    (2) *Objections.* Within 14 days after being served with a copy of the recommended disposition, a party may serve and file specific written objections to the proposed findings and recommendations. A party may respond to another party's objections within 14 days after being served with a copy. Unless the district judge orders otherwise, the objecting party must promptly arrange for transcribing the record, or whatever portions of it the parties agree to or the magistrate judge considers sufficient.

    (3) *Resolving Objections.* The district judge must determine de novo any part of the magistrate judge's disposition that has been properly objected to. The district judge may accept, reject, or modify the recommended disposition; receive further evidence; or return the matter to the magistrate judge with instructions.

Rule 73. Magistrate Judges: Trial by Consent; Appeal

(a) Trial by Consent. When authorized under 28 U.S.C. § 636(c), a magistrate judge may, if all parties consent, conduct a civil action or proceeding, including a jury or nonjury trial. A record must be made in accordance with 28 U.S.C. § 636(c)(5).

(b) Consent Procedure.

    (1) *In General.* When a magistrate judge has been designated to conduct civil actions or proceedings, the clerk must give the parties written notice of their opportunity to consent under 28 U.S.C. § 636(c). To signify their consent, the parties must jointly or separately file a statement consenting to the referral. A district judge or magistrate judge may be informed of a party's response to the clerk's notice only if all parties have consented to the referral.

    (2) *Reminding the Parties About Consenting.* A district judge, magistrate judge, or other court official may remind the parties of the magistrate judge's availability, but must also advise them that they are free to withhold consent without adverse substantive consequences.

    (3) *Vacating a Referral.* On its own for good cause—or when a party shows extraordinary circumstances—the district judge may vacate a referral to a magistrate judge under this rule.

(c) Appealing a Judgment. In accordance with 28 U.S.C. § 636(c)(3), an appeal from a judgment entered at a magistrate judge's direction may be taken to the court of appeals as would any other appeal from a district-court judgment.

Rule 74. [Abrogated.]

Rule 75. [Abrogated.]

Rule 76. [Abrogated.]

TITLE X. DISTRICT COURTS AND CLERKS: CONDUCTING BUSINESS; ISSUING ORDERS

Rule 77. Conducting Business; Clerk's Authority; Notice of an Order or Judgment

(a) When Court Is Open. Every district court is considered always open for filing any paper, issuing and returning process, making a motion, or entering an order.

(b) Place for Trial and Other Proceedings. Every trial on the merits must be conducted in open court and, so far as convenient, in a regular courtroom. Any other act or proceeding may be done or conducted by a judge in chambers, without the attendance of the clerk or other court official, and anywhere inside or outside the district. But no hearing—other than one ex parte—may be conducted outside the district unless all the affected parties consent.

(c) Clerk's Office Hours; Clerk's Orders.

(1) *Hours.* The clerk's office—with a clerk or deputy on duty—must be open during business hours every day except Saturdays, Sundays, and legal holidays. But a court may, by local rule or order, require that the office be open for specified hours on Saturday or a particular legal holiday other than one listed in Rule 6(a)(6)(A).

(2) *Orders.* Subject to the court's power to suspend, alter, or rescind the clerk's action for good cause, the clerk may:

    (A) issue process;

    (B) enter a default;

    (C) enter a default judgment under Rule 55(b)(1); and

    (D) act on any other matter that does not require the court's action.

(d) Serving Notice of an Order or Judgment.

(1) *Service.* Immediately after entering an order or judgment, the clerk must serve notice of the entry, as provided in Rule 5(b), on each party who is not in default for failing to appear. The clerk must record the service on the docket. A party also may serve notice of the entry as provided in Rule 5(b).

(2) *Time to Appeal Not Affected by Lack of Notice.* Lack of notice of the entry does not affect the time for appeal or relieve—or authorize the court to relieve—a party for failing to appeal within the time allowed, except as allowed by Federal Rule of Appellate Procedure (4)(a).

Rule 78. Hearing Motions; Submission on Briefs

(a) Providing a Regular Schedule for Oral Hearings. A court may establish regular times and places for oral hearings on motions.

(b) Providing for Submission on Briefs. By rule or order, the court may provide for submitting and determining motions on briefs, without oral hearings.

Rule 79. Records Kept by the Clerk

(a) Civil Docket.

(1) *In General.* The clerk must keep a record known as the "civil docket" in the form and manner prescribed by the Director of the Administrative Office of the United States Courts with the approval of the Judicial Conference of the United States. The clerk must enter each civil action in the docket. Actions must be assigned consecutive file numbers, which must be noted in the docket where the first entry of the action is made.

(2) *Items to be Entered.* The following items must be marked with the file number and entered chronologically in the docket:

(A) papers filed with the clerk;

(B) process issued, and proofs of service or other returns showing execution; and

(C) appearances, orders, verdicts, and judgments.

(3) *Contents of Entries; Jury Trial Demanded.* Each entry must briefly show the nature of the paper filed or writ issued, the substance of each proof of service or other return, and the substance and date of entry of each order and judgment. When a jury trial has been properly demanded or ordered, the clerk must enter the word "jury" in the docket.

(b) Civil Judgments and Orders. The clerk must keep a copy of every final judgment and appealable order; of every order affecting title to or a lien on real or personal property; and of any other order that the court directs to be kept. The clerk must keep these in the form and manner prescribed by the Director of the Administrative Office of the United States Courts with the approval of the Judicial Conference of the United States.

(c) Indexes; Calendars. Under the court's direction, the clerk must:

(1) keep indexes of the docket and of the judgments and orders described in Rule 79(b); and

(2) prepare calendars of all actions ready for trial, distinguishing jury trials from nonjury trials.

(d) Other Records. The clerk must keep any other records required by the Director of the Administrative Office of the United States Courts with the approval of the Judicial Conference of the United States.

Rule 80. Stenographic Transcript as Evidence

If stenographically reported testimony at a hearing or trial is admissible in evidence at a later trial, the testimony may be proved by a transcript certified by the person who reported it.

TITLE XI. GENERAL PROVISIONS

Rule 81. Applicability of the Rules in General; Removed Actions

(a) Applicability to Particular Proceedings.

(1) *Prize Proceedings.* These rules do not apply to prize proceedings in admiralty governed by 10 U.S.C. §§ 7651–7681.

(2) *Bankruptcy.* These rules apply to bankruptcy proceedings to the extent provided by the Federal Rules of Bankruptcy Procedure.

(3) *Citizenship.* These rules apply to proceedings for admission to citizenship to the extent that the practice in those proceedings is not specified in federal statutes and has previously conformed to the practice in civil actions. The provisions of 8 U.S.C. § 1451 for service by publication and for answer apply in proceedings to cancel citizenship certificates.

(4) *Special Writs.* These rules apply to proceedings for habeas corpus and for quo warranto to the extent that the practice in those proceedings:

(A) is not specified in a federal statute, the Rules Governing Section 2254 Cases, or the Rules Governing Section 2255 Cases; and

(B) has previously conformed to the practice in civil actions.

(5) *Proceedings Involving a Subpoena.* These rules apply to proceedings to compel testimony or the production of documents through a subpoena issued by a United States officer or agency under a federal statute, except as otherwise provided by statute, by local rule, or by court order in the proceedings

(6) *Other Proceedings.* These rules, to the extent applicable, govern proceedings under the following laws, except as these laws provide other procedures:

(A) 7 U.S.C. §§ 292, 499g(c), for reviewing an order of the Secretary of Agriculture;

(B) 9 U.S.C., relating to arbitration;

(C) 15 U.S.C. § 522, for reviewing an order of the Secretary of the Interior;

(D) 15 U.S.C. § 715d(c), for reviewing an order denying a certificate of clearance;

(E) 29 U.S.C. §§ 159, 160, for enforcing an order of the National Labor Relations Board;

(F) 33 U.S.C. §§ 918, 921, for enforcing or reviewing a compensation order under the Longshore and Harbor Workers' Compensation Act; and

(G) 45 U.S.C. § 159, for reviewing an arbitration award in a railway-labor dispute.

(b) **Scire Facias and Mandamus.** The writs of scire facias and mandamus are abolished. Relief previously available through them may be obtained by appropriate action or motion under these rules.

(c) **Removed Actions.**

(1) *Applicability.* These rules apply to a civil action after it is removed from a state court.

(2) *Further Pleading.* After removal, repleading is unnecessary unless the court orders it. A defendant who did not answer before removal must answer or present other defenses or objections under these rules within the longest of these periods:

(A) 21 days after receiving—through service or otherwise—a copy of the initial pleading stating the claim for relief;

(B) 21 days after being served with the summons for an initial pleading on file at the time of service; or

(C) 7 days after the notice of removal is filed.

(3) *Demand for a Jury Trial.*

(A) As Affected by State Law. A party who, before removal, expressly demanded a jury trial in accordance with state law need not renew the demand after removal. If the state law did not require an express demand for a jury trial, a party need not make one after removal unless the court orders the parties to do so within a specified time. The court must so order at a party's request and may so order on its own. A party who fails to make a demand when so ordered waives a jury trial.

(B) Under Rule 38. If all necessary pleadings have been served at the time of removal, a party entitled to a jury trial under Rule 38 must be given one if the party serves a demand within 14 days after:

    (i)   it files a notice of removal; or

    (ii)   it is served with a notice of removal filed by another party.

(d) Law Applicable.

    (1) *"State Law" Defined.* When these rules refer to state law, the term "law" includes the state's statutes and the state's judicial decisions.

    (2) *"State" Defined.* The term "state" includes, where appropriate, the District of Columbia and any United States commonwealth or territory.

    (3) *"Federal Statute" Defined in the District of Columbia.* In the United States District Court for the District of Columbia, the term "federal statute" includes any Act of Congress that applies locally to the District.

Rule 82. Jurisdiction and Venue Unaffected

These rules do not extend or limit the jurisdiction of the district courts or the venue of actions in those courts. An admiralty or maritime claim under Rule 9(h) is governed by 28 U.S.C. § 1390.

Rule 83. Rules by District Courts; Judge's Directives

(a) Local Rules.

    (1) *In General.* After giving public notice and an opportunity for comment, a district court, acting by a majority of its district judges, may adopt and amend rules governing its practice. A local rule must be consistent with—but not duplicate—federal statutes and rules adopted under 28 U.S.C. §§ 2072 and 2075, and must conform to any uniform numbering system prescribed by the Judicial Conference of the United States. A local rule takes effect on the date specified by the district court and remains in effect unless amended by the court or abrogated by the judicial council of the circuit. Copies of rules and amendments must, on their adoption, be furnished to the judicial council and the Administrative Office of the United States Courts and be made available to the public.

    (2) *Requirement of Form.* A local rule imposing a requirement of form must not be enforced in a way that causes a party to lose any right because of a nonwillful failure to comply.

(b) Procedure When There Is No Controlling Law. A judge may regulate practice in any manner consistent with federal law, rules adopted under 28 U.S.C. §§ 2072 and 2075, and the district's local rules. No sanction or other disadvantage may be imposed for noncompliance with any requirement not in federal law, federal rules, or the local rules unless the alleged violator has been furnished in the particular case with actual notice of the requirement.

Note on the 1985 Amendment to Federal Rule 83

The 1985 alteration enhances the local rulemaking process by requiring appropriate public notice of proposed rules and an opportunity to comment on them. It attempts to assure that the expert advice of practitioners and scholars is made available to the district court before local rules are promulgated.

Rule 84. Forms. [Abrogated.]

Note on the Elimination of Federal Rule 84 and the Appendix of Forms

Prior to its abrogation, effective December 1, 2015, Rule 84 read: "The forms in the Appendix suffice under these rules and illustrate the simplicity and brevity that these rules contemplate." The ostensible reason given for abrogation was that the forms were unnecessary. They were, it was said, out of date, little used, and covered by state or other unofficial forms if needed. Many observers, believe that the main reason for abrogation was that the forms that dealt with pleading were considered too general and thus inconsistent with modern Supreme Court decisions requiring more specific allegations in order to withstand motions to dismiss for failure to state a claim. See the cases set out in Part IX, infra. For an analysis of the history and details leading up to the decision to abrogate Rule 84 and the Appendix of Forms, see Coleman, Abrogation Magic: The Rules Enabling Act Process, Civil Rule 84, and the Forms, 15 Nevada L.J. 1093 (2015).

The former forms appear in the Appendix of Abrogated Forms set out following the current rules.

Rule 85. Title

These rules may be cited as the Federal Rules of Civil Procedure.

Rule 86. Effective Dates

(a) In General. These rules and any amendments take effect at the time specified by the Supreme Court, subject to 28 U.S.C. § 2074. They govern:

(1)   proceedings in an action commenced after their effective date; and

(2)   proceedings after that date in an action then pending unless:

(A)   the Supreme Court specifies otherwise; or

(B)   the court determines that applying them in a particular action would be infeasible or work an injustice.

(b) December 1, 2007 Amendments. If any provision in Rules 1–5.1, 6–73, or 77–86 conflicts with another law, priority in time for the purpose of 28 U.S.C. § 2072(b) is not affected by the amendments taking effect on December 1, 2007.

APPENDIX OF ABROGATED FORMS

[Abrogated Effective December 1, 2015.]

[Although all of the forms were eliminated in 2015, at the same time the provisions of Forms 5, 6, and 7 were appended to Rule 4.]

Form 1

CAPTION

(Use on every summons, complaint, answer, motion, or other document.)

United States District Court
for the
_____ District of _____

A B, Plaintiff)	
)	
v.)	
)	Civil Action No. _____
C D, Defendant)	
)	
v.)	
)	
E F, Third-Party Defendant)	
(Use if needed.))	

(Name of Document)

Form 2

DATE, SIGNATURE, ADDRESS, E-MAIL ADDRESS, AND TELEPHONE NUMBER

(Use at the conclusion of pleadings and other papers that require a signature.)

Date _____

_____
(Signature of the attorney or unrepresented party)

_____
(Printed name)

_____
(Address)

_____
(E-mail address)

_____
(Telephone number)

APPENDIX OF ABROGATED FORMS

Form 3

SUMMONS

(Caption—See Form 1.)

To *name the defendant*:

A lawsuit has been filed against you.

Within 21 days after service of this summons on you (not counting the day you received it), you must serve on the plaintiff an answer to the attached complaint or a motion under Rule 12 of the Federal Rules of Civil Procedure. The answer or motion must be served on the plaintiff's attorney, _____, whose address is _____. If you fail to do so, judgment by default will be entered against you for the relief demanded in the complaint. You also must file your answer or motion with the court.

Date _____

_____
Clerk of Court

(Court Seal)

(Use 60 days if the defendant is the United States or a United States agency, or is an officer or employee of the United States allowed 60 days by Rule 12(a)(3).)

Form 4

SUMMONS ON A THIRD-PARTY COMPLAINT

(Caption—See Form 1.)

To *name the third-party defendant*:

A lawsuit has been filed against defendant _____, who as third-party plaintiff is making this claim against you to pay part or all of what [he] may owe to the plaintiff _____.

Within 21 days after service of this summons on you (not counting the day you received it), you must serve on the plaintiff and on the defendant an answer to the attached third-party complaint or a motion under Rule 12 of the Federal Rules of Civil Procedure. The answer or motion must be served on the defendant's attorney, _____, whose address is, _____, and also on the plaintiff's attorney, _____, whose address is, _____. If you fail to do so, judgment by default will be entered against you for the relief demanded in the third-party complaint. You also must file the answer or motion with the court and serve it on any other parties.

A copy of the plaintiff's complaint is also attached. You may—but are not required to—respond to it.

Date _____

_____
Clerk of Court

(Court Seal)

Form 5

NOTICE OF A LAWSUIT AND REQUEST
TO WAIVE SERVICE OF A SUMMONS

(Caption—See Form 1.)

To (*name the defendant—or if the defendant is a corporation, partnership, or association name an officer or agent authorized to receive service*):

Why are you getting this?

A lawsuit has been filed against you, or the entity you represent, in this court under the number shown above. A copy of the complaint is attached.

This is not a summons, or an official notice from the court. It is a request that, to avoid expenses, you waive formal service of a summons by signing and returning the enclosed waiver. To avoid these expenses, you must return the signed waiver within (*give at least 30 days or at least 60 days if the defendant is outside any judicial district of the United States*) from the date shown below, which is the date this notice was sent. Two copies of the waiver form are enclosed, along with a stamped, self-addressed envelope or other prepaid means for returning one copy. You may keep the other copy.

What happens next?

If you return the signed waiver, I will file it with the court. The action will then proceed as if you had been served on the date the waiver is filed, but no summons will be served on you and you will have 60 days from the date this notice is sent (see the date below) to answer the complaint (or 90 days if this notice is sent to you outside any judicial district of the United States).

If you do not return the signed waiver within the time indicated, I will arrange to have the summons and complaint served on you. And I will ask the court to require you, or the entity you represent, to pay the expenses of making service.

Please read the enclosed statement about the duty to avoid unnecessary expenses.

I certify that this request is being sent to you on the date below.

(Date and sign—See Form 2.)

Form 6

WAIVER OF THE SERVICE OF SUMMONS

(Caption—See Form 1.)

To *name the plaintiff's attorney or the unrepresented plaintiff*:

I have received your request to waive service of a summons in this action along with a copy of the complaint, two copies of this waiver form, and a prepaid means of returning one signed copy of the form to you.

I, or the entity I represent, agree to save the expense of serving a summons and complaint in this case.

I understand that I, or the entity I represent, will keep all defenses or objections to the lawsuit, the court's jurisdiction, and the venue of the action, but that I waive any objections to the absence of a summons or of service.

I also understand that I, or the entity I represent, must file and serve an answer or a motion under Rule 12 within 60 days from _____, the date when this request was sent (or 90 days if it was sent outside the United States). If I fail to do so, a default judgment will be entered against me or the entity I represent.

(Date and sign—See Form 2.)

(*Attach the following to Form 6.*)

Duty to Avoid Unnecessary Expenses of Serving a Summons

Rule 4 of the Federal Rules of Civil Procedure requires certain defendants to cooperate in saving unnecessary expenses of serving a summons and complaint. A defendant who is located in the United States and who fails to return a signed waiver of service requested by a plaintiff located in the United States will be required to pay the expenses of service, unless the defendant shows good cause for the failure.

153

"Good cause" does *not* include a belief that the lawsuit is groundless, or that it has been brought in an improper venue, or that the court has no jurisdiction over this matter or over the defendant or the defendant's property.

If the waiver is signed and returned, you can still make these and all other defenses and objections, but you cannot object to the absence of a summons or of service.

If you waive service, then you must, within the time specified on the waiver form, serve an answer or a motion under Rule 12 on the plaintiff and file a copy with the court. By signing and returning the waiver form, you are allowed more time to respond than if a summons had been served.

Form 7

STATEMENT OF JURISDICTION

a.   (*For diversity-of-citizenship jurisdiction.*) The plaintiff is [a citizen of *Michigan*] [a corporation incorporated under the laws of *Michigan* with its principal place of business in *Michigan*]. The defendant is [a citizen of *New York*] [a corporation incorporated under the laws of *New York* with its principal place of business in *New York*]. The amount in controversy, without interest and costs, exceeds the sum or value specified by 28 U.S.C. § 1332.

b.   (*For federal-question jurisdiction.*) This action arises under [the United States Constitution, *specify the article or amendment and the section*] [a United States treaty *specify*] [a federal statute, ___ U.S.C. § ___].

c.   (*For a claim in the admiralty or maritime jurisdiction.*) This is a case of admiralty or maritime jurisdiction. (*To invoke admiralty status under Rule 9(h) use the following:* This is an admiralty or maritime claim within the meaning of Rule 9(h).)

Form 8

STATEMENT OF REASONS FOR OMITTING A PARTY

(*If a person who ought to be made a party under Rule 19(a) is not named, include this statement in accordance with Rule 19(c).*)

This complaint does not join as a party *name* who [is not subject to this court's personal jurisdiction] [cannot be made a party without depriving this court of subject-matter jurisdiction] because *state the reason.*

Form 9

STATEMENT NOTING A PARTY'S DEATH

(Caption—See Form 1.)

In accordance with Rule 25(a) *name the person,* who is [a party to this action] [a representative of or successor to the deceased party] notes the death during the pendency of this action of *name,* [*describe as party* in this action].

(Date and sign—See Form 2.)

Form 10

COMPLAINT TO RECOVER A SUM CERTAIN

(Caption—See Form 1.)

1.   (Statement of Jurisdiction—See Form 7.)

*(Use one or more of the following as appropriate
and include a demand for judgment.)*

(a)   *On a Promissory Note*

     2.   On *date,* the defendant executed and delivered a note promising to pay the plaintiff on *date* the sum of $_____ with interest at the rate of ___ percent. A copy of the note [is attached as Exhibit A] [is summarized as follows: _____.]

     3.   The defendant has not paid the amount owed.

(b)   *On an Account*

     2.   The defendant owes the plaintiff $_____ according to the account set out in Exhibit A.

(c)   *For Goods Sold and Delivered*

     2.   The defendant owes the plaintiff $_____ for goods sold and delivered by the plaintiff to the defendant from *date* to *date.*

(d)   *For Money Lent*

     2.   The defendant owes the plaintiff $_____ for money lent by the plaintiff to the defendant on *date.*

(e)   *For Money Paid by Mistake*

     2.   The defendant owes the plaintiff $_____ for money paid by mistake to the defendant on *date* under these circumstances: *describe with particularity in accordance with Rule 9(b).*

(f)   *For Money Had and Received*

     2.   The defendant owes the plaintiff $_____ for money that was received from *name* on *date* to be paid by the defendant to the plaintiff.

Demand for Judgment

     Therefore, the plaintiff demands judgment against the defendant for $_____, plus interest and costs.

(Date and sign—See Form 2.)

Form 11

COMPLAINT FOR NEGLIGENCE

(Caption—See Form 1.)

     1.   (Statement of Jurisdiction—See Form 7.)

     2.   On *date*, at *place*, the defendant negligently drove a motor vehicle against the plaintiff.

     3.   As a result, the plaintiff was physically injured, lost wages or income, suffered physical and mental pain, and incurred medical expenses of $_____.

     Therefore, the plaintiff demands judgment against the defendant for $_____, plus costs.

(Date and sign—See Form 2).

Comparative State Provision

**North Carolina Rules of Civil Procedure, Rule 84—
[Form] (3) Complaint for Negligence**

     1.   On _____, ___, at [name of place where accident occurred], defendant negligently drove a motor vehicle against plaintiff who was then crossing said street.

155

2. Defendant was negligent in that:

(a) Defendant drove at an excessive speed.

(b) Defendant drove through a red light.

(c) Defendant failed to yield the right-of-way to plaintiff in a marked crosswalk.

3. As a result plaintiff was thrown down and had his leg broken and was otherwise injured, was prevented from transacting his business, suffered great pain of body and mind, and incurred expenses for medical attention and hospitalization [in the sum of one thousand dollars] (or) [in an amount not yet determined].

Wherefore, plaintiff demands judgment against defendant in the sum of _____ dollars and costs.

See also New York Civil Practice Law and Rules 3041, 3043, as set out in connection with Federal Rule 8(a), supra.

Form 12

COMPLAINT FOR NEGLIGENCE WHEN THE PLAINTIFF DOES NOT KNOW WHO IS RESPONSIBLE

(Caption—See Form 1.)

1. (Statement of Jurisdiction—See Form 7.)

2. On *date*, at *place*, defendant *name* or defendant *name* or both of them willfully or recklessly or negligently drove, or caused to be driven, a motor vehicle against the plaintiff.

3. As a result, the plaintiff was physically injured, lost wages or income, suffered mental and physical pain, and incurred medical expenses of $_____.

Therefore, the plaintiff demands judgment against one or both defendants for $_____, plus costs.

(Date and sign—See Form 2.)

Form 13

COMPLAINT FOR NEGLIGENCE UNDER THE FEDERAL EMPLOYERS' LIABILITY ACT

(Caption—See Form 1.)

1. (Statement of Jurisdiction—See Form 7.)

2. At the times below, the defendant owned and operated in interstate commerce a railroad line that passed through a tunnel located at _____.

3. On *date*, the plaintiff was working to repair and enlarge the tunnel to make it convenient and safe for use in interstate commerce.

4. During this work, the defendant, as the employer, negligently put the plaintiff to work in a section of the tunnel that the defendant had left unprotected and unsupported.

5. The defendant's negligence caused the plaintiff to be injured by a rock that fell from an unsupported portion of the tunnel.

6. As a result, the plaintiff was physically injured, lost wages or income, suffered mental and physical pain, and incurred medical expenses of $_____.

Therefore, the plaintiff demands judgment against the defendant for $_____, and costs.

(Date and sign—See Form 2.)

Form 14

COMPLAINT FOR DAMAGES UNDER THE MERCHANT MARINE ACT

(Caption—See Form 1.)

1.   (Statement of Jurisdiction—See Form 7.)

2.   At the times below, the defendant owned and operated the vessel *name* and used it to transport cargo for hire by water in interstate and foreign commerce.

3.   On *date*, at *place*, the defendant hired the plaintiff under seamen's articles of customary form for a voyage from _____ to _____ and return at a wage of $_____ a month and found, which is equal to a shore worker's wage of $_____ a month.

4.   On *date*, the vessel was at sea on the return voyage. (*Describe the weather and the condition of the vessel.*)

5.   (*Describe as in Form 11 the defendant's negligent conduct.*)

6.   As a result of the defendant's negligent conduct and the unseaworthiness of the vessel, the plaintiff was physically injured, has been incapable of any gainful activity, suffered mental and physical pain, and has incurred medical expenses of $_____.

Therefore, the plaintiff demands judgment against the defendant for $_____, plus costs.

(Date and sign—See Form 2.)

Form 15

COMPLAINT FOR THE CONVERSION OF PROPERTY

(Caption—See Form 1.)

1.   (Statement of Jurisdiction—See Form 7.)

2.   On *date*, at *place*, the defendant converted to the defendant's own use property owned by the plaintiff. The property converted consists of *describe*.

3.   The property is worth $_____.

Therefore, the plaintiff demands judgment against the defendant for $_____, plus costs.

(Date and sign—See Form 2.)

Form 16

THIRD-PARTY COMPLAINT

(Caption—See Form 1.)

1.   Plaintiff *name* has filed against defendant *name* a complaint, a copy of which is attached.

2.   (*State grounds entitling defendant's name to recover from third-party defendant's name for (all or an identified share) of any judgment for plaintiff's name against defendant's name.*)

Therefore, the defendant demands judgment against *third-party defendant's name* for *all or an identified share* of sums that may be adjudged against the defendant in the plaintiff's favor.

(Date and sign—See Form 2.)

Form 17

COMPLAINT FOR SPECIFIC PERFORMANCE
OF A CONTRACT TO CONVEY LAND

(Caption—See Form 1.)

1.　(Statement of Jurisdiction—See Form 7.)

2.　On *date*, the parties agreed to the contract [attached as Exhibit A] [summarize the contract].

3.　As agreed, the plaintiff tendered the purchase price and requested a conveyance of the land, but the defendant refused to accept the money or make a conveyance.

4.　The plaintiff now offers to pay the purchase price.

Therefore, the plaintiff demands that:

　　(a)　the defendant be required to specifically perform the agreement and pay damages of $_____, plus interest and costs, or

　　(b)　if specific performance is not ordered, the defendant be required to pay damages of $_____, plus interest and costs.

(Date and sign—See Form 2.)

Form 18

COMPLAINT FOR PATENT INFRINGEMENT

(Caption—See Form 1.)

1.　(Statement of Jurisdiction—See Form 7.)

2.　On *date*, United States Letters Patent No. _____ were issued to the plaintiff for an invention in an *electric motor*. The plaintiff owned the patent throughout the period of the defendant's infringing acts and still owns the patent.

3.　The defendant has infringed and is still infringing the Letters Patent by making, selling, and using *electric motors* that embody the patented invention, and the defendant will continue to do so unless enjoined by this court.

4.　The plaintiff has complied with the statutory requirement of placing a notice of the Letters Patent on all *electric motors* it manufactures and sells and has given the defendant written notice of the infringement.

Therefore, the plaintiff demands:

　　(a)　a preliminary and final injunction against the continuing infringement;

　　(b)　an accounting for damages; and

　　(c)　interest and costs.

(Date and sign—See Form 2.)

Form 19

COMPLAINT FOR COPYRIGHT INFRINGEMENT
AND UNFAIR COMPETITION

(Caption—See Form 1.)

1.　(Statement of Jurisdiction—See Form 7.)

2.   Before *date*, the plaintiff, a United States citizen, wrote a book entitled _____.

3.   The book is an original work that may be copyrighted under United States law. A copy of the book is attached as Exhibit A.

4.   Between *date* and *date*, the plaintiff applied to the copyright office and received a certificate of registration dated _____ and identified as *date, class, number*.

5.   Since *date*, the plaintiff has either published or licensed for publication all copies of the book in compliance with the copyright laws and has remained the sole owner of the copyright.

6.   After the copyright was issued, the defendant infringed the copyright by publishing and selling a book entitled _____, which was copied largely from the plaintiff's book. A copy of the defendant's book is attached as Exhibit B.

7.   The plaintiff has notified the defendant in writing of the infringement.

8.   The defendant continues to infringe the copyright by continuing to publish and sell the infringing book in violation of the copyright, and further has engaged in unfair trade practices and unfair competition in connection with its publication and sale of the infringing book, thus causing irreparable damage.

Therefore, the plaintiff demands that:

(a)   until this case is decided the defendant and the defendant's agents be enjoined from disposing of any copies of the defendant's book by sale or otherwise;

(b)   the defendant account for and pay as damages to the plaintiff all profits and advantages gained from unfair trade practices and unfair competition in selling the defendant's book, and all profits and advantages gained from infringing the plaintiff's copyright (but no less than the statutory minimum);

(c)   the defendant deliver for impoundment all copies of the book in the defendant's possession or control and deliver for destruction all infringing copies and all plates, molds, and other materials for making infringing copies;

(d)   the defendant pay the plaintiff interest, costs, and reasonable attorney's fees; and

(e)   the plaintiff be awarded any other just relief.

(Date and sign—See Form 2.)

Form 20

COMPLAINT FOR INTERPLEADER AND DECLARATORY RELIEF

(Caption—See Form 1.)

1.   (Statement of Jurisdiction—See Form 7.)

2.   On *date*, the plaintiff issued a life insurance policy on the life of *name* with *name* as the named beneficiary.

3.   As a condition for keeping the policy in force, the policy required payment of a premium during the first year and then annually.

4.   The premium due on *date* was never paid, and the policy lapsed after that date.

5.   On *date*, after the policy had lapsed, both the insured and the named beneficiary died in an automobile collision.

6.   Defendant *name* claims to be the beneficiary in place of *name* and has filed a claim to be paid the policy's full amount.

7.   The other two defendants are representatives of the deceased persons' estates. Each defendant has filed a claim on behalf of each estate to receive payment of the policy's full amount.

8.   If the policy was in force at the time of death, the plaintiff is in doubt about who should be paid.

Therefore, the plaintiff demands that:

(a)   each defendant be restrained from commencing any action against the plaintiff on the policy;

(b)   a judgment be entered that no defendant is entitled to the proceeds of the policy or any part of it, but if the court determines that the policy was in effect at the time of the insured's death, that the defendants be required to interplead and settle among themselves their rights to the proceeds, and that the plaintiff be discharged from all liability except to the defendant determined to be entitled to the proceeds; and

(c)   the plaintiff recover its costs.

(Date and sign—See Form 2.)

Form 21

COMPLAINT ON A CLAIM FOR A DEBT AND TO SET ASIDE A FRAUDULENT CONVEYANCE UNDER RULE 18(b)

(Caption—See Form 1.)

1.   (Statement of Jurisdiction—See Form 7.)

2.   On *date*, defendant *name* signed a note promising to pay to the plaintiff on *date* the sum of $_____ with interest at the rate of ___ percent. [The pleader may, but need not, attach a copy or plead the note verbatim.]

3.   Defendant *name* owes the plaintiff the amount of the note and interest.

4.   On *date*, defendant *name* conveyed all defendant's real and personal property *if less than all, describe it fully* to defendant *name* for the purpose of defrauding the plaintiff and hindering or delaying the collection of the debt.

Therefore, the plaintiff demands that:

(a)   judgment for $_____, plus costs, be entered against defendant(s) *name(s)*; and

(b)   the conveyance to defendant *name* be declared void and any judgment granted be made a lien on the property.

(Date and sign—See Form 2.)

Form 30

ANSWER PRESENTING DEFENSES UNDER RULE 12(b)

(Caption—See Form 1.)

Responding to Allegations in the Complaint

1.   Defendant admits the allegations in paragraphs _____.

2.   Defendant lacks knowledge or information sufficient to form a belief about the truth of the allegations in paragraphs _____.

3.   Defendant admits *identify part of the allegation* in paragraph _____ and denies or lacks knowledge or information sufficient to form a belief about the truth of the rest of the paragraph.

Failure to State a Claim

4.   The complaint fails to state a claim upon which relief can be granted.

Failure to Join a Required Party

5.   If there is a debt, it is owed jointly by the defendant and *name* who is a citizen of _____. This person can be made a party without depriving this court of jurisdiction over the existing parties.

Affirmative Defense—Statute of Limitations

6.   The plaintiff's claim is barred by the statute of limitations because it arose more than _____ years before this action was commenced.

Counterclaim

7.   *(Set forth any counterclaim in the same way a claim is pleaded in a complaint. Include a further statement of jurisdiction if needed.)*

Crossclaim

8.   *(Set forth a crossclaim against a coparty in the same way a claim is pleaded in a complaint. Include a further statement of jurisdiction if needed.)*

(Date and sign—See Form 2.)

Form 31

ANSWER TO A COMPLAINT FOR MONEY HAD AND RECEIVED WITH A COUNTERCLAIM FOR INTERPLEADER

(Caption—See Form 1.)

Response to the Allegations in the Complaint

(See Form 30.)

Counterclaim for Interpleader

1.   The defendant received from *name* a deposit of $_____.

2.   The plaintiff demands payment of the deposit because of a purported assignment from *name*, who has notified the defendant that the assignment is not valid and who continues to hold the defendant responsible for the deposit.

Therefore, the defendant demands that:

    (a)   *name* be made a party to this action;

    (b)   the plaintiff and *name* be required to interplead their respective claims;

    (c)   the court decide whether the plaintiff or *name* or either of them is entitled to the deposit and discharge the defendant of any liability except to the person entitled to the deposit; and

    (d)   the defendant recover costs and attorney's fees.

(Date and sign—See Form 2.)

Form 40

MOTION TO DISMISS UNDER RULE 12(b) FOR LACK OF JURISDICTION, IMPROPER VENUE, INSUFFICIENT SERVICE OF PROCESS, OR FAILURE TO STATE A CLAIM

(Caption—See Form 1.)

The defendant moves to dismiss the action because:

1. the amount in controversy is less than the sum or value specified by 28 U.S.C. § 1332;

2. the defendant is not subject to the personal jurisdiction of this court;

3. venue is improper (this defendant does not reside in this district and no part of the events or omissions giving rise to the claim occurred in the district);

4. the defendant has not been properly served, as shown by the attached affidavits of _____; or

5. the complaint fails to state a claim upon which relief can be granted.

(Date and sign—See Form 2.)

Form 41

MOTION TO BRING IN A THIRD-PARTY DEFENDANT

(Caption—See Form 1.)

The defendant, as third-party plaintiff, moves for leave to serve on *name* a summons and third-party complaint, copies of which are attached.

(Date and sign—See Form 2.)

Form 42

MOTION TO INTERVENE AS A DEFENDANT UNDER RULE 24

(Caption—See Form 1.)

1. *Name* moves for leave to intervene as a defendant in this action and to file the attached answer.

(*State grounds under Rule 24(a) or (b).*)

2. The plaintiff alleges patent infringement. We manufacture and sell to the defendant the articles involved, and we have a defense to the plaintiff's claim.

3. Our defense presents questions of law and fact that are common to this action.

(Date and sign—See Form 2.)

[An Intervener's Answer must be attached. See Form 30.]

Form 50

REQUEST TO PRODUCE DOCUMENTS AND TANGIBLE THINGS, OR TO ENTER ONTO LAND UNDER RULE 34

(Caption—See Form 1.)

The plaintiff *name* requests that the defendant *name* respond within _____ days to the following requests:

1. To produce and permit the plaintiff to inspect and copy and to test or sample the following documents, including electronically stored information:

(Describe each document and the electronically stored information, either individually or by category.)

(State the time, place, and manner of the inspection and any related acts.)

2. To produce and permit the plaintiff to inspect and copy—and to test or sample—the following tangible things:

(Describe each thing, either individually or by category.)

(State the time, place, and manner of the inspection and any related acts.)

3. To permit the plaintiff to enter onto the following land to inspect, photograph, test, or sample the property or an object or operation on the property.

(Describe the property and each object or operation.)

(State the time and manner of the inspection and any related acts.)

(Date and sign—See Form 2.)

Form 51

REQUEST FOR ADMISSIONS UNDER RULE 36

(Caption—See Form 1.)

The plaintiff *name* asks the defendant *name* to respond within _____ 30 days to these requests by admitting, for purposes of this action only and subject to objections to admissibility at trial:

1. The genuineness of the following documents, copies of which [are attached] [are or have been furnished or made available for inspection and copying].

(List each document.)

2. The truth of each of the following statements:

(List each statement.)

(Date and sign—See Form 2.)

Form 52

REPORT OF THE PARTIES' PLANNING MEETING

(Caption—See Form 1.)

1. The following persons participated in a Rule 26(f) conference on date by state the method of conferring:

(e.g., name representing the plaintiff.)

2.   Initial Disclosures. The parties [have completed] [will complete by *date*] the initial disclosures required by Rule 26(a)(1).

3.   Discovery Plan. The parties propose this discovery plan:

(Use separate paragraphs or subparagraphs if the parties disagree.)

(a)   Discovery will be needed on these subjects: (*describe.*)

(b)   Disclosure of discovery of electronically stored information should be handled as follows: (briefly describe the parties' proposals, including the form or forms for production.)

(c)   The parties have agreed to an order regarding claims of privilege or of protection as trial-preparation material asserted after production, as follows: (briefly describe the provisions of the proposed order.)

(d)   (Dates for commencing and completing discovery, including discovery to be commenced or completed before other discovery.)

(e)   (Maximum number of interrogatories by each party to another party, along with the dates the answers are due.)

(f)   (Maximum number of requests for admission, along with the dates responses are due.)

(g)   (Maximum number of depositions by each party.)

(h)   (Limits on the length of depositions, in hours.)

(i)   (Dates for exchanging reports of expert witnesses.)

(j)   (Dates for supplementations under Rule 26(e).)

4.   Other Items:

(a)   (A date if the parties ask to meet with the court before a scheduling order.)

(b)   (Requested dates for pretrial conferences.)

(c)   (Final dates for the plaintiff to amend pleadings or to join parties.)

(d)   (Final dates for the defendant to amend pleadings or to join parties.)

(e)   (Final dates to file dispositive motions.)

(f)   (State the prospects for settlement.)

(g)   (Identify any alternative dispute resolution procedure that may enhance settlement prospects.)

(h)   (Final dates for submitting Rule 26(a)(3) witness lists, designations of witnesses whose testimony will be presented by deposition, and exhibit lists.)

(i)   (Final dates to file objections under Rule 26(a)(3).)

(j)   (Suggested trial date and estimate of trial length.)

(k)   (Other matters.)

(Date and sign—see Form 2.)

Form 60

NOTICE OF CONDEMNATION

(Caption—See Form 1.)

To *name the defendant.*

1. A complaint in condemnation has been filed in the United States District Court for the _____ District of _____, to take property to use for *purpose*. The interest to be taken is *describe*. The court is located in the United States courthouse at this address: _____.

2. The property to be taken is described below. You have or claim an interest in it.

(Describe the property.)

3. The authority for taking this property is *cite*.

4. If you want to object or present any defense to the taking you must serve an answer on the plaintiff's attorney within 21 days [after being served with this notice][from (insert the date of the last publication of notice)]. Send your answer to this address: _____.

5. Your answer must identify the property in which you claim an interest, state the nature and extent of that interest, and state all your objections and defenses to the taking. Objections and defenses not presented are waived.

6. If you fail to answer you consent to the taking and the court will enter a judgment that takes your described property interest.

7. Instead of answering, you may serve on the plaintiff's attorney a notice of appearance that designates the property in which you claim an interest. After you do that, you will receive a notice of any proceedings that affect you. Whether or not you have previously appeared or answered, you may present evidence at a trial to determine compensation for the property and share in the overall award.

(Date and sign—See Form 2.)

Form 61

COMPLAINT FOR CONDEMNATION

(Caption—See Form 1; name as defendants the property and at least one owner.)

1. (Statement of Jurisdiction—See Form 7.)

2. This is an action to take property under the power of eminent domain and to determine just compensation to be paid to the owners and parties in interest.

3. The authority for the taking is _____.

4. The property is to be used for _____.

5. The property to be taken is (*describe in enough detail for identification—or attach the description and state "is described in Exhibit A, attached."*)

6. The interest to be acquired is _____.

7. The persons known to the plaintiff to have or claim an interest in the property are: _____. (*For each person include the interest claimed.*)

8. There may be other persons who have or claim an interest in the property and whose names could not be found after a reasonably diligent search. They are made parties under the designation "Unknown Owners."

Therefore, the plaintiff demands judgment:

(a) condemning the property;

(b) determining and awarding just compensation; and

(c) granting any other lawful and proper relief.

(Date and sign—See Form 2.)

Form 70

JUDGMENT ON A JURY VERDICT

(Caption—See Form 1.)

This action was tried by a jury with Judge _____ presiding, and the jury has rendered a verdict.

It is ordered that:

[the plaintiff *name* recover from the defendant name the amount of $ _____ with interest at the rate of ___%, along with costs.]

[the plaintiff recover nothing, the action be dismissed on the merits, and the defendant *name* recover costs from the plaintiff *name*.]

Date _____

_____
Clerk of Court

Form 71

JUDGMENT BY THE COURT WITHOUT A JURY

(Caption—See Form 1.)

This action was tried by Judge _____ without a jury and the following decision was reached:

It is ordered that [the plaintiff *name* recover from the defendant *name* the amount of $ _____, with prejudgment interest at the rate of ___%, postjudgment interest at the rate of ___%, along with costs.] [the plaintiff recover nothing, the action be dismissed on the merits, and the defendant *name* recover costs from the plaintiff *name*.]

Date _____

_____
Clerk of Court

Form 80

NOTICE OF A MAGISTRATE JUDGE'S AVAILABILITY

1. A magistrate judge is available under title 28 U.S.C. § 636(c) to conduct the proceedings in this case, including a jury or nonjury trial and the entry of final judgment. But a magistrate judge can be assigned only if all parties voluntarily consent.

2. You may withhold your consent without adverse substantive consequences. The identity of any party consenting or withholding consent will not be disclosed to the judge to whom the case is assigned or to any magistrate judge.

3. If a magistrate judge does hear your case, you may appeal directly to a United States court of appeals as you would if a district judge heard it.

A form called *Consent to an Assignment to a United States Magistrate Judge* is available from the court clerk's office.

Form 81

CONSENT TO AN ASSIGNMENT TO A MAGISTRATE JUDGE

(Caption—See Form 1.)

I voluntarily consent to have a United States magistrate judge conduct all further proceedings in this case, including a trial, and order the entry of final judgment. (Return this form to the court clerk— not to a judge or magistrate judge.)

Date _____

_____
Signature of the Party

Form 82

ORDER OF ASSIGNMENT TO A MAGISTRATE JUDGE

(Caption—See Form 1.)

With the parties' consent it is ordered that this case be assigned to United States Magistrate Judge _____ of this district to conduct all proceedings and enter final judgment in accordance with 28 U.S.C. § 636(c).

Date _____

_____
United States District Judge

SUPPLEMENTAL RULES FOR ADMIRALTY OR MARITIME CLAIMS AND ASSET FORFEITURE ACTIONS

Rule A. Scope of Rules

(1)   These Supplemental Rules apply to:

(A)   the procedure in admiralty and maritime claims within the meaning of Rule 9(h) with respect to the following remedies:

(i)   maritime attachment and garnishment,

(ii)   actions in rem,

(iii)   possessory, petitory, and partition actions, and

(iv)   actions for exoneration from or limitation of liability;

(B)   forfeiture actions in rem arising from a federal statute; and

(C)   the procedure in statutory condemnation proceedings analogous to maritime actions in rem, whether within the admiralty and maritime jurisdiction or not. Except as otherwise provided, references in these Supplemental Rules to actions in rem include such analogous statutory condemnation proceedings.

(2)   The Federal Rules of Civil Procedure also apply to the foregoing proceedings except to the extent that they are inconsistent with these Supplemental Rules.

Rule B. In Personam Actions: Attachment and Garnishment

(1)   WHEN AVAILABLE; COMPLAINT, AFFIDAVIT, JUDICIAL AUTHORIZATION, AND PROCESS. In an in personam action:

(a)   If a defendant is not found within the district when a verified complaint praying for attachment and the affidavit required by Rule B(1)(b) are filed, a verified complaint may contain a prayer for process to attach the defendant's tangible or intangible personal property—up to the amount sued for—in the hands of garnishees named in the process.

(b)   The plaintiff or the plaintiff's attorney must sign and file with the complaint an affidavit stating that, to the affiant's knowledge, or on information and belief, the defendant cannot be found within the district. The court must review the complaint and affidavit and, if the conditions of this Rule B appear to exist, enter an order so stating and authorizing process of attachment and garnishment. The clerk may issue supplemental process enforcing the court's order upon application without further court order.

(c)   If the plaintiff or the plaintiff's attorney certifies that exigent circumstances make court review impracticable, the clerk must issue the summons and process of attachment and garnishment. The plaintiff has the burden in any post-attachment hearing under Rule E(4)(f) to show that exigent circumstances existed.

(d)(i) If the property is a vessel or tangible property on board a vessel, the summons, process, and any supplemental process must be delivered to the marshal for service.

(ii)   If the property is other tangible or intangible property, the summons, process, and any supplemental process must be delivered to a person or organization authorized to serve it, who may be (A) a marshal; (B) someone under contract with the United States; (C) someone specially appointed by the court for that purpose; or, (D) in an action brought by the United States, any officer or employee of the United States.

(e)   The plaintiff may invoke state-law remedies under Rule 64 for seizure of person or property for the purpose of securing satisfaction of the judgment.

(2)   NOTICE TO DEFENDANT. No default judgment may be entered except upon proof—which may be by affidavit—that:

(a)   the complaint, summons, and process of attachment or garnishment have been served on the defendant in a manner authorized by Rule 4;

(b)   the plaintiff or the garnishee has mailed to the defendant the complaint, summons, and process of attachment or garnishment, using any form of mail requiring a return receipt; or

(c)   the plaintiff or the garnishee has tried diligently to give notice of the action to the defendant but could not do so.

(3)   ANSWER.

(a)   *By Garnishee.* The garnishee shall serve an answer, together with answers to any interrogatories served with the complaint, within 21 days after service of process upon the garnishee. Interrogatories to the garnishee may be served with the complaint without leave of court. If the garnishee refuses or neglects to answer on oath as to the debts, credits, or effects of the defendant in the garnishee's hands, or any interrogatories concerning such debts, credits, and effects that may be propounded by the plaintiff, the court may award compulsory process against the garnishee. If the garnishee admits any debts, credits, or effects, they shall be held in the garnishee's hands or paid into the registry of the court, and shall be held in either case subject to the further order of the court.

(b)   *By Defendant.* The defendant shall serve an answer within 30 days after process has been executed, whether by attachment of property or service on the garnishee.

Note on the 1985 Amendment to Rule B(1)

The 1985 alterations were designed to ensure that the rule is consistent with the principles of procedural due process enunciated by the Supreme Court in *Sniadach v. Family Finance Corp.,* 395 U.S. 337 (1969), and later developed in *Fuentes v. Shevin,* 407 U.S. 67 (1972), *Mitchell v. W.T. Grant Co.,* 416 U.S. 600 (1974), and *North Georgia Finishing, Inc. v. Di-Chem, Inc.,* 419 U.S. 601 (1975).

Rule C. In Rem Actions: Special Provisions

(1)   WHEN AVAILABLE. An action in rem may be brought:

(a)   To enforce any maritime lien;

(b)   Whenever a statute of the United States provides for a maritime action in rem or a proceeding analogous thereto.

Except as otherwise provided by law a party who may proceed in rem may also, or in the alternative, proceed in personam against any person who may be liable.

Statutory provisions exempting vessels or other property owned or possessed by or operated by or for the United States from arrest or seizure are not affected by this rule. When a statute so provides, an action against the United States or an instrumentality thereof may proceed on in rem principles.

(2)   COMPLAINT. In an action in rem the complaint must:

(a)   be verified;

(b)   describe with reasonable particularity the property that is the subject of the action;

(c)   state that the property is within the district or will be within the district while the action is pending.

(3)   JUDICIAL AUTHORIZATION AND PROCESS.

(a)   *Arrest Warrant.*

(i)   The court must review the complaint and any supporting papers. If the conditions for an in rem action appear to exist, the court must issue an order directing the clerk to issue a warrant for the arrest of the vessel or other property that is the subject of the action.

(ii)   If the plaintiff or the plaintiff's attorney certifies that exigent circumstances make court review impracticable, the clerk must promptly issue a summons and a warrant for the arrest of the vessel or other property that is the subject of the action. The plaintiff has the burden in any post-arrest hearing under Rule E(4)(f) to show that exigent circumstances existed.

(b)   *Service.*

(i)   If the property that is the subject of the action is a vessel or tangible property on board a vessel, the warrant and any supplemental process must be delivered to the marshal for service.

(ii)   If the property that is the subject of the action is other property, tangible or intangible, the warrant and any supplemental process must be delivered to a person or organization authorized to enforce it, who may be: (A) a marshal; (B) someone under contract with the United States; (C) someone specially appointed by the court for that purpose; or, (D) in an action brought by the United States, any officer or employee of the United States.

(c)   *Deposit in Court.* If the property that is the subject of the action consists in whole or in part of freight, the proceeds of property sold, or other intangible property, the clerk must issue— in addition to the warrant—a summons directing any person controlling the property to show cause why it should not be deposited in court to abide the judgment.

(d)   *Supplemental Process.* The clerk may upon application issue supplemental process to enforce the court's order without further court order.

(4)   NOTICE. No notice other than execution of process is required when the property that is the subject of the action has been released under Rule E(5). If the property is not released within 14 days after execution, the plaintiff must promptly—or within the time that the court allows—give public notice of the action and arrest in a newspaper designated by court order and having general circulation in the district, but publication may be terminated if the property is released before publication is completed. The notice must specify the time under Rule C(6) to file a statement of interest in or right against the seized property and to answer. This rule does not affect the notice requirements in an action to foreclose a preferred ship mortgage under 46 U.S.C. §§ 31301 et seq., as amended.

(5)   ANCILLARY PROCESS. In any action in rem in which process has been served as provided by this rule, if any part of the property that is the subject of the action has not been brought within the control of the court because it has been removed or sold, or because it is intangible property in the hands of a person who has not been served with process, the court may, on motion, order any person having possession or control of such property or its proceeds to show cause why it should not be delivered into the custody of the marshal or other person or organization having a warrant for the arrest of the property, or paid into court to abide the judgment; and, after hearing, the court may enter such judgment as law and justice may require.

(6)   RESPONSIVE PLEADING; INTERROGATORIES.

(a)   *Statement of Interest; Answer; In an action in rem:*

(i)   A person who asserts a right of possession or any ownership interest in the property that is the subject of the action must file a verified statement of right or interest:

(A)   within 14 days after the execution of process, or

(B)   within the time that the court allows:

(ii)   the statement of right or interest must describe the interest in the property that supports the person's demand for its restitution or right to defend the action;

(iii) an agent, bailee, or attorney must state the authority to file a statement of right or interest on behalf of another; and

(iv) a person who asserts a right of possession or any ownership interest must serve an answer within 21 days after filing the statement of interest or right.

(b) *Interrogatories.* Interrogatories may be served with the complaint in an in rem action without leave of court. Answers to the interrogatories must be served with the answer to the complaint.

Note on the 1985 Amendment to Rule C(3)

The 1985 amendments provide for judicial scrutiny before the issuance of any warrant of arrest. Their purpose is to eliminate any doubt as to the rule's constitutionality under the *Sniadach* line of cases. See 1985 Amendment to Rule B(1), following Rule B, supra.

Rule D. Possessory, Petitory, and Partition Actions

In all actions for possession, partition, and to try title maintainable according to the course of the admiralty practice with respect to a vessel, in all actions so maintainable with respect to the possession of cargo or other maritime property, and in all actions by one or more part owners against the others to obtain security for the return of the vessel from any voyage undertaken without their consent, or by one or more part owners against the others to obtain possession of the vessel for any voyage on giving security for its safe return, the process shall be by a warrant of arrest of the vessel, cargo, or other property, and by notice in the manner provided by Rule B(2) to the adverse party or parties.

Rule E. Actions in Rem and Quasi in Rem: General Provisions

(1) APPLICABILITY. Except as otherwise provided, this rule applies to actions in personam with process of maritime attachment and garnishment, actions in rem, and petitory, possessory, and partition actions, supplementing Rules B, C, and D.

(2) COMPLAINT; SECURITY.

(a) *Complaint.* In actions to which this rule is applicable the complaint shall state the circumstances from which the claim arises with such particularity that the defendant or claimant will be able, without moving for a more definite statement, to commence an investigation of the facts and to frame a responsive pleading.

(b) *Security for Costs.* Subject to the provisions of Rule 54(d) and of relevant statutes, the court may, on the filing of the complaint or on the appearance of any defendant, claimant, or any other party, or at any later time, require the plaintiff, defendant, claimant, or other party to give security, or additional security, in such sum as the court shall direct to pay all costs and expenses that shall be awarded against the party by any interlocutory order or by the final judgment, or on appeal by any appellate court.

(3) PROCESS.

(a) In admiralty and maritime proceedings process in rem or of maritime attachment and garnishment may be served only within the district.

(b) *Issuance and Delivery.* Issuance and delivery of process in rem, or of maritime attachment and garnishment, shall be held in abeyance if the plaintiff so requests.

(4) EXECUTION OF PROCESS; MARSHAL'S RETURN; CUSTODY OF PROPERTY; PROCEDURES FOR RELEASE.

(a) *In General.* Upon issuance and delivery of the process, or, in the case of summons with process of attachment and garnishment, when it appears that the defendant cannot be found within the district, the marshal or other person or organization having a warrant shall forthwith execute the process in accordance with this subdivision (4), making due and prompt return.

(b) *Tangible Property.* If tangible property is to be attached or arrested, the marshal or other person or organization having the warrant shall take it into the marshal's possession for safe custody. If the character or situation of the property is such that the taking of actual possession is impracticable, the marshal or other person executing the process shall affix a copy thereof to the property in a conspicuous place and leave a copy of the complaint and process with the person having possession or the person's agent. In furtherance of the marshal's custody of any vessel the marshal is authorized to make a written request to the collector of customs not to grant clearance to such vessel until notified by the marshal or a deputy marshal or by the clerk that the vessel has been released in accordance with these rules.

(c) *Intangible Property.* If intangible property is to be attached or arrested the marshal or other person or organization having the warrant shall execute the process by leaving with the garnishee or other obligor a copy of the complaint and process requiring the garnishee or other obligor to answer as provided in Rules B(3)(a) and C(6); or the marshal may accept for payment into the registry of the court the amount owed to the extent of the amount claimed by the plaintiff with interest and costs, in which event the garnishee or other obligor shall not be required to answer unless alias process shall be served.

(d) *Directions with Respect to Property in Custody.* The marshal or other person or organization having the warrant may at any time apply to the court for directions with respect to property that has been attached or arrested, and shall give notice of such application to any or all of the parties as the court may direct.

(e) *Expenses of Seizing and Keeping Property; Deposit.* These rules do not alter the provisions of Title 28, U.S.C., § 1921, as amended, relative to the expenses of seizing and keeping property attached or arrested and to the requirement of deposits to cover such expenses.

(f) *Procedure for Release from Arrest or Attachment.* Whenever property is arrested or attached, any person claiming an interest in it shall be entitled to a prompt hearing at which the plaintiff shall be required to show why the arrest or attachment should not be vacated or other relief granted consistent with these rules. This subdivision shall have no application to suits for seamen's wages when process is issued upon a certification of sufficient cause filed pursuant to Title 46, U.S.C. §§ 603 and 604 or to actions by the United States for forfeitures for violation of any statute of the United States.

(5) RELEASE OF PROPERTY.

(a) *Special Bond.* Whenever process of maritime attachment and garnishment or process in rem is issued the execution of such process shall be stayed, or the property released, on the giving of security, to be approved by the court or clerk, or by stipulation of the parties, conditioned to answer the judgment of the court or of any appellate court. The parties may stipulate the amount and nature of such security. In the event of the inability or refusal of the parties so to stipulate the court shall fix the principal sum of the bond or stipulation at an amount sufficient to cover the amount of the plaintiff's claim fairly stated with accrued interest and costs; but the principal sum shall in no event exceed (i) twice the amount of the plaintiff's claim or (ii) the value of the property on due appraisement, whichever is smaller. The bond or stipulation shall be conditioned for the payment of the principal sum and interest thereon at 6 per cent per annum.

(b) *General Bond.* The owner of any vessel may file a general bond or stipulation, with sufficient surety, to be approved by the court, conditioned to answer the judgment of such court in all or any actions that may be brought thereafter in such court in which the vessel is attached or arrested. Thereupon the execution of all such process against such vessel shall be stayed so long as the amount secured by such bond or stipulation is at least double the aggregate amount claimed by plaintiffs in all actions begun and pending in which such vessel has been attached or arrested. Judgments and remedies may be had on such bond or stipulation as if a special bond or stipulation had been filed in each of such actions. The district court may make necessary orders to carry this rule into effect, particularly as to the giving of proper notice of any action against or attachment of a vessel for which a general bond has been filed. Such bond or stipulation shall be indorsed by the clerk with a minute of the actions wherein process is so stayed. Further security may be required by the court at any time.

If a special bond or stipulation is given in a particular case, the liability on the general bond or stipulation shall cease as to that case.

(c) *Release by Consent or Stipulation; Order of Court or Clerk; Costs.* Any vessel, cargo, or other property in the custody of the marshal or other person or organization having the warrant may be released forthwith upon the marshal's acceptance and approval of a stipulation, bond, or other security, signed by the party on whose behalf the property is detained or the party's attorney and expressly authorizing such release, if all costs and charges of the court and its officers shall have first been paid. Otherwise no property in the custody of the marshal, other person or organization having the warrant, or other officer of the court shall be released without an order of the court; but such order may be entered as of course by the clerk, upon the giving of approved security as provided by law and these rules, or upon the dismissal or discontinuance of the action; but the marshal or other person or organization having the warrant shall not deliver any property so released until the costs and charges of the officers of the court shall first have been paid.

(d) *Possessory, Petitory, and Partition Actions.* The foregoing provisions of this subdivision (5) do not apply to petitory, possessory, and partition actions. In such cases the property arrested shall be released only by order of the court, on such terms and conditions and on the giving of such security as the court may require.

(6) REDUCTION OR IMPAIRMENT OF SECURITY. Whenever security is taken the court may, on motion and hearing, for good cause shown, reduce the amount of security given; and if the surety shall be or become insufficient, new or additional sureties may be required on motion and hearing.

(7) SECURITY ON COUNTERCLAIM.

(a) When a person who has given security for damages in the original action asserts a counterclaim that arises from the transaction or occurrence that is the subject of the original action, a plaintiff for whose benefit the security has been given must give security for damages demanded in the counterclaim unless the court for cause shown, directs otherwise. Proceedings on the original claim must be stayed until this security is given unless the court directs otherwise.

(b) The plaintiff is required to give security under Rule E(7)(a) when the United States or its corporate instrumentality counterclaims and would have been required to give security to respond in damages if a private party but is relieved by law from giving security.

(8) RESTRICTED APPEARANCE. An appearance to defend against an admiralty and maritime claim with respect to which there has issued process in rem, or process of attachment and garnishment, may be expressly restricted to the defense of such claim, and in that event shall not constitute an appearance for the purposes of any other claim with respect to which such process is not available or has not been served.

(9) DISPOSITION OF PROPERTY; SALES.

(a) *Interlocutory Sales; Delivery.*

(i) On application of a party, the marshal, or other person having custody of the property, the court may order all or part of the property sold—with the sales proceeds, or as much of them as will satisfy the judgment, paid into court to await further orders of the court—if:

(A) the attached or arrested property is perishable, or liable to deterioration, decay, or injury by being detained in custody pending the action;

(B) the expense of keeping the property is excessive or disproportionate; or

(C) there is an unreasonable delay in securing release of the property.

(ii) In the circumstances described in Rule E(9)(a)(i), the court, on motion by a defendant or a person filing a statement of interest or right under Rule C(6), may order that the property, rather than being sold, be delivered to the movant upon giving security under these rules.

(b) *Sales; Proceeds.* All sales of property shall be made by the marshal or a deputy marshal, or by other person or organization having the warrant, or by any other person assigned by the court where the marshal or other person or organization having the warrant is a party in interest; and the proceeds of sale shall be forthwith paid into the registry of the court to be disposed of according to law.

(10) PRESERVATION OF PROPERTY. When the owner or another person remains in possession of property attached or arrested under the provisions of Rule E(4)(b) that permit execution of process without taking actual possession, the court, on a party's motion or on its own, may enter any order necessary to preserve the property and to prevent its removal.

Note on the 1985 Amendments to Rule E

New Rule E(4)(f), effective August 1, 1985, makes available the type of prompt post-seizure hearing in proceedings under Supplemental Rules B and C that the Supreme Court has called for in a number of cases arising in other contexts. Rule E(4)(f) is based on a proposal by the Maritime Law Association of the United States and on local admiralty rules in the Eastern and Southern Districts of New York.

Rule E(4)(f) will be triggered by the defendant or any other person with an interest in the property seized. Upon an oral or written application similar to that used in seeking a temporary restraining order, see Rule 65(b), the court will be required to hold a hearing as promptly as possible to determine whether to allow the arrest or attachment to stand. The plaintiff has the burden of showing why the seizure should not be vacated.

Rule F. Limitation of Liability

(1) TIME FOR FILING COMPLAINT; SECURITY. Not later than six months after receipt of a claim in writing, any vessel owner may file a complaint in the appropriate district court, as provided in subdivision (9) of this rule, for limitation of liability pursuant to statute. The owner (a) shall deposit with the court, for the benefit of claimants, a sum equal to the amount or value of the owner's interest in the vessel and pending freight, or approved security therefor, and in addition such sums, or approved security therefor, as the court may from time to time fix as necessary to carry out the provisions of the statutes as amended; or (b) at the owner's option shall transfer to a trustee to be appointed by the court, for the benefit of claimants, the owner's interest in the vessel and pending freight, together with such sums, or approved security therefor, as the court may from time to time fix as necessary to carry out the provisions of the statutes as amended. The plaintiff shall also give security for costs and, if the plaintiff elects to give security, for interest at the rate of 6 percent per annum from the date of the security.

(2) COMPLAINT. The complaint shall set forth the facts on the basis of which the right to limit liability is asserted, and all facts necessary to enable the court to determine the amount to which the owner's liability shall be limited. The complaint may demand exoneration from as well as limitation of liability. It shall state the voyage, if any, on which the demands sought to be limited arose, with the date and place of its termination; the amount of all demands including all unsatisfied liens or claims of lien, in contract or in tort or otherwise, arising on that voyage, so far as known to the plaintiff, and what actions and proceedings, if any, are pending thereon; whether the vessel was damaged, lost, or abandoned, and, if so, when and where; the value of the vessel at the close of the voyage or, in case of wreck, the value of her wreckage, strippings, or proceeds, if any, and where and in whose possession they are; and the amount of any pending freight recovered or recoverable. If the plaintiff elects to transfer the plaintiff's interest in the vessel to a trustee, the complaint must further show any prior paramount liens thereon, and what voyages or trips, if any, she has made since the voyage or trip on which the claims sought to be limited arose, and any existing liens arising upon any such subsequent

voyage or trip, with the amounts and causes thereof, and the names and addresses of the lienors, so far as known; and whether the vessel sustained any injury upon or by reason of such subsequent voyage or trip.

(3) CLAIMS AGAINST OWNER; INJUNCTION. Upon compliance by the owner with the requirements of subdivision (1) of this rule all claims and proceedings against the owner or the owner's property with respect to the matter in question shall cease. On application of the plaintiff the court shall enjoin the further prosecution of any action or proceeding against the plaintiff or the plaintiff's property with respect to any claim subject to limitation in the action.

(4) NOTICE TO CLAIMANTS. Upon the owner's compliance with subdivision (1) of this rule the court shall issue a notice to all persons asserting claims with respect to which the complaint seeks limitation, admonishing them to file their respective claims with the clerk of the court and to serve on the attorneys for the plaintiff a copy thereof on or before a date to be named in the notice. The date so fixed shall not be less than 30 days after issuance of the notice. For cause shown, the court may enlarge the time within which claims may be filed. The notice shall be published in such newspaper or newspapers as the court may direct once a week for four successive weeks prior to the date fixed for the filing of claims. The plaintiff not later than the day of second publication shall also mail a copy of the notice to every person known to have made any claim against the vessel or the plaintiff arising out of the voyage or trip on which the claims sought to be limited arose. In cases involving death a copy of such notice shall be mailed to the decedent at the decedent's last known address, and also to any person who shall be known to have made any claim on account of such death.

(5) CLAIMS AND ANSWER. Claims shall be filed and served on or before the date specified in the notice provided for in subdivision (4) of this rule. Each claim shall specify the facts upon which the claimant relies in support of the claim, the items thereof, and the dates on which the same accrued. If a claimant desires to contest either the right to exoneration from or the right to limitation of liability the claimant shall file and serve an answer to the complaint unless the claim has included an answer.

(6) INFORMATION TO BE GIVEN CLAIMANTS. Within 30 days after the date specified in the notice for filing claims, or within such time as the court thereafter may allow, the plaintiff shall mail to the attorney for each claimant (or if the claimant has no attorney to the claimant) a list setting forth (a) the name of each claimant, (b) the name and address of the claimant's attorney (if the claimant is known to have one), (c) the nature of the claim, i.e., whether property loss, property damage, death, personal injury, etc., and (d) the amount thereof.

(7) INSUFFICIENCY OF FUND OR SECURITY. Any claimant may by motion demand that the funds deposited in court or the security given by the plaintiff be increased on the ground that they are less than the value of the plaintiff's interest in the vessel and pending freight. Thereupon the court shall cause due appraisement to be made of the value of the plaintiff's interest in the vessel and pending freight; and if the court finds that the deposit or security is either insufficient or excessive it shall order its increase or reduction. In like manner any claimant may demand that the deposit or security be increased on the ground that it is insufficient to carry out the provisions of the statutes relating to claims in respect of loss of life or bodily injury; and, after notice and hearing, the court may similarly order that the deposit or security be increased or reduced.

(8) OBJECTIONS TO CLAIMS: DISTRIBUTION OF FUND. Any interested party may question or controvert any claim without filing an objection thereto. Upon determination of liability the fund deposited or secured, or the proceeds of the vessel and pending freight, shall be divided pro rata, subject to all relevant provisions of law, among the several claimants in proportion to the amounts of their respective claims, duly proved, saving, however, to all parties any priority to which they may be legally entitled.

(9) VENUE; TRANSFER. The complaint shall be filed in any district in which the vessel has been attached or arrested to answer for any claim with respect to which the plaintiff seeks to limit liability; or, if the vessel has not been attached or arrested, then in any district in which the owner has been sued with respect to any such claim. When the vessel has not been attached or arrested to answer the

matters aforesaid, and suit has not been commenced against the owner, the proceedings may be had in the district in which the vessel may be, but if the vessel is not within any district and no suit has been commenced in any district, then the complaint may be filed in any district. For the convenience of parties and witnesses, in the interest of justice, the court may transfer the action to any district; if venue is wrongly laid the court shall dismiss or, if it be in the interest of justice, transfer the action to any district in which it could have been brought. If the vessel shall have been sold, the proceeds shall represent the vessel for the purposes of these rules.

Rule G. Forfeiture Actions in Rem

(1) SCOPE. This rule governs a forfeiture action in rem arising from a federal statute. To the extent that this rule does not address an issue, Supplemental Rules C and E and the Federal Rules of Civil Procedure also apply.

(2) COMPLAINT. The complaint must:

(a)   be verified;

(b)   state the grounds for subject-matter jurisdiction, in rem jurisdiction over the defendant property, and venue;

(c)   describe the property with reasonable particularity;

(d)   if the property is tangible, state its location when any seizure occurred and—if different—its location when the action is filed;

(e)   identify the statute under which the forfeiture action is brought; and

(f)   state sufficiently detailed facts to support a reasonable belief that the government will be able to meet its burden of proof at trial.

(3) JUDICIAL AUTHORIZATION AND PROCESS.

(a)   *Real Property.* If the defendant is real property, the government must proceed under 18 U.S.C. § 985.

(b)   *Other Property; Arrest Warrant.* If the defendant is not real property:

(i)   the clerk must issue a warrant to arrest the property if it is in the government's possession, custody, or control;

(ii)   the court—on finding probable cause—must issue a warrant to arrest the property if it is not in the government's possession, custody, or control and is not subject to a judicial restraining order; and

(iii)   a warrant is not necessary if the property is subject to a judicial restraining order.

(c)   *Execution of Process.*

(i)   The warrant and any supplemental process must be delivered to a person or organization authorized to execute it, who may be: (A) a marshal or any other United States officer or employee; (B) someone under contract with the United States; or (C) someone specially appointed by the court for that purpose.

(ii)   The authorized person or organization must execute the warrant and any supplemental process on property in the United States as soon as practicable unless:

(A)   the property is in the government's possession, custody, or control; or

(B)   the court orders a different time when the complaint is under seal, the action is stayed before the warrant and supplemental process are executed, or the court finds other good cause.

(iii) The warrant and any supplemental process may be executed within the district or, when authorized by statute, outside the district.

(iv) If executing a warrant on property outside the United States is required, the warrant may be transmitted to an appropriate authority for serving process where the property is located.

(4) NOTICE.

(a) *Notice by Publication.*

(i) When Publication Is Required. A judgment of forfeiture may be entered only if the government has published notice of the action within a reasonable time after filing the complaint or at a time the court orders. But notice need not be published if:

(A) the defendant property is worth less than $1,000 and direct notice is sent under Rule G(4)(b) to every person the government can reasonably identify as a potential claimant; or

(B) the court finds that the cost of publication exceeds the property's value and that other means of notice would satisfy due process.

(ii) Content of the Notice. Unless the court orders otherwise, the notice must:

(A) describe the property with reasonable particularity;

(B) state the times under Rule G(5) to file a claim and to answer; and

(C) name the government attorney to be served with the claim and answer.

(iii) Frequency of Publication. Published notice must appear:

(A) once a week for three consecutive weeks; or

(B) only once if, before the action was filed, notice of nonjudicial forfeiture of the same property was published on an official internet government forfeiture site for at least 30 consecutive days, or in a newspaper of general circulation for three consecutive weeks in a district where publication is authorized under Rule G(4)(a)(iv).

(iv) Means of Publication. The government should select from the following options a means of publication reasonably calculated to notify potential claimants of the action:

(A) if the property is in the United States, publication in a newspaper generally circulated in the district where the action is filed, where the property was seized, or where property that was not seized is located;

(B) if the property is outside the United States, publication in a newspaper generally circulated in a district where the action is filed, in a newspaper generally circulated in the country where the property is located, or in legal notices published and generally circulated in the country where the property is located; or

(C) instead of (A) or (B), posting a notice on an official internet government forfeiture site for at least 30 consecutive days.

(b) *Notice to Known Potential Claimants.*

(i) Direct Notice Required. The government must send notice of the action and a copy of the complaint to any person who reasonably appears to be a potential claimant on the facts known to the government before the end of the time for filing a claim under Rule G(5)(a)(ii)(B).

(ii) Content of the Notice. The notice must state:

(A) the date when the notice is sent;

(B)   a deadline for filing a claim, at least 35 days after the notice is sent;

(C)   that an answer or a motion under Rule 12 must be filed no later than 21 days after filing the claim; and

(D)   the name of the government attorney to be served with the claim and answer.

(iii)   Sending Notice.

(A)   The notice must be sent by means reasonably calculated to reach the potential claimant.

(B)   Notice may be sent to the potential claimant or to the attorney representing the potential claimant with respect to the seizure of the property or in a related investigation, administrative forfeiture proceeding, or criminal case.

(C)   Notice sent to a potential claimant who is incarcerated must be sent to the place of incarceration.

(D)   Notice to a person arrested in connection with an offense giving rise to the forfeiture who is not incarcerated when notice is sent may be sent to the address that person last gave to the agency that arrested or released the person.

(E)   Notice to a person from whom the property was seized who is not incarcerated when notice is sent may be sent to the last address that person gave to the agency that seized the property.

(iv)   When Notice Is Sent. Notice by the following means is sent on the date when it is placed in the mail, delivered to a commercial carrier, or sent by electronic mail.

(v)   Actual Notice. A potential claimant who had actual notice of a forfeiture action may not oppose or seek relief from forfeiture because of the government's failure to send the required notice.

(5)   RESPONSIVE PLEADINGS.

(a)   *Filing a Claim.*

(i)   A person who asserts an interest in the defendant property may contest the forfeiture by filing a claim in the court where the action is pending. The claim must:

(A)   identify the specific property claimed;

(B)   identify the claimant and state the claimant's interest in the property;

(C)   be signed by the claimant under penalty of perjury; and

(D)   be served on the government attorney designated under Rule G(4)(a)(ii)(C) or (b)(ii)(D).

(ii)   Unless the court for good cause sets a different time, the claim must be filed:

(A)   by the time stated in a direct notice sent under Rule G(4)(b);

(B)   if notice was published but direct notice was not sent to the claimant or the claimant's attorney, no later than 30 days after final publication of newspaper notice or legal notice under Rule G(4)(a) or no later than 60 days after the first day of publication on an official internet government forfeiture site; or

(C)   if notice was not published and direct notice was not sent to the claimant or the claimant's attorney:

(1)   if the property was in the government's possession, custody, or control when the complaint was filed, no later than 60 days after the filing, not counting

any time when the complaint was under seal or when the action was stayed before execution of a warrant issued under Rule G(3)(b); or

(2) if the property was not in the government's possession, custody, or control when the complaint was filed, no later than 60 days after the government complied with 18 U.S.C. § 985(c) as to real property, or 60 days after process was executed on the property under Rule G(3).

(iii) A claim filed by a person asserting an interest as a bailee must identify the bailor, and if filed on the bailor's behalf must state the authority to do so.

(b) *Answer.* A claimant must serve and file an answer to the complaint or a motion under Rule 12 within 21 days after filing the claim. A claimant waives an objection to in rem jurisdiction or to venue if the objection is not made by motion or stated in the answer.

(6) SPECIAL INTERROGATORIES.

(a) *Time and Scope.* The government may serve special interrogatories limited to the claimant's identity and relationship to the defendant property without the court's leave at any time after the claim is filed and before discovery is closed. But if the claimant serves a motion to dismiss the action, the government must serve the interrogatories within 21 days after the motion is served.

(b) *Answers or Objections.* Answers or objections to these interrogatories must be served within 21 days after the interrogatories are served.

(c) *Government's Response Deferred.* The government need not respond to a claimant's motion to dismiss the action under Rule G(8)(b) until 21 days after the claimant has answered these interrogatories.

(7) PRESERVING, PREVENTING CRIMINAL USE, AND DISPOSING OF PROPERTY; SALES.

(a) *Preserving and Preventing Criminal Use of Property.* When the government does not have actual possession of the defendant property the court, on motion or on its own, may enter any order necessary to preserve the property, to prevent its removal or encumbrance, or to prevent its use in a criminal offense.

(b) *Interlocutory Sale or Delivery.*

(i) Order to Sell. On motion by a party or a person having custody of the property, the court may order all or part of the property sold if:

(A) the property is perishable or at risk of deterioration, decay, or injury by being detained in custody pending the action;

(B) the expense of keeping the property is excessive or is disproportionate to its fair market value;

(C) the property is subject to a mortgage or to taxes on which the owner is in default; or

(D) the court finds other good cause.

(ii) Who Makes the Sale. A sale must be made by a United States agency that has authority to sell the property, by the agency's contractor, or by any person the court designates.

(iii) Sale Procedures. The sale is governed by 28 U.S.C. § § 2001, 2002, and 2004, unless all parties, with the court's approval, agree to the sale, aspects of the sale, or different procedures.

(iv) Sale Proceeds. Sale proceeds are a substitute res subject to forfeiture in place of the property that was sold. The proceeds must be held in an interest-bearing account maintained by the United States pending the conclusion of the forfeiture action.

(v) Delivery on a Claimant's Motion. The court may order that the property be delivered to the claimant pending the conclusion of the action if the claimant shows circumstances that would permit sale under Rule G(7)(b)(i) and gives security under these rules.

(c) *Disposing of Forfeited Property.* Upon entry of a forfeiture judgment, the property or proceeds from selling the property must be disposed of as provided by law.

(8) MOTIONS.

(a) *Motion To Suppress Use of the Property as Evidence.* If the defendant property was seized, a party with standing to contest the lawfulness of the seizure may move to suppress use of the property as evidence. Suppression does not affect forfeiture of the property based on independently derived evidence.

(b) *Motion To Dismiss the Action.*

(i) A claimant who establishes standing to contest forfeiture may move to dismiss the action under Rule 12(b).

(ii) In an action governed by 18 U.S.C. § 983(a)(3)(D) the complaint may not be dismissed on the ground that the government did not have adequate evidence at the time the complaint was filed to establish the forfeitability of the property. The sufficiency of the complaint is governed by Rule G(2).

(c) *Motion To Strike a Claim or Answer.*

(i) At any time before trial, the government may move to strike a claim or answer:

(A) for failing to comply with Rule G(5) or (6), or

(B) because the claimant lacks standing.

(ii) The motion:

(A) must be decided before any motion by the claimant to dismiss the action; and

(B) may be presented as a motion for judgment on the pleadings or as a motion to determine after a hearing or by summary judgment whether the claimant can carry the burden of establishing standing by a preponderance of the evidence.

(d) *Petition to Release Property.*

(i) If a United States agency or an agency's contractor holds property for judicial or nonjudicial forfeiture under a statute governed by 18 U.S.C. § 983(f), a person who has filed a claim to the property may petition for its release under § 983(f).

(ii) If a petition for release is filed before a judicial forfeiture action is filed against the property, the petition may be filed either in the district where the property was seized or in the district where a warrant to seize the property issued. If a judicial forfeiture action against the property is later filed in another district—or if the government shows that the action will be filed in another district—the petition may be transferred to that district under 28 U.S.C. § 1404.

(e) *Excessive Fines.* A claimant may seek to mitigate a forfeiture under the Excessive Fines Clause of the Eighth Amendment by motion for summary judgment or by motion made after entry of a forfeiture judgment if:

(i) the claimant has pleaded the defense under Rule 8; and

(ii)   the parties have had the opportunity to conduct civil discovery on the defense.

(9)   TRIAL. Trial is to the court unless any party demands trial by jury under Rule 38.

PART II

Selected Provisions of the United States Constitution, Title 28 of the United States Code,

and

Other Federal Statutes

***

TABLE OF CONTENTS

Selected Provisions of the Constitution of the United States

Selected Provisions of Title 28, United States Code— Judiciary and Judicial Procedure

Section

SELECTED PROVISIONS

Selective Provisions of Title 18, United States Code— Criminal Law and Procedure

Selected Provision of Title 42, United States Code— The Public Health and Welfare

Selected Provision of Section 205(c) of the E-Government Act of 2002

Selected Provisions of the Constitution of the United States

ARTICLE I.

Section 8. The Congress shall have Power To lay and collect Taxes, Duties, Imposts and Excises, to pay the Debts and provide for the common Defense and general Welfare of the United States; but all Duties, Imposts and Excises shall be uniform throughout the United States;

To borrow Money on the credit of the United States;

To regulate Commerce with foreign Nations, and among the several States, and with the Indian Tribes;

To establish an uniform Rule of Naturalization, and uniform Laws on the subject of Bankruptcies throughout the United States;

* * *

SELECTED PROVISIONS

To promote the Progress of Science and useful Arts, by securing for limited Times to Authors and Inventors the exclusive Right to their respective Writings and Discoveries;

To constitute Tribunals inferior to the supreme Court;

To define and punish Piracies and Felonies committed on the high seas, and offences against the Law of Nations;

To declare War, grant Letters of Marque and Reprisal, and make Rules concerning Captures on Land and Water;

To raise and support Armies, but no Appropriation of Money to that Use shall be for a longer Term than two Years;

To provide and maintain a Navy;

* * *

To exercise exclusive Legislation in all Cases whatsoever, over such District (not exceeding ten Miles square) as may, by Cession of particular States, and the Acceptance of Congress, become the Seat of the Government of the United States, and to exercise like Authority over all Places purchased by the Consent of the Legislature of the State in which the Same shall be, for the Erection of Forts, Magazines, Arsenals, dock-Yards, and other needful Buildings;—And

To make all Laws which shall be necessary and proper for carrying into Execution the foregoing Powers, and all other Powers vested by this Constitution in the Government of the United States, or in any Department or Officer thereof.

ARTICLE III.

Section 1. The judicial Power of the United States, shall be vested in one supreme Court, and in such inferior Courts as the Congress may from time to time ordain and establish. The Judges, both of the supreme and inferior Courts, shall hold their Offices during good Behaviour, and shall, at stated Times, receive for their Services, a Compensation, which shall not be diminished during their Continuance in Office.

Section 2. The judicial Power shall extend to all Cases, in Law and Equity, arising under this Constitution, the Laws of the United States, and Treaties made, or which shall be made, under their Authority;—to all Cases affecting Ambassadors, other public Ministers and Consuls;—to all Cases of admiralty and maritime Jurisdiction;—to Controversies to which the United States shall be a Party;—to Controversies between two or more States;—between a State and Citizens of another State;—between Citizens of different States;—between Citizens of the same State claiming Lands under Grants of different States, and between a State, or the Citizens thereof, and foreign States, Citizens or Subjects.

In all Cases affecting Ambassadors, other public Ministers and Consuls, and those in which a State shall be Party, the supreme Court shall have original Jurisdiction. In all the other Cases before mentioned, the supreme Court shall have appellate Jurisdiction, both as to Law and Fact, with such Exceptions, and under such Regulations as the Congress shall make.

The Trial of all Crimes, except in Cases of Impeachment, shall be by Jury; and such Trial shall be held in the State where the said Crimes shall have been committed; but when not committed within any State, the Trial shall be at such Place or Places as the Congress may by Law have directed.

* * *

ARTICLE IV.

Section 1. Full Faith and Credit shall be given in each State to the public Acts, Records, and judicial Proceedings of every other State. And the Congress may by general Laws prescribe the Manner in which such Acts, Records and Proceedings shall be proved, and the Effect thereof.

CONSTITUTION OF THE UNITED STATES

Section 2. The Citizens of each State shall be entitled to all Privileges and Immunities of Citizens in the several States.

* * *

ARTICLE VI.

* * *

This Constitution, and the Laws of the United States which shall be made in Pursuance thereof; and all Treaties made, or which shall be made, under the Authority of the United States, shall be the supreme Law of the Land; and the Judges in every State shall be bound thereby, any Thing in the Constitution or Laws of any State to the Contrary notwithstanding.

* * *

AMENDMENT I.

Congress shall make no law respecting an establishment of religion, or prohibiting the free exercise thereof; or abridging the freedom of speech, or of the press; or the right of the people peaceably to assemble, and to petition the Government for a redress of grievances.

AMENDMENT IV.

The right of the people to be secure in their persons, houses, papers, and effects, against unreasonable searches and seizures, shall not be violated, and no Warrants shall issue, but upon probable cause, supported by Oath or affirmation, and particularly describing the place to be searched, and the persons or things to be seized.

AMENDMENT V.

No person shall be held to answer for a capital, or otherwise infamous crime, unless on a presentment or indictment of a Grand Jury, except in cases arising in the land or naval forces, or in the Militia, when in actual service in time of War or public danger; nor shall any person be subject for the same offence to be twice put in jeopardy of life or limb; nor shall be compelled in any criminal case to be a witness against himself, nor be deprived of life, liberty, or property, without due process of law; nor shall private property be taken for public use, without just compensation.

AMENDMENT VII.

In Suits at common law, where the value in controversy shall exceed twenty dollars, the right of trial by jury shall be preserved, and no fact tried by a jury, shall be otherwise re-examined in any Court of the United States, than according to the rules of the common law.

Comparative State Provisions

See the state provisions as set out following Federal Rule of Civil Procedure 38, supra.

AMENDMENT IX.

The enumeration in the Constitution, of certain rights, shall not be construed to deny or disparage others retained by the people.

AMENDMENT X.

The powers not delegated to the United States by the Constitution, nor prohibited by it to the States, are reserved to the States respectively, or to the people.

AMENDMENT XI.

The Judicial power of the United States shall not be construed to extend to any suit in law or equity, commenced or prosecuted against one of the United States by Citizens of another State, or by Citizens or Subjects of any Foreign State.

AMENDMENT XIV.

Section 1. All persons born or naturalized in the United States, and subject to the jurisdiction thereof, are citizens of the United States and of the State wherein they reside. No State shall make or enforce any law which shall abridge the privileges or immunities of citizens of the United States; nor shall any State deprive any person of life, liberty, or property, without due process of law; nor deny to any person within its jurisdiction the equal protection of the laws.

* * *

Section 5. The Congress shall have power to enforce, by appropriate legislation, the provisions of this article.

Selected Provisions of Title 28, United States Code— Judiciary and Judicial Procedure

§ 471. Requirement for a district court civil justice expense and delay reduction plan

There shall be implemented by each United States district court, in accordance with this chapter, a civil justice expense and delay reduction plan. The plan may be a plan developed by such district court or a model plan developed by the Judicial Conference of the United States. The purposes of each plan are to facilitate deliberate adjudication of civil cases on the merits, monitor discovery, improve litigation management, and ensure just, speedy, and inexpensive resolutions of civil disputes.

§ 472. Development and implementation of a civil justice expense and delay reduction plan

(a)   The civil justice expense and delay reduction plan implemented by a district court shall be developed or selected, as the case may be, after consideration of the recommendations of an advisory group appointed in accordance with section 478 of this title.

(b)   The advisory group of a United States district court shall submit to the court a report, which shall be made available to the public and which shall include—

(1)   an assessment of the matters referred to in subsection (c)(1);

(2)   the basis for its recommendation that the district court develop a plan or select a model plan;

(3)   recommended measures, rules and programs; and

(4)   an explanation of the manner in which the recommended plan complies with section 473 of this title.

(c)   (1)   In developing its recommendations, the advisory group of a district court shall promptly complete a thorough assessment of the state of the court's civil and criminal dockets. In performing the assessment for a district court, the advisory group shall—

(A)   determine the condition of the civil and criminal dockets;

(B)   identify trends in case filings and in the demands being placed on the court's resources;

(C)   identify the principal causes of cost and delay in civil litigation, giving consideration to such potential causes as court procedures and the ways in which litigants and their attorneys approach and conduct litigation; and

(D)   examine the extent to which costs and delays could be reduced by a better assessment of the impact of new legislation on the courts.

(2) In developing its recommendations, the advisory group of a district court shall take into account the particular needs and circumstances of the district court, litigants in such court, and the litigants' attorneys.

(3) The advisory group of a district court shall ensure that its recommended actions include significant contributions to be made by the court, the litigants, and the litigants' attorneys toward reducing cost and delay and thereby facilitating access to the courts.

(d) The chief judge of the district court shall transmit a copy of the plan implemented in accordance with subsection (a) and the report prepared in accordance with subsection (b) of this section to—

(1) the Director of the Administrative Office of the United States Courts;

(2) the judicial council of the circuit in which the district court is located; and

(3) the chief judge of each of the other United States district courts located in such circuit.

§ 473. Content of civil justice expense and delay reduction plans

(a) In formulating the provisions of its civil justice expense and delay reduction plan, each United States district court, in consultation with an advisory group appointed under section 478 of this title, shall consider and may include the following principles and guidelines of litigation management and cost and delay reduction:

(1) systematic, differential treatment of civil cases that tailors the level of individualized and case specific management to such criteria as case complexity, the amount of time reasonably needed to prepare the case for trial, and the judicial and other resources required and available for the preparation and disposition of the case;

(2) early and ongoing control of the pretrial process through involvement of a judicial officer in—

(A) assessing and planning the progress of a case;

(B) setting early, firm trial dates, such that the trial is scheduled to occur within eighteen months after the filing of the complaint, unless a judicial officer certifies that—

(i) the demands of the case and its complexity make such a trial date incompatible with serving the ends of justice; or

(ii) the trial court cannot reasonably be held within such time because of the complexity of the case or the number or complexity of pending criminal cases;

(C) controlling the extent of discovery and the time for completion of discovery, and ensuring compliance with appropriate requested discovery in a timely fashion; and

(D) setting, at the earliest practicable time, deadlines for filing motions and a time framework for their disposition;

(3) for all cases that the court or an individual judicial officer determines are complex and any other appropriate cases, careful and deliberate monitoring through a discovery-case management conference or a series of such conferences at which the presiding judicial officer—

(A) explores the parties' receptivity to, and the propriety of, settlement or proceeding with the litigation;

(B) identifies or formulates the principal issues in contention and, in appropriate cases, provides for the staged resolution or bifurcation of issues for trial consistent with Rule 42(b) of the Federal Rules of Civil Procedure;

      (C)   prepares a discovery schedule and plan consistent with any presumptive time limits that a district court may set for the completion of discovery and with any procedures a district court may develop to—

        (i)   identify and limit the volume of discovery available to avoid unnecessary or unduly burdensome or expensive discovery; and

        (ii)   phase discovery into two or more stages; and

      (D)   sets, at the earliest practicable time, deadlines for filing motions and a time framework for their disposition;

    (4)   encouragement of cost-effective discovery through voluntary exchange of information among litigants and their attorneys and through the use of cooperative discovery devices;

    (5)   conservation of judicial resources by prohibiting the consideration of discovery motions unless accompanied by a certification that the moving party has made a reasonable and good faith effort to reach agreement with opposing counsel on the matters set forth in the motion; and

    (6)   authorization to refer appropriate cases to alternative dispute resolution programs that—

      (A)   have been designated for use in a district court; or

      (B)   the court may make available, including mediation, minitrial, and summary jury trial.

(b)   In formulating the provisions of its civil justice expense and delay reduction plan, each United States district court, in consultation with an advisory group appointed under section 478 of this title, shall consider and may include the following litigation management and cost and delay reduction techniques:

    (1)   a requirement that counsel for each party to a case jointly present a discovery-case management plan for the case at the initial pretrial conference, or explain the reasons for their failure to do so;

    (2)   a requirement that each party be represented at each pretrial conference by an attorney who has the authority to bind that party regarding all matters previously identified by the court for discussion at the conference and all reasonably related matters;

    (3)   a requirement that all requests for extensions of deadlines for completion of discovery or for postponement of the trial be signed by the attorney and the party making the request;

    (4)   a neutral evaluation program for the presentation of the legal and factual basis of a case to a neutral court representative selected by the court at a nonbinding conference conducted early in the litigation;

    (5)   a requirement that, upon notice by the court, representatives of the parties with authority to bind them in settlement discussions be present or available by telephone during any settlement conference; and

    (6)   such other features as the district court considers appropriate after considering the recommendations of the advisory group referred to in section 472(a) of this title.

(c)   Nothing in a civil justice expense and delay reduction plan relating to the settlement authority provisions of this section shall alter or conflict with the authority of the Attorney General to conduct litigation on behalf of the United States, or any delegation of the Attorney General.

§ 474. Review of district court action

(a)   (1)   The chief judge of each district court in a circuit and the chief judge of the circuit shall, as a committee—

(A)   review each plan and report submitted pursuant to section 472(d) of this title; and

(B)   make such suggestions for additional actions or modified actions of that district court as the committee considers appropriate for reducing cost and delay in civil litigation in the district court.

(2)   The chief judge of a circuit may designate another judge of the court of appeals of that circuit, and the chief judge of a district court may designate another judge of such court, to perform that chief judge's responsibilities under paragraph (1) of this subsection.

(b)   The Judicial Conference of the United States—

(1)   shall review each plan and report submitted by a district court pursuant to section 472(d) of this title; and

(2)   may request the district court to take additional action if the Judicial Conference determines that such court has not adequately responded to the conditions relevant to the civil and criminal dockets of the court or to the recommendations of the district court's advisory group.

§ 475. Periodic district court assessment

After developing or selecting a civil justice expense and delay reduction plan, each United States district court shall assess annually the condition of the court's civil and criminal dockets with a view to determining appropriate additional actions that may be taken by the court to reduce cost and delay in civil litigation and to improve the litigation management practices of the court. In performing such assessment, the court shall consult with an advisory group appointed in accordance with section 478 of this title.

§ 476. Enhancement of judicial information dissemination

(a)   The Director of the Administrative Office of the United States Courts shall prepare a semiannual report, available to the public, that discloses for each judicial officer—

(1)   the number of motions that have been pending for more than six months and the name of each case in which such motion has been pending;

(2)   the number of bench trials that have been submitted for more than six months and the name of each case in which such trials are under submission; and

(3)   the number and names of cases that have not been terminated within three years after filing.

(b)   To ensure uniformity of reporting, the standards for categorization or characterization of judicial actions to be prescribed in accordance with section 481 of this title shall apply to the semiannual report prepared under subsection (a).

§ 477. Model civil justice expense and delay reduction plan

(a)   (1)   Based on the plans developed and implemented by the United States district courts designated as Early Implementation District Courts pursuant to section 103(c) of the Civil Justice Reform Act of 1990, the Judicial Conference of the United States may develop one or more model civil justice expense and delay reduction plans. Any such model plan shall be accompanied by a report explaining the manner in which the plan complies with section 473 of this title.

(2)   The Director of the Federal Judicial Center and the Director of the Administrative Office of the United States Courts may make recommendations to the Judicial Conference regarding the development of any model civil justice expense and delay reduction plan.

(b)   The Director of the Administrative Office of the United States Courts shall transmit to the United States district courts and to the Committees on the Judiciary of the Senate and the House of Representatives copies of any model plan and accompanying report.

§ 478. Advisory groups

(a)   Within ninety days after the date of the enactment of this chapter, the advisory group required in each United States district court in accordance with section 472 of this title shall be appointed by the chief judge of each district court, after consultation with the other judges of such court.

(b)   The advisory group of a district court shall be balanced and include attorneys and other persons who are representative of major categories of litigants in such court, as determined by the chief judge of such court.

(c)   Subject to subsection (d), in no event shall any member of the advisory group serve longer than four years.

(d)   Notwithstanding subsection (c), the United States Attorney for a judicial district, or his or her designee, shall be a permanent member of the advisory group for that district court.

(e)   The chief judge of a United States district court may designate a reporter for each advisory group, who may be compensated in accordance with guidelines established by the Judicial Conference of the United States.

(f)   The members of an advisory group of a United States district court and any person designated as a reporter for such group shall be considered as independent contractors of such court when in the performance of official duties of the advisory group and may not, solely by reason of service on or for the advisory group, be prohibited from practicing law before such court.

§ 479. Information on litigation management and cost and delay reduction

(a)   Within four years after the date of the enactment of this chapter, the Judicial Conference of the United States shall prepare a comprehensive report on all plans received pursuant to section 472(d) of this title. The Director of the Federal Judicial Center and the Director of the Administrative Office of the United States Courts may make recommendations regarding such report to the Judicial Conference during the preparation of the report. The Judicial Conference shall transmit copies of the report to the United States district courts and to the Committees on the Judiciary of the Senate and the House of Representatives.

(b)   The Judicial Conference of the United States shall, on a continuing basis—

(1)   study ways to improve litigation management and dispute resolution services in the district courts; and

(2)   make recommendations to the district courts on ways to improve such services.

(c)   (1)   The Judicial Conference of the United States shall prepare, periodically revise, and transmit to the United States district courts a Manual for Litigation Management and Cost and Delay Reduction. The Director of the Federal Judicial Center and the Director of the Administrative Office of the United States Courts may make recommendations regarding the preparation of and any subsequent revisions to the Manual.

(2)   The Manual shall be developed after careful evaluation of the plans implemented under section 472 of this title, the demonstration program conducted under section 104 of the Civil Justice Reform Act of 1990, and the pilot program conducted under section 105 of the Civil Justice Reform Act of 1990.

(3)   The Manual shall contain a description and analysis of the litigation management, cost and delay reduction principles and techniques, and alternative dispute resolution programs considered most effective by the Judicial Conference, the Director of the Federal Judicial Center, and the Director of the Administrative Office of the United States Courts.

§ 1251. Original jurisdiction

(a)   The Supreme Court shall have original and exclusive jurisdiction of all controversies between two or more States.

(b)   The Supreme Court shall have original but not exclusive jurisdiction of:

(1)   All actions or proceedings to which ambassadors, other public ministers, consuls, or vice consuls of foreign states are parties;

(2)   All controversies between the United States and a State;

(3)   All actions or proceedings by a State against the citizens of another State or against aliens.

§ 1253. Direct appeals from decisions of three-judge courts

Except as otherwise provided by law, any party may appeal to the Supreme Court from an order granting or denying, after notice and hearing, an interlocutory or permanent injunction in any civil action, suit or proceeding required by any Act of Congress to be heard and determined by a district court of three judges.

§ 1254. Courts of appeals; certiorari; appeal; certified questions

Cases in the courts of appeals may be reviewed by the Supreme Court by the following methods:

(1)   By writ of certiorari granted upon the petition of any party to any civil or criminal case, before or after rendition of judgment or decree;

(2)   By certification at any time by a court of appeals of any question of law in any civil or criminal case as to which instructions are desired, and upon such certification the Supreme Court may give binding instructions or require the entire record to be sent up for decision of the entire matter in controversy.

Related Provisions Regarding Appeals to the Highest Court in a Jurisdiction

(a)   *Discretionary Review*

1.   *Comparative state provisions*

California Constitution Art. 6, § 11(a)

The Supreme Court has appellate jurisdiction when judgment of death has been pronounced. With that exception courts of appeal have appellate jurisdiction when superior courts have original jurisdiction in causes of a type within the appellate jurisdiction of the courts of appeal on June 30, 1995, and in other causes prescribed by statute. * * *

California Constitution Art. 6, § 12

(a)   The Supreme Court may, before decision, transfer to itself a cause in a court of appeal. It may, before decision, transfer a cause from itself to a court of appeal or from one court of appeal or division to another. The court to which a cause is transferred has jurisdiction.

(b)   The Supreme Court may review the decision of a court of appeal in any cause.

(c)   The Judicial Council shall provide, by rules of court, for the time and procedure for transfer and for review, including, among other things, provisions for the time and procedure for transfer with instructions, for review of all or part of a decision, and for remand as improvidently granted.

(d)   This section shall not apply to an appeal involving a judgment of death.

California Rule of Court 8.500(a)(1)

A party may file a petition in the Supreme Court for review of any decision of the Court of Appeal, including any interlocutory order, except the denial of a transfer of a case within the appellate jurisdiction of the superior court.

California Rule of Court 8.500(e)(1) & (2)

(1)   A petition for review must be served and filed within 10 days after the Court of Appeal decision is final in that court * * *.

(2)   * * * [T]he Chief Justice may relieve a party from a failure to file a timely petition for review if the time for the court to order review on its own motion has not expired.

California Rule of Court 8.512(b)

(1)   The court may order review within 60 days after the last petition for review is filed. [Extensions may be ordered to a date not to exceed 90 days after the last petition is filed.] * * *

(2)   If the court does not rule on the petition within the time allowed by (1), the petition is deemed denied.

* * *

California Rule of Court 8.512(c)(1)

If no petition for review is filed, the Supreme Court may, on its own motion, order review of a Court of Appeal decision within 30 days after the decision is final in that court. Before the 30-day period or any extension expires, the Supreme Court may order one or more extensions to a date not later than 90 days after the decision is final in the Court of Appeal. * * *

California Rule of Court 8.512(d)(1)

An order granting review must be signed by at least four justices [out of seven] * * *.

* * *

New York Civil Practice Law and Rules 5602

(a)   Permission of appellate division or court of appeals. An appeal may be taken to the court of appeals by permission of the appellate division granted before application to the court of appeals, or by permission of the court of appeals upon refusal by the appellate division or upon direct application. * * * Permission by the court of appeals for leave to appeal shall be pursuant to rules * * * which shall provide that leave to appeal be granted upon the approval of two judges of the court of appeals. Such appeal may be taken:

1.   in an action originating in the supreme court, a county court, a surrogate's court, the family court, the court of claims or an administrative agency or an arbitration,

(i)   from an order of the appellate division which finally determines the action and which is not appealable as of right, or

(ii)   from a final judgment of such court or final determination of such agency or final arbitration award where the appellate division has made an order on a prior appeal in the action which necessarily affects the final judgment, determination or award and the final judgment or determination or award is not appealable as of right pursuant to subdivision (d) of section 5601 of this article; and

2.   in a proceeding instituted by or against one or more public officers or a board, commission or other body of public officers or a court or tribunal, from an order of the appellate division which does not finally determine such proceeding, except that the appellate division shall not grant permission to appeal from an order granting or affirming the granting of a new trial or hearing.

(b)   Permission of appellate division. An appeal may be taken to the court of appeals by permission of the appellate division:

1.   from an order of the appellate division which does not finally determine an action, except an order described in paragraph two of subdivision (a) or subparagraph (iii) of paragraph two of subdivision (b) of this section or in subdivision (c) of section 5601;

2.   in an action originating in a court other than the supreme court, a county court, a surrogate's court, the family court, the court of claims or an administrative agency,

(i)   from an order of the appellate division which finally determines the action, and which is not appealable as of right pursuant to paragraph one of subdivision (b) of section 5601, or

(ii)   from a final judgment of such court or a final determination of such agency where the appellate division has made an order on a prior appeal in the action which necessarily affects the final judgment or determination and the final judgment or determination is not appealable as of right pursuant to subdivision (d) of section 5601, or

(iii)   from an order of the appellate division granting or affirming the granting of a new trial or hearing where the appellant stipulates that, upon affirmance, judgment absolute shall be entered against him.

2.   *Basis for exercise of discretion*

United States Supreme Court Rule 10

Review on a writ of certiorari is not a matter of right, but of judicial discretion. A petition for a writ of certiorari will be granted only for compelling reasons. The following, although neither controlling nor fully measuring the Court's discretion, indicate the character of the reasons the Court considers:

(a)   a United States court of appeals has entered a decision in conflict with the decision of another United States court of appeals on the same important matter; has decided an important federal question in a way that conflicts with a decision by a state court of last resort; or has so far departed from the accepted and usual course of judicial proceedings, or sanctioned such a departure by a lower court, as to call for an exercise of this Court's supervisory power;

(b)   a state court of last resort has decided an important federal question in a way that conflicts with the decision of another state court of last resort or of a United States court of appeals;

(c)   a state court or a United States court of appeals has decided an important question of federal law that has not been, but should be, settled by this Court, or has decided an important federal question in a way that conflicts with relevant decisions of this Court.

A petition for a writ of certiorari is rarely granted when the asserted error consists of erroneous factual findings or the misapplication of a properly stated rule of law.

California Rule of Court 8.500(b) & (c)

(b)   Grounds for review

The Supreme Court may order review of a Court of Appeal decision:

(1)   When necessary to secure uniformity of decision or to settle an important question of law;

(2)   When the Court of Appeal lacked jurisdiction;

(3)   When the Court of Appeal decision lacked the concurrence of sufficient qualified justices; or

(4)   For the purpose of transferring the matter to the Court of Appeal for such proceedings as the Supreme Court may order.

(c)   Limits of review

(1)   As a policy matter, on petition for review the Supreme Court normally will not consider an issue that the petitioner failed to timely raise in the Court of Appeal.

(2)　A party may petition for review without petitioning for rehearing in the Court of Appeal, but as a policy matter the Supreme Court normally will accept the Court of Appeal opinion's statement of the issues and facts unless the party has called the Court of Appeal's attention to any alleged omission or misstatement of an issue or fact in a petition for rehearing.

(b)　*Mandatory Review*

Georgia Constitution Art. 6, § 1, ¶ VIII

Any court shall transfer to the appropriate court in the state any civil case in which it determines that jurisdiction or venue lies elsewhere.

Georgia Constitution Art. 6, § 5, ¶ V

In the event of an equal division of the Judges when sitting as a body, the case shall be immediately transmitted to the Supreme Court.

Georgia Constitution Art. 6, § 6, ¶ II

The Supreme Court shall be a court of review and shall exercise exclusive appellate jurisdiction in the following cases:

(1)　All cases involving the construction of a treaty or of the Constitution of the State of Georgia or of the United States and all cases in which the constitutionality of a law, ordinance, or constitutional provision has been drawn in question; and

(2)　All cases of election contest.

Georgia Constitution Art. 6, § 6, ¶ III

Unless otherwise provided by law, the Supreme Court shall have appellate jurisdiction of the following classes of cases:

(1)　Cases involving title to land;

(2)　All equity cases;

(3)　All cases involving wills;

(4)　All habeas corpus cases;

(5)　All cases involving extraordinary remedies;

(6)　All divorce and alimony cases;

(7)　All cases certified to it by the Court of Appeals; and

(8)　All cases in which a sentence of death was imposed or could be imposed.

Review of all cases shall be as provided by law.

Georgia Constitution, Art. 6, § 6, ¶ V

The Supreme Court may review by certiorari cases in the Court of Appeals which are of gravity or great public importance.

New York Civil Practice Law and Rules 5601

(a)　Dissent. An appeal may be taken to the court of appeals as of right in an action originating in the supreme court, a county court, a surrogate's court, the family court, the court of claims or an administrative agency, from an order of the appellate division which finally determines the action, where there is a dissent by at least two justices on a question of law in favor of the party taking such appeal.

(b)　Constitutional grounds. An appeal may be taken to the court of appeals as of right:

1.　from an order of the appellate division which finally determines an action where there is directly involved the construction of the constitution of the state or of the United States; and

2.   from a judgment of a court of record of original instance which finally determines an action where the only question involved on the appeal is the validity of a statutory provision of the state or of the United States under the constitution of the state or of the United States.

(c)   From order granting new trial or hearing, upon stipulation for judgment absolute. An appeal may be taken to the court of appeals as of right in an action originating in the supreme court, a county court, a surrogate's court, the family court, the court of claims or an administrative agency, from an order of the appellate division granting or affirming the granting of a new trial or hearing where the appellant stipulates that, upon affirmance, judgment absolute shall be entered against him.

(d)   Based upon non-final determination of appellate division. An appeal may be taken to the court of appeals as of right from a final judgment entered in a court of original instance from a final determination of an administrative agency or from a final arbitration award, or from an order of the appellate division which finally determines an appeal from such a judgment or determination, where the appellate division has made an order on a prior appeal in the action which necessarily affects the judgment, determination or award and which satisfies the requirements of subdivision (a) or of paragraph one of subdivision (b) except that of finality.

§ 1257. State courts; appeal; certiorari

(a)   Final judgments or decrees rendered by the highest court of a State in which a decision could be had, may be reviewed by the Supreme Court by writ of certiorari, where the validity of a treaty or statute of the United States is drawn in question or where the validity of a statute of any State is drawn in question on the ground of its being repugnant to the Constitution, treaties, or laws of the United States, or where any title, right, privilege or immunity is specially set up or claimed under the Constitution or the treaties or statutes of, or any commission held or authority exercised under, the United States.

(b)   For purposes of this section, the term "highest court of a State" includes the District of Columbia Court of Appeals.

Related Provision

[See United States Supreme Court Rule 10 set out in note (a)(2) following § 1254, supra.]

§ 1291. Final decisions of district courts

The courts of appeals (other than the United States Court of Appeals for the Federal Circuit) shall have jurisdiction of appeals from all final decisions of the district courts of the United States, the United States District Court for the District of the Canal Zone, the District Court of Guam, and the District Court of the Virgin Islands, except where a direct review may be had in the Supreme Court * * *.

Comparative State Provision

[See New York Civil Practice Law and Rules 5701 as set out following 28 U.S.C. § 1292, infra.]

§ 1292. Interlocutory decisions

(a)   Except as provided in subsections (c) and (d) of this section, the courts of appeals shall have jurisdiction of appeals from:

(1)   Interlocutory orders of the district courts of the United States, the United States District Court for the District of the Canal Zone, the District Court of Guam, and the District Court of the Virgin Islands, or of the judges thereof, granting, continuing, modifying, refusing or dissolving injunctions, or refusing to dissolve or modify injunctions, except where a direct review may be had in the Supreme Court;

(2)   Interlocutory orders appointing receivers, or refusing orders to wind up receiverships or to take steps to accomplish the purposes thereof, such as directing sales or other disposals of property;

(3)   Interlocutory decrees of such district courts or the judges thereof determining the rights and liabilities of the parties to admiralty cases in which appeals from final decrees are allowed.

(b)   When a district judge, in making in a civil action an order not otherwise appealable under this section, shall be of the opinion that such order involves a controlling question of law as to which there is substantial ground for difference of opinion and that an immediate appeal from the order may materially advance the ultimate termination of the litigation, he shall so state in writing in such order. The Court of Appeals which would have jurisdiction of an appeal of such action may thereupon, in its discretion, permit an appeal to be taken from such order, if application is made to it within ten days after the entry of the order: *Provided, however,* That application for an appeal hereunder shall not stay proceedings in the district court unless the district judge or the Court of Appeals or a judge thereof shall so order.

(c)   The United States Court of Appeals for the Federal Circuit shall have exclusive jurisdiction—

(1)   of an appeal from an interlocutory order or decree described in subsection (a) or (b) of this section in any case over which the court would have jurisdiction of an appeal under section 1295 of this title; and

(2)   of an appeal from a judgment in a civil action for patent infringement which would otherwise be appealable to the United States Court of Appeals for the Federal Circuit and is final except for an accounting.

(d)   (1)   When the chief judge of the Court of International Trade issues an order under the provisions of section 256(b) of this title, or when any judge of the Court of International Trade, in issuing any other interlocutory order, includes in the order a statement that a controlling question of law is involved with respect to which there is a substantial ground for difference of opinion and that an immediate appeal from that order may materially advance the ultimate termination of the litigation, the United States Court of Appeals for the Federal Circuit may, in its discretion, permit an appeal to be taken from such order, if application is made to that Court within ten days after the entry of such order.

(2)   When the chief judge of the United States Court of Federal Claims issues an order under section 798(b) of this title, or when any judge of the United States Court of Federal Claims, in issuing an interlocutory order, includes in the order a statement that a controlling question of law is involved with respect to which there is a substantial ground for difference of opinion and that an immediate appeal from that order may materially advance the ultimate termination of the litigation, the United States Court of Appeals for the Federal Circuit may, in its discretion, permit an appeal to be taken from such order, if application is made to that Court within ten days after the entry of such order.

(3)   Neither the application for nor the granting of an appeal under this subsection shall stay proceedings in the Court of International Trade or in the Court of Federal Claims, as the case may be, unless a stay is ordered by a judge of the Court of International Trade or of the Court of Federal Claims or by the United States Court of Appeals for the Federal Circuit or a judge of that court.

(4)   (A)   The United States Court of Appeals for the Federal Circuit shall have exclusive jurisdiction of an appeal from an interlocutory order of a district court of the United States, the District Court of Guam, the District Court of the Virgin Islands, or the District Court for the Northern Mariana Islands, granting or denying, in whole or in part, a motion to transfer an action to the United States Court of Federal Claims under section 1631 of this title.

(B)   When a motion to transfer an action to the Court of Federal Claims is filed in a district court, no further proceedings shall be taken in the district court until 60 days after the court has ruled upon the motion. If an appeal is taken from the district court's grant or denial of the motion, proceedings shall be further stayed until the appeal has been decided by the Court of Appeals for the Federal Circuit. The stay of proceedings in the district court shall not bar the granting of preliminary or injunctive relief, where appropriate and where expedition is reasonably necessary. However, during the period in which proceedings are stayed as provided in this subparagraph, no transfer to the Court of Federal Claims pursuant to the motion shall be carried out.

(e)   The Supreme Court may prescribe rules, in accordance with section 2072 of this title, to provide for an appeal of an interlocutory decision to the courts of appeals that is not otherwise provided for under subsection (a), (b), (c), or (d).

Comparative Federal and State Provisions

(a)   *Related Federal Rules*

[See Federal Rule of Civil Procedure 23(f), supra, and Federal Rule of Appellate Procedure 5, infra.]

(b)   *Comparative State Provisions*

Minnesota Rules of Civil Appellate Procedure 103.03

An appeal may be taken to the Court of Appeals:

(a)   from a final judgment or from a partial judgment entered pursuant to Minn.R.Civ.P. 54.02;

(b)   from an order which grants, refuses, dissolves or refuses to dissolve, an injunction;

(c)   from an order vacating or sustaining an attachment;

(d)   from an order denying a new trial, or from an order granting a new trial if the trial court expressly states therein, or in a memorandum attached thereto, that the order is based exclusively upon errors of law occurring at the trial, and upon no other ground; and the trial court shall specify such errors in its order or memorandum, but upon appeal, such order granting a new trial may be sustained for errors of law prejudicial to respondent other than those specified by the trial court;

(e)   from an order which, in effect, determines the action and prevents a judgment from which an appeal might be taken;

(f)   from a final order or judgment made or rendered in proceedings supplementary to execution;

(g)   * * *

(h)   * * *

(i)   if the trial court certifies that the question presented is important and doubtful, from an order which denies a motion to dismiss for failure to state a claim upon which relief can be granted or from an order which denies a motion for summary judgment; and

(j)   from such other orders or decisions as may be appealable by statute or under the decisions of the Minnesota appellate courts.

New York Civil Practice Law and Rules 5701

(a)   Appeals as of right. An appeal may be taken to the appellate division as of right in an action, originating in the supreme court or a county court:

1.   from any final or interlocutory judgment except one entered subsequent to an order of the appellate division which disposes of all the issues in the action; or

2.   from an order not specified in subdivision (b), where the motion it decided was made upon notice and it:

(i)   grants, refuses, continues or modifies a provisional remedy; or

    (ii)   settles, grants or refuses an application to resettle a transcript or statement on appeal; or

    (iii)   grants or refuses a new trial; except where specific questions of fact arising upon the issues in an action triable by the court have been tried by a jury, pursuant to an order for that purpose, and the order grants or refuses a new trial upon the merits; or

    (iv)   involves some part of the merits; or

    (v)   affects a substantial right; or

    (vi)   in effect determines the action and prevents a judgment from which an appeal might be taken; or

    (vii)   determines a statutory provision of the state to be unconstitutional, and the determination appears from the reasons given for the decision or is necessarily implied in the decision; or

    (viii) grants a motion for leave to reargue * * * or determines a motion for leave to renew * * * [an earlier motion that resulted in an order].

    3.   from an order, where the motion it decided was made upon notice, refusing to vacate or modify a prior order, if the prior order would have been appealable as of right under paragraph two had it decided a motion made upon notice.

(b)   Orders not appealable as of right. An order is not appealable to the appellate division as of right where it:

    1.   is made in a proceeding against a body or officer pursuant to article 78; or

    2.   requires or refuses to require a more definite statement in a pleading; or

    3.   orders or refuses to order that scandalous or prejudicial matter be stricken from a pleading.

(c)   Appeals by permission. An appeal may be taken to the appellate division from any order which is not appealable as of right in an action originating in the supreme court or a county court by permission of the judge who made the order granted before application to a justice of the appellate division; or by permission of a justice of the appellate division in the department to which the appeal could be taken, upon refusal by the judge who made the order or upon direct application.

§ 1331. Federal question

The district courts shall have original jurisdiction of all civil actions arising under the Constitution, laws, or treaties of the United States.

§ 1332. Diversity of citizenship; amount in controversy; costs

(a)   The district courts shall have original jurisdiction of all civil actions where the matter in controversy exceeds the sum or value of $75,000, exclusive of interest and costs, and is between—

    (1)   citizens of different States;

    (2)   citizens of a State and citizens or subjects of a foreign state, except that the district courts shall not have original jurisdiction under this subsection of an action between citizens of a State and citizens or subjects of a foreign state who are lawfully admitted for permanent residence in the United States and are domiciled in the same State.

    (3)   citizens of different States and in which citizens or subjects of a foreign state are additional parties; and

    (4)   a foreign state * * * as plaintiff and citizens of a State or of different States.

(b)   Except when express provision therefor is otherwise made in a statute of the United States, where the plaintiff who files the case originally in the Federal courts is finally adjudged to be entitled to recover less than the sum or value of $75,000, computed without regard to any setoff or counterclaim to which the defendant may be adjudged to be entitled, and exclusive of interest and costs, the district court may deny costs to the plaintiff and, in addition, may impose costs on the plaintiff.

(c)   For the purposes of this section and section 1441 of this title—

(1)   a corporation shall be deemed to be a citizen of every State and foreign state by which it has been incorporated and of the State or foreign state where it has its principal place of business, except that in any direct action against the insurer of a policy or contract of liability insurance, whether incorporated or unincorporated, to which action the insured is not joined as a party-defendant, such insurer shall be deemed a citizen of—

(A)   every State and foreign state of which the insured is a citizen;

(B)   every State and foreign state by which the insurer has been incorporated; and

(C)   the State or foreign state where the insurer has its principal place of business; and

(2)   the legal representative of the estate of a decedent shall be deemed to be a citizen only of the same State as the decedent, and the legal representative of an infant or incompetent shall be deemed to be a citizen only of the same State as the infant or incompetent.

(d)   (1)   In this subsection—

(A)   the term "class" means all of the class members in a class action;

(B)   the term "class action" means any civil action filed under rule 23 of the Federal Rules of Civil Procedure or similar State statute or rule of judicial procedure authorizing an action to be brought by 1 or more representative persons as a class action;

(C)   the term "class certification order" means an order issued by a court approving the treatment of some or all aspects of a civil action as a class action; and

(D)   the term "class members" means the persons (named or unnamed) who fall within the definition of the proposed or certified class in a class action.

(2)   The district courts shall have original jurisdiction of any civil action in which the matter in controversy exceeds the sum or value of $5,000,000, exclusive of interest and costs, and is a class action in which—

(A)   any member of a class of plaintiffs is a citizen of a State different from any defendant;

(B)   any member of a class of plaintiffs is a foreign state or a citizen or subject of a foreign state and any defendant is a citizen of a State; or

(C)   any member of a class of plaintiffs is a citizen of a State and any defendant is a foreign state or a citizen or subject of a foreign state.

(3)   A district court may, in the interests of justice and looking at the totality of the circumstances, decline to exercise jurisdiction under paragraph (2) over a class action in which greater than one-third but less than two-thirds of the members of all proposed plaintiff classes in the aggregate and the primary defendants are citizens of the State in which the action was originally filed based on consideration of—

(A)   whether the claims asserted involve matters of national or interstate interest;

(B)   whether the claims asserted will be governed by laws of the State in which the action was originally filed or by the laws of other States;

(C)   whether the class action has been pleaded in a manner that seeks to avoid Federal jurisdiction;

(D)　whether the action was brought in a forum with a distinct nexus with the class members, the alleged harm, or the defendants;

(E)　whether the number of citizens of the State in which the action was originally filed in all proposed plaintiff classes in the aggregate is substantially larger than the number of citizens from any other State, and the citizenship of the other members of the proposed class is dispersed among a substantial number of States; and

(F)　whether, during the 3-year period preceding the filing of that class action, 1 or more other class actions asserting the same or similar claims on behalf of the same or other persons have been filed.

(4)　A district court shall decline to exercise jurisdiction under paragraph (2)—

(A)　(i)　over a class action in which—

(I)　greater than two-thirds of the members of all proposed plaintiff classes in the aggregate are citizens of the State in which the action was originally filed;

(II)　at least 1 defendant is a defendant—

(aa)　from whom significant relief is sought by members of the plaintiff class;

(bb)　whose alleged conduct forms a significant basis for the claims asserted by the proposed plaintiff class; and

(cc)　who is a citizen of the State in which the action was originally filed; and

(III)　principal injuries resulting from the alleged conduct or any related conduct of each defendant were incurred in the State in which the action was originally filed; and

(ii)　during the 3-year period preceding the filing of that class action, no other class action has been filed asserting the same or similar factual allegations against any of the defendants on behalf of the same or other persons; or

(B)　two-thirds or more of the members of all proposed plaintiff classes in the aggregate, and the primary defendants, are citizens of the State in which the action was originally filed.

(5)　Paragraphs (2) through (4) shall not apply to any class action in which—

(A)　the primary defendants are States, State officials, or other governmental entities against whom the district court may be foreclosed from ordering relief; or

(B)　the number of members of all proposed plaintiff classes in the aggregate is less than 100.

(6)　In any class action, the claims of the individual class members shall be aggregated to determine whether the matter in controversy exceeds the sum or value of $5,000,000, exclusive of interest and costs.

(7)　Citizenship of the members of the proposed plaintiff classes shall be determined for purposes of paragraphs (2) through (6) as of the date of filing of the complaint or amended complaint, or, if the case stated by the initial pleading is not subject to Federal jurisdiction, as of the date of service by plaintiffs of an amended pleading, motion, or other paper, indicating the existence of Federal jurisdiction.

(8)　This subsection shall apply to any class action before or after the entry of a class certification order by the court with respect to that action.

(9)　Paragraph (2) shall not apply to any class action that solely involves a claim—

(A)   concerning a covered security as defined under 16(f)(3) of the Securities Act of 1933 (15 U.S.C. 78p(f)(3)) and section 28(f)(5)(E) of the Securities Exchange Act of 1934 (15 U.S.C. 78bb(f)(5)(E));

(B)   that relates to the internal affairs or governance of a corporation or other form of business enterprise and that arises under or by virtue of the laws of the State in which such corporation or business enterprise is incorporated or organized; or

(C)   that relates to the rights, duties (including fiduciary duties), and obligations relating to or created by or pursuant to any security (as defined under section 2(a)(1) of the Securities Act of 1933 (15 U.S.C. 77b(a)(1)) and the regulations issued thereunder).

(10)   For purposes of this subsection and section 1453, an unincorporated association shall be deemed to be a citizen of the State where it has its principal place of business and the State under whose laws it is organized.

(11)   (A)   For purposes of this subsection and section 1453, a mass action shall be deemed to be a class action removable under paragraphs (2) through (10) if it otherwise meets the provisions of those paragraphs.

(B)   (i)   As used in subparagraph (A), the term "mass action" means any civil action (except a civil action within the scope of section 1711(2)) in which monetary relief claims of 100 or more persons are proposed to be tried jointly on the ground that the plaintiffs' claims involve common questions of law or fact, except that jurisdiction shall exist only over those plaintiffs whose claims in a mass action satisfy the jurisdictional amount requirements under subsection (a).

(ii)   As used in subparagraph (A), the term "mass action" shall not include any civil action in which—

(I)   all of the claims in the action arise from an event or occurrence in the State in which the action was filed, and that allegedly resulted in injuries in that State or in States contiguous to that State;

(II)   the claims are joined upon motion of a defendant;

(III) all of the claims in the action are asserted on behalf of the general public (and not on behalf of individual claimants or members of a purported class) pursuant to a State statute specifically authorizing such action; or

(IV)   the claims have been consolidated or coordinated solely for pretrial proceedings.

(C)   (i)   Any action(s) removed to Federal court pursuant to this subsection shall not thereafter be transferred to any other court pursuant to section 1407, or the rules promulgated thereunder, unless a majority of the plaintiffs in the action request transfer pursuant to section 1407.

(ii)   This subparagraph will not apply—

(I)   to cases certified pursuant to rule 23 of the Federal Rules of Civil Procedure; or

(II)   if plaintiffs propose that the action proceed as a class action pursuant to rule 23 of the Federal Rules of Civil Procedure.

(D)   The limitations periods on any claims asserted in a mass action that is removed to Federal court pursuant to this subsection shall be deemed tolled during the period that the action is pending in Federal court.

(e)   The word "States", as used in this section, includes the Territories, the District of Columbia, and the Commonwealth of Puerto Rico.

Related Federal Provisions

Congress has provided for an exception to the "complete diversity" requirement of § 1332(a) in 28 U.S.C. § 1369 for certain multiparty, multiforum actions. The latter is augmented by liberal provisions for venue and service of process in §§ 1391(g) and 1697, effectively allowing such cases to be brought in any federal court where any defendant resides or where any substantial part of the action arose. A similar exception exists for certain interpleader cases, see 28 U.S.C. §§ 1335 and 1397, infra.

§ 1333. Admiralty, maritime and prize cases

The district courts shall have original jurisdiction, exclusive of the courts of the States, of:

(1)   Any civil case of admiralty or maritime jurisdiction, saving to suitors in all cases all other remedies to which they are otherwise entitled.

(2)   Any prize brought into the United States and all proceedings for the condemnation of property taken as prize.

§ 1334. Bankruptcy cases and proceedings

(a)   Except as provided in subsection (b) of this section, the district courts shall have original and exclusive jurisdiction of all cases under title 11.

(b)   Except as provided in subsection (e)(2), and notwithstanding any Act of Congress that confers exclusive jurisdiction on a court or courts other than the district courts, the district courts shall have original but not exclusive jurisdiction of all civil proceedings arising under title 11, or arising in or related to cases under title 11.

(c)   (1)   Except with respect to a case under chapter 15 of title 11, nothing in this section prevents a district court in the interest of justice, or in the interest of comity with State courts or respect for State law, from abstaining from hearing a particular proceeding arising under title 11 or arising in or related to a case under title 11.

(2)   Upon timely motion of a party in a proceeding based upon a State law claim or State law cause of action, related to a case under title 11 but not arising under title 11 or arising in a case under title 11, with respect to which an action could not have been commenced in a court of the United States absent jurisdiction under this section, the district court shall abstain from hearing such proceeding if an action is commenced, and can be timely adjudicated, in a State forum of appropriate jurisdiction.

(d)   Any decision to abstain or not to abstain made under subsection (c) (other than a decision not to abstain in a proceeding described in subsection (c)(2)) is not reviewable by appeal or otherwise by the court of appeals under section 158(d), 1291, or 1292 of this title or by the Supreme Court of the United States under section 1254 of this title. Subsection (c) and this subsection shall not be construed to limit the applicability of the stay provided for by section 362 of title 11, United States Code, as such section applies to an action affecting the property of the estate in bankruptcy.

(e)   The district court in which a case under title 11 is commenced or is pending shall have exclusive jurisdiction—

(1)   of all the property, wherever located, of the debtor as of the commencement of such case, and property of the estate, and

(2)   over all claims or causes of action that involve construction of section 327 of title 11, United States Code, or rules relating to disclosure requirements under section 327.

§ 1335. Interpleader

(a)   The district courts shall have original jurisdiction of any civil action of interpleader or in the nature of interpleader filed by any person, firm, or corporation, association, or society having in his or its custody or possession money or property of the value of $500 or more, or having issued a note, bond, certificate, policy of insurance, or other instrument of value or amount of $500 or more, or providing for the delivery or payment or the loan of money or property of such amount or value, or being under any obligation written or unwritten to the amount of $500 or more, if

(1)   Two or more adverse claimants, of diverse citizenship as defined in subsection (a) or (d) of section 1332 of this title, are claiming or may claim to be entitled to such money or property, or to any one or more of the benefits arising by virtue of any note, bond, certificate, policy or other instrument, or arising by virtue of any such obligation; and if (2) the plaintiff has deposited such money or property or has paid the amount of or the loan or other value of such instrument or the amount due under such obligation into the registry of the court, there to abide the judgment of the court, or has given bond payable to the clerk of the court in such amount and with such surety as the court or judge may deem proper, conditioned upon the compliance by the plaintiff with the future order or judgment of the court with respect to the subject matter of the controversy.

(b)   Such an action may be entertained although the titles or claims of the conflicting claimants do not have a common origin, or are not identical, but are adverse to and independent of one another.

§ 1337. Commerce and antitrust regulations

(a)   The district courts shall have original jurisdiction of any civil action or proceeding arising under any Act of Congress regulating commerce or protecting trade and commerce against restraints and monopolies * * *.

Related Federal Provision

United States Code Tit. 15, § 15(a)

Except as provided in subsection (b) [regarding suits by foreign states], any person who shall be injured in his business or property by reason of anything forbidden in the antitrust laws may sue therefor in any district court of the United States in the district in which the defendant resides or is found or has an agent, without respect to the amount in controversy, and shall recover threefold the damages by him sustained, and the cost of suit, including a reasonable attorney's fee. * * *

§ 1338. Patents, plant variety protection, copyrights, mask works, trademarks and unfair competition

(a)   The district courts shall have original jurisdiction of any civil action arising under any Act of Congress relating to patents, plant variety protection, copyrights and trademarks. No State court shall have jurisdiction over any claim for relief arising under any Act of Congress relating to patents, plant variety protection, or copyrights. For purposes of this subsection, the term 'State' includes any State of the United States, the District of Columbia, the Commonwealth of Puerto Rico, the United States Virgin Islands, American Samoa, Guam, and the Northern Mariana Islands.

(b)   The district courts shall have original jurisdiction of any civil action asserting a claim of unfair competition when joined with a substantial and related claim under the copyright, patent, plant variety protection or trademark laws.

(c)   Subsections (a) and (b) apply to exclusive rights in mask works under chapter 9 of title 17, and to exclusive rights in designs under chapter 13 of title 17, to the same extent as such subsections apply to copyrights.

§ 1343. Civil rights and elective franchise

(a)   The district courts shall have original jurisdiction of any civil action authorized by law to be commenced by any person:

(1)   To recover damages for injury to his person or property, or because of the deprivation of any right or privilege of a citizen of the United States, by any act done in furtherance of any conspiracy mentioned in section 1985 of Title 42;

(2)   To recover damages from any person who fails to prevent or to aid in preventing any wrongs mentioned in section 1985 of Title 42 which he had knowledge were about to occur and power to prevent;

(3)   To redress the deprivation, under color of any State law, statute, ordinance, regulation, custom or usage, of any right, privilege or immunity secured by the Constitution of the United States or by any Act of Congress providing for equal rights of citizens or of all persons within the jurisdiction of the United States;

(4)   To recover damages or to secure equitable or other relief under any Act of Congress providing for the protection of civil rights, including the right to vote.

* * *

§ 1345. United States as plaintiff

Except as otherwise provided by Act of Congress, the district courts shall have original jurisdiction of all civil actions, suits or proceedings commenced by the United States, or by any agency or officer thereof expressly authorized to sue by Act of Congress.

§ 1346. United States as defendant

(a)   The district courts shall have original jurisdiction, concurrent with the United States Court of Federal Claims, of:

(1)   Any civil action against the United States for the recovery of any internal-revenue tax alleged to have been erroneously or illegally assessed or collected, or any penalty claimed to have been collected without authority or any sum alleged to have been excessive or in any manner wrongfully collected under the internal-revenue laws;

(2)   Any other civil action or claim against the United States, not exceeding $10,000 in amount, founded either upon the Constitution, or any Act of Congress, or any regulation of an executive department, or upon any express or implied contract with the United States, or for liquidated or unliquidated damages in cases not sounding in tort * * *. For the purpose of this paragraph, an express or implied contract with the Army and Air Force Exchange Service, Navy Exchanges, Marine Corps Exchanges, Coast Guard Exchanges, or Exchange Councils of the National Aeronautics and Space Administration shall be considered an express or implied contract with the United States.

(b)(1)   Subject to the provisions of chapter 171 of this title, the district courts, together with the United States District Court for the District of the Canal Zone and the District Court of the Virgin Islands, shall have exclusive jurisdiction of civil actions on claims against the United States for money damages, accruing on and after January 1, 1945, for injury or loss of property, or personal injury or death caused by the negligent or wrongful act of omission of any employee of the Government while acting within the scope of his office or employment, under circumstances where the United States, if a private person, would be liable to the claimant in accordance with the law of the place where the act or omission occurred.

(2)   No person convicted of a felony who is incarcerated * * * may bring a civil action against the United States or an agency, officer, or employee of the Government, for mental or emotional injury suffered while in custody without a prior showing of physical injury or the commission of a sexual act (as defined in section 2246 of title 18).

(c)   The jurisdiction conferred by this section includes jurisdiction of any set-off, counterclaim, or other claim or demand whatever on the part of the United States against any plaintiff commencing an action under this section.

(d)   The district courts shall not have jurisdiction under this section of any civil action or claim for a pension.

(e)   The district courts shall have original jurisdiction of any civil action against the United States provided in section 6226, 6228(a), 7426, or 7428 * * * or section 7429 of the Internal Revenue Code of 1986.

(f)   The district courts shall have exclusive original jurisdiction of civil actions under section 2409a to quiet title to an estate or interest in real property in which an interest is claimed by the United States.

(g)   * * *

§1359. Parties collusively joined or made

A district court shall not have jurisdiction of a civil action in which any party, by assignment or otherwise, has been improperly or collusively made or joined to invoke the jurisdiction of such court.

§1361. Action to compel an officer of the United States to perform his duty

The district courts shall have original jurisdiction of any action in the nature of mandamus to compel an officer or employee of the United States or any agency thereof to perform a duty owed to the plaintiff.

§1367. Supplemental jurisdiction

(a)   Except as provided in subsections (b) and (c) or as expressly provided otherwise by Federal statute, in any civil action of which the district courts have original jurisdiction, the district courts shall have supplemental jurisdiction over all other claims that are so related to claims in the action within such original jurisdiction that they form part of the same case or controversy under Article III of the United States Constitution. Such supplemental jurisdiction shall include claims that involve the joinder or intervention of additional parties.

(b)   In any civil action of which the district courts have original jurisdiction founded solely on section 1332 of this title, the district courts shall not have supplemental jurisdiction under subsection (a) over claims by plaintiffs against persons made parties under Rule 14, 19, 20, or 24 of the Federal Rules of Civil Procedure, or over claims by persons proposed to be joined as plaintiffs under Rule 19 of such rules, or seeking to intervene as plaintiffs under Rule 24 of such rules, when exercising supplemental jurisdiction over such claims would be inconsistent with the jurisdictional requirements of section 1332.

(c)   The district courts may decline to exercise supplemental jurisdiction over a claim under subsection (a) if—

(1)   the claim raises a novel or complex issue of State law,

(2)   the claim substantially predominates over the claim or claims over which the district court has original jurisdiction,

(3)   the district court has dismissed all claims over which it has original jurisdiction, or

(4)   in exceptional circumstances there are other compelling reasons for declining jurisdiction.

(d)   The period of limitations for any claim asserted under subsection (a), and for any other claim in the same action that is voluntarily dismissed at the same time as or after the dismissal of the claim under subsection (a), shall be tolled while the claim is pending and for a period of 30 days after it is dismissed unless State law provides for a longer tolling period.

(e)   As used in this section, the term "State" includes the District of Columbia, the Commonwealth of Puerto Rico, and any territory or possession of the United States.

§ 1369. Multiparty, multiforum jurisdiction

(a) Subject-Matter Jurisdiction.

(a) IN GENERAL.—The district courts shall have original jurisdiction of any civil action involving minimal diversity between adverse parties that arises from a single accident, where at least 75 natural persons have died in the accident at a discrete location, if—

(1) a defendant resides in a State and a substantial part of accident took place in another State or other location, regardless of whether that defendant is also a resident of the State where a substantial part of the accident took place.

(2) any two defendants reside in different States, regardless of whether such defendants are also residents of the same State or States; or

(3) substantial parts of the accident took place in different States.

(b) LIMITATION OF JURISDICTION OF DISTRICT COURTS.—The district court shall abstain from hearing any civil action described in subsection (a) in which

(1) the substantial majority of all plaintiffs are citizens of a single State of which the primary defendants are also citizens; and

(2) the claims asserted will be governed primarily by the laws of that State.

(c) SPECIAL RULES AND DEFINITIONS.—For purposes of this section—

(1) minimal diversity exists between adverse parties if any party is a citizen of a State and any adverse party is a citizen of another State, a citizen or subject of a foreign state, or a foreign state as defined in section 1603(a) of this title;

(2) a corporation is deemed to be a citizen of any State, and a citizen or subject of any foreign state, in which it is incorporated or has its principal place of business, and is deemed to be a resident of any State in which it is incorporated or licensed to do business or is doing business;

(3) the term "injury" means—

(A) physical harm to a natural person; and

(B) physical damage to or destruction of tangible property, but only if physical harm described in subparagraph (A) exists;

(4) the term "accident" means a sudden accident, or a natural event culminating in an accident, that results in death incurred at a discrete location by at least 75 natural persons; and

(5) the term "State" includes the District of Columbia, the Commonwealth of Puerto Rico, and any territory or possession of the United States.

(d) INTERVENING PARTIES.—In any action in a district court which is or could have been brought, in whole or in part, under this section, any person with a claim arising from the accident described in subsection (a) shall be permitted to intervene as a party plaintiff in the action, even if that person could not have brought an action in a district court as an original matter.

(e) NOTIFICATION OF JUDICIAL PANEL ON MULTIDISTRICT LITIGATION.—A district court in which an action under this section is pending shall promptly notify the judicial panel on multidistrict litigation of the pendency of the action.

§ 1390. Scope

(a) VENUE DEFINED.—As used in this chapter, the term "venue" refers to the geographic specification of the proper court or courts for the litigation of a civil action that is within the subject-matter jurisdiction of the district courts in general, and does not refer to any grant or restriction of subject-matter jurisdiction providing for a civil action to be adjudicated only by the district court for a particular district or districts.

(b) EXCLUSION OF CERTAIN CASES.—Except as otherwise provided by law, this chapter shall not govern the venue of a civil action in which the district court exercises the jurisdiction conferred by section 1333, except that such civil actions may be transferred between district courts as provided in this chapter.

(c) CLARIFICATION REGARDING CASES REMOVED FROM STATE COURTS.—This chapter shall not determine the district court to which a civil action pending in a State court may be removed, but shall govern the transfer of an action so removed as between districts and divisions of the United States district courts.

§ 1391. Venue generally

(a) APPLICABILITY OF SECTION.—Except as otherwise provided by law—

(1) this section shall govern the venue of all civil actions brought in district courts of the United States; and

(2) the proper venue for a civil action shall be determined without regard to whether the action is local or transitory in nature.

(b) VENUE IN GENERAL.—A civil action may be brought in—

(1) a judicial district in which any defendant resides, if all defendants are residents of the State in which the district is located;

(2) a judicial district in which a substantial part of the events or omissions giving rise to the claim occurred, or a substantial part of property that is the subject of the action is situated; or

(3) if there is no district in which an action may otherwise be brought as provided in this section, any judicial district in which any defendant is subject to the court's personal jurisdiction with respect to such action.

(c) RESIDENCY.—For all venue purposes—

(1) a natural person, including an alien lawfully admitted for permanent residence in the United States, shall be deemed to reside in the judicial district in which that person is domiciled;

(2) an entity with the capacity to sue and be sued in its common name under applicable law, whether or not incorporated, shall be deemed to reside, if a defendant, in any judicial district in which such defendant is subject to the court's personal jurisdiction with respect to the civil action in question and, if a plaintiff, only in the judicial district in which it maintains its principal place of business; and

(3) a defendant not resident in the United States may be sued in any judicial district, and the joinder of such a defendant shall be disregarded in determining where the action may be brought with respect to other defendants.

(d) RESIDENCY OF CORPORATIONS IN STATES WITH MULTIPLE DISTRICTS.—For purposes of venue under this chapter, in a State which has more than one judicial district and in which a defendant that is a corporation is subject to personal jurisdiction at the time an action is commenced, such corporation shall be deemed to reside in any district in that State within which its contacts would be sufficient to subject it to personal jurisdiction if that district were a separate State, and, if there is no such district, the corporation shall be deemed to reside in the district within which it has the most significant contacts.

(e) ACTIONS WHERE DEFENDANT IS OFFICER OR EMPLOYEE OF THE UNITED STATES.—

(1) IN GENERAL.—A civil action in which a defendant is an officer or employee of the United States or any agency thereof acting in his official capacity or under color of legal authority, or an agency of the United States, or the United States, may, except as otherwise provided by law, be brought in any judicial district in which (1) a defendant in the action resides, (2) a substantial part of the events or omissions giving rise to the claim occurred, or a substantial part of property that is the subject of the action is situated, or (3) the plaintiff resides if no real property is involved in the action. Additional persons may be joined as parties to any such action in accordance with the Federal Rules of Civil Procedure and with such other venue requirements as would be applicable if the United States or one of its officers, employees, or agencies were not a party.

(2) SERVICE.—The summons and complaint in such an action shall be served as provided by the Federal Rules of Civil Procedure except that the delivery of the summons and complaint to the officer or agency as required by the rules may be made by certified mail beyond the territorial limits of the district in which the action is brought.

(f) CIVIL ACTIONS AGAINST A FOREIGN STATE.—A civil action against a foreign state as defined in section 1603(a) of this title may be brought—

(1) in any judicial district in which a substantial part of the events or omissions giving rise to the claim occurred, or a substantial part of property that is the subject of the action is situated;

(2) in any judicial district in which the vessel or cargo of a foreign state is situated, if the claim is asserted under section 1605(b) of this title;

(3) in any judicial district in which the agency or instrumentality is licensed to do business or is doing business, if the action is brought against an agency or instrumentality of a foreign state as defined in section 1603(b) of this title; or

(4) in the United States District Court for the District of Columbia if the action is brought against a foreign state or political subdivision thereof.

(g) MULTIPARTY, MULTIFORUM LITIGATION.—A civil action in which jurisdiction of the district court is based upon section 1369 of this title may be brought in any district in which any defendant resides or in which a substantial part of the accident giving rise to the action took place.

§ 1397. Interpleader

Any civil action of interpleader or in the nature of interpleader under section 1335 of this title may be brought in the judicial district in which one or more of the claimants reside.

§ 1400. Patents and copyrights, mask works and designs

(a) Civil actions, suits, or proceedings arising under any Act of Congress relating to copyrights or exclusive rights in mask works or designs may be instituted in the district in which the defendant or his agent resides or may be found.

(b) Any civil action for patent infringement may be brought in the judicial district where the defendant resides, or where the defendant has committed acts of infringement and has a regular and established place of business.

§ 1401. Stockholder's derivative action

Any civil action by a stockholder on behalf of his corporation may be prosecuted in any judicial district where the corporation might have sued the same defendants.

§ 1402. United States as defendant

(a) Any civil action in a district court against the United States under subsection (a) of section 1346 of this title may be prosecuted only:

(1)   Except as provided in paragraph (2), in the judicial district where the plaintiff resides;

(2)   In the case of a civil action by a corporation under paragraph (1) of subsection (a) of section 1346, in the judicial district in which is located the principal place of business or principal office or agency of the corporation; or if it has no principal place of business or principal office or agency in any judicial district (A) in the judicial district in which is located the office to which was made the return of the tax in respect of which the claim is made, or (B) if no return was made, in the judicial district in which lies the District of Columbia. Notwithstanding the foregoing provisions of this paragraph a district court, for the convenience of the parties and witnesses, in the interest of justice, may transfer any such action to any other district or division.

(b)   Any civil action on a tort claim against the United States under subsection (b) of section 1346 of this title may be prosecuted only in the judicial district where the plaintiff resides or wherein the act or omission complained of occurred.

(c)   Any civil action against the United States under subsection (e) of section 1346 of this title may be prosecuted only in the judicial district where the property is situated at the time of levy, or if no levy is made, in the judicial district in which the event occurred which gave rise to the cause of action.

(d)   Any civil action under section 2409a to quiet title to an estate or interest in real property in which an interest is claimed by the United States shall be brought in the district court of the district where the property is located or, if located in different districts, in any of such districts.

§ 1404.   Change of venue

(a)   For the convenience of parties and witnesses, in the interest of justice, a district court may transfer any civil action to any other district or division where it might have been brought or to any district or division to which all parties have consented.

* * *

Comparative State Provision

Wisconsin Statutes Annotated § 801.63

(1)   **Stay on initiative of parties.** If a court of this state, on motion of any party, finds that trial of an action pending before it should as a matter of substantial justice be tried in a forum outside this state, the court may in conformity with sub. (3) enter an order to stay further proceedings on the action in this state. A moving party under this subsection must stipulate consent to suit in the alternative forum and waive right to rely on statutes of limitation which may have run in the alternative forum after commencement of the action in this state. A stay order may be granted although the action could not have been commenced in the alternative forum without consent of the moving party.

(2)   **Time for filing and hearing motion.** The motion to stay the proceedings shall be filed prior to or with the answer unless the motion is to stay proceedings on a cause raised by counterclaim, in which instance the motion shall be filed prior to or with the reply. The issues raised by this motion shall be tried to the court in advance of any issue going to the merits of the action and shall be joined with objections, if any, raised by answer or motion pursuant to s. 802.06(2). The court shall find separately on each issue so tried and these findings shall be set forth in a single order.

(3)   **Scope of trial court discretion on motion to stay proceedings.** The decision on any timely motion to stay proceedings pursuant to sub. (1) is within the discretion of the court in which the action is pending. In the exercise of that discretion the court may appropriately consider such factors as:

(a)   Amenability to personal jurisdiction in this state and in any alternative forum of the parties to the action;

(b)   Convenience to the parties and witnesses of trial in this state and in any alternative forum;

(c)   Differences in conflict of law rules applicable in this state and in any alternative forum; or

(d)   Any other factors having substantial bearing upon the selection of a convenient, reasonable and fair place of trial.

(4)   Subsequent modification of order to stay proceedings. Jurisdiction of the court continues over the parties to a proceeding in which a stay has been ordered under this section until a period of 5 years has elapsed since the last order affecting the stay was entered in the court. At any time during which jurisdiction of the court continues over the parties to the proceedings, the court may, on motion and notice to the parties, subsequently modify the stay order and take any further action in the proceeding as the interests of justice require. When jurisdiction of the court over the parties and the proceeding terminates by reason of the lapse of 5 years following the last court order in the action, the clerk of the court in which the stay was granted shall without notice enter an order dismissing the action.

* * *

§ 1406. Cure or waiver of defects

(a)   The district court of a district in which is filed a case laying venue in the wrong division or district shall dismiss, or if it be in the interest of justice, transfer such case to any district or division in which it could have been brought.

(b)   Nothing in this chapter shall impair the jurisdiction of a district court of any matter involving a party who does not interpose timely and sufficient objection to the venue.

* * *

Comparative State Provision

Illinois Compiled Statutes ch. 735, 5/2–104(a), (b)

(a)   No order or judgment is void because rendered in the wrong venue, except in case of judgment by confession as provided in subsection (c) of Section 2–1301 of this Act. No action shall abate or be dismissed because commenced in the wrong venue if there is a proper venue to which the cause may be transferred.

(b)   All objections of improper venue are waived by a defendant unless a motion to transfer to a proper venue is made by the defendant on or before the date upon which he or she is required to appear or within any further time that may be granted him or her to answer or move with respect to the complaint, except that if a defendant upon whose residence venue depends is dismissed upon motion of plaintiff, a remaining defendant may promptly move for transfer as though the dismissed defendant had not been a party.

§ 1407. Multidistrict litigation

[See 28 U.S.C. § 1332(d)(11)(C), supra, limiting transfer under § 1407 in "mass actions."]

(a)   When civil actions involving one or more common questions of fact are pending in different districts, such actions may be transferred to any district for coordinated or consolidated pretrial proceedings. Such transfers shall be made by the judicial panel on multidistrict litigation authorized by this section upon its determination that transfers for such proceedings will be for the convenience of parties and witnesses and will promote the just and efficient conduct of such actions. Each action so transferred shall be remanded by the panel at or before the conclusion of such pretrial proceedings to the district from which it was transferred unless it shall have been previously terminated: *Provided, however,* That the panel may separate any claim, crossclaim, counter-claim, or third-party claim and remand any of such claims before the remainder of the action is remanded.

(b)   Such coordinated or consolidated pretrial proceedings shall be conducted by a judge or judges to whom such actions are assigned by the judicial panel on multidistrict litigation. For this purpose, upon request of the panel, a circuit judge or a district judge may be designated and assigned temporarily for service in the transferee district by the Chief Justice of the United States or the chief judge of the circuit, as may be required, in accordance with the provisions of chapter 13 of this title. With the consent of the transferee district court, such actions may be assigned by the panel to a judge or judges of such district. The judge or judges to whom such actions are assigned, the members of the judicial panel on multidistrict litigation, and other circuit and district judges designated when needed by the panel may exercise the powers of a district judge in any district for the purpose of conducting pretrial depositions in such coordinated or consolidated pretrial proceedings.

(c) Proceedings for the transfer of an action under this section may be initiated by—

(i) the judicial panel on multidistrict litigation upon its own initiative, or

(ii) motion filed with the panel by a party in any action in which transfer for coordinated or consolidated pretrial proceedings under this section may be appropriate. A copy of such motion shall be filed in the district court in which the moving party's action is pending.

The panel shall give notice to the parties in all actions in which transfers for coordinated or consolidated pretrial proceedings are contemplated, and such notice shall specify the time and place of any hearing to determine whether such transfer shall be made. Orders of the panel to set a hearing and other orders of the panel issued prior to the order either directing or denying transfer shall be filed in the office of the clerk of the district court in which a transfer hearing is to be or has been held. The panel's order of transfer shall be based upon a record of such hearing at which material evidence may be offered by any party to an action pending in any district that would be affected by the proceedings under this section, and shall be supported by findings of fact and conclusions of law based upon such record. Orders of transfer and such other orders as the panel may make thereafter shall be filed in the office of the clerk of the district court of the transferee district and shall be effective when thus filed. The clerk of the transferee district court shall forthwith transmit a certified copy of the panel's order to transfer to the clerk of the district court from which the action is being transferred. An order denying transfer shall be filed in each district wherein there is a case pending in which the motion for transfer has been made.

(d) The judicial panel on multidistrict litigation shall consist of seven circuit and district judges designated from time to time by the Chief Justice of the United States, no two of whom shall be from the same circuit. The concurrence of four members shall be necessary to any action by the panel.

(e) No proceedings for review of any order of the panel may be permitted except by extraordinary writ pursuant to the provisions of title 28, section 1651, United States Code. Petitions for an extraordinary writ to review an order of the panel to set a transfer hearing and other orders of the panel issued prior to the order either directing or denying transfer shall be filed only in the court of appeals having jurisdiction over the district in which a hearing is to be or has been held. Petitions for an extraordinary writ to review an order to transfer or orders subsequent to transfer shall be filed only in the court of appeals having jurisdiction over the transferee district. There shall be no appeal or review of an order of the panel denying a motion to transfer for consolidated or coordinated proceedings.

(f) The panel may prescribe rules for the conduct of its business not inconsistent with Acts of Congress and the Federal Rules of Civil Procedure.

(g) Nothing in this section shall apply to any action in which the United States is a complainant arising under the antitrust laws. "Antitrust laws" as used herein include those acts referred to in the Act of October 15, 1914, as amended (38 Stat. 730; 15 U.S.C. 12), and also include the Act of June 19, 1936 (49 Stat. 1526; 15 U.S.C. 13, 13a, and 13b) and the Act of September 26, 1914, as added March 21, 1938 (52 Stat. 116, 117; 15 U.S.C. 56); but shall not include section 4A of the Act of October 15, 1914, as added July 7, 1955 (69 Stat. 282; 15 U.S.C. 15a).

(h) Notwithstanding the provisions of section 1404 or subsection (f) of this section, the judicial panel on multidistrict litigation may consolidate and transfer with or without the consent of the parties, for both pretrial purposes and for trial, any action brought under section 4C of the Clayton Act.

§ 1441. Removal of civil actions

[See 28 U.S.C. § 1453, infra, regarding removal of class actions.]

(a)   GENERALLY.—Except as otherwise expressly provided by Act of Congress, any civil action brought in a State court of which the district courts of the United States have original jurisdiction, may be removed by the defendant or the defendants, to the district court of the United States for the district and division embracing the place where such action is pending.

(b)   REMOVAL BASED ON DIVERSITY OF CITIZENSHIP.—(1) In determining whether a civil action is removable on the basis of the jurisdiction under section 1332(a) of this title, the citizenship of defendants sued under fictitious names shall be disregarded.

(2)   A civil action otherwise removable solely on the basis of the jurisdiction under section 1332(a) of this title may not be removed if any of the parties in interest properly joined and served as defendants is a citizen of the State in which such action is brought.

(c)   JOINDER OF FEDERAL LAW CLAIMS AND STATE LAW CLAIMS.—(1) If a civil action includes—

(A)   a claim arising under the Constitution, laws, or treaties of the United States (within the meaning of section 1331 of this title), and

(B)   a claim not within the original or supplemental jurisdiction of the district court or a claim that has been made nonremovable by statute,

the entire action may be removed if the action would be removable without the inclusion of the claim described in subparagraph (B).

(2)   Upon removal of an action described in paragraph (1), the district court shall sever from the action all claims described in paragraph (1)(B) and shall remand the severed claims to the State court from which the action was removed. Only defendants against whom a claim described in paragraph (1)(A) has been asserted are required to join in or consent to the removal under paragraph (1).

(d)   ACTIONS AGAINST FOREIGN STATES.—Any civil action brought in a State court against a foreign state as defined in section 1603(a) of this title may be removed by the foreign state to the district court of the United States for the district and division embracing the place where such action is pending. Upon removal the action shall be tried by the court without jury. Where removal is based upon this subsection, the time limitations of section 1446(b) of this chapter may be enlarged at any time for cause shown.

(e)   MULTIPARTY, MULTIFORUM JURISDICTION.—(1) Notwithstanding the provisions of subsection (b) of this section, a defendant in a civil action in a State court may remove the action to the district court of the United States for the district and division embracing the place where the action is pending if—

(A)   the action could have been brought in a United States district court under section 1369 of this title; or

(B)   the defendant is a party to an action which is or could have been brought, in whole or in part, under section 1369 in a United States district court and arises from the same accident as the action in State court, even if the action to be removed could not have been brought in a district court as an original matter.

The removal of an action under this subsection shall be made in accordance with section 1446 of this title, except that a notice of removal may also be filed before trial of the action in State court within 30 days after the date on which the defendant first becomes a party to an action under section 1369 in a United States district court that arises from the same accident as the action in State court, or at a later time with leave of the district court.

(2)   Whenever an action is removed under this subsection and the district court to which it is removed or transferred under section 1407(j) has made a liability determination requiring further proceedings as to damages, the district court shall remand the action to the State court from which it

had been removed for the determination of damages, unless the court finds that, for the convenience of parties and witnesses and in the interest of justice, the action should be retained for the determination of damages. [Author's note: Section 1407 does not contain subsection (j).]

(3) Any remand under paragraph (2) shall not be effective until 60 days after the district court has issued an order determining liability and has certified its intention to remand the removed action for the determination of damages. An appeal with respect to the liability determination and the choice of law determination of the district court may be taken during that 60-day period to the court of appeals with appellate jurisdiction over the district court. In the event a party files such an appeal, the remand shall not be effective until the appeal has been finally disposed of. Once the remand has become effective, the liability determination shall not be subject to further review by appeal or otherwise.

(4) Any decision under this subsection concerning remand for the determination of damages shall not be reviewable by appeal or otherwise.

(5) An action removed under this subsection shall be deemed to be an action under section 1369 and an action in which jurisdiction is based on section 1369 of this title for purposes of this section and sections 1407, 1697, and 1785 of this title.

(6) Nothing in this subsection shall restrict the authority of the district court to transfer or dismiss an action on the ground of inconvenient forum.

(f) DERIVATIVE REMOVAL JURISDICTION.—The court to which a civil action is removed under this section is not precluded from hearing and determining any claim in such civil action because the State court from which such civil action is removed did not have jurisdiction over that claim.

§ 1442. Federal officers sued or prosecuted

(a) A civil action or criminal prosecution that is commenced in a State court that is against or directed to any of the following persons may be removed by them to the district court of the United States for the district and division embracing the place wherein it is pending:

(1) The United States or any agency thereof or any officer (or any person acting under that officer) of the United States or of any agency thereof, in an official on individual capacity for, or relating to, any act under color of such office or on account of any right, title or authority claimed under any Act of Congress for the apprehension or punishment of criminals or the collection of the revenue.

(2) A property holder whose title is derived from any such officer, where such action or prosecution affects the validity of any law of the United States.

(3) Any officer of the courts of the United States, for or relating to any Act under color of office or in the performance of his duties.

(4) Any officer of either House of Congress, for or relating to any act in the discharge of his official duty under an order of such House.

(b) A personal action commenced in any State court by an alien against any citizen of a State who is, or at the time the alleged action accrued was, a civil officer of the United States and is a nonresident of such State, wherein jurisdiction is obtained by the State court by personal service of process, may be removed by the defendant to the district court of the United States for the district and division in which the defendant was served with process.

(c) * * *

(d) In this section, the following definitions apply:

(1) The terms "civil action" and "criminal prosecution" include any proceeding (whether or not ancillary to another proceeding) to the extent that in such proceeding a judicial order, including a subpoena for testimony or documents, is sought or issued. If removal is sought for a

proceeding described in the previous sentence, and there is no other basis for removal, only that proceeding may be removed to the district court.

* * *

§ 1443. Civil rights cases

Any of the following civil actions or criminal prosecutions, commenced in a State court may be removed by the defendant to the district court of the United States for the district and division embracing the place wherein it is pending:

(1) Against any person who is denied or cannot enforce in the courts of such State a right under any law providing for the equal civil rights of citizens of the United States, or of all persons within the jurisdiction thereof;

(2) For any act under color of authority derived from any law providing for equal rights, or for refusing to do any act on the ground that it would be inconsistent with such law.

§ 1445. Nonremovable actions

(a) A civil action in any State court against a railroad or its receivers or trustees, arising under * * * [the Federal Employers' Liability Act, 45 U.S.C. §§ 51–60], may not be removed to any district court of the United States.

* * *

(c) A civil action in any State court arising under the workmen's compensation laws of such State may not be removed to any district court of the United States.

(d) A civil action in any State court arising under section 40302 of the Violence Against Women Act of 1994 may not be removed to any district court of the United States.

§ 1446. Procedure for removal of civil actions

(a) GENERALLY.—A defendant or defendants desiring to remove any civil action from a State court shall file in the district court of the United States for the district and division within which such action is pending a notice of removal signed pursuant to Rule 11 of the Federal Rules of Civil Procedure and containing a short and plain statement of the grounds for removal, together with a copy of all process, pleadings, and orders served upon such defendant or defendants in such action.

(b) REQUIREMENTS; GENERALLY.—(1) The notice of removal of a civil action or proceeding shall be filed within 30 days after the receipt by the defendant, through service or otherwise, of a copy of the initial pleading setting forth the claim for relief upon which such action or proceeding is based, or within 30 days after the service of summons upon the defendant if such initial pleading has then been filed in court and is not required to be served on the defendant, whichever period is shorter.

(2)(A) When a civil action is removed solely under section 1441(a), all defendants who have been properly joined and served must join in or consent to the removal of the action.

(B) Each defendant shall have 30 days after receipt by or service on that defendant of the initial pleading or summons described in paragraph (1) to file the notice of removal.

(C) If defendants are served at different times, and a later-served defendant files a notice of removal, any earlier-served defendant may consent to the removal even though that earlier-served defendant did not previously initiate or consent to removal.

(3) Except as provided in subsection (c), if the case stated by the initial pleading is not removable, a notice of removal may be filed within thirty days after receipt by the defendant, through service or otherwise, of a copy of an amended pleading, motion, order or other paper from which it may first be ascertained that the case is one which is or has become removable.

(c) REQUIREMENTS; REMOVAL BASED ON DIVERSITY OF CITIZENSHIP.—(1) A case may not be removed under subsection (b)(3) on the basis of jurisdiction conferred by section 1332 more than 1 year after commencement of the action, unless the district court finds that the plaintiff has acted in bad faith in order to prevent a defendant from removing the action.

(2) If removal of a civil action is sought on the basis of the jurisdiction conferred by section 1332(a), the sum demanded in good faith in the initial pleading shall be deemed to be the amount in controversy, except that—

(A) the notice of removal may assert the amount in controversy if the initial pleading seeks—

(i) nonmonetary relief; or

(ii) a money judgment, but the State practice either does not permit demand for a specific sum or permits recovery of damages in excess of the amount demanded; and

(B) removal of the action is proper on the basis of an amount in controversy asserted under subparagraph (A) if the district court finds, by the preponderance of the evidence, that the amount in controversy exceeds the amount specified in section 1332(a).

(3)(A) If the case stated by the initial pleading is not removable solely because the amount in controversy does not exceed the amount specified in section 1332(a), information relating to the amount in controversy in the record of the State proceeding, or in responses to discovery, shall be treated as an 'other paper' under subsection (b)(3).

(B) If the notice of removal is filed more than 1 year after commencement of the action and the district court finds that the plaintiff deliberately failed to disclose the actual amount in controversy to prevent removal, that finding shall be deemed bad faith under paragraph (1).

(d) NOTICE TO ADVERSE PARTIES AND STATE COURT.—Promptly after the filing of such notice of removal of a civil action the defendant or defendants shall give written notice thereof to all adverse parties and shall file a copy of the notice with the clerk of such State court, which shall effect removal and the State court shall proceed no further unless and until the case is remanded.

(e) * * *

(f) * * *

(g) Where the civil action or criminal prosecution that is removable under section 1442(a) is a proceeding in which a judicial order for testimony or documents is sought or issued or sought to be enforced, the 30-day requirement of subsections (b) and (c) is satisfied if the person or entity desiring to remove the proceeding files the notice of removal not later than 30 days after receiving, through service, notice of any such proceeding.

§ 1447. Procedure after removal generally

(a) In any case removed from a State court, the district court may issue all necessary orders and process to bring before it all proper parties whether served by process issued by the State court or otherwise.

(b) It may require the removing party to file with its clerk copies of all records and proceedings in such State court or may cause the same to be brought before it by writ of certiorari issued to such State court.

(c) A motion to remand the case on the basis of any defect other than lack of subject matter jurisdiction must be made within 30 days after the filing of the notice of removal under section 1446(a). If at any time before final judgment it appears that the district court lacks subject matter jurisdiction, the case shall be remanded. An order remanding the case may require payment of just costs and any actual expenses, including attorney fees, incurred as a result of the removal. A certified copy of the order of remand shall be mailed by the clerk to the clerk of the State court. The State court may thereupon proceed with such case.

(d) An order remanding a case to the State court from which it was removed is not reviewable on appeal or otherwise, except that an order remanding a case to the State court from which it was removed pursuant to section 1442 or 1443 of this title shall be reviewable by appeal or otherwise.

(e) If after removal the plaintiff seeks to join additional defendants whose joinder would destroy subject matter jurisdiction, the court may deny joinder, or permit joinder and remand the action to the State court.

§ 1453. Removal of class actions

(a) Definitions.—In this section, the terms "class", "class action", "class certification order", and "class member" shall have the meanings given such terms under section 1332(d)(1).

(b) In General.—A class action may be removed to a district court of the United States in accordance with section 1446 (except that the 1-year limitation under section 1446(c)(1) shall not apply), without regard to whether any defendant is a citizen of the State in which the action is brought, except that such action may be removed by any defendant without the consent of all defendants.

(c) Review of Remand Orders.—

(1) In general.—Section 1447 shall apply to any removal of a case under this section, except that notwithstanding section 1447(d), a court of appeals may accept an appeal from an order of a district court granting or denying a motion to remand a class action to the State court from which it was removed if application is made to the court of appeals not less than 10 days after entry of the order.

(2) Time period for judgment.—If the court of appeals accepts an appeal under paragraph (1), the court shall complete all action on such appeal, including rendering judgment, not later than 60 days after the date on which such appeal was filed, unless an extension is granted under paragraph (3).

(3) Extension of time period.—The court of appeals may grant an extension of the 60-day period described in paragraph (2) if—

(A) all parties to the proceeding agree to such extension, for any period of time; or

(B) such extension is for good cause shown and in the interests of justice, for a period not to exceed 10 days.

(4) Denial of appeal.—If a final judgment on the appeal under paragraph (1) is not issued before the end of the period described in paragraph (2), including any extension under paragraph (3), the appeal shall be denied.

(d) Exception.—This section shall not apply to any class action that solely involves—

(1) a claim concerning a covered security as defined under section 16(f)(3) of the Securities Act of 1933 (15 U.S.C. 78p(f)(3)) and section 28(f)(5)(E) of the Securities Exchange Act of 1934 (15 U.S.C. 78bb(f)(5)(E));

(2) a claim that relates to the internal affairs or governance of a corporation or other form of business enterprise and arises under or by virtue of the laws of the State in which such corporation or business enterprise is incorporated or organized; or

(3) a claim that relates to the rights, duties (including fiduciary duties), and obligations relating to or created by or pursuant to any security (as defined under section 2(a)(1) of the Securities Act of 1933 (15 U.S.C. 77b(a)(1)) and the regulations issued thereunder).

§ 1631. Transfer to cure want of jurisdiction

Whenever a civil action is filed in a court as defined in section 610 of this title or an appeal, including a petition for review of administrative action, is noticed for or filed with such a court and that court finds that there is a want of jurisdiction, the court shall, if it is in the interest of justice, transfer such action or appeal to any other such court in which the action or appeal could have been brought at the time it was filed or noticed, and the action or appeal shall proceed as if it had been filed in or noticed for the court to which it is transferred on the date upon which it was actually filed in or noticed for the court from which it is transferred.

§ 1651. Writs

(a)   The Supreme Court and all courts established by Act of Congress may issue all writs necessary or appropriate in aid of their respective jurisdictions and agreeable to the usages and principles of law.

(b)   An alternative writ or rule nisi may be issued by a justice or judge of a court which has jurisdiction.

§ 1652. State laws as rules of decision

The laws of the several states, except where the Constitution or treaties of the United States or Acts of Congress otherwise require or provide, shall be regarded as rules of decision in civil actions in the courts of the United States, in cases where they apply.

Related State Provision

Illinois Supreme Court Rule 20

(a)   **Certification.** When it shall appear to the Supreme Court of the United States, or to the United States Court of Appeals for the Seventh Circuit, that there are involved in any proceeding before it questions as to the law of this State, which may be determinative of the said cause, and there are no controlling precedents in the decisions of this court, such court may certify such questions of the laws of this State to this court for instructions concerning such questions of State law, which certificate this court, by written opinion, may answer.

(b)   **Contents of Certification Order.** A certification order shall contain:

(1)   the questions of law to be answered; and

(2)   a statement of all facts relevant to the questions certified and showing fully the nature of the controversy in which the questions arose.

(c)   **Record Before Certifying Court.** This court may require the original or copies of all or of any portion of the record before the certifying court to be filed with it, if, in the opinion of this court, the record or a portion thereof may be necessary in answering the questions.

* * *

§ 1653. Amendment of pleadings to show jurisdiction

Defective allegations of jurisdiction may be amended, upon terms, in the trial or appellate courts.

§ 1655. Lien enforcement; absent defendants

In an action in a district court to enforce any lien upon or claim to, or to remove any incumbrance or lien or cloud upon the title to, real or personal property within the district, where any defendant cannot be served within the State, or does not voluntarily appear, the court may order the absent defendant to appear or plead by a day certain.

Such order shall be served on the absent defendant personally if practicable, wherever found, and also upon the person or persons in possession or charge of such property, if any. Where personal service is not practicable, the order shall be published as the court may direct, not less than once a week for six consecutive weeks.

If an absent defendant does not appear or plead within the time allowed, the court may proceed as if the absent defendant had been served with process within the State, but any adjudication shall, as regards the absent defendant without appearance, affect only the property which is the subject of the action. When a part of the property is within another district, but within the same state, such action may be brought in either district.

Any defendant not so personally notified may, at any time within one year after final judgment, enter his appearance, and thereupon the court shall set aside the judgment and permit such defendant to plead on payment of such costs as the court deems just.

§ 1658. Time limitations on the commencement of civil actions arising under Acts of Congress

(a)   Except as otherwise provided by law, a civil action arising under an Act of Congress enacted after the date of the enactment of this section may not be commenced later than 4 years after the cause of action accrues.

* * *

§ 1693. Place of arrest in civil action

Except as otherwise provided by Act of Congress, no person shall be arrested in one district for trial in another in any civil action in a district court.

§ 1694. Patent infringement action

In a patent infringement action commenced in a district where the defendant is not a resident but has a regular and established place of business, service of process, summons or subpoena upon such defendant may be made upon his agent or agents conducting such business.

§ 1695. Stockholder's derivative action

Process in a stockholder's action in behalf of his corporation may be served upon such corporation in any district where it is organized or licensed to do business or is doing business.

§ 1697. Service in multiparty, multiforum actions

When the jurisdiction of the district court is based in whole or in part upon section 1369 of this title, process, other than subpoenas, may be served at any place within the United States, or anywhere outside the United States if otherwise permitted by law.

§ 1711. Definitions

In this chapter [for purposes of §§ 1712–1715]:

(1)   Class.—The term "class" means all of the class members in a class action.

(2)   Class action.—The term "class action" means any civil action filed in a district court of the United States under rule 23 of the Federal Rules of Civil Procedure or any civil action that is removed to a district court of the United States that was originally filed under a State statute or rule of judicial procedure authorizing an action to be brought by 1 or more representatives as a class action.

(3)   Class counsel.—The term "class counsel" means the persons who serve as the attorneys for the class members in a proposed or certified class action.

(4) Class members.—The term "class members" means the persons (named or unnamed) who fall within the definition of the proposed or certified class in a class action.

(5) Plaintiff class action.—The term "plaintiff class action" means a class action in which class members are plaintiffs.

(6) Proposed settlement.—The term "proposed settlement" means an agreement regarding a class action that is subject to court approval and that, if approved, would be binding on some or all class members.

§ 1712. Coupon settlements

(a) Contingent fees in coupon settlements.—If a proposed settlement in a class action provides for a recovery of coupons to a class member, the portion of any attorney's fee award to class counsel that is attributable to the award of the coupons shall be based on the value to class members of the coupons that are redeemed.

(b) Other attorney's fee awards in coupon settlements.—

(1) In general.—If a proposed settlement in a class action provides for a recovery of coupons to class members, and a portion of the recovery of the coupons is not used to determine the attorney's fee to be paid to class counsel, any attorney's fee award shall be based upon the amount of time class counsel reasonably expended working on the action.

(2) Court approval.—Any attorney's fee under this subsection shall be subject to approval by the court and shall include an appropriate attorney's fee, if any, for obtaining equitable relief, including an injunction, if applicable. Nothing in this subsection shall be construed to prohibit application of a lodestar with a multiplier method of determining attorney's fees.

(c) Attorney's fee awards calculated on a mixed basis in coupon settlements.—If a proposed settlement in a class action provides for an award of coupons to class members and also provides for equitable relief, including injunctive relief—

(1) that portion of the attorney's fee to be paid to class counsel that is based upon a portion of the recovery of the coupons shall be calculated in accordance with subsection (a); and

(2) that portion of the attorney's fee to be paid to class counsel that is not based upon a portion of the recovery of the coupons shall be calculated in accordance with subsection (b).

(d) Settlement valuation expertise.—In a class action involving the awarding of coupons, the court may, in its discretion upon the motion of a party, receive expert testimony from a witness qualified to provide information on the actual value to the class members of the coupons that are redeemed.

(e) Judicial scrutiny of coupon settlements.—In a proposed settlement under which class members would be awarded coupons, the court may approve the proposed settlement only after a hearing to determine whether, and making a written finding that, the settlement is fair, reasonable, and adequate for class members. The court, in its discretion, may also require that a proposed settlement agreement provide for the distribution of a portion of the value of unclaimed coupons to 1 or more charitable or governmental organizations, as agreed to by the parties. The distribution and redemption of any proceeds under this subsection shall not be used to calculate attorneys' fees under this section.

§ 1713. Protection against loss by class members

The court may approve a proposed settlement under which any class member is obligated to pay sums to class counsel that would result in a net loss to the class member only if the court makes a written finding that nonmonetary benefits to the class member substantially outweigh the monetary loss.

§ 1714. Protection against discrimination based on geographic location

The court may not approve a proposed settlement that provides for the payment of greater sums to some class members than to others solely on the basis that the class members to whom the greater sums are to be paid are located in closer geographic proximity to the court.

§ 1715. Notifications to appropriate Federal and State officials

(a) Definitions.—

(1) Appropriate federal official.—In this section, the term "appropriate Federal official" means—

(A) the Attorney General of the United States; or

(B) in any case in which the defendant is a Federal depository institution, a State depository institution, a depository institution holding company, a foreign bank, or a nondepository institution subsidiary of the foregoing (as such terms are defined in section 3 of the Federal Deposit Insurance Act (12 U.S.C. 1813)), the person who has the primary Federal regulatory or supervisory responsibility with respect to the defendant, if some or all of the matters alleged in the class action are subject to regulation or supervision by that person.

(2) Appropriate state official.—In this section, the term "appropriate State official" means the person in the State who has the primary regulatory or supervisory responsibility with respect to the defendant, or who licenses or otherwise authorizes the defendant to conduct business in the State, if some or all of the matters alleged in the class action are subject to regulation by that person. If there is no primary regulator, supervisor, or licensing authority, or the matters alleged in the class action are not subject to regulation or supervision by that person, then the appropriate State official shall be the State attorney general.

(b) In general.—Not later than 10 days after a proposed settlement of a class action is filed in court, each defendant that is participating in the proposed settlement shall serve upon the appropriate State official of each State in which a class member resides and the appropriate Federal official, a notice of the proposed settlement consisting of—

(1) a copy of the complaint and any materials filed with the complaint and any amended complaints (except such materials shall not be required to be served if such materials are made electronically available through the Internet and such service includes notice of how to electronically access such material);

(2) notice of any scheduled judicial hearing in the class action;

(3) any proposed or final notification to class members of—

(A) (i) the members' rights to request exclusion from the class action; or

(ii) if no right to request exclusion exists, a statement that no such right exists; and

(B) a proposed settlement of a class action;

(4) any proposed or final class action settlement;

(5) any settlement or other agreement contemporaneously made between class counsel and counsel for the defendants;

(6) any final judgment or notice of dismissal;

(7) (A) if feasible, the names of class members who reside in each State and the estimated proportionate share of the claims of such members to the entire settlement to that State's appropriate State official; or

(B) if the provision of information under subparagraph (A) is not feasible, a reasonable estimate of the number of class members residing in each State and the estimated proportionate share of the claims of such members to the entire settlement; and

(8) any written judicial opinion relating to the materials described under subparagraphs (3) through (6).

(c) Depository institutions notification.—

(1) Federal and other depository institutions.—In any case in which the defendant is a Federal depository institution, a depository institution holding company, a foreign bank, or a non-depository institution subsidiary of the foregoing, the notice requirements of this section are satisfied by serving the notice required under subsection (b) upon the person who has the primary Federal regulatory or supervisory responsibility with respect to the defendant, if some or all of the matters alleged in the class action are subject to regulation or supervision by that person.

(2) State depository institutions.—In any case in which the defendant is a State depository institution (as that term is defined in section 3 of the Federal Deposit Insurance Act (12 U.S.C. 1813)), the notice requirements of this section are satisfied by serving the notice required under subsection (b) upon the State bank supervisor (as that term is defined in section 3 of the Federal Deposit Insurance Act (12 U.S.C. 1813)) of the State in which the defendant is incorporated or chartered, if some or all of the matters alleged in the class action are subject to regulation or supervision by that person, and upon the appropriate Federal official.

(d) Final approval.—An order giving final approval of a proposed settlement may not be issued earlier than 90 days after the later of the dates on which the appropriate Federal official and the appropriate State official are served with the notice required under subsection (b).

(e) Noncompliance if notice not provided.—

(1) In general.—A class member may refuse to comply with and may choose not to be bound by a settlement agreement or consent decree in a class action if the class member demonstrates that the notice required under subsection (b) has not been provided.

(2) Limitation.—A class member may not refuse to comply with or to be bound by a settlement agreement or consent decree under paragraph (1) if the notice required under subsection (b) was directed to the appropriate Federal official and to either the State attorney general or the person that has primary regulatory, supervisory, or licensing authority over the defendant.

(3) Application of rights.—The rights created by this subsection shall apply only to class members or any person acting on a class member's behalf, and shall not be construed to limit any other rights affecting a class member's participation in the settlement.

(f) Rule of construction.—Nothing in this section shall be construed to expand the authority of, or impose any obligations, duties, or responsibilities upon, Federal or State officials.

§ 1738. State and Territorial statutes and judicial proceedings; full faith and credit

The Acts of the legislature of any State, Territory, or Possession of the United States, or copies thereof, shall be authenticated by affixing the seal of such State, Territory or Possession thereto.

The records and judicial proceedings of any court of any such State, Territory or Possession, or copies thereof, shall be proved or admitted in other courts within the United States and its Territories and Possessions by the attestation of the clerk and seal of the court annexed, if a seal exists, together with a certificate of a judge of the court that the said attestation is in proper form.

Such Acts, records and judicial proceedings or copies thereof, so authenticated, shall have the same full faith and credit in every court within the United States and its Territories and Possessions as they have by law or usage in the courts of such State, Territory or Possession from which they are taken.

§ 1781. Transmittal of letter rogatory or request

(a)   The Department of State has power, directly, or through suitable channels—

(1)   to receive a letter rogatory issued, or request made, by a foreign or international tribunal, to transmit it to the tribunal, officer, or agency in the United States to whom it is addressed, and to receive and return it after execution; and

(2)   to receive a letter rogatory issued, or request made, by a tribunal in the United States, to transmit it to the foreign or international tribunal, officer, or agency to whom it is addressed, and to receive and return it after execution.

(b)   This section does not preclude—

(1)   the transmittal of a letter rogatory or request directly from a foreign or international tribunal to the tribunal, officer, or agency in the United States to whom it is addressed and its return in the same manner; or

(2)   the transmittal of a letter rogatory or request directly from a tribunal in the United States to the foreign or international tribunal, officer, or agency to whom it is addressed and its return in the same manner.

§ 1782. Assistance to foreign and international tribunals and to litigants before such tribunals

(a)   [Subject to any legally applicable privilege] the district court of the district in which a person resides or is found may order him to give his testimony or statement or to produce a document or other thing for use in a proceeding in a foreign or international tribunal * * *. The order may be made pursuant to a letter rogatory issued, or request made, by a foreign or international tribunal or upon the application of any interested person and may direct that the testimony or statement be given, or the document or other thing be produced, before a person appointed by the court. By virtue of his appointment, the person appointed has power to administer any necessary oath and take the testimony or statement. The order may prescribe the practice and procedure, which may be in whole or part the practice and procedure of the foreign country or the international tribunal, for taking the testimony or statement or producing the document or other thing. To the extent that the order does not prescribe otherwise, the testimony or statement shall be taken, and the document or other thing produced, in accordance with the Federal Rules of Civil Procedure.

* * *

Comparative State Provision

Massachusetts General Laws Annotated c. 233, § 45

A person may be summoned and compelled, in like manner and under the same penalties as are provided for a witness before a court, to give his deposition in a cause pending in a court of any other state or government. Such deposition may be taken before a justice of the peace or a notary public in the commonwealth, or before a commissioner appointed under the authority of the state or government in which the action is pending. If the deposition is taken before such commissioner, the witness may be summoned and compelled to appear before him by process from a justice of the peace or a notary public in the commonwealth.

§ 1783. Subpoena of person in foreign country

(a)   A court of the United States may order the issuance of a subpoena requiring the appearance as a witness before it, or before a person or body designated by it, of a national or resident of the United States who is in a foreign country, or requiring the production of a specified document or other thing by him, if the court finds that particular testimony or the production of the document or other thing by him is necessary in the interest of justice, and, in other than a criminal action or proceeding, if the court finds, in addition, that it is not possible to obtain his testimony in admissible form without his personal appearance or to obtain the production of the document or other thing in any other manner.

* * *

§ 1785. Subpoenas in multiparty, multiforum actions

When the jurisdiction of the district court is based in whole or in part upon section 1369 of this title, a subpoena for attendance at a hearing or trial may, if authorized by the court upon motion for good cause shown, and upon such terms and conditions as the court may impose, be served in any place within the United States or anywhere outside the United States if otherwise permitted by law.

§ 1861. Declaration of policy

It is the policy of the United States that all litigants in Federal courts entitled to trial by jury shall have the right to grand and petit juries selected at random from a fair cross section of the community in the district or division wherein the court convenes. It is further the policy of the United States that all citizens shall have the opportunity to be considered for service on grand and petit juries in the district courts of the United States, and shall have an obligation to serve as jurors when summoned for that purpose.

§ 1862. Discrimination prohibited

No citizen shall be excluded from service as a grand or petit juror in the district courts of the United States or in the Court of International Trade on account of race, color, religion, sex, national origin, or economic status.

§ 1863. Plan for random jury selection

(a) Each United States district court shall devise and place into operation a written plan for random selection of grand and petit jurors that shall be designed to achieve the objectives of sections 1861 and 1862 of this title, and that shall otherwise comply with the provisions of this title. The plan shall be placed into operation after approval by a reviewing panel consisting of the members of the judicial council of the circuit and either the chief judge of the district whose plan is being reviewed or such other active district judge of that district as the chief judge of the district may designate. The panel shall examine the plan to ascertain that it complies with the provisions of this title. If the reviewing panel finds that the plan does not comply, the panel shall state the particulars in which the plan fails to comply and direct the district court to present within a reasonable time an alternative plan remedying the defect or defects. Separate plans may be adopted for each division or combination of divisions within a judicial district. The district court may modify a plan at any time and it shall modify the plan when so directed by the reviewing panel. The district court shall promptly notify the panel, the Administrative Office of the United States Courts, and the Attorney General of the United States, of the initial adoption and future modifications of the plan by filing copies therewith. Modifications of the plan made at the instance of the district court shall become effective after approval by the panel. Each district court shall submit a report on the jury selection process within its jurisdiction to the Administrative Office of the United States Courts in such form and at such times as the Judicial Conference of the United States may specify. The Judicial Conference of the United States may, from time to time, adopt rules and regulations governing the provisions and the operation of the plans formulated under this title.

(b) Among other things, such plan shall—

(1) either establish a jury commission, or authorize the clerk of the court, to manage the jury selection process. If the plan establishes a jury commission, the district court shall appoint one citizen to serve with the clerk of the court as the jury commission: *Provided, however,* That

the plan for the District of Columbia may establish a jury commission consisting of three citizens. The citizen jury commissioner shall not belong to the same political party as the clerk serving with him. The clerk or the jury commission, as the case may be, shall act under the supervision and control of the chief judge of the district court or such other judge of the district court as the plan may provide. Each jury commissioner shall, during his tenure in office, reside in the judicial district or division for which he is appointed. Each citizen jury commissioner shall receive compensation to be fixed by the district court plan at a rate not to exceed $50 per day for each day necessarily employed in the performance of his duties, plus reimbursement for travel, subsistence, and other necessary expenses * * *.

(2)   specify whether the names of prospective jurors shall be selected from the voter registration lists or the lists of actual voters of the political subdivisions within the district or division. The plan shall prescribe some other source or sources of names in addition to voter lists where necessary to foster the policy and protect the rights secured by sections 1861 and 1862 of this title. * * *

(3)   specify detailed procedures to be followed by the jury commission or clerk in selecting names from the sources specified in paragraph (2) of this subsection. These procedures shall be designed to ensure the random selection of a fair cross section of the persons residing in the community in the district or division wherein the court convenes. They shall ensure that names of persons residing in each of the counties, parishes, or similar political subdivisions within the judicial district or division are placed in a master jury wheel; and shall insure that each county, parish, or similar political subdivision within the district or division is substantially proportionally represented in the master jury wheel for that judicial district, division, or combination of divisions. For the purposes of determining proportional representation in the master jury wheel, either the number of actual voters at the last general election in each county, parish, or similar political subdivision, or the number of registered voters if registration of voters is uniformly required throughout the district or division, may be used.

(4)   provide for a master jury wheel (or a device similar in purpose and function) into which the names of those randomly selected shall be placed. The plan shall fix a minimum number of names to be placed initially in the master jury wheel, which shall be at least one-half of 1 per centum of the total number of persons on the lists used as a source of names for the district or division; but if this number of names is believed to be cumbersome and unnecessary, the plan may fix a smaller number of names to be placed in the master wheel, but in no event less than one thousand. The chief judge of the district court, or such other district court judge as the plan may provide, may order additional names to be placed in the master jury wheel from time to time as necessary. The plan shall provide for periodic emptying and refilling of the master jury wheel at specified times, the interval for which shall not exceed four years.

(5)   (A)   except as provided in subparagraph (B), specify those groups of persons or occupational classes whose members shall, on individual request therefor, be excused from jury service. Such groups or classes shall be excused only if the district court finds, and the plan states, that jury service by such class or group would entail undue hardship or extreme inconvenience to the members thereof, and excuse of members thereof would not be inconsistent with sections 1861 and 1862 of this title.

(B)   specify that volunteer safety personnel, upon individual request, shall be excused from jury service. For purposes of this subparagraph, the term "volunteer safety personnel" means individuals serving a public agency (as defined in section 1203(6) of title I of the Omnibus Crime Control and Safe Streets Act of 1968) in an official capacity, without compensation, as firefighters or members of a rescue squad or ambulance crew.

(6)   specify that the following persons are barred from jury service on the ground that they are exempt: (A) members in active service in the Armed Forces of the United States; (B) members of the fire or police departments of any State, the District of Columbia, any territory or possession of the United States, or any subdivision of a State, the District of Columbia, or such territory or

possession; (C) public officers in the executive, legislative, or judicial branches of the Government of the United States, or of any State, the District of Columbia, any territory or possession of the United States, or any subdivision of a State, the District of Columbia, or such territory or possession, who are actively engaged in the performance of official duties.

(7) fix the time when the names drawn from the qualified jury wheel shall be disclosed to parties and to the public. If the plan permits these names to be made public, it may nevertheless permit the chief judge of the district court, or such other district court judge as the plan may provide, to keep these names confidential in any case where the interests of justice so require.

(8) specify the procedures to be followed by the clerk or jury commission in assigning persons whose names have been drawn from the qualified jury wheel to grand and petit jury panels.

(c) The initial plan shall be devised by each district court and transmitted to the reviewing panel specified in subsection (a) of this section within one hundred and twenty days of the date of enactment of the Jury Selection and Service Act of 1968. The panel shall approve or direct the modification of each plan so submitted within sixty days thereafter. Each plan or modification made at the direction of the panel shall become effective after approval at such time thereafter as the panel directs, in no event to exceed ninety days from the date of approval. Modifications made at the instance of the district court under subsection (a) of this section shall be effective at such time thereafter as the panel directs, in no event to exceed ninety days from the date of modification.

(d) State, local and Federal officials having custody, possession, or control of voter registration lists, lists of actual voters, or other appropriate records shall make such lists and records available to the jury commission or clerks for inspection, reproduction, and copying at all reasonable times as the commission or clerk may deem necessary and proper for the performance of duties under this title. The district courts shall have jurisdiction upon application by the Attorney General of the United States to compel compliance with this subsection by appropriate process.

§1864. Drawing of names from the master jury wheel; completion of juror qualification form

(a) From time to time as directed by the district court, the clerk or a district judge shall draw at random from the master jury wheel the names of as many persons as may be required for jury service. The clerk or jury commission shall post a general notice for public review in the clerk's office and on the court's website explaining the process by which names are periodically and randomly drawn. The clerk or jury commission may upon order of the court prepare an alphabetical list of the names drawn from the master jury wheel. Any list so prepared shall not be disclosed to any person except pursuant to the district court plan or pursuant to section 1867 or 1868 of this title. The clerk or jury commission shall mail to every person whose name is drawn from the master wheel a juror qualification form accompanied by instructions to fill out and return the form, duly signed and sworn, to the clerk or jury commission by mail within ten days. If the person is unable to fill out the form, another shall do it for him, and shall indicate that he has done so and the reason therefor. In any case in which it appears that there is an omission, ambiguity, or error in a form, the clerk or jury commission shall return the form with instructions to the person to make such additions or corrections as may be necessary and to return the form to the clerk or jury commission within ten days. Any person who fails to return a completed juror qualification form as instructed may be summoned by the clerk or jury commission forthwith to appear before the clerk or jury commission to fill out a juror qualification form. A person summoned to appear because of failure to return a juror qualification form as instructed who personally appears and executes a juror qualification form before the clerk or jury commission may, at the discretion of the district court, except where his prior failure to execute and mail such form was willful, be entitled to receive for such appearance the same fees and travel allowances paid to jurors under section 1871 of this title. At the time of his appearance for jury service, any person may be required to fill out another juror qualification form in the presence of the jury commission or the clerk or the court, at which time, in such cases as it appears warranted, the person may be questioned, but only with regard to his responses to questions contained on the form. Any information thus acquired by the clerk or jury commission may be noted on the juror qualification form and transmitted to the chief judge or such district court judge as the plan may provide.

(b)　Any person summoned pursuant to subsection (a) of this section who fails to appear as directed shall be ordered by the district court forthwith to appear and show cause for his failure to comply with the summons. Any person who fails to appear pursuant to such order or who fails to show good cause for noncompliance with the summons may be fined not more than $1000, imprisoned not more than three days, ordered to perform community service, or any combination thereof. Any person who willfully misrepresents a material fact on a juror qualification form for the purpose of avoiding or securing service as a juror may be fined not more than $1000, imprisoned not more than three days, ordered to perform community service, or any combination thereof.

§ 1865.　Qualifications for jury service

(a)　The chief judge of the district court, or such other district court judge as the plan may provide, on his initiative or upon recommendation of the clerk or jury commission, or the clerk under the supervision of the court if the court's jury selection plan so authorizes, shall determine solely on the basis of information provided on the juror qualification form and other competent evidence whether a person is unqualified for, or exempt, or to be excused from jury service. The clerk shall enter such determination in the space provided on the juror qualification form and in any alphabetical list of names drawn from the master jury wheel. If a person did not appear in response to a summons, such fact shall be noted on said list.

(b)　In making such determination the chief judge of the district court, or such other district court judge as the plan may provide, or the clerk if the court's jury selection plan so provides, shall deem any person qualified to serve on grand and petit juries in the district court unless he—

(1)　is not a citizen of the United States eighteen years old who has resided for a period of one year within the judicial district;

(2)　is unable to read, write, and understand the English language with a degree of proficiency sufficient to fill out satisfactorily the juror qualification form;

(3)　is unable to speak the English language;

(4)　is incapable, by reason of mental or physical infirmity, to render satisfactory jury service; or

(5)　has a charge pending against him for the commission of, or has been convicted in a State or Federal court of record of, a crime punishable by imprisonment for more than one year and his civil rights have not been restored.

§ 1866.　Selection and summoning of jury panels

(a)　The jury commission, or in the absence thereof the clerk, shall maintain a qualified jury wheel and shall place in such wheel names of all persons drawn from the master jury wheel who are determined to be qualified as jurors and not exempt or excused pursuant to the district court plan. From time to time, the jury commission or the clerk shall draw at random from the qualified jury wheel such number of names of persons as may be required for assignment to grand and petit jury panels. The clerk or jury commission shall post a general notice for public review in the clerk's office and on the court's website explaining the process by which names are periodically and randomly drawn. The jury commission or the clerk shall prepare a separate list of names of persons assigned to each grand and petit jury panel.

(b)　When the court orders a grand or petit jury to be drawn the clerk or jury commission or their duly designated deputies shall issue summonses for the required number of jurors.

Each person drawn for jury service may be served personally, or by registered, certified, or first-class mail addressed to such person at his usual residence or business address.

If such service is made personally, the summons shall be delivered by the clerk or the jury commission or their duly designated deputies to the marshal who shall make such service.

If such service is made by mail, the summons may be served by the marshal or by the clerk, the jury commission or their duly designated deputies, who shall make affidavit of service and shall attach thereto any receipt from the addressee for a registered or certified summons.

(c)   Except as provided in section 1865 of this title or in any jury selection plan provision adopted pursuant to paragraph (5) or (6) of section 1863(b) of this title, no person or class of persons shall be disqualified, excluded, excused, or exempt from service as jurors: *Provided*, That any person summoned for jury service may be (1) excused by the court, or by the clerk under supervision of the court if the court's jury selection plan so authorizes, upon a showing of undue hardship or extreme inconvenience, for such period as the court deems necessary, at the conclusion of which such person either shall be summoned again for jury service under subsections (b) and (c) of this section, or if the court's jury selection plan so provides, the name of such person shall be reinserted into the qualified jury wheel for selection pursuant to subsection (a) of this section, or (2) excluded by the court on the ground that such person may be unable to render impartial jury service or that his service as a juror would be likely to disrupt the proceedings, or (3) excluded upon peremptory challenge as provided by law, or (4) excluded pursuant to the procedure specified by law upon a challenge by any party for good cause shown, or (5) excluded upon determination by the court that his service as a juror would be likely to threaten the secrecy of the proceedings, or otherwise adversely affect the integrity of jury deliberations. No person shall be excluded under clause (5) of this subsection unless the judge, in open court, determines that such is warranted and that exclusion of the person will not be inconsistent with sections 1861 and 1862 of this title. The number of persons excluded under clause (5) of this subsection shall not exceed one per centum of the number of persons who return executed jury qualification forms during the period, specified in the plan, between two consecutive fillings of the master jury wheel. The names of persons excluded under clause (5) of this subsection, together with detailed explanations for the exclusions, shall be forwarded immediately to the judicial council of the circuit, which shall have the power to make any appropriate order, prospective or retroactive, to redress any misapplication of clause (5) of this subsection, but otherwise exclusions effectuated under such clause shall not be subject to challenge under the provisions of this title. Any person excluded from a particular jury under clause (2), (3), or (4) of this subsection shall be eligible to sit on another jury if the basis for his initial exclusion would not be relevant to his ability to serve on such other jury.

(d)   Whenever a person is disqualified, excused, exempt, or excluded from jury service, the jury commission or clerk shall note in the space provided on his juror qualification form or on the juror's card drawn from the qualified jury wheel the specific reason therefor.

(e)   In any two-year period, no person shall be required to (1) serve or attend court for prospective service as a petit juror for a total of more than thirty days, except when necessary to complete service in a particular case, or (2) serve on more than one grand jury, or (3) serve as both a grand and petit juror.

(f)   When there is an unanticipated shortage of available petit jurors drawn from the qualified jury wheel, the court may require the marshal to summon a sufficient number of petit jurors selected at random from the voter registration lists, lists of actual voters, or other lists specified in the plan, in a manner ordered by the court consistent with sections 1861 and 1862 of this title.

(g)   Any person summoned for jury service who fails to appear as directed may be ordered by the district court to appear forthwith and show cause for failure to comply with the summons. Any person who fails to show good cause for noncompliance with a summons may be fined not more than $1000, imprisoned not more than three days, ordered to perform community service, or any combination thereof.

§ 1867. Challenging compliance with selection procedures

(a)   In criminal cases, before the voir dire examination begins, or within seven days after the defendant discovered or could have discovered, by the exercise of diligence, the grounds therefor, whichever is earlier, the defendant may move to dismiss the indictment or stay the proceedings against him on the ground of substantial failure to comply with the provisions of this title in selecting the grand or petit jury.

(b)   In criminal cases, before the voir dire examination begins, or within seven days after the Attorney General of the United States discovered or could have discovered, by the exercise of diligence, the grounds therefor, whichever is earlier, the Attorney General may move to dismiss the indictment or stay the proceedings on the ground of substantial failure to comply with the provisions of this title in selecting the grand or petit jury.

(c)   In civil cases, before the voir dire examination begins, or within seven days after the party discovered or could have discovered, by the exercise of diligence, the grounds therefor, whichever is earlier, any party may move to stay the proceedings on the ground of substantial failure to comply with the provisions of this title in selecting the petit jury.

(d)   Upon motion filed under subsection (a), (b), or (c) of this section, containing a sworn statement of facts which, if true, would constitute a substantial failure to comply with the provisions of this title, the moving party shall be entitled to present in support of such motion the testimony of the jury commission or clerk, if available, any relevant records and papers not public or otherwise available used by the jury commissioner or clerk, and any other relevant evidence. If the court determines that there has been a substantial failure to comply with the provisions of this title in selecting a grand jury, the court shall stay the proceedings pending the selection of a grand jury in conformity with this title or dismiss the indictment, whichever is appropriate. If the court determines that there has been a substantial failure to comply with the provisions of this title in selecting the petit jury, the court shall stay the proceedings pending the selection of a petit jury in conformity with this title.

(e)   The procedures prescribed by this section shall be the exclusive means by which a person accused of a Federal crime, the Attorney General of the United States or a party in a civil case may challenge any jury on the ground that such jury was not selected in conformity with the provisions of this title. Nothing in this section shall preclude any person or the United States from pursuing any other remedy, civil or criminal, which may be available for the vindication or enforcement of any law prohibiting discrimination on account of race, color, religion, sex, national origin or economic status in the selection of persons for service on grand or petit juries.

(f)   The contents of records or papers used by the jury commission or clerk in connection with the jury selection process shall not be disclosed, except pursuant to the district court plan or as may be necessary in the preparation or presentation of a motion under subsection (a), (b), or (c) of this section, until after the master jury wheel has been emptied and refilled pursuant to section 1863(b)(4) of this title and all persons selected to serve as jurors before the master wheel was emptied have completed such service. The parties in a case shall be allowed to inspect, reproduce, and copy such records or papers at all reasonable times during the preparation and pendency of such a motion. Any person who discloses the contents of any record or paper in violation of this subsection may be fined not more than $1,000 or imprisoned not more than one year, or both.

§ 1868. Maintenance and inspection of records

After the master jury wheel is emptied and refilled pursuant to section 1863(b)(4) of this title, and after all persons selected to serve as jurors before the master wheel was emptied have completed such service, all records and papers compiled and maintained by the jury commission or clerk before the master wheel was emptied shall be preserved in the custody of the clerk for four years or for such longer period as may be ordered by a court, and shall be available for public inspection for the purpose of determining the validity of the selection of any jury.

§ 1869. Definitions

For purposes of this chapter—

(a)   "clerk" and "clerk of the court" shall mean the clerk of the district court of the United States, any authorized deputy clerk, and any other person authorized by the court to assist the clerk in the performance of functions under this chapter;

(b)   "chief judge" shall mean the chief judge of any district court of the United States;

(c)   "voter registration lists" shall mean the official records maintained by State or local election officials of persons registered to vote in either the most recent State or the most recent Federal general election, or, in the case of a State or political subdivision thereof that does not require registration as a prerequisite to voting, other official lists of persons qualified to vote in such election. The term shall also include the list of eligible voters maintained by any Federal examiner pursuant to the Voting Rights Act of 1965 where the names on such list have not been included on the official registration lists or other official lists maintained by the appropriate State or local officials. With respect to the districts of Guam and the Virgin Islands, "voter registration lists" shall mean the official records maintained by territorial election officials of persons registered to vote in the most recent territorial general election;

(d)   "lists of actual voters" shall mean the official lists of persons actually voting in either the most recent State or the most recent Federal general election;

(e)   "division" shall mean: (1) one or more statutory divisions of a judicial district; or (2) in statutory divisions that contain more than one place of holding court, or in judicial districts where there are no statutory divisions, such counties, parishes, or similar political subdivisions surrounding the places where court is held as the district court plan shall determine: *Provided*, That each county, parish, or similar political subdivision shall be included in some such division;

(f)   "district court of the United States", "district court", and "court" shall mean any district court established by chapter 5 of this title, and any court which is created by Act of Congress in a territory and is invested with any jurisdiction of a district court established by chapter 5 of this title;

(g)   "jury wheel" shall include any device or system similar in purpose or function, such as a properly programmed electronic data processing system or device;

(h)   "juror qualification form" shall mean a form prescribed by the Administrative Office of the United States Courts and approved by the Judicial Conference of the United States, which shall elicit the name, address, age, race, occupation, education, length of residence within the judicial district, distance from residence to place of holding court, prior jury service, and citizenship of a potential juror, and whether he should be excused or exempted from jury service, has any physical or mental infirmity impairing his capacity to serve as juror, is able to read, write, speak and understand the English language, has pending against him any charge for the commission of a State or Federal criminal offense punishable by imprisonment for more than one year, or has been convicted in any State or Federal Court of record of a crime punishable by imprisonment for more than one year and has not had his civil rights restored. The form shall request, but not require, any other information not inconsistent with the provisions of this title and required by the district court plan in the interests of the sound administration of justice. The form also shall elicit the sworn statement that his responses are true to the best of his knowledge. Notarization shall not be required. The form shall contain words clearly informing the person that the furnishing of any information with respect to his religion, national origin, or economic status is not a prerequisite to his qualification for jury service, that such information need not be furnished if the person finds it objectionable to do so, and that information concerning race is required solely to enforce nondiscrimination in jury selection and has no bearing on an individual's qualification for jury service.

(i) "public officer" shall mean a person who is either elected to public office or who is directly appointed by a person elected to public office;

(j) "undue hardship or extreme inconvenience", as a basis for excuse from immediate jury service under section 1866(c)(1) of this chapter, shall mean great distance, either in miles or travel-time, from the place of holding court, grave illness in the family or any other emergency which outweighs in immediacy and urgency the obligation to serve as a juror when summoned, or any other factor which the court determines to constitute an undue hardship or to create an extreme inconvenience to the juror; and in addition, in situations where it is anticipated that a trial or grand jury proceeding may require more than thirty days of service, the court may consider, as a further basis for temporary excuse, severe economic hardship to an employer which would result from the absence of a key employee during the period of such service; and

(k) "jury summons" shall mean a summons issued by a clerk of court, jury commission, or their duly designated deputies, containing either a preprinted or stamped seal of court, and containing the name of the issuing clerk imprinted in preprinted, type, or facsimile manner on the summons or the envelopes transmitting the summons.

§ 1870. Challenges

In civil cases, each party shall be entitled to three peremptory challenges. Several defendants or several plaintiffs may be considered as a single party for the purposes of making challenges, or the court may allow additional peremptory challenges and permit them to be exercised separately or jointly.

All challenges for cause or favor, whether to the array or panel or to individual jurors, shall be determined by the court.

§ 1919. Dismissal for lack of jurisdiction

Whenever any action or suit is dismissed in any district court, the Court of International Trade, or the Court of Federal Claims for want of jurisdiction, such court may order the payment of just costs.

§ 1920. Taxation of costs

A judge or clerk of any court of the United States may tax as costs the following:

(1) Fees of the clerk and marshal;

(2) Fees for printed or electronically recorded transcripts necessarily obtained for use in the case;

(3) Fees and disbursements for printing and witnesses;

(4) Fees for exemplification and the costs of making copies of any materials where the copies are necessarily obtained for use in the case;

(5) Docket fees under section 1923 of this title;

(6) Compensation of court appointed experts, compensation of interpreters, and salaries, fees, expenses, and costs of special interpretation services under section 1828 of this title.

A bill of costs shall be filed in the case and, upon allowance, included in the judgment or decree.

§ 1927. Counsel's liability for excessive costs

Any attorney or other person admitted to conduct cases in any court of the United States or any Territory thereof who so multiplies the proceedings in any case unreasonably and vexatiously may be required by the court to satisfy personally the excess costs, expenses, and attorneys' fees reasonably incurred because of such conduct.

§ 1963. Registration of judgments for enforcement in other districts

A judgment in an action for the recovery of money or property entered in any court of appeals, district court, bankruptcy court, or in the Court of International Trade may be registered by filing a certified copy of such judgment in any other district or, with respect to the Court of International Trade, in any judicial district, when the judgment has become final by appeal or expiration of the time for appeal or when ordered by the court that entered the judgment for good cause shown. Such a judgment entered in favor of the United States may be so registered any time after judgment is entered. A judgment so registered shall have the same effect as a judgment of the district court of the district where registered and may be enforced in like manner.

A certified copy of the satisfaction of any judgment in whole or in part may be registered in like manner in any district in which the judgment is a lien.

The procedure prescribed under this section is in addition to other procedures provided by law for the enforcement of judgments.

Comparative State Provisions

Uniform Enforcement of Foreign Judgments Act (1964 Revised Act) § 2

A copy of any foreign judgment authenticated in accordance with the act of Congress or the statutes of this state may be filed in the office of the Clerk of any [District Court of any city or county] of this state. The Clerk shall treat the foreign judgment in the same manner as a judgment of the [District Court of any city or county] of this state. A judgment so filed has the same effect and is subject to the same procedures, defenses and proceedings for reopening, vacating, or staying as a judgment of a [District Court of any city or county] of this state and may be enforced or satisfied in like manner.

Uniform Enforcement of Foreign Judgments Act (1964 Revised Act) § 6

The right of a judgment creditor to bring an action to enforce his judgment instead of proceeding under this Act remains unimpaired.

§ 2071. Rule-making power generally

(a)   The Supreme Court and all courts established by Act of Congress may from time to time prescribe rules for the conduct of their business. Such rules shall be consistent with Acts of Congress and rules of practice and procedure prescribed under section 2072 of this title.

(b)   Any rule prescribed by a court, other than the Supreme Court, under subsection (a) shall be prescribed only after giving appropriate public notice and an opportunity for comment. Such rule shall take effect upon the date specified by the prescribing court and shall have such effect on pending proceedings as the prescribing court may order.

(c)   (1)   A rule of a district court prescribed under subsection (a) shall remain in effect unless modified or abrogated by the judicial council of the relevant circuit.

(2)   Any other rule prescribed by a court other than the Supreme Court under subsection (a) shall remain in effect unless modified or abrogated by the Judicial Conference.

(d)   Copies of rules prescribed under subsection (a) by a district court shall be furnished to the judicial council, and copies of all rules prescribed by a court other than the Supreme Court under subsection (a) shall be furnished to the director of the Administrative Office of the United States Courts and made available to the public.

(e)   If the prescribing court determines that there is an immediate need for a rule, such court may proceed under this section without public notice and opportunity for comment, but such court shall promptly thereafter afford such notice and opportunity for comment.

(f)   No rule may be prescribed by a district court other than under this section.

§ 2072. Rules of procedure and evidence; power to prescribe

[See Selected Provision of section 205(c) of the E-Government Act of 2002, Enabling the Supreme Court to Prescribe Rules to Protect Privacy and Security Relating to Electronic Filing of Documents, at the end of this Part II, infra.]

(a)   The Supreme Court shall have the power to prescribe general rules of practice and procedure and rules of evidence for cases in the United States district courts (including proceedings before magistrates thereof) and courts of appeals.

(b)   Such rules shall not abridge, enlarge or modify any substantive right. All laws in conflict with such rules shall be of no further force or effect after such rules have taken effect.

(c)   Such rules may define when a ruling of a district court is final for the purposes of appeal under section 1291 of this title.

§ 2111. Harmless error

On the hearing of any appeal or writ of certiorari in any case, the court shall give judgment after an examination of the record without regard to errors or defects which do not affect the substantial rights of the parties.

§ 2201. Creation of remedy

(a)   In a case of actual controversy within its jurisdiction, except with respect to Federal taxes other than actions brought under section 7428 of the Internal Revenue Code of 1986 * * *, any court of the United States, upon the filing of an appropriate pleading, may declare the rights and other legal relations of any interested party seeking such declaration, whether or not further relief is or could be sought. Any such declaration shall have the force and effect of a final judgment or decree and shall be reviewable as such.

* * *

Comparative State Provisions

Connecticut Superior Court Rules of Civil Procedure § 17–55

A declaratory judgment action may be maintained if all of the following conditions have been met:

(1)   The party seeking the declaratory judgment has an interest, legal or equitable, by reason of danger of loss or of uncertainty as to the party's rights or other jural relations;

(2)   There is an actual bona fide and substantial question or issue in dispute or substantial uncertainty of legal relations which requires settlement between the parties; and

(3)   In the event that there is another form of proceeding that can provide the party seeking the declaratory judgment immediate redress, the court is of the opinion that such party should be allowed to proceed with the claim for declaratory judgment despite the existence of such alternate procedure.

Uniform Declaratory Judgments Act § 6

The court may refuse to render or enter a declaratory judgment or decree where such judgment or decree, if rendered or entered, would not terminate the uncertainty or controversy giving rise to the proceeding.

§ 2202. Further relief

Further necessary or proper relief based on a declaratory judgment or decree may be granted, after reasonable notice and hearing, against any adverse party whose rights have been determined by such judgment.

§ 2283. Stay of State court proceedings

A court of the United States may not grant an injunction to stay proceedings in a State court except as expressly authorized by Act of Congress, or where necessary in aid of its jurisdiction, or to protect or effectuate its judgments.

§ 2284. Three-judge court; when required; composition; procedure

(a) A district court of three judges shall be convened when otherwise required by Act of Congress, or when an action is filed challenging the constitutionality of the apportionment of congressional districts or the apportionment of any statewide legislative body.

(b) In any action required to be heard and determined by a district court of three judges under subsection (a) of this section, the composition and procedure of the court shall be as follows:

(1) Upon the filing of a request for three judges, the judge to whom the request is presented shall, unless he determines that three judges are not required, immediately notify the chief judge of the circuit, who shall designate two other judges, at least one of whom shall be a circuit judge. The judges so designated, and the judge to whom the request was presented, shall serve as members of the court to hear and determine the action or proceeding.

* * *

§ 2361. Process and procedure

In any civil action of interpleader or in the nature of interpleader under section 1335 of this title, a district court may issue its process for all claimants and enter its order restraining them from instituting or prosecuting any proceeding in any State or United States court affecting the property, instrument or obligation involved in the interpleader action until further order of the court. Such process and order shall be returnable at such time as the court or judge thereof directs, and shall be addressed to and served by the United States marshals for the respective districts where the claimants reside or may be found.

Such district court shall hear and determine the case, and may discharge the plaintiff from further liability, make the injunction permanent, and make all appropriate orders to enforce its judgment.

§ 2403. Intervention by United States or a State; constitutional question

(a) In any action, suit or proceeding in a court of the United States to which the United States or any agency, officer or employee thereof is not a party, wherein the constitutionality of any Act of Congress affecting the public interest is drawn in question, the court shall certify such fact to the Attorney General, and shall permit the United States to intervene for presentation of evidence, if evidence is otherwise admissible in the case, and for argument on the question of constitutionality. The United States shall, subject to the applicable provisions of law, have all the rights of a party and be subject to all liabilities of a party as to court costs to the extent necessary for a proper presentation of the facts and law relating to the question of constitutionality.

(b) In any action, suit, or proceeding in a court of the United States to which a State or any agency, officer, or employee thereof is not a party, wherein the constitutionality of any statute of that State affecting the public interest is drawn in question, the court shall certify such fact to the attorney general of the State, and shall permit the State to intervene for presentation of evidence, if evidence is otherwise admissible in the case, and for argument on the question of constitutionality. The State shall, subject to the applicable provisions of law, have all the rights of a party and be subject to all liabilities of a party as to court costs to the extent necessary for a proper presentation of the facts and law relating to the question of constitutionality.

Selected Provisions of Title 18, United States Code—
Criminal Law and Procedure

§ 2333. Civil remedies

(a) **Action and Jurisdiction**—Any national of the United States injured in his or her person, property, or business by reason of any act of international terrorism, or his or her estate, survivors, or heirs, may sue therefor in any appropriate district court of the United States and shall recover threefold the damages he or she sustains and the cost of the suit, including attorney's fees.

* * *

§ 2334. Jurisdiction and venue

* * *

(e) **Consent of certain parties to personal jurisdiction [for civil actions under § 2333(a)]**

(1) In general—Except as provided in paragraph (2), for purposes of any civil action under section 2333 of this title, a defendant shall be deemed to have consented to personal jurisdiction in such civil action if, regardless of the date of the occurrence of the act of international terrorism upon which such civil action was filed, the defendant

(A) . . .accepts. . .any form of assistance, however provided, under. . .[various specified acts] of the Foreign Assistance Act of 1961; or

(B) . . .[benefits] from a waiver or suspension of section 1003 of the Anti-Terrorism Act of 1987. . .and continues to maintain. . .or. . .establishes or procures any office, headquarters, premises, or other facilities or establishments within the jurisdiction of the United States.

(2) Applicability—Paragraph (1) shall not apply to any defendant who ceases to engage in the conduct described in paragraphs (1)(A) and (1)(B) for 5 consecutive calendar years.

Selected Provision of Title 42, United States Code—
The Public Health and Welfare

§ 1983. Civil action for deprivation of rights

Every person who, under color of any statute, ordinance, regulation, custom, or usage, of any State or Territory or the District of Columbia, subjects, or causes to be subjected, any citizen of the United States or other person within the jurisdiction thereof to the deprivation of any rights, privileges, or immunities secured by the Constitution and laws, shall be liable to the party injured in an action at law, suit in equity, or other proper proceeding for redress, except that in any action brought against a judicial officer for an act or omission taken in such officer's judicial capacity, injunctive relief shall not be granted unless a declaratory decree was violated or declaratory relief was unavailable. For the purposes of this section, any Act of Congress applicable exclusively to the District of Columbia shall be considered to be a statute of the District of Columbia.

Selected Provision of § 205(c) of the E-Government Act of 2002, Enabling
the Supreme Court to Prescribe Rules to Protect Privacy and
Security Relating to Electronic Filing of Documents

[See Rule 5.2 in Part I, supra.]

(3) Privacy and security concerns.—

(A) (i) The Supreme Court shall prescribe rules, in accordance with sections 2072 and 2075 of title 28, United States Code, to protect privacy and security concerns relating to electronic filing of documents and the public availability under this subsection of documents filed electronically.

(ii)   Such rules shall provide to the extent practicable for uniform treatment of privacy and security issues throughout the Federal courts.

(iii)   Such rules shall take into consideration best practices in Federal and State courts to protect private information or otherwise maintain necessary information security.

(iv)   Except as provided in clause (v), to the extent that such rules provide for the redaction of certain categories of information in order to protect privacy and security concerns, such rules shall provide that a party that wishes to file an otherwise proper document containing such protected information may file an unredacted document under seal, which shall be retained by the court as part of the record, and which, at the discretion of the court and subject to any applicable rules issued in accordance with chapter 131 of title 28, United States Code, shall be either in lieu of, or in addition to, a redacted copy in the public file.

(v)   Such rules may require the use of appropriate redacted identifiers in lieu of protected information described in clause (iv) in any pleading, motion, or other paper filed with the court (except with respect to a paper that is an exhibit or other evidentiary matter, or with respect to a reference list described in this subclause), or in any written discovery response—

(I)   by authorizing the filing under seal, and permitting the amendment as of right under seal, of a reference list that—

(aa) identifies each item of unredacted protected information that the attorney or, if there is no attorney, the party, certifies is relevant to the case; and

(bb) specifies an appropriate redacted identifier that uniquely corresponds to each item of unredacted protected information listed; and

(II)   by providing that all references in the case to the redacted identifiers in such reference list shall be construed, without more, to refer to the corresponding unredacted item of protected information.

(B)   (i)   Subject to clause (ii), the Judicial Conference of the United States may issue interim rules, and interpretive statements relating to the application of such rules, which conform to the requirements of this paragraph and which shall cease to have effect upon the effective date of the rules required under subparagraph (A).

(ii)   Pending issuance of the rules required under subparagraph (A), any rule or order of any court, or of the Judicial Conference, providing for the reaction of certain categories of information in order to protect privacy and security concerns arising from electronic filing or electronic conversion shall comply with, and be construed in conformity with, subparagraph (A)(iv).

(C)   Not later than 1 year after the rules prescribed under subparagraph (A) take effect, and every 2 years thereafter, the Judicial Conference shall submit to Congress a report on the adequacy of those rules to protect privacy and security.

PART III

Selected State Personal Jurisdictional Statutes

and

Selected State Constitutional Provisions Governing a State's Court System

plus

Selected State Statutes Governing the Powers of Appellate Courts

---

TABLE OF CONTENTS

Selected State Personal Jurisdictional Statutes

Selected State Constitutional Provisions Governing a State's Court System

Selected State Statutes Governing the Powers of Appellate Courts

---

SELECTED STATE STATUTES

Selected State Personal Jurisdictional Statutes

New York Civil Practice Law and Rules 302(a)

(a)   Acts which are the basis of jurisdiction. As to a cause of action arising from any of the acts enumerated in this section, a court may exercise personal jurisdiction over any non-domiciliary, or his executor or administrator, who in person or through an agent:

    1.   transacts any business within the state or contracts anywhere to supply goods or services in the state; or

    2.   commits a tortious act within the state, except as to a cause of action for defamation of character arising from the act; or

    3.   commits a tortious act without the state causing injury to person or property within the state, except as to a cause of action for defamation of character arising from the act, if he

        (i)   regularly does or solicits business, or engages in any other persistent course of conduct, or derives substantial revenue from goods used or consumed or services rendered, in the state, or

        (ii)   expects or should reasonably expect the act to have consequences in the state and derives substantial revenue from interstate or international commerce; or

    4.   owns, uses or possesses any real property situated within the state.

(b)   Personal jurisdiction over non-resident defendant in matrimonial actions or family court proceedings. A court in any matrimonial action or family court proceeding involving a demand for support, alimony, maintenance, distributive awards or special relief in matrimonial actions may exercise personal jurisdiction over the respondent or defendant notwithstanding the fact that he or she no longer is a resident or domiciliary of this state, or over his or her executor or administrator, if the party seeking support is a resident of or domiciled in this state at the time such demand is made, provided that this state was the matrimonial domicile of the parties before their separation, or the defendant abandoned the plaintiff in this state, or the claim for support, alimony, maintenance, distributive awards or special relief in matrimonial actions accrued under the laws of this state or under an agreement executed in this state. The family court may exercise personal jurisdiction over a non-resident respondent to the extent provided in sections one hundred fifty-four and one thousand thirty-six and article five-B of the family court act and article five-A of the domestic relations law.

(c)   Effect of appearance. Where personal jurisdiction is based solely upon this section, an appearance does not confer such jurisdiction with respect to causes of action not arising from an act enumerated in this section.

* * *

North Carolina General Statutes § 1–75.2

Definitions.—In this article the following words have the designated meanings:

(1)   "Person" means any natural person, partnership, corporation, body politic, and any unincorporated association, organization, or society which may sue or be sued under a common name.

* * *

North Carolina General Statutes § 1–75.4

Personal jurisdiction, grounds for generally.—A court of this State having jurisdiction of the subject matter has jurisdiction over a person served in an action pursuant to Rule 4(j), Rule 4(j1) or 4(j3) of the Rules of Civil Procedure under any of the following circumstances:

SELECTED STATE PERSONAL JURISDICTIONAL STATUTES

(1) Local Presence or Status.—In any action, whether the claim arises within or without this State, in which a claim is asserted against a party who when service of process is made upon such party:

    a. Is a natural person present within this State; or

    b. Is a natural person domiciled within this State; or

    c. Is a domestic corporation; or

    d. Is engaged in substantial activity within this State, whether such activity is wholly interstate, intrastate, or otherwise.

(2) Special Jurisdiction Statutes.—In any action which may be brought under statutes of this State that specifically confer grounds for personal jurisdiction.

(3) Local Act or Omission.—In any action claiming injury to person or property or for wrongful death within or without this State arising out of an act or omission within this State by the defendant.

(4) Local Injury; Foreign Act.—In any action for wrongful death occurring within this State or in any action claiming injury to person or property within this State arising out of an act or omission outside this State by the defendant, provided in addition that at or about the time of the injury either:

    a. Solicitation or services activities were carried on within this State by or on behalf of the defendant; or

    b. Products, materials or things processed, serviced or manufactured by the defendant were used or consumed within this State in the ordinary course of trade; or

    c. Unsolicited bulk mail was sent into or within this State by the defendant using a computer, computer network, or the computer services of an electronic mail service provider in contravention of the authority granted by or in violation of the policies set by the electronic mail service provider. Transmission of commercial electronic mail from an organization to its members shall not be deemed to be unsolicited bulk commercial electronic mail.

(5) Local Services, Goods or Contracts.—In any action which:

    a. Arises out of a promise, made anywhere to the plaintiff or to some third party for the plaintiff's benefit, by the defendant to perform services within this State or to pay for services to be performed in this State by the plaintiff; or

    b. Arises out of services actually performed for the plaintiff by the defendant within this State, or services actually performed for the defendant by the plaintiff within this State if such performance within this State was authorized or ratified by the defendant; or

    c. Arises out of a promise, made anywhere to the plaintiff or to some third party for the plaintiff's benefit, by the defendant to deliver or receive within this State, or to ship from this State goods, documents of title, or other things of value; or

    d. Relates to goods, documents of title, or other things of value shipped from this State by the plaintiff to the defendant on his order or direction; or

    e. Relates to goods, documents of title, or other things of value actually received by the plaintiff in this State from the defendant through a carrier without regard to where delivery to the carrier occurred.

(6) Local Property.—In any action which arises out of:

    a. A promise, made anywhere to the plaintiff or to some third party for the plaintiff's benefit, by the defendant to create in either party an interest in, or protect, acquire, dispose of, use, rent, own, control or possess by either party real property situated in this State; or

b. A claim to recover for any benefit derived by the defendant through the use, ownership, control or possession by the defendant of tangible property situated within this State either at the time of the first use, ownership, control or possession or at the time the action is commenced; or

c. A claim that the defendant return, restore, or account to the plaintiff for any asset or thing of value which was within this State at the time the defendant acquired possession or control over it; or

d. A claim related to a loan made in this State or deemed to have been made in this State under G.S.24–2.1, regardless of the situs of the lender, assignee, or other holder of the loan note and regardless of whether the loan repayment or fee is received through a loan servicer, provided that: (i) the loan was made to a borrower who is a resident of the State, (ii) the loan is incurred by the borrower primarily for personal, family, or household purposes, and (iii) the loan is secured by a mortgage or deed of trust on real property situated in this State upon which there is located or there is to be located a structure or structures designed principally for occupancy of from one to four families.

(7) Deficiency Judgment on Local Foreclosure or Resale.—In any action to recover a deficiency judgment upon an obligation secured by a mortgage, deed of trust, conditional sale, or other security instrument executed by the defendant or his predecessor to whose obligation the defendant has succeeded and the deficiency is claimed either:

a. In an action in this State to foreclose such security instrument upon real property, tangible personal property, or an intangible represented by an indispensable instrument, situated in this State; or

b. Following sale of real or tangible personal property or an intangible represented by an indispensable instrument in this State under a power of sale contained in any security instrument.

(8) Director or Officer of a Domestic Corporation.—In any action against a defendant who is or was an officer or director of a domestic corporation where the action arises out of the defendant's conduct as such officer or director or out of the activities of such corporation while the defendant held office as a director or officer.

(9) Taxes or Assessments.—In any action for the collection of taxes or assessments levied, assessed or otherwise imposed by a taxing authority of this State after the date of ratification of this act.

(10) Insurance or Insurers.—In any action which arises out of a contract of insurance as defined in G.S. 58–1–10 made anywhere between the plaintiff or some third party and the defendant and in addition either:

a. The plaintiff was a resident of this State when the event occurred out of which the claim arose; or

b. The event out of which the claim arose occurred within this State, regardless of where the plaintiff resided.

(11) Personal Representative.—In any action against a personal representative to enforce a claim against the deceased person represented, whether or not the action was commenced during the lifetime of the deceased, where one or more of the grounds stated in subdivisions (2) to (10) of this section would have furnished a basis for jurisdiction over the deceased had he been living.

SELECTED STATE PERSONAL JURISDICTIONAL STATUTES

(12) **Marital Relationship.**—In any action under Chapter 50 that arises out of the marital relationship within this State, notwithstanding subsequent departure from the State, if the other party to the marital relationship continues to reside in this State.

North Carolina General Statutes § 1–75.7

Personal jurisdiction—Grounds for without service of summons.—A court of this State having jurisdiction of the subject matter may, without serving a summons upon him, exercise jurisdiction in an action over a person:

(1) Who makes a general appearance in an action; * * * or

(2) With respect to any counterclaim asserted against that person in an action which he has commenced in the State.

North Carolina General Statutes § 1–75.8

Jurisdiction in rem or quasi in rem—Grounds for generally.—A court of this State having jurisdiction of the subject matter may exercise jurisdiction in rem or quasi in rem on the grounds stated in this section. A judgment in rem or quasi in rem may affect the interests of a defendant in a status, property or thing acted upon only if process has been served upon the defendant pursuant to Rule 4(k) of the Rules of Civil Procedure. Jurisdiction in rem or quasi in rem may be invoked in any of the following cases:

(1) When the subject of the action is real or personal property in this State and the defendant has or claims any lien or interest therein, or the relief demanded consists wholly or partially in excluding the defendant from any interest or lien therein. This subdivision shall apply whether any such defendant is known or unknown.

(2) When the action is to foreclose, redeem from or satisfy a deed of trust, mortgage, claim or lien upon real or personal property in this State.

(3) When the action is for a divorce or for annulment of marriage of a resident of this State.

(4) When the defendant has property within this State which has been attached or has a debtor within the State who has been garnished. Jurisdiction under this subdivision may be independent of or supplementary to jurisdiction acquired under subdivisions (1), (2) and (3) of this section.

[Authors' Note: In Balcon, Inc. v. Sadler, 36 N.C.App. 322, 244 S.E.2d 164 (1978), the court held that subdivision (4) fails to meet standards set forth in Shaffer v. Heitner, 433 U.S. 186, 97 S. Ct. 2569, 53 L. Ed.2d 683 (1977), and is therefore unconstitutional.]

(5) In any other action in which in rem or quasi in rem jurisdiction may be constitutionally exercised.

Rhode Island General Laws Annotated § 9–5–33(a)

Every foreign corporation, every individual not a resident of this state or his or her executor or administrator, and every partnership or association, composed of any person or persons not such residents, that shall have the necessary minimum contacts with the state of Rhode Island, shall be subject to the jurisdiction of the state of Rhode Island, and the courts of this state shall hold such foreign corporations and such nonresident individuals or their executors or administrators, and such partnerships or associations amenable to suit in Rhode Island in every case not contrary to the provisions of the constitution or laws of the United States.

Uniform Interstate and International Procedure Act § 1.02

A court may exercise personal jurisdiction over a person domiciled in, organized under the laws of, or maintaining his or its principal place of business in, this state as to any [cause of action] [claim for relief].

SELECTED STATE STATUTES

Uniform Interstate and International Procedure Act § 1.05

When the court finds that in the interest of substantial justice the action should be heard in another forum, the court may stay or dismiss the action in whole or in part on any conditions that may be just.

Uniform Parentage Act § 8(b) (1973 Act)

A person who has sexual intercourse in this State thereby submits to the jurisdiction of the courts of this State as to an action brought under this Act with respect to a child who may have been conceived by that act of intercourse. * * *

Selected State Constitutional Provisions
Governing a State's Court System

California Constitution Article 6, § 1

The judicial power of this State is vested in the Supreme Court, courts of appeal, and superior courts, all of which are courts of record.

Georgia Constitution Article 6, § 1, ¶ I

The judicial power of the state shall be vested exclusively in the following classes of courts: magistrate courts, probate courts, juvenile courts, state courts, superior courts, Court of Appeals, and Supreme Court. Magistrate courts, probate courts, juvenile courts, and state courts shall be courts of limited jurisdiction. In addition, the General Assembly may establish or authorize the establishment of municipal courts and may authorize administrative agencies to exercise quasi-judicial powers. * * *

Pennsylvania Constitution Article 5, § 1

The judicial power of the Commonwealth shall be vested in a unified judicial system consisting of the Supreme Court, the Superior Court, the Commonwealth court, courts of common pleas, community courts, municipal and traffic courts in the City of Philadelphia, such other courts as may be provided by law and justices of the peace. All courts and justices of the peace and their jurisdiction shall be in this unified judicial system.

Selected State Statutes Governing
the Powers of Appellate Courts

Alabama Code § 12–2–13

The Supreme Court, in deciding each case when there is a conflict between its existing opinion and any former ruling in the case, must be governed by what, in its opinion, at that time is law, without any regard to such former ruling on the law by it; but the right of third persons, acquired on the faith of the former ruling, shall not be defeated or interfered with by or on account of any subsequent ruling.

Comparative Provision

See Georgia Code Annotated § 9–11–60(h), supra, following Federal Rule 60.

California Civil Procedure Code § 909

In all cases where trial by jury is not a matter of right or where trial by jury has been waived, the reviewing court may make factual determinations contrary to or in addition to those made by the trial court. The factual determinations may be based on the evidence adduced before the trial court either with or without the taking of evidence by the reviewing court. The reviewing court may for the purpose of making the factual determinations or for any other purpose in the interests of justice, take additional evidence of or concerning facts occurring at any time prior to the decision of the appeal, and may give or direct the entry of any judgment or order and may make any further or other order as the case may require. This section shall be liberally construed to the end among others that, where feasible, causes may be finally disposed of by a single appeal and without further proceedings in the trial court except where in the interests of justice a new trial is required on some or all of the issues.

PART IV

Selected Portions of the Federal Rules of Appellate Procedure

---

Note that the Supreme Court has approved alterations of Rules 3(d), 5(a), 21(a) and (c), 25(d)(1), 26(c), 26.1, 32(f), and 39(d), and has transmitted them to Congress. Generally the changes appear in brackets; the changes to Rule 26.1 appear in italics after the current rule.

Unless Congress intervenes, the changes are effective December 1, 2019.

TABLE OF CONTENTS

Title I.   Applicability of Rules

Title II.   Appeal From a Judgment or Order of a District Court

Title III.   Appeals from the United States Tax Court [Omitted]

Title IV.   Review or Enforcement of an Order of an Administrative Agency, Board, Commission, or Officer

Title V.   Extraordinary Writs

RULES OF APPELLATE PROCEDURE

Title VI. Habeas Corpus; Proceedings in Forma Pauperis

Title VII. General Provisions

[The Appellate Forms are omitted.]

TITLE I. APPLICABILITY OF RULES

Rule 1. Scope of Rules; Definition; Title

(a) Scope of Rules.

(1) These rules govern procedure in the United States courts of appeals.

(2) When these rules provide for filing a motion or other document in the district court, the procedure must comply with the practice of the district court.

(b) Definition: In these rules "state" includes the District of Columbia and any United States commonwealth or territory.

(c) Title. These rules are to be known as the Federal Rules of Appellate Procedure.

Rule 2. Suspension of Rules

On its own or a party's motion, a court of appeals may—to expedite its decision or for other good cause—suspend any provision of these rules in a particular case and order proceedings as it directs, except as otherwise provided in Rule 26(b).

TITLE II. APPEAL FROM A JUDGMENT
OR ORDER OF A DISTRICT COURT

Rule 3. Appeal as of Right—How Taken

Note that proposed changes to Rule 3(d)(1) and (3) have been approved by the Supreme Court. The changes appear in brackets within the current rule.

Unless Congress intervenes, the changes are effective December 1, 2019.

(a) Filing the Notice of Appeal.

(1)   An appeal permitted by law as of right from a district court to a court of appeals may be taken only by filing a notice of appeal with the district clerk within the time allowed by Rule 4. At the time of filing, the appellant must furnish the clerk with enough copies of the notice to enable the clerk to comply with Rule 3(d).

(2)   An appellant's failure to take any step other than the timely filing of a notice of appeal does not affect the validity of the appeal, but is ground only for the court of appeals to act as it considers appropriate, including dismissing the appeal.

(3)   An appeal from a judgment by a magistrate judge in a civil case is taken in the same way as an appeal from any other district court judgment.

(4)   An appeal by permission under 28 U.S.C. § 1292(b) or an appeal in a bankruptcy case may be taken only in the manner prescribed by Rules 5 and 6, respectively.

(b) Joint or Consolidated Appeals.

(1)   When two or more parties are entitled to appeal from a district-court judgment or order, and their interests make joinder practicable, they may file a joint notice of appeal. They may then proceed on appeal as a single appellant.

(2)   When the parties have filed separate timely notices of appeal, the appeals may be joined or consolidated by the court of appeals.

(c) Contents of the Notice of Appeal.

(1)   The notice of appeal must:

(A)   specify the party or parties taking the appeal by naming each one in the caption or body of the notice, but an attorney representing more than one party may describe those parties with such terms as "all plaintiffs," "the defendants," "the plaintiffs A, B, et al.," or "all defendants except X";

(B)   designate the judgment, order, or part thereof being appealed; and

(C)   name the court to which the appeal is taken.

(2)   A pro se notice of appeal is considered filed on behalf of the signer and the signer's spouse and minor children (if they are parties), unless the notice clearly indicates otherwise.

(3)   In a class action, whether or not the class has been certified, the notice of appeal is sufficient if it names one person qualified to bring the appeal as representative of the class.

(4)   An appeal must not be dismissed for informality of form or title of the notice of appeal, or for failure to name a party whose intent to appeal is otherwise clear from the notice.

(5)   Form 1 in the Appendix of Forms is a suggested form of a notice of appeal.

(d)   Serving the Notice of Appeal.

(1)   The district clerk must serve notice of the filing of a notice of appeal by [mailingsending] a copy to each party's counsel of record—excluding the appellant's—or, if a party is proceeding pro se, to the party's last known address. When a defendant in a criminal case appeals, the clerk must also serve a copy of the notice of appeal on the defendant [, either by personal service or by mail addressed to the defendant]. The clerk must promptly send a copy of the notice of appeal and of the docket entries—and any later docket entries—to the clerk of the court of appeals named in the notice. The district clerk must note, on each copy, the date when the notice of appeal was filed.

(2)   If an inmate confined in an institution files a notice of appeal in the manner provided by Rule 4(c), the district clerk must also note the date when the clerk docketed the notice.

(3)   The district clerk's failure to serve notice does not affect the validity of the appeal. The clerk must note on the docket the names of the parties to whom the clerk [mailssends] copies, with the date of [mailingsending]. Service is sufficient despite the death of a party or the party's counsel.

(e)   Payment of Fees. Upon filing a notice of appeal, the appellant must pay the district clerk all required fees. The district clerk receives the appellate docket fee on behalf of the court of appeals.

Rule 4.   Appeal as of Right—When Taken

(a)   Appeal in a Civil Case.

(1)   *Time for Filing a Notice of Appeal.*

(A)   In a civil case, except as provided in Rules 4(a)(1)(B), 4(a)(4), and 4(c), the notice of appeal required by Rule 3 must be filed with the district clerk within 30 days after entry of the judgment or order appealed from.

(B)   The notice of appeal may be filed by any party within 60 days after entry of the judgment or order appealed from if one of the parties is:

     (i)   the United States;

     (ii)   a United States agency;

     (iii)   a United States officer or employee sued in an official capacity; or

     (iv)   a current or former United States officer or employee sued in an individual capacity for an act or omission occurring in connection with duties performed on the United States' behalf—including all instances in which the United States represents that person when the judgment or order is entered or files the appeal for that person.

     (C)   * * *

(2)   *Filing Before Entry of Judgment.* A notice of appeal filed after the court announces a decision or order—but before the entry of the judgment or order—is treated as filed on the date of and after the entry.

(3)   *Multiple Appeals.* If one party timely files a notice of appeal, any other party may file a notice of appeal within 14 days after the date when the first notice was filed, or within the time otherwise prescribed by this Rule 4(a), whichever period ends later.

(4)   *Effect of a Motion on a Notice of Appeal.*

(A)   If a party files in the district court any of the following motions under the Federal Rules of Civil Procedure—and does so within the time allowed by those rules—the time to file an appeal runs for all parties from the entry of the order disposing of the last such remaining motion:

     (i)   for judgment under Rule 50(b);

(ii) to amend or make additional factual findings under Rule 52(b), whether or not granting the motion would alter the judgment;

(iii) for attorney's fees under Rule 54 if the district court extends the time to appeal under Rule 58;

(iv) to alter or amend the judgment under Rule 59;

(v) for a new trial under Rule 59; or

(vi) for relief under Rule 60 if the motion is filed no later than 28 days after the judgment is entered.

(B) (i) If a party files a notice of appeal after the court announces or enters a judgment—but before it disposes of any motion listed in Rule 4(a)(4)(A)—the notice becomes effective to appeal a judgment or order, in whole or in part, when the order disposing of the last such remaining motion is entered.

(ii) A party intending to challenge an order disposing of any motion listed in Rule 4(a)(4)(A), or a judgment altered or amended upon such a motion, must file a notice of appeal, or an amended notice of appeal—in compliance with Rule 3(c)—within the time prescribed by this Rule measured from the entry of the order disposing of the last such remaining motion.

(iii) No additional fee is required to file an amended notice.

(5) *Motion for Extension of Time.*

(A) The district court may extend the time to file a notice of appeal if:

(i) a party so moves no later than 30 days after the time prescribed by this Rule 4(a) expires; and

(ii) that party shows excusable neglect or good cause.

(B) A motion filed before the expiration of the time prescribed in Rule 4(a)(1) or (3) may be ex parte unless the court requires otherwise. If the motion is filed after the expiration of the prescribed time, notice must be given to the other parties in accordance with local rules.

(C) No extension under this Rule 4(a)(5) may exceed 30 days after the prescribed time or 14 days after the date when the order granting the motion is entered, whichever is later.

(6) *Reopening the Time to File an Appeal.* The district court may reopen the time to file an appeal for a period of 14 days after the date when its order to reopen is entered, but only if all the following conditions are satisfied:

(A) the court finds that the moving party did not receive notice under Federal Rule of Civil Procedure 77(d) of the entry of the judgment or order sought to be appealed within 21 days after entry;

(B) the motion is filed within 180 days after the judgment or order is entered or within 14 days after the moving party receives notice under Federal Rule of Civil Procedure 77(d) of the entry, whichever is earlier; and

(C) the court finds that no party would be prejudiced.

(7) *Entry Defined.*

(A) A judgment or order is entered for purposes of this Rule 4(a):

(i) if Federal Rule Civil Procedure 58(a) does not require a separate document, when the judgment or order is entered in the civil docket under Federal Rule of Civil Procedure 79(a); or

(ii) if Federal Rule Civil Procedure 58(a) requires a separate document, when the judgment or order is entered in the civil docket under Federal Rule of Civil Procedure 79(a) and when the earlier of these events occurs:

- the judgment or order is set forth on a separate document, or

- 150 days have run from entry of the judgment or order in the civil docket under Federal Rule of Civil Procedure 79(a).

(B) A failure to set forth a judgment or order on a separate document when required by Federal Rule of Civil Procedure 58(a) does not affect the validity of an appeal from that judgment or order.

(b) Appeal in a Criminal Case.

(1) *Time for Filing a Notice of Appeal.* * * *

(c) Appeal by an Inmate Confined in an Institution. * * *

(1) If an institution has a system designed for legal mail, an inmate confined there must use that system to receive the benefit of this Rule 4(c)(1). If an inmate files a notice of appeal in either a civil or a criminal case, the notice is timely if it is deposited in the institution's internal mail system on or before the last day for filing and:

(A) it is accompanied by:

(i) a declaration in compliance with 28 U.S.C. § 1746—or a notarized statement—setting out the date of deposit and stating that first-class postage is being prepaid; or

(ii) evidence (such as a postmark or date stamp) showing that the notice was so deposited and that postage was prepaid; or

(B) the court of appeals exercises its discretion to permit the later filing of a declaration or notarized statement that satisfies Rule 4(c)(1)(A)(i).

(2) If an inmate files the first notice of appeal in a civil case under this Rule 4(c), the 14-day period provided in Rule 4(a)(3) for another party to file a notice of appeal runs from the date when the district court dockets the first notice.

(3) When a defendant in a criminal case files a notice of appeal under this Rule 4(c), the 30-day period for the government to file its notice of appeal runs from the entry of the judgment or order appealed from or from the district court's docketing of the defendant's notice of appeal, whichever is later.

(d) Mistaken Filing in the Court of Appeals. If a notice of appeal in either a civil or a criminal case is mistakenly filed in the court of appeals, the clerk of that court must note on the notice the date when it was received and send it to the district clerk. The notice is then considered filed in the district court on the date so noted.

Rule 5. Appeal by Permission

Note that proposed changes to Rule 5(a)(1) have been approved by the Supreme Court. The changes appear in brackets within the current rule.

Unless Congress intervenes, the changes are effective December 1, 2019.

(a) Petition for Permission to Appeal.

(1) To request permission to appeal when an appeal is within the court of appeals' discretion, a party must file a petition [for permission to appeal. The petition must be filed] with the circuit clerk [with proof of serviceand serve it] on all other parties to the district-court action.

(2) The petition must be filed within the time specified by the statute or rule authorizing the appeal or, if no such time is specified, within the time provided by Rule 4(a) for filing a notice of appeal.

(3)   If a party cannot petition for appeal unless the district court first enters an order granting permission to do so or stating that the necessary conditions are met, the district court may amend its order, either on its own or in response to a party's motion, to include the required permission or statement. In that event, the time to petition runs from entry of the amended order.

(b)   Contents of the Petition; Answer or Cross-Petition; Oral Argument.

(1)   The petition must include the following:

    (A)   the facts necessary to understand the question presented;

    (B)   the question itself;

    (C)   the relief sought;

    (D)   the reasons why the appeal should be allowed and is authorized by a statute or rule; and

    (E)   an attached copy of:

        (i)   the order, decree, or judgment complained of and any related opinion or memorandum, and

        (ii)   any order stating the district court's permission to appeal or finding that the necessary conditions are met.

(2)   A party may file an answer in opposition or a cross-petition within 10 days after the petition is served.

(3)   The petition and answer will be submitted without oral argument unless the court of appeals orders otherwise.

(c)   Form of Papers; Number of Copies. All papers must conform to Rule 32(a)(1). An original and 3 copies must be filed unless the court requires a different number by local rule or by order in a particular case.

[Rule 5(c) would normally limit documents produced by computer to 5,200 words or handwritten or typed documents to 20 pages. See Rule 32(e), (f), and (g) for details of the requirements.]

(d)   Grant of Permission; Fees; Cost Bond; Filing the Record.

(1)   Within 14 days after the entry of the order granting permission to appeal, the appellant must:

    (A)   pay the district clerk all required fees; and

    (B)   file a cost bond if required under Rule 7.

(2)   A notice of appeal need not be filed. The date when the order granting permission to appeal is entered serves as the date of the notice of appeal for calculating time under these rules.

(3)   The district clerk must notify the circuit clerk once the petitioner has paid the fees. Upon receiving this notice, the circuit clerk must enter the appeal on the docket. The record must be forwarded and filed in accordance with Rules 11 and 12(c).

Rule 7.   Bond for Costs on Appeal in a Civil Case

In a civil case, the district court may require an appellant to file a bond or provide other security in any form and amount necessary to ensure payment of costs on appeal. Rule 8(b) applies to a surety on a bond given under this rule.

Rule 8.   Stay or Injunction Pending Appeal

(a)   Motion for Stay.

(1)   *Initial Motion in the District Court.* A party must ordinarily move first in the district court for the following relief:

    (A)   a stay of the judgment or order of a district court pending appeal;

    (B)   approval of a supersedeas bond or other security to obtain a stay of judgment; or

    (C)   an order suspending, modifying, restoring, or granting an injunction while an appeal is pending.

    (2)   *Motion in the Court of Appeals; Conditions on Relief.* A motion for the relief mentioned in Rule 8(a)(1) may be made to the court of appeals or to one of its judges.

        (A)   The motion must:

            (i)   show that moving first in the district court would be impracticable; or

            (ii)   state that, a motion having been made, the district court denied the motion or failed to afford the relief requested and state any reasons given by the district court for its action.

        (B)   The motion must also include:

            (i)   the reasons for granting the relief requested and the facts relied on;

            (ii)   originals or copies of affidavits or other sworn statements supporting facts subject to dispute; and

            (iii)   relevant parts of the record.

        (C)   The moving party must give reasonable notice of the motion to all parties.

        (D)   A motion under this Rule 8(a)(2) must be filed with the circuit clerk and normally will be considered by a panel of the court. But in an exceptional case in which time requirements make that procedure impracticable, the motion may be made to and considered by a single judge.

        (E)   The court may condition relief on a party's filing a bond or other security in the district court.

  (b)   Proceeding Against a Surety. * * *

  (c)   Stay in a Criminal Case. * * *

Rule 10. The Record on Appeal

  (a)   Composition of the Record on Appeal. The following items constitute the record on appeal:

    (1)   the original papers and exhibits filed in the district court;

    (2)   the transcript of proceedings, if any; and

    (3)   a certified copy of the docket entries prepared by the district clerk.

  (b)   The Transcript of Proceedings.

    (1)   *Appellant's Duty to Order.* Within 14 days after filing the notice of appeal or entry of an order disposing of the last timely remaining motion of a type specified in Rule 4(a)(4)(A), whichever is later, the appellant must do either of the following:

        (A)   order from the reporter a transcript of such parts of the proceedings not already on file as the appellant considers necessary, subject to a local rule of the court of appeals and with the following qualifications:

            (i)   the order must be in writing;

            (ii)   if the cost of the transcript is to be paid by the United States under the Criminal Justice Act, the order must so state; and

(iii)   the appellant must, within the same period, file a copy of the order with the district clerk; or

(B)   file a certificate stating that no transcript will be ordered.

(2)   *Unsupported Finding or Conclusion.* If the appellant intends to urge on appeal that a finding or conclusion is unsupported by the evidence or is contrary to the evidence, the appellant must include in the record a transcript of all evidence relevant to that finding or conclusion.

(3)   *Partial Transcript.* Unless the entire transcript is ordered:

(A)   the appellant must—within the 14 days provided in Rule 10(b)(1)—file a statement of the issues that the appellant intends to present on the appeal and must serve on the appellee a copy of both the order or certificate and the statement;

(B)   if the appellee considers it necessary to have a transcript of other parts of the proceedings, the appellee must, within 14 days after the service of the order or certificate and the statement of the issues, file and serve on the appellant a designation of additional parts to be ordered; and

(C)   unless within 14 days after service of that designation the appellant has ordered all such parts, and has so notified the appellee, the appellee may within the following 14 days either order the parts or move in the district court for an order requiring the appellant to do so.

(4)   *Payment.* At the time of ordering, a party must make satisfactory arrangements with the reporter for paying the cost of the transcript.

(c)   Statement of the Evidence When the Proceedings Were Not Recorded or When a Transcript Is Unavailable. If the transcript of a hearing or trial is unavailable, the appellant may prepare a statement of the evidence or proceedings from the best available means, including the appellant's recollection. The statement must be served on the appellee, who may serve objections or proposed amendments within 14 days after being served. The statement and any objections or proposed amendments must then be submitted to the district court for settlement and approval. As settled and approved, the statement must be included by the district clerk in the record on appeal.

(d)   Agreed Statement as the Record on Appeal. In place of the record on appeal as defined in Rule 10(a), the parties may prepare, sign, and submit to the district court a statement of the case showing how the issues presented by the appeal arose and were decided in the district court. The statement must set forth only those facts averred and proved or sought to be proved that are essential to the court's resolution of the issues. If the statement is truthful, it—together with any additions that the district court may consider necessary to a full presentation of the issues on appeal—must be approved by the district court and must then be certified to the court of appeals as the record on appeal. The district clerk must then send it to the circuit clerk within the time provided by Rule 11. A copy of the agreed statement may be filed in place of the appendix required by Rule 30.

(e)   Correction or Modification of the Record.

(1)   If any difference arises about whether the record truly discloses what occurred in the district court, the difference must be submitted to and settled by that court and the record conformed accordingly.

(2)   If anything material to either party is omitted from or misstated in the record by error or accident, the omission or misstatement may be corrected and a supplemental record may be certified and forwarded:

(A)   on stipulation of the parties;

(B)   by the district court before or after the record has been forwarded; or

(C)   by the court of appeals.

(3)   All other questions as to the form and content of the record must be presented to the court of appeals.

Rule 11. Forwarding the Record

(a) **Appellant's Duty.** An appellant filing a notice of appeal must comply with Rule 10(b) and must do whatever else is necessary to enable the clerk to assemble and forward the record. If there are multiple appeals from a judgment or order, the clerk must forward a single record.

(b) **Duties of Reporter and District Clerk.**

(1) *Reporter's Duty to Prepare and File a Transcript.* The reporter must prepare and file a transcript as follows:

(A)   Upon receiving an order for a transcript, the reporter must enter at the foot of the order the date of its receipt and the expected completion date and send a copy, so endorsed, to the circuit clerk.

(B)   If the transcript cannot be completed within 30 days of the reporter's receipt of the order, the reporter may request the circuit clerk to grant additional time to complete it. The clerk must note on the docket the action taken and notify the parties.

(C)   When a transcript is complete, the reporter must file it with the district clerk and notify the circuit clerk of the filing.

(D)   If the reporter fails to file the transcript on time, the circuit clerk must notify the district judge and do whatever else the court of appeals directs.

(2) *District Clerk's Duty to Forward.* When the record is complete, the district clerk must number the documents constituting the record and send them promptly to the circuit clerk together with a list of the documents correspondingly numbered and reasonably identified. Unless directed to do so by a party or the circuit clerk, the district clerk will not send to the court of appeals documents of unusual bulk or weight, physical exhibits other than documents, or other parts of the record designated for omission by local rule of the court of appeals. If the exhibits are unusually bulky or heavy, a party must arrange with the clerks in advance for their transportation and receipt.

(c) **Retaining the Record Temporarily in the District Court for Use in Preparing the Appeal.** The parties may stipulate, or the district court on motion may order, that the district clerk retain the record temporarily for the parties to use in preparing the papers on appeal. In that event the district clerk must certify to the circuit clerk that the record on appeal is complete. Upon receipt of the appellee's brief, or earlier if the court orders or the parties agree, the appellant must request the district clerk to forward the record.

(d) **[Abrogated.]**

(e) **Retaining the Record by Court Order.**

(1)   The court of appeals may, by order or local rule, provide that a certified copy of the docket entries be forwarded instead of the entire record. But a party may at any time during the appeal request that designated parts of the record be forwarded.

(2)   The district court may order the record or some part of it retained if the court needs it while the appeal is pending, subject, however, to call by the court of appeals.

(3)   If part or all of the record is ordered retained, the district clerk must send to the court of appeals a copy of the order and the docket entries together with the parts of the original record allowed by the district court and copies of any parts of the record designated by the parties.

(f) **Retaining Parts of the Record in the District Court by Stipulation of the Parties.** The parties may agree by written stipulation filed in the district court that designated parts of the record be retained in the district court subject to call by the court of appeals or request by a party. The parts of the record so designated remain a part of the record on appeal.

(g) Record for a Preliminary Motion in the Court of Appeals. If, before the record is forwarded, a party makes any of the following motions in the court of appeals:

- for dismissal;

- for release;

- for a stay pending appeal;

- for additional security on the bond on appeal or on a bond or other security provided to obtain a stay of judgment; or

- for any other intermediate order—

the district clerk must send the court of appeals any parts of the record designated by any party.

Rule 12. Docketing the Appeal; Filing a Representation Statement; Filing the Record

(a) Docketing the Appeal. Upon receiving the copy of the notice of appeal and the docket entries from the district clerk under Rule 3(d), the circuit clerk must docket the appeal under the title of the district-court action and must identify the appellant, adding the appellant's name if necessary.

(b) Filing a Representation Statement. Unless the court of appeals designates another time, the attorney who filed the notice of appeal must, within 14 days after filing the notice, file a statement with the circuit clerk naming the parties that the attorney represents on appeal.

(c) Filing the Record, Partial Record, or Certificate. Upon receiving the record, partial record, or district clerk's certificate as provided in Rule 11, the circuit clerk must file it and immediately notify all parties of the filing date.

Rule 12.1. Remand After an Indicative Ruling by the District Court on a Motion for Relief That Is Barred by a Pending Appeal

(a) Notice to the Court of Appeals. If a timely motion is made in the district court for relief that it lacks authority to grant because of an appeal that has been docketed and is pending, the movant must promptly notify the circuit clerk if the district court states either that it would grant the motion or that the motion raises a substantial issue.

(b) Remand After an Indicative Ruling. If the district court states that it would grant the motion or that the motion raises a substantial issue, the court of appeals may remand for further proceedings but retains jurisdiction unless it expressly dismisses the appeal. If the court of appeals remands but retains jurisdiction, the parties must promptly notify the circuit clerk when the district court has decided the motion on remand.

TITLE IV. REVIEW OR ENFORCEMENT OF AN ORDER OF AN ADMINISTRATIVE AGENCY, BOARD, COMMISSION, OR OFFICER

Rule 15. Review or Enforcement of an Agency Order—How Obtained; Intervention

(a) Petition for Review; Joint Petition.

(1)   Review of an agency order is commenced by filing, within the time prescribed by law, a petition for review with the clerk of a court of appeals authorized to review the agency order. If their interests make joinder practicable, two or more persons may join in a petition to the same court to review the same order.

(2)   The petition must:

(A)   name each party seeking review either in the caption or the body of the petition—using such terms as "et al.," "petitioners," or "respondents" does not effectively name the parties;

(B)   name the agency as a respondent (even though not named in the petition, the United States is a respondent if required by statute); and

(C)   specify the order or part thereof to be reviewed.

(3)   Form 3 in the Appendix of Forms is a suggested form of a petition for review.

(4)   In this rule "agency" includes an agency, board, commission, or officer; "petition for review" includes a petition to enjoin, suspend, modify, or otherwise review, or a notice of appeal, whichever form is indicated by the applicable statute.

(b)   Application or Cross-Application to Enforce an Order; Answer; Default.

(1)   An application to enforce an agency order must be filed with the clerk of a court of appeals authorized to enforce the order. If a petition is filed to review an agency order that the court may enforce, a party opposing the petition may file a cross-application for enforcement.

(2)   Within 21 days after the application for enforcement is filed, the respondent must serve on the applicant an answer to the application and file it with the clerk. If the respondent fails to answer in time, the court will enter judgment for the relief requested.

(3)   The application must contain a concise statement of the proceedings in which the order was entered, the facts upon which venue is based, and the relief requested.

(c)   Service of the Petition or Application. The circuit clerk must serve a copy of the petition for review, or an application or cross-application to enforce an agency order, on each respondent as prescribed by Rule 3(d), unless a different manner of service is prescribed by statute. At the time of filing, the petitioner must:

(1)   serve, or have served, a copy on each party admitted to participate in the agency proceedings, except for the respondents;

(2)   file with the clerk a list of those so served; and

(3)   give the clerk enough copies of the petition or application to serve each respondent.

(d)   Intervention. Unless a statute provides another method, a person who wants to intervene in a proceeding under this rule must file a motion for leave to intervene with the circuit clerk and serve a copy on all parties. The motion—or other notice of intervention authorized by statute—must be filed within 30 days after the petition for review is filed and must contain a concise statement of the interest of the moving party and the grounds for intervention.

(e)   Payment of Fees. When filing any separate or joint petition for review in a court of appeals, the petitioner must pay the circuit clerk all required fees.

Rule 18. Stay Pending Review

(a)   Motion for a Stay.

(1)   *Initial Motion Before the Agency.* A petitioner must ordinarily move first before the agency for a stay pending review of its decision or order.

(2)   *Motion in the Court of Appeals.* A motion for a stay may be made to the court of appeals or one of its judges.

(A)   The motion must:

(i)   show that moving first before the agency would be impracticable; or

(ii)   state that, a motion having been made, the agency denied the motion or failed to afford the relief requested and state any reasons given by the agency for its action.

(B)   The motion must also include:

(i)   the reasons for granting the relief requested and the facts relied on;

(ii)   originals or copies of affidavits or other sworn statements supporting facts subject to dispute; and

(iii)   relevant parts of the record.

(C)   The moving party must give reasonable notice of the motion to all parties.

(D)   The motion must be filed with the circuit clerk and normally will be considered by a panel of the court. But in an exceptional case in which time requirements make that procedure impracticable, the motion may be made to and considered by a single judge.

(b) Bond. The court may condition relief on the filing of a bond or other appropriate security.

Rule 19. Settlement of a Judgment Enforcing an Agency Order in Part

When the court files an opinion directing entry of judgment enforcing the agency's order in part, the agency must within 14 days file with the clerk and serve on each other party a proposed judgment conforming to the opinion. A party who disagrees with the agency's proposed judgment must within 10 days file with the clerk and serve the agency with a proposed judgment that the party believes conforms to the opinion. The court will settle the judgment and direct entry without further hearing or argument.

TITLE V. EXTRAORDINARY WRITS

Rule 21. Writs of Mandamus and Prohibition, and Other Extraordinary Writs

Note that proposed changes to Rule 21(a) and (c) have been approved by the Supreme Court. The changes appear in brackets within the current rule.

Unless Congress intervenes, the changes are effective December 1, 2019.

(a) Mandamus or Prohibition to a Court: Petition, Filing, Service, and Docketing.

(1)   A party petitioning for a writ of mandamus or prohibition directed to a court must file [athe] petition with the circuit clerk [with proof of serviceand serve it] on all parties to the proceeding in the trial court. The party must also provide a copy to the trial-court judge. All parties to the proceeding in the trial court other than the petitioner are respondents for all purposes.

(2)   (A)   The petition must be titled "In re [name of petitioner]."

(B)   The petition must state:

(i)   the relief sought;

(ii)   the issues presented;

(iii)   the facts necessary to understand the issue presented by the petition; and

(iv)   the reasons why the writ should issue.

(C)   The petition must include a copy of any order or opinion or parts of the record that may be essential to understand the matters set forth in the petition.

(3)   Upon receiving the prescribed docket fee, the clerk must docket the petition and submit it to the court.

(b) Denial; Order Directing Answer; Briefs; Precedence.

(1)   The court may deny the petition without an answer. Otherwise, it must order the respondent, if any, to answer within a fixed time.

(2)   The clerk must serve the order to respond on all persons directed to respond.

(3)   Two or more respondents may answer jointly.

(4)   The court of appeals may invite or order the trial-court judge to address the petition or may invite an amicus curiae to do so. The trial-court judge may request permission to address the petition but may not do so unless invited or ordered to do so by the court of appeals.

(5)   If briefing or oral argument is required, the clerk must advise the parties, and when appropriate, the trial-court judge or amicus curiae.

(6)   The proceeding must be given preference over ordinary civil cases.

(7)   The circuit clerk must send a copy of the final disposition to the trial-court judge.

(c)   Other Extraordinary Writs. An application for an extraordinary writ other than one provided for in Rule 21(a) must be made by filing a petition with the circuit clerk [~~with proof of service~~and serve it] on the respondents. Proceedings on the application must conform, so far as is practicable, to the procedures prescribed in Rule 21(a) and (b).

(d)   Form of Papers; Number of Copies. All papers must conform to Rule 32(a)(1). An original and 3 copies must be filed unless the court requires the filing of a different number by local rule or by order in a particular case.

[Rule 21(d) would normally restrict documents produced by computer to 7,800 words or handwritten or typed documents to 30 pages. See Rules 32(e), (f), and (g) for details of the requirements.]

TITLE VI. HABEAS CORPUS; PROCEEDINGS IN FORMA PAUPERIS

Rule 24. Proceeding in Forma Pauperis

(a)   Leave to Proceed in Forma Pauperis.

(1)   *Motion in the District Court.* Except as stated in Rule 24(a)(3), a party to a district-court action who desires to appeal in forma pauperis must file a motion in the district court. The party must attach an affidavit that:

    (A)   shows in the detail prescribed by Form 4 of the Appendix of Forms, the party's inability to pay or to give security for fees and costs;

    (B)   claims an entitlement to redress; and

    (C)   states the issues that the party intends to present on appeal.

(2)   *Action on the Motion.* If the district court grants the motion, the party may proceed on appeal without prepaying or giving security for fees and costs, unless a statute provides otherwise. If the district court denies the motion, it must state its reasons in writing.

(3)   *Prior Approval.* A party who was permitted to proceed in forma pauperis in the district-court action, or who was determined to be financially unable to obtain an adequate defense in a criminal case, may proceed on appeal in forma pauperis without further authorization, unless:

    (A)   the district court—before or after the notice of appeal is filed—certifies that the appeal is not taken in good faith or finds that the party is not otherwise entitled to proceed in forma pauperis and states in writing its reasons for the certification or finding; or

    (B)   a statute provides otherwise.

(4)   *Notice of District Court's Denial.* The district clerk must immediately notify the parties and the court of appeals when the district court does any of the following:

    (A)   denies a motion to proceed on appeal in forma pauperis;

    (B)   certifies that the appeal is not taken in good faith; or

    (C)   finds that the party is not otherwise entitled to proceed in forma pauperis.

(5) *Motion in the Court of Appeals.* A party may file a motion to proceed on appeal in forma pauperis in the court of appeals within 30 days after service of the notice prescribed in Rule 24(a)(4). The motion must include a copy of the affidavit filed in the district court and the district court's statement of reasons for its action. If no affidavit was filed in the district court, the party must include the affidavit prescribed by Rule 24(a)(1).

(b) Leave to Proceed in Forma Pauperis on Appeal or Review of an Administrative-Agency Proceeding. When an appeal or review of a proceeding before an administrative agency, board, commission, or officer (including for the purpose of this rule the United States Tax Court) proceeds directly in a court of appeals, a party may file in the court of appeals a motion for leave to proceed on appeal in forma pauperis with an affidavit prescribed by Rule 24(a)(1).

(c) Leave to Use Original Record. A party allowed to proceed on appeal in forma pauperis may request that the appeal be heard on the original record without reproducing any part.

TITLE VII. GENERAL PROVISIONS

Rule 25. Filing and Service

Note that a proposed addition to Rule 25(d)(1) has been approved by the Supreme Court. The addition appears in brackets within the current rule.

Unless Congress intervenes, the addition is effective December 1, 2019.

(a) Filing.

(1) *Filing with the Clerk.* A paper required or permitted to be filed in a court of appeals must be filed with the clerk.

(2) *Filing: Method and Timeliness.*

(A) *Nonelectronic Filing.*

(i) In general. For a paper not filed electronically, filing may be accomplished by mail addressed to the clerk, but filing is not timely unless the clerk receives the papers within the time fixed for filing.

(ii) A Brief or Appendix. A brief or appendix not filed electronically is timely filed, however, if on or before the last day for filing, it is:

- mailed to the clerk by first-class mail, or other class of mail that is at least as expeditious, postage prepaid; or

- dispatched to a third-party commercial carrier for delivery to the clerk within 3 days.

(iii) Inmate Filing. * * *

(B) *Electronic Filing and Signing.*

(i) By a Represented Person—Generally Required; Exceptions. A person represented by an attorney must file electronically, unless nonelectronic filing is allowed by the court for good cause or is allowed or required by local rule.

(ii) By an Unrepresented Person—When Allowed or Required. A person not represented by an attorney:

- may file electronically only if allowed by court order or by local rule; and

- may be required to file electronically only by court order, or by a local rule that includes reasonable exceptions.

(iii) Signing. A filing made through a person's electronic-filing account and authorized by that person, together with that person's name on a signature block, constitutes the person's signature.

(iv) Same as a Written Paper. A paper filed electronically is a written paper for purposes of these rules.

(3) *Filing a Motion with a Judge.* If a motion requests relief that may be granted by a single judge, the judge may permit the motion to be filed with the judge; the judge must note the filing date on the motion and give it to the clerk.

(4) *Clerk's Refusal of Documents.* The clerk must not refuse to accept for filing any paper presented for that purpose solely because it is not presented in proper form as required by these rules or by any local rule or practice.

(5) *Privacy Protection.* An appeal in a case whose privacy protection was governed by Federal Rule of Bankruptcy Procedure 9037, Federal Rule Civil Procedure 5.2, or Federal Rule of Criminal Procedure 49.1 is governed by the same rule on appeal. * * *

(b) Service of All Papers Required. Unless a rule requires service by the clerk, a party must, at or before the time of filing a paper, serve a copy on the other parties to the appeal or review. Service on a party represented by counsel must be made on the party's counsel.

(c) Manner of Service.

(1) Nonelectronic service may be any of the following:

(A) personal, including delivery to a responsible person at the office of counsel;

(B) by mail; or

(C) by third-party commercial carrier for delivery within 3 days.

(2) Electronic service of a paper may be made (A) by sending it to a registered user by filing it with the court's electronic-filing system or (B) by sending it by other electronic means that the person to be served consented to in writing.

(3) When reasonable considering such factors as the immediacy of the relief sought, distance, and cost, service on a party must be by a manner at least as expeditious as the manner used to file the paper with the court.

(4) Service by mail or by commercial carrier is complete on mailing or delivery to the carrier. Service by electronic means is complete on filing or sending, unless the party making service is notified that the paper was not received by the party served.

(d) Proof of Service.

(1) A paper presented for filing must contain either of the following [if it was served other than through the court's electronic-filing system]:

(A) an acknowledgment of service by the person served; or

(B) proof of service consisting of a statement by the person who made service certifying:

(i) the date and manner of service;

(ii) the names of the persons served; and

(iii) their mail or electronic addresses, facsimile numbers, or the addresses of the places of delivery.

(2) When a brief or appendix is filed by mailing or dispatch in accordance with Rule 25(a)(2)(B), the proof of service must also state the date and manner by which the document was mailed or dispatched to the clerk.

(3)   Proof of service may appear on or be affixed to the papers filed.

(e)   Number of Copies. When these rules require the filing or furnishing of a number of copies, a court may require a different number by local rule or by order in a particular case.

Rule 26. Computing and Extending Time

Note that proposed changes to Rule 26(c) have been approved by the Supreme Court. The changes appear in brackets within the current rule.

Unless Congress intervenes, the changes are effective December 1, 2019.

(a)   Computing Time. The following rules apply in computing any time period specified in these rules, in any local rule or court order, or in any statute that does not specify a method of computing time.

(1)   **Period Stated in Days or a Longer Unit.** When the period is stated in days or a longer unit of time:

(A)   exclude the day of the event that triggers the period;

(B)   count every day, including intermediate Saturdays, Sundays, and legal holidays; and

(C)   include the last day of the period, but if the last day is a Saturday, Sunday, or legal holiday, the period continues to run until the end of the next day that is not a Saturday, Sunday, or legal holiday.

(2)   **Period Stated in Hours.** When the period is stated in hours:

(A)   begin counting immediately on the occurrence of the event that triggers the period;

(B)   count every hour, including hours during intermediate Saturdays, Sundays, and legal holidays; and

(C)   if the period would end on a Saturday, Sunday, or legal holiday, the period continues to run until the same time on the next day that is not a Saturday, Sunday, or legal holiday.

(3)   **Inaccessibility of the Clerk's Office.** Unless the court orders otherwise, if the clerk's office is inaccessible:

(A)   on the last day for filing under Rule 26(a)(1), then the time for filing is extended to the first accessible day that is not a Saturday, Sunday, or legal holiday; or

(B)   during the last hour for filing under Rule 26(a)(2), then the time for filing is extended to the same time on the first accessible day that is not a Saturday, Sunday, or legal holiday.

(4)   **"Last Day" Defined.** Unless a different time is set by a statute, local rule, or court order, the last day ends:

(A)   for electronic filing in the district court, at midnight in the court's time zone;

(B)   for electronic filing in the court of appeals, at midnight in the time zone of the circuit clerk's principal office;

(C)   for filing under Rules 4(c)(1), 25(a)(2)(B), and 25(a)(2)(C)—and filing by mail under Rule 13(a)(2)—at the latest time for the method chosen for delivery to the post office, third-party commercial carrier, or prison mailing system; and

(D)   for filing by other means, when the clerk's office is scheduled to close.

(5)   **"Next Day" Defined.** The "next day" is determined by continuing to count forward when the period is measured after an event and backward when measured before an event.

(6)   **"Legal Holiday" Defined.** "Legal holiday" means:

(A)   the day set aside by statute for observing New Year's Day, Martin Luther King Jr.'s Birthday, Washington's Birthday, Memorial Day, Independence Day, Labor Day, Columbus Day, Veterans' Day, Thanksgiving Day, or Christmas Day;

(B)   any day declared a holiday by the President or Congress; and

(C)   for periods that are measured after an event, any other day declared a holiday by the state where either of the following is located: the district court that rendered the challenged judgment or order, or the circuit clerk's principal office.

(b)   Extending Time. For good cause, the court may extend the time prescribed by these rules or by its order to perform any act, or may permit an act to be done after that time expires. But the court may not extend the time to file:

(1)   a notice of appeal (except as authorized in Rule 4) or a petition for permission to appeal; or

(2)   a notice of appeal from or a petition to enjoin, set aside, suspend, modify, enforce, or otherwise review an order of an administrative agency, board, commission, or officer of the United States, unless specifically authorized by law.

(c)   Additional Time [a(A)]fter Service. When a party may or must act within a specified time after being served, [and the paper is not served electronically on the party on the date stated in the proof of service,] 3 days are added after the period would otherwise expire under Rule 26(a) [, unless the paper is delivered on the date of service stated in the proof of service. For purposes of this Rule 26(c), a paper that is served electronically is not treated as delivered on the date of service stated in the proof of service].

Rule 26.1. Corporate Disclosure Statement

Note that a number of changes to Rule 26.1 have been approved by the Supreme Court. They involve changing the title of Rule 26.1, changes to 26.1(a), addition of new parts (b) and (c) regarding criminal law and bankruptcy appeals, and changes to original parts (b) and (c) which would be redesignated as parts (d) and (e). The proposed rule, as altered by the proposed changes, appears in italics, following the current rule.

Unless Congress intervenes, the amended rule is effective December 1, 2019.

(a)   Who Must File. Any nongovernmental corporate party to a proceeding in a court of appeals must file a statement that identifies any parent corporation and any publicly held company that owns 10% or more of the stock or states that there is no such corporation.

(b)   Time for Filing; Supplemental Filing. A party must file the Rule 26.1(a) statement with the principal brief or upon filing a motion, response, petition, or answer in the court of appeals, whichever occurs first, unless a local rule requires earlier filing. Even if the statement has already been filed, the party's principal brief must include the statement before the table of contents. A party must supplement its statement whenever the information that must be disclosed under Rule 26.1(a) changes.

(c)   Number of Copies. If the Rule 26.1 statement is filed before the principal brief, or if a supplemental statement is filed, the party must file an original and 3 copies unless the court requires a different number by local rule or by order in a particular case.

Proposed Amended Rule 26.1 as Approved by the Supreme Court

Rule 26.1. Disclosure Statement

(a)   *Nongovernmental Corporations.*

Any nongovernmental corporation that is a party to a proceeding in a court of appeals must file a statement that identifies any parent corporation and any publicly held corporation that owns 10% or more of its stock or states that there is no such corporation. The same requirement applies to a nongovernmental corporation that seeks to intervene.

(b) **[Criminal Cases—omitted]**

(c) **[Bankruptcy Cases—omitted]**

(d) **Time for Filing; Supplemental Filing.** *The Rule 26.1 state must*

(1) be filed with the principal brief or upon filing a motion, response, petition or answer in the court of appeals, whichever occurs first, unless a local rule require earlier filing;

(2) be included before the table of contents in the principal brief; and

(3) be supplemented whenever the information required under Rule 26.1 changes.

(e) **Number of Copies.** *If the Rule 26.1 statement is filed before the principal brief, or if a supplemental statement is filed, an original and 3 copies must be filed unless the court requires a different number by local rule or by order in a particular case.*

Rule 27. Motions

(a) In General.

(1) *Application for Relief.* An application for an order or other relief is made by motion unless these rules prescribe another form. A motion must be in writing unless the court permits otherwise.

(2) *Contents of a Motion.*

(A) Grounds and Relief Sought. A motion must state with particularity the grounds for the motion, the relief sought, and the legal argument necessary to support it.

(B) Accompanying Documents.

(i) Any affidavit or other paper necessary to support a motion must be served and filed with the motion.

(ii) An affidavit must contain only factual information, not legal argument.

(iii) A motion seeking substantive relief must include a copy of the trial court's opinion or agency's decision as a separate exhibit.

(C) Documents Barred or not Required.

(i) A separate brief supporting or responding to a motion must not be filed.

(ii) A notice of motion is not required.

(iii) A proposed order is not required.

(3) *Response.*

(A) Time to File. Any party may file a response to a motion; Rule 27(a)(2) governs its contents. The response must be filed within 10 days after service of the motion unless the court shortens or extends the time. A motion authorized by Rules 8, 9, 18, or 41 may be granted before the 10-day period runs only if the court gives reasonable notice to the parties that it intends to act sooner.

(B) Request for Affirmative Relief. A response may include a motion for affirmative relief. The time to respond to the new motion, and to reply to that response, are governed by Rule 27(a)(3)(A) and (a)(4). The title of the response must alert the court to the request for relief.

(4) *Reply to Response.* Any reply to a response must be filed within 7 days after service of the response. A reply must not present matters that do not relate to the response.

(b) Disposition of a Motion for a Procedural Order. The court may act on a motion for a procedural order—including a motion under Rule 26(b)—at any time without awaiting a response, and may, by rule or by order in a particular case, authorize its clerk to act on specified types of procedural motions. A party adversely affected by the court's, or the clerk's, action may file a motion to reconsider, vacate, or modify that action. Timely opposition filed after the motion is granted in whole or in part does not constitute a request to reconsider, vacate, or modify the disposition; a motion requesting that relief must be filed.

(c) Power of a Single Judge to Entertain a Motion. A circuit judge may act alone on any motion, but may not dismiss or otherwise determine an appeal or other proceeding. A court of appeals may provide by rule or by order in a particular case that only the court may act on any motion or class of motions. The court may review the action of a single judge.

(d) Form of Papers; Page Limits; and Number of Copies.

(1) *Format.*

(A) Reproduction. A motion, response, or reply may be reproduced by any process that yields a clear black image on light paper. The paper must be opaque and unglazed. Only one side of the paper may be used.

(B) Cover. A cover is not required but there must be a caption that includes the case number, the name of the court, the title of the case, and a brief descriptive title indicating the purpose of the motion and identifying the party or parties for whom it is filed. If a cover is used, it must be white.

(C) Binding. The document must be bound in any manner that is secure, does not obscure the text, and permits the document to lie reasonably flat when open.

(D) Paper Size, line spacing, and margins. The document must be on 8½ by 11 inch paper. The text must be double-spaced, but quotations more than two lines long may be indented and single-spaced. Headings and footnotes may be single-spaced. Margins must be at least one inch on all four sides. Page numbers may be placed in the margins, but no text may appear there.

(E) Typeface and type styles. The document must comply with the typeface requirements of Rule 32(a)(5) and the type-style requirements of Rule 32(a)(6).

(2) *Page Limits.* [The following restrictions apply: (A) on a motion or response thereto, 5,200 words produced by computer, or (B) on a handwritten or typed motion or response thereto, 20 pages, or (C) on a reply, 2,600 words produced by computer or (D) on a handwritten or typed reply, 10 pages. See Rules 32(e), (f), and (g) for details of the requirements.]

(3) *Number of Copies.* An original and 3 copies must be filed unless the court requires a different number by local rule or by order in a particular case.

(e) Oral Argument. A motion will be decided without oral argument unless the court orders otherwise.

Rule 30. Appendix to the Briefs

(a) Appellant's Responsibility.

(1) *Contents of the Appendix.* The appellant must prepare and file an appendix to the briefs containing:

(A) the relevant docket entries in the proceeding below;

(B) the relevant portions of the pleadings, charge, findings, or opinion;

(C) the judgment, order, or decision in question; and

(D) other parts of the record to which the parties wish to direct the court's attention.

(2) *Excluded Material.* Memoranda of law in the district court should not be included in the appendix unless they have independent relevance. Parts of the record may be relied on by the court or the parties even though not included in the appendix.

(3) *Time to File; Number of Copies.* Unless filing is deferred under Rule 30(c), the appellant must file 10 copies of the appendix with the brief and must serve one copy on counsel for each party separately represented. An unrepresented party proceeding in forma pauperis must file 4 legible copies with the clerk, and one copy must be served on counsel for each separately represented party. The court may by local rule or by order in a particular case require the filing or service of a different number.

(b) All Parties' Responsibilities.

(1) *Determining the Contents of the Appendix.* The parties are encouraged to agree on the contents of the appendix. In the absence of an agreement, the appellant must, within 14 days after the record is filed, serve on the appellee a designation of the parts of the record the appellant intends to include in the appendix and a statement of the issues the appellant intends to present for review. The appellee may, within 14 days after receiving the designation, serve on the appellant a designation of additional parts to which it wishes to direct the court's attention. The appellant must include the designated parts in the appendix. The parties must not engage in unnecessary designation of parts of the record, because the entire record is available to the court. This paragraph applies also to a cross-appellant and a cross-appellee.

(2) *Costs of Appendix.* Unless the parties agree otherwise, the appellant must pay the cost of the appendix. If the appellant considers parts of the record designated by the appellee to be unnecessary, the appellant may advise the appellee, who must then advance the cost of including those parts. The cost of the appendix is a taxable cost. But if any party causes unnecessary parts of the record to be included in the appendix, the court may impose the cost of those parts on that party. Each circuit must, by local rule, provide for sanctions against attorneys who unreasonably and vexatiously increase litigation costs by including unnecessary material in the appendix.

(c) Deferred Appendix.

(1) *Deferral Until After Briefs Are Filed.* The court may provide by rule for classes of cases or by order in a particular case that preparation of the appendix may be deferred until after the briefs have been filed and that the appendix may be filed 21 days after the appellee's brief is served. Even though the filing of the appendix may be deferred, Rule 30(b) applies; except that a party must designate the parts of the record it wants included in the appendix when it serves its brief, and need not include a statement of the issues presented.

(2) *References to the Record.*

(A) If the deferred appendix is used, the parties may cite in their briefs the pertinent pages of the record. When the appendix is prepared, the record pages cited in the briefs must be indicated by inserting record page numbers, in brackets, at places in the appendix where those pages of the record appear.

(B) A party who wants to refer directly to pages of the appendix may serve and file copies of the brief within the time required by Rule 31(a), containing appropriate references to pertinent pages of the record. In that event, within 14 days after the appendix is filed, the party must serve and file copies of the brief, containing references to the pages of the appendix in place of or in addition to the references to the pertinent pages of the record. Except for the correction of typographical errors, no other changes may be made to the brief.

(d) Format of the Appendix. The appendix must begin with a table of contents identifying the page at which each part begins. The relevant docket entries must follow the table of contents. Other parts of the record must follow chronologically. When pages from the transcript of proceedings are placed in the appendix, the transcript page numbers must be shown in brackets immediately before the included pages. Omissions in the text of papers or of the transcript must be indicated by asterisks. Immaterial formal matters (captions, subscriptions, acknowledgments, etc.) should be omitted.

(e) Reproduction of Exhibits. Exhibits designated for inclusion in the appendix may be reproduced in a separate volume, or volumes, suitably indexed. Four copies must be filed with the appendix, and one copy must be served on counsel for each separately represented party. If a transcript of a proceeding before an administrative agency, board, commission, or officer was used in a district-court action and has been designated for inclusion in the appendix, the transcript must be placed in the appendix as an exhibit.

(f) Appeal on the Original Record Without an Appendix. The court may, either by rule for all cases or classes of cases or by order in a particular case, dispense with the appendix and permit an appeal to proceed on the original record with any copies of the record, or relevant parts, that the court may order the parties to file.

Rule 31. Serving and Filing Briefs

(a) Time to Serve and File a Brief.

(1)   The appellant must serve and file a brief within 40 days after the record is filed. The appellee must serve and file a brief within 30 days after the appellant's brief is served. The appellant may serve and file a reply brief within 21 days after service of the appellee's brief but a reply brief must be filed at least 7 days before argument, unless the court, for good cause, allows a later filing.

(2)   A court of appeals that routinely considers cases on the merits promptly after the briefs are filed may shorten the time to serve and file briefs, either by local rule or by order in a particular case.

(b) Number of Copies. Twenty-five copies of each brief must be filed with the clerk and 2 copies must be served on counsel for each separately represented party. An unrepresented party proceeding in forma pauperis must file 4 legible copies with the clerk, and one copy must be served on counsel for each separately represented party. The court may by local rule or by order in a particular case require the filing or service of a different number.

(c) Consequence of Failure to File. If an appellant fails to file a brief within the time provided by this rule, or within an extended time, an appellee may move to dismiss the appeal. An appellee who fails to file a brief will not be heard at oral argument unless the court grants permission.

Rule 32. Form of Briefs, Appendices, and Other Papers

Note that proposed changes to Rule 32(f) have been approved by the Supreme Court. The changes appear in brackets within the current rule.

Unless Congress intervenes, the changes are effective December 1, 2019.

(a) Form of a Brief.

(1)   *Reproduction.*

(A)   A brief may be reproduced by any process that yields a clear black image on light paper. The paper must be opaque and unglazed. Only one side of the paper may be used.

(B)   Text must be reproduced with a clarity that equals or exceeds the output of a laser printer.

(C)   Photographs, illustrations, and tables may be reproduced by any method that results in a good copy of the original; a glossy finish is acceptable if the original is glossy.

(2)   *Cover.* Except for filings by unrepresented parties, the cover of the appellant's brief must be blue; the appellee's, red; an intervenor's or amicus curiae's, green; and any reply brief, gray. The front cover of a brief must contain:

(A)   the number of the case centered at the top;

(B)   the name of the court;

(C)   the title of the case (see Rule 12(a));

(D)   the nature of the proceeding (e.g., Appeal, Petition for Review) and the name of the court, agency, or board below;

(E)   the title of the brief, identifying the party or parties for whom the brief is filed; and

(F)   the name, office address, and telephone number of counsel representing the party for whom the brief is filed.

(3)   *Binding.* The brief must be bound in any manner that is secure, does not obscure the text, and permits the brief to lie reasonably flat when open.

(4)   *Paper Size, Line Spacing, and Margins.* The brief must be on 8½ by 11 inch paper. The text must be double-spaced, but quotations more than two lines long may be indented and single-spaced. Headings and footnotes may be single-spaced. Margins must be at least one inch on all four sides. Page numbers may be placed in the margins, but no text may appear there.

(5)   *Typeface.* Either a proportionally spaced or a monospaced face may be used.

(A)   A proportionally spaced face must include serifs, but sans-serif type may be used in headings and captions. A proportionally spaced face must be 14-point or larger.

(B)   A monospaced face may not contain more than 10½ characters per inch.

(6)   *Type Styles.* A brief must be set in a plain, roman style, although italics or boldface may be used for emphasis. Case names must be italicized or underlined.

(7)   *Length.*

(A)   Page limitation. A principal brief may not exceed 30 pages, or a reply brief 15 pages, unless it complies with Rule 32(a)(7)(B).

(B)   Type-volume limitation.

(i)   A principal brief is acceptable if:

- it contains no more than 13,000 words; or

- it uses a monospaced face and contains no more than 1,300 lines of text.

(ii)   A reply brief is acceptable if it contains no more than half of the type volume specified in Rule 32(a)(7)(B)(i).

(iii)   Headings, footnotes, and quotations count toward the word and line limitations. The corporate disclosure statement, table of contents, table of citations, statement with respect to oral argument, any addendum containing statutes, rules or regulations, and any certificates of counsel do not count toward the limitation.

(b)   Form of an Appendix. An appendix must comply with Rule 32(a)(1), (2), (3), and (4), with the following exceptions:

(1)   The cover of a separately bound appendix must be white.

(2)   An appendix may include a legible photocopy of any document found in the record or of a printed judicial or agency decision.

(3)   When necessary to facilitate inclusion of odd-sized documents such as technical drawings, an appendix may be a size other than 8½ by 11 inches, and need not lie reasonably flat when opened.

(c)   Form of Other Papers.

(1)   *Motion.* The form of a motion is governed by Rule 27(d).

(2) *Other Papers.* Any other paper, including a petition for rehearing and a petition for rehearing en banc, and any response to such a petition, must be reproduced in the manner prescribed by Rule 32(a), with the following exceptions:

  (A) a cover is not necessary if the caption and signature page of the paper together contain the information required by Rule 32(a)(2); and

  (B) Rule 32(a)(7) does not apply.

(d) Signature. Every brief, motion, or other paper filed with the court must be signed by the party filing the paper or, if the party is represented, by one of the party's attorneys.

(e) Local Variation. Every court of appeals must accept documents that comply with the form requirements of this rule and the length limits set by these rules. By local rule or order in a particular case a court of appeals may accept documents that do not meet all of the form requirements of this rule or the length limits set by these rules.

(f) Items Excluded from Length. In computing any length limit, headings, footnotes, and quotations count toward the limit but the following items do not:

- [the] cover page;
- [a corporate] disclosure statement;
- [a] table of contents;
- [a] table of citations;
- [a] statement regarding oral argument;
- [an] addendum containing statutes, rules, or regulations;
- certificates of counsel;
- [the] signature block;
- [the] proof of service; and
- any item specifically excluded by these rules or by local rule.

(g) Certificate of Compliance

(1) **Briefs and Papers That Require a Certificate.** A brief submitted under Rules 28.1(e)(2), 29(b)(4), or 32(a)(7)(B)—and a paper submitted under Rules 5(c)(1), 21(d)(1), 27(d)(2)(A), 27(d)(2)(C), 35(b)(2)(A), or 40(b)(1)—must include a certificate by the attorney, or an unrepresented party, that the document complies with the type-volume limitation. The person preparing the certificate may rely on the word or line count of the word-processing system used to prepare the document. The certificate must states the number of words—or the number of lines of monospaced type—in the document.

(2) **Acceptable Form.** Form 6 in the Appendix of Forms meets the requirements for a certificate of compliance.

Note: Form 6 reads as follows:

Certification of Compliance With Type-Volume Limit, Typeface Requirements, and Type-Style Requirements

1. This document complies with [the type-volume limit of Fed. R. App. P. [*insert Rule citation; e.g. 32(a)(7)(B)*]] [the word limit of Fed. R. App. P. [*insert Rule citation; e.g. 5(c)(1)*]] because, excluding the parts of the document exempted by Fed. R. App. P. 32(f) [and [*insert applicable Rule citation, if any*]]:

  ☐ this document contains [*state the number of*] words, **or**

  ☐ this brief uses a monospaced typeface and contains [*state the number of*] lines of text.

2. This document complies with the typeface requirements of Fed. R. App. P. 32(a)(5) and type-style requirements of Fed. R. App. P. 32(a)(6) because:

☐   this document has been prepared in a proportionally spaced typeface using [*state name and version of word-processing program*] in [*state font size and name of type style*], **or**

☐   this document has been prepared in a monospaced typeface using [*state name and version of word-processing program*] with [*state number of characters per inch and name of type*].

(s)_____

Attorney for _____

Dated: _____

Rule 32.1. Citing Judicial Dispositions

(a) Citation Permitted. A court may not prohibit or restrict the citation of federal judicial opinions, orders, judgments, or other written dispositions that have been:

(i)   designated as "unpublished," "not for publication," "non-precedential," "not precedent," or the like; and

(ii)   issued on or after January 1, 2007.

(b) Copies Required. If a party cites a federal judicial opinion, order, judgment, or disposition that is not available in a publicly accessible electronic database, the party must file and serve a copy of that opinion, order, judgment, or disposition with the brief or other paper in which it is cited.

Rule 33. Appeal Conferences

The court may direct the attorneys—and, when appropriate, the parties—to participate in one or more conferences to address any matter that may aid in disposing of the proceedings, including simplifying the issues and discussing settlement. A judge or other person designated by the court may preside over the conference, which may be conducted in person or by telephone. Before a settlement conference, the attorneys must consult with their clients and obtain as much authority as feasible to settle the case. The court may, as a result of the conference, enter an order controlling the course of the proceedings or implementing any settlement agreement.

Rule 34. Oral Argument

(a) In General.

(1)   *Party's Statement.* Any party may file, or a court may require by local rule, a statement explaining why oral argument should, or need not, be permitted.

(2)   *Standards.* Oral argument must be allowed in every case unless a panel of three judges who have examined the briefs and record unanimously agrees that oral argument is unnecessary for any of the following reasons:

(A)   the appeal is frivolous;

(B)   the dispositive issue or issues have been authoritatively decided; or

(C)   the facts and legal arguments are adequately presented in the briefs and record, and the decisional process would not be significantly aided by oral argument.

(b) Notice of Argument; Postponement. The clerk must advise all parties whether oral argument will be scheduled, and, if so, the date, time, and place for it, and the time allowed for each side. A motion to postpone the argument or to allow longer argument must be filed reasonably in advance of the hearing date.

(c) Order and Contents of Argument. The appellant opens and concludes the argument. Counsel must not read at length from briefs, records, or authorities.

(d) Cross-Appeals and Separate Appeals. If there is a cross-appeal, Rule 28(h) determines which party is the appellant and which is the appellee for purposes of oral argument. Unless the court directs otherwise, a cross-appeal or separate appeal must be argued when the initial appeal is argued. Separate parties should avoid duplicative argument.

(e) Nonappearance of a Party. If the appellee fails to appear for argument, the court must hear appellant's argument. If the appellant fails to appear for argument, the court may hear the appellee's argument. If neither party appears, the case will be decided on the briefs, unless the court orders otherwise.

(f) Submission on Briefs. The parties may agree to submit a case for decision on the briefs, but the court may direct that the case be argued.

(g) Use of Physical Exhibits at Argument; Removal. Counsel intending to use physical exhibits other than documents at the argument must arrange to place them in the courtroom on the day of the argument before the court convenes. After the argument, counsel must remove the exhibits from the courtroom, unless the court directs otherwise. The clerk may destroy or dispose of the exhibits if counsel does not reclaim them within a reasonable time after the clerk gives notice to remove them.

Rule 35. En Banc Determination

(a) When Hearing or Rehearing En Banc May Be Ordered. A majority of the circuit judges who are in regular active service and who are not disqualified may order that an appeal or other proceeding be heard or reheard by the court of appeals en banc. An en banc hearing or rehearing is not favored and ordinarily will not be ordered unless:

(1) en banc consideration is necessary to secure or maintain uniformity of the court's decisions; or

(2) the proceeding involves a question of exceptional importance.

(b) Petition for Hearing or Rehearing En Banc. A party may petition for a hearing or rehearing en banc.

(1) The petition must begin with a statement that either:

(A) the panel decision conflicts with a decision of the United States Supreme Court or of the court to which the petition is addressed (with citation to the conflicting case or cases) and consideration by the full court is therefore necessary to secure and maintain uniformity of the court's decisions; or

(B) the proceeding involves one or more questions of exceptional importance, each of which must be concisely stated; for example, a petition may assert that a proceeding presents a question of exceptional importance if it involves an issue on which the panel decision conflicts with the authoritative decisions of other United States Courts of Appeals that have addressed the issue.

(2) [Subject to the court's permission, Rule 35(b)(2) would normally restrict documents produced by computer to 3,900 words. Handwritten and typewritten documents would be limited to 15 pages. See Rules 32(e), (f), and (g) for details of the requirements.]

(3) For purposes of the limit in Rule 35(b)(2), if a party files both a petition for panel rehearing and a petition for rehearing en banc, they are considered a single document even if they are filed separately, unless separate filing is required by local rule.

(c) Time for Petition for Hearing or Rehearing En Banc. A petition that an appeal be heard initially en banc must be filed by the date when the appellee's brief is due. A petition for a rehearing en banc must be filed within the time prescribed by Rule 40 for filing a petition for rehearing.

(d) Number of Copies. The number of copies to be filed must be prescribed by local rule and may be altered by order in a particular case.

(e)   **Response.** No response may be filed to a petition for an en banc consideration unless the court orders a response.

(f)   **Call for a Vote.** A vote need not be taken to determine whether the case will be heard or reheard en banc unless a judge calls for a vote.

Rule 36.   Entry of Judgment; Notice

(a)   **Entry.** A judgment is entered when it is noted on the docket. The clerk must prepare, sign, and enter the judgment:

(1)   after receiving the court's opinion—but if settlement of the judgment's form is required, after final settlement; or

(2)   if a judgment is rendered without an opinion, as the court instructs.

(b)   **Notice.** On the date when judgment is entered, the clerk must mail to all parties a copy of the opinion—or the judgment, if no opinion was written—and a notice of the date when the judgment was entered.

Rule 37.   Interest on Judgment

(a)   **When the Court Affirms.** Unless the law provides otherwise, if a money judgment in a civil case is affirmed, whatever interest is allowed by law is payable from the date when the district court's judgment was entered.

(b)   **When the Court Reverses.** If the court modifies or reverses a judgment with a direction that a money judgment be entered in the district court, the mandate must contain instructions about the allowance of interest.

Rule 38.   Frivolous Appeal—Damages and Costs

If a court of appeals determines that an appeal is frivolous, it may, after a separately filed motion or notice from the court and reasonable opportunity to respond, award just damages and single or double costs to the appellee.

Rule 39.   Costs

Note that a proposed change to Rule 39(d)(1) has been approved by the Supreme Court. The change appears in brackets within the current rule.

Unless Congress intervenes, the change is effective December 1, 2019.

(a)   **Against Whom Assessed.** The following rules apply unless the law provides or the court orders otherwise:

(1)   if an appeal is dismissed, costs are taxed against the appellant, unless the parties agree otherwise;

(2)   if a judgment is affirmed, costs are taxed against the appellant;

(3)   if a judgment is reversed, costs are taxed against the appellee;

(4)   if a judgment is affirmed in part, reversed in part, modified, or vacated, costs are taxed only as the court orders.

(b)   **Costs For and Against the United States.** Costs for or against the United States, its agency, or officer will be assessed under Rule 39(a) only if authorized by law.

(c)   **Costs of Copies.** Each court of appeals must, by local rule, fix the maximum rate for taxing the cost of producing necessary copies of a brief or appendix, or copies of records authorized by Rule

30(f). The rate must not exceed that generally charged for such work in the area where the clerk's office is located and should encourage economical methods of copying.

(d) Bill of Costs: Objections; Insertion in Mandate.

(1) A party who wants costs taxed must—within 14 days after entry of judgment—file with the circuit clerk [, with proof of service, and serve] an itemized and verified bill of costs.

(2) Objections must be filed within 14 days after service of the bill of costs, unless the court extends the time.

(3) The clerk must prepare and certify an itemized statement of costs for insertion in the mandate, but issuance of the mandate must not be delayed for taxing costs. If the mandate issues before costs are finally determined, the district clerk must—upon the circuit clerk's request—add the statement of costs, or any amendment of it, to the mandate.

(e) Costs on Appeal Taxable in the District Court. The following costs on appeal are taxable in the district court for the benefit of the party entitled to costs under this rule:

(1) the preparation and transmission of the record;

(2) the reporter's transcript, if needed to determine the appeal;

(3) premiums paid for a bond or other security to preserve rights pending appeal; and

(4) the fee for filing the notice of appeal.

Rule 40. Petition for Panel Rehearing

(a) Time to File; Contents; Answer; Action by the Court if Granted.

(1) *Time.* Unless the time is shortened or extended by order or local rule, a petition for panel rehearing may be filed within 14 days after entry of judgment. But in a civil case, unless an order shortens or extends the time, the petition may be filed by any party within 45 days after entry of judgment if one of the parties is:

(A) the United States;

(B) a United States agency;

(C) a United States officer or employee sued in an official capacity; or

(D) a current or former United States officer or employee sued in an individual capacity for an act or omission occurring in connection with duties performed on the United States' behalf—including all instances in which the United States represents that person when the court of appeals' judgment is entered or files the petition for that person.

(2) *Contents.* The petition must state with particularity each point of law or fact that the petitioner believes the court has overlooked or misapprehended and must argue in support of the petition. Oral argument is not permitted.

(3) *Answer.* Unless the court requests, no answer to a petition for panel rehearing is permitted. But ordinarily rehearing will not be granted in the absence of such a request.

(4) *Action by the Court.* If a petition for panel rehearing is granted, the court may do any of the following:

(A) make a final disposition of the case without reargument;

(B) restore the case to the calendar for reargument or resubmission; or

(C) issue any other appropriate order.

(b)   Form of Petition; Length. * * * [Rule 40(b) would normally restrict a petition produced by computer to 3,900 words. A handwritten or typed petition would be limited to 15 pages. See Appellate Rules 32(e), (f), and (g), supra, for details of the requirements.]

Rule 41. Mandate: Contents; Issuance and Effective Date; Stay

(a)   Contents. Unless the court directs that a formal mandate issue, the mandate consists of a certified copy of the judgment, a copy of the court's opinion, if any, and any direction about costs.

(b)   When Issued. The court's mandate must issue 7 days after the time to file a petition for rehearing expires, or 7 days after entry of an order denying a timely petition for panel rehearing, petition for rehearing en banc, or motion for stay of mandate, whichever is later. The court may shorten or extend the time by order.

(c)   Effective Date. The mandate is effective when issued.

(d)   Staying the Mandate Pending a Petition for Certiorari.

(1)   *Motion to Stay.* A party may move to stay the mandate pending the filing of a petition for a writ of certiorari in the Supreme Court. The motion must be served on all parties and must show that the petition would present a substantial question and that there is good cause for a stay.

(2)   *Duration of Stay; Extensions.* The stay must not exceed 90 days, unless:

(A)   the period is extended for good cause; or

(B)   the party who obtained the stay notifies the circuit court in writing within the period of the stay:

(i)   that the time for filing the petition has been extended, in which case the stay continues for the extended period; or

(ii)   that the petition has been filed, in which case the stay continues until the Supreme Court's final disposition.

(3)   *Security.* The court may require a bond or other security as a condition to granting or continuing a stay of the mandate.

(4)   *Issuance of the Mandate.* The court of appeals must issue the mandate immediately on receiving a copy of a Supreme Court order denying the petition, unless extraordinary circumstances exist.

Rule 42. Voluntary Dismissal

(a)   Dismissal in the District Court. Before an appeal has been docketed by the circuit clerk, the district court may dismiss the appeal on the filing of a stipulation signed by all parties or on the appellant's motion with notice to all parties.

(b)   Dismissal in the Court of Appeals. The circuit clerk may dismiss a docketed appeal if the parties file a signed dismissal agreement specifying how costs are to be paid and pay any fees that are due. But no mandate or other process may issue without a court order. An appeal may be dismissed on the appellant's motion on terms agreed to by the parties or fixed by the court.

Rule 43. Substitution of Parties

(a)   Death of a Party.

(1)   *After Notice of Appeal Is Filed.* If a party dies after a notice of appeal has been filed or while a proceeding is pending in the court of appeals, the decedent's personal representative may be substituted as a party on motion filed with the circuit clerk by the representative or by any party. A party's motion must be served on the representative in accordance with Rule 25. If the decedent has

no representative, any party may suggest the death on the record, and the court of appeals may then direct appropriate proceedings.

(2) *Before Notice of Appeal Is Filed—Potential Appellant.* If a party entitled to appeal dies before filing a notice of appeal, the decedent's personal representative—or, if there is no personal representative, the decedent's attorney of record—may file a notice of appeal within the time prescribed by these rules. After the notice of appeal is filed, substitution must be in accordance with Rule 43(a)(1).

(3) *Before Notice of Appeal Is Filed—Potential Appellee.* If a party against whom an appeal may be taken dies after entry of a judgment or order in the district court, but before a notice of appeal is filed, an appellant may proceed as if the death had not occurred. After the notice of appeal is filed, substitution must be in accordance with Rule 43(a)(1).

(b) Substitution for a Reason Other Than Death. If a party needs to be substituted for any reason other than death, the procedure prescribed in Rule 43(a) applies.

(c) Public Officer: Identification; Substitution.

(1) *Identification of Party.* A public officer who is a party to an appeal or other proceeding in an official capacity may be described as a party by the public officer's official title rather than by name. But the court may require the public officer's name to be added.

(2) *Automatic Substitution of Officeholder.* When a public officer who is a party to an appeal or other proceeding in an official capacity dies, resigns, or otherwise ceases to hold office, the action does not abate. The public officer's successor is automatically substituted as a party. Proceedings following the substitution are to be in the name of the substituted party, but any misnomer that does not affect the substantial rights of the parties may be disregarded. An order of substitution may be entered at any time, but failure to enter an order does not affect the substitution.

Rule 44. Case Involving a Constitutional Question When the United States or the Relevant State Is Not a Party

(a) Constitutional Challenge to Federal Statute. If a party questions the constitutionality of an Act of Congress in a proceeding in which the United States or its agency, officer, or employee is not a party in an official capacity, the questioning party must give written notice to the circuit clerk immediately upon the filing of the record or as soon as the question is raised in the court of appeals. The clerk must then certify that fact to the Attorney General.

(b) Constitutional Challenge to State Statute. If a party questions the constitutionality of a statute of a State in a proceeding in which that State or its agency, officer, or employee is not a party in an official capacity, the questioning party must give written notice to the circuit clerk immediately upon the filing of the record or as soon as the question is raised in the court of appeals. The clerk must then certify that fact to the attorney general of the State.

Rule 45. Clerk's Duties

(a) General Provisions.

(1) *Qualifications.* The circuit clerk must take the oath and post any bond required by law. Neither the clerk nor any deputy clerk may practice as an attorney or counselor in any court while in office.

(2) *When Court Is Open.* The court of appeals is always open for filing any paper, issuing and returning process, making a motion, and entering an order. The clerk's office with the clerk or a deputy in attendance must be open during business hours on all days except Saturdays, Sundays, and legal holidays. A court may provide by local rule or by order that the clerk's office be open for specified hours on Saturdays or on legal holidays other than New Year's Day, Martin Luther King, Jr.'s Birthday,

Washington's Birthday, Memorial Day, Independence Day, Labor Day, Columbus Day, Veterans' Day, Thanksgiving Day, and Christmas Day.

(b) Records.

(1) *The Docket.* The circuit clerk must maintain a docket and an index of all docketed cases in the manner prescribed by the Director of the Administrative Office of the United States Courts. The clerk must record all papers filed with the clerk and all process, orders, and judgments.

(2) *Calendar.* Under the court's direction, the clerk must prepare a calendar of cases awaiting argument. In placing cases on the calendar for argument, the clerk must give preference to appeals in criminal cases and to other proceedings and appeals entitled to preference by law.

(3) *Other Records.* The clerk must keep other books and records required by the Director of the Administrative Office of the United States Courts, with the approval of the Judicial Conference of the United States, or by the court.

(c) Notice of an Order or Judgment. Upon the entry of an order or judgment, the circuit clerk must immediately serve by mail a notice of entry on each party to the proceeding, with a copy of any opinion, and must note the mailing on the docket. Service on a party represented by counsel must be made on counsel.

(d) Custody of Records and Papers. The circuit clerk has custody of the court's records and papers. Unless the court orders or instructs otherwise, the clerk must not permit an original record or paper to be taken from the clerk's office. Upon disposition of the case, original papers constituting the record on appeal or review must be returned to the court or agency from which they were received. The clerk must preserve a copy of any brief, appendix, or other paper that has been filed.

Rule 46. Attorneys

(a) Admission to the Bar.

(1) *Eligibility.* An attorney is eligible for admission to the bar of a court of appeals if that attorney is of good moral and professional character and is admitted to practice before the Supreme Court of the United States, the highest court of a state, another United States court of appeals, or a United States district court (including the district courts for Guam, the Northern Mariana Islands, and the Virgin Islands).

(2) *Application.* An applicant must file an application for admission, on a form approved by the court that contains the applicant's personal statement showing eligibility for membership. The applicant must subscribe to the following oath or affirmation:

> "I, _____, do solemnly swear [or affirm] that I will conduct myself as an attorney and counselor of this court, uprightly and according to law; and that I will support the Constitution of the United States."

(3) *Admission Procedures.* On written or oral motion of a member of the court's bar, the court will act on the application. An applicant may be admitted by oral motion in open court. But, unless the court orders otherwise, an applicant need not appear before the court to be admitted. Upon admission, an applicant must pay the clerk the fee prescribed by local rule or court order.

(b) Suspension or Disbarment.

(1) *Standard.* A member of the court's bar is subject to suspension or disbarment by the court if the member:

(A) has been suspended or disbarred from practice in any other court; or

(B) is guilty of conduct unbecoming a member of the court's bar.

(2) *Procedure.* The member must be given an opportunity to show good cause, within the time prescribed by the court, why the member should not be suspended or disbarred.

(3) *Order.* The court must enter an appropriate order after the member responds and a hearing is held, if requested, or after the time prescribed for a response expires, if no response is made.

(c) Discipline. A court of appeals may discipline an attorney who practices before it for conduct unbecoming a member of the bar or for failure to comply with any court rule. First, however, the court must afford the attorney reasonable notice, an opportunity to show cause to the contrary, and, if requested, a hearing.

Rule 47. Local Rules by Courts of Appeals

(a) Local Rules.

(1) Each court of appeals acting by a majority of its judges in regular active service may, after giving appropriate public notice and opportunity for comment, make and amend rules governing its practice. A generally applicable direction to parties or lawyers regarding practice before a court must be in a local rule rather than an internal operating procedure or standing order. A local rule must be consistent with—but not duplicative of—Acts of Congress and rules adopted under 28 U.S.C. § 2072 and must conform to any uniform numbering system prescribed by the Judicial Conference of the United States. Each circuit clerk must send the Administrative Office of the United States Courts a copy of each local rule and internal operating procedure when it is promulgated or amended.

(2) A local rule imposing a requirement of form must not be enforced in a manner that causes a party to lose rights because of a nonwillful failure to comply with the requirement.

(b) Procedure When There Is No Controlling Law. A court of appeals may regulate practice in a particular case in any manner consistent with federal law, these rules, and local rules of the circuit. No sanction or other disadvantage may be imposed for noncompliance with any requirement not in federal law, federal rules, or the local circuit rules unless the alleged violator has been furnished in the particular case with actual notice of the requirement.

Rule 48. Masters

(a) Appointment; Powers. A court of appeals may appoint a special master to hold hearings, if necessary, and to recommend factual findings and disposition in matters ancillary to proceedings in the court. Unless the order referring a matter to a master specifies or limits the master's powers, those powers include, but are not limited to, the following:

(1) regulating all aspects of a hearing;

(2) taking all appropriate action for the efficient performance of the master's duties under the order;

(3) requiring the production of evidence on all matters embraced in the reference; and

(4) administering oaths and examining witnesses and parties.

(b) Compensation. If the master is not a judge or court employee, the court must determine the master's compensation and whether the cost is to be charged to any party.

PART V

Selected Sample Court Orders and Notices for Controlling Discovery, Pretrial Conferences, *and* Settlement of Class Actions

---

TABLE OF CONTENTS

Stipulation and Order Governing Discovery and the Protection and Exchange of Confidential Information[1]

It is hereby stipulated and agreed by and between the undersigned parties to this action that the following restrictions and procedures shall apply to all documents, testimony, interrogatories, and other information produced, given or exchanged by any party or non-party in the course of pretrial discovery in this action (hereinafter collectively referred to as "Pre-trial Information").

1. All Pre-trial Information shall be treated and deemed as confidential and protected within the meaning of Chancery Court Rule 26(c). In addition to the foregoing, any party or non-party may designate any Pre-trial Information that reflects sensitive internal business or competitive information not relating to proposed transactions or negotiations between or among the parties as "Confidential—Attorneys Only."

2. Unless otherwise ordered by the Court in this proceeding, all Pre-trial Information will be held by the receiving party solely for use in connection with the above-captioned action.

3. Pre-trial Information shall not be disclosed to any person, except:

    (a) outside counsel and to house counsel for the parties;

    (b) employees of such counsel assigned to and necessary to assist such counsel in the preparation of this litigation;

    (c) officers, directors, or employees of the parties, to the extent deemed necessary by counsel for the prosecution or defense of this litigation;

    (d) consultants or experts, to the extent deemed necessary by counsel for the prosecution or defense of the litigation; and

    (e) the Court.

4. Pre-trial Information designated "Confidential-Attorneys Only" shall not be disclosed to any person other than those persons included in paragraphs 3(a), 3(b) and 3(c) above.

---

[1] Sussman & Sussman, "Confidentiality Agreements Help Protect Clients," Legal Times of New York, September 1984, p. 6, 36 (reproducing protective order entered by a state court in Pennzoil Co. v. Getty Oil Co., No. 7425 (Del. Ch. Jan. 24, 1984)).

5. Any person given access to Pre-trial Information pursuant to the terms hereof shall be advised that the documents, material or information are being disclosed pursuant to and subject to the terms of this Stipulation and Order and may not be disclosed other than pursuant to the terms hereof.

6. Pre-trial Information used in connection with any pleading, motion, hearing or trial or otherwise submitted to the Court shall be filed under seal.

7. Inadvertent production of any document or other information during discovery in this action shall be without prejudice to any claim that such material is privileged or protected from discovery as work product within the meaning of Chancery Court Rule 26, and no party shall be held to have waived any rights under Rule 26 by such inadvertent production. Any document or information so produced and subject to a claim of privilege or work product subsequently made shall immediately be returned to the producing party, or expunged, and, in either event, such document or information shall not be introduced into evidence in this or any other proceeding by any person without the consent of the producing party or by order of the Court, nor will such document or information be subject to production in any proceeding by virtue of the fact that it was inadvertently produced in this proceeding.

8. Nothing herein shall preclude any of the parties from, upon twenty-four (24) hours notice to the other parties, making application to the Court for an order modifying any of the terms hereof or contesting or seeking designation of any information as "Confidential—Attorneys Only."

9. The parties agree forthwith to submit this Stipulation and Order to the Court to be "So Ordered" and further agree that, prior to approval by the Court, this Stipulation and Order shall be effective as if approved and, specifically, that any violation of its terms shall be subject to the same sanctions and penalties, including those under Chancery Court Rule 37 as if this Stipulation and Order had been entered by the Court.

10. At the conclusion of the litigation, all Pre-trial Information and all copies thereof, and all documents designated "Confidential-Attorneys Only" and all copies thereof, shall be promptly returned to the producing parties or, at their written request, destroyed. The return or destruction of such documents shall be certified by the receiving persons.

11. This Stipulation and Order shall inure to the benefit of and be enforceable by non-parties with respect to information produced, given, or exchanged by them in the course of pre-trial discovery.

Pretrial Order Establishing Schedules for Completion of All Subsequent Steps in a Case

Part I. Second Wave and Completion of Discovery[2]

Part II. Designation of Deposition Evidence and Documents for Objections Thereto

Part III. Final Pretrial Briefs, Written Offers of Proof, Written Narrative Summaries of Expert Testimony, and Statements of Uncontroverted Facts

Part IV. Listing of Trial Witnesses

Part V. Filing of Proposed Voir Dire Questions

Part VI. Scheduling Final Pretrial Conference

Part VII. Setting Trial Date

---

[2] Adaptation of Pretrial Order, except for Part VII, from "Manual for Complex Litigation," Fifth Edition, For Use With Federal Practice and Procedure by Charles Alan Wright and Arthur R. Miller (West Publishing Co. 1982).

SAMPLE COURT ORDERS & NOTICES

Part I.   Second Wave and Completion of Discovery

A.   The following interrogatories on behalf of plaintiffs were approved and ordered answered on or before the _____ day of _____, 20__ [*list interrogatories*].

B.   The following requests for production of documents on behalf of plaintiffs were granted and the documents were ordered produced at [*insert location*] on or before the _____ day of _____, 20__ [*list motions approved*].

C.   Depositions on behalf of plaintiffs of the following persons, at the places and times designated, were approved:

Witness	Company	Location	Date
_____	_____	_____	_____
_____	_____	_____	_____
_____	_____	_____	_____

D.   The following interrogatories on behalf of defendants were approved and ordered answered on or before the _____ day of _____, 20__ [*list interrogatories*].

E.   The following requests for production of documents on behalf of defendants were granted and the documents were ordered produced at [*insert location*] on or before the _____ day of _____, 20__ [*list motions approved*].

F.   Depositions on behalf of defendants of the following persons, at the places and times designated, were approved:

Witness	Company	Location	Date
_____	_____	_____	_____
_____	_____	_____	_____
_____	_____	_____	_____

G.   Except as may hereafter be ordered by the Court for good cause shown and in the interest of the just determination of this cause, no discovery in addition to the discovery heretofore ordered shall be taken in this cause.

Part II.   Designation of Deposition Testimony, Documents, and Objections Thereto

H.   On or before the _____ day of _____, 20__, plaintiffs shall designate those portions of deposition testimony that plaintiffs desire to offer in evidence at the trial.

I.   On or before the _____ day of _____, 20__, defendants (1) shall designate the parts of the depositions designated by plaintiffs that defendants seek to require plaintiffs to introduce under Federal Rule of Civil Procedure 32(a)(4), and (2) shall designate such portions of depositions as defendants desire to offer in evidence at the trial.

J.   On or before the _____ day of _____, 20__, plaintiffs (1) shall designate the part of the depositions designated by defendants that plaintiffs seek to require defendants to introduce under Federal Rule of Civil Procedure 32(a)(4), and (2) shall counter-designate such portions of the depositions designated by defendants as plaintiffs desire to offer in evidence at the trial.

K.   On or before the _____ day of _____, 20__, plaintiffs shall designate those documents they desire to introduce at trial and shall provide each defendant with a copy of each such document.

L.   On or before the _____ day of _____, 20__, defendants shall designate those documents they desire to introduce at trial and shall provide each plaintiff with a copy of each such document.

M.   On or before the _____ day of _____, 20__, plaintiffs and defendants shall file all objections to designated deposition testimony and exhibits.

Part III.   Final Pretrial Briefs, Written Offers of Proof, Written Narrative Summaries of Expert Testimony, and Statements of Uncontroverted Facts

N.[3]   Plaintiffs and defendants shall each file two detailed, written pretrial briefs constructed as hereinafter provided. The first such brief shall be filed by the plaintiffs on or before the _____ day of _____, 20__, and shall relate to the claims for relief by plaintiffs against defendants. The second such brief shall be filed by the defendants on or before the _____ day of _____, 20__, and shall relate to the defenses, including affirmative defenses, of the defendants to plaintiffs' claims for relief, and, in a separate section, to the defendants' claims for relief on their counterclaims herein. The third such brief shall be filed by the plaintiffs on or before the _____ day of _____, 20__, and shall relate to plaintiffs' reply to the affirmative matter in the defenses of defendants to plaintiffs' claims for relief, and to plaintiffs' defenses, including affirmative defenses, to defendants' counterclaims for relief. The fourth such brief shall be filed by the defendants on or before the _____ day of _____, 20__, and shall relate to the reply of the defendants to any affirmative matter in the defenses of plaintiffs to the counterclaims of defendants.

Each of the four briefs required to be filed as hereinafter provided shall consist of (1) a detailed narrative statement of the facts proposed to be proved by the party filing the brief, and (2) concise statements of legal contentions of the party filing the brief in support of any affirmative matter contained in the brief and in response to legal contentions made by the adverse party in the next preceding brief. In sections of the pretrial brief there shall be a narrative statement or statement of facts and statements of legal contentions. Neither shall be commingled with the other, and they shall be in the following form:

(1)   In support of each claim for relief, whether contained in the complaint or the counterclaim, the party or parties asserting the claim for relief shall set forth in simple declarative sentences, separately numbered, the narration of all facts relied upon in support of the claim or claims for relief herein. Each narrative statement of facts shall be in a separate section and shall be complete in itself and shall contain no recitation of what any witness testified to, or what the adverse party or parties stated or admitted in these or other proceedings, and no reference to the pleadings or other documents or schedules as such; provided, however, that at the option of a party or parties, any narrative statement of facts may contain references in parentheses to the names of witnesses, depositions, pleadings, exhibits, or other documents, but no party or parties shall be required to admit or deny the accuracy of such references. No narrative statement of facts shall, so far as possible, contain any color words, labels, or legal conclusions; and in no event shall any color word, label, or legal conclusion be commingled with any statement of fact in any sentence or paragraph. Each narrative statement of facts shall be constructed, to the best of the ability of plaintiffs' counsel, so that the opposite party will be able to admit or deny each separate sentence of the statement of facts. Each separate sentence of the statement of facts shall be separately and consecutively numbered.

(2)   In each separate section of the pretrial brief containing the statement of legal contentions and authorities in support thereof, all legal contentions and authorities in support of the claim or claims for relief that are the subject for the foregoing narrative statement of facts, necessary to demonstrate the liability of the adverse party or parties to the party or parties filing the brief, shall be separately, clearly, and concisely stated in separately numbered

---

[3]   This paragraph of Part III is based upon a pretrial order entered by Chief Judge William H. Becker on June 21, 1967, in Johnson v. Tri-State Motor Transit Co., Civil Action No. 15974–3 (W.D.Mo.), in which both a complaint and a counterclaim were filed.

paragraphs. Each such paragraph shall be followed by a citation of authorities in support thereof without quotations therefrom.

(3)   The party or parties filing a pretrial brief in defense of a claim or claims for relief shall set forth in a separate section, in separate simple declarative sentences, factual statements admitting or denying each separate sentence contained in the narrative statement of facts of the adverse party in support of its claim for relief, except in instances where a portion of a sentence can be admitted and a portion denied. In those instances the brief shall state clearly the portion of the sentence admitted and the portion denied. Each separate sentence of a brief in response to a narrative statement of facts in support of a claim for relief shall bear the same number as the corresponding sentence in the narrative statement of facts in support of the claim for relief. In a separate portion of the narrative fact statement in response to a narrative fact brief in support of a claim for relief, the responding party shall set forth in a separate narrative statement all affirmative matters of a factual nature relied upon by it in defense (in whole or in part) against the claim or claims for relief. This separate narrative statement of affirmative matters shall be contained in a narrative statement of facts constructed in the same manner as hereinabove provided for a narrative statement of facts in support of a claim for relief.

(4)   In response to a brief in support of a claim for relief, the party or parties responding shall, in a separate section of the pretrial brief, set forth a statement of legal contentions and authorities in defense (in whole or in part) against the claim for relief to which the response is made. In this separate section the party or parties shall set forth its legal contentions and authorities in support thereof, directly responding to the legal contentions of the adverse party in support of the claim for relief, and shall separately set forth such additional contentions of the party or parties as may be necessary to demonstrate the nonliability (in whole or in part) of the party or parties filing the brief or briefs. The statement of legal contentions in a brief responding to a brief in support of a claim for relief shall be constructed in the same manner as provided in subparagraph (2) hereinabove for the statement of legal contentions of a party or parties in support of a claim for relief.

(5)   Within _____ days after the service of defendant's pretrial brief containing statements of affirmative matter, the plaintiff shall file a reply pretrial brief containing factual statements admitting or denying each separate sentence of the separate narrative statement of affirmative matters of the defendant. This portion of the plaintiff's reply brief shall be constructed in the same manner provided in subparagraph (3) above for defendant's factual statements responding to plaintiff's narrative statement of facts, and shall be in a separate portion of the reply brief.

(6)   Within _____ days after the service of defendant's statement of additional legal contentions and authorities in support thereof, plaintiff shall file, in a separate part of its reply brief, its separate statement of additional legal contentions and authorities in support thereof, which shall directly respond to the additional legal contentions of defendant. The statement of legal contentions and authorities in support thereof shall be constructed in the same manner provided in subparagraph (4) above for defendant's pretrial brief, and shall be in a separate portion of the reply brief.

(7)   Any factual contention, any legal contention, any claim for relief or defense (in whole or in part), or any affirmative matter not set forth in detail as provided hereinabove shall be deemed abandoned, uncontroverted, or withdrawn in future proceedings, notwithstanding the contents of any pleadings or other papers on file herein, except for factual contentions, legal contentions, claims for relief or defenses thereto, and affirmative matters of which a party may not be aware and could not be aware in the exercise of reasonable diligence at the time of filing the briefs hereinabove provided for. Any matters of which a party was not aware at the time of filing and of which he could not have been aware in the exercise of

diligence at the time of the filing of a brief may be supplemented by a supplemental brief by leave of Court for good cause shown on timely motion therefor.

O. On or before the _____ day of _____, 20__, each plaintiff and each defendant herein shall serve and file written offers of proof on the following issues: (list)

P. On or before the _____ day of _____, 20__, each plaintiff and each defendant herein shall serve and file written narrative summaries setting forth in detail the testimony of each expert whom the party so filing will employ at trial, including a complete listing of all documents, data, and authorities studied by each such expert.

Q. On or before the _____ day of _____, 20__, the parties shall confer and attempt to agree on a joint statement of those factual issues that are without substantial controversy, and agree upon forms of statements of factual issues that are controverted. If the parties are unable to agree upon the uncontroverted factual issues or upon the forms of statements of the controverted factual issues, each party shall separately prepare on or before the _____ day of _____, 20__, a proposed statement thereof.

Part IV. Listing of Trial Witnesses

R. On or before the _____ day of _____, 20__, each plaintiff shall identify each witness it intends to call at trial in its case in chief and state whether such witness will appear in person or by deposition.

S. On or before the _____ day of _____, 20__, each defendant shall identify each witness it intends to call at trial in its case in chief and state whether such witness will appear in person or by deposition.

Part V. Filing of Proposed Voir Dire Questions

T. On or before the _____ day of _____, 20__, all parties shall file in writing (1) proposed topics for questions for voir dire examination of the jury, and (2) separate written requests for instructions to the jury and for special interrogatories. On each request for an instruction to the jury, there shall be noted the source of authorities from which it is derived or on which it is based.

Part VI. Scheduling Final Pretrial Conference

U. A final pretrial conference is set for the _____ day of _____, 20__, beginning at the hour of _____ o'clock, __.m.

V. At the pretrial conference set in paragraph U, final trial plans will be developed and, among other things, the following matters will be considered:

(1) The then undetermined issues of fact and law will be delineated and, to the extent feasible, simplified;

(2) The reception in evidence of documentary matters not precluded by stipulation of fact, subject to such objections, if any, as may be reserved for the trial;

(3) The identity and scope of testimony of witnesses to be called at time of trial and their possible limitation will be considered;

(4) An agreement upon a trial schedule;

(5) The handling of documentary evidence;

(6) Authentication of documents;

(7) Witness lists;

(8) Spokesmen;

(9) Examination of witnesses;

(10) Use of written narrative statements of expert witnesses;

(11) Use of depositions, including the possible use of narrative summaries or verbatim extracts;

(12) Final pretrial briefs filed pursuant to this pretrial order;

(13) Limitation of opening statements;

(14) Current index of the record;

(15) Daily transcripts;

(16) Instructions;

(17) Separation of issues;

(18) Use of and mechanics for special jury verdict, or general verdict with interrogatories;

(19) Possibility of settlement.

Part VII. Setting Trial Date

W.   Trial of the above-captioned case shall begin on the _____ day of _____, 20__, at _____ o'clock, __.m.

Dated this _____ day of _____, 20__.

JUDGE

Final Pretrial Order[4]

A final pretrial conference was held in this cause on the _____ day of _____, 20__, wherein the following proceedings were had:

A.   The following counsel were present representing the plaintiffs: (list).

B.   The following counsel were present representing the defendants: (list).

C.   The following issues of fact and law were framed, and the following witnesses who may be called at trial and exhibits that may be offered at trial were identified (list):

    (1)   Jurisdiction and venue

    (2)   Admitted facts

    (3)   Plaintiffs' contentions on disputed facts

    (4)   Defendants' contentions on disputed facts

    (5)   Plaintiffs' contentions on the principal issues of law

    (6)   Defendants' contentions on the principal issues of law

    (7)   Plaintiffs' exhibits

Exhibit No.	Identification (Description)
_____	_____
_____	_____

---

[4]   Adapted from "Manual for Complex Litigation," Fifth Edition, For Use With Federal Practice and Procedure by Charles Alan Wright and Arthur R. Miller (West Publishing Co. 1982). This order is based on a final pretrial order developed by Judge George H. Boldt for use in Public Utility District No. 2 v. General Elec. Co., Civil Action No. 5380 (W.D.Wash.).

SAMPLE COURT ORDERS & NOTICES

(8) Defendants' exhibits

Exhibit No.

Identification
(Description)

_____   _____

_____   _____

(9) Plaintiffs' witness list

Name

Live or Deposition
Testimony

_____   _____

_____   _____

(10) Defendants' witness list

Name

Live or Deposition
Testimony

_____   _____

_____   _____

D. Trial in this cause shall commence on the _____ day of _____, 20__. Court sessions will be held from _____ o'clock a.m. to _____ o'clock p.m. on _____.

(1) Plaintiffs shall, to the extent possible, present separately the evidence regarding each issue following the order set forth below: (list).

(2) When plaintiffs' case is completed, defendants shall, to the extent possible, present separately the evidence regarding each issue following the order set forth below: (list).

(3) Each defendant shall present its evidence in the order in which defendants are named in the caption of this case.

(4) When defendants' case is completed, plaintiffs shall present their rebuttal evidence.

(5) None of the provisions herein shall require witnesses to make multiple appearances to maintain the order of presentation set forth above.

(6) The Court will not receive evidence relating to the period prior to _____ or subsequent to _____.

(7) _____, of counsel for plaintiffs, and _____, of counsel for defendants, are designated to represent all counsel of the parties as liaison counsel to receive notifications and act as spokesmen for co-counsel.

(8) Each motion by any defendant (or any plaintiff) on each objection shall be considered as made by each defendant (or plaintiff) in the same manner and to the same extent as though made separately by each such party, unless otherwise stated.

(9) Unless otherwise authorized by the Court, only one counsel for each party shall examine any witness. Counsel for the respective defendants shall attempt to designate one of their number to handle the cross-examination of any witness. Cross-examination of witnesses shall follow the direct examination, unless otherwise authorized by the Court.

(10) Plaintiffs' opening statements shall be limited to _____. Defendants' opening statements shall be limited to _____. Plaintiffs' and defendants' counsel respectively shall agree on the division of time. If necessary, the Court will make the division.

(11) Daily transcript shall be delivered after adjournment of the Court each day. Corrections shall be suggested at the opening of Court on the second following morning.

(12) (Jury Case) A jury of twelve jurors and _____ alternates shall be selected. Each plaintiff is permitted _____ peremptory challenges. Each defendant is permitted _____ peremptory challenges. The voir dire examination initially shall be conducted on the basis of the following questions:

(Questions (a)–(o) to be asked of the entire panel as a group.)

(a) This trial in all probability will be a lengthy one. While it is not possible to make a precise estimate, it may last as long as _____ months or more. Is there any reason why you cannot serve as a juror for that duration? What is it?

(b) Are you or any of your immediate family (spouse, children, parents, or brothers and sisters) or have you or any of your immediate family ever been employed by or represented any of the following: (list plaintiffs)?

(c) Are you or are any of your immediate family (spouse, children, parents, or brothers and sisters) or have you or any of your immediate family ever been employed by or represented any of the following: (list defendants)?

(d) Are you or any of your immediate family stockholders or holders of any other securities or obligations, or have you or any of your immediate family ever been stockholders or holders of any other securities or obligations, of any of the above companies?

(e) Do you or any of your immediate family have any business connections or dealings, or have you or any of your immediate family ever had any business connections or dealings, with any of the above companies? (If so, elicit details.)

(f) Have you or any of your immediate family or any organization you have been associated with ever had any dispute or unpleasantness with any of the above-named companies? If so, was it resolved to your satisfaction?

(g) Do you know any lawyers who are or ever have been associated with any of the following firms: (list)?

(h) Do you have any relatives or friends who are lawyers? (If so, elicit details.)

(i) Have you ever worked for a lawyer or law firm? (If so, elicit details.)

(j) Have you ever served on a federal jury in the past year?

(k) Have you or any of your immediate family ever been involved in a lawsuit as a plaintiff or a defendant? (If so, elicit details.)

(l) Has any one among you ever heard or read anything concerning any proceeding in this cause?

(m) Have you ever discussed this case with anyone?

(n) Would the fact that the defendant (or defendants) in a prior federal criminal proceeding entered a plea of guilty make it difficult or impossible for you to find for the defendants if the evidence shows that plaintiffs were not injured?

(o) Have you formed or expressed an opinion who should prevail in this controversy?

(Questions (p)–(u) to be asked of each juror individually.)

(p) What is your name?

(q)   What is your home address?

(r)   Are you married? If so: (a) How many children do you have? How old are they? What are the occupations of each of your adult children, and by whom are they employed? What is the occupation of your spouse? Who is his (her) employer?

(s)   Who is your employer?

(t)   Briefly describe the work you do.

(u)   How long have you been with your present employer? (a) (If less than 10 years:) Would you describe what jobs you have had since 20__?

It is hereby so ORDERED.

Dated this _____ day of _____, 20__.

JUDGE

Notice of Settlement of Class Action With Proof of Claim Form[5]

NOTICE OF CLASS ACTION DETERMINATION AND SETTLEMENT HEARING TO PURCHASERS OF THE FOLLOWING SECURITIES OF THE SINGER COMPANY BETWEEN JANUARY 20, 2006 AND DECEMBER 29, 2008 (INCLUSIVE): (i) SINGER'S COMMON STOCK, PAR VALUE $10 PER SHARE, (ii) SINGER'S $3.50 CUMULATIVE PREFERRED STOCK, STATED VALUE $13 PER SHARE AND (iii) SINGER'S 8% SINKING FUND DEBENTURES DUE JANUARY 15, 2010

AND

PROOF OF CLAIM UNITED STATES DISTRICT COURT
FOR THE DISTRICT OF NEW JERSEY

THIS NOTICE IS GIVEN pursuant to Rule 23 of the Federal Rules of Civil Procedure and pursuant to an Order of the United States District Court for the District of New Jersey (hereinafter sometimes called the "Court") entered November 14, 2009, to all persons who, during the period from January 20, 2006 through December 29, 2008 purchased (i) shares of Common Stock, par value $10 per share of The Singer Company (hereinafter called the "Company"), or (ii) shares of the Company's $3.50 Cumulative Preferred Stock, stated value $13 per share, or (iii) any of the Company's 8% Sinking Fund Debentures due January 15, 2010 (hereinafter sometimes called the "Class Securities"). Such persons who are not employees of the Company purchasing their shares pursuant to a stock option plan, stock purchase plan or executive incentive plan sponsored or adopted by the Company, and who are not individual defendants in the action or a spouse, child, parent, brother or sister of such defendants, are herein collectively called the "Class."

NATURE OF THE ACTION

The above action entitled Thomas Bullock v. Donald P. Kircher, et al., asserts a claim on behalf of the Class against the Company and certain of its officers and directors. The consolidated complaint, which is brought under the provisions of the Securities Exchange Act of 1934 and Rule 10b–5 adopted by the Securities and Exchange Commission thereunder, alleges, *inter alia*, that the defendants conspired to and did cause certain of the Company's financial statements and other publicly disseminated information to contain material untrue statements and omissions concerning the assets and net worth of the Company and the Company's business generally. Damages are sought on behalf of the members of the Class.

---

[5]   Adapted from "Manual for Complex Litigation," Fifth Edition, For Use With Federal Practice and Procedure, by Charles Alan Wright and Arthur R. Miller (West Publishing Co. 1982). This type of notice and proof of claim form were used by the Honorable Stanley S. Brotman in Bullock v. Kircher, Civil Action No. 76–1173 (D.N.J.), and published in the *Wall Street Journal* (Jan. 8, 1979).

SAMPLE COURT ORDERS & NOTICES

FURTHER PROCEEDINGS

The defendants have filed answers denying, and continue to deny, any liability or any wrongdoing whatever in connection with claims in the action and have asserted various defenses. The Court has not yet passed on the merits of the claims or of any defenses thereto. The giving of this notice is not meant to imply that there has been any violation of the law, or that a recovery after a trial could be had if the action is not settled. Following the joinder of issues in the action, the attorneys for plaintiff engaged in extensive pre-trial discovery, including the review and analysis of tens of thousands of documents produced by defendants and third parties and the taking of in excess of twenty depositions. On the basis of their detailed investigation of the facts and the law relating to the issues involved in this action, they have concluded that the proposed settlement described below is fair to the members of the Class.

THE CLASS

The Court has ruled that the action may, pursuant to Rule 23 of the Federal Rules of Civil Procedure, proceed and be maintained as a class action on behalf of all persons who purchased any of the Class Securities described in the first paragraph of this Notice during the period January 20, 2006 through December 29, 2008.

If you purchased shares of the Company's Common Stock or $3.50 Cumulative Preferred Stock or any of the Company's 8% Sinking Fund Debentures due January 15, 2010 during the period January 20, 2006 through December 29, 2008 and are not related to or affiliated with any of the defendants, and are not an employee of the Company who purchased securities through a plan sponsored or adopted by the Company, you are a member of the Class. Any Class member may, however, request the Court to exclude him from the Class, provided that such request is made in writing, postmarked on or before March 15, 2010, addressed to:

Singer Settlement Administration Committee
c/o Heffler & Company
P.O. Box 30
Philadelphia, Pennsylvania 19105

setting forth the name and number of this case (Bullock v. Kircher, Civ. 76–1173); your name and present address; the number of shares, and/or amount of debentures, included in the Class Securities which were purchased by you between January 20, 2006 and December 29, 2008, inclusive; the date(s) of purchase; your address on the date of purchase if the Class Securities were registered in your own name; if the Class Securities were not so registered, the name and address on the date of purchase of the person who was the registered holder of such Class Securities on such date; and your request to be excluded from the Class (all joint owners must sign this request and provide such information). A Class member who has excluded himself from the Class in the manner above specified will not share in the benefits of any favorable judgment or settlement and will not be affected by the proposed settlement described below or bound by any adverse judgment which may be rendered. Any judgment, whether or not favorable to the members of the Class, will include all Class members who have not requested exclusion, whether or not they join or intervene in the action. Any Class member who does not request exclusion may, if he desires, enter an appearance in the action through counsel of his own choice. If he does so, he may be responsible for the fees, costs and disbursements resulting therefrom or relating thereto. Any Class member who does not request exclusion and who does not enter an appearance through his own counsel will be represented by Mssrs. Barrack, Rodos & McMahon, 2000 Market Street, Philadelphia, Pennsylvania 19103, counsel for plaintiff Thomas Bullock in this action.

THE PROPOSED SETTLEMENT

An agreement of settlement has been reached in the action between counsel for the plaintiff and counsel for the defendants, which is embodied in a Stipulation and Agreement of Compromise and Settlement dated November 10, 2009 (the "Settlement Agreement") on file with the Court. As noted above, the attorneys for plaintiff, on the basis of an extensive investigation of the facts and the law relating to the matters complained of, have concluded that the proposed settlement is fair to, and in the best interests of, the Class. While defendants deny all charges of wrongdoing and do not concede liability, they desire to settle the action on the basis proposed in order to put to rest all further controversy, and to avoid substantial expenses and the inconvenience and distraction of burdensome and protracted litigation. The following description of the proposed settlement is a summary only, and reference is made to the text of the Settlement Agreement for a full statement of the provisions thereof:

1. The Company has established a Settlement Fund of $4,400,000 which has been invested in interest bearing obligations. Such interest will, if the settlement is approved by the Court, inure to the benefit of the Class.

2. The Company has established an Administration Fund of $175,000.

3. The Administration Fund will be used to pay the costs of administering the settlement provided for in the Settlement Agreement, including costs of compiling lists of holders of Class Securities, costs of identifying through informal requests or judicial proceedings beneficial owners of Class Securities, expenses of publishing and mailing notices of the settlement and hearings thereon, and the fees and disbursements of accountants and disbursing agents retained to administer claims of, and payments to, holders of Class Securities.

4. The Settlement Fund and all interest earned thereon will be distributed under the Court's direction and supervision, as follows: (i) in payment of all expenses in excess of $175,000 incurred in the administration of the settlement; (ii) to the extent approved by Order of the Court in payment of the fees, allowances and disbursements of counsel for plaintiff; (iii) the balance (the "Net Settlement Fund") to the members of the Class who file valid Proofs of Claim in accordance with the procedure set forth below in proportion to the Recognized Loss incurred by each such member.

5. *The Recognized Loss* of a member of the Class shall be measured as follows: the actual cost of all shares of the Company's Common Stock, par value $10 per share, and the actual cost of all shares of the Company's $3.50 Cumulative Preferred Stock, stated value $13 per share, and the actual cost of all of the Company's 8% Sinking Fund Debentures due January 15, 2010 purchased by him during the period from January 20, 2006 through December 29, 2008 less the total of: (i) the actual sales price received for such shares or debentures sold on or prior to October 16, 2009, and (ii) as to any such shares or debentures still held after October 16, 2009, (a) the number of such shares of Common Stock multiplied by $18.375 (the closing price for such Common Stock of the Company on October 16, 2009), (b) the number of such shares of Cumulative Preferred Stock multiplied by $35.50 (the closing price for such Cumulative Preferred Stock of the Company on October 16, 2009), and (c) the number of $1,000 multiples of such Sinking Fund Debentures multiplied by $852.50 (the closing price for each $1,000 of such Sinking Fund Debentures on October 16, 2009). The terms "actual cost" and "actual sales price" shall be deemed to include brokerage commissions, stock transfer taxes and other miscellaneous charges (excepting accrued interest) usually incurred in connection with a purchase or sale. The date of purchase or sale shall be the "contract" or "trade" date, as distinguished from the "settlement" date. Any member of the Class who acquired shares of such Common Stock or shares of such Cumulative Preferred Stock or any such Sinking Fund Debentures by gift or bequest or operation of law shall assume the actual cost of his transferor for the purpose of this paragraph.

6. Any Class member who excludes himself from the Class by following the procedure described above shall not be entitled to any distribution from the Net Settlement Fund.

7. If the proposed settlement is approved by the Court, there will be a dismissal on the merits of all claims, demands and causes of action, without limitation and whether or not heretofore asserted, which plaintiff and each member of the Class (except those who exclude themselves from the Class as provided above) have or may have, or which have been or might have been asserted on their behalf, against the defendants, or any of them, or which have been or might have been asserted against the officers, directors, employees, agents, attorneys, and representatives of the Company and/or the individual defendants, or any of them, in connection with or arising out of any of the matters, transactions and occurrences recited, described or referred to in the pleadings and proceedings herein,

and with prejudice to all members of the Class except those Class members who exclude themselves from the Class as provided above.

8.   By filing a Proof of Claim, a member of the Class will thereby submit himself to the jurisdiction of the Court, and each Proof of Claim shall be subject to investigation and discovery if deemed necessary by the Settlement Administration Committee pursuant to the Federal Rules of Civil Procedure.

9.   Plaintiff or defendants may withdraw from the Settlement Agreement under certain circumstances described in the Settlement Agreement, in which event the Settlement Fund and all interest thereon and the Administration Fund and all interest therein, less any amounts incurred for administering the settlement, shall be returned to the Company.

NOTICE TO BROKERS AND OTHER NOMINEES

The Court has directed each brokerage house, bank and other institutional nominee which purchased Class Securities to forward a copy of the Notice and Proof of Claim to all persons who were the beneficial owners of any Class Securities purchased in your record name during the period January 20, 2006 through January 15, 2008. Adequate quantities of the Notice and Proof of Claim will be mailed to you by the Settlement Administration Committee upon your request.

ATTORNEYS' FEES AND COSTS

Messrs. Barrack, Rodos & McMahon, attorneys for plaintiff Thomas Bullock, and other associated plaintiff's counsel, will apply to the Court, at the hearing described below, for an award of counsel fees not to exceed 25% of the total of the Settlement Fund and the Administration Fund and all interest earned on those funds, plus litigation expenses and disbursements actually incurred. Such award as may be granted by the Court will be paid from the Settlement Fund.

THE HEARING

Pursuant to an order of the Court filed November 14, 2009, a hearing will be held before The Honorable Stanley S. Brotman, or Magistrate Stephen M. Oriofsky to whom this matter may be referred, United States Court House, Fourth and Market Streets, Camden, New Jersey 08101 at 10 a.m. on April 9, 2010 for the purpose of determining whether the proposed settlement is fair, reasonable and adequate and whether it should be approved by the Court and the action dismissed on the merits and with prejudice as provided above and for the purpose of considering plaintiff's counsel's application for fees, allowances and disbursements. The hearing may be adjourned from time to time by the Court at the hearing or at any adjourned session thereof without further notice.

Any member of the Class who has not requested exclusion therefrom may appear at the hearing and show cause, if any he has, why the proposed settlement should not be approved and the action should not be dismissed on the merits and with prejudice and/or present any opposition to the application of plaintiff's counsel for fees, allowances and disbursements, provided that no such person shall be heard, except by special permission of the Court, unless his objection or opposition is made in writing and is filed together with copies of all other papers and briefs to be submitted by him to the Court at the hearing with the Court on or before March 15, 2010, and showing due proof of service on Barrack, Rodos & McMahon, 2000 Market Street, Philadelphia, Pennsylvania 19103; Riker, Danzig, Scherer, Debevoise & Hyland, 744 Broad Street, Newark, New Jersey 07102; and Pitney, Hardin & Kipp, 163 Madison Avenue, Morristown, New Jersey 07960. Any member of the Class who does not make his objection in the manner provided above shall be deemed to have waived such objection and shall be forever foreclosed from making any objection to the fairness or adequacy of the proposed settlement or to the request of plaintiff's counsel for fees, allowances and disbursements.

EXAMINATION OF PAPERS AND INQUIRIES

For a more detailed statement of the matters involved in the above-entitled action, reference is made to the pleadings, to the Stipulation and Agreement of Compromise and Settlement, and to the other papers filed in this action, all of which may be inspected at the Office of the Clerk of the United

SAMPLE COURT ORDERS & NOTICES

States District Court for the District of New Jersey, Fourth and Market Streets, Camden, New Jersey 08101, during the hours of each business day.

The Court has appointed a settlement administration committee consisting of Leonard Barrack, Dickinson R. Debevoise and William D. Hardin. Any contact by members of the Class should be with the Committee through the office of Heffler & Company, P.O. Box 30, Philadelphia, Pennsylvania 19105 (Tel. 215–665–8870). No inquiry should be directed to the Clerk of the Court or to Judge Stanley S. Brotman.

PROOF OF CLAIM

1.   TO RECEIVE ANY PAYMENTS FROM THIS SETTLEMENT, YOU MUST SIGN AND HAVE NOTARIZED THE ATTACHED PROOF OF CLAIM FORM, AND SUBMIT PROPER DOCUMENTATION SUPPORTING YOUR CLAIM.

2.   Distribution of the proceeds of any settlement or of any judgment is subject to Court Approval.

3.   You must file your completed and signed Proof of Claim on or before March 15, 2010 addressed as follows:

Singer Settlement Administration Committee
c/o Heffler & Company
P.O. Box 30
Philadelphia, Pennsylvania 19105
Tel. 215–665–8870

Your Proof of Claim form shall be deemed to have been filed when posted, if mailed by registered or certified mail, postage prepaid, addressed in accordance with the instructions given therein. A Proof of Claim filed otherwise shall be deemed to be filed at the time it is actually received by the person or office designated to receive it in the Proof of Claim.

4.   The claim must be filed in the name, or names, of the actual beneficial owner, or owners, of the securities upon which the claim is based. All joint owners must sign this Proof of Claim. Executors, administrators, guardians, and trustees may complete and sign the form on behalf of persons represented by them, but must identify the beneficial owners. Proof of their authority need not accompany the Proof of Claim but their titles or capacities must be stated.

5.   You must list all acquisitions of any Class Securities on or after January 20, 2006 through December 29, 2008 and all dispositions of any Class Securities at any time.

6.   If you acquired any Class Securities by gift, inheritance or operation of law, you are to report them as if you acquired them at the actual cost of your transferor.

7.   Brokerage commissions, stock transfer taxes or other miscellaneous charges (excepting accrued interest) usually incurred in connection with either a purchase or a sale of the Class Securities shall be included in the cost and the sales price of such Class Securities.

8.   Your Proof of Claim must be under oath, and must be accompanied by the documents called for therein.

Dated this _____ day of _____, _____.

JUDGE

THIS ENTIRE FORM (OTHER THAN SIGNATURES)
MUST BE TYPED OR PRINTED

UNITED STATES DISTRICT COURT

FOR THE DISTRICT OF NEW JERSEY

SAMPLE COURT ORDERS & NOTICES

THOMAS BULLOCK, on behalf of himself and all others similarly situated,

Plaintiff,

vs.

DONALD P. KIRCHER, JOSEPH B. FLAVIN, GILBERT W. FITZHUGH, ARTHUR H. FREDSTON, EDWIN J. GRAF, WILLIAM G. HAMILTON, JR., LLOYD L. KELLEY, IAN K. MacGREGOR, JAMES W. McKEE, JR., DONALD E. MEADS, WILLIAM H. MORTON, DONALD G. ROBBINS, JR., ARTHUR J. SANTRY, JR., F. WAYNE VALLEY, THE SINGER COMPANY,

Defendants.

_____

_____

Herein designated as the "Claimant"

The undersigned, being duly sworn, deposes and says that the following is true, correct and complete to the best of his knowledge, information and belief.

I. IDENTITY OF CLAIMANT:

   A. Claimant's name,* mailing address and telephone number are as follows:

   _____

   _____

   B. Claimant is (check one)—

   _____ An Individual

   _____ Two or more persons holding stock or debentures jointly

   _____ Partnership

   _____ Corporation

   _____ Executor or Administrator

   _____ Trustee

   _____ Other (specify) _____

* If stock or debentures are held jointly, give the names of all persons interested in the stock or debentures.

II. STATEMENT OF CLAIM:

   A. Claimant (or person from whom Claimant acquired shares by gifts or inheritance, or deceased person for whom Claimant is acting as executor or administrator) made the following purchases of (i) Common Stock of The Singer Company, par value $10 per share, (ii) $3.50 Cumulative Preferred Stock of The Singer Company, stated value $13 per share and (iii) The Singer Company's 8% Sinking Fund Debentures due January 15, 2010, during the period January 20, 2006 through December 29, 2008. *Claimant has included information as to all such purchases made during such period.*

Number of shares and amount of debentures purchased (list each type of security separately)	Date of purchase (trade date)	Price for the purchases, shares or debentures (including commissions)

SAMPLE COURT ORDERS & NOTICES

<table>
<tr><td rowspan="2">Name in which shares or debentures registered</td><td colspan="3" align="center">Type of Security</td></tr>
<tr><td align="center">Common</td><td align="center">Preferred</td><td align="center">Debenture</td></tr>
</table>

B.   Claimant sold the following (i) Common Stock of The Singer Company, par value $10 per share, (ii) $3.50 Cumulative Preferred Stock of The Singer Company, stated value $13 per share and (iii) The Singer Company's 8% Sinking Fund Debentures due January 15, 2010, referred to Paragraph II A above. *Claimant has included information with respect to all such sales, and such shares and debentures are still held by the Claimant to the extent that their sale is not listed below.*

Number of shares and amount of debentures sold (list each type of security separately)	Date of sale (trade date)	Price for the sold shares or debentures (including commissions and expenses)

<table>
<tr><td rowspan="2">Name in which shares or debentures registered at time of sale</td><td colspan="3" align="center">Type of Security</td></tr>
<tr><td align="center">Common</td><td align="center">Preferred</td><td align="center">Debenture</td></tr>
</table>

III.   ADDITIONAL PROOF REQUIRED:

CLAIMANT MUST ANNEX TO THIS PROOF OF CLAIM COPIES OF BROKER'S CONFIRMATION, MONTHLY ACCOUNT STATEMENTS, DELIVERY RECEIPTS, OR OTHER DOCUMENTATION ESTABLISHING EVIDENCE OF ALL PURCHASES AND SALES INCLUDED IN PARAGRAPH II OF THIS PROOF OF CLAIM.

IV.   THE FOLLOWING PARAGRAPHS APPLY TO ALL CLAIMANTS:

A.   By the filing of this Proof of Claim, Claimant hereby submits to the jurisdiction of the United States District Court for the District of New Jersey.

B.   Claimant understands that the information contained in this Proof of Claim is subject to investigation and discovery pursuant to the Federal Rules of Civil Procedure and that Claimant may be required to furnish additional information to support this Proof of Claim.

C.   Claimant hereby certifies that neither he (it) nor any purchaser of shares or debentures of The Singer Company which are the subject of this Proof of Claim was (i) an employee of The Singer Company who purchased his shares pursuant to a stock option plan, stock purchase plan or executive incentive plan sponsored or adopted by Singer, or (ii) an individual defendant in this action, or (iii) a spouse, child, parent, brother, sister, officer, director, partner, or controlling person of any named defendant or a subsidiary or affiliate of a named defendant, or (iv) an underwriter, purchasing for its own beneficial account, with respect to any of the securities which are the subject of this Proof of Claim.

D.   By the filing of this Proof of Claim, and in consideration of the right to participate in the distribution of the Settlement Fund, Claimant hereby waives and releases all claims and demands which he (it) may have against any defendant in the Action, or against the officers, directors, employees, agents, attorneys and representatives of any of such defendants, or against any other person or business entity, arising from or related to the matters complained of in the above-entitled action or the consummation of the terms of the Stipulation and Agreement of Compromise and Settlement entered into in said action.

Sworn to before me this   Signed _____

_____ day of 20__.   (Name(s)—all registered joint owners must sign)

_____   _____

        Notary Public   (Address)

THIS PROOF OF CLAIM MUST BE FILED NO LATER THAN MARCH 15, 20__ AND MUST BE MAILED TO:

Singer Settlement Administration Committee
c/o Heffler & Company
P.O. Box 30
Philadelphia, Pennsylvania 19105**

1.45. Additional Sample Sections That May Be Used in Settlement Notices

In addition to the sections contained in the sample notices of settlement set out above, the Court may desire to use one or more of the following sections:

(a)   Section on reasons for settlement[6]

REASONS FOR SETTLEMENT: Defendants disclaim any liability and any wrongdoing of any kind whatsoever and have denied the allegations in both actions and have asserted defenses that they believe are meritorious, but they consider it desirable that this action and the claims alleged therein be settled upon the terms and conditions set forth in the Settlement Agreement, in order to avoid further expenses, and burdensome, protracted litigation, and to put at rest all claims that have been or might be asserted by any member of either class arising from the subject matter of the complaints herein. The proposed settlements and this Notice are not to be construed as admissions of liability of any kind whatsoever by any of the defendants.

Counsel for plaintiffs and the classes represented by them have thoroughly investigated the facts and circumstances underlying the issues raised by the pleadings herein and the law applicable thereto, have conducted extensive discovery, and have concluded that, taking into account the risks involved in establishing, in whole or in part, a right to recovery on behalf of the named plaintiffs and the classes they represent against the defendants and the likelihood that this litigation will be further protracted and expensive, it would be in the best interests of the named plaintiffs and the classes they represent to settle these actions upon the terms and conditions set forth in the Settlement Agreement and that such terms are fair, adequate, and reasonable.

Once again, the Court has not expressed any opinion concerning the merits of the claims or defenses herein.

(b)   Section on effect of failure to file proof of claim form[7]

If you do not exclude yourself and also do not file a valid Claim Form, you will be included in the Class, but you will not receive any portion of the Net Settlement Fund, and you will be bound by the Final Judgment in this Litigation, the Settlement Stipulation, and the releases therein, and you will be barred from any further assertion of released and settled claims. To receive a portion of the

---

** A Proof of Claim shall be deemed to have been filed when posted, if mailed by registered or certified mail, postage prepaid. A Proof of Claim filed otherwise shall be deemed to be filed at the time it is actually received by the Singer Settlement Administration Committee at the address set forth above.

6   From an order used in Weisberg v. APL Corp., Civil Action No. 74-C-1794 (E.D.N.Y.).

7   Adapted from an order used in Friedman v. Zale Corp., Civil Action No. 3-77-0850-C (N.D.Tex.).

Settlement Fund you must file a Claim Form in a proper manner and mail it so that it is received on or before _____ _____, 20__.

(c)   Section on effect of failure to file proof of claim form and filing objections to settlement[8]

TO ALL PERSONS WHO PURCHASED COMMON STOCK OF GIANT STORES CORP. DURING THE PERIOD APRIL 16, 2005 THROUGH AND INCLUDING MAY 23, 2007.

PLEASE TAKE NOTICE that a hearing will be held on May 9, 2010 at 9:30 a. m. before the Honorable Charles M. Metzner, Judge of the United States District Court for the Southern District of New York, at the United States Courthouse, Foley Square, New York, New York in Room 519. The purpose of the hearing is to determine whether the two proposed settlements of the above-entitled Consolidated Class Action for sums aggregating $4,750,000, which will constitute the entire recovery to the class members, pursuant to two Stipulations of Settlement, should be approved by the Court as fair, reasonable, and adequate, and to consider the application of plaintiffs for the award of counsel fees and expenses. If you have not excluded yourself from the class, you may be entitled to share in the distribution of the settlement fund. TO SHARE IN THE DISTRIBUTION OF THE SETTLEMENT FUND, YOU MUST FILE A PROOF OF CLAIM ON OR BEFORE JUNE 15, 2010, establishing that you purchased common stock of Giant Stores Corp. during the period April 16, 2005 through and including May 23, 2007.

Objections to the settlement or the award of counsel fees, expenses, and disbursements must be filed no later than April 27, 2010 as provided in the detailed notice referred to below.

A more detailed notice describing the proposed settlements of this consolidated class action, the fees and expenses requested, the hearing thereon, and the requirement that a proof of claim be filed, has been mailed to all persons appearing on the transfer records of Giant Stores Corp. as record purchasers during the period April 16, 2005 through and including May 23, 2007. If you have not received a copy of that notice, *you may obtain one and a Proof of Claim form by making a written request to* Clerk of the Court, P.O. Box 1220, General Post Office, New York, New York 10001.

Re: Giant Stores Corp., *or* Attorneys for Plaintiffs,

One Pennsylvania Plaza, New York, New York 10001

Attention: Jared Specthrie, Esq.

---

[8]   Adapted from an order used in Goldberg v. Touche Ross & Co., Civil Action No. 74 Civ. 1483 (S.D.N.Y.).

PART VI

Illustrative Litigation Problem
with
Sample Documents

Introduction

The purpose of the illustrative problem is three-fold: to give a general picture of the flow of litigation; to present a series of sample documents in the context of a factual setting; and, finally, to demonstrate how specific procedural matters may arise during the course of an actual case. The problem is broken into four sections: Jurisdiction, Pleadings, Pretrial Discovery and Motions, and Trial, Verdict, and Attacks on Verdict. Each section contains a number of questions to focus attention on the problems raised.

Stage I. Jurisdiction

Plaintiff Thomas A_____, filed an action in a state court. The complaint read as follows:

IN THE SUPERIOR COURT, DELTA COUNTY, STATE OF ARVADA

Thomas A_____,	)	
Plaintiff	)	
	)	
vs.	)	Civil P 15163
	)	COMPLAINT
Reginald B_____, Daniel C_____,	)	
and D_____ Corporation,	)	
Defendants	)	

COUNT ONE

I

On or about June 1, 2017, plaintiff Thomas A_____ was involved in a motor vehicle collision with an automobile driven by defendant Reginald B_____ and with a bulldozer operated by defendant Daniel C_____ who was acting within the scope of his employment with defendant D_____ Corporation. The collision occurred on Public Highway 10 in the state of Arvada, approximately twenty miles east of the City of Diego.

II

Defendants and each of them have informed plaintiff that they suffered injuries to persons and property in a total amount of $100,000 and have demanded that plaintiff remit the amount of such damages or face institution of legal action against him for their recovery.

ILLUSTRATIVE LITIGATION PROBLEM

III

Defendants have informed plaintiff that their injuries are proximately due to the plaintiff's negligence in that at the time of the collision, plaintiff was operating his vehicle in excess of the speed limit.

IV

Plaintiff is an agent of the Federal Bureau of Investigation. At the time of the collision he was proceeding at a speed of 80 miles per hour along Public Highway 10 pursuant to orders, duly issued, to assist in the apprehension of escaped federal prisoners. Plaintiff's speed, although in excess of the state speed limit, was necessary in order for him to carry out his assigned duties.

WHEREFORE, Plaintiff prays for a declaration:

(1)   That he was not negligent at the time of the collision.

(2)   That he is immune from liability because his acts were required within the scope of his federal duties.

(3)   Awarding him such other relief to which he is entitled.

James L. W_____
Attorney for Plaintiff

——————

Question:

On the basis of facts stated in the complaint could plaintiff have maintained suit in a federal district court?

——————

Plaintiff A_____ is a citizen of the State of Mindon, defendant B_____ is a citizen of the State of Arvada, defendant C_____ is a citizen of the State of Lamar, and the D_____ Corporation, which does considerable business in all three states is incorporated in Lamar where its equipment is housed and where all of its 2000 workmen reside. Its administrative offices, however, are located in Mindon, which is the residence of its 10 executive officers and 25 office workers.

——————

Questions:

1.   **How does the information regarding the citizenship and activities of the parties affect the ability of plaintiff to bring his action in a federal court? In the federal court of Arvada?**

2.   **Assuming that Arvada has enacted the broadest possible statutes permitting service of process on out-of-state residents, can the courts of Arvada constitutionally assert personal jurisdiction over all the defendants in this action by personally serving them where they reside? Is the extension of jurisdiction to cover such a case a wise policy?**

——————

After filing his action, but prior to attempting service of process, plaintiff's attorney called defendant C_____ at his house, informed him of the pending suit, and requested a meeting in Arvada in order to arrange a settlement. The attorney promised that C_____ would be paid a substantial sum but only if he tacitly agreed to take a job in another part of the country and to resist all efforts by

ILLUSTRATIVE LITIGATION PROBLEM

his codefendants to induce him to testify against plaintiff. C_____ agreed to the meeting. Immediately upon his arrival in Arvada, however, he was greeted by a process server who handed him a summons to appear in plaintiff's action. When C_____ arrived at the attorney's office, he was told by the secretary there that the scheduled meeting was canceled and would be rescheduled. C_____, justifiably angry, stormed out of the office to return home. Before leaving Arvada, however, he tarried long enough to look at 100 acres of unimproved real estate that was for sale. Several days after returning home, he purchased the property for $50,000 in a transaction handled through the mail.

Questions:

1.   Is the service made on C_____ in Arvada sufficient to bring him before the state courts? What arguments might he make if he wishes to avoid being sued in Arvada?

2.   May C_____'s purchase of the property in any way assist plaintiff in bringing his action against C_____?

The original complaint was served on all defendants on June 30, 2017. On July 31, 2017, prior to the filing of any response by defendants, and without leave of court, plaintiff filed a "First Amended Complaint" containing all the information in the original complaint and adding the following new counts:

COUNT TWO

I

Plaintiff incorporates herein the allegations contained in paragraphs I and IV of Count One.

II

Defendant C_____ negligently stopped the bulldozer along the side of Public Highway 10. As a direct and proximate result thereof, plaintiff was unable to avoid striking the vehicle driven by defendant B_____ which in turn caused plaintiff to strike the bulldozer.

III

As a direct and proximate result of defendant C_____'s negligence, plaintiff suffered severe physical injuries involving his head and right shoulder. Plaintiff has endured great pain and suffering and will have large hospital and doctor bills in an amount as yet unascertained.

WHEREFORE, Plaintiff prays for damages in the amount of $160,000 against defendant C_____ and such other relief to which plaintiff is entitled.

COUNT THREE

I

On July 13, 2017, plaintiff deposited the sum of $2,500 cash with the Efficiency Bank of Mindon as trustee, to deliver said sum to defendant B_____ upon his execution of a release form provided by plaintiff.

II

On July 17, 2017, the Efficiency Bank paid B_____ $2,500 cash. The Bank did not receive the executed form from defendant B_____ then or at any subsequent time.

WHEREFORE, Plaintiff prays that the court order defendant B_____ to execute such release form or in the alternative to hold the $2,500 as a constructive trustee for plaintiff or for any other relief to which plaintiff is entitled.

ILLUSTRATIVE LITIGATION PROBLEM

Attached to the amended complaint and labeled "Exhibit" was the following document:

RELEASE FORM

Whereas B_____ is alleging a claim for personal injury and property damage against A_____ arising from a vehicle collision, and whereas both parties wish to avoid litigation,

B_____ hereby acknowledges receipt of $2,500 from A_____ and in consideration therefor, forever releases A_____ from any and all liability to B_____ arising from any cause whatsoever occurring on or before the date of this instrument.

_____   _____
Date   Signature

_____

Question:

May defendants, or any one of them, when served with the amended complaint have the entire case removed to the federal court in Arvada?

_____

Stage II. Pleadings

Five days after receiving the amended complaint, defendant B_____'s attorney filed the following document and sent a copy to each of the parties through their attorneys:

IN THE SUPERIOR COURT, DELTA COUNTY STATE OF ARVADA

Thomas A_____,	)	
Plaintiff	)	
	)	Civil P 15163
vs.	)	
	)	NOTICE OF MOTION
Reginald B_____, Daniel C_____	)	TO STRIKE
and D_____ Corporation,	)	
Defendants	)	

To Thomas A_____, plaintiff, and to his attorney, James L. W_____.

You and each of you will please take notice that on August 10, 2017, at the hour of 9:00 A.M. in the above entitled court, defendant Reginald B_____ will move to strike the First Amended Complaint. The motion is made on the ground that the said Amended Complaint was filed without leave of court as required by Rule 15 of the Arvada Rules of Civil Procedure.

In the alternative, defendant B_____ will move to strike Count Three of the First Amended Complaint on the ground that it is improperly joined with Counts One and Two in violation of section 20 of the Arvada Civil Practice Act.

Louisa F_____

Attorney for Defendant B_____

Attached to the motion was the following supporting document which is required of all motions to strike in Arvada courts:

ILLUSTRATIVE LITIGATION PROBLEM

STATEMENT OF POINTS AND AUTHORITIES
SUPPORTING MOTION TO STRIKE

I

1.   Rule 15(a) of the Arvada Rules of Civil Procedure provides that a complaint cannot be amended without leave of court "after defendant's answer has been filed."

2.   This rule should logically be interpreted to prohibit amendment without leave of court if the normal time for answer has elapsed, whether or not such answer is filed.

3.   Under Rule 12(a) of the Arvada Rules of Civil Procedure the time for answer is twenty-one days after service. Plaintiff's First Amended Complaint was filed on July 29, 2017, whereas the original complaint was served on June 29, 2017.

II

1.   Section 20 of the Arvada Civil Practice Act permits joinder of causes all of which fall within one of the following classes:

    (1)   Contracts, express or implied

    (2)   Physical injury to person

    (3)   Injury to property

    (4)   Injury to character

    (5)   Matters arising out of the same transactions or occurrences.

2.   Count Three of plaintiff's First Amended Complaint does not appear in any of the statutory categories in which Counts One and Two appear.

Questions:

1.   How likely is it that the court will grant the motion to strike the entire complaint? See Federal Rule 15(a) and the comparative state materials, supra.

2.   What chance does defendant have on his motion to strike Count Three? Note Federal Rule 18(a) and the comparative state materials, supra.

At the same time that she filed her notice of motion, defendant B_____'s attorney filed and served on all parties the following:

IN THE SUPERIOR COURT, DELTA COUNTY, STATE OF ARVADA

Thomas A_____,	)
Plaintiff	)
	) Civil P 15163
vs.	)
	) DEMURRER
Reginald B_____, Daniel C_____	)
and D_____ Corporation,	)
Defendants	)

Defendant B_____ demurs to the First Amended Complaint on file herein as follows:

I

Count One does not state facts sufficient to constitute a cause of action.

ILLUSTRATIVE LITIGATION PROBLEM

II

Count Three does not state facts sufficient to constitute a cause of action.

III

There is a defect of parties in plaintiff's Count Three.

IV

The court has no jurisdiction over the matters in Count Three because an Indispensable Party has not been joined.

Louisa F_____

Attorney for Defendant B_____

Under Arvada rules, defendant need not set the date for the demurrer; instead the clerk of the court must notify all parties as to the time the hearing will be held.

Questions:

1. Assuming that this case, if properly pleaded, would justify declaratory relief under Arvada law, and further assuming that Arvada follows the classic rules of code pleading, what chance does defendant B_____ have on his challenge to the sufficiency of Counts One and Three? What possible defects may he point to in arguing that the demurrer should be sustained? Would the result be different if the court was operating under the Federal Rules of Civil Procedure?

2. How successful will B_____ be regarding his challenges as to joinder of parties? Does anything turn on whether or not the Efficiency Bank is subject to personal jurisdiction in Arvada? See Federal Rule 19.

After hearing arguments on both the motion to strike and the demurrer, the trial judge issued the following order, which was prepared at his direction by defendant B_____'s attorney:

IN THE SUPERIOR COURT, DELTA COUNTY STATE OF ARVADA

Thomas A_____,	)	
Plaintiff	)	
	)	Civil P 15163
vs.	)	
	)	ORDER
Reginald B_____, Daniel C_____	)	
and D_____ Corporation,	)	
Defendants	)	

The motion of defendant Reginald B_____ to strike the First Amended Complaint or in the alternative to strike parts therefrom and his demurrer to counts One and Three having come on regularly for hearing before the undersigned this 10th day of August, 2017, at the hour of 10 A.M., upon notice duly and regularly served and plaintiff Thomas A_____ appearing by his counsel James. L. W_____ and defendant Reginald B_____, appearing by his counsel, Louisa F_____, and no

ILLUSTRATIVE LITIGATION PROBLEM

appearance having been made on behalf of the other named defendants and the matter having been argued and submitted and good cause appearing therefore,

IT IS HEREBY ORDERED, AS FOLLOWS:

(1) That defendant's motion to strike be denied in all particulars.

(2) That defendant's demurrer to Count One be denied.

(3) That defendant's demurrer to Count Three be sustained on the ground that it fails to state facts constituting a cause of action.

(4) That the demurrer otherwise be denied in all particulars.

(5) That plaintiff has leave to file an amended complaint in ten days from the date hereof and that defendant is granted twenty days from the date hereof to file his Answer.

Dated: August 10, 2017

Learned W_____

Judge of the Superior Court

Questions:

1. **What choices does plaintiff now have with regard to the Court's ruling on Count Three of his complaint? What will be the consequences of an amendment if he later wishes to claim that the trial court erred? If he fails to amend, will he be prohibited from bringing any new action against B_____ for the same loss?**

2. **What chance does plaintiff have to appeal immediately the ruling as to Count Three? If it is within the trial or appellate court's discretion to permit an amendment, should it be allowed?**

On August 22, 2017, plaintiff filed a Second Amended Complaint changing only the allegations of Count Three as follows:

COUNT THREE

I

On July 13, 2017, plaintiff deposited the sum of $2,500 cash with the Efficiency Bank of Mindon. The money was held in trust to deliver said sum to defendant B_____ upon his execution of a specific release form provided by plaintiff. The release form is attached to this complaint as an "Exhibit" and is made a part hereof as if set forth in full herein.

II

On July 17, 2017, the Efficiency Bank paid the $2,500 held in trust to defendant B_____. The Bank did not receive the executed form from defendant B_____ then or at any subsequent time.

WHEREFORE, Plaintiff prays that the court order defendant B_____ to execute such release form or in the alternative to hold the $2,500 as a constructive trustee for plaintiff or for any other relief to which plaintiff is entitled.

Once again defendant B_____ demurred to the complaint on the ground that Count Three failed to state a cause of action. The demurrer was overruled.

ILLUSTRATIVE LITIGATION PROBLEM

Questions:

1. To what extent does this amendment cure any defects in the prior complaint?

2. What choices does B_____ have with regard to the court's ruling on Count Three? If he answers does he waive the defense that Count Three doesn't state a valid cause of action? What if he fails to answer? See Federal Rule 8(d).

3. What opportunity does B_____ have to appeal immediately the overruling of his demurrer to Count Three? Should a trial or appellate court in its discretion permit the appeal?

On August 23, 2017, defendant C_____ filed and served on all other parties the following Answer and Crossclaim:

IN THE SUPERIOR COURT, DELTA COUNTY STATE OF ARVADA

Thomas A_____,	)	
Plaintiff	)	
	)	Civil P 15163
vs.	)	
	)	ANSWER AND
Reginald B_____, Daniel C_____	)	CROSSCLAIM
and D_____ Corporation,	)	
Defendants	)	

Defendant Daniel C_____ Answers and alleges as follows:

I

Admits the allegations of paragraph I of Count One of plaintiff's complaint.

II

Admits the allegations of paragraphs II and III of Count One of plaintiff's complaint and alleges the truth of those facts in paragraph III of Count One of which plaintiff alleges defendant C_____ informed him and further alleges that defendant C_____ was severely injured, endured great pain and suffering and medical expenses, none of which can presently be ascertained with certainty but which will amount at a minimum to $25,000.

III

Admits so much of paragraph IV of Count One of plaintiff's complaint that alleges that plaintiff drove in excess of the state speed limit; has no information as to plaintiff's employment at the time of the collision and on that ground denies the allegation relating to plaintiff's employment as an FBI agent; and denies that a speed of 80 miles per hour was required by defendant's duties or was in any way reasonable or non-negligent.

IV

Refuses to admit or deny each and every allegation of paragraph II of Count Two of plaintiff's complaint and demands that plaintiff be put to his proof.

V

Has no information or belief as to the allegations of paragraph III of Count Two of plaintiff's complaint, and on that ground denies the allegations of said paragraph III.

ILLUSTRATIVE LITIGATION PROBLEM

CROSSCLAIM

Defendant C_____ as a Crossclaim alleges as follows:

I

At the time of the collision which is the subject of plaintiff's action, defendant Daniel C_____ was stopping his bulldozer on the shoulder of Public Highway 10 in the State of Arvada, to assist defendant Reginald B_____ whose vehicle had stalled on the highway.

II

Defendant B_____ was instructing and directing defendant C_____ in parking the bulldozer in order that it would not be a hazard to vehicles approaching along the highway. Defendant C_____ followed such instructions as given by defendant B_____. C_____'s reliance on such instructions was reasonable.

III

Plaintiff in this action seeks damages from defendant C_____ on the grounds that said bulldozer was improperly stopped so as to create an unreasonable risk to passing traffic. The position of the bulldozer when stopped was the direct and proximate result of defendant B_____'s negligence in giving the aforesaid instructions.

WHEREFORE, Defendant C_____ prays as follows:

1. That plaintiff take nothing by his action.

2. That defendant B_____ be held liable to indemnify defendant C_____ for all amounts, if any, which defendant C_____ is ordered to pay plaintiff on the basis of his complaint herein.

3. That defendant C_____ be awarded such damages and other relief to which he is entitled.

Samuel R_____

Attorney for Defendant C_____

Questions:

1. **Could plaintiff successfully move for a judgment on the pleadings against defendant C_____? What arguments does plaintiff have that all of the essential elements of his case have been admitted?**

2. **Suppose the case had been brought in a federal court and that B_____ had not been named as a codefendant by plaintiff. Could the crossclaim still have been maintained by defendant C_____? See Federal Rule 14. How would your answer be affected if the Arvada law, on the basis of the facts alleged, clearly prohibited C_____'s claim against B_____ for indemnity but permitted C_____ to recover damages for his own personal injuries from B_____? Could C_____ sue for such injuries on a crosscomplaint? See Federal Rules 13(g) and (h).**

Shortly after defendant C_____ filed his Answer and Crossclaim, defendants B_____ and D_____ Corporation filed separate answers to Counts One and Two of plaintiff's complaint, asserting that the sole cause of the accident was plaintiff's negligence. Both B_____ and D_____ Corporation demanded, by way of counterclaim, payment for the damages they suffered. In addition defendant B_____ generally denied allegations in Count Three of the complaint.

ILLUSTRATIVE LITIGATION PROBLEM

B_____ then filed an answer to defendant C_____'s Crossclaim as follows:

IN THE SUPERIOR COURT, DELTA COUNTY STATE OF ARVADA

Thomas A_____,	)	
Plaintiff	)	
	)	Civil P 15163
vs.	)	
	)	ANSWER TO
Reginald B_____, Daniel C_____	)	CROSSCLAIM
and D_____ Corporation,	)	
Defendants	)	

Defendant B_____ for an Answer to the Crossclaim filed by Defendant C_____:

I

Denies each and every allegation therein stated.

II

Alleges that defendant C_____ was negligent in stopping the bulldozer and that said negligence was a direct and proximate cause of plaintiff's injuries.

WHEREFORE, Defendant B_____ prays that defendant C_____ take nothing from defendant B_____ on his cross-action.

Louisa F_____

Attorney for Defendant B_____

Question:

Should any of the parties file further pleadings? To what extent are they permitted to do so? See Federal Rule 7(a), supra.

Stage III.   Pretrial Discovery and Motions

On September 1, 2017, defendant B_____ filed and served on all parties the following document:

IN THE SUPERIOR COURT, DELTA COUNTY STATE OF ARVADA

Thomas A_____,	)	
Plaintiff	)	
	)	Civil P 15163
vs.	)	
	)	NOTICE OF MOTION
Reginald B_____, Daniel C_____	)	
and D_____ Corporation,	)	
Defendants	)	

To plaintiff Thomas A_____ and his attorney, James L. W_____:

You are hereby notified that on September 6, 2017, at the hour of 10 A.M. in the courtroom of the above entitled court, defendant Reginald B_____ will move this court for an order directing plaintiff to submit to a physical examination by Dr. William M_____, whose office is at 420 D_____ Avenue,

ILLUSTRATIVE LITIGATION PROBLEM

in the City of Diego, State of Arvada. The purpose of the examination is to determine the state of plaintiff's mental health at the time of the collision described in the Complaint herein. The motion is based upon Rule 35 of the Arvada Rules of Civil Procedure. The examination is necessary to determine whether plaintiff was mentally capable of safely operating a motor vehicle at a speed of 80 miles per hour; whether he was aware of his ability or inability to do so; and whether he is capable of truthful testimony. The motion is made upon the affidavit of Louisa F_____, Attorney for defendant Reginald B_____, and upon evidence, oral and documentary, to be presented at the hearing of this motion.

Louisa F_____

Attorney for Defendant B_____

AFFIDAVIT

STATE OF ARVADA)
               ss.)   Civil P 15163
COUNTY OF DELTA)

Louisa F_____, being first duly sworn, states that she is attorney for defendant Reginald B_____ herein and is familiar with the issues to be tried.

In this action plaintiff seeks a declaration that he was not negligent in operating a vehicle although he was traveling at a high rate of speed in excess of the state speed laws. The ability of an individual to control a motor vehicle at high speeds depends upon his individual psychological make-up which determines his reaction time. Defendant is without expert information as to these matters regarding plaintiff.

Plaintiff further alleges that his speeding was reasonable. This will in part depend on whether plaintiff knew he created an unreasonable risk by driving much faster than was necessary under the circumstances. Defendant B_____ can ascertain such knowledge on the part of plaintiff only through an examination by an expert.

The undersigned is informed and believes that plaintiff will testify during trial on his own behalf. Defendant B_____ is unable without the examination here requested, to obtain evidence as to whether plaintiff is a pathological liar or is otherwise psychologically unable or unlikely to tell the truth.

Dr. M_____ is a practicing clinical psychologist, with a Ph.D. degree from Midwestern University. He is licensed to practice under the laws of the State of Arvada and has been practicing in the State for the past 12 years and enjoys an excellent reputation in his field.

Louisa F_____

Subscribed and sworn to before me this First day of September, 2017.

[Signed] Rita N_____
Notary Public In and For the
State of Arvada, Delta County

[Notary Seal
of the State
of Arvada]

Questions:

How likely is the court to grant the motion? Assuming that Federal Rule 35 is applicable, what arguments could be made by A_____ to avoid such examination?

ILLUSTRATIVE LITIGATION PROBLEM

Defendant B_____'s attorney subsequently learned that the lawyer for defendant D_____ Corporation has done considerable investigation of every aspect of the case. B_____'s attorney therefore sent the following interrogatories to D_____ Corporation:

IN THE SUPERIOR COURT, DELTA COUNTY STATE OF ARVADA

Thomas A_____,	)
Plaintiff	)
	) Civil P 15163
vs.	)
	) INTERROGATORIES
Reginald B_____, Daniel C_____	)
and D_____ Corporation,	)
Defendants	)

To D_____ Corporation:

Please take notice that the following interrogatories are submitted pursuant to Rule 33 of the Arvada Rules of Civil Procedure; answers are required by said Rule 33 within 30 days of the receipt hereof:

1. What are the names and addresses of persons, if any, other than the named parties to this action, from whom you have obtained written statements regarding the activities of plaintiff and defendant C_____ just prior to, at the time of, and immediately subsequent to the collision which is the subject of plaintiff's action?

2. What are the names and addresses of those persons, if any, other than the parties named in this action, whom you have interviewed regarding the activities of defendant B_____ just prior to, at the time of, and immediately subsequent to the collision which is the subject of plaintiff's action and defendant C_____'s counterclaim?

3. What information concerning the events in this action has D_____ Corporation or its attorneys voluntarily turned over to defendant C_____ or his attorneys?

4. What is the nature of the conspiracy, if any, between defendant C_____ and defendant D_____ Corporation or their attorneys regarding a concerted effort to avoid liability by placing all blame for the accident on plaintiff and defendant B_____?

5. Is it true that two days after the collision defendant C_____ told an investigating attorney for D_____ Corporation that the only instruction given by him by B_____ just prior to the accident was "Get the hell off of the road!"?

6. What is the substance of the reports of any experts hired by defendant D_____ Corporation, other than those already turned over to plaintiff, regarding the speed and exact location of the vehicles involved in the accident just prior to and at the time of the collision?

7. What are the names and addresses of any experts referred to in Interrogatory 6 above?

Louisa F_____

Attorney for Defendant B_____

D_____ Corporation responded to these interrogatories as follows:

ILLUSTRATIVE LITIGATION PROBLEM

IN THE SUPERIOR COURT, DELTA COUNTY STATE OF ARVADA

Thomas A_____,   )
                    Plaintiff   )
)   Civil P 15163
              vs.   )
)   OBJECTIONS TO
Reginald B_____, Daniel C_____   )   INTERROGATORIES
    and D_____ Corporation,)
                    Defendants)

To defendant Reginald B_____ and Louisa F_____, his attorney:

Please take notice that defendant D_____ Corporation, objects to the interrogatories which were served by you on September 8, 2017, and said defendant will on September 15, 2017, at the hour of 10 A.M. in the above entitled Court, move for an order striking said interrogatories for the following reasons:

1. Interrogatories may not be served by one defendant on a codefendant in an action.

2. Interrogatory Number 2 is irrelevant as to matters between D_____ Corporation and B_____.

3. Each of the interrogatories request information within the work-product privilege.

Paul Y_____

Attorney for Defendant
D_____Corporation

Question:

Assume that the Arvada discovery rule regarding interrogatories is the same as the federal rule. What are defendant D_____ Corporation's chances on its motion? See Federal Rule 26(b)(1), (b)(2), and (b)(4) and Federal Rule 33(a) and (b).

On September 12, 2017, defendant B_____ moved for summary judgment on the crossclaim filed by defendant C_____. The motion was supported by an affidavit of one William G_____, which read as follows:

AFFIDAVIT

STATE OF ARVADA   )
) ss.)   Civil P 15163
COUNTY OF DELTA   )

William G_____, being first duly sworn deposes and says:

That on June 1, 2017, he was a passenger in a vehicle driven by Reginald B_____; that said vehicle was involved in a collision on Public Highway 10, East of the City of Diego; that just prior to the collision, the vehicle driven by B_____ was required to stop on the highway because the pavement was blocked by a bulldozer crossing over the road; that B_____ had shouted a few words to the bulldozer operator; that said operator had shouted back and waved his fist in an angry manner; that B_____ had then said, "I told him to get the hell out of the middle of the road"; that thereupon

ILLUSTRATIVE LITIGATION PROBLEM

another vehicle approaching from the opposite direction at a high rate of speed struck the bulldozer and careened into the car driven by B_____.

William G_____

Subscribed and sworn to before me this First day of September, 2017.

[*Signed*] Rita N_____
Notary Public In and For the
State of Arvada, Delta County

[*Notary Seal
of the State of
Arvada*]

Defendant C_____ filed no answering affidavits; at the hearing his attorney argued that the affidavit was insufficient to justify summary judgment, that the failure of B_____ to file his own affidavit was in itself sufficient reason to deny the motion, and that C_____'s pleadings clearly contradicted the statements in the affidavit. The court took the matter under advisement and one week later signed an order granting the motion in favor of B_____.

Questions:

Was the decision of the trial judge appropriate? Should it be reversed on appeal?

The filing of G_____'s affidavit was the first notice to defendant D_____ Corporation that G_____ had been a witness to the collision. The Corporation's attorney sent copies of the following document to all other parties:

IN THE SUPERIOR COURT, DELTA COUNTY STATE OF ARVADA

Thomas A_____,	)	
Plaintiff	)	Civil P 15163
	)	
vs.	)	NOTICE OF TIME
	)	AND PLACE OF
Reginald B_____, Daniel	)	DEPOSITION
C_____		
and D_____ Corporation,	)	
Defendants	)	

To Thomas A_____, plaintiff, and to James L. W_____, his Attorney; to Reginald B_____, defendant and Louisa F_____, his Attorney; to Daniel C_____, defendant, and Samuel R_____, his Attorney:

YOU AND EACH OF YOU will please take notice that on September 19, 2017, at the hour of 9 a.m., at the office of Irma W_____, Notary Public, whose address is 13 W_____ Drive, City of Diego, State of Arvada, defendant D_____ Corporation will take the deposition of William G_____, whose address is 280 F_____ Street, City of Diego, State of Arvada, upon oral examination before the above named Irma W_____, Notary Public said deposition to continue from day to day until completed.

Paul Y_____

Attorney for Defendant
D_____Corporation

ILLUSTRATIVE LITIGATION PROBLEM

The following document was prepared by D_____ Corporation's attorney for service on William G_____:

IN THE SUPERIOR COURT, DELTA COUNTY STATE OF ARVADA

Thomas A_____,   )
                    Plaintiff)
)   Civil P 15163
            vs.   )
)   SUBPOENA
Reginald B_____, Daniel   )
C_____   )
    and D_____ Corporation,   )
            Defendants   )

The People of the State of Arvada to

William G_____

280 F_____ Street

Diego, Arvada

GREETING:

You are commanded to appear and attend proceedings of the above entitled Court to be held on September 19, 2017, at the hour of 9 A.M. at the office of Irma W_____, Notary Public, whose address is 13 W_____ Drive, City of Diego, State of Arvada, then and there to give testimony on deposition as a witness produced by defendant D_____ Corporation in said action now pending in said Court.

And you are advised that disobedience of said subpoena may be punished as a contempt by the above entitled Court and for such disobedience you will also forfeit to any party or parties aggrieved thereby the sum of all damages suffered due to your failure so to attend.

September 13, 2017

Angus B_____
(Clerk)

By Solomon D_____
(Deputy Clerk)

Questions:

Is it necessary to subpoena every witness for deposition? Is it wise to do so? See Federal Rule 30(g)(2).

Stage IV.   Trial, Verdict, and Attacks on Verdict

After all of the parties engaged in and completed their discovery and defendants B_____ and C_____ submitted voluntarily to physical examinations by plaintiff's doctor, defendant B_____ filed the following document on November 10, 2016:

ILLUSTRATIVE LITIGATION PROBLEM

Thomas A_____,	)	
Plaintiff	)	Civil P 15163
	)	
vs.	)	MEMORANDUM TO
	)	SET FOR TRIAL AND
Reginald B_____, Daniel	)	DEMAND FOR JURY
C_____	)	
and D_____ Corporation,	)	TRIAL
Defendant	)	

The Court is requested to set the above entitled case for trial. Jury is hereby demanded on all factual issues.

I hereby represent to the Court that this cause is at issue; that all affirmative pleadings have been answered; that to my knowledge no new parties will be served with summons prior to time of trial, and I know of no further pleading to be filed and know of no reason why the cause should not be tried as soon as the calendar of the Court will permit. I certify that the party filing this memorandum has completed all discovery proceedings.

November 14, 2017

Louisa F_____

Attorney for Defendant B_____

———————

Plaintiff then filed a special memorandum taking the position that a jury trial was not appropriate on the issued involved in Count Three of his complaint. The trial court, on January 10, 2018, issued an order setting the case for trial by jury on March 1, 2018. The order specified that jury trial was denied as to the issues contained in Count Three.

———————

Questions:

If the case had been brought in a federal court would the Constitutional right to trial by jury extend to the issues in Count Three? Would the demand for jury trial have been adequate?

———————

At the trial testimony was given by A_____, B_____, C_____ and their medical experts, the highway patrolmen who arrived at the scene shortly after the accident, and G_____. The evidence, in addition to bearing on the question of which of the parties was at fault and the purported settlement agreement between A_____ and B_____, showed that all three participants, A_____, B_____, and C_____ had suffered serious personal injuries and that both the bulldozer and B_____'s car had been badly damaged. In addition, on cross-examination, A_____'s attorney adduced the following testimony from one of the highway patrolmen who had been called as a witness by C_____'s attorney:

Q.   Now you say that plaintiff's car struck the bulldozer head-on?

A.   Yes.

Q.   Are you certain that the car didn't hit the side of the bulldozer which was projecting out toward the roadway?

A.   I don't think it did.

ILLUSTRATIVE LITIGATION PROBLEM

Q. How do you know?

A. Well, plaintiff's car appeared to have struck something head-on; the impact was directly in front. I looked at the wreck.

Q. Did you see evidence of a second impact?

A. No.

Q. You mean to say that you disagree with the testimony of every participant in the collision that plaintiff's car hit the bulldozer and bounced into the automobile driven by B_____?

A. I guess so. The car was in awful shape. Really too bad. It was a brand new model. I have one just like it myself. Worth $23,800. Total wreck.

Court: Just answer the questions please.

Q. Then you really couldn't tell where the initial impact was?

A. I guess not.

After all parties had rested and the final arguments were about to begin, defendant B_____ requested that the court reopen the case to take additional testimony from witnesses on a "new" point. On the promise that the new presentation would take no more than one hour, the court granted permission, subject to a motion to strike if the evidence was unfair to any of the other parties. B_____'s attorney first called to the stand the owner of the largest construction company in Arvada who testified that the custom of every local construction company was to plant flares to warn approaching traffic when a piece of heavy equipment was crossing the road. Then three people testified. Each was the driver of a vehicle that had preceded plaintiff's car by a few minutes on Highway 10 on the day of the accident. Each remembered passing the site where the accident subsequently took place. They remembered seeing a huge bulldozer as it was moving along the road. The testimony of witness H_____ is typical.

Q. As you approached the area where the bulldozer was located did you see a warning flare?

A. No. Not that I recall. I don't remember seeing it.

Cross-examination by C_____'s attorney.

Q. How far had you driven?

A. 200 miles.

Q. Had you passed other construction sites?

A. Sure.

Q. Did you see flares there?

A. I may have. I guess I did.

Q. Were you looking to see if flares were or were not present at construction sites?

A. No, of course not. If a flare was present, I'd slow down.

Q. Was there anything unusual about the construction site in question here?

A. No.

Q. How much farther did you drive after you passed the site?

A. About 150 miles.

Q. When did you realize that an accident occurred there shortly after you passed?

A. Not until a few days ago when one of the lawyers here tracked us down. I'll never know how he did it!

ILLUSTRATIVE LITIGATION PROBLEM

—————

After this evidence was presented, defendant C_____'s attorney moved to strike on the ground that it raised a new issue regarding the use of flares, that he was unable, because of such short notice, to "scour the countryside" for other witnesses to rebut the testimony given, and that since none of the parties had mentioned the seeing of or the setting of flares in their testimony, the new evidence was all improper. He rejected the judge's offer to grant a two-day continuance on the ground that it would be "futile."

The trial court denied the motion. Each of the parties then made final arguments, and moved for directed verdicts, which were denied; and the court then gave its instructions. The instructions on negligence, causation, and respondeat superior were general in form but correct, and no specific instructions were requested. After instructing on how to compute damages the court added the following as Instruction 46:

Ladies and gentlemen of the jury. You will be given a number of verdict forms. One asks whether or not plaintiff should collect from defendant C_____, and if so how much. Another does the same regarding defendant D_____ Corporation. Then you have three other forms asking whether any of the three defendants should collect on counterclaims against plaintiff. You must answer each of these. If you find liability, there is a place where you set down the amount of damages. You are required to decide how much is for personal injury and how much for property damage. These forms are to aid you in making a proper verdict; you may write additional information on them as you wish.

Defendant C_____ objected to the instruction insofar as it permitted plaintiff to collect damages for his vehicle on the ground that such damages had never been pleaded or proved. Plaintiff objected to that part of the instruction permitting defendant C_____ to collect any damages whatsoever against plaintiff on the ground that defendant C_____ had failed to file a counterclaim therefor.

Defendant B_____ objected on the ground that the court should have left to the jury those issues involved in Count Three of plaintiff's complaint.

The Court denied the objections of C_____ and B_____, but granted plaintiff's motion and ordered the jury to find that in no event would plaintiff A_____ be liable to Defendant C_____.

While the jury was debating the court said: "I find for plaintiff on Count Three of his complaint. However, the equitable relief sought by plaintiff is totally inappropriate. There is clearly an adequate remedy at law. Defendant B_____ never intended to sign a release of liability. Therefore I find that defendant B_____ has been unjustly enriched by the amount of $2,500 and I hereby award plaintiff that sum against defendant B_____."

The jury then returned with its verdict. It found for plaintiff on all points, awarding $150,000 for physical injuries and $23,800 for property damage against C_____ and D_____ Corporation. The jury foreman wrote on the verdict sheet, "We find defendant C_____ negligent because of his failure to set out warning flares. Since defendant C_____ was operating within the scope of his employment with D_____ Corporation, we find against D_____ Corporation too. Everybody else seemed reasonable to us."

—————

Defendant C_____ then filed the following motion:

ILLUSTRATIVE LITIGATION PROBLEM

IN THE SUPERIOR COURT, DELTA COUNTY STATE OF ARVADA

Thomas A_____,   )
                  Plaintiff   )   Civil P 15163
)
         vs.   )   NOTICE OF MOTION
)   FOR JUDGMENT
Reginald B_____, Daniel C_____   )   N.O.V. AND FOR
     and D_____ Corporation,   )   NEW TRIAL
               Defendants   )

To plaintiff A_____, and his Attorney James W_____:

YOU AND EACH OF YOU ARE NOTIFIED that on the 27th day of March, 2018, at the hour of 10 A.M. in the above entitled Court, defendant Daniel C_____ will move for an order for judgment notwithstanding the verdict on Counts One and Two of the Complaint, and if the same be denied, for a new trial. In addition defendant C_____ will move for a new trial for the purposes of collecting damages for his injuries as alleged in his Answer and Crossclaim. Said motions are based on the insufficiency of the evidence to sustain or legally justify a ruling that defendant was negligent on the ground specified by the jury in its special verdict, that it was error for the court at the end of trial to admit and not to strike the evidence pertaining to the use of flares, that it was error to instruct the jury that plaintiff could collect damages for his vehicle, and that the Court erred in instructing the jury that defendant C_____ failed to state a valid claim for damages against plaintiff.

                              Samuel R_____

                              Attorney for Defendant C_____

Defendant B_____ filed his own motion for new trial as to Count Three on the ground that he was denied his constitutional right to a trial by jury.

Defendant D_____ Corporation filed a motion to dismiss the action for failure of the complaint to state a cause of action for collection of damages against the corporation. In the alternative it requested a new trial on the same ground.

All of the motions were consolidated for hearing.

Questions:

1.   What argument does defendant C_____ have to support his motion for a judgment as a matter of law? Is he likely to be successful? Has C_____ failed to include any significant error in the trial as a basis for seeking a new trial?

2.   What arguments will the various parties make regarding the other motions? In considering defendant B_____'s motion assume that the right to jury trial in Arvada is identical to that in the federal courts.

ILLUSTRATIVE LITIGATION PROBLEM

Shortly after arguments on these motions the court made the following order:

IN THE SUPERIOR COURT, DELTA COUNTY STATE OF ARVADA

Thomas A_____,	)	
Plaintiff	)	
	)	Civil P 15163
vs.	)	
	)	ORDER
Reginald B_____, Daniel C_____	)	
and D_____ Corporation,	)	
Defendants	)	

The motion of defendant C_____ for a judgment N.O.V. and for a new trial and the motions of defendants B_____ and D_____ Corporation for a new trial and dismissal having come on regularly for hearing before the undersigned on the 27th day of March, 2018, at the hour of 10 A.M., upon notice duly and regularly served and plaintiff A_____ appearing by James L. W_____, his counsel, and defendant C_____ appearing by Samuel R_____, his counsel, and defendant B_____ appearing by Louisa F_____, his counsel, and defendant D_____ Corporation appearing by Paul Y_____, its counsel, and the matter having been argued and submitted and good cause appearing therefor,

IT IS HEREBY ORDERED that defendant C_____'s motion for judgment notwithstanding the verdict be denied, and that defendant C_____'s motion and defendant B_____'s motion for new trial be denied.

IT IS FURTHER ORDERED that defendant D_____ Corporation's motion to dismiss plaintiff's complaint for failure of plaintiff to allege a claim for damages against D_____ Corporation is granted without leave to amend.

Dated: April 16, 2018

Learned W_____

Judge of the Superior Court

————————

The Court then rendered the following judgment:

IN THE SUPERIOR COURT, DELTA COUNTY STATE OF ARVADA

Thomas A_____,	)	
Plaintiff	)	
	)	Civil P 15163
vs.	)	
	)	JUDGMENT
Reginald B_____, Daniel C_____,	)	
and D_____ Corporation,	)	
Defendants	)	

The above entitled cause came on regularly for trial before the undersigned sitting with a jury on March 1, 2018. Upon the jury being duly sworn and impaneled, evidence was presented, the matter argued and the jury instructed by the undersigned.

The Court, after deliberation, rendered the following verdict on issues not triable to a jury: that plaintiff recover the sum of $2,500 from defendant B_____.

The jury, after deliberation, rendered the following verdict: We the jury find for the plaintiff and against defendants Reginald B_____, Daniel C_____ and D_____ Corporation, and declare that

ILLUSTRATIVE LITIGATION PROBLEM

plaintiff was not negligent. We further find that plaintiff suffered damages against defendants C_____ and D_____ Corporation in the amount of $150,000 for personal injuries and $23,800 for property damage.

The Court then dismissed plaintiff's claim for damages against defendant D_____ Corporation on the ground that the complaint failed to state a claim for such relief.

IT IS HEREBY ORDERED ADJUDGED AND DECREED that plaintiff have judgment as follows:

1. Plaintiff is declared to have been not negligent in his conduct toward defendants B_____, C_____ and D_____ Corporation.

2. Plaintiff is entitled to damages against defendant B_____ in the amount of $2,500, plus interest thereon at the rate of 7% per annum, and for his costs of action.

3. Plaintiff is entitled to damages against defendant C_____ in the amount of $163,800 plus interest thereon at the rate of 7% per annum, and for his costs of suit.

Dated: April 30, 2018

Learned W_____

Judge of the Superior Court

_____

Defendants C_____ and D_____ Corporation decided to appeal this decision. Their attorneys filed the following documents which were duly served on plaintiff:

IN THE SUPERIOR COURT, DELTA COUNTY STATE OF ARVADA

Thomas A_____,	)
Plaintiff	)
	) Civil P 15163
vs.	)
	) NOTICE OF APPEAL
Reginald B_____, Daniel C_____,	)
D_____ Corporation,	)
Defendants	)

To Angus B_____, County Clerk;

Notice is hereby given that defendants Daniel C_____ and D_____ Corporation appeal from that part of the judgment relating to Counts One and Two of plaintiff's Complaint and also to that part of the judgment denying to said defendants Daniel C_____ and D_____ Corporation damages for their injuries to person and property.

Dated: June 27, 2018.

Samuel R_____

Attorney for Defendant Daniel C_____

Paul Y_____

Attorney for Defendant D_____Corporation

ILLUSTRATIVE LITIGATION PROBLEM

IN THE SUPERIOR COURT, DELTA COUNTY STATE OF ARVADA

Thomas A_____,	)	
Plaintiff	)	Civil P 15163
	)	
vs.	)	NOTICE TO PREPARE
Reginald B_____, Daniel C_____,	)	TRANSCRIPT
and D_____ Corporation,	)	
Defendants	)	

To Angus B_____, Clerk of the above entitled Court:

Please take notice that defendants Daniel C_____ and D_____ Corporation have commenced an appeal and in connection therewith require a reporter's transcript of the proceedings and testimony in the above entitled case which transcript shall also include the instructions to the jury which were given and those which were refused, all statements, orders, requests, rulings and remarks of the court, counsel, the parties or any witnesses, and all exhibits introduced into evidence during the course of trial.

Samuel R_____

Attorney for Defendant Appellant Daniel
C_____

Paul Y_____

Attorney for Defendant Appellant
D____Corporation

While the appeal was pending plaintiff brought a new action against D_____ Corporation for damages of $163,800, alleging the negligence of C_____ and the fact that C_____ had been acting within the scope of his employment. The Corporation filed an answer denying both these allegations, alleging that plaintiff had been contributorily negligent, and that the action was barred by res judicata. Both parties then moved for summary judgment in their favor on the entire case or as to those issues which could be so decided. Each party supported its case solely with a certified copy of the entire record in the first suit.

Question:

Should the court grant a full summary judgment to either party? If not, to what extent, if any, is a partial summary judgment appropriate?

The trial court, after a hearing, rendered a decision granting summary judgment for the plaintiff. Shortly thereafter the appeal in the first action was argued and submitted. Within two weeks the appellate court handed down a decision setting aside the verdict in the first action and ordering a new trial on all issues.

Question:

What steps should D_____ Corporation's lawyer now take with regard to the summary judgment rendered in the second action? See Federal Rule 60(b)(5).

PART VII

Local Rules of the United States District Courts for the Southern and Eastern Districts of New York

Effective April 8, 2019

TABLE OF CONTENTS

Rule 1.1. Application of Rules

These Local Civil Rules apply in all civil actions and proceedings governed by the Federal Rules of Civil Procedure.

Rule 1.2. Night Depository

A night depository with an automatic date stamp shall be maintained by the Clerk of the Southern District in the Pearl Street Courthouse and by the Clerk of the Eastern District in the Brooklyn Courthouse. After regular business hours, papers for the District Court only may be deposited in the night depository. Such papers will be considered as having been filed in the District Court as of the time and date stamped thereon, which shall be deemed presumptively correct.

Rule 1.3. Admission to the Bar

(a) A member in good standing of the bar of the state of New York, or a member in good standing of the bar of the United States District Court in Connecticut or Vermont and of the bar of the State in which such district court is located, provided such district court by its rule extends a corresponding privilege to members of the bar of this Court, may be admitted to practice in this Court on compliance with the following provisions:

* * * After submitting the application in electronic form, each applicant for admission shall file with the Clerk, at least ten (10) days prior to hearing (unless, for good cause shown, the Judge shall shorten the time), the signed paper copy of the verified written petition for admission stating: (1) applicant's residence and office address; (2) the time when, and courts where, admitted; (3) applicant's legal training and experience; (4) whether applicant has ever been held in contempt of court, and, if

so, the nature of the contempt and the final disposition thereof; (5) whether applicant has ever been censured, suspended, disbarred or denied admission or readmission by any court, and, if so, the facts and circumstances connected therewith; (6) that applicant has read and is familiar with (a) the provisions of the Judicial Code (Title 28, U.S.C.) which pertain to the jurisdiction of, and practice in, the United States District Courts; (b) the Federal Rules of Civil Procedure; (c) the Federal Rules of Criminal Procedure; (d) the Federal Rules of Evidence; (e) the Local Rules of the United States District Court for the Southern and Eastern Districts of New York; and (f) the New York State Rules of Professional Conduct as adopted from time to time by the Appellate Divisions of the State of New York; and (7) that applicant will faithfully adhere to all rules applicable to applicant's conduct in connection with any activities in this Court.

The petition shall be accompanied by a certificate of the clerk of the court for each of the states in which the applicant is a member of the bar, which has been issued within thirty (30) days of filing and states that the applicant is a member in good standing of the bar of that state court. The petition shall also be accompanied by an affidavit of an attorney of this Court who has known the applicant for at least one year, stating when the affiant was admitted to practice in this Court, how long and under what circumstances the attorney has known the applicant, and what the attorney knows of the applicant's character and experience at the bar. Such petition shall be placed at the head of the calendar and, on the call thereof, the attorney whose affidavit accompanied the petition shall personally move the admission of the applicant. If the petition is granted, the applicant shall take the oath of office and sign the roll of attorneys.

* * *

(b)   A member in good standing of the bar of either the Southern or Eastern District of New York may be admitted to the bar of the other district without formal application (1) upon filing in that district a certificate of the Clerk of the United States District Court for the district in which the applicant is a member of the bar, which has been issued within thirty (30) days of filing and states that the applicant is a member in good standing of the bar of that Court; (2) an affidavit by the applicant stating (a) whether the applicant has ever been convicted of a felony, (b) whether the applicant has ever been censured, suspended, disbarred or denied admission or readmission by any court, (c) whether there are any disciplinary proceedings presently against the applicant and (d) the facts and circumstances surrounding any affirmative responses to (a) through (c); and (3) upon taking the oath of office, signing the roll of attorneys of that district, and paying the fee required in that district. Each district retains the right to deny admission based upon the content of the affidavit in response to item (2).

(c)   A member in a good standing of the bar of any state or of any United States District Court may be permitted to argue or try a particular case in whole or in part as counsel or advocate, upon motion (which may be made by the applicant) and (1) upon filing with the Clerk of the District Court a certificate of the court for each of the states in which the applicant is a member of the bar, which has been issued for thirty (30) days of filing and states that the applicant is a member in good standing of the bar of that state court, and an affidavit by the applicant stating (a) whether the applicant has ever been convicted of a felony, (b) whether the applicant has ever been censured, suspended, disbarred or denied admission or readmission by any court, (c) whether there are any disciplinary proceedings presently against the applicant and (d) the facts and circumstances surrounding any affirmative responses to (a) through (c); and (2) upon paying the required fee. Attorneys appearing for the Department of Justice may appear before the Court without requesting pro hac vice admission. Attorneys appearing for other federal agencies must move for pro hac vice admission but the fee requirement is waived and the certificate(s) of good standing may have been issued within one year of filing. Only an attorney who has been so admitted or who is a member of the bar of this Court may enter appearances for parties, sign stipulations or receive payments upon judgments, decrees or orders.

(d)   If an attorney who is a member of the bar of this Court, or who has been authorized to appear in a case in this Court, changes his or her residence or office address, the attorney shall immediately notify the Clerk of the Court, in addition to serving and filing a notice of change of address in each pending case in which the attorney has appeared.

Rule 1.4.   Withdrawal or Displacement of Attorney of Record

An attorney who has appeared as attorney of record for a party may be relieved or displaced only by order of the Court and may not withdraw from a case without leave of the Court granted by order. Such an order may be granted only upon a showing by affidavit or otherwise of satisfactory reasons for withdrawal or displacement and the posture of the case, including its position, if any, on the calendar, and whether or not the attorney is asserting a retaining or charging lien. All applications to withdraw must be served upon the client and (unless excused by the Court) upon all other parties.

Rule 1.5.   Discipline of Attorneys

(a) Committee on Grievances. The Chief Judge shall appoint a committee of the Board of Judges known as the Committee on Grievances, which under the direction of the Chief Judge shall have charge of all matters relating to the discipline of attorneys. The Chief Judge shall appoint a panel of attorneys who are members of the bar of this Court to advise or assist the Committee on Grievances. At the direction of the Committee on Grievances or its chair, members of this panel of attorneys may investigate complaints, may prepare and support statements of charges, or may serve as members of hearing panels.

(b) Grounds for Discipline or Other Relief. Discipline or other relief, of the types set forth in paragraph (c) below, may be imposed, by the Committee on Grievances, after notice and opportunity to respond as set forth in paragraph (d) below, if any of the following grounds is found by clear and convincing evidence:

(1) Any member of the bar of this Court has been convicted of a felony or misdemeanor in any federal court, or in a court of any state or territory.

(2) Any member of the bar of this Court has been disciplined by any federal court or by a court of any state or territory.

(3) Any member of the bar of this Court has resigned from the bar of any federal court or of a court of any state or territory while an investigation into allegations of misconduct by the attorney was pending.

(4) Any member of the bar of this Court has an infirmity which prevents the attorney from engaging in the practice of law.

(5) In connection with activities in this Court, any attorney is found to have engaged in conduct violative of the New York State Rules of Professional Conduct as adopted from time to time by the Appellate Divisions of the State of New York. In interpreting the Code, in the absence of binding authority from the Supreme Court or the United States Court of Appeals for the Second Circuit, this Court, in the interests of comity and predictability, will give due regard to decisions of the New York Court of Appeals and other New York State courts, absent significant federal interests.

(6) Any attorney not a member of the bar of this Court has appeared at the bar of this Court without permission to do so.

(c) Types of Discipline or Other Relief.

(1) In the case of an attorney admitted to the bar of this Court, discipline imposed pursuant to paragraph (b)(1), (b)(2), (b)(3), or (b)(5) above may consist of a letter of reprimand or admonition, censure, suspension, or an order striking the name of the attorney from the roll of attorneys admitted to the bar of this Court.

(2)   In the case of an attorney not admitted to the bar of this Court, discipline imposed pursuant to paragraph (b)(5) or (b)(6) above may consist of a letter of reprimand or admonition, censure, or an order precluding the attorney from again appearing at the bar of this Court.

(3)   Relief required pursuant to paragraph (b)(4) above shall consist of suspending the attorney from practice before this Court.

(d)   Procedure.

(1)   If it appears that there exists a ground for discipline set forth in paragraph (b)(1), (b)(2), or (b)(3), notice thereof shall be served by the Committee on Grievances upon the attorney concerned by first class mail, directed to the address of the attorney as shown on the rolls of this court and to the last known address of the attorney (if any) as shown in the complaint and any materials submitted therewith. Service shall be deemed complete upon mailing in accordance with the provisions of this paragraph.

In all cases in which any federal court or a court of any state or territory has entered an order disbarring or censuring an attorney or suspending the attorney from practice, whether or not on consent, the notice shall be served together with an order by the Clerk of this Court, to become effective twenty-four days after the date of service upon the attorney, disbarring or censuring the attorney or suspending the attorney from practice in this Court upon terms and conditions comparable to those set forth by the other court of record. In all cases in which an attorney has resigned from the bar of any federal court or of a court of any state or territory while an investigation into allegations of misconduct by the attorney was pending, even if the attorney remains admitted to the bar of any other court, the notice shall be served together with an order entered by the Clerk of this Court, to become effective twenty-four days after the date of service upon the attorney, deeming the attorney to have resigned from the bar of this Court. Within twenty days of the date of service of either order, the attorney may file a motion for modification or revocation of the order. Any such motion shall set forth with specificity the facts and principles relied upon by the attorney as showing cause why a different disposition should be ordered by this Court. The timely filing of such a motion will stay the effectiveness of the order until further order by this Court. If good cause is shown to hold an evidentiary hearing, the Committee on Grievances may direct such a hearing pursuant to paragraph (d)(4) below. If good cause is not shown to hold an evidentiary hearing, the Committee on Grievances may proceed to impose discipline or to take such other action as justice and this rule may require. If an evidentiary hearing is held, the Committee may direct such interim relief pending the hearing as justice may require.

In all other cases, the notice shall be served together with an order by the Committee on Grievances directing the attorney to show cause in writing why discipline should not be imposed. If the attorney fails to respond in writing to the order to show cause, or if the response fails to show good cause to hold an evidentiary hearing, the Committee on Grievances may proceed to impose discipline or to take such other action as justice and this rule may require. If good cause is shown to hold an evidentiary hearing, the Committee on Grievances may direct such a hearing pursuant to paragraph (d)(4) below. If an evidentiary hearing is held, the Committee may direct such interim relief pending the hearing as justice may require.

(2)   In the case of a ground for discipline set forth in paragraph (b)(2) or (b)(3) above, discipline may be imposed unless the attorney concerned establishes by clear and convincing evidence (i) that there was such an infirmity of proof of misconduct by the attorney as to give rise to the clear conviction that this Court could not consistent with its duty accept as final the conclusion of the other court, or (ii) that the procedure resulting in the investigation or discipline of the attorney by the other court was so lacking in notice or opportunity to be heard as to constitute a deprivation of due process, or (iii) that the imposition of discipline by this Court would result in grave injustice.

(3) Complaints in writing alleging any ground for discipline or other relief set forth in paragraph (b) above shall be directed to the Chief Judge, who shall refer such complaints to the Committee on Grievances. The Committee on Grievances, by its chair, may designate an attorney, who may be selected from the panel of attorneys established pursuant to paragraph (a) above, to investigate the complaint, if it deems investigation necessary or warranted, and to prepare a statement of charges, if the Committee deems that necessary or warranted. Complaints, and any files based on them, shall be treated as confidential unless otherwise ordered by the Chief Judge for good cause shown.

(4) A statement of charges alleging a ground for discipline or other relief set forth in paragraph (b)(4), (b)(5), or (b)(6) shall be served upon the attorney concerned by certified mail, return receipt requested, directed to the address of the attorney as shown on the rolls of this Court and to the last known address of the attorney (if any) as shown in the complaint and any materials submitted therewith, together with an order by the Committee on Grievances directing the attorney to show cause in writing why discipline or other relief should not be imposed. Upon the respondent attorney's answer to the charges the matter will be designated by the Committee on Grievances for a prompt evidentiary hearing before a Magistrate Judge of the Court or before a panel of three attorneys, who may be selected from the panel of attorneys established pursuant to paragraph (a) above. The Magistrate Judge or panel of attorneys conducting the hearing may grant such pre-hearing discovery as they determine to be necessary, shall hear witnesses called by the attorney supporting the charges and by the respondent attorney, and may consider such other evidence included in the record of the hearing as they deem relevant and material. The Magistrate Judge or panel of attorneys conducting the hearing shall report their findings and recommendations in writing to the Committee on Grievances and shall serve them upon the respondent attorney and the attorney supporting the charges. After affording the respondent attorney and the attorney supporting the charges an opportunity to respond in writing to such report, or if no timely answer is made by the respondent attorney, or if the Committee on Grievances determines that the answer raises no issue requiring a hearing, the Committee on Grievances may proceed to impose discipline or to take such action as justice and this rule may require.

(e) Reinstatement. Any attorney who has been suspended or precluded from appearing in this Court or whose name has been struck from the roll of the members of the bar of this Court may apply in writing to the Chief Judge, for good cause shown, for the lifting of the suspension or preclusion or for reinstatement to the rolls. The Chief Judge shall refer such application to the Committee on Grievances. The Committee on Grievances may refer the application to a Magistrate Judge or hearing panel of attorneys (who may be the same Magistrate Judge or panel of attorneys who previously heard the matter) for findings and recommendations, or may act upon the application without making such a referral. * * *

(f) Remedies for Misconduct. The remedies provided by this rule are in addition to the remedies available to individual District Judges and Magistrate Judges under applicable law with respect to lawyers appearing before them. Individual District Judges and Magistrate Judges may also refer any matter to the Chief Judge for referral to the Committee on Grievances to consider the imposition of discipline or other relief pursuant to this rule.

(g) Notice to Other Courts. When an attorney is known to be admitted to practice in the court of any state or territory, or in any other federal court, and has been convicted of any crime or disbarred, precluded from appearing, suspended or censured in this Court, the Clerk shall send to such other court or courts a certified copy of the judgment of conviction or order of disbarment, preclusion, suspension or censure, a certified or electronic copy of the Court's opinion, if any, and a statement of the attorney's last known office and residence address.

(h) Duty of Attorney to Report Discipline.

(1) In all cases in which any federal, state or territorial court, agency or tribunal has entered an order disbarring or censuring an attorney admitted to the bar of this Court, or

suspending the attorney from practice, whether or not on consent, the attorney shall deliver a copy of said order to the Clerk of this Court within fourteen days after the entry of the order.

(2)   In all cases in which any member of the bar of this Court has resigned from the bar of any federal, state or territorial court, agency or tribunal while an investigation into allegations of misconduct against the attorney was pending, the attorney shall report such resignation to the Clerk of this Court within fourteen days after the submission of the resignation.

(3)   In all cases in which this Court has entered an order disbarring or censuring an attorney, or suspending the attorney from practice, whether or not on consent, the attorney shall deliver a copy of said order within fourteen days after the entry of the order to the clerk of each federal, state or territorial court, agency and tribunal in which such attorney has been admitted to practice.

(4)   Any failure of an attorney to comply with the requirements of this Local Civil Rule 1.5(h) shall constitute a basis for discipline of said attorney pursuant to Local Civil Rule 1.5(c).

Rule 1.6.   Duty of Attorneys in Related Cases

(a)   It shall be the continuing duty of each attorney appearing in any civil or criminal case to bring promptly to the attention of the Court all facts which said attorney believes are relevant to a determination that said case and one or more pending civil or criminal cases should be heard by the same Judge, in order to avoid unnecessary duplication of judicial effort. As soon as the attorney becomes aware of such relationship, said attorney shall notify the Judges to whom the cases has been assigned.

(b)   If counsel fails to comply with Local Civil Rule 1.6(a), the Court may assess reasonable costs directly against counsel whose action has obstructed the effective administration of the Court's business.

Rule 1.7.   Fees of Court Clerks and Reporters

(a)   The Clerk shall not be required to render any service for which a fee is prescribed by statute or by the Judicial Conference of the United States unless the fee for the particular service is paid to the Clerk in advance or the Court orders otherwise.

(b)   Every attorney appearing in any proceeding who orders a transcript of any trial, hearing, or any other proceeding, is obligated to pay the cost thereof to the court reporters of the Court upon rendition of the invoice unless at the time of such order, the attorney, in writing, advises the court reporter that only the client is obligated to pay.

Rule 1.8.   Photographs, Radio, Recordings, Television

Unless authorized to do so by an administrative order of each respective Court, no one other than Court officials engaged in the conduct of Court business shall (a) bring any camera, transmitter, receiver, recording device, cellular telephone, computer or other electronic device into any courthouse; or (b) make an audio or video recording of any proceeding or any communication with the Court, an employee of the Court or any person acting at the direction of the Court, including a mediator.

Rule 1.9.   Acceptable Substitutes for Affidavits

In situations in which any Local Rule provides for an affidavit or a verified statement, the following are acceptable substitutes: (a) a statement subscribed under penalty of perjury as prescribed in 28 U.S.C. § 1746; or (b) if accepted by the Court as a substitute for an affidavit or a verified statement, (1) a statement signed by an attorney or by a party not represented by an attorney pursuant to Federal Rule of Civil Procedure 11, or (2) an oral representation on the record in open court.

Rule 5.1.   Filing of Discovery Materials

A party seeking or opposing relief under Fed. R. Civ. P. 26 through 37 inclusive, or making or opposing any other motion or application, shall quote or attach only those portions of the depositions, interrogatories, requests for documents, requests for admissions, or other discovery or disclosure materials, together with the responses and objections thereto, that are the subject of the discovery motion or application, or are cited in papers submitted in connection with any other motion or application. See also Civil Local Rule 37.1.

Rule 5.2.   Electronic Service and Filing of Documents

(a)   Parties serving and filing papers shall follow the instructions regarding Electronic Case Filing (ECF) published on the website of each respective Court. A paper served and filed by electronic means in accordance with such instructions is, for purposes of Fed. R. Civ. P. 5, served and filed in compliance with the Local Civil Rules of the Southern and Eastern Districts of New York.

* * *

Rule 5.3.   Service by Overnight Delivery

Service upon an attorney may be made by overnight delivery service. "Overnight delivery service" means any delivery service which regularly accepts items for overnight delivery. Overnight delivery service shall be deemed service by mail for purposes of Fed. R. Civ. P. 5 and 6.

Rule 6.1.   Service and Filing of Motion Papers

Except for letter-motions as permitted by Local Rule 7.1(d), and unless otherwise provided by statute or rule, or by the Court in a Judge's Individual Practice or in a direction in a particular case, upon any motion, the notice of motion, supporting affidavits, and memoranda shall be served and filed as follows:

(a)   On all motions and applications under Fed. R. Civ. P. 26 through 37 inclusive and 45(d)(3), (1) the notice of motion, supporting affidavits, and memoranda of law shall be served by the moving party on all other parties that have appeared in the action, (2) any opposing affidavits and answering memoranda of law shall be served within seven days after service of the moving papers, and (3) any reply affidavits and reply memoranda of law shall be served within two days after service of the answering papers. In computing periods of days, refer to Fed. R. Civ. P. 6 and Local Civil Rule 6.4.

(b)   On all civil motions, petitions and applications, other than those described in Rule 6.1(a), and other than petitions for writs of habeas corpus, (1) the notice of motion, supporting affidavits, and memoranda of law shall be served by the moving party on all other parties that have appeared in the action, (2) any opposing affidavits and answering memoranda shall be served within fourteen days after service of the moving papers, and (3) any reply affidavits and memoranda of law shall be served within seven days after service of the answering papers. In computing periods of days, refer to Fed. R. Civ. P. 6 and Local Civil Rule 6.4.

(c)   The parties and their attorneys shall only appear to argue the motion if so directed by the Court by order or by a Judge's Individual Practice.

(d)   No *ex parte* order, or order to show cause to bring on a motion, will be granted except upon a clear and specific showing by affidavit of good and sufficient reasons why a procedure other than by notice of motion is necessary, and stating whether a previous application for similar relief has been made.

Rule 6.2.   Orders on Motions

A memorandum signed by the Court of the decision on a motion that does not finally determine all claims for relief, or an oral decision on such a motion, shall constitute the order unless the memorandum or oral decision directs the submission or settlement of an order in more extended form. The notation in the docket of a memorandum or oral decision that does not direct the submission or settlement of an order in more extended form shall constitute the entry of the order. Where an order in more extended form is required to be submitted or settled, the notation in the docket of such order shall constitute the entry of the order.

Rule 6.3. Motions for Reconsideration or Reargument

Unless otherwise provided by the Court or by statute or rule (such as Fed. R. Civ. P. 50, 52, and 59), a notice of motion for reconsideration or reargument of a Court order determining a motion shall be served within fourteen (14) days after the entry of the Court's determination of the original motion, or in the case of a Court order resulting in a judgment, within fourteen (14) days after the entry of the judgment. There shall be served with the notice of motion a memorandum setting forth concisely the matters or controlling decisions which counsel believes the Court has overlooked. The time periods for the service of answering and reply memoranda, if any, shall be governed by Local Civil Rule 6.1(a) or (b), as in the case of the original motion. No oral argument shall be heard unless the Court directs that the matter shall be reargued orally. No affidavits shall be filed by any party unless directed by the Court.

Rule 6.4. Computation of Time

In computing any period of time prescribed or allowed by the Local Civil Rules or the Local Admiralty and Maritime Rules, the provisions of Fed. R. Civ. P. 6 shall apply unless otherwise stated.

* * *

Rule 7.1. Motion Papers

(a) Except for letter-motions as permitted by Local Rule 7.1(d) or as otherwise permitted by the Court, all motions shall include the following motion papers:

(1) A notice of motion, or an order to show cause signed by the Court, which shall specify the applicable rules or statutes pursuant to which the motion is brought, and shall specify the relief sought by the motion;

(2) A memorandum of law, setting forth the cases and other authorities relied upon in support of the motion, and divided, under appropriate headings, into as many parts as there are issues to be determined; and

(3) Supporting affidavits and exhibits thereto containing any factual information and portions of the record necessary for the decision of the motion.

(b) Except for letter-motions as permitted by Local Rule 7.1(d) or as otherwise permitted by the Court, all oppositions and replies with respect to motions shall comply with Local Civil Rule 7.1(a)(2) and (3) above, and an opposing party who seeks relief that goes beyond the denial of the motion shall comply as well with Local Civil Rule 7.1(a)(1) above.

(c) Unless otherwise ordered by the District Judge to whom the appeal is assigned, appellate briefs on bankruptcy appeals shall comply with * * * Federal Rules of Bankruptcy Procedure 8015 to 8017.

(d) Applications for extensions or adjournments, applications for a pre-motion conference, and similar non-dispositive matters as permitted by the instructions regarding ECF published on the website of each respective Court and any pertinent Individual Judge's Practices, may be brought by letter-motion filed via ECF pursuant to Local Civil Rule 5.2(b).

Rule 7.1.1.   Disclosure Statement

For purposes of Fed. R. Civ. P. 7.1(b)(2), "promptly" shall mean "within fourteen days," that is, parties are required to file a supplemental disclosure statement within fourteen days of the time there is any change in the information required in a disclosure statement filed pursuant to those rules.

Rule 7.2.   Authorities to Be Provided to Pro Se Litigants

In cases involving a pro se litigant, counsel shall, when serving a memorandum of law (or other submissions to the Court), provide the pro se litigant (but not other counsel or the Court) with copies of cases and other authorities cited therein that are unpublished or reported exclusively on computerized databases. Upon request, counsel shall provide the pro se litigant with copies of such unpublished cases and other authorities as are cited in a decision of the Court and were not previously cited by any party.

Rule 11.1.   Form of Pleadings, Motions, and Other Papers

(a)   Every pleading, written motion, and other paper must (1) be plainly written, typed, printed, or copied without erasures or interlineations which materially deface it, (2) bear the docket number and the initials of the District Judge and any Magistrate Judge before whom the action or proceeding is pending, and (3) have the name of each person signing it clearly printed or typed directly below the signature.

* * *

Rule 12.1.   Notice to Pro Se Litigant Who Opposes a Rule 12 Motion Supported by Matters Outside the Pleadings

A represented party moving to dismiss or for judgment on the pleadings against a party proceeding pro se, who refers in support of the motion to matters outside the pleadings as described in Fed. R. Civ. P. 12(b) or 12(c), shall serve and file the following notice with the full text of Fed. R. Civ. P. 56 attached at the time the motion is served. If the Court rules that the motion to dismiss or for judgment on the pleadings will be treated as one for summary judgment pursuant to Fed. R. Civ. P. 56, and the movant has not previously served and filed the notice required by this rule, the movant shall amend the form notice to reflect that fact and shall serve and file the amended notice within fourteen days of the Court's ruling.

* * *

[A copy of the required notice appears in connection with Rule 56.2, infra.]

Rule 16.1.   Exemptions From Mandatory Scheduling Order

Matters involving habeas corpus petitions, social security disability cases, motions to vacate sentences, forfeitures, and reviews from administrative agencies are exempted from the mandatory scheduling order required by Fed. R. Civ. P. 16(b).

Rule 16.2.   Entry and Modification of Mandatory Scheduling Orders by Magistrate Judges

In any case referred to a Magistrate Judge, the Magistrate Judge may issue or modify scheduling orders pursuant to Fed. R. Civ. P. 16(b).

Rule 23.1.   Fees in Class Action and Shareholder Derivative Actions

Fees for attorneys or others shall not be paid upon recovery or compromise in a class action or a derivative action on behalf of a corporation except as allowed by the Court after a hearing upon such notice as the Court may direct. The notice shall include a statement of the names and addresses of the applicants for such fees and the amounts requested respectively and shall disclose any fee sharing agreements with anyone. Where the Court directs notice of a hearing upon a proposed voluntary dismissal or settlement of a class action or a derivative action, the above information as to the applications shall be included in the notice.

Rule 26.1.   **Address of Party and Original Owner of Claim to Be Furnished**

A party shall furnish to any other party, within seven (7) days after a demand, a verified statement setting forth:

(a)   If the responding party is a natural person, that party's residence and domicile, and any state or other jurisdiction of which that party is a citizen for purposes of 28 U.S.C. § 1332;

(b)   If the responding party is a partnership, limited liability partnership, limited liability company, or other unincorporated association, like information for all of its partners or members, as well as the state or other jurisdiction of its formation;

(c)   If the responding party is a corporation, its state or other jurisdiction of incorporation, principal place of business, and any state or other jurisdiction of which that party is a citizen for purposes of 28 U.S.C. § 1332; and

(d)   In the case of an assigned claim, corresponding information for each original owner of the claim and for any assignee.

Rule 26.2.   **Assertion of Claim of Privilege**

(a)   Unless otherwise agreed by the parties or directed by the Court where a claim of privilege is asserted in objecting to any means of discovery or disclosure, including but not limited to a deposition, and an answer is not provided on the basis of such assertion,

(1)   the attorney asserting the privilege shall identify the nature of the privilege (including work product) which is being claimed and, if the privilege is governed by state law, indicate the state's privilege rule being invoked; and

(2)   the following information shall be provided in the objection, or (in the case of a deposition) in response to questions by the questioner, unless divulgence of such information would cause disclosure of the allegedly privileged information:

(A)   For documents: (i) the type of document, e.g., letter or memorandum; (ii) the general subject matter of the document; (iii) the date of the document; and (iv) the author of the document, the addressees of the document, and any other recipients, and, where not apparent, the relationship of the author, addressees, and recipients to each other;

(B)   For oral communications: (i) the name of the person making the communication and the names of persons present while the communication was made and, where not apparent, the relationship of the persons present to the person making the communication; (ii) the date and place of communication; and (iii) the general subject matter of the communication.

(b)   Where a claim of privilege is asserted in response to discovery or disclosure other than a deposition, and information is not provided on the basis of such assertion, the information set forth in paragraph (a) above shall be furnished in writing at the time of the response to such discovery or disclosure, unless otherwise ordered by the Court.

(c)   Efficient means of providing information regarding claims of privilege are encouraged, and parties are encouraged to agree upon measures that further this end. For example, when asserting privilege on the same basis with respect to multiple documents, it is presumptively proper to provide the information required by this rule by group or category. A party receiving a privilege log that groups documents or otherwise departs from a document-by-document or communication-by-communication listing may not object solely on that basis, but may object if the substantive information required by this rule has not been provided in a comprehensible form.

Rule 26.3.   Uniform Definitions in Discovery Requests

(a)   The full text of the definitions and rules of construction set forth in paragraphs (c) and (d) is deemed incorporated by reference into all discovery requests. No discovery request shall use broader definitions or rules of construction than those set forth in paragraphs (c) and (d). This rule shall not preclude (1) the definition of other terms specific to the particular litigation, (2) the use of abbreviations, or (3) a more narrow definition of a term defined in paragraph (c).

(b)   This rule is not intended to broaden or narrow the scope of discovery permitted by the Federal Rules of Civil Procedure.

(c)   The following definitions apply to all discovery requests:

(1)   *Communication.* The term "communication" means the transmittal of information (in the form of facts, ideas, inquiries or otherwise).

(2)   *Document.* The term "document" is defined to be synonymous in meaning and equal in scope to the usage of the term "documents or electronically stored information" in Fed. R. Civ. P. 34(a)(1)(A). A draft or non-identical copy is a separate document within the meaning of this term.

(3)   *Identify (with respect to persons).* When referring to a person, "to identify" means to give, to the extent known, the person's full name, present or last known address, and when referring to a natural person, additionally, the present or last known place of employment. Once a person has been identified in accordance with this subparagraph, only the name of that person need be listed in response to subsequent discovery requesting the identification of that person.

(4)   *Identify (with respect to documents).* When referring to documents, "to identify" means to give, to the extent known, the (i) type of document; (ii) general subject matter; (iii) date of the document; and (iv) author(s), addressee(s) and recipient(s). In the alternative, the responding party may produce the documents, together with identifying information sufficient to satisfy Fed. R. Civ. P. 33(d).

(5)   *Parties.* The terms "plaintiff" and "defendant" as well as a party's full or abbreviated name or a pronoun referring to a party mean the party and, where applicable, its officers, directors, employees, partners, corporate parent, subsidiaries or affiliates. This definition is not intended to impose a discovery obligation on any person who is not a party to the litigation.

(6)   *Person.* The term "person" is defined as any natural person or any legal entity, including, without limitation, any business or governmental entity or association.

(7)   *Concerning.* The term "concerning" means relating to, referring to, describing, evidencing or constituting.

(d)   The following rules of construction apply to all discovery requests:

(1)   *All/Any/Each.* The terms "all", "any" and "each" shall be construed as encompassing any and all.

(2)   *And/Or.* The connectives "and" and "or" shall be construed either disjunctively or conjunctively as necessary to bring within the scope of the discovery request all responses that might otherwise be construed to be outside of its scope.

(3)   *Number.* The use of the singular form of any word includes the plural and vice versa.

Rule 26.4.   Cooperation Among Counsel in Discovery

(a)   Counsel are expected to cooperate with each other, consistent with the interests of their clients, in all phases of the discovery process and to be courteous in their dealings with each other, including in matters relating to scheduling and timing of various discovery procedures.

(b)   Discovery requests shall be read reasonably in the recognition that the attorney serving them generally does not have the information being sought and the attorney receiving them generally does have such information or can obtain it from the client.

Rule 26.5.   Form Discovery Requests

Attorneys using form discovery requests shall review them to ascertain that they are consistent with the scope of discovery under Fed. R. Civ. P. 26(b)(1). Non-compliant requests shall not be used.

Rule 30.1.   Counsel Fees on Taking Depositions More Than 100 Miles From Courthouse

When a deposition upon oral examination is to be taken at a place more than one hundred (100) miles from the courthouse, any party may request the Court to issue an order providing that prior to the examination, another party shall pay the expense (including a reasonable counsel fee) of the attendance of one attorney for each other party at the place where the deposition is to be taken. The amounts so paid, unless otherwise directed by the Court, may be taxed as a cost at the conclusion of the action or proceeding.

Rule 30.2.   Telephonic and Other Remote Depositions

The motion of a party to take the deposition of an adverse party by telephone or other remote means will presumptively be granted. Where the opposing party is a corporation, the term "adverse party" means an officer, director, managing agent or corporate designee pursuant to Fed. R. Civ. P. 30(b)(6).

Rule 30.3.   Persons Attending Depositions

A person who is a party in the action may attend the deposition of a party or witness. A witness or potential witness in the action may attend the deposition of a party or witness unless otherwise ordered by the Court.

Rule 30.4.   Conferences Between Deponent and Defending Attorney

An attorney for a deponent shall not initiate a private conference with the deponent while a deposition question is pending, except for the purpose of determining whether a privilege should be asserted.

Rule 33.2.   Standard Discovery in Prisoner Pro Se Actions

(a)   This rule shall apply in any action commenced pro se in which the plaintiff's complaint includes any claim described in paragraph (b) of this rule, in which the events alleged in the complaint occurred while the plaintiff was in custody of [any prison, jail, or correctional facility within the state of New York.] * * *

(b)   The claims to which the standard discovery requests shall apply are Use of Force Cases, Inmate Against Inmate Assault Cases and Disciplinary Due Process Cases, as defined below.

(1)   "Use of Force Case" refers to an action in which the complaint alleges that an employee of the Department or Facility used physical force against the plaintiff in violation of the plaintiff's rights.

(2)   "Inmate against Inmate Assault Case" refers to an action in which the complaint alleges that an employee of the Department or Facility was responsible for the plaintiff's injury resulting from physical contact with another inmate.

(3)   "Disciplinary Due Process Case" refers to an action in which (i) the complaint alleges that an employee of the Department or Facility violated or permitted the violation of a right or

rights in a disciplinary proceeding against the plaintiff, and (ii) the punishment imposed upon plaintiff as a result of that proceeding was placement in a special housing unit for more than 30 days.

(c)   * * *

(d)   The requests, denominated "Plaintiff's Local Civil Rule 33.2 Interrogatories and Requests for Production of Documents," shall be answered within 120 days of service of the complaint on any named defendant except (i) as otherwise ordered by the Court, for good cause shown, which shall be based upon the facts and procedural status of the particular case and not upon a generalized claim of burden, expense or relevance or (ii) if a dispositive motion is pending. The responses to the requests shall be served upon the plaintiff and shall include verbatim quotation of the requests. Copies of the requests are available from the Court, including the Court's website.

(e)   Except upon permission of the Court, for good cause shown, the requests shall constitute the sole form of discovery available to plaintiff during the 120-day period designated above.

Rule 33.3. Interrogatories (Southern District Only)

(a)   Unless otherwise ordered by the Court, at the commencement of discovery, interrogatories will be restricted to those seeking names of witnesses with knowledge of information relevant to the subject matter of the action, the computation of each category of damage alleged, and the existence, custodian, location and general description of relevant documents, including pertinent insurance agreements, and other physical evidence, or information of a similar nature.

(b)   During discovery, interrogatories other than those seeking information described in paragraph (a) above may only be served (1) if they are a more practical method of obtaining the information sought than a request for production or a deposition, or (2) if ordered by the Court.

(c)   At the conclusion of other discovery, and at least 30 days prior to the discovery cut-off date, interrogatories seeking the claims and contentions of the opposing party may be served unless the Court has ordered otherwise.

Rule 37.1. Verbatim Quotation of Discovery Materials

Upon any motion or application involving discovery or disclosure requests or responses under Fed. R. Civ. P. 37, the moving party shall specify and quote or set forth verbatim in the motion papers each discovery request and response to which the motion or application is addressed. The motion or application shall also set forth the grounds upon which the moving party is entitled to prevail as to each request or response. Local Civil Rule 5.1 also applies to the motion or application.

Rule 37.2. Mode of Raising Discovery Disputes With the Court (Southern District Only)

No motion under Rules 26 through 37 inclusive of the Federal Rules of Civil Procedure shall be heard unless counsel for the moving party has first requested an informal conference with the Court by letter-motion for a pre-motion discovery conference * * * and such request has either been denied or the discovery dispute has not been resolved as a consequence of such a conference.

Rule 37.3. Mode of Raising Discovery and Other Non-Dispositive Pretrial Disputes With the Court (Eastern District Only)

(a) Good Faith Effort to Resolve. Prior to seeking judicial resolution of a discovery or non-dispositive pretrial dispute, the attorneys for the affected parties or non-party witness shall attempt to confer in good faith in person or by telephone in an effort to resolve the dispute in conformity with Fed. R. Civ. P. 37(a)(1).

(b) Disputes Arising During Depositions. Where the attorneys for the affected parties or a non-party witness cannot agree on a resolution of a discovery dispute that arises during a deposition, they shall, to the extent practicable, notify the Court by telephone and seek a ruling while the deposition is in progress. If a prompt ruling cannot be obtained, and the dispute involves an instruction to the witness not to answer a question, the instruction not to answer may stand and the deposition shall continue until a ruling is obtained pursuant to the procedure set forth in paragraph (c) below.

(c) Other Discovery and Non-Dispositive Pretrial Disputes. Where the attorneys for the affected parties or non-party witness cannot agree on a resolution of any other discovery dispute or non-dispositive pretrial dispute, or if they are unable to obtain a telephonic ruling on a discovery dispute that arises during a deposition as provided in paragraph (b) above, they shall notify the Court by letter not exceeding three pages in length outlining the nature of the dispute and attaching relevant materials. Within four days of receiving such a letter, any opposing affected party or non-party witness may submit a responsive letter not exceeding three pages attaching relevant materials. Except for the letters and attachments authorized herein, or where a ruling which was made exclusively as a result of a telephone conference is the subject of *de novo* review pursuant to paragraph (d) hereof, papers shall not be submitted with respect to a dispute governed by this rule unless the Court has so directed.

(d) Motion for Reconsideration. A ruling made exclusively as a result of a telephone conference may be the subject of *de novo* reconsideration by a letter not exceeding five pages in length attaching relevant materials submitted by any affected party or non-party witness. Within four days of receiving such a letter, any other affected party or non-party witness may submit a responsive letter not exceeding five pages in length attaching relevant materials.

(e) Decision of the Court. The Court shall record or arrange for the recording of the Court's decision in writing. Such written order may take the form of an oral order read into the record of a deposition or other proceeding, a handwritten memorandum, a handwritten marginal notation on a letter or other document, or any other form the Court deems appropriate.

Rule 39.1. Custody of Trial and Hearing Exhibits

(a) Unless the Court orders otherwise, trial and hearing exhibits shall not be filed with the Clerk, but shall be retained in the custody of the respective attorneys who produced them in court.

(b) Trial and hearing exhibits which have been filed with the Clerk shall be removed by the party responsible for them (1) if no appeal is taken, within ninety (90) days after a final decision is rendered, or (2) if an appeal has been taken, within thirty (30) days after the final disposition of the appeal. Parties failing to comply with this rule shall be notified by the Clerk to remove their exhibits and upon their failure to do so within thirty (30) days, the Clerk may dispose of them as the Clerk may see fit.

Rule 39.2. Order of Summation

After the close of evidence in civil trials, the order of summation shall be determined in the discretion of the Court.

Rule 47.1. Assessment of Jury Costs

All counsel in civil cases shall seriously discuss the possibility of settlement a reasonable time prior to trial. The Court may, in its discretion, assess the parties or counsel with the cost of one day's attendance of the jurors if a case is settled after the jury has been summoned or during trial, the amount to be paid to the Clerk of the Court. For purposes of this rule, a civil jury is considered summoned for a trial as of Noon one day prior to the designated date of the trial.

Rule 53.1.   Masters

(a) Oath. Every person appointed pursuant to Rule 53 shall, before entering upon his or her duties, take and subscribe an oath, which, except as otherwise prescribed by statute or rule, shall be the same as the oath prescribed for Judges pursuant to 28 U.S.C. § 453, with the addition of the words "in conformance with the order of appointment" after the words "administer justice." Such an oath may be taken before any federal or state officer authorized by federal law to administer oaths, and shall be filed in the office of the Clerk.

(b) May Sit Outside District. A person appointed pursuant to Rule 53 may sit within or outside the district. When the person appointed is requested to sit outside the district for the convenience of a party and there is opposition by another party, he or she may make an order for the holding of the hearing, or a part thereof, outside the district, upon such terms and conditions as shall be just. Such order may be reviewed by the Court upon motion of any party, served within twenty-one (21) days after service on all parties by the master of the order.

Rule 54.1.   Taxable Costs

(a) Notice of Taxation of Costs. Within thirty (30) days after the entry of final judgment, or, in the case of an appeal by any party, within thirty (30) days after the final disposition of the appeal, unless this period is extended by the Court for good cause shown, any party seeking to recover costs shall file with the Clerk a notice of taxation of costs * * * , indicating the date and time of taxation * * * and annexing a bill of costs. Costs will not be taxed during the pendency of any appeal, motion for reconsideration, or motion for new trial. * * * Any party failing to file a request to tax costs within this thirty (30) day period will be deemed to have waived costs. The notice of taxation of costs shall be served upon each other party, and shall specify the date and time fixed for taxation, which shall comply with the notice period prescribed by Fed. R. Civ. P. 54. The bill of costs shall include an affidavit that the costs claimed are allowable by law, are correctly stated and were necessarily incurred. Bills for the costs claimed shall be attached as exhibits.

(b) Objections to Bill of Costs. A party objecting to any cost item shall serve objections prior to the date and time scheduled for taxation. The parties need not appear at the date and time scheduled for taxation unless requested by the Clerk. The Clerk will proceed to tax costs at the time scheduled and allow such items as are properly taxable. In the absence of written objection, any item listed may be taxed within the discretion of the Clerk.

(c) Items Taxable as Costs.

(1) *Transcripts.* The cost of any part of the original trial transcript that was necessarily obtained for use in this Court or on appeal is taxable. Convenience of counsel is not sufficient. The cost of a transcript of Court proceedings prior to or subsequent to trial is taxable only when authorized in advance or ordered by the Court.

(2) *Depositions.* Unless otherwise ordered by the Court, the original transcript of a deposition, plus one copy, is taxable if the deposition was used or received in evidence at the trial, whether or not it was read in its entirety. Costs for depositions are also taxable if they were used by the Court in ruling on a motion for summary judgment or other dispositive substantive motion. Costs for depositions taken solely for discovery are not taxable. Counsel's fees and expenses in attending the taking of a deposition are not taxable except as provided by statute, rule (including Local Civil Rule 30.1), or order of the Court. Fees, mileage, and subsistence for the witness at the deposition are taxable at the same rates as for attendance at trial if the deposition taken was used or received in evidence at the trial.

(3) *Witness Fees, Travel Expenses and Subsistence.* Witness fees and travel expenses authorized by 28 U.S.C. § 1821 are taxable if the witness testifies. Subsistence pursuant to 28 U.S.C. § 1821 is taxable if the witness testifies and it is not practical for the witness to return to his or her residence from day to day. No party to the action may receive witness fees, mileage, or

subsistence. Fees for expert witnesses are taxable only to the extent of fees for ordinary witnesses unless prior Court approval was obtained.

(4) *Interpreting Costs.* The reasonable fee of a competent interpreter is taxable if the fee of the witness involved is taxable.

(5) *Exemplifications and Copies of Papers.* A copy of an exhibit is taxable if the original was not available and the copy was used or received in evidence. The cost of copies used for the convenience of counsel or the Court are not taxable. The fees for a search and certification or proof of the non-existence of a document in a public office is taxable.

(6) *Maps, Charts, Models, Photographs and Summaries.* The cost of photographs, 8″ × 10″ in size or less, is taxable if used or received in evidence. Enlargements greater than 8″ × 10″ are not taxable except by order of the Court. Costs of maps, charts, and models, including computer generated models, are not taxable except by order of the Court. The cost of compiling summaries, statistical comparisons and reports is not taxable.

(7) *Attorney Fees and Related Costs.* Attorney fees and disbursements and other related fees and paralegal expenses are not taxable except by order of the Court. A motion for attorney fees and related non-taxable expenses shall be made within the time period prescribed by Fed. R. Civ. P. 54.

(8) *Fees of Masters, Receivers, Commissioners and Court Appointed Experts.* Fees of masters, receivers, commissioners, and court appointed experts are taxable as costs, unless otherwise ordered by the Court.

(9) *Costs for Title Searches.* A party is entitled to tax necessary disbursements for the expenses of searches made by title insurance, abstract or searching companies.

(10) *Docket and Miscellaneous Fees.* Docket fees, and the reasonable and actual fees of the Clerk and of a marshal, sheriff, and process server, are taxable unless otherwise ordered by the Court.

Rule 54.2. Security for Costs

The Court, on motion or on its own initiative, may order any party to file an original bond for costs or additional security for costs in such an amount and so conditioned as it may designate. For failure to comply with the order the Court may make such orders in regard to noncompliance as are just, and among others the following: an order striking out pleadings or staying further proceedings until the bond is filed or dismissing the action or rendering a judgment by default against the non-complying party.

Rule 54.3. Entering Satisfaction of Money Judgment

Satisfaction of a money judgment entered or registered in this district shall be entered by the Clerk as follows:

(a) upon the payment into the Court of the amount thereof, plus interest, and the payment of the Clerk's and marshal's fees, if any;

(b) upon the filing of a satisfaction executed and acknowledged by: (1) the judgment creditor; or (2) the judgment creditor's legal representatives or assigns, with evidence of their authority; or (3) the judgment creditor's attorney if within ten (10) years of the entry of the judgment or decree;

(c) if the judgment creditor is the United States, upon the filing of a satisfaction executed by the United States Attorney;

(d) pursuant to an order of satisfaction entered by the Court; or

(e) upon the registration of a certified copy of a satisfaction entered in another court.

Rule 55.1.   Certificate of Default

A party applying for entry of default under Fed. R. Civ. P. 55(a) shall file:

(a)   a request for a Clerk's Certificate of Default; and

(b)   an affidavit demonstrating that:

     (1)   the party against whom a notation of default is sought is not an infant, in the military, or an incompetent person;

     (2)   the party has failed to plead or otherwise defend the action; and

     (3)   the pleading to which no response has been made was properly served.

A proposed Clerk's Certificate of Default form must be attached to the affidavit.

Rule 55.2.   Default Judgment

(a)   By the Clerk. Upon issuance of a Clerk's certificate of default, if the claim to which no response has been made only sought payment of a sum certain, and does not include a request for attorney's fees or other substantive relief, and if a default judgment is sought against all remaining parties to the action, the moving party shall submit an affidavit showing the principal amount due and owing, not exceeding the amount sought in the claim to which no response has been made, plus interest, if any, computed by the party, with credit for all payments received to date clearly set forth, and costs, if any, pursuant to 28 U.S.C. § 1920.

(b)   By the Court. In all other cases the party seeking a judgment by default shall apply to the Court as described in Fed. R. Civ. P. 55(b)(2), and shall append to the application (1) the Clerk's certificate of default, (2) a copy of the claim to which no response has been made, and (3) a proposed form of default judgment.

(c)   Mailing of Papers. Unless otherwise ordered by the Court, all papers submitted to the Court pursuant to Local Civil Rule 55.2(a) or (b) above shall simultaneously be mailed to the party against whom a default judgment is sought at the last known residence of such party (if an individual) or the last known business address of such party (if a person other than an individual). Proof of such mailing shall be filed with the Court. If the mailing is returned, a supplemental affidavit shall be filed with the Court setting forth that fact, together with the reason provided for return, if any.

Rule 56.1.   Statements of Material Facts on Motion for Summary Judgment

(a)   Upon any motion for summary judgment pursuant to Rule 56 of the Federal Rules of Civil Procedure, there shall be annexed to the notice of motion a separate, short and concise statement, in numbered paragraphs, of the material facts as to which the moving party contends there is no genuine issue to be tried. Failure to submit such a statement may constitute grounds for denial of the motion.

(b)   The papers opposing a motion for summary judgment shall include a correspondingly numbered paragraph responding to each numbered paragraph in the statement of the moving party, and if necessary, additional paragraphs containing a separate, short and concise statement of the additional material facts as to which it is contended that there exists a genuine issue to be tried.

(c)   Each numbered paragraph in the statement of material facts required to be served by the moving party will be deemed to be admitted for purposes of the motion unless specifically controverted by a correspondingly numbered paragraph in the statement required to be served by the opposing party.

(d)   Each statement by the movant or opponent pursuant to Rule 56.1(a) and (b), including each statement controverting any statement of material fact, must be followed by citation to evidence which would be admissible, set forth as required by Fed. R. Civ. P. 56(c).

Rule 56.2. Notice to Pro Se Litigant Who Opposes a Summary Judgment

Any represented party moving for summary judgment against a party proceeding *pro se* shall serve and file as a separate document, together with the papers in support of the motion, the following "Notice To Pro Se Litigant Who Opposes a Motion For Summary Judgment" with the full text of Fed. R. Civ. P. 56 and Local Civil Rule 56.1 attached. Where the pro se party is not the plaintiff, the movant shall amend the form notice as necessary to reflect that fact.

Notice to Pro Se Litigant Who Opposes a Motion for Summary Judgment

The defendant in this case has moved for summary judgment pursuant to Rule 56 of the Federal Rules of Civil Procedure. This means that the defendant has asked the court to decide this case without a trial, based on written materials, including affidavits, submitted in support of the motion. THE CLAIMS YOU ASSERT IN YOUR COMPLAINT MAY BE DISMISSED WITHOUT A TRIAL IF YOU DO NOT RESPOND TO THIS MOTION ON TIME by filing sworn affidavits and/or other papers as required by Rule 56(c) of the Federal Rules of Civil Procedure and by Local Civil Rule 56.1. The full text of Rule 56 of the Federal Rules of Civil Procedure and Local Civil Rule 56.1 is attached.

In short, Rule 56 provides that you may NOT oppose summary judgment simply by relying upon the allegations in your complaint. Rather, you must submit evidence, such as witness statements or documents, countering the facts asserted by the defendant and raising specific facts that support your claim. If you have proof of your claim, now is the time to submit it. Any witness statements must be in the form of affidavits. An affidavit is a sworn statement of fact based on personal knowledge stating facts that would be admissible at trial. You may submit your own affidavit and/or the affidavits of others. You may submit affidavits that were prepared specifically in response to defendant's motion for summary judgment.

If you do not respond to the motion for summary judgment on time with affidavits and/or documents contradicting the material facts asserted by the defendant, the Court may accept defendant's factual assertions as true. Judgment may then be entered in defendant's favor without a trial.

If you have any questions, you may direct them to the Pro Se Office.

Rule 58.1. Remand by an Appellate Court

Any mandate, order, or judgment of an appellate court, when filed in the office of the Clerk of the District Court, shall automatically become the order or judgment of the District Court and be entered as such by the Clerk without further order, except if such mandate, order, or judgment of the appellate court requires further proceedings in the District Court other than a new trial, an order shall be entered making the order or judgment of the appellate court the order or judgment of the District Court.

Rule 65.1.1. Sureties

(a) Whenever a bond, undertaking or stipulation is required, it shall be sufficient, except as otherwise prescribed by law, if the instrument is executed by the surety or sureties only.

(b) Except as otherwise provided by law, every bond, undertaking or stipulation must be secured by: (1) the deposit of cash or government bonds in the amount of the bond, undertaking or stipulation; or (2) the undertaking or guaranty of a corporate surety holding a certificate of authority from the Secretary of the Treasury; or (3) the undertaking or guaranty of two individual residents of the district in which the case is pending, each of whom owns real or personal property within the district worth double the amount of the bond, undertaking or stipulation, over all his or her debts and liabilities, and over all obligations assumed by said surety on other bonds, undertakings or stipulations, and exclusive of all legal exemptions.

(c) Except as otherwise provided by law, all bonds, undertakings and stipulations of corporate sureties holding certificates of authority from the Secretary of the Treasury, where the amount of such bonds or undertakings has been fixed by a Judge or by Court rule or statute, may be approved by the Clerk.

(d) In the case of a bond, or undertaking, or stipulation executed by individual sureties, each surety shall attach the surety's affidavit of justification, giving the surety's full name, occupation, residence and business addresses, and showing that the surety is qualified as an individual surety under paragraph (b) of this rule.

(e) Members of the bar who have appeared in the case shall not act as a surety in the case. Administrative officers and employees of the Court, the marshal, and the marshal's deputies and assistants, shall not act as a surety in any suit, action or proceeding pending in this Court.

(f) Whenever a notice of motion to enforce the liability of a surety upon a bond is served upon the Clerk pursuant to Fed. R. Civ. P. 65.1 or Fed. R. App. P. 8(b), the party making such motion shall deposit with the Clerk the original, three copies, and one additional copy for each surety to be served.

Rule 67.1.   Order for Deposit in Interest-Bearing Account

(a) Whenever a party seeks a court order for money to be deposited by the Clerk in an interest-bearing account, the party shall file the proposed order. The Clerk shall inspect the proposed order for proper form and content and compliance with this rule prior to submission to the judge for signature.

(b) Proposed orders directing the Clerk to invest such funds in an interest-bearing account or other instrument shall include the following:

    (1) the exact United States dollar amount of the principal sum to be invested; and

    (2) wording which directs the Clerk to deduct from the income on the investment a fee consistent with that authorized by the Judicial Conference of the United States and set by the Director of the Administrative Office.

(c) Unless ordered by the court, interpleader funds shall be deposited in the Disputed Ownership Fund in an interest-bearing account. Income generated from fund investments in each case will be distributed after the appropriate fee has been applied and tax withholdings have been deducted from the fund.

Rule 72.1.   Powers of Magistrate Judges

In addition to other powers of Magistrate Judges:

(a) Full-time Magistrate Judges are hereby specially designated to exercise the jurisdiction set forth in 28 U.S.C. § 636(c).

(b) Magistrate Judges are authorized to entertain *ex parte* applications by appropriate representatives of the United States government for the issuance of administrative inspection orders or warrants.

(c) Magistrate Judges may issue subpoenas, *writs of habeas corpus ad testificandum* or *ad prosequendum* or other orders necessary to obtain the presence of parties or witnesses or evidence needed for court proceedings, and may sign in forma pauperis orders.

(d) Matters arising under 28 U.S.C. §§ 2254 and 2255 or challenging the conditions of the confinement of prisoners may be referred to a Magistrate Judge by the District Judge to whom the case has been assigned. A Magistrate Judge may perform any or all of the duties imposed upon a District Judge by the rules governing such proceedings in the United States district courts. In so doing, a Magistrate Judge may issue any preliminary orders and conduct any necessary evidentiary hearing or other appropriate proceeding and shall submit to a District Judge a report containing proposed findings of fact and recommendations for disposition of the matter by the District Judge.

Rule 72.2. Reference to Magistrate Judge (Eastern District Only)

A Magistrate Judge shall be assigned to each case upon the commencement of the action, except in those categories of actions set forth in Local Civil Rule 16.1. In any courthouse in this District in which there is more than one Magistrate Judge such assignment shall be at random on a rotating basis. Except in multi-district cases and antitrust cases, a Magistrate Judge so assigned is empowered to act with respect to all non-dispositive pretrial matters unless the assigned District Judge orders otherwise.

Rule 73.1. Consent Jurisdiction Procedure

(a)   When a civil action is filed with the Clerk, the Clerk shall give the filing party notice of the Magistrate Judge's consent jurisdiction in a form approved by the Court, with sufficient copies to be served with the complaint on adversary parties. A copy of such notice shall be attached to any third-party complaint served by a defendant.

(b)   When a completed consent form has been filed, the Clerk shall forward the form for final approval to the District Judge to whom the case was originally assigned. Once the District Judge has approved the transfer and returned the consent form to the Clerk for filing, the Clerk shall reassign the case for all purposes to the Magistrate Judge previously designated to receive any referrals or to whom the case has previously been referred for any purpose, except that in the Eastern District of New York, upon application of the parties, the Clerk shall select a new Magistrate Judge at random. If no designation or referral has been made, the Clerk shall select a new Magistrate Judge at random.

Rule 77.1. Submission of Orders, Judgments and Decrees

Proposed orders, judgments and decrees shall be presented as directed by the ECF rules published on the website of each respective Court. Unless the form of order, judgment or decree is consented to in writing, or unless the Court otherwise directs, four (4) days' notice of settlement is required. One (1) day's notice is required of all counter-proposals.

Rule 81.1. Removal of Cases From State Courts

If the Court's jurisdiction is based upon diversity of citizenship, and regardless of whether or not service of process has been effected on all parties, the notice of removal shall set forth (1) in the case of each individual named as a party, that party's residence and domicile and any state or other jurisdiction of which that party is a citizen for purposes of 28 U.S.C. § 1332; (2) in the case of each party that is a partnership, limited liability partnership, limited liability company, or other unincorporated association, like information for all of its partners or members, as well as the state or other jurisdiction of its formation; (3) in the case of each party that is a corporation, its state or other jurisdiction of incorporation, principal place of business, and any state or other jurisdiction of which that party is a citizen for purposes of 28 U.S.C. § 1332; (4) in the case of an assigned claim, corresponding information for each original owner of the claim and for each assignee; and (5) the date on which each party that has been served was served. If such information or a designated part is unknown to the removing party, the removing party may so state, and in that case plaintiff within twenty-one (21) days after removal shall file in the office of the Clerk a statement of the omitted information.

Rule 83.1. Transfer of Cases to Another District

In a case ordered transferred from this District, the Clerk, unless otherwise ordered, shall upon the expiration of seven (7) days effectuate the transfer of the case to the transferee court.

Rule 83.2.   Settlement of Actions by or on Behalf of Infants or Incompetents, Wrongful Death Actions and Actions for Conscious Pain and Suffering of the Decedent

(a) Settlement of Actions by or on Behalf of Infants or Incompetents.

(1)   An action by or on behalf of an infant or incompetent shall not be settled or compromised, or voluntarily discontinued, dismissed or terminated, without leave of the Court embodied in an order, judgment or decree. The proceeding upon an application to settle or compromise such an action shall conform, as nearly as may be, to the New York State statutes and rules, but the Court, for cause shown, may dispense with any New York State requirement.

(2)   The Court shall authorize payment to counsel for the infant or incompetent of a reasonable attorney's fee and proper disbursements from the amount recovered in such an action, whether realized by settlement, execution or otherwise and shall determine the said fee and disbursements, after due inquiry as to all charges against the fund.

(3)   The Court shall order the balance of the proceeds of the recovery or settlement to be distributed as it deems may best protect the interest of the infant or incompetent.

(b) Settlement of Wrongful Death Actions and Actions for Conscious Pain and Suffering of the Decedent. In an action for wrongful death or conscious pain and suffering of the decedent:

(1)   Where required by statute or otherwise, the Court shall apportion the avails of the action, and shall approve the terms of any settlement.

(2)   The Court shall approve an attorney's fee only upon application in accordance with the provisions of the New York State statutes and rules.

Rule 83.3.   Habeas Corpus

Unless otherwise provided by statute, applications for a writ of habeas corpus made by persons under the judgment and sentence of a court of the State of New York shall be filed, heard and determined in the District Court for the district within which they were convicted and sentenced; provided, however, that if the convenience of the parties and witnesses requires a hearing in a different district, such application may be transferred to any district which is found by the assigned Judge to be more convenient. The Clerks of the Southern and Eastern District Courts are authorized and directed to transfer such applications to the District herein designated for filing, hearing and determination.

Rule 83.4.   Publication of Advertisements

(a)   Unless otherwise provided by statute, rule, or order of the Court, all advertisements except notices of sale of real estate or of any interest in land shall be published in a newspaper which has a general circulation in this district or a circulation reasonably calculated to give public notice of a legal publication. The Court may direct the publication of such additional advertisement as it may deem advisable.

(b)   Unless otherwise ordered, notices for the sale of real estate or of any interest in land shall be published in a newspaper of general circulation in the county in which the real estate or the land in question is located.

Rule 83.5.   Notice of Sale

In any civil action, the notice of any proposed sale of property directed to be made by any order or judgment of the Court, unless otherwise ordered by the Court, need not set out the terms of sale specified in the order or judgment, and the notice will be sufficient if in substantially the following form:

UNITED STATES DISTRICT COURT
. . . . District of New York

[Docket No. and Judge's Initials]

[CAPTION],

NOTICE OF SALE

Pursuant to. . . . .(Order or Judgment). . . . . .of the United States District Court for the . . . . District of New York, filed in the office of the clerk on . . . . (Date) . . . . .in the case entitled . . . . (Name and Docket Number) . . . . .the undersigned will sell at . . . . (Place of Sale) . . . . .on. . . . . (Date and Hour of Sale) . . . . the property in said . . . . (Order or Judgment) . . . . .described and therein directed to be sold, to which . . . . (Order or Judgment) . . . . reference is made for the terms of sale and for a description of the property which may be briefly described as follows:

Dated:

_____
Signature and Official Title

The notice need not describe the property by metes and bounds or otherwise in detail and will be sufficient if in general terms it identifies the property by specifying its nature and location. However, it shall state: the approximate acreage of any real estate outside the limits of any town or city; the street, lot and block number of any real estate within any town or city; and a general statement of the character of any improvements upon the property.

Rule 83.6.   Contempt Proceedings in Civil Cases

(a)   A proceeding to adjudicate a person in civil contempt, including a case provided for in Fed. R. Civ. P. 37(b)(1) and 37(b)(2)(A)(vii), shall be commenced by the service of a notice of motion or order to show cause. The affidavit upon which such notice of motion or order to show cause is based shall set out with particularity the misconduct complained of, the claim, if any, for damages occasioned thereby and such evidence as to the amount of damages as may be available to the moving party. A reasonable counsel fee, necessitated by the contempt proceedings, may be included as an item of damage. Where the alleged contemnor has appeared in the action by an attorney, the notice of motion or order to show cause and the papers upon which it is based may be served upon said attorney; otherwise service shall be made personally, together with a copy of this Local Civil Rule 83.6, in the manner provided for by the Federal Rules of Civil Procedure for the service of a summons. If an order to show cause is sought, such order may, upon necessity shown, embody a direction to the United States marshal to arrest the alleged contemnor and hold such person unless bail is posted in an amount fixed by the order, conditioned on the appearance of such person in all further proceedings on the motion, and further conditioned that the alleged contemnor will hold himself or herself amenable to all orders of the Court for surrender.

(b)   If the alleged contemnor puts in issue his or her alleged misconduct or the damages thereby occasioned, said person shall upon demand be entitled to have oral evidence taken, either before the Court or before a master appointed by the Court. When by law such alleged contemnor is entitled to a trial by jury, said person shall make written demand before the beginning of the hearing on the application; otherwise the alleged contemnor will be deemed to have waived a trial by jury.

(c)   If the alleged contemnor is found to be in contempt of Court, an order shall be entered (1) reciting or referring to the verdict or findings of fact upon which the adjudication is based; (2) setting forth the amount of damages, if any, to which the complainant is entitled; (3) fixing the fine, if any, imposed by the Court, which fine shall include the damages found and naming the person to whom such fine shall be payable; (4) stating any other conditions, the performance of which will operate to purge the contempt; and (5) directing, where appropriate, the arrest of the contemnor by the United States marshal and confinement until the performance of the condition fixed in the order and the payment of the fine, or until the contemnor be otherwise discharged pursuant to law. A certified copy of the order committing the contemnor shall be sufficient warrant to the marshal for the arrest and confinement of the contemnor. The complainant shall also have the same remedies against the property of the contemnor as if the order awarding the fine were a final judgment.

(d)   If the alleged contemnor is found not guilty of the charges, said person shall be discharged from the proceedings and, in the discretion of the Court, may have judgment against the complainant for costs and disbursements and a reasonable counsel fee.

Rule 83.7.   Court-Annexed Arbitration (Eastern District Only)

* * *

[Parts (a), (b), and (c) refer to the selection, compensation and immunity of arbitrators.]

(d)   Civil Cases Eligible for Compulsory Arbitration.

(1)   The Clerk of Court shall, as to all cases filed after January 1, 1986, designate and process for compulsory arbitration all civil cases (excluding social security cases, tax matters, prisoners' civil rights cases and any action based on an alleged violation of a right secured by the Constitution of the United States or if jurisdiction is based in whole or in part on Title 28, U.S.C. § 1343) wherein money damages only are being sought in an amount not in excess of $150,000.00 exclusive of interest and costs.

(2)   The parties may by written stipulation agree that the Clerk of Court shall designate and process for court-annexed arbitration any civil case that is not subject to compulsory arbitration hereunder.

(3)   For purposes of this Rule only, in all civil cases damages shall be presumed to be not in excess of $150,000.00 exclusive of interest and costs, unless:

(A)   Counsel for plaintiff, at the time of filing the complaint, or in the event of the removal of a case from state court or transfer of a case from another district to this Court, within thirty (30) days of the docketing of the case in this district, files a certification with the Court that the damages sought exceed $150,000.00, exclusive of interest and costs; or

(B)   Counsel for a defendant, at the time of filing a counterclaim or crossclaim files a certification with the Court that the damages sought by the counter-claim or crossclaim exceed $150,000.00 exclusive of interest and costs.

(e)   Referral to Arbitration.

(1)   After an answer is filed in a case determined eligible for arbitration, the arbitration clerk shall send a notice to counsel setting the date and time for the arbitration hearing. The date of the arbitration hearing set forth in the notice shall be approximately four months but in no event later than 120 days from the date the answer was filed, except that the arbitration proceeding shall not, in the absence of the consent of the parties, commence until 30 days after the disposition by the District Court of any motion to dismiss the complaint, motion for judgment on the pleadings, motion to join necessary parties, or motion for summary judgment, if the motion was filed during a time period specified by the District Court. The 120-day and 30-day periods specified in the preceding sentence may be modified by the Court for good cause shown. The notice shall also advise counsel that they may agree to an earlier date for the arbitration hearing provided the arbitration clerk is notified within 30 days of the date of the notice. The notice shall also advise counsel that they have 90 days to complete discovery unless the Judge to whom the case has been assigned orders a shorter or longer period for discovery. The Judge may refer the case to a Magistrate Judge for purposes of discovery. In the event

a third party has been brought into the action, this notice shall not be sent until an answer has been filed by the third party.

(2)   The Court shall, *sua sponte,* or on motion of a party exempt any case from arbitration in which the objectives of arbitration would not be realized

    (A)   because the case involves complex or novel issues,

    (B)   because legal issues predominate over factual issues, or

    (C)   for other good cause.

Application by a party for an exemption from compulsory arbitration shall be made by written letter to the court not exceeding three pages in length, outlining the basis for the request and attaching relevant materials, which shall be submitted no later than 21 days after receipt of the notice to counsel setting forth the date and time for the arbitration hearing. Within four days of receiving such a letter, any opposing affected party may submit a responsive letter not exceeding three pages attaching relevant materials.

(3)   Cases not originally designated as eligible for compulsory arbitration, but which in the discretion of the assigned Judge, are later found to qualify, may be referred to arbitration. A U.S. District Judge or a U.S. Magistrate Judge, in cases that exceed the arbitration ceiling of $150,000 exclusive of interest and costs, in their discretion, may suggest that the parties should consider arbitration. If the parties are agreeable, an appropriate consent form signed by all parties or their representatives may be entered and filed in the case prior to scheduling an arbitration hearing.

(4)   The arbitration shall be held before one arbitrator unless a panel of three arbitrators is requested by a party, in which case one of them shall be designated as chairperson of the panel. If the amount of controversy, exclusive of interest and costs, if $5,000 or less, the arbitration shall be held before a single arbitrator. The arbitration panel shall be chosen at random by the Clerk of the Court from the lawyers who have been duly certified as arbitrators. The arbitration panel shall be scheduled to hear not more than three cases.

(5)   The Judge to whom the case has been assigned shall, 30 days prior to the date scheduled for the arbitration hearing, sign an order setting forth the date and time of the arbitration hearing and the names of the arbitrators designated to hear the case. If a party has filed a motion for judgment on the pleadings, summary judgment or similar relief, the Judge shall not sign the order before ruling on the motion, but the filing of such a motion on or after the date of the order shall not stay the arbitration unless the Judge so orders.

(6)   Upon entry of the order designating the arbitrators, the arbitration clerk shall send to each arbitrator a copy of all pleadings, including the order designating the arbitrators, and the guidelines for arbitrators.

(7)   Persons selected to be arbitrators shall be disqualified for bias or prejudice as provided in Title 28, U.S.C. § 144, and shall disqualify themselves in any action which they would be required under title 28, U.S.C. § 455 to disqualify themselves if they were a justice, judge, or magistrate.

(f)   Arbitration Hearing.

(1)   The arbitration hearing shall take place in the United States Courthouse in a courtroom assigned by the arbitration clerk on the date and at the time set forth in the order of the Court. The arbitrators are authorized to change the date and time of the hearing provided the hearing is commenced within 30 days of the hearing date set forth in the order of the Court. Any continuance beyond this 30 day period must be approved by the Judge to whom the case has been assigned. The arbitration clerk must be notified immediately of any continuance.

(2)   Counsel for the parties shall report settlement of the case to the arbitration clerk and all members of the arbitration panel assigned to the case.

(3)   The arbitration hearing may proceed in the absence of any party who, after notice, fails to be present. In the event, however, that a party fails to participate in the arbitration process in a meaningful manner, the Court may impose appropriate sanctions, including, but not limited to, the striking of any demand for a trial de novo filed by that party.

(4)   Rule 45 of the Federal Rules of Civil Procedure shall apply to subpoenas for attendance of witnesses and the production of documentary evidence at an arbitration hearing under this Rule. Testimony at an arbitration hearing shall be under oath or affirmation.

(5)   The Federal Rules of Evidence shall be used as guides to the admissibility of evidence. Copies or photographs of all exhibits, except those intended solely for impeachment, must be marked for identification and delivered to adverse parties at least fourteen (14) days prior to the hearing. The arbitrators shall receive exhibits in evidence without formal proof unless counsel has been notified at least seven (7) days prior to the hearing that the adverse party intends to raise an issue concerning the authenticity of the exhibit. The arbitrators may refuse to receive in evidence any exhibit, a copy or photograph of which has not been delivered to the adverse party as provided herein.

(6)   A party may have a recording and transcript made of the arbitration hearing, but that party shall make all necessary arrangements and bear all expenses thereof.

(g)   Arbitration Award and Judgment.

(1)   The arbitration award shall be filed with the Court promptly after the hearing is concluded and shall be entered as the judgment of the court after the 30 day period for requesting a trial de novo pursuant to Section (h) has expired, unless a party has demanded a trial de novo. The judgment so entered shall be subject to the same provisions of law and shall have the same force and effect as a judgment of the Court in a civil action, except that it shall not be appealable. In a case involving multiple claims and parties, any segregable part of an arbitration award as to which an aggrieved party has not timely demanded a trial de novo shall become part of the final judgment with the same force and effect as a judgment of the Court in a civil action, except that it shall not be appealable.

(2)   The contents of any arbitration award shall not be made known to any Judge who might be assigned the case,

(A)   except as necessary for the Court to determine whether to assess costs or attorneys fees,

(B)   until the District Court has entered final judgment in the action or the action has been otherwise terminated, or

(C)   except for purposes of preparing the report required by section 903(b) of the Judicial Improvement and Access to Justice Act.

(3)   Costs may be taxed as part of any arbitration award pursuant to Title 28, U.S.C. § 1920.

(h)   Trial De Novo.

(1)   Within 30 days after the arbitration award is entered on the docket, any party may demand in writing a trial de novo in the District Court. Such demand shall be filed with the arbitration clerk, and served by the moving party upon all counsel of record or other parties. Withdrawal of a demand for a trial de novo shall not reinstate the arbitrators' award and the case shall proceed as if it had not been arbitrated.

(2)   Upon demand for a trial de novo and the payment to the Clerk required by paragraph (4) of this section, the action shall be placed on the calendar of the Court and treated for all purposes as if it had not been referred to arbitration, and any right of trial by jury that a party would otherwise have shall be preserved inviolate.

(3)   At the trial de novo, the Court shall not admit evidence that there had been an arbitration proceeding, the nature or amount of the award, or any other matter concerning the conduct of the arbitration proceeding.

(4) Upon making a demand for trial de novo the moving party shall, unless permitted to proceed in forma pauperis, deposit with the Clerk of the Court an amount equal to the arbitration fees of the arbitrators as provided in Section (b). The sum so deposited shall be returned to the party demanding a trial de novo in the event that party obtains a final judgment, exclusive of interest and costs, more favorable than the arbitration award. If the party demanding a trial de novo does not obtain a more favorable result after trial or if the Court determines that the party's conduct in seeking a trial de novo was in bad faith, the sum so deposited shall be paid by the Clerk to the Treasury of the United States.

Rule 83.8. Court-Annexed Mediation (Eastern District Only)

(a) Description. Mediation is a process in which parties and counsel agree to meet with a neutral mediator trained to assist them in settling disputes. The mediator improves communication across party lines, helps parties articulate their interests and understand those of the other party, probes the strengths and weaknesses of each party's legal positions, and identifies areas of agreement and helps generate options for a mutually agreeable resolution to the dispute. In all cases, mediation provides an opportunity to explore a wide range of potential solutions and to address interests that may be outside the scope of the stated controversy or which could not be addressed by judicial action. A hallmark of mediation is its capacity to expand traditional settlement discussions and broaden resolution options, often by exploring litigant needs and interests that may be formally independent of the legal issues in controversy.

(b) Mediation Procedures.

(1) *Eligible cases.* Judges and Magistrate Judges may designate civil cases for inclusion in the mediation program, and when doing so shall prepare an order to that effect. Alternatively, and subject to the availability of qualified mediators, the parties may consent to participation in the mediation program by preparing and executing a stipulation signed by all parties to the action and so-ordered by the Court.

    (A) Mediation deadline. Any court order designating a case for inclusion in the mediation program, however arrived at, may contain a deadline not to exceed six months from the date of entry on the docket of that order. This deadline may be extended upon motion to the Court for good cause shown.

[Authors' note: there is no section (b)(1)(B).]

(2) *Mediators.* Parties whose case has been designated for inclusion in the mediation program shall be offered the options of (a) using a mediator from the Court's panel, a listing of which is available in the Clerk's Office; (b) selecting a mediator on their own; or (c) seeking the assistance of a reputable neutral ADR organization in the selection of a mediator. * * *

(3) *Scheduling the mediation.* The mediator, however chosen, will contact all attorneys to fix the date and place of the first mediation session, which shall be held within thirty days of the date the mediator was appointed or at such other time as the Court may establish.

    (A) The Clerk's Office will provide counsel with copies of the Judge's order referring the case to the mediation program, the Clerk's Office notice of appointment of mediator (if applicable), and a copy of the program procedures.

[Authors' note: there is no section (b)(3)(B).]

(4) *Written mediation statements.* No less than fourteen days prior to the first mediation session, each party shall submit directly to the mediator a mediation statement not to exceed ten pages double-spaced, not including exhibits, outlining the key facts and legal issues in the case. The statement will also include a description of motions filed and their status, and any other information that will advance settlement prospects or make the mediation more productive. Mediation statements are not briefs and are not filed with the Court, nor shall the assigned Judge or Magistrate Judge have access to them.

(5) *Mediation session(s).* The mediator meets initially with all parties to the dispute and their counsel in a joint session. The mediator may hold mediation sessions in his/her office, or at the Court, or at such other place as the parties and the mediator shall agree. At this meeting, the mediator explains the mediation process and gives each party an opportunity to explain his or her views about the matters in dispute. There is then likely to be discussion and questioning among the parties as well as between the mediator and the parties.

    (A) Separate caucuses. At the conclusion of the joint session, the mediator will typically caucus individually with each party. Caucuses permit the mediator and the parties to explore more fully the needs and interests underlying the stated positions. In caucuses the mediator strives to facilitate settlement on matters in dispute and the possibilities for settlement. In some cases the mediator may offer specific suggestions for settlement; in other cases the mediator may help the parties generate creative settlement proposals.

    (B) Additional sessions. The mediator may conduct additional joint sessions to promote further direct discussion between the parties, or she/he may continue to work with the parties in private caucuses.

    (C) Conclusion. The mediation concludes when the parties reach a mutually acceptable resolution, when the parties fail to reach an agreement, on the date the Judge or Magistrate Judge specified as the mediation deadline in their designation order, or in the event no such date has been specified by the Court, at such other time as the parties and/or the mediator may determine. The mediator has no power to impose settlement and the mediation process is confidential, whether or not a settlement is reached.

(6) *Settlement.* If settlement is reached, in whole or in part, the agreement, which shall be binding upon all parties, will be put into writing and counsel will file a stipulation of dismissal or such other document as may be appropriate. If the case does not settle, the mediator will immediately notify the Clerk's Office, and the case or the portion of the case that has not settled will continue in the litigation process.

(c) Attendance at Mediation Sessions.

(1) In all civil cases designated by the Court for inclusion in the mediation program, attendance at one mediation session shall be mandatory: thereafter, attendance shall be voluntary. The Court requires of each party that the attorney who has primary responsibility for handling the trial of the matter attend the mediation sessions.

(2) In addition, the Court may require, and if it does not, the mediator may require the attendance at the mediation session of a party or its representative in the case of a business or governmental entity or a minor, with authority to settle the matter and to bind the party. This requirement reflects the Court's view that the principal values of mediation include affording litigants with an opportunity to articulate their positions and interests directly to the other parties and to a mediator and to hear, first hand, the other party's version of the matters in dispute. Mediation also enables parties to search directly with the other party for mutually agreeable solutions.

(d) Confidentiality.

(1) The parties will be asked to sign an agreement of confidentiality at the beginning of the first mediation session to the following effect:

    (A) Unless the parties otherwise agree, all written and oral communications made by the parties and the mediator in connection with or during any mediation session are confidential and may not be disclosed or used for any purpose unrelated to the mediation.

    (B) The mediator shall not be called by any party as a witness in any court proceeding related to the subject matter of the mediation unless related to the alleged misconduct of the mediator.

(2)   Mediators will maintain the confidentiality of all information provided to, or discussed with, them. The Clerk of Court and the ADR Administrator are responsible for program administration, evaluation, and liaison between the mediators, and the Court and will maintain strict confidentiality.

(3)   No papers generated by the mediation process will be included in Court files, nor shall the Judge or Magistrate Judge assigned to the case have access to them. Information about what transpires during mediation sessions will not at any time be made known to the Court, except to the extent required to resolve issues of noncompliance with the mediation procedures. However, communications made in connection with or during a mediation may be disclosed if all parties and, if appropriate as determined by the mediator, the mediator so agree. Nothing in this section shall be construed to prohibit parties from entering into written agreements resolving some or all of the case or entering and filing with the Court procedural or factual stipulations based on suggestions or agreements made in connection with a mediation.

(e) Oath and Disqualification of Mediator.

(1)   Each individual certified as a mediator shall take the oath or affirmation prescribed by 28 U.S.C. § 453 before serving as a mediator.

(2)   No mediator may serve in any matter in violation of the standards set forth in 28 U.S.C. § 455. If a mediator is concerned that a circumstance covered by subparagraph (a) of that section might exist, e.g., if the mediator's law firm has represented one or more of the parties, or if one of the lawyers who would appear before the mediator at the mediation session is involved in a case on which an attorney in the mediator's firm is working, the mediator shall promptly disclose that circumstance to all counsel in writing. A party who believes that the assigned mediator has a conflict of interest shall bring this concern to the attention of the Clerk's Office in writing, within fourteen (14) days of learning the source of the potential conflict or the objection to such a potential conflict shall be deemed to have been waived. Any objections that cannot be resolved by the parties in consultation with the Clerk's Office shall be referred to the Judge or Magistrate Judge who has designated the case for inclusion in the mediation program.

(3)   A party who believes that the assigned mediator has engaged in misconduct in such capacity shall bring this concern to the attention of the Clerk's Office in writing, within fourteen (14) days of learning of the alleged misconduct or the objection to such alleged misconduct shall be deemed to have been waived. Any objections that cannot be resolved by the parties in consultation with the Clerk's Office shall be referred to the Judge who has designated the case for inclusion in the mediation program.

(f) Services of the Mediators.

(1)   Participation by mediators in the program is on a voluntary basis. Each mediator shall receive a fee of $600 for the first four hours or less of the actual mediation. Time spent preparing for the mediation will not be compensated. Thereafter, the mediator shall be compensated at the rate of $250 per hour. The mediator's fee shall be paid by the parties to the mediation. Any party that is unable or unwilling to pay the fee may apply to the referring judge for a waiver of the fee, with a right of appeal to the district judge in the event the referral was made by a magistrate judge. Each member of the panel will be required to mediate a maximum of two cases pro bono each year, if requested by the Court. Attorneys serving on the Court's panel will be given credit for pro bono work.

(2)   Appointment to the Court's panel is for a three year term, subject to renewal. A panelist will not be expected to serve on more than two cases during any twelve month period and will not be required to accept each assignment offered. Repeated rejection of assignments will result in the attorney being dropped from the panel.

(g) Immunity of the Mediators. Mediators shall be immune from liability or suit with respect to their conduct as such to the maximum extent permitted by applicable law.

Rule 83.9.   Alternative Dispute Resolution (Southern District Only)

(a) Alternative Dispute Resolution Options:

The U.S. District Court for the Southern District of New York provides litigants with opportunities to discuss settlement through judicial settlement conferences and mediation.

(b) Definition of Mediation

In mediation, parties and counsel meet, sometimes collectively and sometimes individually, with a neutral third party (the mediator) who has been trained to facilitate confidential settlement discussions. The parties articulate their respective positions and interests and generate options for a mutually agreeable resolution to the dispute. The mediator assists the parties in reaching their own negotiated settlement by defining the issues, probing and assessing the strengths and weaknesses of each party's legal positions, and identifying areas of agreement and disagreement. The main benefits of mediation are that it can result in an expeditious and less costly resolution of the litigation, and can produce creative solutions to complex disputes often unavailable in traditional litigation.

(c) Administration of the Mediation Program

(1)   The Mediation Supervisor, appointed by the Clerk of the Court, shall administer the Court's mediation program. The Chief Judge shall appoint one or more District Judges or Magistrate Judges to oversee the program.

(2)   The Mediation Supervisor, in consultation with other Court personnel, shall ensure that information about the Court's mediation program is available on the Court's website which will be updated as needed.

(3)   The mediation program shall be governed by the "Procedures of the Mediation Program for the Southern District of New York," which sets forth specific and more detailed information regarding the mediation program, and which is available on the Court's official website (www.nysd.uscourts.gov) or from the Mediation Office.

(4)   In no event is the scheduling of mediation to interfere with any scheduling order of the Court.

(d) Consideration of Alternative Dispute Resolution

In all civil cases including those eligible for mediation pursuant to paragraph (e), each party shall consider the use of mediation or a judicial settlement conference and shall report to the assigned Judge at the initial Rule 16(b) case management conference, or subsequently, whether the party believes mediation or a judicial settlement conference may facilitate the resolution of the lawsuit. Judges are encouraged to note the availability of the mediation program and/or a judicial settlement conference before, at, or after the initial Rule 16(b) case management conference.

(e) Mediation Program Eligibility

(1)   All civil cases other than social security, habeas corpus, and tax cases are eligible for mediation, whether assigned to Manhattan or White Plains.

(2)   The Board of Judges may, by Administrative Order, direct that certain specified categories of cases shall automatically be submitted to the mediation program. The assigned District Judge or Magistrate Judge may issue a written order exempting a particular case with or without the request of the parties.

(3)   For all other cases, the assigned District Judge or Magistrate Judge may determine that a case is appropriate for mediation and may order that case to mediation, with or without the consent of the parties, before, at, or after the initial Rule 16(b) case management conference. Alternatively, the parties should notify the assigned Judge at any time of their desire to mediate.

(f)   Judicial Settlement Conferences

Judicial settlement conferences may be ordered by District Judges or Magistrate Judges with or without the request or consent of the parties.

PART VIII

Proposed Federal Statutes Regulating Civil Procedure

TABLE OF CONTENTS

Proposed Equality Act (Section 12. Juries)

S. 788, 116th Cong., 1st Sess. was introduced in the Senate on March 13, 2019. The purpose of Section 12 of the bill is to eliminate discrimination based on a person's sexual orientation or gender identity with respect to jury service in federal court.

The bill would amend Title 28, section 1862 by adding the words "including sexual orientation and gender identity" after the word "sex." If the bill were to be enacted, the statute would read as follows:

Section 1862: No citizen shall be excluded from service as a grand or petit juror in the district courts of the United States or in the Court of International Trade on account of race, color, religion, sex (including sexual orientation and gender identity), national origin, or economic status.

Proposed Federal Courts Access Act of 2019

S. 297, 116th Cong., 1st Sess. was introduced in the Senate on January 31, 2019. The bill was earlier introduced on July 19, 2018, in a previous session of Congress, but was not enacted. One purpose of the bill is to reduce the volume of cases in the federal courts based on diversity of citizenship. Another purpose is to ease removal of class actions from state courts to federal courts. The stated general purposes of the bill are to "assure fairer and more efficient civil litigation and prompt recoveries for claimants and defendants"; to diminish litigation abuses; and to "restore the intent of the framers of the Constitution of the United States by ensuring Federal court consideration of major controversies, consistent with diversity jurisdiction principles."

The bill would alter Title 28, section 1332(a) to raise the required amount in controversy for diversity jurisdiction to exceed $125,000. Currently, the statute requires the amount to exceed $75,000. It also would amend 28 U.S.C. § 1332(a)(1) to require the action to be between "not less than 1 plaintiff and 1 defendant who are citizens of different states." Currently the statute requires only that the action be between "citizens of different states."

With reference to class actions now dealt with in 28 U.S.C. § 1332(d), the bill would reduce the required amount in controversy from exceeding $5,000,000 to exceeding $125,000. Accordingly, in 28 U.S.C. § 1332(d)(6) it would reduce the required aggregate amount of claims of individual class members from over $5,000,000 to over $125,000. The bill also would eliminate current provisions § 1332(b)(3) and (4) under which the federal court can or must decline jurisdiction in cases in which class treatment is inappropriate.

The bill would dramatically alter removal from state courts of cases based on diversity of citizenship. Under the current law, Title 28, section 1441(b), a state court case cannot be removed if "any" defendant is a citizen of the state in which the action is brought. Under the proposed bill, removal

PROPOSED FEDERAL STATUTES

is barred only if "all" defendants are citizens of the state. Note that with respect to removable class actions, Title 28, section 1453(b) of the bill continues to allow any defendant to remove without the consent of all defendants.

Proposed Litigation Funding Transparency Act of 2019

S. 471, 116th Cong., 1st Sess. was introduced in the Senate on February 13, 2019. The purpose of the bill is to increase transparency and oversight of third-party litigation funding of class actions.

The bill would add Title 28, section 1716 as follows:

Section 1716. Third-party litigation funding disclosure

 (a) In General. In any class action, class counsel shall—

  (1) disclose in writing to the court and all other named parties to the class action the identity of any commercial enterprise, other than a class member or class counsel of record, that has a right to receive payment that is contingent on the receipt of monetary relief in the class action by settlement, judgment, or otherwise; and

  (2) produce for inspection and copying, except as otherwise stipulated or ordered by the court, any agreement creating the contingent right.

 (b) Timing. The disclosure required by subsection (a) shall be made not later than the later of—

  (1) 10 days after execution of any agreement described in subsection (a)(2); or

  (2) the time of service of the action.

The bill also would amend Title 28, section 1407 by redesignating subsections (g) and (h) as subsections (h) and (i) respectively, and insert after subsection (f) the following:

Section 1407(g)(1): In any coordinated or consolidated pretrial proceedings conducted pursuant to this section, counsel for a party asserting a claim whose civil action is assigned to or directly filed in the proceedings shall—

 (A) disclose in writing to the court and all other parties the identity of the commercial enterprise, other than the named parties of counsel, that has a right to receive payment that is contingent on the receipt of monetary relief in the civil action by settlement, judgment, or otherwise; and

 (B) produce for inspection and copying, except as otherwise stipulated or ordered by the court, any agreement creating the contingent right.

(2) The disclosure required by paragraph (1) shall be made not later than the later of—

 (A) 10 days after execution of any agreement described in paragraph (1)(B); or

 (B) the time the civil action becomes subject to this section.

Proposed Protect the Gig Economy Act of 2019

H.R. 76, 116th Cong., 1st Sess. was introduced in the House of Representatives on January 3, 2019. The primary purpose of the bill is to protect the "gig economy" and small businesses that operate in large part through free-lance contractor services from threats of class-action litigation.

The bill would add a new paragraph (5) to Federal Rule of Civil Procedure 23(a) expanding the preliminary requirements for class certification to include a new requirement, stating:

5. the claim does not allege the misclassification of employees as independent contractors.

PROPOSED FEDERAL STATUTES

Proposed Stopping Foreign Businesses Sanctuary Act of 2019

H.R. 702, 116th Cong., 1st Sess. was introduced in the House of Representatives on January 22, 2019. The purpose of the bill is to provide for jurisdiction of federal and state courts over foreign state-owned or state-controlled entities that conduct commercial activity in the United States.

The bill would add sections 1605(e) and 1603(d)(2) of Title 28 as follows:

Section 1605(e). Notwithstanding any other provision of law, an entity is not immune from the jurisdiction of the courts of the United States or of the States if the entity—

(1) is incorporated in a foreign state in which state-owned or state-controlled entities commonly engage in commercial activity; and

(2) conducts commercial activity in the United States.

Section 1603(d)(2). For purposes of this chapter, a commercial activity of an agency or instrumentality of a foreign state, or an entity described in section 1605(e), shall be attributable to any corporate affiliate of the agency, instrumentality, or entity that—

(A) directly or indirectly owns a majority of the shares of the agency, instrumentality, or entity; and

(B) is also an agency or instrumentality of a foreign state, or an entity described in section 1605(e).

PART IX

Plaintiffs' Complaints

in

Bell Atlantic Corp. v. Twombly,

in

Ashcroft v. Iqbal,

and in

Erickson v. Pardus

TABLE OF CONTENTS

Complaint in Bell Atlantic Corp. v. Twombly

UNITED STATES DISTRICT COURT

SOUTHERN DISTRICT OF NEW YORK

No. 02 CIV. 10220 (GEL.)

William Twombly and Lawrence Marcus, individually and
on behalf of all others similarly situated, Plaintiffs,

v.

Bell Atlantic Corporation, BellSouth Corporation, Qwest Communications International
Inc., SBC Communications Inc., and Verizon Communications Inc.,

Defendants.

CONSOLIDATED AMENDED CLASS ACTION
COMPLAINT JURY TRIAL DEMANDED

Plaintiffs, by and through their undersigned attorneys, for their Amended Class Action Complaint allege the claims set forth herein. Plaintiffs' claim as to themselves and their own actions, as set forth in ¶¶ 9 and 10 are based upon their own knowledge. All other allegations are based upon information and belief pursuant to the investigation of counsel.

I.

NATURE OF THE ACTION

1.   This lawsuit is brought as a class action on behalf of all individuals and entities who purchased local telephone and/or high speed internet services in the continental United States (excluding Alaska and Hawaii) from at least as early as February 8, 1996 and continuing to present (the "Class Period").

2.   The Telecommunications Act of 1996, 47 U.S.C. §§ 151 to 614 (the "Act") was designed to promote competition for local telephone services by opening the markets to effective competition. The purpose, intent and requirements of the Act are to create competition without delay in the local telephone services markets so that the public's local telephone bills and charges will be reduced as soon as possible by virtue of such competition.

3.   Local telephone services include traditional dial tone primarily used to make or receive voice, fax, or analog modem calls from a residence or business and exchange access services which allow long distance carriers to use their local exchange facilities to originate and terminate long distance calls to end users. Local telephone services also include, but are not limited to, custom calling services such as Caller ID, Call Waiting, Voice Mail and other advanced services. High speed internet services include circuits that connect customers to the internet at speeds in excess of 56K such as, but not limited to, T1 lines, asynchronous transfer mode circuits, frame relay circuits, ISDN, and digital subscriber lines ("DSL"). The rates concerning certain features or services are either not subject to tariff filing requirements and/or are not subject to any meaningful review.

4.   Plaintiffs allege that Defendants entered into a contract, combination or conspiracy to prevent competitive entry in their respective local telephone and/or high speed internet services markets by, among other things, agreeing not to compete with one another and to stifle attempts by others to compete with them and otherwise allocating customers and markets to one another.

5.   As a direct and proximate result of Defendants' unlawful contract, combination or conspiracy, Plaintiffs and members of the Class allege that Defendants have hindered the development of the local telephone and/or high speed internet services markets. Plaintiffs and members of the Class further allege that they have been and continue to be denied the benefits of free and unrestrained competition for local telephone and/or high speed internet services. Plaintiffs and members of the Class

have, therefore, been forced to pay supracompetitive prices for such services causing them to sustain injury to their business or property.

II.

JURISDICTION AND VENUE

6.   Plaintiffs bring this class action under Sections 4 and 16 of the Clayton Act, 15 U.S.C. §§ 15 and 26, to recover treble damages and injunctive relief as well as reasonable attorneys' fees and costs with respect to injuries arising from violations by Defendants of the federal antitrust laws, including Section 1 of the Sherman Act. 15 U.S.C. § 1.

7.   The Court has federal question subject matter jurisdiction over this matter pursuant to 28 U.S.C. §§ 1331, 1337(a) and Sections 4 and 16 of the Clayton Act, 15 U.S.C. §§ 15(a) and 26. The Court has supplemental jurisdiction over the state antitrust law claims pursuant to 28 U.S.C. § 1367.

8.   Venue in this district is proper pursuant to 28 U.S.C. § 1391(b)(2) because a part of the events or omissions giving rise to the claims occurred in this district, and pursuant to 28 U.S.C. § 1391(b)(3) and 15 U.S.C. §§ 15 and 22 because Defendants Bell Atlantic and Verizon have maintained or maintain a principal place of business within this district.

III.

PARTIES

9.   Plaintiff William Twombly is a resident of Bethel, Connecticut. At times relevant herein, William Twombly was a resident of New York, New York and purchased local telephone and/or high speed internet services from Defendants Bell Atlantic Corporation or Verizon Communications, Inc.

10.   Plaintiff Lawrence Marcus is a resident of Maple Glen, Pennsylvania. At times relevant herein, Lawrence Marcus purchased local telephone and/or high speed internet services from Defendants Bell Atlantic Corporation or Verizon Communications, Inc.

11.   Defendant Bell Atlantic Corporation is a Delaware corporation with its principal place of business at 1095 Avenue of Americas, New York, New York. Bell Atlantic Corporation is a telecommunications company with principal operating subsidiaries (together with the parent company "Bell Atlantic") that provide local telephone and/or high speed internet services to subscribers in Connecticut, Delaware, Maryland, Massachusetts, Maine, New Hampshire, New York, New Jersey, Pennsylvania, Rhode Island, Vermont, Virginia, West Virginia and the District of Columbia.

12.   Defendant BellSouth Corporation is a Delaware corporation with its principal place of business at 1155 Peachtree Street, N.E., Atlanta, Georgia. BellSouth Corporation is a telecommunications company that, through its wholly owned subsidiaries, including but not limited to Bell South Telecommunications, Inc. (together with the parent company "BellSouth"), provides local telephone and/or high speed internet services to millions of subscribers in Alabama, Florida, Georgia, Kentucky, Louisiana, Mississippi, North Carolina, South Carolina and Tennessee ("BellSouth").

13.   Defendant Qwest Communications International, Inc., is a Delaware corporation with its principal place of business at 1801 California Street, Denver, Colorado. Qwest Communications International, Inc., is a telecommunications company that, through its wholly-owned subsidiaries including but not limited to Qwest Corporation, Inc. (together with the parent company "Qwest"), provides local telephone and/or high speed internet services in fourteen states, including Arizona, Colorado, Idaho, Iowa, Minnesota, Montana, Nebraska, New Mexico, North Dakota, Oregon, South Dakota, Utah, Washington, and Wyoming ("Qwest").

14.   Defendant SBC Communications, Inc., is a Delaware corporation with its principal place of business at 175 East Houston, San Antonio, Texas. SBC Communications, Inc., is a telecommunications company that, through its operating subsidiaries including but not limited to SBC Ameritech, SBC Nevada Bell, SBC Pacific Bell, SBC SNET and SBC Southwestern Bell (together with the parent company "SBC"), provides local telephone and/or high speed internet services to subscribers

in Arkansas, California, Connecticut, Florida, Illinois, Indiana, Kansas, Michigan, Missouri, Nevada, Ohio, Oklahoma, Texas and Wisconsin.

15. Defendant Verizon Communications, Inc. ("Verizon") is a Delaware corporation with its principal place of business at 1095 Avenue of Americas, New York, New York. GTE Corporation ("GTE") merged with and became a wholly-owned subsidiary of Bell Atlantic. Bell Atlantic now does business as Verizon Communications, Inc.

IV.

CO-CONSPIRATORS

16. Various other persons, firms, corporations and associations, not named in this Complaint, have participated in the violations alleged herein and have performed acts and made statements in furtherance thereof.

V.

BACKGROUND

A. The Bell Operating System and Divestiture

17. During the early part of its approximately 120-year history, the telephone industry experienced varying periods of competition, monopolization and regulation. By 1934, the Bell System, consisting of Bell Operating Companies, along with American Telephone and Telegraph Company ("AT&T"), owned 80 percent of all the local telephone lines and services in the United States and owned a monopoly long-distance network. The Bell Operating Companies were wholly-owned subsidiaries of AT&T.

18. In 1934, the Communications Act of 1934 was adopted. That act severed regulation of the telephone industry from the Interstate Commerce Commission and provided for the creation of the Federal Communications Commission ("FCC") to regulate interstate telephone, telegraph and radio companies. Interstate and international telephone services fell under the aegis of the FCC, and intrastate telephone services became regulated under the auspices of respective state commissions. Once a telephone communications service crossed a state line, it fell under the jurisdiction of the FCC.

19. In 1974, the United States filed a lawsuit against AT&T alleging that it had monopolized and conspired to restrain trade in the manufacture, distribution, sale and installation of telephones, telephone apparatus equipment and materials and supplies in violation of §§ 1, 2, and 3 of the Sherman Act, 15 U.S.C. §§ 1, 2, and 3. The basic theory of the government's case, as explained by the District Court, was that AT&T had unlawfully used its control of local exchange facilities to suppress competition in related markets, such as the markets for long distance services, which are dependent upon access to the local exchange to originate and terminate calls. United States v. AT&T, 524 F.Supp. 1336, 1352 (D.D.C. 1981).

20. In 1982, the United States and AT&T agreed to settle the case through the entry of a consent decree. In 1982, United States District Court Judge Harold H. Greene signed the Modified Final Judgment, settling the antitrust suit against AT&T. The Modified Final Judgment was based on divestiture; AT&T was required to divest itself of its twenty-two Bell Operating Companies ("BOCs"). The BOCs provided the means by which local telephone service was furnished, Bell customers gained access to the network for both local and long distance telecommunications services through the BOCs. The Modified Final Judgment, however, imposed certain business restrictions on the newly divested BOCs. Specifically, the BOCs were prohibited from providing inter-LATA services (which are long distance services involving calls that terminated outside the "local access and transport area" in which they originate, as defined in the Modified Final Judgment), or any non-telecommunications services, and from manufacturing telecommunications equipment. In addition, the Modified Final Judgment required the BOCs to provide all interexchange carriers (i.e., long distance providers) with exchange access that was equal in type, quality and price to the access provided to AT&T. United States v.

COMPLAINT IN BELL ATLANTIC CORP. V. TWOMBLY

AT&T, 552 F.Supp. 131, 227 (D.D.C. 1982), aff'd sub nom., Maryland v. United States, 460 U.S. 1001, 103 S.Ct. 1240, 75 L.Ed.2d 472 (1983).

21.   On January 1, 1984, divestiture of the Bell System by AT&T divested the seven Regional Bell Operating Companies ("RBOCs") and exited the local telephone business. The RBOCs were barred from providing long distance services. The seven RBOCs became known as the Baby Bells and included: Ameritech; SBC Communications; Pacific Telesis; Bell South; US West; Bell Atlantic; and NYNEX. SBC became the parent corporation of Southwestern Bell, and Pacific Telesis became the parent corporation of Pacific Bell and Nevada bell. SBC and Pacific Telesis merged in early 1997. NYNEX and Bell Atlantic merged in mid-1997 and became known as Bell Atlantic Corporation. Bell Atlantic later merged with GTE Corporation and is now doing business as Verizon Communications, Inc.

22.   Local telephone companies such as the Bell Operating Companies are commonly referred to as local exchange carriers ("LECs") and provide business and residential customers with local telephone and/or high speed internet services.

23.   In addition to the Bell Operating Companies, there are hundreds of other local exchange carriers operating in the United States. These local exchange carriers generally offer the same services as the Bell Operating Companies. Although GTE was not one of the original Bell Operating Companies, prior to merging with Bell Atlantic it acquired local telephone systems in 28 states and was one of the largest local phone companies in the nation in terms of telephone lines. Local exchange carriers historically operated in their local franchise areas free of competition, pursuant to exclusive franchises granted by state regulatory authorities.

24.   A consent decree also was entered against GTE in 1984. United States v. GTE Corp., 1985–1 Trade Cas. (CCH) § 66.355 (D.D.C. 1984) ("GTE Consent Decree"). The GTE Consent Decree was prompted by GTE's acquisition of one of the largest long-distance companies in the United States, and was based upon the same concerns underlying the AT&T consent decree with the United States. Under the GTE Consent Decree, operating companies (i.e., the local exchange providers) were prohibited from providing long distance services, but GTE Corporation itself was permitted to provide long distance services through other subsidiaries. GTE was required to maintain total separation between its long distance operations and the GTE operating companies, so that those companies could not use their position as exclusive local telephone service providers within their franchised areas to lessen competition in long distance services.

B.   The Telecommunications Act of 1996

25.   On February 8, 1996, the Telecommunications Act of 1996 became law when it was signed by President Clinton. Pub. L. No. 104, 110 Stat. 56. The Act amends the Communications Act of 1934. (See 47 U.S.C. § 609, Historical and Statutory Notes.) The Act changed the landscape of federal and state telecommunications regulatory policies and the telecommunications industry.

26.   The Act adopts a pro-competitive framework for the telecommunications industry in the United States. It opens the markets for both local telephone and long-distance services to effective competition.

27.   Because of their prior unique existence as government granted monopolies and the benefits that they enjoyed as government granted monopolies, the Act requires that the LECs, including Defendants, must provide potential competitors access and connections to their lines and equipment on just, reasonable and non-discriminatory terms.

28.   The Act also requires the incumbent local exchange companies ("ILEC") to provide competitors with the same quality of service that the incumbent local exchange carriers provide to themselves or their own customers. The Act specifically defines an ILEC as follows: "With respect to an area, the local exchange carrier that on February 8, 1996, provided telephone exchange service in such area." 47 U.S.C. § 251. The seven original RBOCs, GTE and Defendants herein are ILECs.

29. With respect to long-distance service, the Act establishes a detailed mechanism for the RBOCs to compete for the first time in the long distance business. Unlike the RBOCs, GTE was allowed to expand into long-distance telephone service as soon as the Act became law on February 8, 1996.

30. Pursuant to the Act, before the respective RBOCs can offer long-distance telephone service, they must, inter alia, satisfy a 14-point checklist of requirements and demonstrate that there is a competition in their respective local markets. It is up to the FCC in coordination with the Department of Justice and various state public utilities commissions to decide, upon request by an RBOC, when the RBOC has met the requirements.

31. Section 251 of the Act (47 U.S.C. § 251) imposes certain obligations on ILECs designed to permit new entrants to use some or all of the ILECs' networks to offer local-exchange services.

32. Section 251 of the Act requires an ILEC to: (1) allow a competitor to interconnect with its network so that the competitor can provide calls to and from that network; (2) sell to competitors access to components of its network, called network elements, on an unbundled or individual basis; and (3) sell its retail telephone services to competitors at wholesale prices. All of these requirements of an ILEC are to be provided by the ILEC "on rates, terms, and conditions that are just, reasonable, and nondiscriminatory." Id. Section 251 imposes specific obligations on telecommunications carriers designed to promote competition in local exchange markets across the country. Federal Register/Vol. 61, No. 169, August 29, 1996, at 45476.

33. The Act directed the FCC to establish regulations to implement § 251's requirements within six months of its enactment. On August 8, 1996, the FCC released its Report and Order ("Report and Order").

34. The Report and Order promulgated "national rules and regulations implementing the statutory requirements of the Act intended to encourage the development of competition in local exchange and exchange access markets." Federal Register/Vol. 61, No. 169, August 29, 1996, at 45476.

35. GTE and the RBOCs appealed the Report and Order to the 8th Circuit, and on October 15, 1996, the 8th Circuit stayed the Report and Order, including its pricing rules and regulations, pending a decision on the merits. Iowa Utils. Bd. v. FCC, 109 F.3d 418 (8th Cir. 1996). The group defending the Report and Order included, among others, the FCC and the U.S. Department of Justice.

36. On July 18, 1997, the U.S. Court of Appeals for the Eighth Circuit filed its Opinion in the Iowa Utilities Board v. FCC case. Iowa Utils. Bd. v. FCC, 120 F.3d 753 (8th Cir. 1997). The Court vacated certain provisions of the FCC's Report and Order and upheld the remainder. Specifically, the Court stated: "We decline the petitioners' request to vacate the FCC's entire First Report and Order and limit our rejection of FCC rules only to those that we have specifically overturned in this opinion." Id. At 819. In a footnote, the Court stated: "In total we vacate the following provisions: 47 C.F.R. §§ 51.303, 51.305(a)(4), 51.311(c)–f51.317 (vacated only to the extent this rule establishes a presumption that a network element must be unbundled if it is technically feasible to do so), 51.405, 51.501–51.515 (inclusive except for 51.515(b), 51.601–51.611 (inclusive), 51.701–51.717 (inclusive except for 51.701) 51.703 51.709(b), 51.7119a0910, 51.7159d0 and 51.717 but only as they apply to CMRS providers), 51.809 First Report and Order ¶¶ 101–103, 121–128, 180. We also vacate the proxy range for line ports used in the delivery of basic residential and business exchange services established in the FCC's Order on Reconsideration dated September 27 1996." Id.

C. The RBOCs' Market Allocation and Refusal to Compete

37. The 1996 Telecommunications Act authorized RBOCs to offer local telephone and/or high speed internet services in each other's territories, yet they have stayed almost completely out of one another's markets. Indeed, "[t]he major telephone companies have not sought to provide local telephone service outside of their home territories." Consumer Federation of America, Lessons From 1996 Telecommunications Act: Deregulation Before Meaningful Competition Spells Consumer Disaster, February 2001, p. 2. "Major incumbent service providers have failed to attack markets within

their industry . . . [m]ajor incumbent service providers have failed to use their facilities to attack cross markets." Id. at 20.

38. "It was hoped that the large incumbent local monopoly companies (RBOCs) might attack their neighbors' service areas, as they are the best situated to do so. But such competition has not happened. The incumbent local exchange carriers (RBOCs) have simply not tried to enter each other's service territories in any significant way." Consumer Federation of America, Lessons From 1996 Telecommunications Act: Deregulation Before Meaningful Competition Spells Consumer Disaster, February 2001, p. 13.

39. Although the RBOCs contend that CLECs are hurting them by leasing network components at below-cost rates, the RBOCs have refrained from engaging in meaningful head-to-head competition in each other's markets. For example, "[i]n New York, SBC served a grand total of six residential lines at the end of 2001." Joan Campion, Competition Is Vital For Phone Customers, Chicago Tribune, Nov. 11, 2002, Commentary pg. 20.

40. The failure of the RBOCs to compete with one another would be anomalous in the absence of an agreement among the RBOCs not to compete with one another in view of the fact that in significant respects, the territories that they service are non-contiguous. As reflected in Exhibit A hereto, SBC serves most of the State of Connecticut even though Verizon rather than SBC serves the surrounding states. SBC serves California and Nevada, even though Qwest serves the other surrounding states. Similarly, there are many relatively small areas within the States of California, Texas, Illinois, Michigan, Ohio, Wisconsin, Indiana and other states that are served by Verizon, even though SBC serves all surrounding territories, as illustrated in Exhibit B hereto,[1] The failure of the RBOCs that serve the surrounding territories to make significant attempts to compete in the surrounded territories is strongly suggestive of conspiracy, since the service of such surrounded territories presents the RBOC serving surrounding territories with an especially attractive business opportunity that such RBOCs have not meaningfully pursued.

41. In competing for business in Connecticut, Verizon's predominance in the surrounding states would have provided it with substantial competitive advantages. In competing for business in California and Nevada, Qwest's predominance in surrounding states would have given it substantial competitive advantages. In competing for the business in the many smaller territories that Verizon serves that are surrounded by territories served by other RBOCs, the dominance of those other RBOCs in surrounding areas would have given them substantial competitive advantages. Nevertheless, Verizon has not sought to compete in a meaningful manner with SBC in Connecticut, Qwest has not sought to compete meaningfully with SBC in California and Nevada, and the RBOCs that serve the areas surrounding the smaller areas served by Verizon, as illustrated in Exhibit B hereto, have not sought to compete meaningfully with Verizon in those smaller areas. In the absence of an agreement not to compete, it is especially unlikely that there would have been no efforts by surrounding and dominant RBOCs to compete in such surrounded territories.

42. On October 31, 2002, Richard Notebaert, the former Chief Executive Officer of Ameritech, who sold the company to Defendant SBC in 1999 and who currently serves as the Chief Executive Officer of Defendant Qwest, was quoted in a Chicago Tribune article as saying it would be fundamentally wrong to compete in the SBC/Ameritech territory, adding "it might be a good way to turn a quick dollar but that doesn't make it right." Jon Van, Ameritech Customers Off Limits: Notebaert, Chicago Tribune, Oct. 31, 2002 Business, pg. 1.

---

[1] On information and belief, all or substantially all of the small areas served by Verizon that are surrounded by territories served by other RBOCs, as illustrated in Exhibit B hereto, were acquired by Verizon not as the result of competition by it with other RBOCs since the time of enactment of the Telecommunications Act, but rather through acquisition of territories served by Verizon's corporate predecessors-in-interest who served those areas prior to that time. [Note that exhibit B is not included in this excerpt.]

43.   The pronouncement that Qwest would forgo lucrative opportunities in its sister monopoly markets and in its principal line of business came as Qwest announced a Third Quarter loss of $214 million and 13% fall in revenue.

44.   On November 8, 2002, in response to Notebaert's remarks, the Illinois Coalition For Competitive Telecom called Notebaert's statement "evidence of potential collusion among regional Bell phone monopolies to not compete against one another and kill off potential competitors in local phone service." Illinois CLECS Assail Notebaert, State Telephone Regulation Report, Comment, Vol. 20, No. 22. According to the article, "[t]he CLEC group said Notebaert indicated that the Bells' strategy was to divide the country into local phone 'fiefdoms,' not to compete against each other, and to devote their collective efforts to 'eliminating would-be competitors in local service.'" Id.

45.   On December 18, 2002, United States Representatives John Conyers, Jr. of Michigan and Zoe Lofgren of California sent a letter to United States Attorney General John Ashcroft requesting that the U.S. Department of Justice, Antitrust Division investigate whether the RBOCs are violating the antitrust laws by carving up their market territories and deliberately refraining from competing with one another. Jon Van, Lawmakers Seek Probe of Bells; Do Firms Agree Not To Compete, Chicago Tribune, Dec. 19, 2002, Business, pg. 2; James S. Granelli, Federal Probe of Baby Bells Urged; Comments By Chairman of Qwest Raise Questions About the Competitive Zeal of the Regional Phone Companies, Los Angeles Times, Dec. 19, 2002, Business, Part 3, Pg. 3; Conyers Asks Justice Dept. To Investigate Bells On Anticompetitive Practices, Communications Daily, Dec. 20, 2002, Today's News. Representatives Conyers and Lofgren questioned the extent to which the ROBCs' "very apparent noncompetition policy in each others' markets is coordinated." Letter to The Honorable John D. Ashcroft dated December 18, 2002, p. 2.

46.   The RBOCs do indeed communicate amongst themselves through a myriad of organizations, including but not limited to the United States Telecom Association, the Tele-Messaging Industry Association, the Alliance for Telecommunications Industry Solutions, Telecordia, Alliance for Public Technology, the Telecommunications Industry Association and the Progress and Freedom Foundation.

47.   Defendants have engaged in parallel conduct in order to prevent competition in their respective local telephone and/or high speed internet service markets. "They have refused to open their markets by dragging their feet in allowing competitors to interconnect, refusing to negotiate in good faith, litigating every nook and cranny of the law, and avoiding head-to-head competition like the plague." Consumer Federation of America, Lessons From 1996 Telecommunications Act: Deregulation Before Meaningful Competition Spells Consumer Disaster, February 2001, p. 1. Defendants also have engaged and continue to engage in unanimity of action by committing one or more of the following wrongful acts in furtherance of a common anticompetitive objective to prevent competition from Competitive Local Exchange Carriers ("CLECs") in the their respective local telephone and/or high speed internet services markets:

   (a)   Defendants have failed to provide the same quality of service to competitors that Defendants provided to their own retail customers;

   (b)   Defendants have failed to provide access to their operational support systems ("OSS"), including on-line customer service records ("CSRs"), on a nondiscriminatory basis that places competitors at parity. Moreover, competitors do not have access to unbundled elements on the same basis on which Defendants accessed the same elements;

   (c)   Defendants' competitors have experienced undue delays in the provisioning of unbundled elements. Such delays are discriminatory and preclude competitors from offering service as attractive to customers as Defendants' services and on a basis that places competitors at parity with a respective Defendant;

   (d)   Defendants have billed customers of competitors who are converted from Defendants' retail service. As a result of Defendants' practices, customers of competitors are double-billed. Defendants' practices have severely impacted competitors' relationships with customers;

(e)   Defendants have failed to provide interconnection between the network and those of competitors that is equal in quality to the interconnection that each provided itself;

(f)   Defendants have refused to sell to competitors, on just, reasonable, and non-discriminatory terms, access to components of the network on an unbundled or individual basis;

(g)   Defendants have refused to sell to competitors local telephone and/or high speed internet services at wholesale prices that are just, reasonable and nondiscriminatory, thereby preventing Defendants' competitors from being able to competitively resell the services to Plaintiffs and members of the Class;

(h)   Defendants have refused to allow competitors to connect to essential facilities, consisting of, but not limited to, local telephone lines, equipment, transmission and central switching stations (central office) and "local loop" on just, reasonable and non-discriminatory terms;

(i)   Defendants have used discriminatory and error filled methods to bill local telephone service competitors in order to discourage competition by making it virtually impossible for competitors to audit the bills they received from Defendants;

(j)   Defendants have imposed slow and inaccurate manual order processing causing competitors to devote significant time, effort and expense to identify and rectify problems to ensure that orders were ultimately processed correctly;

(k)   Defendants have used monopoly power in their respective wholesale local telephone and/or high speed internet services market in order to gain or maintain a competitive advantage in the retail market for the provision of local telephone and/or high speed internet services; and

(l)   Defendants have used their respective monopoly power and exclusive control over essential facilities consisting of, but not limited to, local telephone lines, equipment, transmission and central switching stations (central office) and "local loop" to negotiate agreements on unfair terms with competitors who were seeking access to their respective local telephone networks. Each Defendant, possessing the exclusive and sole source of entry into its own local telephone and/or high speed internet services market, was in a superior bargaining position to competitors and potential competitors and used that superior bargaining position to dictate unfair terms upon competitors.

48.   The structure of the market for local telephone services is such as to make a market allocation agreement feasible, in that the four defendants, taken together, account for as much as ninety percent or more of the markets for local telephone services within the 48 contiguous states. Elaborate communications thus would not have been necessary in order to enable Defendants to agree to allocate territories and to refrain from competing with one another. A successful conspiracy among the Defendants to allocate territories would not require such frequent communications as to make prompt detection likely.

49.   If one of the Defendants had broken ranks and commenced competition in another's territory the others would quickly have discovered that fact. The likely immediacy of such discovery makes a territorial allocation agreement among the Defendants more feasible, more readily enforceable, and more probable. In this respect as well, the structure of the market was conducive to an agreement among the Defendants to allocate territories to one another.

50.   Had any one of the Defendants not sought to prevent CLECs (other than the other Defendants) from competing effectively within that Defendant's allocated territory in the ways described above, the resulting greater competitive inroads into that Defendant's territory would have revealed the degree to which competitive entry by CLECs would have been successful in the other territories in the absence of such conduct. In addition, the greater success of any CLEC that made substantial competitive inroads into one Defendant's territory would have enhanced the likelihood that such a CLEC might present a competitive threat in other Defendants' territories as well. In these respects as well as others, Defendants had compelling common motivations to include in their unlawful

horizontal agreement an agreement that each of them would engage in a course of concerted conduct calculated to prevent effective competition from CLECs in each of the allocated territories.

51. In the absence of any meaningful competition between the RBOCs in one another's markets, and in light of the parallel course of conduct that each engaged in to prevent competition from CLECs within their respective local telephone and/or high speed internet services markets and the other facts and market circumstances alleged above, Plaintiffs allege upon information and belief that Defendants have entered into a contract, combination or conspiracy to prevent competitive entry in their respective local telephone and/or high speed internet services markets and have agreed not to compete with one another and otherwise allocated customers and markets to one another.

VI.

INTERSTATE TRADE AND COMMERCE

52. At times relevant herein, Defendants and/or their subsidiaries provided local and regional telephone and/or high speed internet services across state lines, and regularly and frequently solicited customers and sent bills and received payments via the mail throughout the United States. The marketing, sale and provision of local telephone and/or high speed internet services regularly occurs in and substantially affects interstate trade and commerce.

VII.

CLASS ACTION ALLEGATIONS

53. Plaintiffs bring this action pursuant to Rule 23 of the Federal Rules of Civil Procedure on behalf of the following class:

> All persons or entities who reside or resided in the continental United States (excluding Alaska and Hawaii) and are or were subscribers of local telephone and/or high speed internet services (the "Class") from February 8, 1996 to present (the "Class Period"). Excluded from the Class are the Defendants and any parent, subsidiary, corporate affiliate, officer, director or employee of a Defendant and any judge or magistrate judge assigned to entertain any portion of this case.

54. The members of the Class are so numerous and geographically dispersed that joinder of all members is impracticable. The exact number and identity of Class members is unknown to Plaintiffs but can readily be ascertained from books and records maintained by Defendants or their agents. Upon information and belief, there are millions of local telephone and/or high speed internet services subscribers in the United States who are within the defined Class.

55. There are questions of law or fact common to the Class members concerning:

(a) whether Defendants and their co-conspirators engaged in a contract, combination or conspiracy to prevent competitive entry in their respective local telephone and/or high speed internet services markets by, among other things, agreeing not to compete with one another and otherwise allocating customers and markets to one another;

(b) the duration and extent of the contract, combination or conspiracy alleged herein;

(c) whether the Defendants were participants in the contract, combination or conspiracy alleged herein;

(d) whether the alleged contract, combination or conspiracy violated Section 1 of the Sherman Act, 15 U.S.C. § 1;

(e) whether the alleged contract, combination or conspiracy caused injury and damage to Plaintiffs and members of the Class and the appropriate measure of damages;

(f) whether a Defendant's conduct violated state antitrust laws;

(g) whether Plaintiffs and members of the Class are entitled to injunctive and other equitable relief; and

(h)   whether Defendants and their co-conspirators fraudulently concealed the conspiracy alleged herein.

56.   The claims of Plaintiffs are typical of the claims of each of the members of the Class. Plaintiffs and members of the Class purchased local telephone and/or high speed internet services from a Defendant or a competitor of a Defendant in the continental United States.

57.   Plaintiffs will fairly and adequately protect the interests of the Class. There is no conflict of interest between Plaintiffs and other members of the Class and Plaintiffs are represented by experienced class action counsel.

58.   Defendants have acted in an unlawful manner on grounds generally applicable to all members of the Class.

59.   The questions of law or of fact common to the claims of the Class predominate over any questions affecting only individual class members, so that the certification of this case as a class action is superior to other available methods for the fair and efficient adjudication of the controversy.

60.   For these reasons, the proposed Class may be certified under Fed. R. Civ. P. 23.

VIII.

FRAUDULENT CONCEALMENT

61.   Plaintiffs and members of the Class had no knowledge of the contract, combination or conspiracy or any facts alleged herein which might have led to the discovery thereof until shortly before the filing of this Complaint. Plaintiffs and members of the Class could not have discovered the contract, combination or conspiracy at an earlier date by the exercise of due diligence because of the affirmative, deceptive practices and techniques of secrecy employed by Defendants. Through these acts of secrecy and deception, which included affirmative acts to hide their wrongdoing, Defendants actively misled Plaintiffs and the Class about the existence and terms of their contract, combination or conspiracy to prevent competitive entry in their respective local telephone and/or high speed internet services markets by, among other things, agreeing not to compete with one another and to stifle attempts by others to compete with them and otherwise allocating customers and markets to one another.

COUNT I

Violation of Sherman Act 15 U.S.C. § 1

62.   Plaintiffs repeat and reallege the allegations contained in paragraphs 1 through 61 as if fully set forth herein.

63.   Defendants and their co-conspirators have engaged in a horizontal contract, combination or conspiracy in unreasonable restraint of trade in violation of Section 1 of the Sherman Act. 15 U.S.C. § 1.

64.   Beginning at least as early as February 6, 1996, and continuing to the present, the exact dates being unknown to Plaintiffs, Defendants and their co-conspirators engaged in a contract, combination or conspiracy to prevent competitive entry in their respective local telephone and/or high speed internet services markets by, among other things, agreeing not to compete with one another and to stifle attempts by others to compete with them and otherwise allocating customers and markets to one another in violation to Section 1 of the Sherman Act. 15 U.S.C. § 1.

65.   The contract, combination or conspiracy has had and will continue to have the following effects:

(a)   competition in the local telephone and/or high speed internet services markets have been unlawfully restrained, suppressed or eliminated;

(b)   Plaintiffs and members of the Class have been denied the benefits of free, open and unrestricted competition in the local telephone and/or high speed internet services markets; and

COMPLAINT IN BELL ATLANTIC CORP. V. TWOMBLY

(c)   the prices of local telephone and/or high speed internet services in the United States have been fixed, raised, maintained or stabilized at artificially high and noncompetitive levels.

66.   As a direct and proximate result of Defendants' unlawful conduct, Plaintiffs and members of the Class have suffered injury to their business or property and have paid supracompetitive prices for local telephone and/or high speed internet services.

67.   If not permanently enjoined, the unlawful contract, combination or conspiracy will continue and cause irreparable harm to Plaintiffs and members of the Class who have no adequate remedy at law.

COUNT II

Violation of State Antitrust Laws

68.   Plaintiffs repeat and reallege the allegations contained in paragraphs 1 through 67 as if fully set forth herein.

69.   As described above, Defendants have engaged in a contract, combination or conspiracy to prevent competitive entry in their respective local telephone and/or high speed internet services markets by, among other things, agreeing not to compete with one another and to stifle attempts by others to compete with them and otherwise allocating customers and markets to one another in violation of the following state antitrust laws.

70.   Defendants have unlawfully entered into a contract, combination or conspiracy in unreasonable restraint of trade in violation of Arizona Revised Stat. §§ 44–1401, et seq.

71.   Defendants have unlawfully entered into a contract, combination or conspiracy in unreasonable restraint of trade in violation of Cal. Bus. & Prof. Code §§ 16700, et seq., and Cal. Bus. & Prof. Code § 17200.

72.   Defendants have unlawfully entered into a contract, combination or conspiracy in unreasonable restraint of trade in violation of D.C. Code Ann. §§ 28–45031, et seq.

73.   Defendants have unlawfully entered into a contract, combination or conspiracy in unreasonable restraint of trade in violation of Fla. Stat. §§ 501, Part II, et seq.

74.   Defendants have unlawfully entered into a contract, combination or conspiracy in unreasonable restraint of trade in violation of Iowa Code §§ 553.4 et seq.

75.   Defendants have unlawfully entered into a contract, combination or conspiracy in unreasonable restraint of trade in violation of Kan. Stat. Ann. §§ 50–101, et seq.

76.   Defendants have unlawfully entered into a contract, combination or conspiracy in unreasonable restraint of trade in violation of La. Rev. Stat. §§ 51:137, et seq.

77.   Defendants have unlawfully entered into a contract, combination or conspiracy in unreasonable restraint of trade in violation of Me. Rev. Stat. Ann. 10, § 1101, et seq.

78.   Defendants have unlawfully entered into a contract, combination or conspiracy in unreasonable restraint of trade in violation of Mass. Ann. Laws ch. 93, et seq.

79.   Defendants have unlawfully entered into a contract, combination or conspiracy in unreasonable restraint of trade in violation of Mich. Comp. Laws Ann. §§ 445.771, et seq.

80.   Defendants have unlawfully entered into a contract, combination or conspiracy in unreasonable restraint of trade in violation of Minn. Stat. §§ 325D.52, et seq.

81.   Defendants have unlawfully entered into a contract, combination or conspiracy in unreasonable restraint of trade in violation of Miss. Code Ann. §§ 75–21–1, et seq.

82.   Defendants have unlawfully entered into a contract, combination or conspiracy in unreasonable restraint of trade in violation of Nev. Rev. Stat. Ann. § 598A, et seq.

83. Defendants have unlawfully entered into a contract, combination or conspiracy in unreasonable restraint of trade in violation of New Jersey Consumer Fraud Act, N.J. Stat. Ann. §§ 56:8–1 et seq.

84. Defendants have unlawfully entered into a contract, combination or conspiracy in unreasonable restraint of trade in violation of N.M. Stat. Ann. §§ 57–1–1 et seq.

85. Defendants have unlawfully entered into a contract, combination or conspiracy in unreasonable restraint of trade in violation of New York General Business Law §§ 340, et seq. and § 349 et seq.

86. Defendants have unlawfully entered into a contract, combination or conspiracy in unreasonable restraint of trade in violation of N.C. Gen. Stat. §§ 75–1, et seq.

87. Defendants have unlawfully entered into a contract, combination or conspiracy in unreasonable restraint of trade in violation of N.D. Cent. Code § 51.08.1–01, et seq.

88. Defendants have unlawfully entered into a contract, combination or conspiracy in unreasonable restraint of trade in violation of S.D. Codified Laws Ann. § 37–1, et seq.

89. Defendants have unlawfully entered into a contract, combination or conspiracy in unreasonable restraint of trade in violation of Tenn. Code Ann. §§ 47–25–101, et seq.

90. Defendants have unlawfully entered into a contract, combination or conspiracy in unreasonable restraint of trade in violation of Vt. Stat. Ann. 9, § 2453, et seq.

91. Defendants have unlawfully entered into a contract, combination or conspiracy in unreasonable restraint of trade in violation of W.Va. Code §§ 47–18–1, et seq.

92. Defendants have unlawfully entered into a contract, combination or conspiracy in unreasonable restraint of trade in violation of Wis. Stat. § 133.01, et seq.

93. Plaintiffs and members of the Class have been injured in their business or property by reason of Defendants' antitrust violations alleged in this Count. Their injury consists of paying higher prices for local telephone and/or high speed internet services than they would have paid in the absence of the violations alleged herein. This injury is of the type the antitrust laws of the above States and the District of Columbia were designed to prevent and flows from that which makes Defendants' conduct unlawful.

COUNT III

Unjust Enrichment

94. Plaintiffs repeat and reallege the allegations contained in paragraphs 1 through 93 as if fully set forth herein.

95. Defendants have benefitted from their unlawful acts through the overpayments from Plaintiffs and other Class members and the increased profits resulting from such overpayments. It would be inequitable for Defendants to be permitted to retain the benefit of these overpayments, which were conferred by Plaintiffs and the other class members and retained by Defendants.

96. Plaintiffs and members of the Class are entitled to the establishment of a constructive trust consisting of the benefit to Defendants of such overpayments, from which Plaintiffs and the other Class members may make claims on a pro-rata basis for restitution.

PRAYER FOR RELIEF

WHEREFORE, Plaintiffs and members of the Class pray that the Court enter judgment in their favor as follows:

A. Declaring this action to be a proper class action and certifying Plaintiffs as the representative of the Class pursuant to Rule 23 of the Federal Rules of Civil Procedure;

B. Declaring that Defendants violated and are in violation of the Sherman Act § 1 and the various state antitrust statutes alleged herein;

C. Awarding threefold the damages sustained by Plaintiffs and members of the Class as a result Defendants' violations;

D. Ordering injunctive relief preventing and restraining Defendants and all persons acting on their behalf from engaging in the unlawful acts alleged herein;

["E" omitted in original]

F. Awarding Plaintiffs and members of the Class the costs, expenses, and reasonable attorneys' fees and experts' fees for bringing and prosecuting this action; and

G. Awarding Plaintiffs and members of the Class such other and further relief as the Court may deem just and proper.

JURY DEMAND

Pursuant to Rule 38(h) of the Federal Rules of Civil Procedure, Plaintiffs hereby demand a jury trial on all issues so triable.

Dated: April 11, 2003

_____

First Amended Complaint in Ashcroft v. Iqbal

UNITED STATES DISTRICT COURT

EASTERN DISTRICT OF NEW YORK

No. 04 CV 1809 (JG) (JA)

Ehab Elmaghraby and Javaid Iqbal, Plaintiffs

v.

John Ashcroft, Attorney General of the United States; Robert Mueller, Director of the Federal Bureau of Investigation, and [31 other named individuals, 19 unknown persons sued as "John Doe" 1–19] and the United States of America, Defendants

[NOTE: Although the complaint involves claims against the many named defendants, the Supreme Court case, Ashcroft v. Iqbal, 556 U.S. 607, 129 S.Ct. 1937 (2009), concerns only the sufficiency of the allegations against defendants Ashcroft and Mueller. As a result, many allegations that do not involve defendants Ashcroft or Mueller have been omitted except when necessary to provide appropriate background and to give a flavor to the case.]

NATURE OF ACTION

1.   This is an action brought by Plaintiffs EHAB ELMAGHRABY and JAVAID IQBAL to remedy the brutal mistreatment and discrimination each Plaintiff suffered while in the care, custody, and control of Defendants. Plaintiffs ELMAGHRABY and IQBAL are Muslim men from Egypt and Pakistan, respectively. In the months after September 11, 2001, Plaintiffs were detained at the Metropolitan Detention Center ("MDC") in Brooklyn, New York. Plaintiffs were arbitrarily classified as being "of high interest" to the government's terrorism investigation after September 11th, and accordingly were housed in the MDC's Administrative Maximum ("ADMAX") Special Housing Unit ("SHU").

2.   While in the ADMAX SHU, Plaintiffs were subjected to a pattern and practice of cruel, inhuman, and degrading treatment in violation of the First, Fourth, Fifth, Sixth, and Eighth Amendments to the United States Constitution, federal statutory law, and customary international law. Among other things, they were deliberately and cruelly subjected to numerous instances of excessive force and verbal abuse, unlawful strip and body cavity-searches, the denial of medical treatment, the denial of adequate nutrition, extended detention in solitary confinement, the denial of adequate exercise, and deliberate interference with their rights to counsel and to exercise of their sincere religious beliefs. They were placed in tiny cells for more than 23 hours per day, and strip-searched, manacled and shackled when removed from their cells. Plaintiffs were housed in the ADMAX SHU in the absence of adequate standards or procedures for determining that such a classification was appropriate, or that the classification should continue, in violation of the Fifth Amendment to the United States Constitution.

3.   Plaintiffs were singled out for such mistreatment because of their race, national origin, and religion. Defendants, by creating, participating in, and endorsing Plaintiffs' systematic mistreatment, violated the principles enunciated in *Bivens v. Six Unknown Named Agents of Federal Bureau of Narcotics*, 403 U.S. 388 (1971), the Alien Tort Claims Act ("ATCA"), 28 U.S.C. § 1350, the Religious Freedom Restoration Act ("RFRA"), 42 USC § 2000bb, the civil rights conspiracy statute, 42 U.S.C. § 1985(3), and the Federal Tort Claims Act ("FTCA"), 28 U.S.C. § 2671 et seq.

4.   As a result of Defendants' misconduct, Plaintiffs suffered severe and permanent physical injuries, and severe emotional distress and humiliation. Plaintiffs now bring this lawsuit to redress these wrongs and to seek just and fair compensation.

FIRST AMENDED COMPLAINT IN ASHCROFT V. IQBAL

JURISDICTION AND VENUE

5. This action is brought pursuant to *Bivens*, under the First, Fourth, Fifth, Sixth, and Eighth Amendments to the United States Constitution, 28 U.S.C. § 1346(b), 28 U.S.C. § 1350, and 42 U.S.C. §§ 1985(3) and 2000bb.

6. This Court has jurisdiction under 28 U.S.C. §§ 1331, 1346(b), and 1350.

7. Venue is proper in the United States District Court for the Eastern District of New York pursuant to 28 U.S.C. § 1391(b), as the events giving rise to this action occurred within this district.

PARTIES

8. Plaintiff EHAB ELMAGHRABY is a native and citizen of Egypt, where he currently resides. He was detained in the MDC from on or about October 1, 2001 to on or about August 28, 2002.

9. Plaintiff JAVAID IQBAL is a native and citizen of Pakistan, where he currently resides. He was detained in the MDC from on or about November 5, 2001 to on or about January 15, 2003.

10. Defendant JOHN ASHCROFT is the Attorney General of the United States. As Attorney General, Defendant ASHCROFT has ultimate responsibility for the implementation and enforcement of the immigration and federal criminal laws. He is a principal architect of the policies and practices challenged here. He authorized, condoned, and/or ratified the unreasonable and excessively harsh conditions under which Plaintiffs were detained.

11. Defendant ROBERT MUELLER is the Director of the Federal Bureau of Investigation ("FBI"). As FBI Director, he was instrumental in the adoption, promulgation, and implementation of the policies and practices challenged here.

12. Defendant MICHAEL ROLINCE was at all relevant times the Chief of the FBI's International Terrorism Operations Section, Counterterrorism Division, and as such was instrumental in the implementation of the policies and practices challenged here.

13. Defendant KENNETH MAXWELL was at all relevant times the Assistant Special Agent in Charge, New York Field Office, FBI and as such was instrumental in the implantation of the policies and practices challenged here.

14. Defendant KATHLEEN HAWK SAWYER was at all relevant times the Director of the Federal Bureau of Prisons. As such, Defendant SAWYER was responsible for the custody, care and control of the individuals detained in the MDC, including Plaintiffs, and was instrumental in the adoption, promulgation, and implementation of the policies and practices challenged here. She authorized, condoned and/or ratified the unreasonable and excessively harsh conditions under which Plaintiffs were detained.

15. Defendant DAVID RARDIN was at all relevant times the Director of the Northeast Region of the Bureau of Prisons. As such, Defendant RARDIN was responsible for the custody, care and control of the individuals detained in the MDC, including Plaintiffs, and was instrumental in the adoption, promulgation, and implementation of the policies and practices challenged here. He authorized, condoned and/or ratified the unreasonable and excessively harsh conditions under which Plaintiffs were detained.

16. Defendant MICHAEL COOKSEY was at all relevant times the Assistant Director for Correctional Programs of the Bureau of Prisons. As such, Defendant COOKSEY was responsible for ensuring a safe and secure institutional environment for the individuals detained in the MDC, including Plaintiffs, and was instrumental in the adoption, promulgation, and implementation of the policies and practices challenged here. He authorized, condoned and/or ratified the unreasonable and excessively harsh conditions under which Plaintiffs were detained.

17. Defendant DENNIS HASTY was at some relevant times the Warden of the MDC. While Warden, Defendant HASTY was responsible for the terms and conditions under which Plaintiffs were confined at the MDC, and for supervising, hiring, and training officers who brutalized and mistreated

Plaintiffs. While Warden, Defendant HASTY subjected Plaintiffs to unreasonable and excessively harsh conditions of confinement.

18. Defendant MICHAEL ZENK is currently the Warden of the MDC. As Warden, Defendant ZENK was responsible at some relevant times for the terms and conditions under which Plaintiffs were confined at the MDC, and for supervising, hiring, and training officers who brutalized and mistreated Plaintiffs. As Warden, Defendant ZENK subjected Plaintiffs to unreasonable and excessively harsh conditions of confinement.

19. Defendant LINDA THOMAS is the former Associate Warden of Programs of the MDC and was at all relevant times the Associate Warden of Programs of the MDC. While Associate Warden, Defendant THOMAS was responsible for the terms and conditions under which Plaintiffs were confined at the MDC, and for supervising, hiring, and training officers who brutalized and mistreated Plaintiffs. As Associate Warden, Defendant THOMAS subjected Plaintiffs to unreasonable and excessively harsh conditions of confinement.

20. Defendant SHERMAN is the Associate Warden of Custody of the MDC and was at all relevant times the Associate Warden of Custody of the MDC. While Associate Warden, Defendant SHERMAN was responsible for the terms and conditions under which Plaintiffs were confined at the MDC, and for supervising, hiring, and training officers who brutalized and mistreated Plaintiffs. As Associate Warden, Defendant SHERMAN subjected Plaintiffs to unreasonable and excessively harsh conditions of confinement.

21. Defendant Captain SALVATORE LOPRESTI is and was at all relevant times employed at the MDC. While Captain, Defendant LOPRESTI was responsible for the terms and conditions under which Plaintiffs were confined at the MDC, and for supervising and training officers who brutalized and mistreated Plaintiffs. As Captain, Defendant LOPRESTI subjected Plaintiffs to unreasonable and excessively harsh conditions of confinement.

* * *

[Paragraphs 22–44 name additional defendants each of whom, other than a defendant named in paragraph 43, is charged with subjecting "Plaintiffs to unreasonable and exceptionally harsh conditions of confinement." Paragraph 45 names the United states as a defendant and paragraph 46 alleges that all defendants acted under color of federal law.]

STATEMENT OF FACTS

General Background

47. In the months after September 11, 2001, the Federal Bureau of Investigation ("FBI"), under the direction of Defendant MUELLER, arrested and detained thousands of Arab Muslim men, designated herein as "post-September 11th detainees," as part of its investigation of the events of September 11.

48. Many of these men, including Plaintiffs, were classified as being "of high interest" to the government's post-September-11th investigation by the FBI without specific criteria or a uniform classification system.

* * *

51. Defendants ROLINCE and/or MAXWELL classified Mr. Elmaghraby and Mr. Iqbal as "of high interest" to the post-September-11th investigation because of their race, religion, and national origin, and not because of any evidence that Plaintiffs were involved in terrorist activity.

* * *

53. Those post-September 11th detainees classified by the FBI as being "of high interest" were confined at the MDC in Brooklyn, New York, in the ADMAX SHU, which is the Federal Bureau of Prisons' ("BOP") most restrictive type of confinement.

FIRST AMENDED COMPLAINT IN ASHCROFT V. IQBAL

* * *

59.   The ADMAX SHU enforced a four-man hold restraint policy, the use of hand-held cameras to record detainee movements, cameras in each cell to monitor detainees, and physical security enhancements.

60.   Post-September 11th detainees in the ADMAX SHU were subjected to highly restrictive conditions of confinement. They were not permitted to move about the unit, use the telephone freely, nor were they permitted any electronic equipment in their cells, such as small radios. Post-September 11th detainees moved outside their cells only when they were restrained with handcuffs and leg irons and escorted by four staff members.

61.   For many weeks, post-September 11th detainees in the ADMAX SHU were subjected to a communications blackout that barred them from receiving telephone calls, visitors, mail, and from placing telephone calls. During this period, the post-September 11th detainees, including Plaintiff ELMAGHRABY, were unable to make any contact with their attorneys or families.

62.   Compounding this situation, MDC employees often turned away lawyers and family members who came to visit individual post-September 11th detainees by falsely stating that the individual detainee was no longer detained in the MDC.

* * *

64.   Because of the highly restrictive nature of the ADMAX SHU, BOP regulations require an employee known as the Segregation Review Official to conduct a weekly review of the status of each inmate housed in the SHU after he has spent seven days in administrative detention or disciplinary segregation. The Segregation Review Official is also required to conduct a formal hearing every 30 days assessing the inmate's status. The Segregation Review Official's finding must be approved by the Reviewing Authority.

* * *

67.   The appropriate review processes were never provided to the post-September 11th detainees, including Plaintiffs. Instead, the detainees were held in the ADMAX SHU until the FBI approved their release to the general population unit.

68.   Until the FBI approved the release of a particular detainee, MDC policy was to automatically annotate the detainee status with the phrase "continue high security." The post-September 11th detainees were not afforded any hearings, and they remained under restrictive detention in the ADMAX SHU as a matter of policy until defendant COOKSEY issued a memorandum approving their release to general population.

69.   The policy of holding post-September-11th detainees in highly restrictive conditions of confinement until they were "cleared" by the FBI was approved by Defendants ASHCROFT and MUELLER in discussions in the weeks after September 11, 2001.

* * *

74.   * * * Defendants ASHCROFT, MUELLER, and ROLINCE never imposed deadlines for the "clearance" process, and many detainees were held in the ADMAX SHU even after they were approved for release to the general population unit by the FBI.

75.   As a result numerous detainees, including Plaintiffs, were held in ADMAX SHU for extended periods of time, although there was no evidence linking them to terrorist activity.

* * *

FIRST AMENDED COMPLAINT IN ASHCROFT V. IQBAL

Cruel and Inhumane Conditions of Confinement in the ADMAX SHU

* * *

[Plaintiff Elmaghraby was alleged to have been detained in the ADMAX SHU from about October 1, 2001 until August 28, 2002. Plaintiff Iqbal allegedly was retained in the ADMAX SHU from about January 8, 2002 until the end of July 2002.]

82. While detained in the ADMAX SHU, Plaintiffs were kept in solitary confinement, not permitted to leave their cells for more than one hour each day with few exceptions, verbally and physically abused, routinely subjected to humiliating and unnecessary strip and body-cavity searches, denied access to basic medical care, denied access to legal counsel, denied adequate exercise and nutrition, and subjected to cruel and inhumane conditions of confinement.

83. The conditions of Plaintiffs' confinement incited fear and anguish, exacerbated their physical pain and emotional distress, and subjected them to embarrassment and humiliation.

84. Plaintiffs were housed in small cells with the lights on almost 24 hours per day until in or about March 2002. MDC staff deliberately turned on the air conditioner throughout the winter months, and turned on the heat during the summer months.

85. Plaintiffs were not provided with adequate bedding and personal hygiene items. Until in or about January 2002, Mr. ELMAGHRABY was not given a blanket, pillow, mattress, or any toilet paper. Similarly, Mr. IQBAL was never provided with pillows or more than one blanket.

86. Whenever Plaintiffs were removed from their cells, they were hand cuffed and shackled around their legs and waist.

87. Plaintiffs were subjected to continuous verbal abuse from the MDC staff, demonstrating their animus towards Plaintiffs. Such statements included Mr. IQBAL being called "a terrorist" by Defendant ZENK, "a terrorist and a killer" by Defendant GUSSAK, a "Muslim bastard" by Defendant COTTON, and a "Muslim killer" by Defendant PEREZ. Mr. ELMAGHRABY was called a "terrorist" by Defendant SHACKS; when Mr. ELMAGHRABY requested a pair of shoes, Defendant THOMAS responded with a statement, "No shoes for a terrorist"; Defendant COTTON expressed the same animus when he said, "a terrorist should not ask for anything" to Mr. ELMAGHRABY.

88. Plaintiffs were rarely permitted to exercise, and the conditions under which they were permitted to exercise were punitive in effect and intent. For instance, when permitted to exercise in the winter, Plaintiffs were taken to the recreation areas in the ADMAX SHU, which were on the top floor of the MDC in the open-air, in early winter mornings without proper jackets and shoes.

89. On certain days when it rained, MDC officers took Mr. IQBAL to the recreation areas for exercise, and left him in the open-air for hours until he was completely drenched. When Mr. IQBAL was brought back to his cell, the officers deliberately turned on the air conditioner, causing him severe physical discomfort.

90. As the weather became milder, MDC officers permitted Mr. ELMAGHRABY to go to the recreation areas for his exercise. However, the officers permitted him to remain outside for only 15 minutes, in contrast to the cold winter months where the officers left Mr. ELMAGHRABY in the open-air for hours. In the summer months, when it was extremely hot and humid, MDC officers again left Mr. ELMAGHRABY outside for hours.

91. Moreover, Plaintiffs were not provided with adequate food. As a result of the harassment they experienced in the ADMAX SHU, and nutritionally inadequate food, Plaintiffs lost a significant amount of weight. While in custody, Mr. IQBAL lost over 40 pounds, and Mr. ELMAGHRABY lost over 20 pounds. Furthermore, as a result of not having adequate food for a prolonged period of time, Mr. IQBAL currently suffers from persistent digestive problems, causing him to require medical treatment.

92. Such conditions of confinement were punitive in intent and effect.

93. Such conditions of confinement were not related to any legitimate penological interest.

94. Such conditions of confinement were imposed without any individualized determination as to whether they were appropriate for Plaintiffs.

95. Indeed, the MDC's Segregation Review Officials, Defendants BLEDSOE, BECK, and ORTIZ, never conducted a weekly review of Plaintiffs' status regarding whether or not it was appropriate to continue to detain them in the ADMAX SHU. In addition, during the entire time Plaintiffs were housed in the ADMAX SHU, they never received a formal hearing to determine whether such confinement was appropriate. The MDC's Reviewing Authority, Defendant LOPRESTI, nonetheless continued to approve Plaintiffs' confinement in ADMAX SHU.

96. Defendants ASHCROFT, MUELLER, SAWYER, RARDIN, COOKSEY, HASTY, ZENK, THOMAS, SHERMAN, LOPRESTI, and SHACKS each knew of, condoned, and willfully and maliciously agreed to subject Plaintiffs to these conditions of confinement as a matter of policy, solely on account of their religion, race, and/or national origin and for no legitimate penological interest.

97. Defendants ASHCROFT, MUELLER, SAWYER, RARDIN, COOKSEY, HASTY, ZENK, THOMAS, SHERMAN, and LOPRESTI willfully and maliciously designed a policy whereby individuals such as Plaintiffs were arbitrarily designated to be confined in the ADMAX SHU without providing any individual determination as to whether such designation was appropriate or should continue.

98. Keeping Plaintiffs in isolation for nearly 24 hours per day, without access to fresh air and light, adequate bedding, adequate heat, and without adequate recreation or exercise, bore no relationship to legitimate security concerns, constituted unjustified punishment, deprived Plaintiffs of their right to liberty, and amounted to the willful, malicious, and unnecessary infliction of pain and suffering.

99. As a result of Defendants' imposition of unlawful conditions of confinement, Plaintiffs suffered permanent physical injury and emotional distress.

* * *

[Paragraphs 100–200 provide details of alleged physical and emotional abuse of plaintiffs by named defendants other than defendants Ashcroft and Mueller. Paragraphs 100–152 include allegations of assaults, beatings, verbal abuse, and unjustified strip and body-cavity searches. Paragraphs 153–200 allege additional facts of abuse, including interference with plaintiffs practice of their religion, interference with their consultation with legal counsel, and "indifference" to their medical needs. It is alleged that plaintiffs were targeted "for mistreatment because of Plaintiffs' race religion, and/or national origin."]

In paragraphs 201–270, plaintiffs assert twenty-one causes of action against various defendants, often referring to or repeating allegations stated in prior paragraphs. Of these twenty-one causes, seven include the names of defendants Ashcroft and Mueller. These seven causes are set out below.]

SECOND CAUSE OF ACTION

(Assignment to ADMAX SHU—Fifth Amendment Due Process)

204. Plaintiffs repeat and reallege as if fully set forth herein the allegations contained in paragraphs numbered 1 through 203.

205. By willfully and maliciously adopting, promulgating and implementing the policy and practice under which Plaintiffs were confined to solitary confinement in the ADMAX SHU in an arbitrary and unreasonable manner, without any defined criteria, contemporaneous review, or process of any sort, and by which classifications Plaintiffs experienced unnecessary and unreasonable restrictions on their liberty that were atypical and significant departures from the restrictions imposed upon detainees in general population, Defendants ASHCROFT, MUELLER, ROLINCE, MAXWELL, SAWYER, RARDIN, COOKSEY, HASTY, ZENK, THOMAS, SHERMAN, LOPRESTI, BECK, BLEDSOE, ORTIZ, and SHACKS, acting under color of law and their authority as federal officers,

have intentionally or recklessly deprived Plaintiffs of liberty without due process of law in violation of the Fifth Amendment to the United States Constitution.

206. As a result of Defendants' unlawful conduct, Plaintiffs suffered emotional distress humiliation, and embarrassment, and accordingly each Plaintiff is entitled to compensatory damages against ASHCROFT, MUELLER, ROLINCE, MAXWELL, SAWYER, RARDIN, COOKSEY, HASTY, ZENK, THOMAS, SHERMAN, LOPRESTI, BECK, BLEDSOE, ORTIZ, and SHACKS, jointly and severally in an amount to be determined at trial and punitive damages against each Defendant in an amount to be determined at trial.

* * *

ELEVENTH CAUSE OF ACTION

(Discrimination Against Muslims—First Amendment)

231. Plaintiffs repeat and reallege as if fully set forth herein the allegations contained in paragraphs numbered 1 through 230.

232. Defendants ASHCROFT, MUELLER, ROLINCE, MAXWELL, SAWYER, RARDIN, COOKSEY, HASTY, ZENK, THOMAS, SHERMAN, LOPRESTI, BARRERE, TORRES, COTTON, DEFRANCISCO, PEREZ, and SHACKS, by adopting, promulgating, failing to prevent, failing to remedy, and/or implementing a policy and practice of imposing harsher conditions of confinement on Plaintiffs because of Plaintiffs' sincere religious beliefs violated Plaintiffs' rights under the First Amendment to the United States Constitution.

233. As a result, Plaintiffs suffered extreme physical injuries and emotional distress, including permanent injuries, and accordingly are entitled to compensatory damages against ASHCROFT, MUELLER, ROLINCE, MAXWELL, SAWYER, RARDIN, COOKSEY, HASTY, ZENK, THOMAS, SHERMAN, LOPRESTI, BARRERE, TORRES, COTTON, DEFRANCISCO, PEREZ, and SHACKS, jointly and severally in an amount to be determined at trial and punitive damages against each Defendant in an amount to be determined at trial.

TWELFTH CAUSE OF ACTION

(Race Discrimination—Fifth Amendment Equal Protection)

234. Plaintiffs repeat and reallege as if fully set forth herein the allegations contained in paragraphs numbered 1 through 233.

235. Defendants ASHCROFT, MUELLER, ROLINCE, MAXWELL, SAWYER, RARDIN, COOKSEY, HASTY, ZENK, THOMAS, SHERMAN, LOPRESTI, BARRERE, BECK, BLEDSOE, CUCITI, CUSH, GUSSAK, MUNDO, ORTIZ, TORRES, ALAMO, CHASE, CLARDY, COTTON, DEFRANCISCO, DIAZ, JAIKISSON, MOORE, OSTEEN, PEREZ, ROSEBERRY, SHACKS, LORENZO, and DOE Nos. 1–19, by adopting, promulgating, failing to prevent, failing to remedy, and/or implementing a policy and practice of imposing harsher conditions of confinement on Plaintiffs because of Plaintiffs' race violated Plaintiffs' rights under the Fifth Amendment to the United States Constitution.

236. As a result, Plaintiffs suffered extreme physical injuries and emotional distress, including permanent injuries, and accordingly are entitled to compensatory damages against ASHCROFT, MUELLER, ROLINCE, MAXWELL, SAWYER, RARDIN, COOKSEY, HASTY, ZENK, THOMAS, SHERMAN, LOPRESTI, BARRERE, BECK, BLEDSOE, CUCITI, CUSH, GUSSAK, MUNDO, ORTIZ, TORRES, ALAMO, CHASE, CLARDY, COTTON, DEFRANCISCO, DIAZ, JAIKISSON, MOORE, OSTEEN, PEREZ, ROSEBERRY, SHACKS, LORENZO, and DOE Nos. 1–19, jointly and severally in an amount to be determined at trial and punitive damages against each Defendant in an amount to be determined at trial.

FIRST AMENDED COMPLAINT IN ASHCROFT V. IQBAL

THIRTEENTH CAUSE OF ACTION

(Conditions of Confinement—RFRA)

237. Plaintiffs repeat and reallege as if fully set forth herein the allegations contained in paragraphs numbered 1 through 236.

238. Defendants ASHCROFT, MUELLER, ROLINCE, MAXWELL, SAWYER, RARDIN, COOKSEY, HASTY, ZENK, THOMAS, SHERMAN, LOPRESTI, BARRERE, BECK, BLEDSOE, CUCITI, CUSH, GUSSAK, MUNDO, ORTIZ, TORRES, ALAMO, CHASE, CLARDY, COTTON, DEFRANCISCO, DIAZ, JAIKISSON, MOORE, OSTEEN, PEREZ, ROSEBERRY, SHACKS, LORENZO, and DOE Nos. 1–19, by adopting, promulgating, failing to prevent, failing to remedy, and/or implementing a policy and practice of imposing harsher conditions of confinement on Plaintiffs because of Plaintiffs' sincere religious beliefs, substantially burdened Plaintiffs' religious exercise and belief, without any legitimate justification, in violation of 42 U.S.C. § 2000bb–1.

239. As a result, Plaintiffs suffered extreme physical injuries and emotional distress, including permanent injuries, and accordingly are entitled to compensatory damages against ASHCROFT, MUELLER, ROLINCE, MAXWELL, SAWYER, RARDIN, COOKSEY, HASTY, ZENK, THOMAS, SHERMAN, LOPRESTI, BARRERE, BECK, BLEDSOE, CUCITI, CUSH, GUSSAK, MUNDO, ORTIZ, TORRES, ALAMO, CHASE, CLARDY, COTTON, DEFRANCISCO, DIAZ, JAIKISSON, MOORE, OSTEEN, PEREZ, ROSEBERRY, SHACKS, LORENZO, and DOE Nos. 1–19, jointly and severally in an amount to be determined at trial and punitive damages against each Defendant in an amount to be determined at trial.

* * *

SIXTEENTH CAUSE OF ACTION

(Religious Discrimination—42 U.S.C. § 1985(3))

246. Plaintiffs repeat and reallege as if fully set forth herein the allegations contained in paragraphs numbered 1 through 245.

247. Defendants, by engaging in the following conduct, agreed to deprive Plaintiffs of the equal protection of the laws and of equal privileges and immunities of the laws of the United States because of Plaintiffs' sincere religious belief, resulting in injury to Plaintiffs' person and property, in violation of 42 U.S.C. § 1985(3): Defendants ASHCROFT, MUELLER, SAWYER, RARDIN, COOKSEY, HASTY, ZENK, THOMAS, SHERMAN, LOPRESTI, and SHACKS's agreement to subject Plaintiffs to unnecessarily harsh conditions of confinement in ADMAX SHU without due process of law; Defendants BARRERE, BECK, BLEDSOE, ORTIZ, MUNDO, ALAMO, CHASE, CLARDY, DEFRANCISCO, DIAZ, JAIKISSON, MOORE, and OSTEEN's agreement to brutally mistreat Mr. ELMAGHRABY on or about October 1, 2001; Defendants DOE Nos. 2–16's agreement to brutally assault Mr. IQBAL on or about January 8, 2002; Defendants CUSH, DEFRANCISCO, OSTEEN, and DOE Nos. 17–18's agreement to subject Mr. IQBAL to unnecessary strip and body-cavity searches on or about March 20, 2002, and brutally beat him in response to his peaceful protest of the searches; Defendants BECK, ORTIZ, BARRERE, MUNDO, and OSTEEN's agreement on or about October 1, 2001 to conduct an extreme and cruel body-cavity search of Mr. ELMAGHRABY during which Defendant BARRERE willfully and maliciously inserted a flashlight into Mr. ELMAGHRABY's anal cavity; Defendants MUNDO, COTTON, DEFRANCISCO, and OSTEEN's agreement on or about January 8, 2002 to conduct an extreme and cruel strip search of Mr. ELMAGHRABY in which Defendant COTTON willfully and maliciously pushed a pencil into Mr. ELMAGHRABY's anal cavity; Defendants SAWYER, RARDIN, COOKSEY, HASTY, ZENK, THOMAS, SHERMAN, LOPRESTI, and SHACKS's agreement to subject Plaintiffs to unnecessary and extreme strip and body-cavity searches as a matter of policy; Defendants SHACKS, PEREZ, DEFRANCISCO, TORRES, and COTTON's agreement to routinely confiscate Mr. IQBAL's Koran; and Defendants THOMAS, HASTY, ZENK, SHACKS, COTTON, and BARRERE's agreement to substantially burden Mr. ELMAGHRABY's religious practice while he was housed in ADMAX SHU.

FIRST AMENDED COMPLAINT IN ASHCROFT V. IQBAL

248. As a result, Plaintiffs suffered extreme physical injuries and emotional distress, including permanent injuries, and accordingly are entitled to compensatory damages against ASHCROFT, MUELLER, SAWYER, RARDIN, COOKSEY, HASTY, ZENK, THOMAS, SHERMAN, LOPRESTI, BARRERE, BECK, BLEDSOE, CUSH, GUSSAK, MUNDO, ORTIZ, TORRES, ALAMO, CHASE, CLARDY, COTTON, DEFRANCISCO, DIAZ, JAIKISSON, MOORE, PEREZ, SHACKS, and DOE Nos. 2–18 jointly and severally in an amount to be determined at trial and punitive damages against each Defendant in an amount to be determined at trial.

SEVENTEENTH CAUSE OF ACTION

(Race and National Origin Discrimination—42 U.S.C. § 1985(3))

249. Plaintiffs repeat and reallege as if fully set forth herein the allegations contained in paragraphs numbered 1 through 248.

250. Defendants, by engaging in the following conduct, agreed to deprive Plaintiffs of the equal protection of the laws and of equal privileges and immunities of the laws of the United States because of Plaintiffs' race and/or national origin, resulting in injury to Plaintiffs' person and property, in violation of 42 U.S.C. § 1985(3): Defendants ASHCROFT, MUELLER, SAWYER, RARDIN, COOKSEY, HASTY, ZENK, THOMAS, SHERMAN, LOPRESTI, and SHACKS's agreement to subject Plaintiffs to unnecessarily harsh conditions of confinement in ADMAX SHU without due process of law; Defendants BARRERE, BECK, BLEDSOE, ORTIZ, MUNDO, ALAMO, CHASE, CLARDY, DEFRANCISCO, DIAZ, JAIKISSON, MOORE, and OSTEEN's agreement to brutally mistreat Mr. ELMAGHRABY on or about October 1, 2001; Defendants DOE Nos. 2–16's agreement to brutally assault Mr. IQBAL on or about January 8, 2002; Defendants CUSH, DEFRANCISCO, OSTEEN, and DOE Nos. 17–18's agreement to subject Mr. IQBAL to unnecessary strip and body-cavity searches on or about March 20, 2002, and brutally beat him in response to his peaceful protest of the searches; Defendants BECK, ORTIZ, BARRERE, MUNDO, and OSTEEN's agreement on or about October 1, 2001 to conduct an extreme and cruel body-cavity search of Mr. ELMAGHRABY during which Defendant BARRERE willfully and maliciously inserted a flashlight into Mr. ELMAGHRABY's anal cavity; Defendants MUNDO, COTTON, DEFRANCISCO, and OSTEEN's agreement on or about January 8, 2002 to conduct an extreme and cruel strip search of Mr. ELMAGHRABY in which Defendant COTTON willfully and maliciously pushed a pencil into Mr. ELMAGHRABY's anal cavity; Defendants SAWYER, RARDIN, COOKSEY, HASTY, ZENK, THOMAS, SHERMAN, LOPRESTI, and SHACKS's agreement to subject Plaintiffs to unnecessary and extreme strip and body-cavity searches as a matter of policy; Defendants SHACKS, PEREZ, DEFRANCISCO, TORRES, and COTTON's agreement to routinely confiscate Mr. IQBAL's Koran; and Defendants THOMAS, HASTY, ZENK, SHACKS, COTTON, and BARRERE's agreement to substantially burden Mr. ELMAGHRABY's religious practice while he was housed in ADMAX SHU.

251. As a result, Plaintiffs suffered extreme physical injuries and emotional distress, including permanent injuries, and accordingly are entitled to compensatory damages against ASHCROFT, MUELLER, SAWYER, RARDIN, COOKSEY, HASTY, ZENK, THOMAS, SHERMAN, LOPRESTI, BARRERE, BECK, BLEDSOE, CUSH, GUSSAK, MUNDO, ORTIZ, TORRES, ALAMO, CHASE, CLARDY, COTTON, DEFRANCISCO, DIAZ, JAIKISSON, MOORE, PEREZ, SHACKS, and DOE Nos. 2–18 jointly and severally in an amount to be determined at trial and punitive damages against each Defendant in an amount to be determined at trial.

* * *

TWENTY-FIRST CAUSE OF ACTION

(Cruel, Inhuman, or Degrading Treatment—Customary International Law:)

266. Plaintiffs repeat and reallege as if fully set forth herein the allegations contained in paragraphs numbered 1 through 265.

FIRST AMENDED COMPLAINT IN ASHCROFT V. IQBAL

267. The acts described herein had the intent and the effect of grossly humiliating Plaintiffs, forcing them to act against their will and conscience, inciting fear and anguish, and breaking their physical and moral resistance.

268. The acts described herein constituted cruel, inhuman or degrading treatment in violation of the law of the nations under the Alien Tort Claims Act, 28 U.S.C. § 1350, in that the acts violated customary international law prohibiting cruel, inhuman or degrading treatment as reflected, expressed, and defined in multilateral treaties and other international treatments, international and domestic judicial decisions.

269. Defendants ASHCROFT, MUELLER, ROLINCE, MAXWELL, SAWYER, RARDIN, COOKSEY, HASTY, ZENK, THOMAS, SHERMAN, LOPRESTI, BARRERE, BECK, BLEDSOE, CUCITI, CUSH, GUSSAK, MUNDO, ORTIZ, TORRES, ALAMO, CHASE, CLARDY, COTTON, DEFRANCISCO, DIAZ, JAIKISSON, MOORE, OSTEEN, PEREZ, ROSEBERRY, SHACKS, LORENZO, and DOE Nos. 1–19 are liable for said conduct in that Defendants, acting under the color of law and their authority as federal officers, directed, ordered, confirmed, ratified and/or conspired to cause cruel, inhuman or degrading treatment of Plaintiffs.

270. Plaintiffs were forced to suffer severe physical and psychological abuse and emotional distress and are entitled to monetary damages.

JURY DEMAND

Plaintiffs demand a trial by jury. Plaintiff IQBAL does not demand trial by jury for his claims arising under the FTCA.

PRAYER FOR RELIEF

WHEREFORE Plaintiffs respectfully request that a judgment be granted as follows:

a.   Awarding compensatory and punitive damages to Plaintiffs for Defendants' violations of constitutional law, federal statutory law, customary international law, and local law, which caused Plaintiffs to suffer physical and emotional harm, in an amount that is fair, just, reasonable and in conformity with the evidence;

b.   Awarding Plaintiffs attorney's fees and costs pursuant to 42 U.S.C. § 1988 and N.Y.C. Code § 8–502; and,

c.   Such other relief as this Court deems just and proper.

Dated: New York, New York
          September 30, 2004

THE URBAN JUSTICE CENTER and
KOOB & MAGOOLAGHAN

By: _____

Alexander A. Reinert (AR-1740)
Koob & Magoolaghan
South Street Seaport
19 Fulton Street, suite 408
New York, New York 10038
Tel: 212-406-3095

–and–

FIRST AMENDED COMPLAINT IN ASHCROFT V. IQBAL

Haeyoung Yoon (HY-8962)
Urban Justice Center
666 Broadway, 10th Floor
New York, New York 10012
Tel: 646-459-3003

Attorneys for Plaintiffs

Complaint in Erickson v. Pardus

**IN THE UNITED STATES DISTRICT COURT
FOR THE DISTRICT OF COLORADO**

05- -405

Civil Action No. _____

(To be supplied by the court)

_____ William Erickson, _____, Plaintiff,

V.

_____ Barry J. Pardus, Assist. Clinical Dir., C.D.O.C., _____

_____ Dr. Anita Bloor, L.C.F. Medical Staff, _____

_____ (All defendants named in their individual and official capacities). _____

_____

_____

_____

_____

_____, Defendant(s).

(List each named defendant on a separate line.)

PRISONER COMPLAINT

COMPLAINT IN ERICKSON V. PARDUS

A. PARTIES

1. William Erickson, #59295, Limon Correctional Facility, 49030 St. Hwy. 71,
   (Plaintiff's name, prisoner identification number, and complete mailing address)
   Limon, CO. 80826

2. Barry J. Pardus, Assistant Director of Clinical Services, Colorado Dept.
   (Name, title, and address of first defendant)
   of Corrections, 2862 South Circle Drive, Colorado Springs, CO 80906

   At the time the claim(s) alleged in this complaint arose, was this defendant acting under color of state law? _xx_ Yes __ No (CHECK ONE). Briefly explain your answer.
   Mr. Pardus is the Assistant Director of Clinical Services for the Colo. Dept. of Corrections.
   As such, he is vested with the authority to Act under the color of State law. See § 17-1-103
   C.R.S.. Mr. Pardus is responsible for enactment of the new C.D.O.C. policy which
   excessively charges C.D.O.C. inmates fees for medical visits.

3. Dr. Anita Bloor, L.C.F. Clinical Director, 49030 St. Hwy. 71, Limon, CO 80826
   (Name, title, and address of second defendant)
   Dr. Bloor is also granted authority to act under the color of State law. See

   At the time the claim(s) alleged in this complaint arose, was this defendant acting under color of state law? _xx_ Yes __ No (CHECK ONE). Briefly explain your answer.
   § 17-1-103 C.R.S. Dr. Bloor had me removed from my hepatitis C treatment for a class
   II C.O.P.D conviction that is not listed in the C.D.O.C treatment protocol for treatment of
   this disease, thus endangering my life and violating my procedural due process protections.

4. _____
   (Name, title, and address of third defendant)

   At the time the claim(s) alleged in this complaint arose, was this defendant acting under color of state law? __ Yes __ No (CHECK ONE). Briefly explain your answer.

(If you are suing more than three defendants, use extra paper to provide the information requested above for each additional defendant. The information about additional defendants should be labeled "A. PARTIES.")

COMPLAINT IN ERICKSON V. PARDUS

B. JURISDICTION

1. I assert jurisdiction over my civil rights claim(s) pursuant to: (check one if applicable)

   __xx__   28 U.S.C § 1343 and 42 U.S.C. § 1983 (state prisoners)

   _____   28 U.S.C § 1331 and *Bivens v. Six Unknown Named Agents of Fed. Bureau of Narcotics*, 403 U.S. 388 (1971) (federal prisoners)

2. I assert jurisdiction pursuant to the following additional or alternative statutes (if any):

   __N/A__

C. NATURE

BRIEFLY state the background of your case. If more space is needed to describe the nature of the case, use extra paper to complete this section. The additional allegations regarding the nature of the case should be labeled "C. NATURE OF THE CASE."

The nature of this case involves two separate Eighth Amendment claims and one Fourteenth Amendment claim. The first of these claims involves me being removed from the Hepatitis C treatment I had begun, because a syringe came up missing from L.C.F. medical on the day myself and several other inmates received our weekly pegylated interferon shot. In a nutshell, I was diagnosed as needing treatment for Hepatitis C. I completed the required classes, etc., had a liver biopsy, and was assessed as needing treatment. I started treatment and shortly after beginning treatment, (which would require 1 year), a syringe came up missing at medical following the Friday afternoons shots for those on treatment. The pod I lived in was shaken down the same day (within 20 minutes of the discovery), and a syringe was found in the trashcan. This syringe was cut-down and could not have possibly been the syringe that was missing from medical as there would not have been time to have facilitated this type of conversion. Nevertheless, I was taken to segregation and written up. I was also removed from the treatment immediately. My arguments are simple: 1) that Dr. Bloor (who removed me from treatment), is being deliberately indifferent to my serious medical needs in violation of my Eighth Amendment protections; and 2) that the C.D.O.C. protocol for treatment of Hepatitis C does not allow for me to be removed fro the reason I was removed and hence my Fourteenth Amendment procedural due process protections have been violated.

The second claim involves C.D.O.C.'s enactment of a medical policy which requires co-pays ($5.00 to see the nurse and $10.00 dollars to see the doctor, $5.00 per visit to the dentist and $5.00 per visit to mental health), for medical visits. I contend that the co-pays are excessive and violate my Eight Amendment protections against cruel and unusual punishment as the visits cost more than I make in a month and C.D.O.C takes these deductions first forcing me to choose between hygienic needs and medical treatment.

COMPLAINT IN ERICKSON V. PARDUS

D. CAUSE OF ACTION

State concisely every claim that you wish to assert in this action. For each claim, specify the right that allegedly has been violated and state all supporting facts that you consider important, including the date(s) on which the incident(s) occurred, the name(s) of the specific person(s) involved in each claim, and the specific facts that show how each person was involved in each claim. You do not need to cite specific cases to support your claim(s). If additional space is needed to describe any claim or to assert more than three claims, use extra paper to continue that claim or to assert the additional claim(s). the additional pages regarding the cause of action should be labeled "D. CAUSE OF ACTION."

1. **Claim One:**   Violation of Eighth Amendment protections against cruel and unusual punishment, i.e., deliberate indifference to my serious medical needs.

Supporting Facts:

1) Pursuant to current Colorado Dept. of Corrections (CDOC), treatment protocols, I was assessed as needing treatment for the disease Hepatitis C, I currently suffer from. As a result, I signed a contract with L.C.F. medical officials where I completed the requisite treatment protocol requirements, such as one year of classes, a liver biopsy (which indicated that I was at the required stages for treatment, etc. As a result, I was placed on treatment. Treatment entailed me receiving medication in the form of pills (3 capsules of Ribavirin twice a day), and a shot of PEGYLATED Interferon, once a week. I received my medications and shot the same time as all other inmates on treatment in the facility. At the same time I was on treatment there were about 5 of us receiving the medications.

2) One Friday afternoon when all of us receiving treatment were at L.C.P. medical, a syringe came up missing. The syringe was one which was used to give us the pegylated interferon shots. As a result, the unit I live in was shook down, and in my living pod, in a communal trashcan, a syringe was discovered. This syringe was not the same type as used in giving the Pegylated Interferon shots, and it had been altered. Due to this discovery, I was immediately removed from the Hepatitis C treatment, even though the pod I lived in houses 52 men, the syringe was not the type used in giving the Interferon shots, the syringe had been altered (and it would have been physically impossible for anyone to do this within 20 minutes of discovery that the syringe was missing), and the CDOC treatment protocol does not allow for removal from treatment for this type of infraction.

3) Dr. Anita Bloor is the one who removed me from the treatment and hence she is personally involved in being deliberately indifferent to my serious medical need. I am still in need of treatment for this disease and CDOC will not treat me, even though I meet the requsite treatment criteria. As such, I contend that Dr. Anita Bloor has violated my Eight Amendment protections against cruel and unusual punishment by refusing me treatment for a disease I suffer from, i.e., through denying me constitutionally mandated medical care.

381

COMPLAINT IN ERICKSON V. PARDUS

2. Claim Two: <u>Violation of Fourteenth Amendment procedural due process</u>
<u>through refusing to treat me even thought the CDOC protocol</u>
<u>mandates I be treated.</u>

Supporting Facts:

1) Once again I state that Dr. Anita Bloor had me removed from the Hepatitis C treatment because a syringe was discovered in my living unit pod. See Claim One. It is my contention that a procedural due process protection was created by CDOC in implementation of the treatment protocol that requires I be treated for Hepatitis C, so long as I meet the pre-requisites of the protocol. See Exhibit A. I thus contend that Dr. Anita Bloor has violated my procedural due process protections by removing me from treatment from Hepatitis C.

3. Claim Three: <u>Violation of Eighth Amendment protections against cruel and</u>
<u>unusual punishment through enactment of an excessive co-pay</u>
<u>policy.</u>

Supporting Facts:

1) On July 26, 2004, Defendant Pardus enacted a new CDOC policy which implements co-pay charges for all inmates. These charges are $5.00 dollars to see a nurse practioner, or physician's assistant and $10.00 dollars to see a doctor. In addition, if an inmate declares an emergency, he/she will be charged $10.00 for the emergency visit unless it is declared a true emergency, then the co-pay is dropped at $5.00 dollars.

2) my only source of income comes from my CDOC job. As of July 1, 2003, this worker's pay was reduced to .60 cents a day. I am not paid for holidays, days the institution is on lockdown, days I am sick, or any other day I do not work for whatever the reason. Moreover, this pay; approxiamtley $10.00 a month, is subject to a 20% deduction for court ordered restitution/costs that were entered on my judgment and sentence under § 16-18.5-106 C.R.S.. This means I actually receive about $8.00 a month in total inmate pay. Of this $8.00 a month, .23 cents a day is given to all inmates as CDOC's obligation to fulfill constitutionally mandated hygienic supplies, etc., for indigent inmates. CDOC does not provide indigent supplies and instead chooses to give each inmate .23 cents a day in order to allow them to purchase the supplies they need from the inmate canteen. This amounts to about $4.75 a month for those non-working inmates or to each inmate. As a result, I receive approximately $3.00 a month for working, of which they want me to pay $5.00 to see a nurse and $10.00 to see a doctor.

3) I contend that this violates my constitutional protections against cruel and unusual punishment, as CDOC does not distinguish any amount of funds on my account as being indigent and if I visit a doctor or see the dentist, etc., they take their co-pay first leaving me nothing to purchase hygiene supplies. Moreover, I contend that the co-pay is excessive in nature.

4) Defendant Pardus enacted this new co-pay policy and as a result is personally involved/responsible.

382

COMPLAINT IN ERICKSON V. PARDUS

E. PREVIOUS LAWSUITS

Have you ever filed a lawsuit, other than this lawsuit, in any federal or state court while you where incarcerated? __xx__ Yes ___ No (CHECK ONE). If you answer "Yes," complete this section of the form. If you have filed more than one lawsuit in the past, use extra paper to provide the necessary information for each additional lawsuit. The information about additional lawsuits should be labeled "E. PREVIOUS LAWSUITS."

1. Name(s) of the defendants lawsuit:

Barry J. Pardus Ast. Dir. Clinical Services
Dr. Anita Bloor, & Anthony A. DeCesaro

2. Docket number and court name:

U.S. District Court of Colo.
Civ. Action No. 04-ES-2376

3. Claims raised in prior lawsuit.

Same as this suit.

4. Disposition of prior lawsuit (for example, is the prior lawsuit still pending? Was it dismissed?)

Dismissed without prejudice.

5. If the prior lawsuit was dismissed, when was it dismissed and why?

I failed to timely respond to a court order, which I stated I never received. I cannot control delivery of the mail in this facility or in this country. Mail goes missing all the time.

6. Result(s) of any appeal in the prior lawsuit:

N/A

F. ADMINISTRATIVE RELIEF

1. Is there a formal grievance procedure at the institution in which you are confined?
   __xx__ Yes ___ No

2. Have you exhausted the available administrative remedies? Attach copies, if available.
   __xx__ Yes ___ No

   See attached grievances.

COMPLAINT IN ERICKSON V. PARDUS

G. REQUEST FOR RELIEF

State the relief you are requesting. If you need more space to complete this section, use extra paper. The additional requests for relief should be labeled "G. REQUEST FOR RELIEF."

Declarative Relief: I seek an Order declaring that my Eighth and Fourteenth Amendment rights have been violated.

Injunction Relief: I seek a permanent injunction requiring CDOC to cease from taking the excessive co-pays and a temporary injunction requiring CDOC to treat me for Hepatitis C under the standards of the treatment protocol established by them.

Compensatory Damages: I seek reimbursement for all costs of this action, to include filing fees, postage costs, copying costs, attorney fees, etc.

Nominal Damages: I see nominal damages of $1.00 from each Defendant.

Punitive Damages: I seek punitive damages in the amount equal to all co-pays collected by CDOC to date and a requirement that CDOC return all co-pays to each inmate where possible.

DECLARATION UNDER PENALTY OF PERJURY

I declare under penalty of perjury that I am the plaintiff in this action, that I have read this complaint, and that the information in this complaint is true and correct. *See* 28 U.S.C. §1746;18 U.S.C. § 1621.

Executed on _____2-22-05_____

_____/s/ William Erickson 59295_____
(Prisoner's Original Signature)

William Erickson, #59295
Limon Correctional Facility
49030 State Highway 71
Limon, CO 80826

PART X

Recent Cases of the United States Supreme Court

Decisions of Note

Epic Systems Corp. v. Lewis, 584 U.S. ___, 138 S.Ct. 1612, 200 L.Ed.2d 889 (2018).

Plaintiff employees sought redress in federal courts in three class actions against their employers alleging their employers' violations of the Fair Labor Standards Act. Defendant employers argued that because the employees had each signed a contract specifying arbitration on an individual basis, under the Federal Arbitration Act (FAA) each employee's case would have to proceed to arbitration on its own. This meant, of course, that because of the cost, few employees could pursue individual actions especially since the decision would have no precedential value. The employees responded with two major arguments. First, the contracts prohibiting class treatment were illegal and thus revocable and specifically exempt from the FAA. Second, to the extent that it prohibited class treatment in these cases, the FAA had been supplanted by language in the later enacted National Labor Relations Act (NLRA). The Supreme Court split five-to-four in deciding the case. The majority emphasized that the FAA was to be strictly applied to contractual agreements "save upon such grounds as exist in law or in equity for the revocation of any contract." FAA § 2. Those grounds include such defenses as fraud, duress, or unconscionability. They do not include situations when a defense is directly or indirectly based on the injustice of the arbitration agreement itself. Here where employees were free to agree or reject the terms of the agreement, even though rejection could determine whether they would obtain or continue to hold a job, the agreement was enforceable. The dissenting Justices argued that by coercing employees to sign an agreement that interfered with their rights under the NLRA, employers made the contract illegal and thus unenforceable, not as a challenge to employers but as to the formation of the contract itself. A more telling argument made by the dissent is that the NLRA is inconsistent with the FAA and the later enacted NLRA must prevail. Section 7 of the NLRA guarantees that employees have the right to organize, engage in collective bargaining, "and to engage in other concerted activities for the purpose of collective bargaining or other mutual aid or protection." Section 8(1) in effect prohibits employers from interfering with, restraining, or coercing employees in the exercise of their rights under NLRA § 7. The majority met this argument by noting that the NLRA dealt at length with the right to organize and bargain and did not deal at all with the methods of adjudicating labor disputes. The right "to engage in other concerted activities" for the purpose of "mutual aid or protection" came at the end of a list of specific rights and is said only to refer to "things employees 'just do' for themselves." Thus there is no true conflict between the FAA and the NLRA. But even if a conflict exists, it is up to the courts to do their best to harmonize the statutes to carry out the intentions of Congress. Here the majority found that a policy of protecting employers from costly class actions was more important than a policy of providing employees with a meaningful method of redressing violations of employment regulations.

Henry Schein, Inc. v. Archer and White Sales, Inc., 586 U.S. ___, 139 S.Ct. 524, 202 L.Ed.2d 480 (2019).

Respondent Archer and White Sales Inc. and petitioner Henry Schein, Inc. entered into a contract that contained a provision requiring arbitration of disputes under or related to the contract except for actions seeking injunctive relief. Respondent brought suit in federal district court against petitioner alleging violations of federal and state antitrust laws and seeking both money damages and injunctive relief. Petitioner moved the court to compel arbitration pursuant to the Federal Arbitration Act. Respondent argued that the case was not subject to arbitration because, in part, it sought injunctive relief. Petitioner claimed that the arbitrator, and not the court, should decide the threshold question of whether the case is subject to arbitration. The court, without deciding if the contract called for arbitration of the threshold question, denied arbitration on the ground that respondent's arguments for arbitration were "wholly groundless," and the Court of Appeals affirmed. In a unanimous opinion, the Supreme Court vacated and remanded the lower court's decision, holding that when a contract delegates the question of whether a dispute is subject to arbitration to an arbitrator, the court may not override the contract, even if it thinks that the argument that the agreement requires arbitration is "wholly groundless." According to the Court, a "wholly groundless" determination, which some lower courts had recognized, was inconsistent with the Federal Arbitration Act. It therefore remanded the case to permit the Fifth Circuit to determine whether the arbitration contract, by its terms, delegated the threshold issue of whether the case is subject to arbitration to an arbitrator.

Nutraceutical Corp. v. Lambert, 586 U.S. ___, 139 S.Ct. 710, 203 L.Ed.2d 43 (2019).

Plaintiff's class action was decertified by the federal district court on February 20, 2015. Under Federal Rule 23(f), plaintiff had 14 days to file a petition for permission to appeal. He failed to do so. Instead, within 10 days he notified the trial court that it was his intention to file a motion for reconsideration of the decertification order. The court ordered him to do so by March 12, which he did, but that was some 20 days after the decertification order. The trial court denied the motion for reconsideration on June 24, and 14 days later plaintiff, for the first time, sought permission to appeal. The Court of Appeals held that despite the 14-day requirement, the appeal was timely. It relied on the fact that because the time limit was set out in a rule, and not a statute, it was not jurisdictional and so was subject to "tolling" based on equitable considerations. The Court of Appeals found that plaintiff had acted "diligently." In a unanimous opinion, the Supreme Court reversed and remanded. It relied primarily on Federal Rule of Appellate Procedure 26(b) that generally allows for extensions of time limits for good cause, but specifically prohibits an extension of time to file for permission to appeal. It distinguished cases allowing appeals when a motion for reconsideration had been filed within 14 days of the decertification decision on the ground that until such a motion was decided, there was no final determination by the trial court to trigger the start of the 14-day period. The Court noted that on remand there was an open question whether the trial court's order that allowed plaintiff to file for reconsideration by March 12 should itself delay the start of the 14-day period until reconsideration was denied.

Republic of Sudan v. Harrison, 587 U.S. ___, 139 S.Ct. 1048, ___ L.Ed.2d ___ (2019).

Victims of the bombing of the USS *Cole*, and their relatives, brought suit against the Republic of Sudan in federal district court under the Foreign Sovereign Immunities Act. The clerk of the court, at plaintiffs' request, addressed the service packet to Sudan's minister of foreign affairs at the Sudan Embassy in the United States, and later certified that a signed receipt had been returned. Sudan failed to appear and the court entered a default judgment plus orders to effect payment of the judgment. Sudan moved to set aside the court's orders, arguing that the district court lacked personal jurisdiction because the method of service was defective under 28 U.S.C. § 1608(3). Section 1608(3) allows service "by any form of mailing requiring a signed receipt, to be addressed and dispatched . . . to the head of the ministry of foreign affairs of the foreign state concerned." Sudan argued that this provision required service to be sent to Sudan's foreign minister at his principal office in Sudan. Plaintiffs argued that all the statute required was a method reasonably calculated to give actual notice. The lower courts held that service had been appropriate, noting that the statute did not state where service was to be made. In an eight-to-one opinion, the Supreme Court reversed. It held that the statute, by using the words "addressed and dispatched," meant that service must be sent to a foreign minister's business office in the foreign state, not to some office in the United States where the minister might rarely be found. The Court also relied on the fact that a signed receipt was required, noting that it would normally be signed by a person in the minister's office who was instructed on how to handle the minister's mail, not by an ordinary mail clerk in a different facility. Finally, the Court noted that service under the statute should be consistent with Federal Rules of Civil Procedure 4(f)(2)(C)(ii) and 4(*l*)(2)(B) requiring evidence of direct delivery of service to a citizen of the United States being sued abroad.

RECENT SUPREME COURT CASES

Justice Thomas dissented on the ground that delivery of service to a country's embassy was within the terms of the statute and a reasonable means of notifying the country's foreign minister, and that the majority's bright-line rule of service "at the minister's office in the foreign state" lacked textual support in the statute.

Lamps Plus, Inc. v. Varela, 2019 WL 1780275, 587 U.S. ___, 139 S.Ct. 1407, ___ L.Ed.2d ___ (2019).

Plaintiff, an employee of the defendant company, filed a class action in a federal court against the company for damages, alleging that tax information of a number of defendant's employees had improperly been disclosed because of hacking. Defendant sought to compel arbitration relying on an arbitration agreement in plaintiff's employment contract. It also argued that arbitration should only be allowed on an individual rather than on a class basis. The trial court authorized class-wide arbitration, the appeals court affirmed, and the company sought reversal in the Supreme Court. A majority of the Court took the position that unless there is clear, express language in the arbitration agreement requiring class arbitration, the Federal Arbitration Act (FAA), as a matter of policy, mandates individual arbitration. In particular, the FAA provides the default rule for resolving contractual ambiguity, and any state law to the contrary cannot be enforced if it presents a barrier to enforcement of the FAA. Since the agreement did not mention class arbitration, the Court reversed, citing Stolt-Nielsen, S.A. v. AnimalFeeds Int'l Corp., 559 U.S. 662, 130 S.Ct. 1758, 176 L.Ed.2 605 (2010). The Court emphasized that the FAA clearly favors individual arbitration as a simple, informal method of settling disputes that is quite different from a more complex process that was presumed to be slower and to increase risks to defendants, as well as to absentee class members, relying on AT&T Mobility v. Concepcion, 563 U.S. 333, 131 S.Ct. 1740, 179 L.Ed.2d 742 (2011).

Justice Thomas, concurring, would have vacated only on the ground that an ambiguous contract provides no basis for finding consent to class-wide arbitration, and expressed skepticism regarding the majority's implied preemption analysis of state law.

The four dissenting Justices agreed that the arbitration agreement should govern, but that the agreement was at best ambiguous regarding class arbitration. In such a case, they argued, state law is applicable to interpreting the agreement and, under the applicable state law, an ambiguous agreement is to be read against the party who drafted it, in this case the defendant employer. In a separate dissent, Justice Ginsburg, joined by Justices Breyer and Sotomayor, countered the notion that arbitration as interpreted today is simply a matter of consent. The dissenters emphasized that employees and consumers often have no true choice regarding arbitration agreements that are forced upon them if they want to maintain their jobs or be able to afford necessary goods. Moreover, the cost of vindicating identical rights of many individuals one person at a time when individual recovery is far too small to justify the cost of going forward is simply a means of denying rights. The Court's precedents enforcing mandatory arbitration agreements against parties with no bargaining power, the dissenters argued, "thwart 'effective access to justice' for those encountering diverse violations of their legal rights," and run counter to Congress's intent when it enacted the FAA of providing parties of roughly equal bargaining power a mechanism to resolve commercial disputes, citing, inter alia, Miller, Simplified Pleading, Meaningful Days in Court, and Trials on the Merits: Reflections on the Deformation of Federal Procedure, 88 N.Y.U. L. Rev. 286, 323 (2013) (stating that the FAA was "enacted in 1925 with the seemingly limited purpose of overcoming the then existing 'judicial hostility' to the arbitration of contract disputes between businesses.").

In addition, at the outset, the Court considered an argument, first raised before the Court, that it lacked jurisdiction because the district court decision was interlocutory, not final. That argument was based on the fact that Lamps Plus filed its suit seeking an order that arbitration proceed and that that order was granted, albeit as a class-wide arbitration, and not the individual arbitration that Lamps Plus wanted. The appeal of an arbitration order is governed by 9 U.S.C. § 16, and sub-provision (b)(2) specifically denies review of orders granting arbitration. The majority, in its opinion upholding jurisdiction, responded with several arguments. First, it pointed out that the trial judge in its order had also dismissed the underlying case, rendering it a final judgment subject to appeal as permitted under 9 U.S.C. § 16(a)(3). Next the Court relied on the fact that Lamps Plus had been denied the relief it sought, namely, individual arbitration; on the view that individual arbitration is fundamentally different from class-wide arbitration, the denial amounted to a final decision that was subject to appeal. Justice Breyer, in a separate dissent, disagreed with the majority's jurisdictional analysis, arguing, that the FAA "limited interlocutory review of orders concerning arbitration in a way that favors arbitration," and that an order directing arbitration—as the district court did in this case—was an interlocutory order not subject to review. Further, in his view, dismissal of the case, as requested by Lamps Plus, had been improper since the pending arbitration had yet to be held.

Biestek v. Berryhill, 587 U.S. ___, 139 S.Ct. 1148, ___ L.Ed.2d ___ (2019).

Petitioner, a former construction worker, applied for social security disability benefits, claiming that he could no longer work. Under the Social Security Act, the agency assigned an Administrative Law Judge (ALJ) to receive evidence and examine witnesses about contested issues in petitioner's case. Such hearings before an ALJ are to be conducted in an informal, non-adversarial manner, and the ALJ is under a statutory duty to develop the factual record. The agency had the burden of showing what, if any, jobs petitioner could now hold and whether those jobs exist in significant numbers in the national economy. The ALJ sought evidence on these questions from a knowledgeable vocational expert who testified, on the basis of her own labor market surveys, that within the national economy there were 240,000 "bench assembler jobs" and 120,000 "sorter jobs" that petitioner could handle. On cross-examination, petitioner's counsel asked to see the surveys. The expert refused on the ground that they were part of her confidential client files. Counsel then suggested that the clients' names could be redacted, but the ALJ held that he would not require the files to be produced in any form. Petitioner's counsel asked no further questions about the supporting data. On the basis of the expert's testimony, the ALJ held that petitioner was not entitled to benefits.

Such an ALJ decision is binding if supported by "substantial evidence." 42 U.S.C. § 405(g). Petitioner filed suit arguing for a categorical rule that an expert's testimony cannot alone constitute "substantial evidence" if the expert refuses a request to provide supporting data. The lower courts, as well as the Supreme Court, affirmed the ALJ's decision. In a majority opinion for six members, Justice Kagan noted that on the total evidence in a case, a cogent opinion of an expert could, along with other reliable information, indeed constitute "substantial evidence," even in the absence of the expert's private data. As a result, petitioner's argument, based solely on a categorical rule, failed.

Justice Gorsuch, in a dissenting opinion joined by Justice Ginsburg, argued that petitioner did not rely on a categorical rule that would eliminate in every case consideration of an expert's opinion when background information was not produced. He agreed that in a hypothetical situation detailed information and the circumstances of the case could result in a finding of "substantial evidence." But the Court must look only to the facts of the case presented where all that the ALJ had before him was the testimony in which the expert stated unsupported conclusions plus the expert's refusal to produce back-up data. In such a situation, the dissenting opinion stated, "an agency expert's bottom-line conclusion, supported only by a claim of readily available evidence that she refuses to produce on request, fails to satisfy the government's statutory burden of producing substantial evidence of available other work." The contrary rule, in the dissenters' view, permits the government to reach decisions based on "secret evidence," and leaves claimants, like petitioner in this case, "to the mercy of a bureaucrat's caprice."

Justice Sotomayor provided a separate dissenting opinion. She agreed with Justice Gorsuch that the question presented in the case did not limit the Court's inquiry to the propriety of a categorical rule, but also encompassed whether the substantial-evidence standard was met where the vocational evidence provided only "conclusory" testimony. Justice Sotomayor emphasized that the ALJ failed to "take steps to ensure that the claimant had a basis from which effective cross-examination could be made," and that the record as developed failed to provide any support for the expert's conclusion. Without that additional evidence, the conclusory testimony alone did not, in her view, meet the substantial-evidence standard.

RECENT SUPREME COURT CASES

Herrera v. Wyoming, 587 U.S. ___, ___ S.Ct. ___, ___ L.Ed.2d ___ (2019).

Petitioner, a member of the Crow Tribe, was convicted in a Wyoming state court of taking elk off season and without a Wyoming hunting license. His defense was based on an 1868 Treaty in which the Crow Indian Nation ceded lands to the United States in exchange for rights of the Indians to hunt on unoccupied portions of the lands. Herrera appealed. Wyoming argued that petitioner's rights under the treaty had expired in 1890 when Wyoming was admitted as a state. It also argued that the land in question, now Bighorn National Forest, was not "unoccupied" as required by the treaty. Subsequently, it also relied on the doctrine of issue preclusion on the ground that the matters had been litigated to a final judgment in Crow Tribe of Indians v. Repsis, 73 F.3d 982 (10th Cir. 1995), a case that involved the same treaty as that before the Court and had been argued on behalf of the Crow Tribe.

Justice Sotomayor delivered the opinion of the Court, joined by Justices Ginsburg, Breyer, Kagan, and Gorsuch. The majority held that *Repsis* did not preclude petitioner from asserting a defense under the 1868 Treaty. To be sure, *Repsis* involved the same treaty and the same tribe. However, it relied upon the reasoning of an older Supreme Court case, Ward v. Race Horse, 163 U.S. 504, 16 S.Ct. 1076, 41 L.Ed.2d 244 (1896), which the Court had since repudiated in Minnesota v. Mille Lac Band of Chippewa Indians, 526 U.S. 172, 119 S.Ct. 1187, 143 L.Ed.2d 270 (1999). The Court explained that under the change-in-law exception to issue preclusion, *Repsis* was not a bar to litigating whether the treaty granting rights "to hunt on the unoccupied lands of the United States" survived Wyoming's statehood:

> Because this Court's intervening decision in *Mille Lacs* repudiated the reasoning on which the Tenth Circuit relied in *Repsis*, *Repsis* does not preclude Herrera from arguing that the 1868 Treaty right survived Wyoming's statehood.

> Under the doctrine of issue preclusion, "a prior judgment . . . foreclos[es] successive litigation of an issue of fact or law actually litigated and resolved in a valid court determination essential to the prior judgment." *New Hampshire* v. *Maine*, 532 U. S. 742, 748–749 (2001). Even when the elements of issue preclusion are met, however, an exception may be warranted if there has been an intervening " 'change in [the] applicable legal context.' " *Bobby* v. *Bies*, 556 U. S. 825, 834 (2009) (quoting Restatement (Second) of Judgments § 28, Comment *c* (1980)); see *Limbach*, 466 U. S., at 363 (refusing to find a party bound by "an early decision based upon a now repudiated legal doctrine"); see also *Montana* v. *United States*, 440 U. S. 147, 155 (1979) (asking "whether controlling facts or legal principles ha[d] changed significantly" since a judgment before giving it preclusive effect); *id.*, at 157–158 (explaining that a prior judgment was conclusive "[a]bsent significant changes in controlling facts or legal principles" since the judgment); *Commissioner* v. *Sunnen*, 333 U. S. 591, 599 (1948) (issue preclusion "is designed to prevent repetitious lawsuits over matters which have once been decided and which have remained substantially static, factually and legally"). The change-in-law exception recognizes that applying issue preclusion in changed circumstances may not "advance the equitable administration of the law." *Bobby*, 556 U. S., at 836–837.[2]

> We conclude that a change in law justifies an exception to preclusion in this case. There is no question that the Tenth Circuit in *Repsis* relied on this Court's binding decision in *Race Horse* to conclude that the 1868 Treaty right terminated upon Wyoming's statehood. See 73 F. 3d, at 994. When the Tenth Circuit reached its decision in *Repsis*, it had no authority to disregard this Court's holding in *Race Horse* and no ability to predict the analysis this Court would adopt in *Mille Lacs*. *Mille Lacs* repudiated *Race Horse*'s reasoning. Although we recognize that it may be difficult at the margins to discern whether a particular legal shift warrants an exception to issue preclusion, this is not a marginal case. At a minimum, a repudiated decision does not retain preclusive force.

In a footnote, the Court also considered, and rejected, the argument that *Repsis* had relied on a second ground of decision, namely, that the lands in question were occupied and so the hunting rights no longer applied:

Wyoming argues that the judgment below should be affirmed because the Tenth Circuit held in *Repsis* that the creation of the forest rendered the land "occupied," see 73 F. 3d, at 994, and thus Herrera is precluded from raising this issue. We did not grant certiorari on the question of how preclusion principles would apply to the alternative judgment in *Repsis*, and—although our dissenting colleagues disagree, * * *—the decision below did not address that issue.

* * * Context thus makes clear that the state court gave issue-preclusive effect only to *Repsis'* holding that the 1868 Treaty was no longer valid, not to *Repsis'* independent, narrower holding that Bighorn National Forest in particular was "occupied" land.

The dissent, written by Justice Alito and joined by Chief Justice Roberts and Justices Thomas and Kavanaugh, emphasized this second ground of decision in *Repsis*, and argued that petitioner's defense was issue precluded by the prior judgment. It considered a conflict of authorities when a case turns on two separate issues as to whether a decision binds the parties on both. The dissent preferred the argument in the First Restatement of Judgments which holds that both are binding. By contrast, the Second Restatement says that neither can be relied upon. The dissent argued that the Second Restatement may be based on the notion that in deciding the issues a court may have concentrated on one rather than the other and the fact that a party that prevails on one issue may not have the incentive to appeal the decision on the other. In the present case, however, the issues arose in a claim for declaratory judgments which would cause the parties to concentrate on both. The dissent also explained that while the Court is cautious in applying declaratory judgments in cases involving criminal cases, it is appropriate to declare what conduct is permissible in order that a would-be offender will be aware of the law in advance. As to the scope of the change-in-law exception, the dissenting opinion stated:

> There is support in the Restatement (Second) of Judgments for the general proposition that a change in law may alter a judgment's preclusive effect, § 28, Comment *c*, p. 276 (1980), and in a prior case, *Bobby* v. *Bies*, 556 U. S. 825, 834 (2009), we invoked that provision. But we have never actually held that a prior judgment lacked preclusive effect on this ground. Nor have we ever defined how much the relevant "legal context" must change in order for the exception to apply. If the exception is applied too aggressively, it could dangerously undermine the important interests served by issue preclusion. So caution is in order in relying on that exception here.

The majority thinks that the exception applies because *Mille Lacs* effectively overruled *Race Horse*, even though it did not say that in so many words. But that is a questionable interpretation. The fact of the matter is that the *Mille Lacs* majority held back from actually overruling *Race Horse*, even though the dissent claimed that it had effectively done so. * * * And while the opinion of the Court repudiated one of the two grounds that the *Race Horse* Court gave for its decision (the equal-footing doctrine), it is by no means clear that *Mille Lacs* also rejected the second ground (the conclusion that the terms of the Act admitting Wyoming to the Union manifested a congressional intent not to burden the State with the right created by the 1868 Treaty). With respect to this latter ground, the *Mille Lacs* Court characterized the proper inquiry as follows: "whether Congress (more precisely, because this is a treaty, the Senate) intended the rights secured by the 1837 Treaty to survive statehood." 526 U. S., at 207. And the Court then went on to analyze the terms of the particular treaty at issue in that case and to contrast those terms with those of the treaty in *Race Horse*. *Mille Lacs*, supra, at 207.

On this reading, it appears that *Mille Lacs* did not reject the second ground for the decision in *Race Horse* but simply found it inapplicable to the facts of the case at hand. I do not claim that this reading of *Mille Lacs* is indisputable, but it is certainly reasonable, and if it is correct, *Mille Lacs* did not change the legal context as much as the majority suggests. It knocked out some of *Race Horse*'s reasoning but did not effectively overrule the decision. Is that enough to eliminate the preclusive effect of the first ground for the *Repsis* judgment?

The majority cites no authority holding that a decision like *Mille Lacs* is sufficient to deprive a prior judgment of its issue-preclusive effect. * * *

In its bottom line, the dissent emphasized that in any future litigation of the "occupied land" argument, the court would be free to and should hold that petitioner is bound by the preclusion doctrine. Thus, in the dissent's view, the majority, by avoiding the threshold question of issue preclusion, had offered a "pointless disquisition on the proper interpretation of the 1868 Treaty."

Merck Sharp & Dohme Corp. v. Albrecht, 587 U.S. ___, ___ S.Ct. ___ L.Ed.2d ___ (2019).

Petitioner (Merck) is the manufacturer of a drug that treats and prevents osteoporosis. Respondents are a group of more than 500 consumers who were prescribed the drug between 1999 and 2010 and who, as a result, suffered atypical femoral fractures. They brought separate suits alleging that petitioner had a duty under state law to warn users of the risk of such a serious injury and that it had failed to do so, despite knowing about the danger as early as 1995. Merck defended the lawsuits arguing that federal law preempted the state duty-to-warn claims. In 2008, Merck had applied to the Federal Food and Drug Administration (FDA) for pre-approval to change the drug label to add a warning of a risk of "stress fractures." The FDA rejected the proposed change as inadequate because "stress fractures" did not clearly relate to atypical femoral fractures. The FDA invited Merck to resubmit its application to address its deficiencies but Merck withdrew its application. In 2011, the FDA, based on its own analysis, ordered that petitioner change the drug label to warn of the risk of atypical femoral fractures.

In a prior case, *Wyeth* v. *Levine*, 555 U.S. 555, 129 S.Ct. 1187, 173 L.Ed.2d 51 (2009), the Court had held that for preemption to apply there must be "clear evidence" that the FDA would not have approved a change in a label required by state law. That in turn left open the question whether such a decision should be considered one of fact for a jury or one of law for a judge. The trial judge in the *Merck* case held that it was for the judge; the Court of Appeals reversed, holding it was a question for the jury. Nine members of the Supreme Court agreed that the question was for the judge, vacated the judgment of the Court of Appeals, and remanded for further proceedings. In an opinion by Justice Breyer, joined by Justices Thomas, Ginsburg, Sotomayor, Kagan, and Gorsuch, the Court noted that such a question is complex, falling somewhere between a clear legal standard and a simple historical fact. The Court analyzed the situation as follows:

> We turn now to what is the determinative question before us: Is the question of agency disapproval primarily one of fact, normally for juries to decide, or is it a question of law, normally for a judge to decide without a jury?

> The complexity of the * * * law [pertaining to when federal law preempts state law] helps to illustrate why we answer this question by concluding that the question is a legal one for the judge, not a jury. The question often involves the use of legal skills to determine whether agency disapproval fits facts that are not in dispute. Moreover, judges, rather than lay juries, are better equipped to evaluate the nature and scope of an agency's determination. Judges are experienced in "[t]he construction of written instruments," such as those normally produced by a federal agency to memorialize its considered judgments. *Markman* v. *Westview Instruments, Inc.*, 517 U. S. 370, 388, 116 S.Ct. 1384, 134 L.Ed.2d 577 (1996). And judges are better suited than are juries to understand and to interpret agency decisions in light of the governing statutory and regulatory context. * * * To understand the question as a legal question for judges makes sense given the fact that judges are normally familiar with principles of administrative law. Doing so should produce greater uniformity among courts; and greater uniformity is normally a virtue when a question requires a determination concerning the scope and effect of federal agency action. * * *

> We understand that sometimes contested brute facts will prove relevant to a court's legal determination about the meaning and effect of an agency decision. For example, if the FDA rejected a drug manufacturer's supplemental application to change a drug label on the ground that the information supporting the application was insufficient to warrant a

labeling change, the meaning and scope of that decision might depend on what information the FDA had before it. Yet in litigation between a drug consumer and a drug manufacturer (which will ordinarily lack an official administrative record for an FDA decision), the litigants may dispute whether the drug manufacturer submitted all material information to the FDA.

But we consider these factual questions to be subsumed within an already tightly circumscribed legal analysis. And we do not believe that they warrant submission alone or together with the larger pre-emption question to a jury. Rather, in those contexts where we have determined that the question is "for the judge and not the jury," we have also held that "courts may have to resolve subsidiary factual disputes" that are part and parcel of the broader legal question. *Teva Pharmaceuticals USA, Inc.* v. *Sandoz, Inc.*, 574 U. S. ___, 135 S.Ct. 831, 838, ___ L.Ed.2d ___ (2015). And, as in contexts as diverse as the proper construction of patent claims and the voluntariness of criminal confessions, they create a question that " 'falls somewhere between a pristine legal standard and a simple historical fact.' " *Markman*, 517 U. S. at 388, 116 S.Ct. 1384 (quoting *Miller* v. *Fenton*, 474 U. S. 104, 114, 106 S.Ct. 445, 88 L.Ed.2d 405 (1985)). In those circumstances, " 'the fact/law distinction at times has turned on a determination that, as a matter of the sound administration of justice, one judicial actor is better positioned than another to decide the issue in question.' " *Markman*, 517 U. S. at 388, 116 S.Ct. 1384 (quoting *Miller*, 474 U. S. at 114, 106 S.Ct. 445). In this context, that "better positioned" decisionmaker is the judge.

Separate concurring opinions by Justice Alito and Justice Thomas addressed the factors to be considered for preemption to apply.

Home Depot U.S.A., Inc. v. Jackson, 587 U.S. ___, ___ S.Ct. ___, ___ L.Ed.2d ___ (2019).

A bank filed a debt-collection action in state court, alleging that the consumer-respondent was liable for charges he had incurred on a Home Depot credit card. The consumer responded by filing third-party class-action claims against petitioner Home Deport U. S. A., Inc., and Carolina Water Systems, Inc., alleging that they had engaged in practices that violated state law. Petitioner filed a notice to remove the case from state to federal court, but respondent moved to remand, arguing that under Shamrock Oil & Gas Corp. v. Sheets, 313 U.S. 100, 61 S.Ct. 868, 85 L.Ed.2d 1214 (1941), removal by a third-party counterclaim defendant was barred in these circumstances. The lower court granted the motion to remand, and the Fourth Circuit affirmed, holding that neither the general removal provision, 28 U. S. C. § 1441(a), nor the removal provision in the Class Action Fairness Act of 2005, § 1453(b), allowed Home Depot to remove the class-action claims filed against it. Justice Thomas delivered the opinion of the Court for a five-to-four majority, and affirmed, explaining that "in the context of these removal provisions the term 'defendant' refers only to the party sued by the original plaintiff." Moreover, *Shamrock Oil*, which held that "an original plaintiff may not remove a counterclaim against it" controlled the question whether a third-party defendant should be able to remove, and similarly barred the court from exercising jurisdiction. Justice Thomas explained:

We agree with Home Depot that *Shamrock Oil* does not specifically address whether a party who was not the original plaintiff can remove a counterclaim filed against it. And we acknowledge, as Home Depot points out, that a third-party counterclaim defendant, unlike the original plaintiff, has no role in selecting the forum for the suit. But the text of § 1441(a) simply refers to "the defendant or the defendants" in the civil action. If a counterclaim defendant who was the original plaintiff is not one of "the defendants," we see no textual reason to reach a different conclusion for a counterclaim defendant who was not originally part of the lawsuit. In that regard, *Shamrock Oil* did not view the counterclaim as a separate action with a new plaintiff and a new defendant. Instead, the Court highlighted that the original plaintiff was still "the plaintiff." * * * Similarly here, the filing of counterclaims that included class-action allegations against a third party did not create a new "civil action" with a new "plaintiff" and a new "defendant."

Nor did CAFA's removal provision change the analysis. "[T]the context here," the Court wrote, "demonstrates that Congress did not expand the types of parties eligible to remove a class action under § 1453(b) beyond § 1441(a)'s limits. If anything, that the language of § 1453(b) mirrors the language in the statutory provisions it is amending suggests that the term 'defendant' is being used consistently across all provisions." Ascribing the word "defendant" different meaning in the two removal contexts "would render the removal provisions incoherent." Finally, the Court argued that any potential gamesmanship was a consequence of the statutory language, and that, if Congress shared the dissent's "disapproval of certain litigation 'tactics.' " Congress could amend the statute.

Justice Alito wrote a dissent, joined by Chief Justice Roberts and Justices Gorsuch and Kavanaugh. The dissent emphasized that a third-party defendant, like an original defendant, did not choose to litigate in state court, and "might face bias there, and with it the potential for crippling unjust losses." Looking to the text and history of CAFA, the dissent argued that Congress specifically sought to end gamesmanship by plaintiffs' lawyers by making it "easier for defendants to remove to federal court." Moreover, in the dissent's view, a third-party counterclaimant defendant could remove under the general removal statute, and *Shamrock Oil*, far from raising a bar, supported removal by an involuntary defendant such as the third-party counterclaimant in this case.

PART XI

Index to Comparative Provisions

Federal Provisions

State Provisions

INDEX TO COMPARATIVE PROVISIONS

INDEX TO COMPARATIVE PROVISIONS

INDEX TO COMPARATIVE PROVISIONS